THE
FRENCH COUNTRY HOUSEWIFE

THE FIRST VOLUME OF
Maison rustique des dames
(1859)

MAISON RUSTIQUE

DES DAMES

PAR

Mᵐᵉ C. MILLET-ROBINET

MEMBRE CORRESPONDANT DE LA SOCIÉTÉ IMPÉRIALE ET CENTRALE D'AGRICULTURE

QUATRIÈME ÉDITION

TOME PREMIER

PARIS

LIBRAIRIE AGRICOLE DE LA MAISON RUSTIQUE

RUE JACOB, 26

1859

Frontispiece. The title page of the fourth edition of Maison rustique des dames.

THE
FRENCH COUNTRY HOUSEWIFE

THE FIRST VOLUME OF

Maison rustique des dames

FOURTH EDITION

(1859)

Cora Millet-Robinet

TRANSLATED INTO ENGLISH,

WITH AN INTRODUCTION

BY

TOM JAINE

PROSPECT BOOKS

2017

First published in Great Britain in 2017 by Prospect Books,
26 Parke Road, London SW13 9NG.
(https://prospectbooks.co.uk)

Maison rustique des dames was first published by the Librairie agricole de la Maison rustique, Paris, in 1845; this translation is of the fourth edition, 1859.

BRITISH LIBRARY CATALOGUING IN PUBLICATION DATA:
A catalogue entry of this book is available from the British Library.

Typeset and designed by Tom Jaine.

ISBN 978-1-909248-52-6

Printed and bound in Malta by the Gutenberg Press Ltd, Malta.

PART II
KITCHEN MANUAL

Figure 1. Cora Millet-Robinet, a portrait painted by her brother-in-law Hippolyte Bruyères. (Courtesy of M. Stéphane Robinet.)

INTRODUCTION

The expectation of coming across a farmhouse in France or, even more, in Britain, where the decoration, furnishings and household equipment date from no later than the 1920s or '30s has perhaps reached vanishing point. Were you fortunate enough to light upon an example, this book would be a fine *vade mecum* to its intricacies. If, however, such a place now burns bright only in your memories of childhood, then it will serve to explain much that was then a mystery. Its author first wrote her book, in fact, in 1845, and this version dates from 1859, but there are many points of contact with the ways of our grandparents, although they may have lived a half-century later. It also lays bare aspects of that much-loved style of cookery, *cuisine bourgeoise*, with recipes that are at once simple and fully explained. My aim with this translation was both to make the book better known and to salute Cora Millet-Robinet, its author, a remarkable woman deserving our admiration.

What follows is a long introduction. Too long, perhaps, for the reader eager to sample the delights of the book itself, but necessary to place it in some context and to give details of a life hitherto obscure. It may be ignored at the start and act as a reservoir of information once curiosity is piqued by the memorable pages of Mme Millet-Robinet's own composition.

THE LIFE AND TIMES OF THE *MAISON RUSTIQUE DES DAMES*

This is a translation of the first volume of *Maison rustique des dames* ('The lady's country house', although I have given a more authentically English-sounding title for the purposes of sale today), a manual of domestic economy, cookery, household medicine, gardening and the distaff side of farming written by Cora Élisabeth Millet-Robinet (1798–1890) and first published in Paris in 1845 (although bibliographers point out its actual date was 1844, despite the evidence of the title page). It was perhaps the most

23

widely read of all such guides in France and was still in print as late as 1944. The issue in question here is the fourth, appearing in 1859.

Although we can trace the outlines of Madame Millet-Robinet's career from official records, her books and her journalism, few letters and no diaries or memoirs of her own have so far come to light, nor does she figure in the reminiscences or the manuscript archives yet discovered of her contemporaries. Any portrait, therefore, lacks a degree of nuance or a strong sense of personality, although she is free enough with her opinions in her published works to allow us to catch some impression of what she must have been like in life. What's more, for an author who was so greatly esteemed in her day, there has been surprisingly little attention paid her by the modern French academic community or indeed by historians of food and domestic management. So the reader who comes across her for the first time will be at a loss to place her achievements in some sort of context. This introduction is couched with this in mind, for Mme Millet-Robinet was a formidable woman and her books of lasting significance.

The *Maison rustique des dames* was an extensive guide to the practical aspects of life a young wife might encounter when first moving to the country. Some advice is offered for almost everything, be it childcare, education, reading-matter, musical taste, entertaining, hiring and keeping staff, cookery, interior design, architecture, heating, lighting or cleaning – and that's before we've stepped outside the house to discuss the garden, the poultry-run or the farm. Elizabeth David remarked that 'judging from the manner of its arrangement and content, [it] may well have had some influence on our own Mrs. Beeton,' but there were many differences between the two writers. Although both women were mindful of the need to instruct their readers on ways to better themselves, Mrs Beeton addressed a largely urban audience while Millet-Robinet speaks only to country-dwellers – the fact that these may well have been city-bred neophytes to the world of ditch and hedgerow merely added spice to her counsels. Another way they differed was in their approach to crafting a book. Mrs Beeton gathered her recipes from hither and yon, many via the pages of her husband's *Englishwoman's Domestic Magazine*. These she then fleshed out with sound advice and information, much of it encyclopaedic and culled from a variety of sources. Cora Millet-Robinet's work feels much more grounded in personal experience. She certainly did draw on other people and other authors, but an arid repertoire of facts is not her style. Her book is a manifesto of right-living, proved by example. Another important distinction is that while the English author died shortly after her first appearance in print, Mme Millet-Robinet lived on for almost half a century. Over more than a dozen editions, she was able to make changes and improvements, as well as comment on technical developments in household equipment which she had put to the test herself.

Maison rustique des dames was first published in 1845 by the Librairie agricole de la Maison rustique, 26 rue Jacob, Paris. All subsequent editions were issued by the same house. The Librairie was founded in 1834, in the first instance to produce an agricultural encyclopaedia under the general title of *Maison rustique du XIXe siècle*. It then developed an extensive catalogue relating to agriculture, gardening, viticulture and domestic matters. *Maison rustique des dames* went through at least twenty-one editions (it gets a little hazy after the First World War). Mme Millet-Robinet had to wait ten years before the second edition was issued in 1855 but thereafter a new version appeared every four years or thereabouts until 1914, the date of the eighteenth edition. The core of the book remained stable, but elements did change: the menus that appeared in 1859 were a new feature; suggestions for a model library were soon suppressed; changes in laundry equipment provoked variation in advice from one edition to the next; but the repertoire of recipes, for example, was surprisingly constant. After the First World War, the book was remodelled, but by no means shortened, by Madame L. Babet-Charton, a director of the École Normale Supérieure of agriculture and domestic science at Grignon (the oldest agricultural college in France), and later the founding director of the first agricultural college for girls at Coëtlogon in Brittany. Mme Babet-Charton wrote the deathless handbook *Blanchissage, repassage* (Laundry, ironing) in 1909. Her daughter Henriette also wrote on domestic topics: a good book on French cheese, one about preparing skins and furs, and one on charcuterie. This revised version of *Maison rustique* was last issued (according to the catalogue of the Bibliothèque nationale) in 1944, although it probably first saw the light of day in about 1920–25. There have been no subsequent editions, but the culinary sections were offered up as *Les Recettes de cuisine de ma grand-mère d'après Madame Millet-Robinet*, published by J.M. Williamson at Nantes in 1995. It was based on the same fourth edition that is translated here.

There was one translation made of this book, into Spanish in 1932 (using the Babet-Charton revision). Entitled *El ama de casa en el campo: Consejero de la mujer en la granja* it was published in Barcelona and appeared as a single volume of 917 pages.

Despite the most recent version made up entirely of recipes, *Maison rustique* was far more than a cookery book and to better understand its place in the literature of domestic economy in the first half of the nineteenth century we might look at several tendencies that seem to come together in its creation. The first thing to remark is that Cora Millet-Robinet was part of a movement – it seems like that at least – of women writers tackling for the first time this broad topic of household management, from the point of view of living in the country, furnishing a house, cooking good meals and preserving a range of foodstuffs. A second strand is how her work reflected the general enthusiasm in the country for agricultural improvement and for the better acceptance of farming and food production as worthy of social status and respect. This was as true of Mme Millet-Robinet's own life as it was of the content of her books, as well as those of her fellow-writers. Contingent on this was the eloquent case she and others made for improving the education of young women so as to fit them for more useful roles in agriculture and around the house and kitchen. A final element in the success, indeed the existence, of the *Maison rustique* was the arrival of a handful of publishing houses on the Paris scene devoted to technical education and instruction. All these possible influences on Mme Millet-Robinet's work depended of course on the radical transformation of French society in the years after the Revolution: on the emergence of a dominant middle class, a certain emancipation of women, the greater part played by the press and publishers, the improvement of agricultural practice, the growth of industry and technological change.

It may be wondered at this point why Cora Millet-Robinet felt moved to write this book. Some lines towards an answer are sketched out in the ensuing pages but a premature conclusion might be attempted. Mme Millet-Robinet did not start writing books until she was in her fortieth year, as the 1830s drew to a close. The early years after her marriage in 1823 saw her move from Paris to a country estate, give birth to and raise a handful of children and set about learning the business of farming. Her husband, an old soldier, was new to this activity too, and felt his work was a mission: to improve his land and act as a model for others to emulate. Added to plain farming, the couple took on the specific venture of sericulture and production of silk thread, again, as a model for the locality, not merely an income. In the 1830s, they were joined in the business by Cora's scientist-brother Stéphane Robinet and made a formidable team that wrote up their activities, submitted them for prizes and medals and all in all acted as a lighthouse of agricultural reform and rural renewal. Note Cora's own comments in the opening pages of the *Maison rustique*: 'To all these satisfactions, there's the success of the farm to which we devote our time; the improvements we describe then see imitated in the district, spreading affluence…. Finally, is it not true to say that the repute that our efforts may bestow on a farm, which then may become a model for the whole district, brings with it that sense of reward that accompanies any useful undertaking brought to a happy conclusion?' Cora was very much involved in all aspects of the work, particularly as her husband was often away performing official military duties. He retired in about 1840 and was thus able to undertake all the supervision himself. Perhaps it was at this juncture that Cora decided her most productive role would be that of writer: pouring all her experience (of both motherhood and running house and farm) into instructions for the next generation.

THE LITERARY CONTEXT

French women came later than their equivalents in England or Germany to writing on cookery or household management. In France, most cookery books had been written by men for male cooks, with a few exceptions (often quite early ones concerning sugar and sweetmeats) addressing women directly. The most celebrated of these exceptions was the founding text *La Cuisinière bourgeoise* (The bourgeois woman-cook) by Menon, a man of course, first published in 1746. Another exception, from not many years later, was Louis Rose's *La Bonne Fermière, ou Élémens économiques, utiles aux jeunes personnes destinées à cet état* (The good farmer's wife, or aspects of household management useful to young people intended for this role) – a study of household management with comments on food and feeding but few recipes – published at Lille in 1765. The steady output in Georgian England of works such as Hannah Glasse's *The Art of Cookery, Made Plain and Easy* (1747), Elizabeth Raffald's *The Experienced English Housekeeper*

(1769) or Martha Bradley's *The British Housewife* (1756) was never matched by the French. In general, the French audience for cookery books consisted of male cooks in noble or gentry households, not the middle-class town-dwellers of England. Nor was domestic economy as important a topic in *ancien régime* France as it was in Britain. It took the Revolution to make a difference.

The first French cookery book written by a woman and addressing female readers was *La Cuisinière républicaine* (The republican woman-cook) of 1795, by Mme Mérigot: her chosen topic was cooking the potato. Thereafter, women did begin to take up the pen, an early example being Louise Béate Augustine Utrecht-Friedel, whose first book was about sweet things, but who then wrote *Le Petit Cuisinier habile* (The small book for the skilful man-cook) in 1814, changing its name to *La Petite Cuisinière habile* (The small book for the skilful woman-cook) in 1821 and for subsequent editions (it found its way to America, as their first 'French' cookbook). More relevant to Mme Millet-Robinet's approach, however, are the books written by Marie Armande Jeanne Gacon-Dufour, dame d'Humières (1753–1835), whose early forays into print antedate the Revolution but whose first manuals of household management, *Recueil pratique d'économie rurale et domestique* (Useful compendium of rural and domestic economy) and *Manuel de la ménagère à la ville et à la campagne, et de la femme de basse-cour* (Town and country housewife and poultrywoman's manual) were published in 1804 and 1805. Subsequently, she composed *Manuel du pâtissier et de la pâtissière, à l'usage de la ville et de la campagne* (Man- and woman-pastrycook's manual, for use in town and country), 1825, and *Manuel des habitants de la campagne et de la bonne fermière* (Manual for countrydwellers and the good woman-farmer), 1826, as well as a score of novels and historical works and more practical books on agriculture, animal husbandry, perfumery and soap-making. The American scholar Valérie Lastinger makes an eloquent case for her scientific achievements in her essay, 'The Laboratory, the Boudoir and the Kitchen'. Mme Gacon-Dufour was a product of the Enlightenment, rationalist, republican, embracing the improving aims of the Physiocrats, strongly feminist (e.g. in her *Dangers d'un mariage forcé* [Risks of forced marriage], 1801) and an advocate of better female education (e.g. in *De la Nécessité de l'instruction pour les femmes* [On the need to educate women], 1805). Her works on domestic economy have a bias towards farming matters, but included much on the preservation of foods and the exploitation of the holding to make readers more self-sufficient. She was, for example, in favour of bee-keeping as a useful income for the housewife, and inventive in her food substitutions to cope with deficiencies in supply of foreign imports during the Napoleonic wars: ways to make apples taste like pineapples, using chillies instead of pepper, and the dried petals of pinks (*Dianthus caryophyllus*) instead of cloves (after all, the English called them clove gilliflowers). She justifies her down-to-earth style and simple vocabulary in terms very reminiscent of Hannah Glasse, in England half a century earlier, who had said, 'I have not wrote in the high, polite stile ... for my Intention is to instruct the lower sort'. All these broader intentions, first seen in Mme Gacon-Dufour, of instruction, improvement, female betterment, autarchy, and good agricultural and domestic practice are taken up again by Millet-Robinet. And similarly, although the older writer sometimes includes townspeople in her titles and her comments, the general drift of much of her work is to glorify country ways over those of the enervated city. Her somewhat combative feminism did not endear her to the male critical establishment, one of whom memorably commented, 'I would rather her *ratafias* than her books.'

Mme Gacon-Dufour has a place in the career of Cora Millet-Robinet thanks to a striking coincidence. In 1820, the botanist, physician and explorer Armand Havet (1795–1820) published the impressive *Dictionnaire des ménages: ou, Recueil de recettes et d'instructions pour l'économie domestique* (Household dictionary: or, compilation of recipes and instructions in domestic economy). Then, unfortunately, he died while on an expedition to Madagascar. A second edition was issued in 1822 but for the third of 1826 the publisher recruited Mme Gacon-Dufour to correct and improve those articles relating to domestic economy and Cora's older brother (and future business partner) Stéphane Robinet, then just qualified as a pharmacist, to look after the scientific matter. You might see there the outline of an apostolic succession of lady writers on household management.

In the first quarter of the nineteenth century, a handful of female authors explored similar fields. Perhaps the highest in social status, though a liberal at heart, was Madame de Genlis (1746–1830), a positive blue-stocking, the governess of the future king Louis-Philippe, who published a *Manuel de la jeune femme: Guide Complet de la maîtresse de maison* (The young lady's manual: a complete guide for the mistress of the house) in 1829. Its instructions were sketchy at best and its recipes a ladylike collection of sweet things and still-room items. Élisabeth-Félicie Bayle-Mouillard (1796–1865), under the name Élisabeth Celnart, was responsible for a dozen more useful manuals published by Roret on subjects as diverse as pork butchery, animal husbandry, good manners, household management and perfumery. She was sometimes accused of plagiarism, particularly of the work of Gacon-Dufour, but her books were widely read from their first appearance in the mid-1820s. She was a native of Moulins, in the Bourbonnais, and was allowed a good education by her schoolmaster father before marrying an Auvergnat lawyer. The publisher Roret later issued Celnart together with Gacon-Dufour and a third writer, Mme Pariset in a single volume. Mme Pariset first wrote *Manuel de la maîtresse de maison, ou Lettres sur l'économie domestique* (Manual for the mistress of the house, or letters on domestic economy) for the publisher Audot in 1821, its last issue by Roret being in 1852. She spoke to the urban bourgeoisie and hardly ruffled the hierarchies of gender. Nor did she write much about cookery (suggesting that hiring a good woman cook was the mistress's first priority), concentrating on management of the house, keeping servants in check and, prescriptively, interior decoration. When most of these women wrote on food, their emphasis was on conservation and preserves and their repertoire was never very systematic, more a miscellany. Millet-Robinet may have drawn on them for inspiration and sometimes attitude, but was somewhat ahead of them in culinary efficiency and range.

Allusion to the Bourbonnais must bring to mind George Sand, her château of Nohant and her novels of country life. On the level of the day-to-day – the scale of their country houses, for example, and their undoubted feminism – there are many parallels that could be drawn with the career of Cora Millet-Robinet, even though Sand was emphatically of higher social status, somewhat more bohemian in conduct and touched only on the practical via her works of fiction. Another writer from that region, however, might be proposed as a better reflection in every sense. Aglaé Adanson (1775–1852) was the daughter of the famous botanist, Michel Adanson, described by some as a 'precursor of evolutionism'. Convent educated, twice married and twice divorced, Aglaé fled the salons of Paris at the turn of the century for her mother's lover's property in Villeneuve-sur-Allier just north of Moulins. Here she reclaimed the estate, fashioned a garden and park, and planted a remarkable collection of trees in an arboretum that survives to the present day (still in the hands of her descendants). She condensed her knowledge into two volumes of excellence called *La Maison de campagne, ouvrage qui peut aussi, en ce qui concerne l'économie domestique, être utile aux personnes qui habitent la ville* (The country house, a work which can also be useful, insofar as it concerns domestic economy, to those who live in town). First published by Audot in 1822, it went through six editions to 1852. The first third of the first volume is a survey of planning, furnishing and management of a small country house (but never a château), the arrangement of the poultry yard and ancillary buildings and ways to handle staff; then there is a short but comprehensive set of recipes; finally an alphabetical miscellany of factual articles on everything from cement to medications. The second volume is a manual of gardening, again suitable for the modest country property, not rolling acres. The *leitmotif* of the book is a wholehearted embrace of country life, the celebration of a decision to quit the city for the sake of personal renewal and rebirth. There is little here about families and offspring: it reads almost as a late-twentieth-century declaration of womanly independence. Mme Adanson (she retook her maiden name in 1808) cites with approval the works of Mesdames Pariset and Gacon-Dufour. Although she was a prize-winner at the Société centrale d'Agriculture de Paris (as was Mme Millet-Robinet), there is no hint in Cora's writings of their having ever met or corresponded. But Aglaé's evangelical approach to country living, her insistence on writing for people of modest means, and her emphasis on practical not theoretical experience would have met Cora's entire approval.

Although all the works alluded to had some culinary content, they were not principally cookery books. But just as advice on household management had flourished, so too had sensible kitchen manuals, addressing a readership not so very distant from that of Gacon-Dufour, Pariset or Adanson. The latter was clear that there were two sorts of cookery books. 'I do not pretend,' she wrote in her *Maison de campagne* (1822), 'to rival *Le Cuisinier*, once *impérial*, but actually *royal*, of M. Viart. On the contrary, I would make a most definite distinction between his work and mine: he has worked for very rich people, and I write for modest country-dwellers.' Just such a distinction is also drawn by Cora Millet-

Robinet, referring to the same book, written by one A. Viard or Viart, first published in 1806 and reaching its thirty-second edition by 1875.[1] If Viard was for the rich, Carême's *L'Art de la cuisine française au dix-neuvième siècle* (The art of French cookery in the nineteenth century), 1835–47, was for the richer, as were later books by the chefs Jules Gouffé (*Le Livre de cuisine* [Cookery book], 1867) and Urbain Dubois (*La Cuisine classique* [Classic cookery], 1856) – although the latter did write a *Nouvelle Cuisine bourgeoise pour la ville et pour la campagne* (New bourgeois cookery for the town and the country) in 1878. Another important general work for either the (male) cooking professional or the moneyed classes was Antoine Beauvilliers's *L'Art du cuisinier* (The man-cook's art), 1814, though criticized as a blatant imitation of Viard. These books may occasionally be mentioned by our domestic economists, but only to be dismissed as not for the likes of their readers. Nor, indeed, was the burgeoning literature of gastronomy – exemplified by Grimod de la Reynière and Brillat-Savarin – anything to do with them. It gets never, or at least very rarely, a mention.

More relevant were books of recipes for the bourgeoisie that began to come off the press with the new century. Not only were they for the middle classes, but they were also for women. Pride of place must be accorded to *La Cuisinière de la Campagne et de la Ville* (The woman-cook in the country and the town) first issued anonymously in 1818, but later over the initials or the name of Louis-Eustache Audot (1783–1870), an important Paris bookseller and publisher. This achieved its hundredth edition in 1928, completely revised by Henriette Babet-Charton, whose mother had reworked the *Maison rustique des dames*. In a note about the origin of the book which he appended to later editions, Audot claimed to be an amateur cook who had perfected his own skills while living in the country (guided, he admitted, by Menon's *Cuisinière bourgeoise*). He certainly borrowed recipes from Menon and, later, a fair few from Aglaé Adanson, whom he had himself published. He kept his methods simple, decoration low-key, ingredients affordable and eschewed, while respecting, the ambitions of Viard and Carême. His book was the foundation of French modern *cuisine bourgeoise*. It was translated into many European languages. Audot

1. Thanks to the vagaries of French politics, its simple title went through several changes to reflect the constitution: *impérial, royal, national, impérial* again, before finally settling with *national* on the fall of Louis-Napoleon. It had also nearly doubled in length.

was not without his imitators and competitors. He complained his success engendered a host of masquerades and re-titlings, that *cuisiniers*, hitherto *impérials*, had suddenly become *campagnards*. Among his *bona fide* competitors was a book published by Roret over the name of P. Cardelli, *Manuel du cuisinier et de la cuisinière à l'usage de la ville et de la campagne* (The man-cook's and woman-cook's manual for use in town and country) which went through a score of editions from 1822. Cardelli was in fact M.H. Duval, former secretary to the Marquis de Las Cases, who had accompanied Napoleon to St Helena. His book was distinguished by a note after each recipe indicating its digestibility: veal cutlets braised with truffles were reckoned heating or liable to cause constipation, pig's kidneys were thought a 'bad food' (*mauvais aliment*) and salmis of woodcock, good.

As more and more cookery books were addressed directly to the female cook and the mistress of the house, rather than to the steward of the household or the gourmandizing master as had been the pre-revolutionary case, so the authors of these books assumed a feminine guise. Often enough, they were in point of fact male: thus the *Cordon Bleu, … par mademoiselle Marguerite* (The professional woman-cook, by Miss Marguerite), 1827, was written by Horace Raisson, who used the pseudonym A.B. de Périgord for other gastronomic titles. A scholar of oriental languages, one J.-J. Mayeux, wrote first *Le Petit Cuisinier français* (The small book of French cookery – though literally, one might suggest, 'The small French man-cook') in 1823, turning it into the *Manuel Complet de la cuisinière bourgeoise* (A complete manual for the bourgeois woman-cook) by 'Mlle Catherine' in 1839. It was reissued constantly throughout the century. These demoiselles were but the first in a line that stretched to 'Tante Marie', the supposed author of *La Véritable Cuisine de famille* (Real family cooking) published by Taride in 1925 and still going strong ('Uncle Paul' wrote Taride's guide to home medicine, while 'Uncle Peter' dispensed knowledge of fishing). Today, the gold-standard of *cuisine bourgeoise* is often deemed *Le Livre de cuisine de Madame E. Saint-Ange*, indeed a woman and the maiden name of Marie Ébrard (adopted for fear that her son would be teased at school), first published in 1927. While it is sometimes difficult to trace borrowings from one book to another, at least if the borrower was linguistically adept, it is plain that this group of books, over more than a century, was working with an identical repertoire. Sequences of recipes in Cora Millet-Robinet can be matched to similar runs in Audot and others. Often the methods and the detail of Cora's instructions indicate individual preference or direct experience, but the palette was not hers, even if the picture was.

There is a revealing paragraph in the collection of recipes from Mmes Pariset, Gacon-Dufour, and Celnart published by Roret. 'The cook as well as the mistress should know most ordinary dishes off by heart; but it is good, not to say essential, to have cookery books to show you a wider variety of things, especially for days when you have guests. There are many such books: I know them all and can guide the mistress towards the best choice. *La Cuisinière bourgeoise* is too old-fashioned; *Le Cuisinier royal, Le Cusinier impérial, Le Cuisinier des Cuisiniers*, the *Art du Cuisinier, Le Manuel des Amphytrions*, are only suitable for restaurateurs or chefs to millionaires. *Le Cuisinier économe*, even if it barely deserves its title, is more useful; but the best, in my view, is the *Manuel du Cuisinier et de la Cuisinière*, by Cardelli (part of Roret's encyclopedia).' It's little wonder that she should recommend a Roret publication, but the other titles are instructive. The first is Menon; then comes Viard's work (in two versions); then there is reference to another long-lived occupant of chefs' shelves, *Le Cuisinier des Cuisiniers*, which first appeared anonymously in 1825 and then (throughout the century) over the name of Jourdan Lecointe, who claimed to be a physician and whose first book was issued in 1790; the *Art du Cuisinier* and *Le Manuel des Amphytrions* are by Beauvilliers and Grimod de la Reynière respectively; and *Le Cuisinier économe* was by 'the late' Archambault, a former restaurateur, and first appeared in 1821.

The very existence of these practical manuals depended on the immense expansion of the printed word, whether in books, magazines, journals or newspapers. Its most eloquent witness is perhaps Gustave Flaubert's final, unfinished, novel *Bouvard et Pécuchet* which appeared in 1881 but described France in the 1840s. The protagonists are two Parisian bachelors earning a humdrum living as copy-clerks, thanks to good handwriting if but little education. A fortunate legacy spurs them to leave the city for the country, buying a small farm in Normandy. Here, straightaway, we meet the idea (though reality was somewhat different) of the rural idyll, so strenuously promoted by Millet-Robinet and her predecessors. Once installed in their ramshackle property, our two heroes set about improvement, both to it and their own fund of knowledge. Step by step, their failing in one branch of expertise leads them to investigate another to explain their lack of success in the first – thus the explosion of their alcohol still demands that they should study chemistry. From small, practical beginnings, their intellectual quest leads them ineluctably towards the great imponderables. Flaubert perhaps intended his narrative as a satire on man's fatuities and baseless presumptions (an incomplete conclusion to the novel contained a 'Dictionary of Received Ideas'), but we may take it as a portrait of a society in which all knowledge was accessible: you only had to buy a book, and Bouvard and Pécuchet accumulated thousands of them. On their first night, 'they took out from their library the four volumes of the *Maison rustique*, sent for Gasparin's course, and took out a subscription to an agricultural journal'. The volumes referred to here are the first issue of the *Maison rustique du XIXe siècle*, an encyclopaedia of agriculture issued by Millet-Robinet's own publisher (a fifth, on horticulture, was to follow); 'Gasparin's course', from the same publisher, was a six-volume instructional manual published from 1843 by a former minister of the interior and, briefly, of agriculture; and of agricultural journals for our student-farmers, there was legion to choose from as each provincial agricultural society had its own publication and the same house that supplied them the *Maison rustique* and Gasparin could also provide the *Journal d'Agriculture pratique.* Millet-Robinet's own *Maison rustique*, for women, was written with the Bouvards and Pécuchets in mind: women need no longer depend on word-of-mouth instruction that probably enshrined the ignorance and prejudice of older generations. They could drink from a pure source, unbiased, experienced, and freighted with every modern invention.

Three Parisian publishing houses were especially relevant to Mme Millet-Robinet's work. First in point of time was Audot, run by Louis-Eustache Audot of *La Cuisinière de la Campagne*. His business was set up in his own name in 1809, having wisely married the boss's daughter. Audot himself was interested in horticulture, as well as cooking, and had early identified women as a target market. His *Encyclopédie des dames* from 1821 gathered a miscellany of improving titles, from histories of dance and music, to Aglaé Adanson's domestic economy and his own plain cookery. Other titles covered pâtisserie and other culinary specialities, as well as home crafts and hobbies ('recreational chemistry'), agriculture and estate management (how to kill moles, for instance), and several trade manuals.

The firm of Roret was founded in 1822 by Nicolas-Edme Roret (1797–1860), himself related to earlier publishers who had specialized in works of natural history (Buffon) and had issued versions of *La Nouvelle Maison rustique* (The new book of the country house) written by Louis Liger in 1702. Roret's great achievement was the *Encyclopédie Roret*, a series of 300 technical descriptive manuals produced over the century on every possible industrial or artisanal process: from bread ovens to drinking fountains. The *Manuels Roret* encompassed cookery (Cardelli, above) and household economy (Mme Celnart, for instance, composed a dozen texts on animal husbandry, artificial flowers, raising children, perfumery, cosmetics, sewing and manners). Their portraits of artisanal skills were, as pointed out by the scholar Anne-Françoise Garçon, useful raw material for realist novelists such as Émile Zola.

The third company we should notice was Cora Millet-Robinet's own Librairie agricole de la Maison rustique. This functioned as an independent publisher from 1834 until the end of the century when it was transferred to Flammarion, now part of Éditions Gallimard. It continued as a bookshop, at the same address, until 2012. The impetus for the Librairie came from a group of farm and garden improvers anxious to translate best English practice, exemplified by the works of John Claudius Loudon (1783–1843) particularly his *Encyclopaedia of Agriculture* of 1825 and *Encyclopaedia of Gardening* of 1823, for the benefit of French reformers. Their most important production was the *Maison rustique du XIXe siècle* in five volumes from 1834 to 1843. The publishing professional responsible in the first instance was Rosalie Huzard (1767–1849) who had established her own firm in 1798 specializing in veterinary and agricultural books. It was she who published Cora Millet-Robinet's first book on the nursing of infants in 1841. Another link that Cora had with the enterprise was the person of Alexandre Bixio (1808–1865), one of the founders and later chief editor. Of Italian origin, this politician and reforming agronomist served briefly as minister of agriculture at the fall of the July Monarchy in 1848 but saw his career cut short by the Second Empire. He was a founder of the *Journal d'Agriculture pratique, de jardinage et d'économie domestique* (Journal of practical agriculture, gardening and domestic economy) in 1837 and one of his colleagues in this venture was Cora's brother Stéphane Robinet. Some of the Librairie's titles were the product of a partnership with the ministry of agriculture under the rubric *Bibliothèque du cultivateur* (Farmer's library). Mme Millet-Robinet contributed books to this series. The direction of the Librairie was taken over by M. Dusacq in the 1850s and then by Léon-Joseph-Elisée Bourguignon through to the last years of the century. Bourguignon was the subject of many of Cora's complaints late in her life as she battled to see new versions of her work come back into print.

THE AGRICULTURAL CONTEXT

We have already made many references to the state of agriculture in France at this time and how efforts were under way to improve it. They were not without precedent. *L'Agriculture et maison rustique* (Agriculture and the country house) by Charles Estienne and Jean Liébault of 1564, the *Théâtre d'agriculture* of 1600 by Olivier de Serres, and the *Nouvelle maison rustique* of 1700 by Louis Liger, which was reworked by Jean-François Bastien in 1798, contribute to an impressive roll-call of encyclopaedic and practical literature from earlier centuries. The repeated use of the title *Maison rustique* by these first theorists goes some way towards explaining why those of the nineteenth century recycled it in their own work, to reinforce a sense of continuity as well as commitment to reform. Add to these the achievements of the encyclopaedists and physiocratic political economists of the eighteenth century and it would be unfair to dismiss all French agriculture as primitive. But primitive it often was, and unproductive. It seemed not to measure up to the progress being made in northern Europe, in Germany, the Low Countries, and Great Britain, hence the labour of translation and interpretation by agronomists such as Mathieu de Dombasle and the Comte de Gasparin whose course of agriculture was devoured by Bouvard and Pécuchet.

Many factors contributed to perceived inefficiencies of French agriculture: the size of the country, the lack of transport infrastructure, the various forms of holdings and the multiplicity of small or peasant farms. Some regions were impressive, especially if they had large urban markets easily accessible, others backward. This was a great educational challenge, as well as economic. Cora Millet-Robinet, her husband and her brother were all in the thick of it, and the *Maison rustique des dames* was intended as a mighty blow for enlightenment, specifically in the agricultural sphere, even if much of its advice concerned the household alone.

An article in the *Revue des deux Mondes* in 1846 is a good account of the movement for agricultural reform in the first half of the century. Its few paragraphs describe accurately the world in which the Millets and Robinets were working, as each of them – Cora, her husband François and her brother Stéphane – was an eager correspondent and contributor to the periodical literature that underpinned the movement, and were proud winners of the various prizes and trophies distributed. It runs thus:

> In the middle of the eighteenth century, France did not yet possess a single agricultural society, and the first was only founded in 1751. ... The French Revolution changed everything. On the one hand, it brought, so to speak, land into the public domain; and on the other, the revolutionary wars and those of the Empire, in spreading our armies across Europe, brought the agricultural practices of various countries to the notice of those of our soldiers who were versed in these matters, and the lessons learned and imparted by these men of action underpinned many aspects of our future prosperity. Under the restored monarchy, the efforts of M. Mathieu de Dombasle and the creation of the model farm at Roville in 1823 quickened progress, and one could say that we owe the new directions taken by agriculture to M. de Dombasle. Since 1830, much activity is plain to see. Forty years ago, there were about fifteen agricultural societies or associations; now they number eight-hundred and twenty-five, if you include local agricultural shows. Membership totals one-hundred thousand. ... Many provincial scientific, literary and cultural academies have their agricultural sections; some societies are specifically agricultural and publish their own bulletins or journals. ... The agricultural shows, which date from no earlier than 1835, are above all practical ... it is remarkable that in less than twelve years these institutions have spread throughout France.

CORA MILLET-ROBINET

Cora Élisabeth Robinet was born in Paris at the end of 1798, the year of Napoleon's Egyptian campaign and the Battle of the Nile. Her parents were Joachim Étienne Robinet (1768–1858) and Agathe Eulalie Laure, née Millet (1775–1810). Her father was variously described in the official record as a merchant's agent, a *négociant* or merchant in his own right, and as an *agent de change* or stockbroker (but this last was struck through on his death certificate). He was born in Mâcon on the Rhône, where his father was clerk to the civil tribunal. His inclusion in a government list of people who had suffered losses or been forced to flee from the French Caribbean colony of Saint-Domingue, now Haiti, on the island of Hispaniola, after the rebellion led by Toussaint Louverture which culminated in independence in 1804, links his early career to that island and doubtless explains his marriage to Laure Millet in 1795.

She – Laure Millet – came from a family of sailors and merchants in Nantes, at the mouth of the Loire. Her own father had started out as a privateer but had given up the sea upon marriage and settled in Saint-Domingue. Laure was born on the island but probably moved to Nantes with her own mother when she came back from the colony in the 1780s. (Although of no relevance here, some of her mother's letters to her sister back home in Nantes have been printed by Guy Debien, see the bibliography below.) Laure's father was a plantation manager and a coffee plantation owner on his own account in Saint-Domingue but did not survive the conflicts and political manoeuvrings that followed the French Revolution, dying in 1792. In France, the Millets were a large clan in southern Brittany. Whether Laure was a close relative of those Millets who in 1810 were the first recorded producers of tinned sardines in the town of Port-Louis, along the coast from Nantes, is not known. Cora's enthusiasm for canned preserves would make it a fitting connection.

Until at least 1810, the Robinet parents were noted as living in the rue des Petits-Augustins (now the rue Bonaparte) in Paris, which ran from the left bank of the Seine up to the rue Jacob. After that, they seem to have moved to the faubourg Saint-Honoré, most often placed at 19 rue Duphot, running from the rue Saint-Honoré to the place de la Madeleine.

Cora had three siblings: her elder brother Stéphane (1796–1869); an elder sister Laure who was born in 1797 but died at the age of twelve in 1809; and a younger sister Marie (1804–1882).

Beyond the dry twigs of bureaucratic record-keeping, we know little of Cora's upbringing. But one document has survived from these years, as if a searing comet traversing an inscrutable sky. It is in a small folder with letters of the 1870s and '80s from Cora and her sister Marie to their

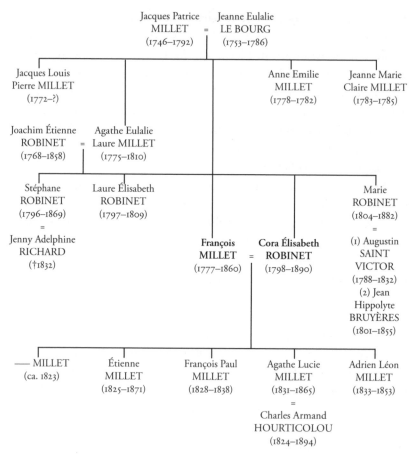

The Millet-Robinet family tree.

great-nephew's wife Isaure Schéfer, née Bachellery. It is a letter from Cora's mother to '*maman*' – which, although undated, must have been written before 1810 (when Cora would have been twelve). The identity of *maman* is not easy to establish: Laure's own mother had died in 1786; it is possibly an unidentified step-mother. The drift of the letter reflects the eternal tensions of family life. *Maman* has evidently found fault with almost everyone: but particularly Cora. Laure pleads that she does not take her behaviour amiss, that she really is a loveable girl. *Maman* obviously treated Stéphane little better (but, the implication seems to be, he has now left home for school and Cora bears the brunt of her resentment). She would appear to be more lenient towards Marie (who, of course, was four years younger). Nor were the parents immune from *maman*'s whiplash tongue, but she assures her they have only her best interests at heart. Her husband may have his moods, which she should forgive, but he has business worries.

Three dates in Cora's early years are evidently significant. In 1809 her older sister died; in 1810 her mother died; and in 1823 she was married. Her husband was her mother's brother, her uncle in other words, François Millet (1777–1860), twenty-one years her senior, a divorcé with two male children, a serving officer in the military administration, with a country property in Poitou. This fact is so arresting that we naturally seek an explanation. All one might observe is that the Millets and the Robinets were a close family. After the death of her mother, Cora would have been the oldest female in the family and as she grew up, presumably took on more household responsibilities. At some stage, they moved from rue des Petits-Augustins to the rue Duphot. This was also the address (no. 19) given as the residence of her uncle François Millet in 1821, two years before his marriage to Cora. One might posit, therefore, a grouping of two older males, one widowed, the other divorced; two sons of the divorced François Millet; and two daughters of the widowed Joachim Robinet (their brother Stéphane having left home). As events turned out, the youngest sister Marie ended up looking after their father. At a later date, he moved to the village of Quinçay in Poitou to be close to her, dying there in 1858. Perhaps Cora 'looked after' her uncle. The dispensations that would have been required for this marriage, both from church and state, have not yet been discovered. (Avunculate marriage is illegal in Great Britain but permissible in France with presidential – or at this stage royal – dispensation.) To continue this theme of family cohesion, when François and Cora moved to Poitou soon after their marriage, they were to be joined by Cora's brother Stéphane, after being widowed in 1832, and his three children. Cora, François and Stéphane were business partners for the next decade at least. Meanwhile, Cora's younger sister Marie married Hippolyte Bruyères in 1834 and moved to a small country house in Quinçay not more than 30 kilometres distant from Cora, where she was joined by her father.

Cora and François Millet had five children. The first died shortly after birth, and there were three other sons and a daughter, each born a couple of years apart after 1825. Not one outlived their mother. The second son died aged ten; the third son died while at agricultural college, aged twenty; their daughter died at thirty-three, but had married and given birth to three daughters of her own; and their eldest son, a bachelor, died at the age of forty-five in 1871. Cora found this difficult to bear. In a letter to her great-niece Isaure written some time in the early 1880s, she scrawled across the top of the sheet: 'Je suis bien malheureuse – je suis seule!' (I am really unhappy – I am alone!).

FRANÇOIS MILLET

As François was her mother's brother, Cora's maternal grandparents were his parents too, and we have already noticed that they hailed from Nantes in Brittany and had been plantation managers and owners in the Caribbean. Both François and his sister were born at Jérémie on the westernmost promontory of Saint-Domingue (the birthplace of Alexandre Dumas' father, the first black general in the French army). As François was orphaned by the age of fifteen, his grandfather Pierre Millet took on the role of guardian. Pierre was a man of some heft in Breton affairs: merchant, shipowner, plantation owner on Saint-Domingue, consul and alderman of the town of Nantes, sometime representative of Nantais mercantile interests at the *conseil du roi* at Versailles and *fermier général*, tax farmer, of the customs and excise for Brittany.

François first enters the official record with his marriage at the age of nineteen to Bonne Angélique Giroud in 1796. She too was the offspring of a mercantile family in Nantes. On his wedding-day François was living on the island of Belle-Isle in Quiberon Bay off the coast of Vannes. The young couple had two sons. Although no documentation has yet been discovered, the marriage did not prosper. A genealogical note survives among the papers of Cora's great-niece Isaure Schéfer that states it ended in divorce. François seems to have cared for his children himself and they remained in contact with their step-mother Cora (who was no more than two years older than them) until the end of their lives.

As he came to maturity at a time of almost constant warfare, it is hardly surprising that François opted for a military career. However, rather than a front-line role, he was employed in the commissariat. He served in Spain during the Peninsular War as adjutant to the *Commissaires des guerres*, the department charged with every aspect of support, payment and supply of the army – an office filled by Stendhal when serving in Germany in 1806–08. Millet's Spanish campaign was crowned by appointment as governor of the Catalan city of Gerona in 1814, although his tenure was brief, the French being ousted from the province in the spring of that year. His commander-in-chief, and Governor General of the province in 1810–11, was Marshal Étienne MacDonald, Duke of Taranto, although ill-health soon forced him to give up these posts (his next field of battle being Russia). Catalonia must have been the occasion of the two men meeting and some years afterwards the association was resumed. After the Marshal had safely navigated the regime-change that occurred with the Bourbon restoration and was appointed a major-general of the royal bodyguard, he continued to serve the Bourbons until the July Revolution of 1830. François Millet, meanwhile, remained in military administration, the *Commissaires des guerres* being reconstituted by Louis XVIII as the *Intendance militaire*. During the 1820s he may have served in Saverne in Alsace and in Limoges, but more importantly he was secretary to Marshal MacDonald in his capacity as Grand Chancellor of the Legion of Honour and from 1823, *chef de bureau* of the Legion (François was himself an officer of the Legion). The connection with MacDonald has some bearing on the *Maison rustique* because one of its very few recipes having reference to an identifiable person is one for Marshal MacDonald's coffee creams in the chapter on home-made sweets. In the 1830s, François served as *sous-intendant militaire de première classe* (in military rank, equivalent to lieutenant-colonel, hitherto he had been an *adjoint* or adjutant) first at Châtellerault, then at Poitiers, before retirement to his own estate. *Sous-intendants* were on post in their localities to look after all aspects of military administration: payment, billetting, uniforms, camps, saddlery, subsistence, transport.

The article in the *Revue des deux Mondes* regarding agricultural improvement that was quoted earlier remarked that 'the revolutionary wars and those of the Empire, in spreading our armies across Europe, brought the agricultural practices of various countries to the notice of those of our soldiers who were versed in these matters, and the lessons learned and imparted by these men of action underpinned many aspects of our future prosperity.' François Millet was a case in point. His brother-in-law recalled that when he returned from the war in 1814, his curiosity turned to agriculture and he took every opportunity to improve his knowledge.

Figure 2. Château de la Cataudière, a postcard of the entrance front, 1906.

Figure 3. Château de la Cataudière, the garden front today.

The works of Mathieu de Dombasle became his favourite reading and although he never received direct instruction from the master, he entered into correspondence with him and was the first to introduce the reforms promoted at Dombasle's model farm and school at Roville into Poitou. Later on, he sent both his sons to the agricultural school of Grand-Jouan, north of Nantes, which emulated Roville and was founded by Dombasle's disciple Jules Rieffel (for whom Cora wrote almost her first essay in print).

This new enthusiasm needed an outlet and five years after the war's end, François bought the small property (100 hectares) of la Cataudière in the commune of Availles-en-Châtellerault. This was to be his and Cora's home until the end of the 1840s.

CHÂTEAU DE LA CATAUDIÈRE

La Cataudière is a charming *gentilhommière* rather than a mansion of the nobility. Externally, it is much the same today as it was in the nineteenth century, although the offices and appurtenances have changed somewhat since a plan of the curtilage was drawn for the cadastral survey of 1810. The core of the building dates from 1663, and the handsome chapel at one end of the range marks it as some degree more elaborate a property than those described by Mme Millet-Robinet in her chapters on the ideal farmhouse. The estate lies at the wooded edge of the commune, in the village of Prinçay, which was absorbed by Availles in 1818. A Gallo-Roman tomb was discovered in fields north of the château by François Millet in 1841, doubtless an unintended consequence of agricultural improvement. The area is now designated an official archaeological zone by the commune.

Availles and Prinçay boast other estates, both older and more distinguished than la Cataudière. The earliest, dating from the twelfth century, is la Tour d'Oyré, founded by Raoul le Faye, younger son of Viscount Aimery of Châtellerault, uncle of Eleanor of Aquitaine and seneschal of Aquitaine. Owners of the château in the later nineteenth century included the dramatist Ludovic Halévy (father of the historian Élie Halévy) and the composer Charles Gounod. The property now known as the Pigeonnier du Perron was inherited by the philosopher René Descartes, who liked to style himself Sieur du Perron. His father was from Châtellerault. Le Perron was no more than a farmhouse, a *métairie*, held on a basis of crop-sharing. Meanwhile, in the same hamlet of Prinçay as

la Cataudière, the central range of Château de la Doubtière was built in
the eighteenth century by Joseph François Dupleix, the French Governor-
General of India who was worsted by Clive in the Carnatic Wars. La
Doubtière is close to deep quarries that were once used to grow mushrooms
and are home to several species of bats, not least the greater horseshoe.

The subsequent history of la Cataudière has left it in fine condition but
with signs of previous occupants altered or suppressed. It was not helped
in this regard by being a private secondary school for the latter part of
the twentieth century and then being occupied by a new-age community
originating in Belgium. It is now back in private, family hands.

The first child born to Cora and François, who survived but a few brief
days, was born in Paris; all her four others saw the first light of day at la
Cataudière. Meanwhile, François was occupied in Paris at the chancery
of the Legion of Honour and it was only with his appointment as *sous-
intendant militaire* at Châtellerault in 1830 that he was able to devote all
his energies to agricultural improvement in Poitou. His brother-in-law
catalogued some of his activities: sowing grassland leys; cultivating root
crops (he was a pioneer of Jerusalem artichokes for example); introduction
of improved breeds of livestock and better housing for them; changing over
to four-field rotations rather than the traditional system of leaving land
to lie fallow; using modern ploughs, as had been developed by Mathieu
de Dombasle, and harrows with iron tines; employing stone rollers and
rolling ploughland; deep ploughing; and using scythes rather than sickles
for harvesting. All these, he commented, transformed what up to that date
had been standard practice in the region. His work did not go unnoticed:
prizes and awards were accorded him by the Société centrale d'agriculture
de Paris as well as the societies of Tours, Poitiers and Châtellerault. That
farming was relatively backward in Poitou is confirmed by a tract written
by one Alix Sauzeau, 'farmer at Granzay' (a village near Niort, south-west
of Poitiers) in 1844 called *Agriculture de partie du Poitou* (Agriculture of
part of Poitou), in which he celebrates recent progress but draws attention
to much conservatism and bad practice. Cora Millet-Robinet herself tells a
story of her close encounter with ignorance when exploring a district with a
view to buying a new estate in the late 1840s. They visited a domaine owned
by a peasant couple that were not so plumb stupid as their neighbours but
who had none the less let the house collapse around them and apparently

encouraged nothing but weeds of the worst sort in the orchard, garden and home fields. When taxed with this neglect, the farmer replied that his wife preferred the weeds to cultivated leys and that the ivy choking the fruit trees was grand fodder for the cattle in winter.

While applauding François Millet for his initiatives, Cora Millet-Robinet interests us the more. She was ever insistent of the significant role that a woman must play in a farming household. It was not the same as in town, she once wrote, where the wife had no practical function in household matters (neither earning money nor undertaking the day-to-day labour). In the country, 'if the man is the great wheel which drives the mill, then the woman is the millstone and nothing will be achieved without her action.' How true this was at la Cataudière. Her husband was often absent on official duties and it fell to her to implement his proposals on the ground. This close involvement in running the enterprise was, she admitted, the impetus and the necessary understanding she needed to be able to write. Without it, she would have known nothing: 'This is how I learnt to be a farmer and acquire the agricultural expertise which allowed me to publish my *Maison rustique des dames*. That work is the fruit of my experience, not just something learned from books.'

OF SILK AND SILKWORMS

Although the intention at la Cataudière was one of broad agricultural improvement, a specific aspect came to occupy centre-stage, silk. Silk had been produced in France since the fifteenth century when Louis XI had invited weavers from Italy and Greece to set up in Tours. White mulberries were needed to feed the silkworms (they eat little else) so the early history of silk in France is the establishment of the mulberry, by such people as François Traucat, Olivier de Serres, and Louis XIV's minister Colbert. The centre of gravity of the nascent industry drifted southwards from the Touraine in the seventeenth and eighteenth centuries, not least because those climes were extremely well suited to the mulberry. Numbers of trees increased greatly, for example in the Cévennes, after the great frost of 1709 wiped out whole tracts of chestnuts. The mulberry was called 'the golden tree' (*l'arbre d'or*) thanks to its utility as a marginal cash crop for peasants and small farmers. The silk industry was set back by the departure of Huguenots after the revocation of the Edict of Nantes in 1685 (to the benefit of Spitalfields) but began to grow again, especially with improved machinery, during the next century. At first, home production of silk was unable to keep up with the expansion of weaving, but output of silk cocoons rose dramatically in the first half of the nineteenth century, from about 4–5,000 tons in 1804 to over 25,000 tons in 1853. To this expanding industry, the Millets wished to contribute. Their achievements would have been less, however, had it not been for the encouragement and co-operation of Cora's brother Stéphane.

STÉPHANE ROBINET

Stéphane (1796–1869) was the eldest child of Joachim and Laure Robinet. He had a long and successful career as a chemist, pharmacist and freelance expert in the production of silk. He was also an accomplished amateur sculptor, exhibiting at the Paris Salons of 1834 and 1835, and making the bust of Cora illustrated here (figure 4). Even though we know nothing of Cora's intellectual formation as a young girl, if her brother's is anything to go by, she did not lack for the right company or cast of mind. His parents sent him in 1807 to Worms in Germany for his schooling. Displaying an aptitude for science, his family's acquaintance with the widow of the celebrated chemist Antoine-François de Fourcroy (d. 1809) gained him admittance in 1812 to the laboratory of Fourcroy's associate Louis-Nicolas Vauquelin (1763–1829), sometime president of the Pharmaceutical Society of Paris and professor of chemistry at the Collège de France. It is worth noting that Cora makes one of her few personal interventions à propos Fourcroy in chapter IX of *Maison rustique*. She describes a fireplace designed by him and remarks, 'I have seen it in action in the home of the sainted chemist's widow and in those of her friends.'

In 1816, Stéphane decided that he should pursue a more commercial line of work and transferred from Vauquelin's laboratory in the Jardin des Plantes (the Paris botanic garden) to the celebrated pharmacy kept by the widow of Bertrand Pelletier in the rue Jacob. Six years of study enabled him to qualify in 1822, in which year he married, set up shop on his own account, and was received as a full member into the Société de pharmacie – he was to become its president in 1832 and 1862. The next few years saw a stream of publications, for instance on the chemical analysis of plants. He was secretary of the Société de chimie médicale in 1824 and elected member

Figure 4. A bust of Cora Millet-Robinet by her brother Stéphane.

of the Académie royale de médécine (section de pharmacie) in 1825 – he was to be vice-president in 1860 and president in 1861. In 1825, with Vauquelin and others, he founded the *Journal de chimie médicale* (Journal of medical chemistry), which he then edited for ten years. He was also a good friend of the group of agricultural theorists and educators behind the *Maison rustique du XIXe siècle* and joined them in the production of the *Journal d'Agriculture pratique*. He was appointed to the Legion of Honour in 1831 – and, while on a quasi-military theme, he was also battalion commander in the 10th legion of the National Guard in Paris from 1830 to 1848.

His steady progress through life came to an abrupt halt with the death of his wife, Jenny Richard, in 1832, leaving him bereft with three children under seven. He sought a radical change of direction, gave up his dispensary and eventually joined his sister in Poitou in 1836 or 1837. He also turned his focus towards a single object: the improvement of the silk industry in France. His success was such as to earn the honorific 'professor' for his free public lectures in Paris and Poitiers on silk production from 1838 to 1843, although he held no official post. For the next ten years he was a partner in the enterprise at la Cataudière and a driving force in its involvement in silk and silkworms. When the Millets moved from la

Cataudière to their new property near Loches after 1847, Stéphane Robinet resumed his engagement with the wider world of science. At the end of his life, his most important contribution was as member of a commission overseeing the construction of an aqueduct bringing water from the River Dhuis in the Aisne to a thirsty Paris 131 kilometres to the east. He died leaving unfinished his hydrographic dictionary for the whole of France.

MORE SILKWORMS

This small family group, therefore, set about demonstrating to all Poitou the virtues of silk production. The first thing to do was to plant mulberry trees. In 1834, more than 20,000 were set in 2 hectares of ground at la Cataudière (to obtain 46 kilograms of cocoons, silkworms might consume 1,000 kilograms of white mulberry leaves). Then there needed to be the buildings in which to raise the silkworms: they did not hang off twigs in the open air, but were carefully housed and fed harvested leaves – although, in fact, Cora did attempt one cycle in the open air in 1838. A magnanery (the building for keeping and breeding silkworms, from the French *magnanerie* which derives in turn from the Occitan for silkworm, *magnan*) was built in Poitiers as a model establishment for the department of the Vienne in 1836 and a second one was developed at la Cataudière which came to be Cora's specific responsibility. At the same time, Stéphane began producing a host of publications and inventions concerning the inner workings of the magnanery, spinning thread and processing the silkworms' food. All his inventions were placed in the public domain for the benefit of all, he took out no patents. Their work involved improvements and experiments with the process of bringing silkworms to maturity, as well as breeding new varieties such as the one named after its creator, Cora. It encompassed not only the worms and their cocoons, but the production of the thread itself. Many were the prizes accorded the partnership by agricultural societies in Paris and the provinces; perhaps most impressive were the bronze and silver medals at the Industrial Exhibitions of 1839 and 1844 respectively, as well as a gold medal from the Société royale et centrale d'agriculture.

There were many reasons why they might have thought silk worth all this time and trouble. It was a growing market, a useful source of cash for the agricultural sector. It was also a very technical process, which repaid study and improvement. The risks of disease and losses were manifold, usually stemming from bad practice. While the Millets may have seen silk as an income stream, their role was educational: the Poitiers magnanery was a 'model' installation for the department as a whole.

To Cora Millet-Robinet, silkworms offered her readers another source of independent income or route to self-sufficiency. Keeping bees was another solution. Earlier writers, for instance Mme Gacon-Dufour, were very keen on bees and honey. But in fact Cora had no chapters devoted to bees or silkworms in her earlier editions, only with the tenth issue of 1877 do they get a mention. There, she speaks fondly of her involvement in silk production and urges her readers to take it up, to provide an income from the fruits of their labour in which they can take a justifiable pride. She had already made this claim to the Société agricole of Poitiers in 1838 when she wrote that small family magnaneries were particularly suited to female direction (exploiting the maternal instinct) and that the income deriving from them was of especial value to the womenfolk.

The Millets established a third magnanery at Loches, a town in the Indre-et-Loire department to the north-east of Châtellerault, in 1847. This was clearly in response to their planned sale of la Cataudière for it was but a few miles distant from their new property, the Domaine de Pont in the commune of Genillé close to the small town of Montrésor. The next year, Stéphane took himself off on a winter's sojourn in Egypt, having given the last of his public lectures on sericulture. This appears to be the moment when he returned to wider scientific studies. In 1853, the departmental magnanery at Poitiers closed its doors. This was at a critical juncture in French silk production. Over-exuberance in the market had given rise to a series of crippling diseases. Some of these stemmed from bad management either in the magnaneries themselves or in the quality of feed provided. Eventually, the government called in Louis Pasteur to advise on the matter, but not before production was reduced to a fraction of its peak. Whether problems such as these had anything to do with the Millets' removal from la Cataudière is not known.

DOMAINE DE PONT

The Domaine de Pont is now sometimes called the Château de Pont. Today, the estate is largely devoted to the vine. When the Millets bought the property in 1847, if Cora's account is to be believed, much was in ruins,

Figure 5. Château de Pont, the original part of the house, as it is today.

Figure 6. Château de Pont, the front added by François Millet, ca. 1847.

dating back to the sixteenth century. They wrapped a new house around what remained of the original structure. They do not appear to have put la Cataudière on the market until the end of 1849, when it was advertised as having a net income of 5,600 francs, two farmyards, a handsome family dwelling, beautiful views, hunting and fishing, vineyards and excellent soils. Their address by the time of this advertisement was Château de Pont, so the building work must have been rapidly undertaken.

We are fortunate to have a series of articles that Cora wrote in 1871 for *Le Magasin pittoresque*, an illustrated miscellany that had great sale from its foundation (in emulation of the English *Penny Magazine*) in 1833. Her object was to explain to an imaginary correspondent how best she should arrange matters when effecting a move from the city to the country. Happily for us, she offered sketch plans of possible residences. Two are for substantial farmhouses such as she describes in the opening chapters of the *Maison rustique*; then there are plans for something altogether more impressive which, she confesses, is the house she had built for herself: in other words, the Château de Pont at Genillé (figures 5 and 6). The present house conforms to her drawings (figures 7 and 8). This was no mean undertaking, especially as her husband François was by this time over 70 years-old, however their eldest son Étienne had been recruited to help run the estate – in 1852 he won a second prize from the departmental agricultural society for best-managed enterprise. The parish history of Genillé by Christophe Meunier makes clear that the Millets were still closely involved in silk production, even if M. Meunier does ignore the fact that so glorious an ornament of French practical literature once lived in his native village. There was, of course, the magnanery they had established at Loches, and then there was the record of the principal landowner in the commune: an improving landlord, once a medical man, Jacques-Philippe Dubreuil-Charmontel. François Millet made an extensive report to the Société royale et centrale d'agriculture in 1848 on the doctor's efforts to bring his holding up to modern standards, noting among other things the planting of 12,000 white mulberry trees to supply leaves to the producers of Loches.

François Millet died in 1860. Cora had two children still living, but her son Étienne who had been helping on the estate, had by this time moved to the Landes in Gascony – this may be why Cora was able to write a short

GROUND FLOOR

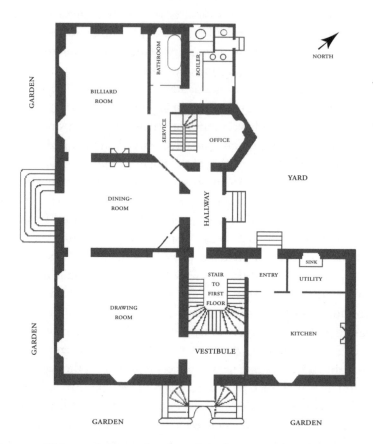

Figure 7. Château de Pont, the plan of the house as printed in Le Magasin pittoresque *in 1871, the ground floor.*

contribution to the *Petite bibliothèque économique et rurale* in 1869 on *foie gras* in the Landes. Her daughter Lucie had married a lawyer and had a house in Poitiers. It is not known where Cora settled immediately after her loss. She may have lived with one of her relations, but her name does not appear on the census lists for any of the likely candidates. We do not find her in the official record again until the census of 1876, when she was identified as the owner of a small farm, la Bernonnière (now Berlonnière), in the village of Saint-Benoît, just south of Poitiers. Before the Revolution, the village had the name of Saint-Benoît-de-Quinçay and was home to an

FIRST FLOOR

Figure 8. Château de Pont, the plan of the house as printed in Le Magasin pittoresque *in 1871, the first floor.*

ancient abbey. La Bernonnière was once part of the abbey's estate (figure 9). After the Revolution, the abbey dissolved, the parishioners renamed the village Quinçay-les-Plaisirs before it reverted to Saint-Benoît *tout court*. Cora remained here until her death in 1890.

It is from these years that a few letters from Cora have survived. They show her feeling slightly isolated from the world, a situation not helped by a progressive loss of sight, so that her letters, had to be written by an amanuensis after 1880, though she could still pen the odd scrawled phrase or scribble her signature. But she was still active. In the autumn of

Figure 9. La Bernonnière, Saint-Benoît, where Cora spent the last years of her life.

1881 she's packing chestnuts off to her great-niece, bottling tomatoes and harvesting cauliflowers. All through these years she is supervising revisions to the *Maison rustique* (largely the work of, or organized by, her great-niece and nephew) and chivvying her publisher for a new version of her *Conseils aux jeunes femmes sur leur condition et leurs devoirs de mère*. Nor does she let up on arranging a new contract with the Librairie agricole to ensure that matters are in order at the end of her life. But she does feel isolated; her house, she complains, is not as comfortable as her sister Marie's, nor the company as stimulating.

That sister lived in the village of Quinçay (another Quinçay) about 15 kilometres away. Her house, the Château Gaillard, had been the property of her second husband, Hippolyte Bruyères, who had died in 1855. Her two children had predeceased their father. Bruyères was a painter. His portrait of Cora is the frontispiece to this book, and prints of his paintings (largely historical and genre) can still be purchased. He wrote and illustrated a treatise on phrenology, *La Phrénologie: Le Geste et la physionomie mis en scène* ([Phrenology: gesture and physionomy displayed], Aubert, 1847). His qualification was that he was the stepson of Johann Gaspar Spurzheim (1766–1832), the founder, with Franz Joseph Gall, of the science of phrenology (and the coiner of the word itself).

Figure 10. Cora Millet-Robinet's gravestone today, in the cemetery at Quinçay, Vienne.

As Cora's life drew to a close, she was accorded her greatest honour by the French state, being made a *chevalier de l'ordre du Mérite agricole* in December 1884. The Order had been created by the French minister of agriculture twelve months before and Cora was one of the first two women *chevaliers*, cited for her agricultural activities and her writings. The other was Marie-Anne Thomas from the village of Penhars in Finistère, whose contribution to farming matters has not so far been identified.

After her death in December 1890, her publisher Louis Bourguignon wrote a heartfelt tribute for the pages of the *Journal d'Agriculture pratique*. Self-interest might have some bearing on his views, but his words reflect the esteem France had for her:

> We had the honour of knowing this worthy woman for the last twenty years, and the memory of her remarkable qualities will live long with us. She worked up until the last day, alert to any developments, always seeking some improvement to incorporate in each new edition of her masterpiece, the *Maison rustique des dames*, which has been and

remains the best of guides for the housewife. You needed to witness just how passionate she was about any new invention that might have bearing on domestic economy, whenever she thought them practical and useful, but also how careful she was to evaluate them before recommending them.

No one understood better, nor explained better than Mme Millet-Robinet, the significant part of women in modern society.... What particularly distinguishes [her] books is that from the first line to the last, the author has a single thought and a single end in sight: instructing women in the duties that flow from their roles as mother and mistress of the house.

Cora was buried next to other members of her family, all in identical tombs, in the cemetery at Quinçay (figure 10).

CORA MILLET-ROBINET: A BIBLIOGRAPHY

Cora Millet-Robinet wrote extensively, both books and contributions to agricultural journals, with a certain amount of freelance journalism elsewhere. Many of her more substantial pieces for journals found their way into print for separate sale. Almost without exception, her books appeared under the imprint of the Librairie agricole de la Maison rustique or its affiliates.

Her first essays into print were not until she had reached her fortieth birthday, when she joined with her husband and brother in accounts of their efforts to raise silkworms in Poitiers and at la Cataudière in 1838–41, delivered in the first instance to various agricultural journals. Had she had her own way, her first appearance would have been entirely on her own account. In 1839, she 'threw a few words on paper,' as she put it, on the subject of education to better fit girls for a life agricultural. She felt strongly, and the matter is constantly returned to in her *Maison rustique*, that they were taught mere fripperies and extravagances and thus had no desire at all to marry farmers. As a result, she concluded, all the young farmers were unhappy with their lot and deprived of fitting helpmeets. Far better that girls should be taught the realities, and joys, of country life, of raising healthy and right-thinking children, of looking after animals. She showed her essay to her brother and he tried to get it published in several agricultural journals. To no avail, until 1846 when the great improver Jules Rieffel, one of Mathieu de Dombasle's principal disciples, printed it in his *Agriculture de l'Ouest de la France*. Her educational syllabus, it has to be said, read very like a table of contents for her first two published books.

Cora's proper debut was her *Conseils aux jeunes femmes sur leur condition et leurs devoirs de mère, pendant l'allaitement* (Advice to young women on their maternal condition and duties when breast-feeding) of 1841. This is an attractive book, drawing closely on her own experience as a nursing mother, which guides the novice through infancy (taking in teething and walking) but no further. She was not the only one to urge mothers to nurse their offspring: Rousseau had made a good start and several of her female domestic-economy predecessors had advocated breast-feeding. But among the middle classes, the wet-nurse was still in demand, even if the usual thing was to have her at home under your own supervision, rather than merely sending the infant off to who knows what squalid circumstance. Emmanuelle Romanet points out that at the end of the century, in France, 2.8 per cent of all births in Lille were suckled by wet-nurses, 9.6 per cent in Bordeaux, 29.3 per cent in Paris and 47.9 per cent in Lyon.

A variant title was given to the same book (*Conseils aux jeunes femmes sur l'éducation de la première enfance* [Advice to young women on bringing up a newborn child]) in 1855, but reverted to the original for a second edition in 1862. It does not seem to have been reissued. However, the Librairie agricole recognized its value and wished to produce a thorough revision some time in the 1870s. Judging from Cora's letters to her great-niece, some of this work was done by herself, but Louis Bourguignon wanted a medical contribution to make it both more extensive and more reliable. He asked Émile Allix to undertake the work. Allix was Victor Hugo's doctor during his exile in Jersey. He had already written a book on the physiology of infants and was medical inspector of child protection and nurseries in Paris. (His brother Jules was an eccentric of the first rank. Imprisoned for his republican sympathies by Napoleon III, he was not only somewhat mad but an advocate of the 'snail telegraph' whereby snails could transmit messages anywhere in the world thanks to their 'sympathetic communication'.) Allix took a very long time to finish his contribution, much to Cora's frustration. The reissue, under the new title of *Le Livre des jeunes mères, la nourrice et le nourrisson* (The book for young mothers, breastfeeding and the baby at the breast), appeared in 1884 and went through twelve editions until 1922, the last being revised yet again by Mme Le Bihan-Rolland. This book had an unexpected transatlantic ripple. Cora Millet Holden was an artist born in Cleveland, Ohio in 1895. Her mother, a doctor, was born Cora Millet Babb. Her grandmother was also a doctor and a feminist. It must have been in homage to an admirable French feminist that these women took her name.

Cora signed her first book 'Cora Millet, née Robinet', as she did too the first edition of her *Maison rustique* in 1845. Subsequent issues, and all her other books, were signed 'Mme Millet-Robinet' or 'Mme Cora Millet-Robinet'. In the census return for 1856, she is listed as Cora Robinet, '*auteur*', as well as wife to François. As the success of *Maison rustique* became more assured as the years passed, so she too became more confident of her status. In venting her spleen at Louis Bourguignon's delays at issuing a new version of her *Conseils* in 1881, she protested that his behaviour was unpardonable given he was dealing with the author of *Maison rustique* that had earned him so much money over the decades.

After *Conseils…*, Cora's next book was indeed the *Maison rustique* in 1844/5. The series of editions over more than seventy years has already been sketched in. It was in every sense her *magnum opus*. Much of her subsequent output depended on it for content and approach.

A book that appeared in the early 1850s was *Le jardinier des fenêtres, des appartements et des petits jardins* (Gardening for window-boxes, apartments and small gardens). This is listed in the catalogue of the Bibliothèque nationale, but undated. A third edition was listed by the Librairie agricole in 1853 and the title crops up again as an Italian translation in about 1870 from a Milanese publisher. By the end of the 1850s, the Librairie agricole published something with the same title, but over the name of Jules Rémy, with a fourth edition coming out in 1861. (Window boxes were quite a popular subject in nineteenth-century France. Other books on the topic are recorded by P. Boitard [Audot, 1823] and Maurice Cristal [Garnier, 1865].)

Definitely from Cora's pen is the *Manuel de l'éleveur des oiseaux de basse-cour et du lapin domestique* (Poultry- and domestic rabbit-keeper's manual) which was first printed after 1850 with a second edition dated 1853 as part of the Librairie agricole's co-operative venture with the ministry of agriculture in their series *Bibliothèque du cultivateur*. The book went through several editions and impressions with a major revision by René Girardeau just before the First World War, which then went through another four editions until 1944. By this time the poultry and rabbits had been joined by pigeons in the title. Understandably, there was much from the *Maison rustique* in the text, but extra material was incorporated – for example, details of slaughter, and some new species of poultry. The book was translated into Danish under the title *Fjerkræets Opdrætning* in 1865; there was a further version in 1881.

Another recycling of her *Maison rustique* was also part of the *Bibliothèque du cultivateur*. This was *Économie domestique* (Domestic economy), first appearing in 1853 and going through at least four editions until 1872. The book was essentially the first half of the first volume of the *Maison rustique*, the text hardly changed. This was translated into Italian in 1891 in Turin.

In the same collection, Cora wrote an excellent guide to conserving fruit (including many fruit-based products such as drinks and ices), *Conservation des fruits* (Preserving fruits). This came out in a single edition in 1854. The core of the work might well have been the *Maison rustique*, but it was not a slavish copy.

At the end of the 1850s, Mme Millet-Robinet wrote two books for the Poitiers publisher G. Hilleret. Both allowed her space to expand her original approach. The first was a manual for servants, *Le Bon domestique, instructions pratiques sur la manière de bien servir, à l'usage des maîtres et des domestiques* (The good servant, useful instructions on good service, for the use of masters and servants). Her second title was *La Routine vaincue par le progrès, histoire agricole et morale* (Routine overcome by progress, an agricultural moral tale), 1860, described as a practical guide for the farmer and the farmer's wife, and an annex to the *Maison rustique des dames*. Practical indeed it was, for the form of an allegorical tale was highjacked by an informative, though hardly gripping, account of improved agriculture. M. Progrès vanquished, and ultimately converted, the stick-in-the-mud M. Routineau thanks to his his go-ahead approach to farming. It all ended happily.

Cora's final book was published in 1868, thereafter it was either journalism or reissues. This was *Maison rustique des enfants* (The children's country house), in quarto, not the usual compact duodecimo. Print, margins and production were generous and its didactic purpose sums up her larger intentions: to bring the joys of country life to all. She wrote it for her grandchildren. Once again, it is an account of good agricultural practice, charmingly and instructively told. It also revisits the household of M. Progrès. Rather endearingly, both these fictional narratives feature an old soldier who takes up the cause of modern agriculture with enthusiasm.

Cora proudly wore her membership of various agricultural societies like medals on her chest, crowned by the foreign decoration from the royal academy in Turin. Women were rarely admitted as full members, permitted only to be correspondents, and she doubtless recalled the difficulties she met trying to place her first contribution on women's education, when she had to rely on the intercession of her brother. Her name crops up frequently in their various bulletins and proceedings, often to do with her work with silkworms, but she wrote most often for the *Journal d'Agriculture pratique* with which Stéphane Robinet was closely associated (and which, of course, came from the same publisher as her own books). We have referred earlier to some pieces she had in *Le Magasin pittoresque* in the years 1870–1872. The editorial footnote to her first appearance is some measure of the world's respect: 'The author of the much-esteemed book *La Maison rustique des dames*, which most of our readers will certainly know. We are happy to announce that Mme Cora Millet is willing to share in our work: we hold her co-operation in the highest regard.' At about the same time, she was contributing articles to the Québécois weekly paper, the *Gazette des campagnes*, on the role of women in agriculture. This was a hot topic among the Canadian farming community and a study by Martine Tremblay makes clear the weight accorded her opinions.

CORA MILLET-ROBINET'S REPUTATION

Cora's appointment as a chevalier of the order of Mérite agricole was sign enough of her standing in the world at large, or at least in the world of France. But other indications abound. In the 1960s and '70s a remarkable investigation was undertaken of the Burgundian village of Minot by a small group of ethnographers, the most famous of whom was the incomparable Yvonne Verdier. One of her colleagues, Françoise Zonabend, wrote about how gardening was always thought women's work and how the grandmothers would teach their children's offspring all they knew of the art. 'Rural ladies at the beginning of the century,' she commented, 'derived all their knowledge from the same bible, *La Maison rustique des dames* by Madame Millet-Robinet.' Another modern testimony to its ubiquity is an attractive essay on how changes in French domestic economy can be traced through the various editions of the *Maison rustique*. The author was Georges-Henri Bousquet and while noting that the book was meant for farming families, he observed that plenty of townsfolk relied on it too. 'My grandmother Bousquet,' he recalled, 'who settled in the Batignolles district of Paris after her marriage in 1868, possessed it, although she certainly had nothing to do with the rural economy.' He goes on to aver that all 'the generation of a certain age … remember the book perfectly.' This earlier universal acquaintance is not matched by that of their descendants. It is not easy today to find a Frenchman who knows the name Millet-Robinet at all, be they farmer, gardener, cook, *boulevardier* or scholar.

Some ten years before Madame Bousquet's marriage, Cora had been awarded a first-class medal for her writings at the Paris Universal Exhibition of 1855. Just a year before those nuptials, the fledgling mathematician Henri Poincaré gave his doting mother a copy of the *Maison rustique*, which must have been about the time that Colette's mother Sidonie was relying on Cora's instructions for the house, kitchen and garden at every turn. Colette herself came to value the *Maison rustique*: 'Mme Millet-Robinet and her sweet science of housewifery, of grafting, of cooking and of keeping animals is always to hand.' Her English biographer, Margaret Crosland, described Colette's enthusiastic gardening and over-enthusiastic dressmaking at her summer house near Saint-Malo, both activities guided – more or less successfully – by Millet-Robinet: 'Colette prided herself on her practical touch, but no amount of reading how to do it books can teach some things. Her domestic bible was *La Maison Rustique des Dames*, by Madame Millet-Robinet, a delightful old book describing the perfect housewife.' Today, the restoration of Colette's birthplace in Burgundy goes on apace, with Millet-Robinet the constant resource for reconstructing the garden.

Mme Cora is less well remembered for her cookery than for her precepts of family life and household management. Competition at the kitchen hearth was perhaps more intense, other authorities took precedence. None the less, Georges Vicaire, in his *Bibliographie gastronomique* of 1890 was minded to comment, 'This work has become an absolute classic and is a complete small encyclopedia of great utility to many housewives. The culinary part is very important and takes up, without any other matter, a good half of the first volume.' Praise indeed.

Cora was not without her English admirers. One was a painter, Philip Gilbert Hamerton, married to a Frenchwoman and occupying a small farm in Scotland in the 1860s. His book, *A Painter's Camp in the Highlands and Thoughts about Art* (1862) opened with a discussion of whether painters should write about art themselves or leave it to more intelligent outside critics. He mused on whether tradesmen ever had the mental equipment to write about their lives: 'Illiterate farmers not only *will* not, but really *cannot* explain their most habitual occupations.... The author of a popular little book, "Our Farm of Four Acres", found that it was useless to consult farmers' wives on the important subject of butter-making.... But when intelligent ladies take to farming, as Madame Millet-Robinet has done, it is astonishing how many things *they* find means to explain, and how lucidly they explain them.' He was lucky, his wife was a friend of Alexandre Bixio, one of the founders of the *Maison rustique du XIXe siècle*, and he had sent them a copy of Cora's book to help these unlikely farmers on their smallholding. Hamerton's wife wrote her own memoirs, including an account of their farming in the north and their proposed migration to southern France to set up closer to her father. 'I had diligently applied myself to our small farm and garden, with the help of a most valuable and simple guide, "La Maison Rustique des Dames," by Madame Millet-Robinet, ... and I had often thought that if my efforts were not always thwarted by the inclemency of the weather, I might count upon a fair return.' She had to persuade her father, a gasworks manager, that country life would be possible, explaining that 'there were now many gentlemen-farmers who did not neglect either their work on the land or their own culture – M. and Madame Millet-Robinet might be cited as examples.' Just as Cora intended, her life and work showed that people could flee the town for a rural idyll – so long as they were properly equipped with instruction.

Another warm testimonial comes from Mrs C.W. Earle, a gardening writer who put together some pleasing essays in *Pot-Pourri from a Surrey Garden* (1897). 'The real fault,' she remarked, 'of all the houses I go into to-day, my own included, though less so than some, is that they are far too full. Things are sure to accumulate. Avoid rubbish, frills and valances, draperies and bows, and all the terrible devices of the modern upholsterer. … I have a French domestic book which I think fascinating and instructive, just because it is French, and much less showy and more primitive than English books of the same kind. It is in two volumes, is called "Maison Rustique des Dames" and is by Madame Millet Robinet. It has had an immense sale in France, and all the little details of household life seem more dignified and less tiresome when read in excellent French.'

Apart from these enthusiastic endorsements, I have not identified any obvious connection between the growing number of English cookery books that purported to describe French cookery for people of modest income and the specific content of the *Maison rustique*. Menon's *Cuisinière bourgeoise* was translated as early as 1793 (as *The French Family Cook*). Audot was Englished in 1846 (as *French Domestic Cookery Combining Elegance with Economy*). A very similarly titled work, *French Domestic Cookery Combining Economy with Elegance*, 'by an English physician many years resident in France', which came out in 1825 does not seem to depend on Audot at all. Anne Cobbett, William's daughter, wrote an excellent handbook, *The English Housekeeper: or, Manual of Domestic Management* in 1835 which includes more general advice on the household than most, including an eloquent descant on female education that Cora would have wholly endorsed. She even included advice on the garden and admits she was inspired by *La Maison de campagne* by Aglaé Adanson, a book she once thought of translating but reckoned it too French for her fellow Britons. A book that is imbued with everything French is *Cookery for English Households*, 'by a French Lady' (Macmillan, 1864). The only comment she makes about French cookery books is that most of what Alexis Soyer suggests is too elaborate for the likes of her readers. Her recipes have points of similarity with those of Mme Millet-Robinet both in method, ingredients and that they both espouse simplicity before show. They are also quite close in their choice of repertoire.

MAISON RUSTIQUE DES DAMES

While most attention has so far been paid to the circumstances surrounding the composition of the *Maison rustique*, some few remarks regarding its contents may be apposite, while not wishing to compromise any reader's approach to the text itself.

For whom was Mme Millet-Robinet writing, and why did she think it necessary to write? In her opening comments, she does not mince her words, agriculture was in crisis: 'A seventh of France is uncultivated, and a significant proportion of the land in hand is so badly worked that yields are low and quality poor.' With her book, she aimed to equip a new generation of female readers with sufficient agricultural knowledge and enthusiasm to make them want to join with a freshly educated male workforce (which had been fleeing the land in unprecedented numbers) and render French farming worthwhile once more. 'I will speak of what experience has taught me; it will be a first stone laid in the great edifice of agricultural education for women.'

She did not merely wish to purvey information, however, but rather to impart a love of a whole situation, a location, a status: '[I will] try hard to portray both the charm and powerful appeal that I have found in my new way of life. I will tell of my activities, my pleasures, the duties I have mapped out for myself.' Even at their most mundane, the two volumes of the *Maison rustique* exude affection for the country and, by implication, for the act of leaving the town for pastures new. Rarely are towns mentioned save with disdain (unless the reader has to obtain some useful supply); never are the charms of urban society preferred over country pursuits:

> The pleasures of the summer months are so varied: walks, meals taken under spreading boughs in a beauty spot, rides out in a carriage, on a horse, even on a donkey; fishing, shooting: all these diversions, so costly to townspeople, can be had for next to nothing if you live in the country. Village fiestas, where you go to dance, rackety country weddings, celebrated in the midst of plenty, are sweet delights to be savoured with friends and relations. If these affairs have none of the show of those in town, nor do they have their stiffness and ceremony.

While there can be no doubt as to the gender of her audience, its affluence and social standing may be slightly less certain. Millet-Robinet's instructions are all-embracing, descending to such relative simplicities as how best to express oneself in the metric system. She had no illusions about the pretensions of many of her readers: 'I am going to give a few details about service at table which both masters and servants may find profitable. If these details seem overly fussy, or even superfluous, to those women who have always lived in good society and know them already, they will be, I think, of great utility to women who have come out of boarding school to get married or who, never having been in the world, know nothing of how guests are received.' She knew that many would know nothing of what she wrote, that their education was almost nil, their experience less than that. This may explain why she was so prescriptive, and certainly often literal-minded in her expressions: they knew nothing at all, a *tabula rasa*.

Did Cora Millet-Robinet patronize her readers? On the one hand her background was both urban and intelligent, and on the other she lived in houses (see above) that were generally a cut above those of her audience. In that series of articles she wrote for *Le Magasin pittoresque* she included plans of two ideal farmhouses (figures 11 and 12). They accord closely with the descriptions in the *Maison rustique* (although she eschewed giving plans in the book, advising readers to apply to an architect). While not nearly so grand as her own places, neither are they farmworkers' cottages. She presumes her readers to be proprietors, or at least substantial tenants, with dining arrangements that do not include the outside labour force – none of those hierarchical tables with farmer at the head, shepherd to one side and herdsman to the other. She expects her audience to go on country walks, to take carriage drives, to have guests for dinner and winter evening parties. Equally, she expects them to be able and willing to cook, to sew, to cast up accounts, and to go into the fields, discuss farming policy with the husband and supervise the labour when he has to be absent. The world she imagines is quite a modern one: servants are certainly essential, but the mistress is no mere ornament:

A mistress of the house has many obligations. The order and perfection she brings to their accomplishment contributes much to the prosperity of the family. She should understand the importance of her role and be resolute in pursuing it; she will find true joy in its performance, stemming from a conviction of her usefulness. She will never be bored, for that stems from idleness or from the futility of our actions; and, once she has banished boredom, content is there to take its place. The slightest act can provoke or renew a sense of enjoyment and, once achieved, life passes so much more rapidly, with that delight that is the true companion of truth and utility.

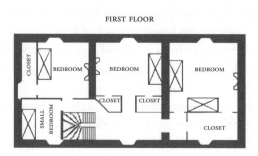

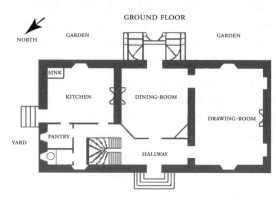

Figure 11. Sketch plan of the smaller of two ideal farmhouses included in an article by Cora in Le Magasin pittoresque *in 1871.*

A young girl you wish to educate so as to equip her to run a farming household must neglect nothing which might improve her mind and allow her to acquire the attributes of society. These attributes will be just as valuable to her in the country as in the town and, as they are more rarely encountered there, they will be the more remarked; careful study will give her more confidence and allow her to converse with her husband on all those topics that only menfolk are interested in; because, if she wishes to please her husband, who is often her only companion, she must endeavour to think as he does. As she should try to make their spare time together a delight, she can quite reasonably give up learning many of the finer and insignificant details of needlework – and be less preoccupied with her personal appearance – so she may pursue those studies her position requires.'

This is a portrait of a woman as a productive economic unit, quite different from the drones of the urban bourgeoisie, and not one who depends on

Figure 12. Sketch plan of the larger of two ideal farmhouses included in an article by Cora in Le Magasin pittoresque *in 1871.*

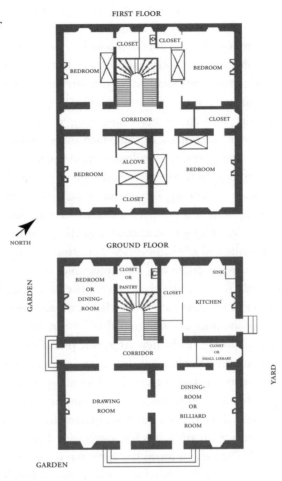

sexual allure as a source of profit: 'Any woman who decides to live in the country, and who takes her duties seriously, must never hesitate to put her hand to the wheel.'

Despite the relative size of the houses she occupied, Cora Millet-Robinet's own establishment appears quite modest, perhaps implying that she lived up to her own ideals of self-reliance. The census return for la Cataudière in 1836 lists only four servants: one bachelor of 30, a married couple of 39 and 33 respectively, with three small children and their grandmother, a 68 year-old widow. Twenty years later, the household at the Château de Pont was not much larger: three single men in their twenties, a female cook, one other female servant and a boy of thirteen. In her old age at la Bernonnière, her servants numbered an old couple and a very young girl.

If she wrote at a critical moment for agriculture, when every sinew of progressives was strained to promote better management and practice, she also stood at a significant juncture in the life domestic. The historian Suzanne Tardieu, in her pioneering analysis of the furnishings and equipment of houses in the Mâconnais *'préindustriel'*, demonstrates how material culture broadened and deepened in the years around 1850. Industrial production provoked a great accumulation of objects, from tableware to bedding, ornaments to lighting, floor-coverings to window-hangings. One reason that nineteenth-century interiors were so cluttered is that shopping was so easy, and so cheap. Mme Millet-Robinet set out to describe and assess these new opportunities to consume, to place them in the context of the well-run household, to suggest how best they might be used. We have already seen that she developed her content from one edition to the next to take novelties into account, thus, a small example, in 1845 she does not mention matches; in 1859 she urges caution in the use and storage of the new strikeable phosphorous matches; in 1893 'she' (posthumously) points out that these dangers can be avoided by the use of safety matches; and in 1920 'she' does not mention matches at all.

In her advice, Mme Millet-Robinet leans vertiginously towards the practical. Not for her random ornament, of dress or of furnishings. Durability, with grace, was her watchword. Mud and dirt were ever-present foes. Realism also informs her approach to man and God. There is almost no mention of the divine in her text, nor of political matters. And man, as opposed to woman, is accorded his customary place at the top of the hierarchy, but it is one which admits the possibility of partnership, not mere command. Her women have an executive role that extends beyond the kitchen and nursery, but they also have their own resorts: 'A lady's bedroom should be a refuge from disturbance, a place of rest and recuperation respected even by the family; in keeping with this, the furniture ought to be of useful simplicity, cleanliness its only ornament. It should include a bed, a mirrored wardrobe or a chest of drawers, a *secrétaire* or small desk, a wooden chest, a comfortable armchair, some more chairs, a stool and a carpet.'

Cora's approach to human relationships other than man and wife is refreshing: her treatment of children is firm but looks forward to independence; her dealings with servants seem exemplary – an element of paternalism such as you might expect, but also a degree of respect for their privacy and identity. She was in favour of allowing some economic participation on the part of servants, for example bonuses or profit-sharing for producing livestock or commodities; she encourages social activities outside the house; she does not insist on burdensome arrangements such as the servants paying for breakages and so forth. The treatment of servants, here as in England, was always a bone of contention, but the depths to which some families might sink, as portrayed in memoirs such as *Jean et Yvonne, domestiques en 1900* (Jean and Yvonne, servants in 1900), are not glimpsed in the pages of the *Maison rustique*.

Of a piece with Millet-Robinet's vision of the role of the mistress in her own household, she expects her to know how to cook, even if not called upon to do so with too great a frequency. The mistress, after all, is already sewing for the family, teaching the children, doing the accounts, supervising the *basse-cour*, dispensing medicine and charity and a host of other things. Her remarks at the beginning of the Kitchen Manual that forms the second half of this volume of *Maison rustique* are to the point:

It is absolutely essential that the mistress of the house knows how to cook. A thousand entirely predictable circumstances may make it necessary for even a rich woman to have to cook at some stage, especially in the country where no opportunity exists, as it does in town, of obtaining supplies from a restaurateur. Even if she does have somewhere to go for help, is it not a great blessing for the mistress who is not wealthy to be able to stand in for her cook at a moment's notice? She will thereby study economy, and avoid imposing on her family a strange and sometimes unwholesome diet; for restaurateurs of the second rank abuse their spices and seasonings to mask the poor quality of the raw materials they employ. And finally, is it not necessary to be able to give helpful advice to an ignorant cook? One can only demand what one knows how to do. The mistress will have only herself to blame for poor food being served if she knows no more than her cook. What can she answer this poor girl when she says, 'Madame, I am doing my best; I don't know how to do otherwise?' Furthermore, a whole host of little expedients may exist in a household that, when properly handled, will result in excellent foodstuffs at very little cost. It is rare that a cook knows how to take advantage of these, and even rarer that thoughts of economy will occur to her spontaneously.

Anyone reading the Kitchen Manual will be struck by its relative conservatism, especially in equipment, and the simplicity of its recipes. We have mentioned earlier that Millet-Robinet and her fellow recipe writers for the bourgeoisie had the more modest segment of that social class in mind. Rich urbanites could consult their Viards or, later, their Dubois, but Millet-Robinet does not even – at least to some extent – come up to Audot's standards. The number of stages to a recipe, the added aromatics, are more at the level of *La Petite Cuisinière habile* than Audot or his ilk. That's not to say that in the lavish deployment of certain ingredients, truffles for instance, Cora has not a more relaxed approach to good value than does the modern cook – but inflation has a way with such things. Conservative too is her relative lack of detail as to quantities (these are particularly nebulous in baking), were we to compare her recipes to her English contemporary Eliza Acton. But the recipes may still, with a little effort, be followed by a modern cook.

On the point of conservatism, Millet-Robinet mentions new developments in kitchen equipment such as the cast-iron range, the Harel stove or the economic stove (*fourneau économique*), but in large part she seems to suggest her recipes be cooked on an open hearth or on the old-fashioned brick- or stone-built charcoal stoves that were current in the eighteenth century. Another feature that may be unfamiliar to the modern reader is Cora's frequent injunction to give a dish top and bottom heat. This may be a tart which is placed on the open hearth beneath a *four de campagne* or Dutch oven, or it is a braise of meat, for example the breast and shoulder of veal on page 469, which is cooked in a pan with top and bottom heat. In this case, the pan has a lid with a raised edge to it (or, more exactly in some examples, a depressed centre) so that embers can be piled on its surface. The modern solution is to place the pan in an oven.

Where Mme Millet-Robinet is nicely up-to-date in her thinking is her advice on family meals. These by no means fit the protein-rich, unbalanced stereotype we hold dear for nineteenth-century dining. Her thoughts about feeding children are also sensible, though we might go easy in introducing them to wine, and her closing remarks on her intended audience in this short extract cannot be repeated too often:

> As a general rule, I do advise a household to adopt the practice of serving two dishes at dinner, or three at the most; one of meat, the other of vegetables, to which can sometimes be joined something from the dairy or a sweet dish. This economical and simple manner of feeding offers more than one advantage: in the first place I think it conducive to good health, of which there is no better protector than moderation – too much variety in food over-excites the stomach; and then it is rare that one does not serve too much food and I am convinced that the slight fatigue provoked each day by so doing is the source of many ailments which are otherwise ascribed to quite different causes; and finally, it spares the servants much time and effort.
>
> Luncheon can be made from the remains of dinner, if there is insufficient left over to provide another dinner. You can add something to that if necessary. I even advise you to accustom the children to a simple lunch, composed of a soup of some sort, usually milk-based, and a nice dish of vegetables or eggs. I am of the opinion that once wine is part of the diet, it is enough to eat meat once a day, although there are many who do not share my views. Very tasty food does not encourage child development or make them vigorous, that will come from simple, healthy food, combined with lots of exercise. As a final point, I would suggest it is good for the children to get used to being less well provided for than their parents, so long as you do it without fuss or severity.
>
> My advice might be criticized by those people who are used to the ways of opulent households, in which the mistress is not concerned with such details, which are entrusted to able servants and performed with more ceremony; but, as I have written already, I do not address these people: they have no need for my humble knowledge; I write for good and simple housewives; I wish to be useful to them, and I hope they welcome my counsels.

While Cora Millet-Robinet seems to have stayed resolutely in Poitou during her working life, her book was intended to be used more widely. She is frank enough about local practices, or differences to the rest of France, but she does not make a point of offering regional dishes in her recipe collection, nor of ignoring other people's habits – for example she cites Flemish and Belgian ways of cooking a number of times. Nor does she personalize her information by name-dropping, anecdote or other means. She refers once to her place of residence (then, in 1859, Genillé in the canton of Montrésor), and she has one recipe linked to a specific individual (Marshal MacDonald, see above). There are a very few Poitevin things, the most obvious being the 'Jaw breaker' or *casse-museau* cake or biscuit on page 632.

THE TRANSLATION AND THE TRANSLATOR'S ACKNOWLEDGEMENTS

Cora Millet-Robinet was careful in her choice of words and clear in her expression of them. She would have made a fine parliamentary draftsman for her clarity and economy. She has a tendency to repeat words for good measure, to ensure she is not misunderstood at any point. Generally, her vocabulary is either accurate or, in the case of adjectives, limited. I have not taken too many liberties, nor attempted to introduce colour or variety where she has eschewed them. Any footnotes in the text which follows are written by the translator.

Millet-Robinet today is most often discussed with reference to her views on child-rearing, the treatment of servants and her dispensing of home-medicines. A measured assessment of her whole output has not yet been undertaken. The single individual deserving most credit for maintaining and increasing Cora's modern reputation is Mme Gloria Godard, a resident also of Availles-en-Châtellerault. Her blogs and her genealogical work on Cora's family (geneanet.org) have been the twin rocks on which this introduction is constructed. Mme Godard has been generous with her information and assistance. I am also grateful for M. Stéphane Robinet for permission to reproduce the portrait of his ancestor. My thanks to Françoise Bérard, Librarian, and her colleagues at the Institut de France, as well as to the unnamed staff at the Bibliothèque nationale de France and their matchless digital programme Gallica (gallica.bnf.fr). Philip and Mary Hyman have been, as ever, ready with their co-operation and willingness to share their infinite knowledge of French culinary literature and food history. Barbara Santich and Caroline Davidson have been generous as audience and commentators, while my wife Sally has put up with a lot. Brendan King's perceptive comments and corrections rendered signal improvements. Catheryn Kilgarriff has been kind enough to publish this wonderful work; I hope it repays her faith.

BIBLIOGRAPHY

(Unless otherwise stated, the French books were published in Paris and the English in London.)

Adanson, Aglaé, *La Maison de campagne* (Audot, 1822).

Audot, Louis-Eustache, *La Cuisinière de la Campagne et de la Ville* (1st ed., Audot, 1818; 15th ed., Audot, 1834; translated as *French Domestic Cookery ... in Twelve Hundred Receipts* published by David Bogue, London, and Harper Bros., New York, 1846).

Baroli, Marc, *La Vie quotidienne en Berry au temps de George Sand* (Hachette, 1982).

Béguin, Maurice, *La Cuisine en Poitou* (Lib. Saint-Denis, Niort, [1932]).

Brioist, Pascal and Fichou, Jean-Christophe, 'La sardine à l'huile ou le premier aliment industriel', *Annales de Bretagne et des Pays de l'Ouest*, vol. 119–4 (2012), pp. 69-80.

Bousquet, Georges-Henri, 'Quelques remarques sur l'évolution de l'économie domestique en France depuis Louis-Philippe', *Revue d'histoire économique et sociale*, Vol. 45, No. 4 (1967), pp. 509–538.

Cardelli, P., pseud. of M.H. Duval, *Manuel du cuisinier et de la cuisinière à l'usage de la ville et de la campagne* (Roret, 1822).

Celnart, Mme [Élisabeth-Félicie Bayle-Mouillard], *Nouveau Manuel complet d'économie domestique* (3rd ed., Roret, 1837).

Chauvaud, Frédéric, ed., *La Société agricole de la Vienne au XIXe et XXe siècles: Guide de recherche* (Geste éditions, La Crèche, 2001).

Chabot, Paul, *Jean et Yvonne, domestiques en 1900* (Tema-éditions, 1977).

David, Elizabeth, *French Provincial Cooking* (Michael Joseph, 1960).

——, *South Wind Through the Kitchen* (Michael Joseph, 1997).

Debien, G., 'Une Nantaise à Saint-Domingue (1782–1786) [Jeanne Eulalie Lebourg, the wife of Jacques Patrice Millet],' *Revue du Bas-Poitou et des Provinces de l'Ouest*, no. 6, 1972, pp. 413–436.

Demonet, Michel, *Tableau de'Agriculture Française au milieu du 19e siècle. L'enquête de 1852* (École des Hautes Études en Sciences Sociales, 1990).

Flaubert, Gustave, *Bouvard et Pécuchet* (first published in 1881; English translation by A.J. Krailsheimer, Penguin Books, 1976).

Gacon-Dufour, Marie Armande Jeanne, *Manuel de la ménagère à la ville et à la campagne, et de la femme de basse-cour* (Buisson, 1805).

——, *Manuel du pâtissier et de la pâtissière, à l'usage de la ville et de la campagne* (Roret, 1825).

——, *Manuel des habitants de la campagne et de la bonne fermière* (Roret, 1826).

Garçon, Anne-Françoise, 'Innover dans le texte. L'Encyclopédie Roret et la vulgarisation des techniques, 1830–1880', *Colloque Les Archives de l'Invention*, May 2003, Paris.

Guérin, André, *La Vie quotidienne en Normandie au temps de Madame Bovary* (Hachette, 1975).

Genlis, Stéphanie-Félicité Du Crest, Comtesse de [Mme de Genlis], *Manuel de la jeune femme: Guide Complet de la maîtresse de maison* (Bouchet, 1829).

Guiral, Pierre, and Thuillier, Guy, *La Vie quotidienne des domestiques en France au XIXe siècle* (Hachette, 1978).

Heywood, Colin, *The Development of the French Economy, 1750–1914* (Cambridge University Press, 1995),

Lastinger, Valérie, 'The Laboratory, the Boudoir and the Kitchen' in A.K. Doig, F.B. Sturzer, eds., *Women, Gender and Disease in Eighteenth-Century England and France* (Cambridge Scholars Publishing, 2014).

Lehmann, Gilly, *The British Housewife: Cookery Books, Cooking and Society in Eighteenth-Century Britain* (Prospect Books, Blackawton, 2003).

Madame Mérigot, *La Cuisinière républicaine* (Mérigot jeune, 1794–1795).

Menon, *La Cuisinière bourgeoise* (Pierre Guillyn, 1746; modern facsimile, edited by Alice Peeters, Temps Actuels, 1981).

Meunier, Christophe, *Genillé…au fil des temps* (Éditions Hugues de Chivré, Chemillé-sur-Indrois, 2006).

Pariset, Mme, *Nouveau Manuel complet de la maîtresse de maison…suivi par une appendice par Mesdames Gacon-Dufour, Celnart, &c* (Roret, 1852 ed.; Pariset first published by Audot, 1821).

Perrot, Marguerite, *Le Mode de vie des familles bourgeoises, 1873–1953* (Presses de la Fondation Nationale des Sciences Politiques, 1982 ed.).

Price, Roger, *An Economic History of Modern France, 1730–1914* (Macmillan, 1981).

Robinet, Stéphane, Obituary notice of François Millet, *Journal d'Agriculture pratique*, 1860, vol. II, July–December.

Romanet, Emmanuelle, 'La mise en nourrice, une pratique répandue en France au XIXe siècle', *Transtext(e)s Transcultures*, 8, 2013.

Rose, Louis, *La Bonne Fermière, ou élémens économiques, utiles aux jeunes personnes destinées à cet état* (J.-B. Henry, Lille, 1765).

Simon-Hiernard, D., 'Les tombes sous tuiles du Bas-Empire de la Cataudière (Availles-en-Châtellerault, Vienne)', in Boissavit-Camus, B., Rérolle, M., *Romains et Barbares entre Loire et Gironde – IVe–Xe siècles*, Catalogue de l'exposition de Poitiers, 6 oct. 1989–28 févr. 1990, Poitiers, 1989.

Tardieu, Suzanne, *La Vie domestique dans le Mâconnais rural préindustriel* (Université de Paris, Travaux et mémoires de l'Institut d'Ethnologie, LXIX, Musée de l'Homme, 1964).

Thuillier, Guy, *Pour une histoire du quotidien au XIXe siècle en Nivernais* (École des Hautes Études en Sciences Sociales, 1977).

Tremblay, Martine, *La Représentation de l'idéal féminin en milieu rural Québécois au XIXe siècle* (MA thesis, Université de Québec, 1987).

Utrecht-Friedel, Louise Béate Augustine, *Le Petit Cuisinier habile* (the author, 1814).

——, *La Petite Cuisinière habile* (Friedel et Gasc, 1821).

Viard, A., *Le Cuisinier Royale* (11th ed., Barba, 1822).

Vicaire, Georges, *Bibliographie gastronomique* (Rouquette et fils, 1890).

Wheaton, Barbara Ketcham, 'The Endangered Cuisinière Bourgeoise', in Harlan Walker ed., *Disappearing Foods: Studies in Foods and Dishes at Risk. Proceedings of the Oxford Symposium on Food and Cookery 1994* (Prospect Books, 1995), pp. 221–226.

Zeldin, Theodore, *France, 1848–1945* (Oxford University Press, 1973–1977).

Zonabend, Françoise, trans. Anthony Forster, *The enduring memory. Time and history in a french village* (Manchester University Press, 1979).

THE FRENCH COUNTRY HOUSEWIFE

Maison rustique des dames

FOREWORD

Knowledge and enlightenment are spreading rapidly through France and all classes of society are bound to share in the benefits of their dissemination. Each day, the country-dweller is less of a stranger to progress; unfortunately the education that his children will receive in towns has little relevance to their future situation. It removes them from the paternal hearth and instils misplaced ambitions in them – which will be their undoing – by glorifying certain social conditions which they will not hesitate to view, quite wrongly in my opinion, as preferable to their parents' profession. It is tragic to see this younger generation abandoning agriculture, and such a state of affairs cannot long continue without precipitating the decay of our society. However, this trend is universal; even in towns, workmen's children – whose fathers have sacrificed everything to provide more than an elementary education – soon recoil in disgust at their parents' condition and chase dreams, invariably deceptive, of immediate fortune. We all know the disastrous consequences of an over-supply of candidates for careers that offer no guarantee of success either now or in the future.

Industry, despite immense development, cannot possibly employ all those who seek a living from it.

In the liberal arts, the bar and medicine, only the most exceptional talent will assure the future of a handful of the young men pursuing these professions. The number remaining unemployed grows every day, and this state of affairs, worsening all the time, can only result in social breakdown. A reaction is essential; come it certainly will, and we will see intelligent young people demand from agriculture legitimate satisfaction of their needs and desires. Make no mistake: if working the soil is sometimes hard, it also offers compensations and benefits for everyone. A seventh of France is uncultivated, and a significant proportion of the land in hand is so badly worked that yields are low and quality poor. An increase in the labour force would immediately have tremendous effect, and consumption would increase in step with production.

The government makes commendable efforts to extend education; but is it not evident that education itself may become a source of unhappiness for those who receive it if they cannot find, once educated, an honourable way of profiting from it? Agriculture offers this way; it is in truth the only career varied enough to present a satisfying future to our eager young people.

If, then, circumstances have it that young men's prospects tend towards agriculture, their wives' life-choices deserve serious consideration more than ever before. Nowadays, men with a taste for farming hold back from this career thanks to difficulties finding a companion who can throw herself into his work while shouldering responsibilities that are the woman's sphere: for young women, to an even greater extent than men, receive an education that leaves them total strangers to the farming life. The habits and tastes imbibed at boarding-school[1] have little to do with the life they might lead married to a farmer. I would not hesitate to state that farmers' daughters are in general less suitable to the role of country housewife than many young town girls brought up by sensible mothers. In point of fact, the useless education farmers' daughters receive in most boarding-schools encourages nothing more than vanity, they forget their country ways, nurturing, if not contempt for them, then at least dislike. And young girls who have never left the countryside are all too often totally unfit to be companions to young men whose good education has fostered taste and the intellect.

I therefore believe it absolutely essential that the aptitudes and skills which make a woman the worthy companion of a highly educated man should not be neglected when preparing young girls to be good country housewives. I bring this serious subject of women's agricultural education to the attention of the government and of those who love their country. They should clearly understand that women in general lack any agricultural instruction and that the greatest number look upon country life with horror – even if a few have enough good sense to realize how pleasant and honourably profitable it can be. Which old soldier, which man of parts, disillusioned by the hustle of everyday life and distanced from the unruly

1.   In French, *pension.*

ambitions that plagued their youth, would not turn their sights towards a country life, where their efforts would gain just reward, if their wives were not invincibly alienated from a mode of existence of which they lack the knowledge to appreciate its felicities? Ah! if they were willing to adopt it, they would see how great was their error! The loneliness they fear would be subdued by constant activity, and the boredom that stems from idleness would be banished forever. Soon they would experience that inexpressible delight of being useful to one's family and to society. And then, far from disapproving of their husband's scheme, they would be the first to applaud it and carry it through. And straightaway, the isolation they so mistakenly dread would be feared no longer, for the countryside, more populous from day to day, will soon offer all of town's pleasures while suffering none of its inconveniences.

So I think that we should actively encourage the introduction of at least some of the skills and knowledge needed for country living into female education, and seek to extend this to girls with an urban background. Although I myself possess neither the knowledge nor the talent to write a work that might encompass the double point of view I refer to, I will attempt to sketch a small part of it and try hard to portray both the charm and powerful appeal that I have found in my new way of life. I will tell of my activities, my pleasures, the duties I have mapped out for myself. I will make clear the means I employ to supervise and supply this small realm to which I now devote my life.

This sketch will, I know, leave much to be desired; but I will speak of what experience has taught me; it will be a first stone laid in the great edifice of agricultural education for women, leaving other more able hands to bring the work to a sound conclusion.

INTRODUCTION

The responsibilities of a woman who lives in the country wishing to participate fully in her situation are far more significant and extensive than those of a woman living in town. This last has only her household to manage and has to hand a thousand ways of providing education for her children; but in the country a woman must not only be the mother but also the teacher of her children; it is not enough that she looks after the house, but she must also play her part in the oversight and operations of the farm itself. No sensible woman will protest at this overload of activities – sweet pleasures will be their yield – it will only seem tedious to those who, finding themselves as it were by accident in this situation, are unable to discern the satisfaction always offered by things you have created yourself, that you have undertaken single-mindedly, and which have a useful and purposeful goal.

The sheer variety of these activities should alarm no woman; she would be wrong to be thus flustered: a busy life satisfies everyone and passes with a speed which lends its own inexpressible charm. Friendly good neighbours are to be found more and more in the country and even if the pleasure of their company is not quite the same as the town's distractions, it has its particular appeal. Talents will out; why is it less pleasing to let them shine in front of sympathetic people anxious to enjoy them than to flaunt them before people bored by such amusements and little disposed to appreciate them? In this last case, your gifts do no more than satisfy your vanity, while in the first they let you savour that content that comes from genuinely pleasing your friends. There is a sense of intimacy to receptions held in the country which gives them their special charm and is hardly ever found in town. Everybody knows each other and loneliness is a common foe. Less attention is paid to inequality of fortune and inequality of rank less emphasized. In the country, it is talent that marks out a man, and the healthy competition this provokes is good for everyone, not at the expense of a few. In industry, the triumph of one business can mean the ruin of a rival; but in agriculture you can never produce enough and the success we achieve for ourselves can only encourage our neighbours.

The pleasures of the summer months are so varied: walks, meals taken under spreading boughs in a beauty spot, rides out in a carriage, on a horse, even on a donkey; fishing, shooting: all these diversions, so costly to townspeople, can be had for next to nothing if you live in the country. Village fiestas, where you go to dance, rackety country weddings, celebrated in the midst of plenty, are sweet delights to be savoured with friends and relations. If these affairs have none of the show of those in town, nor do they have their stiffness and ceremony.

The long winter evenings are far from lacking charm; they are devoted to needlework or reading. A wise housewife will use this time of year to make the outfits to clothe her and her children during the fine days and high days of summer. In the country too, the more intellectual will find the leisure to keep up with arts and literature and abreast of trends in human knowledge. In fact, one soon gets used to the rigours of the season and is not often denied an outing and the pleasure of visiting one's neighbours. A few poor roads will never scotch the chance of a carnival; while the *veillées*,[1] enlivened by a good fire and the solace of company – a solace all the more piquant as it becomes more uncommon – may be the spark that gives rise to a modest party, offered with joy and none of those second-thoughts, often so troubling, provoked by large expense. A careful manager

1.   Mme Millet-Robinet has used the word *veillée* twice so far in this paragraph. The first I have translated as 'the long winter evenings', for that is what she means. The second use refers to the French, and western European, custom of friends and family sitting round a fire, often but not invariably in some neutral territory such as a barn, for long hours of a winter night engaged in some repetitive task (such as spinning), telling tales, conversing, even dancing, eating and drinking. Something of the same ritual and pattern of behaviour, but among the younger generation, is seen in the courtship rite of bundling, known to British and American rural communities at this time. Mme Millet-Robinet rightly mentions that the custom of the *veillée* was on the wane. It is also more usually thought of as a peasant custom, although Madame is writing here for substantial tenant or freehold farmers. She later qualifies her interpretation of the word to bring it closer to an evening party as might be enjoyed by readers today. A good account of *veillées* in the Mâconnais is given by Suzanne Tardieu in her book *La Vie domestique dans le Mâconnais rural préindustriel* (1964).

will know how to marshal all the resources the countryside can offer and to secure that abundance, which is inexpensive there but nowhere else, which is one of the delights of life. It is especially at these winter parties that we appreciate a woman of musical ability or an attractive woman of parts; if the circle of friends is small, it is now that rewarding conversations are to be had about pastimes the winter months permit us, about the tasks of the year just past and the year to come, or the books we have just read, or the delights we have savoured or anticipate enjoying. Everyone is involved in the exchange, because everyone has their own special interest, and the intimate circle forms a sort of family, sharing the same worries and concerns. If the company is larger, the aptitudes of each participant, harnessed to the greater good, will soon transform the reception into a cheerful dance, where each does what they like without fear of criticism from idlers or fools. And finally, games of chess, cards, dominoes and draughts can offer amusement without fear that unfortunate losses will vitiate a simple pleasure that needs no stimulus from raising the stakes. Etiquette has no place in country gatherings, where nothing is done for form's sake: rather than turning up at the neighbours' at ten in the evening, we arrive at six; and the *veillée* doesn't go on all night so people are ready for work the next day; the regular succession of daily tasks never changes, which would be regrettable, but the time for leisure is never diminished.

Still other gratifications await the country dweller, gratifications for which there are no regrets, and of which there is an inexhaustible supply. Charity, a thousand times more satisfying to undertake when you can see the results, takes many forms in the countryside: the works a wife can urge her husband to allocate to the poor; the advice she can give them on how to bring up their families, where disorder is the source of such misery; the help and consolation she can dispense to them when ill; the resignation she can teach them when they suffer reverses; the practical care she can offer to a multitude of small injuries or fleeting ailments, where intelligent intervention brings rapid relief but which, left to fester may worsen and sometimes be fatal; the improvements she can bring to the education of the young folk; the need to combat the prejudices surrounding childbirth that so many women suffer from; the alms distributed in a timely fashion: these are the source of enduring pleasures and are available to even the most modest fortunes. To all these satisfactions, there's the success of the farm to which we devote our time; the improvements we describe then see imitated in the district, spreading affluence; the progress we make by our own efforts in the instruction of our children, their intelligence and physical development. Finally, is it not true to say that the repute that our efforts may bestow on a farm, which then may become a model for the whole district, brings with it that sense of reward that accompanies any useful undertaking brought to a happy conclusion? Since the beginning, the best minds have accorded the first place to agriculture because it has the most decisive influence on the happiness and well-being of humanity.

PART ONE

KEEPING HOUSE

CHAPTER I

THE DUTIES AND RESPONSIBILITIES OF A MISTRESS OF THE HOUSE

A mistress of the house has many obligations. The order and perfection she brings to their accomplishment contributes much to the prosperity of the family. She should understand the importance of her role and be resolute in pursuing it; she will find true joy in its performance, stemming from a conviction of her usefulness. She will never be bored, for that stems from idleness or from the futility of our actions; and, once she has banished boredom, content is there to take its place. The slightest act can provoke or renew a sense of enjoyment and, once achieved, life passes so much more rapidly, with that delight that is the true companion of truth and utility.

A young girl you wish to educate so as to equip her to run a farming household must neglect nothing which might improve her mind and allow her to acquire the attributes of society. These attributes will be just as valuable to her in the country as in the town and, as they are more rarely encountered there, they will be the more remarked; careful study will give her more confidence and allow her to converse with her husband on all those topics that only menfolk are interested in; because, if she wishes to please her husband, who is often her only companion, she must endeavour to think as he does. As she should try to make their spare time together a delight, she can quite reasonably give up learning many of the finer and insignificant details of needlework – and be less preoccupied with her personal appearance – so she may pursue those studies her position requires.

It is quite possible the world thinks the study of agriculture and farm management unsuitable for a young woman, but are grammar, arithmetic, history or geography any more relevant? If you give farming matters equal status, there will be no fear in tackling them, they will be pursued with just as much determination, and these subjects will be the source of real satisfaction.

A woman who has embraced her situation will find much to please her in such studies, not least the charm of novelty, but also the sense of satisfaction in an active life that is useful to everyone. The minor role which our modern way of life sees fit to allow women excludes them from that place in society they could occupy were they more positive and active. Husbands will find those women brought up in the ways we suggest are real colleagues; this in turn will be a further claim on their affection and, given that the head of a family cannot have a better counsellor than his spouse, whose interests are so intimately entangled with his, the partnership will benefit in every way.

In the country, a woman has two households to manage: her own family and the farm; they are never identical, and she needs to devote the same degree of attention and oversight to each of them. If the ideal is sometimes vitiated by practicalities, they should not detract from the overarching requirements of economy and order in both her spheres.

The mistress has all the female farm servants under her control. Their sphere is the farmyard, that is, the dairy, the pigsties and the poultry run. The gardens and the orchards, as well as animals kept for their wool, are also her responsibility. She should also be aware of the jobs needing to be done on the farm as a whole, so that she can act instead of her husband if he be absent or unwell. It is therefore essential that she should be acquainted with all the fields and their cultivation. She should maintain an exact account of outgoings and receipts in all the departments in her care so she can quickly assess their loss or profit, and she should keep track of all expenses whether in the house or the farm.

A mistress should also look after the health of everyone in the household; it is her task to dispense any medicines recommended by the doctor and she should be attentive to his prescriptions and their execution. It is thus absolutely necessary that she acquires some knowledge of domestic healthcare so she can treat simple cases from the outset, both so they do not worsen and that she can assess the right moment when the doctor should be called out.

The distribution of alms is her exclusive role; it is a fitting yet sweet recompense for the cares she has expended.

She should exercise careful supervision of the moral character of all the household servants, gently bringing them back, with reasoned arguments, to the straight and narrow whenever they have strayed, but ensuring their dismissal should they ignore her observations. She should neglect no measure which ensures the proper performance of all religious duties.

A woman who is at once mistress of the household and of the farm as well must exercise active oversight of everything going on in the home and outdoors. She must never ignore what is going on, and when she has issued her instructions, she must make sure they are adhered to. To make the work run more smoothly it is best to give orders for the morrow on the evening of the day before. By looking in unannounced, she will keep everyone on the *qui vive* and it is much better to prevent trouble than to have to solve it.

CHAPTER II

HOW TO TREAT AND MANAGE SERVANTS

I will mention at the outset the qualities you require from a servant: honesty, energy, willingness, tidiness and cleanliness. Honesty is essential; as to the others, you should leave no stone unturned to promote them and make them second nature to your servants. From the moment they enter your service you must familiarize them with all the equipment they will be using and insist they always put it back where it belongs once they have done with it.

Every servant should be spotless, in her person as well as wherever her duties lie; clothing and linen should always be in good condition.

The mistress of the household should treat her servants kindly, but never weakly; she should look to gain their confidence as well as their affection and be ready with good counsel, but should not be over familiar nor, above all, let them into the intimate affairs of the family itself. She would be well advised to give guidance in matters of money. Usually country folk spend the little money they have on buying a small trifle of land, for which they usually pay two or three times over the odds and which earns them a meagre portion so long as they remain in service. The mistress should explain how they would be much better advised to save every penny until they are married; it is the fear of losing the savings they have so painfully acquired that leads servants to invest it all in land; savings banks are entirely worry-free and are the best place for their investment.

You should guard against servants succumbing to the temptations of excessive personal grooming and the insane expense that may entail; rather, you should insist on cleanliness and tidiness. Once you have persuaded them to deposit a small sum with the savings bank, they will be eager to add to their nest egg with further economies. This will give them strength to resist any temptation to waste their money.

So that servants don't go off in search of amusement in unseemly locales, where they will pick up bad habits and waste their time, you should study to divert them, seizing any convenient opportunity to afford them suitable recreation that does not detract from their duties.

As a general rule when hiring servants, it should be agreed at the outset that none of them can absent themselves from the house, even on high days and holidays, without the permission of the master or mistress. You should allow them to go to weddings and feast-days in neighbouring villages, where the family will doubtless go too; indeed, the fear that master and mistress might turn up at any time will inhibit them from making fools of themselves, either in unseemly high jinks or from excessive drinking. When you are happy with your servants, it is sensible to let them have a party at home every now and then; the pleasure it gives them, especially being able to invite their friends along, strengthens the bonds of attachment. Such parties are not costly: a violin, a few cakes, and some bottles of wine is the sum of it. It is best if the family takes part too: their presence imposes a little order on the event and adds to the general enjoyment, but they should not overstay their welcome – eventually they will become a bore and a blight on proceedings.

Every so often, a mistress should *treat* her people. The rigours of their life ensure that they will take enormous pleasure in a more succulent meal than usual. So it should be that when you kill a pig, given that a good housewife gets as much out of it as possible, you take advantage of the event to treat the servants, whose pleasure will be the greater because they owe it to the generosity and canny management of the mistress. On a feast-day, some chicken will always be acceptable: it is a rich man's meat, they'll say, and that thought means there is no better dish to offer them. And a glass of wine from the master's table, offered while they're finishing off an arduous task, will both stimulate and please the servants.

These gestures should always bear fruit: your servants have to be fairly ungrateful not to repay your kindness and solicitude with both zeal and devotion. It is a mistake to think you will achieve the same ends by merely putting up their wages. While never forgetting their interests, you have to engage their emotions if you want to gain their affection. A devotion that stems from monetary considerations is no more than ephemeral, vanishing should payments dry up, or even if they are not regularly augmented; loyalty that comes from the heart is the more genuine and long-lasting.

A housewife should take steps to know everything going on around her and, to that end, she should take great pains to be fair and impartial, even if she does have favourites. If ever a difference does arise between two servants, she should listen carefully to each side and keep a coolness of judgement even while they are losing theirs: that way she will preserve her dignity; she should pause before rushing to judgement in favour of one or the other and, once she has made her decision, she must use her influence and reason to calm the offended party and to persuade the other to initiate a reconciliation. If they refuse, she should take each to one side to impose an agreement and dissipate any traces of rancour that persist. The satisfactory conclusion of tasks undertaken jointly depends, in large part, on there being harmony and understanding.

A mistress should insist her servants address her with respect and that no male servant keeps his hat on in the house. By the same token, she will treat them kindly and politely, and should she ever find herself in the room where they are eating – and they rise to their feet in acknowledgement – that she will always pray them to be seated immediately. If any among them do not treat her with the deference expected and so necessary for good order, she may gently remonstrate and, if that's to no avail, mention it to her husband so he can crack the whip of discipline. If that fails, there is no alternative but dismissal. This should not often occur if the mistress studies to maintain her dignity and calm at every turn.

If a servant has had to be dealt with by the master, but none the less there is some fair excuse for their conduct, the mistress should make every effort to obtain a reprieve (while not forgetting the error which provoked it); she must be the guardian angel of all she surveys.

On new year's day, she should distribute the customary presents discerningly, so as not to excite any envy or jealousy.

One of the best ways of keeping servants enthusiastic and loyal is to give them a stake in any proceeds arising from their activities. We all wish servants would take the interests of their employers to heart and do nothing to damage them, but they have to be fairly special to come up to the mark at every turn. You can secure their affections by right and proper behaviour, but you should consider their interest as well as their wellbeing so they don't look around for a better paid situation. No matter how good and loyal they are, it's always best to appeal to that most powerful motive in the affairs of man, personal profit, as well as to the heart and the affections.

I think any well-managed farm should allow its servants a small percentage on all produce stemming from their labours; the value of this bonus will be multiplied a hundredfold as they strive to increase output in what they now see as theirs.

Thus the shepherdess should receive a bonus for every lamb that lives to an agreed age, and another for every fat lamb sold.

The dairymaid should get the same for every veal calf and for her butter.

The girl in charge of the farmyard should get a bonus for any poultry, piglets or fattened pigs either sold out or consumed in the house itself.

In just the same way, the farmhands should get a bonus on cereals, oilseeds and fatstock. The foreman should get an additional percentage on any stock he buys or sells at a profit.

This moderate consideration, the scale of which will depend on the success of the harvest, will increase the servants' earnings without you having to put up the actual wages (something you only do advisedly). It will also promote their enthusiasm. They will defend your interests as if they were their own and they will strive mightily to increase the yields on everything.

You should keep hold of your servants as long as possible. You should hire them young and get them used to your ways so that in a manner of speaking they feel *at home*.

When you take them on, it should be at as low a wage as possible, with the promise of gradual increments until they get to the standard rate – not ignoring the bonuses I have mentioned, or any other extra tips they may deserve for that assiduity or loyalty which every good employer should seek to recognize and reward.

A small gift wisely and judiciously dispensed, when the occasion merits it, will touch the heart of most servants and encourage their devotion. Your concern for their health, their interests and their pleasures; the bonus on the profits of the farm; the consistency of performance you insist upon; the firmness of direction, but not harshness, that you show; and the impartiality and good judgement with which you treat them; these are the best means of securing good servants. Those who fail to appreciate your methods will soon leave, and you won't regret them. Those who stay will be truly attached to the family and household because they find you offer affection and self-respect. You too, the masters, will conceive an affection for them, and from this concord will flow a perfect harmony which can only enhance the prosperity of all.

Where we live, in the canton of Montrésor (Indre-et-Loire),[1] salaries are reasonable. This is how we have fixed the servants' bonuses on any income arising from produce sold or consumed within the household:

When the foreman sells working animals, he gets what we call *la pièce*. He shares with the other labourers, who have been with us for at least a year, a bonus of 25 centimes for every hectolitre of wheat, oilseed rape and other grain of similar value, and 15 centimes for every hectolitre of rye, spring barley and similar crops.

A junior herdsman looking after the donkeys and the cows and their sheds, shares with the dairymaid all the tips paid by the purchasers of any of these animals.

The shepherd gets 15 centimes for every lamb that survives to St John's day (24 June), which is when they are weaned, and the same amount for every fat sheep sold to the butcher.

The woman in charge of the farmyard, who looks after the pigs and the poultry, gets 50 centimes for every sucking pig, 1 franc for every porker sold, and 5 centimes per head of every fowl killed for the household or sold in the market. You may think these last payments quite high, but if you take into account the great care needed to ensure the chicken are well fattened, and the myriad chances they have of sickening and dying, it ceases to appear so generous.

The dairymaid tasked with milking the cows and making butter gets 10 centimes for every kilogram.

The housemaids under the direction of the mistress should, so long as the husband agrees, be paid by the mistress and get their orders from her.

---

1.   Mme Millet-Robinet moved from the Château de la Cataudière in Availles-en-Châtellerault, just to the south-east of Châtellerault, to the Domaine de Pont in Genillé, next to Montrésor (these are both now in the canton of Loches, south of Tours) in 1847. She lived there until the death of her husband in 1860.

On this matter, I insist on the vital necessity of perfect concord between husband and wife on everything pertaining to the management of the family, farm and household. Once given, the orders of one should never be countermanded by the other, unless, in cases of misunderstanding or disagreement, these matters are first discussed out of everyone's hearing – never in front of the children or servants. It is best, therefore, that husband and wife alert the other to any instructions they are about to issue so they never risk contradiction.

The sensible employer will sometimes consult the servants on the execution of those tasks that lie within their special competence; this will boost their self-esteem, concentrate their minds and urge them to a better performance; indeed, they can often identify aspects of the job that would otherwise escape your attention.

An agricultural business depends in large part on the wise direction of its servants and the means employed to ensure their loyalty and good conduct. You should never forget that good masters engender good servants.

If by dint of decent treatment a master earns his house a fair reputation, he will be sure to get the best recruits. Generous wages and a stake in the profits will be to the benefit of the master's purse at the same time that they put his employees a notch above others in the district. To reap you must sow.

CHAPTER III

HOW TO USE YOUR TIME — SUPERVISION

How to use your time. — A housewife's most important quality is knowing how to use her time. Should she acquire this aptitude, all too rare in the world at large, she will be surprised by the good things that flow from it.

Once a mistress has established a proper routine she should abide by it, not, though, quite so strictly as that she imposes on the children or the servants.

Rising. — She should rise early in the morning: the day's work and routine depend entirely on getting a good start. A farmer's wife should be up in the summer months by five o'clock at the latest, and by seven in the winter, altering the exact time of rising to the length of the days.

Going to bed. — Whenever the day has been profitably spent in work and supervision, sleep is never a problem. As you should go to bed early, even if you have to get up at the break of day you will have had ample rest. Six or seven hours' sleep is quite enough. Never the less, workers who undertake really strenuous tasks will not recover their strength, at any time of the year, without an equivalent period of repose. It is well known that a siesta is universal in southern countries, and the custom answers a real need. In the country, a couple of hours' sleep in the middle of the day, especially during the high summer season (harvest and haymaking), are essential to workers who have risen at the crack of dawn and are exhausted by their labours.

And in similar fashion, working animals need rest. You will ruin even the best of teams in no more than a season if you aren't careful, during the hot summer months, to harness them before the break of day and unhitch them when the sun is at its highest.

People of leisure, of course, need just as much rest, but they will succumb the more willingly to the attractions of a warm bed during the cold months, while getting up betimes in the summer heat to enjoy the freshness of the early morning.

Visiting the kitchen and the farm. — If a mistress has risen early, she will have plenty of time available before breaking her fast. As soon as she is up, she should go to the kitchen and the servants' hall to give her orders for the day and confirm that her instructions of the day before were carried out properly.

Dressing and childcare. — After this, you can dress and attend to the children; dress them and give them jobs they can do on their own, while seeing yourself to household duties. If the children are too young for you to have started on their education, you will have some spare time to devote yourself to reading, artistic endeavour, or overseeing any work going on in the garden or the farm.

Visiting the poor and the sick. — After breakfast, you should fill your time with lessons and homework for the children, or other wifely duties, and take advantage of any spare time to do the round, with all the family, of any ongoing work on the farm. In this way, everyone will be up-to-date with what's going on, and it will give some point to your afternoon walk. You can also, at this point of the day, call on the poor and any sick people you are looking after.

You should organize your time so that you are free towards three o'clock in the afternoon. This is the moment when you can please yourself: receive visits from friends or make visits yourself; go out into the fields and encourage the workers; put in train, or even undertake yourself, some small job in house or farm; any of which should be a pleasing distraction.

Any woman who decides to live in the country, and who takes her duties seriously, must never hesitate to put her hand to the wheel.

Accounts. — Every day, without fail, morning or evening, a mistress will take a moment to put in order her daily accounts, tally up accounts with any servants to whom she has entrusted money, and note the hours of all those she employs on tasks in her purview. This rule must always be observed.

The evening hours. — In summertime, the evening will be spent in looking after the children, supervising the garden, having a walk, reading, playing music, and just doing nothing – something which is so delicious of a warm summer's evening.

In winter, needlework, reading, music and drawing should occupy any spare time.

Sundays and Thursdays. — On Sunday, when church is done, and on Thursday, when the children will have no lessons, the mistress will have some free time when she can please herself. This will be all the more delightful because she has worked for it.

Overseeing the garden. — The garden is within the purview of the mistress of the house. If she doesn't have a gardener, she must direct the gardening. She must, therefore, be well acquainted with the subject so that she can ensure that an inexperienced workforce of day labourers and household servants can undertake the work she requires. This will be quite time-consuming, but everything that results from her efforts will be the more worthwhile.

Overseeing the farm. — A mistress must also plan what is needed from the farm itself and ensure that all the vegetables required for the large workforce that is inevitable in a successful undertaking are sown and cultivated in a timely fashion. She will find it an immense economy to feed her servants plenty of nourishing vegetables: after bread, they should form the largest part of their diet. It is the day-labourers and servants who are charged with this work, so that you do not trouble the gardener himself.

During the major tasks of summertime the mistress must often be on the spot because her husband can't be everywhere and nothing replaces the eye of the master.

Good management is at the heart of a farm's success and intelligent deployment of the workforce is one of its essential foundations. Work undertaken during the summer will absorb much of the farm's costs and oversight of this work is of the first importance.

The moment when the harvest is brought home is no less critical. Someone not actually getting their hands dirty will often be mindful of problems that even the best servants will not anticipate. It will be down to the mistress, should there be imminent disaster, to take the critical decision that may save the harvest at risk, something that can never be left to the farmworkers. At these times of the year, a farmer's wife will probably neglect some of her work indoors in favour of being out in the fields. She will have plenty of time to catch up in the dead season. This is why she needs to know how to do every job on the farm and why she should know the correct terms and language to describe it. She should understand what makes for good tillage, how to harrow, how to weed, when hay or corn is dry enough, when vegetables are ripe for picking and how to store vegetables and fruit.

Flocks. — On farms where sheep are not a principal source of income, the flock and its feeding will belong in the mistress's realm. She should learn, therefore, everything about its requirements.

The success of the dairy will hinge on the choice of cows and their feeding. It is up to the mistress to obtain good stock and to remind her husband to grow the right crops for their nourishment, because the dairy lies entirely within her remit. She is also in charge of raising and fattening the pigs. If these two departments are well run, they will contribute useful profits and much produce for the household. Breeding, too, should have her attention, for the quality and quantity of produce depend on careful feeding and intelligent husbandry.

The poultry-yard. — Finally, the mistress should obtain fine poultry of all sorts for her runs so that from their sale she can cover the costs of feeding all the birds, including those consumed by the household itself.

The hives. — She is in charge of the beehives as well. As a well-run farm will support any number of flowering crops that the bees require for their sustenance, so a good set of hives will produce a useful income.

Domestic economy. — A host of considerations and canny receipts that hardly add at all to the running costs will greatly improve a family's ease and well-being. My aim is to initiate my readers into all these details.

CHAPTER IV

THE MISTRESS'S WARDROBE

Dress and grooming are the principal activities of women living in towns; they have their place, too, in the country. But they should only take up a few minutes of the precious time of a farmer's wife, whose appearance should show that simple good taste, which ignores neither quality nor beauty, which marks every woman of upbringing.

The mistress of the house, in the country, should dress for the whole day, once she has made her toilet and that of her children, and visited the kitchen and the yard outside. Towards the middle of the day she should tidy her hair again and her appearance.

I advise her never to be a slave to fashion, but to choose clothing that, while reflecting changes in style, never makes her look ridiculous. Ignore those fleeting extremes of fashion, which will invariably be in bad taste.

If she is wealthy, I counsel her to buy good fabrics which hold their value and can be worn at all times, rather than anything flashy which is never worth the price once novelty has worn off. If she isn't wealthy, she should always take care to use good quality fabrics but at a lower cost. Trinkets and baubles should never be part of a countrywoman's apparel.

1. Winter clothing.

Dresses and skirts. — For winter wear, a well-lined woollen dress that you can brush or even wash, either check or just one colour, is the most suitable. Merino fabrics will not be thick enough; a nicely coloured woollen twill, well made and worn with a dash, will always be better than a faded silk. The quilted or lined petticoat should be a black wool that can be brushed or washed. White petticoats show the dirt too much in winter and any other colour is ugly.

Aprons. — An apron in silk, filoselle,[1] or woollen twill should be black or something dark, have plenty of pockets, and perhaps a kerchief. It should wash easily and will last a long while if it's good quality. It sits well on a good wool dress.

Collars. — A nice white starched or embroidered collar with a black tie is the only suitable dress for winter. It should be linen or cotton cambric (muslin creases too readily). Cuffs to match the collar look good.

Bonnets. — If you like to wear a bonnet, the best taste is muslin, or jaconet,[2] with little frill of muslin trimmed with lace. This is better than one made of net with an embroidered edging, even if it has lots of ribbons. This looks cheap, does not fit with life in the country and, frankly, is probably more expensive than something in better taste.

Hats, hoods. — When she wants to go out, a farmer's wife should be dressed in a black hat (no patterns or colours) made from something that will cope with a little rain and will cover the ears. Black beaver is perfect, but sometimes is so out of fashion that even in the country it looks ridiculous. An alternative is a black merino hood, lined with a woollen muslin. When it's really cold, you should tuck the hood under the coat so that you are nice and snug.

Stockings. — Stockings should be black wool or good quality white cotton. Black silk or filoselle stockings are expensive and don't last. White stockings are easy and inexpensive to launder. Coloured cotton hose, once it's worn, shows the dirt just as much as white stockings and doesn't suit a woman. When the feet are worn out, rather than darning the soles and heels, which is always unsightly, the best thing is to replace the whole foot, especially if there is a hosiery knitter in the district. If none exists, then you can cut off the foot and sew the stocking top onto a sock designed for the purpose. This will cost half as much as new stockings.

Gaiters. — Cloth gaiters with an understrap that goes under the arch of the foot and will not therefore touch the ground are an excellent means of protecting your stockings, keeping your feet warm and your shoes clean. These gaiters have a buttoned strap across the bridge of the foot; they

1.   Filoselle is a mixture of silk and cotton, used for bonnets, curtains, etc.
2.   Jaconet is a lightweight cotton with a smooth and stiffened finish.

are easy to put on and off and are stylish. You can get them in a light leather which is somewhat more sturdy and better for bad weather. They are quite easy to make yourself, or you can get them made up by a country seamstress if you can get a good pattern.

Shoes, short boots. — Shoes ought be made from horsehide, well-laced brogues with stout soles, styled somewhat like men's shoes. The foot will be more comfortable and have better poise in a shoe of this sort. It is quite wrong to think you'll be better off with a lighter lady's shoe; on the contrary, when the shoe does not press too much, it allows the foot more freedom, copes better with rough and stony ground, and is less tiring. In any case, a stout shoe is essential for the winter as it allows you to go out into the yard or walk on muddy paths without your feet getting damp or cold. If the shoes are well made they will also be elegant. You can have shoes like this in waterproof patent leather; all you have to do is wash them for their shine to be restored. Well-soled cloth boots can replace shoes and gaiters, but they are much more expensive than gaiters.

Clogs. — When it's muddy, you have to wear a light clog. It's possible to put them over the shoe. They are indispensable in the country. With stout shoes, the clogs can have less in the way of uppers so they won't be as heavy. It's likely that you'll suffer a few splashes and flecks of mud, but no matter. If your shoes are thin and insubstantial, on the other hand, or if you insist on wearing slippers, your feet will be wet in an instant.

Gloves. — A farmer's wife should always have gloves in her pocket, and put them on whenever she leaves the house. Even if she can never hope to have hands as pale as those of a woman who lives in her *boudoir*, she ought to pay some attention to their appearance – always the sign of a well-bred woman. I advise that you look after your hands, without too much fuss, and avoid anything that will spoil them unnecessarily. A pretty hand, or at least a cared-for hand, is a charming feature for a woman. Doeskin or kid gloves are the best; they are dearer, but they don't tear. There are several sorts of woollen gloves made nowadays, which are very good for winter. Cotton gloves are nice for summer; they wear well and wash easily. Indoors, a woman can wear mittens, which allow the hands a certain freedom of movement.

Coat. — A well-lined coat of just one colour, made of cloth or plaid twill, is essential. It should have a hood that can be put on or off at will, and sleeves. It should be short enough so that it never hinders walking.

A lighter coat worn with a separate waterproof cape is also a really useful combination. As you will often be riding around in an open carriage, even in winter, you will always be caught by a shower. In these circumstances, nothing is better than rubber.

Jackets. — Short jackets were made for the countrywoman. She should have several, lighter or heavier, depending on the season. It is the most useful of garments, especially for an active woman. A jerkin can be worn instead, if the sleeves of your dress are so bulky that they stop you putting on or off your jacket with ease.

Holiday dress. — On Sundays and holidays, a farmer's wife can wear something a little more elegant than on days of work; but I cannot emphasize enough how important it is that she should study simplicity in all she wears, for that is the mark of good taste, no matter how wealthy she may be.

2. Summer dress.

Dresses. — In summer, a farmer's wife should wear paler dresses, but still of only one colour. If she is young, and it's the fashion, she can wear something with a low neck, with a simple fichu, in muslin or jaconet. Come the autumn, her dresses should be a shade darker. Silk and fabrics that don't wash easily are not suitable for work days; they will soon get stained and be fit for nothing.

Stockings, shoes and gaiters. — In summer, stockings will be white; shoes, the same style as winter, will be either patent leather or an unwaxed skin left in its natural yellowish colour (what we call *veau retourné*[1]); this is supple, strong and doesn't show the dust. A grey or black beaver is also suitable. Blacked shoes will dirty stockings and light-coloured dresses and will always look out of place in summer; the soles should be less substantial than on a winter shoe, but light pumps or shoes made from fabric are not suitable for walking over fields. It's best to wear canvas gaiters (either grey or the same colour as your shoes) so that the dust is kept out of the shoe altogether.

Bonnets. — Summer headwear is always a problem as it should answer the following requirements: it should protect the face and shoulders from

1.   Reversed calf, calf skin which is worn flesh side out, to resemble doeskin.

Figure 1. Jacket and bonnet.

the sun and any sharp summer shower; it should neither be too warm, nor blow off in the slightest breeze, which is really inconvenient; be sturdy enough so that it doesn't have to be fiddled with all day; and finally not be too expensive. For the country, we have adopted a hooded sun-bonnet which is excellent headgear, not dear, and very easy to wear. White bonnets are the best taste and cost no more. You insert bone in the ruffs through a sort of buttonhole sewn on the backside of the hem and you keep the bone in place by tacking it at each end. This is easy to unpick whenever you need to launder it. You keep the ruffs open with tape when you are ironing the bonnet. Wired bonnets are not expensive either and are elegant enough.

Straw hats. — Hats made of so-called Swiss straw [plaited] look well on a younger woman and on children, and can serve instead of these bonnets.

Dressing gown. — A dressing gown is indispensable, in winter well lined and even quilted, and something lighter for the summer. A woman can't do without it in the country, especially if she leaves her room immediately she rises.

3. Advice on personal care and appearance.

If on the one hand I advise women who think of nothing else than their appearance to moderate this tendency, I urge those who neglect this side of things to make every effort to look smart and cared for. A woman whose dress and appearance draw the slightest criticism is certainly at fault. Both her dress and her person should be exquisitely clean.

Her hair should always be tidy and sleek. If she curls it, she should use blotting paper to roll it, which will cost her no more than two francs a year. Curling papers of old newspaper or plain paper are hideous.

The figure should always be supported by a good corset, but not as tightly as some foolish women presume. A tight corset will damage grace and suppleness, inhibit easy movement and ruin a woman's health, without in any way promoting that ideal beauty to which she aspires.

Shoes, even if they lack glamour and are even a mite clumsy, should always be in perfect condition; slippers, even elegant slippers, should never be seen outside the bedroom. Some women have the repellent habit of using old shoes as slippers; my readers have taste enough to know that this sordid economy is beneath them.

Finally, a well-bred woman knows that first appearances – in dress, cleanliness, good taste and tidiness – count for a great deal. At any age, and in any station, a woman should be able to show herself before strangers without a second thought. Is there anything more ridiculous than a woman who flees to her room as soon as she spies a visitor? And she should bear in mind that her appearance matters to her husband just as much as to strangers; if she wishes to hold on to his affections, she must study to please him, in such a way that he never blushes at the thought of her.

CHAPTER V

OCCASIONAL FURNITURE NECESSARY FOR THE MISTRESS OF THE HOUSE

I. — A box for haberdashery. — A holder for yarn. — A cutting-out board, etc.

Making and mending clothes. — A good housewife who is handy with the needle, such an important part of her education, will be able to make many of her own and her children's clothes, as well as keep her husband's in good condition and maintain all the household linen. Needlework is so enjoyable to any woman with the aptitude for it that she will prefer it to all her other jobs and will derive a real sense of pleasure when she makes or mends a piece of linen or a garment. This pleasure is much deeper than a woman who fritters her time away on vanities can ever imagine.

A good housewife will get particular satisfaction from viewing her workbox because everything it contains is so appropriate to her needs.

A box for haberdashery. — It's difficult in the country to assure supplies of every piece of haberdashery at the moment you need it, and at the same time it will be cheaper if you buy in bulk; a workbox or, for want of a better description, a small haberdasher's store is therefore a necessity. The box should be lockable, for nothing tempts a servant girl, even a loyal one, so much as these little lady's essentials. The box should have a double bottom, divided into several sections, so that everything will have its place and you can find what you need with ease and dispatch.

Yarn and cotton. — Each sort of yarn should be wrapped in a slip of parchment tied with a ribbon. The number of the thread contained should be noted on the outside so that whenever you run out you can replace it with exactly the same item. In this manner you will always have a complete set. All you have to do is tell the shop which number thread you desire. When a woman is sewing, she soon knows which is the correct number thread for her task. Cottons, whether for sewing, embroidery or darning, which come either on a card or in a skein, should be arranged in the workbox by thickness. The cottons that are said to be *à la croix* [for embroidery], marked with a cross on the packet, are the best.

Needles. — Needles should always be of the best quality (essential for good work, and faster too) and be bought in packets. They are numbered according to thickness; starting with the thickest. A woman can mix the sizes in her needle case, but only there. The case should be made of wood because wood doesn't blunt them.

Pins. — Pins should be bought by weight, by the thousand or by the box, never by the handful. You can mix different sizes together. The so-called English pins with a flat head are the best but are more expensive than others.

Ribbons, cotton or otherwise. — These should be bought severally, but be sure to get several widths so that you have a complete set. Before putting them away in your workbox, you should wind them flat round a small oblong of strong but thin card. Laces should be stored in the same way.

Silk. — Black sewing silk or cord can be bought as needed and when you use a coloured silk, if it's not sold on cards, as it is in many districts, you should cut any that's left over into convenient lengths for the needle and put them away in folds of paper so that, whenever you need a little, you can find it easily in your store. Bits and pieces, arranged in this manner, won't get in a muddle.

Hooks. — Hooks are bought by weight and stored in a box. So are buttons, which you buy by the gross or the card.

Cards of cotton or yarn. — Cards of cotton should be kept in their own compartment and not mixed with other yarns.

Bobbins. — So that your cotton or thread does not get tangled you should always have wooden bobbins with a nick cut in the flange into which you can slip one end of the thread. This will stop it unwinding and getting dirty. A star-shaped card is also serviceable, but a ball wound round a slip of paper will unwind and get in a tangle.

Yarn holder. — If a woman is used to winding her own yarn and cutting it into skeins, she will need a sheath or roll to store them in. This is made

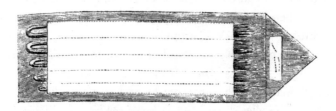

Figure 2. Yarn holder.

with a piece of cloth, folded over, measuring about 25 centimetres long and 10 or 15 centimetres wide. This is divided into ribs by means of simple seams. Each rib or tube should be large enough to accommodate a skein of yarn cut into lengths suitable for a single needleful. You start, on one side of the fabric, with the largest rib or tube you would need for the thickest yarn, and you reduce the size of each rib as you go across the fabric. In this way the yarn is graded by size, which will be helpful at the point of use. Make a small pocket at one end of this yarn-holder, for any little things you may require while sewing. You also can stitch a little piece of flannel on it to act as a pin-cushion. At the pointed end of the fabric, you make a buttonhole, and add a button at the other end on the reverse side. Then

Figure 3. Worktable.

Figure 4. Workbasket.

you can button the whole thing up when you roll it. You should take great care never to leave yarn in plaits or braids because, no matter how carefully done, it's bound to get dirty and tangled.

Cutting board. — You should find a thin pine cutting board 50 centimetres wide and 75 centimetres long, edged in oak at either end. You have it on your knees whenever cutting the bodice of a dress or any other small piece of work.

Worktable. — A little worktable with a lockable drawer is a fine alternative to a workbox, which is often too small for all you need. A hinged lid, with a mirror on the inside, covers a cabinet divided into compartments for all your sewing necessities. The central compartment, larger and deeper than the others, is designed to hold all your work in progress on smaller items. The table should be on casters and should be solid enough to support a lamp.

2. — Patterns. — Workbasket. — Sewing kit.

Patterns. — A large box in the form of a folder is necessary to hold all the paper patterns which a woman should always keep of any clothing she may have made herself, so that she can repeat them without wasting material. I do not hold with anyone cutting without a pattern; they run the risk of never achieving what they want. With a pattern you can be sure of using any fabric to its best advantage. Every pattern should be identified and the date of first use recorded.

Workbasket. — A nice workbasket, lined out in silk and with lots of

Figure 5. Sewing kit.

pockets, is very convenient, especially in the country, where you will often find yourself working outdoors. You load it with everything you need for the work in hand, and with all the things you need most frequently. If you are going from room to room, or going out in the garden to work, you can take the basket with you and have everything at your elbow.

Sewing kit. — A little sewing kit in a case holding scissors, a thimble, a card of needles, etc., is even more portable than a basket. While indispensable, it cannot replace the workbasket.

3. — A work cupboard.

A mistress should also have a press or cupboard where she can store any linen or clothing that needs repair, as well as any new garments she wishes to make up and which she has had first to cut out. They will thus be kept clean and tidy, ready for whenever she may have time to sew them. She can also store any left-over fabric, or pieces taken from a worn-out garment, that might come in handy for certain things. This press will ensure that she does not muddle clothes that need mending with those that do not, and that everything is to hand when she needs it. In addition, she may find a large basket helpful, where she can put anything bulky that she is working on. That way she won't have to throw everything over chairbacks here and there, which only makes her room look a mess.

CHAPTER VI

HOUSEHOLD ROUTINE

1. — General tidiness.

When discussing a topic as important as household management, I urge from the outset that a mistress should insist on perfect tidiness and utter cleanliness. If her house is not in this condition when she reads this chapter, we expect it soon to be. However much she dislikes the thought of embarking on this task, she must accept its necessity. Once done, she will feel a satisfaction that more than repays the effort made. Once everything has been cleaned, tidied and arranged in perfect order, it is but a moment's work to replace each object where it belongs whenever you use it, so it all remains neat and tidy without much extra work. A woman should make every effort to ensure her children and her servants absorb this precious lesson of tidiness: to succeed in this, however, she must have learnt it first herself.

She ought, therefore to make her dispositions, and insist that others do too, to ensure that dirt is not carried through the house. But she should do this without becoming a martyr to cleanliness, unpleasantly house-proud.

Simplicity should reign in the house; luxury is an anomaly in country districts, it is merely clutter which demands constant attention and is quite incompatible with country life. Let every object, every piece of furniture, have its place and its purpose; don't let your linen press hold clothing; don't store scraps of fabric in your wardrobe, etc.; never muddle or mix categories in your cupboards.

A mistress should never put off a job that can be done there and then; there is no greater fault than putting off to the morrow the task that can be done today. Such negligence only leads to general disarray, to uncleanliness, to ruin; it should never be tolerated. If you can't do something immediately, do not put it out of mind, but make sure you turn to it as soon as possible.

In the normal course of events, you should make sure the servants have cleaned and tidied all the rooms before breakfast. If this is not possible during the shortest days of winter, then they should leave the bedrooms and turn to them as soon as possible after breakfast.

2. — Children's and servants' rising and retiring.

The hours of servants' rising and retiring are a matter of regulation. It is often difficult to stop servants breaking the rules but the mistress should assure herself every so often that they are not ignoring them altogether. So that they all get up betimes in the morning, she will have to limit any tendency to sit up together through the nights at *veillées* or work-bees. These night-time sessions have their disadvantages: if you have lots of servants, they waste hours laughing and chatting together; if you have just one, she will probably fall asleep. Suppressing the practice altogether is probably advisable from the point of view of hygiene; and it certainly results, in winter at any rate, in saving heat and light.

When the children rise and go to bed should not be a matter of discussion; this is simple to enforce because the mother, who is also the teacher, puts them to bed and wakes them herself. It is advisable for even the youngest children to get used to a routine and to get themselves up in the morning: habits such as these will stand them in good stead for the rest of their lives.

3. — The children's studies.

A mother should be scrupulous in making sure her children do their lessons regularly. If she is slack or desultory in her oversight, any point of teaching them will be lost. Once a daily routine of study and tuition has been established, it must always be adhered to.

4. — Meals and meal times of the family and the servants.

The number and sequence of meals. — In the country, especially where there are children, three meals are best. Meal times should be regular and invariable.

At those times of the year when farm work is at its most demanding, it is often essential that the master and even the mistress should stay outside to supervise the work in hand; and as the workers' meal times are not the same as the master's, he will be unable to dine at his usual hour. This delay will have a terrible effect on some of the dishes that you may have had prepared and will waste a lot of the servants' time. At these seasons, therefore, I advise that meals are taken in step with those of the workforce and that normal hours are resumed once the more important field tasks have been completed.

If either the children, someone in the household or a servant wants to eat between meals, you should allow them nothing but dry bread, save in exceptional circumstances. An infinity of snacks is contrary to good health and can lead to waste and even abuse.

The family's meals. — When days are longer and you have risen early, breakfast should be at 8.30. The rest of the year it should be at 9 or 10 o'clock.

At midday or one o'clock, depending when you have breakfasted, you may take a *collation* or second breakfast. This light meal should consist of something that occupies but one plate.

Dinner can be at 6 o'clock in the winter and 5 o'clock in the summer, especially in the autumn, so that you have plenty of time before sunset to take a walk.

The servants' meals. — The servants should eat immediately after the family. However, when outside work is at its highest and some of the servants are out in the fields or the garden, it's best to delay the kitchen's dinner until well into the evening, when everyone is indoors. That way, they will all eat together. In this case, the cook and the indoor servants should get on with their evening tasks immediately the family has dined, i.e. washing the dishes, cleaning the pots and pans, getting the bedrooms ready, etc.

You should not interrupt the servants while they are eating; this is their moment of relaxation and they ought not to be disturbed. A mistress can often pass by the servants' hall, but for a moment only, just to see that everything is as it should be, that they have something decent to eat and that the food that she intended is actually on the table.

The crockery. — All the crockery, casseroles, etc., used at the family table, or in the servants' hall, should be cleaned and tidied away the same evening. There is plenty of work of a morning without wasting time on jobs from the night before.

5. — Household expenses.

There are several ways that a master and mistress can deal with household expenses. The best, there's no denying, is that money is held in common, so that husband and wife can spend it as each may wish, just accounting to each other for their actions. However, apart from some husbands not liking this arrangement, it may not always be possible, for instance if he is also a dealer, or if he is working to develop the estate, which is much the same.

In that situation, the husband can make a fixed allowance to his wife for household expenses. For her personal expenditure, he can pay her as and when she needs something, which she will then account for. It is only right in this case that the husband too, when he spends money on himself, accounts to her for his actions. However, as most men don't find this to their liking, fair and equitable though it may be, the wisest course, in my view, is that he makes a fixed allowance and the wife can spend anything left over on herself. If he doesn't allow this small concession, then he denies her the pleasure of discreet charity, or of buying gifts for her husband, children, family or friends.

At the same time, as a good housewife contributes a great deal to the prosperity of the household and even to the farming business, it strikes me as only fair that she should share in some of the profits stemming from her labours: this will be a great encouragement to her.

It is much more difficult to forecast the expenses of a household in the country than one in the town. They fluctuate according to the season, the work in hand, the success of the harvests, and the energy of the household servants. If, as I have mentioned, the husband makes a fixed allowance for household expenses, the wife will always render him a detailed account; at the end of each month, he can make whatever suggestions on the wisdom of her expenditure that he sees fit to make.

In like manner, it is fair and reasonable to allow the wife to cast her eye over the farming accounts, and for her to make her own observations thereon. Women often have an eye for detail that men do not have. Details are important in the success of a farm, in every branch of its operations, and a woman's advice will therefore be timely.

6. — Paying the servants.

You must pay the servants regularly and at the same time as the rest of the district. It is better to pay them every month, or at least every quarter, rather than annually, which is the usual custom in many provinces.

Businessmen and merchants will perhaps disagree with this statement, for they reckon it better to delay any payment; but in a private household, where money destined for one purpose or another will stay put in the cash box until it is needed, it is much wiser to pay out anything that one owes as soon as possible. Otherwise, if you have money lying around, you will only spend it on something other than the reason it was put aside in the first place; and then you will be embarrassed. Anyway, it is only fair that the servants wait no longer than necessary for their wages.

CHAPTER VII

ACCOUNTS. — THE METRIC SYSTEM OF WEIGHTS AND MEASURES. — BAROMETER. — THERMOMETER.

I. — Accounts.

The benefits of good accounts. — Detailed and regular accounts are essential to the good management of a household. It is the foundation of good order and economy; I cannot therefore recommend highly enough that the mistress pays every attention to their regularity and exactitude.

She must make time, morning or evening, for this work which, once mastered, will never take more than fifteen minutes or half an hour. Such accounts will permit her to identify those areas of expenditure which are open to economies: only by doing this will she understand where the money goes and how to best plan her expenses. However, if she neglects her accounts for just one day, she will find everything in a muddle, that the work is so much harder, that she gets bored and disenchanted with the whole affair, and then abandons it altogether or at the most keeps them badly. I can't repeat too often that this way lies ruin and distress.

Account books. — Six books of account are required, as follows: notebook, kitchen account book, general receipts and expenditure, wage book, general memorandum book, letter book.

Notebook. — You should always carry a notebook in your pocket in which you can write any items of expenditure or receipt, as well as just general memoranda. It is a sort of *aide-mémoire*; every entry is dated, and then crossed out once it has been written up or is no longer relevant. Entries should be made whenever necessary and, should you forget to do this, whenever they come to mind later on. As soon as you turn to your proper accounts, you can refer to this journal and extract each item into the apposite book.

Kitchen accounts. — In these are written all food costs. Divide them into three columns; in the first you note the costs of any foodstuffs bought; in the second you record the price of any supplies taken from the farm itself, according them the value they would have fetched had they been sold at market; the third column gives the total of the first two. You total each column at the bottom of the page. This way you will always know your food costs, whether purchased or reared by your own efforts. That second category forms part of the general receipts of the farming business. Here follows an example

KITCHEN ACCOUNTS

DATES	JANUARY, 1859	EXPENSES		
		IN CASH	IN KIND	TOTALS
1st	Bread	1.80	»	1.80
	Milk	»	0.60	0.60
	Butcher's meat	3.50	»	3.50
	Chicken	»	2.50	2.50
	Vegetables	»	1.75	1.75
	Totals	5.30	4.85	10.15

Book of general receipts and expenditure. — In this book are entered all sorts of receipt and expenditure. The account is divided into two sections, which should be kept quite separate: the accounts of the farming business, and the household accounts. The following example gives some idea of how the household account should be arranged.

You can find account books at the stationer's which will have columns and headings already printed; these are easily adjusted to suit your own circumstances.

For reasons of space, I have had to leave out several columns in the figure below, so that the arrangement of income and expenditure can be easily understood. The headings of the columns I have omitted should be: taxes, alms, repairs, furnishings, equipment, healthcare.

MASTER'S

GENERAL RECEIPTS

| DATES | RECEIPTS
JANUARY, 1859 | RECEIPTS | | PRODUCT
OF
SALES | TOTAL
RECEIPTS |
		IN CASH	IN KIND		
1	Rec'd for the household	300 »	» »	» »	300 »
6	Quarter's rent	250 »	» »	» »	250 »
9	Sale of vegetables	» »	» »	15 »	15 »
15	Rec'd from the farmyard, for poultry	» »	25 »	» »	25 »
	— from garden, for vegetables	» »	15 »	» »	15 »
		550 »	40 »	15 »	605 »

The left-hand page, as shown here, is given over to income, and the right to expenditure. The two can be read at a single glance.

You should enter each item of expenditure as soon as you pay it, or whenever you go through your notebook in the manner I have previously described. Every month, you also enter the totals from the kitchen accounts, under two heads: the first including everything paid for in cash, the second including anything supplied by the farm, costed at its market value. By entering your outgoings in their several columns on the page devoted to expenditure you will be able to see at a glance the totals in each category.

On the other page, you enter the value of all your hypothetical income from materials supplied by the farm itself, for example: *received from the garden, for vegetables, … francs; received from the poultry yard, for chicken, … francs;* etc. In addition, you enter receipts from any sales, and moneys received from your husband.

Every month, when balancing up receipts and expenditure, you count up what cash you have in your cash box. This sum, plus the total of your expenses should equal the total of your receipts. Once you have struck your balance, any cash remaining is then carried over to your receipts for the next month.

HOUSE

AND EXPENDITURE

DATES	EXPENSES JANUARY, 1859	MISC EXPENSES	FOOD		HEATING, LIGHTING	LAUNDRY, LINEN	SERVANTS	MASTER	MISTRESS	CHILDREN	TOTAL EXPEND.
			IN CASH	IN KIND							
3	4 kilogr. oil	» »	» »	» »	4 80	» »	»	»	» »	»	4 80
4	20 met. calico	» »	» »	» »	» »	» »	»	»	25 »	»	25 »
9	2 pairs sheets	» »	» »	» »	» »	72 »	»	»	» »	»	72 »
	Haberdashery	6 75	» »	» »	» »	» »	»	»	» »	»	6 75
15	15 steres of wood	» »	» »	» »	180 »	» »	»	»	» »	»	180 »
	Postage stamps	2 30	» »	» »	» »	» »	»	»	» »	»	2 30
	Food	» »	198 »	80 »	» »	» »	»	»	» »	»	278 »
		9 05	198 »	80 »	184 80	72 »	»	»	25 »	»	568 85

If your totals do not agree, it is because there is an error, either in your adding up, or in your record of incomings and outgoings. It is usually that you either failed to make an entry, or you entered an item twice, or you entered the wrong figure. First, you should verify your figures, then check your arithmetic; if everything seems correct, try to recall your dealings. If you can't trace the mistake, as it will never be very large, and as it is hardly necessary that household books should be so officiously correct as those of a business, just make a note of any overspend under the heading 'forgotten revenue' or, if the error is on the expenditure side, 'expenditure not noted'. Then you will have a balance and you can carry on, while resolving always to enter every receipt and every expense.

You can use a part of this same book to open an account for each of the servants. The first entry will be their conditions of employment. If the servant undertakes any dealings on behalf of the household, then the account should have two columns; in one you note the cash he or she has received, and in the second you enter any wages due and the value of the purchases he or she has made. Every time you enter up these accounts, you total the two columns to check the balance. In this way, you will always know if he or she is in debit or credit.

WAGES BOOK

NAMES OF WORKERS	DAILY RATE		MONDAY	TUESDAY	WEDNESDAY	THURSDAY	FRIDAY	SATURDAY	WEEKLY SALARY	
Jean	2	»	—	—	»	—	—	—	10	»
François	2	50	—	—	—	—	—	»	12	50
Catherine	1	25	—	»	»	—	—	»	3	75

Wages book. — This is the account in which the mistress enters the wages due to any workers she employs that are paid by the day. Each week she totals up the amount owing to any worker, she pays him or her, then she strikes through the week's note. If she doesn't actually pay him, she still closes the week's account, so that she knows what is owing, but she does not strike it through.

Each page of this account is divided into nine columns. The first is for the name of the journeyman and the second is for the sum agreed for a day's work. The next six columns are for each day of the working week. On a day when the labourer has worked, you put a small dash. This is fast and simple to execute. In the ninth column, you enter the total, either of wages due (as I have done in the example above) or of days worked.

General memorandum book. — In this book you make a note of the date that you put your flock to the ram, when lambing started, how many lambs were born and their sex, etc.

You can also use it to note the dates when you issued certain instructions – when the date matters: for example, when vegetables were sown in the garden so that you will know in the future whether this was the correct season and can draw the right lesson for future sowings. You can also use this book to make a succinct record of the day's events. It can be extremely useful to have these notes to hand when memory fails you.

Letter book. — In this book you make a register of all the letters you write, adding a précis of their contents where necessary, and making a full copy of business letters which you may need to refer to, or even produce, later on. An alphabetical index will make reference easier. This will allow you to see the state of your correspondence at a glance; you will always be up to date, and you will not be liable to repeat yourself.

2. — The metric system of weights and measures.

The metric system, prescribed by law in place of any ancient weights and measures, is now universal, adopted even by the country labourer. A wife who has to secure or approve any sort of work must therefore be quite at ease with metric measures or else she will be for ever at a disadvantage in carrying out her responsibilities. I take from M. Borie[1] this lucid explanation of the system, and I have printed conversion tables which should cover most calculations that you are likely to require.[2]

A. — An explanation of the metric system.

Metre. — By a decree of 8 May 1790, the Constituent Assembly sought to eliminate abuses arising from so many different weights and measures being employed in commerce. To that end, the Académie des sciences was charged to fix upon a single length as the basis for all weights and measures. The Académie determined that this length should be the *ten-millionth* part of the distance from the pole to the equator, that is to say, a quarter of the circumference of the globe.

Two laws, of 18 Germinal year III and 19 Frimaire year VIII, laid the framework by which France was equipped with a system of measurement founded on scientific method.[3]

1. This is Victor Borie (1818–1880), secretary and sometime lover of George Sand, and a politician, journalist and writer on agricultural matters (he was published by the same house as Mme Millet-Robinet). One of his most famous books is *Les Travaux des champs, éléments d'agriculture pratique*, 1857, but he wrote many others on farming and political subjects.

2. The modern reader may be surprised that such detailed instruction was required, even in 1859. By later editions, for example that of 1893, these details were omitted. Although the metric system was introduced soon after the Revolution, the final statute being enacted in 1799, the old measures remained in use, especially in country districts. The confusion was so great that in 1812 a compromise arrangement was adopted whereby the old names were retained, but with metric values (I depend here on Philip Rush and John O'Keefe, *Weights and Measures*, 1962). Thus the *toise* was 2 metres, the *aune* (ell) 1 metre 20 centimetres, the bushel one-eighth of a hectolitre and the pound (*livre*) half a kilogram. This arrangement was not outlawed until 1840, when metric measures were made compulsory under legislation enacted in 1837. However, in deepest France, where much of the population was illiterate and unschooled, the new system took an age to be accepted.

3. 18 Germinal year III and 19 Frimaire year VIII correspond to 7 April 1795 and 9 December 1799.

The length was named the **Metre.**

So that this process need not be repeated at frequent intervals, a metre cast in platinum was deposited with the legislative body. It was dubbed the *prototype*.

Once the **metre** had been established as the fixed and invariable standard, it could be extended to other weights and measures.

The are. — For measures of extent, i.e. for land, they created a basic unit called the **are**, which was a square of 10 metres on each side.

The stere, or cubic metre. — For measures of volume, particularly of firewood, they created a unit of one metre in three directions: length, breadth and height, which they called a **stere**. This is none other than a **cubic metre.**

Litre. — For liquids, grains and other dry goods, they created a measure which equals a cubic decimetre. This they called a **litre.**

Gram. — It is not difficult to understand how the **metre**, a measure of *length*, could give rise to units that measure *area*, *mass* and *capacity*; but how that same measure can also be adapted to weight may seem at first surprising. Any difficulty was quickly overcome by the calculation that the **gram**, the basic unit of weight, is equal to one cubic centimetre of water at its highest density, i.e. when it has been distilled and heated to a temperature of 4 degrees centigrade.

The names of the units. — I summarize:

The unit of length is therefore called the **Metre.**

—	of area	**Are.**
—	of mass	**Stere.**
—	of capacity	**Litre.**
—	of weight	**Gram.**

These measures can be applied to every sort of quantity.

Multiples of units of weight and measure. — We must now look at certain terms which can seem difficult at first simply because they are unfamiliar. There are **seven** of them: they are the multiples and divisions of the essential units of weight and measure that I have explained above. Although deriving from a foreign language, they are not impossible to remember.

First the multiples: their names derive from Greek, and they are **four in** number, i.e.:

Deca, which means *Ten.*		10
Hecto, —	*Hundred.*	100
Kilo, —	*Thousand.*	1000
Myria. —	*Ten thousand.*	10,000

These four words are called multiples because when they are joined either to the basic unit, the **metre**, or to the secondary measures, **are, stere, litre, gram**, they make up a word that describes those units multiplied by the amount specified, i.e. **deca** ten, **hecto** hundred, **kilo** thousand, **myria** ten thousand. Therefore:

Decametre	means	*ten metres.*
Decalitre	means	*ten litres.*
Decagram	means	*ten grams.*
Hectometre	means	*one hundred metres.*
Hectogram	means	*one hundred grams.*
Hectolitre	means	*one hundred litres.*
Kilometre	means	*one thousand metres.*
Kilolitre	means	*one thousand litres.*
Kilogram	means	*one thousand grams.*
Myriametre	means	*ten thousand metres.*
Myrialitre	means	*ten thousand litres.*
Myriagram	means	*ten thousand grams.*

If these words are applied to these quantities and any quantities which follow, so that the gaps between the various divisions are filled, then the principle – given that the law allows that each weight and measure should have its half and its double – permits the rapid expression of any multiple or subdivision of any weight and any measure.

Divisions of units of weight and measure. — The subdivisions or diminutives are so called because, when joined to the basic unit, they express the fractions of these units: one-tenth, one-hundredth or one-thousandth part of the whole. These fractions are **three** only, thus:

Deci (tenth), the diminutive of **Deca;**
Centi (hundredth), — **Hecto;**
Milli (thousandth), — **Kilo.**

These three words come from the Latin. If they are joined to the units **metre, are, stere, litre** and **gram**, they give a new word indicating fractions of one-tenth, one-hundredth and one-thousand part of a *metre, are, stere, litre* or *gram*. (There is an exception for the *are* and the *stere*. It has been agreed to restrict certain combinations and to use only the following expressions as a matter of course: *Hecto-are*, or the syncope *Hectare*, one hundred ares, or one hundred metres squared, or ten-thousand square metres; *Are*, one hundred square metres, or a square of ten metres; *Centiare*, one-hundredth of an are, or one square metre; *Decastere*, ten steres; *Demi-decastere*, five steres; *Double stere*, two steres; *Stere*, one cubic metre; *Demi-stere*, half a stere; *Decistere*, one-tenth of a stere.)

Thus **decimetre** describes a fraction ten times smaller than a metre, that is, one-tenth of a metre.

Decilitre, a fraction ten times smaller than a litre, that is, a tenth of a litre, etc., etc.

It is the same with **centi** and **milli**, which indicate a hundredth or a thousandth part of whichever unit they are attached to.

Classification of terms used in the metric system. — So that you can always recall what has just been explained, it should be repeated that the decimal metric system is entirely founded on only **twelve** expressions; to make the simplicity of the system even clearer, these terms can be grouped as follows.

They can be divided into three categories:

The *first* is the *five* generic units of weight and measure: **metre, are, stere, litre, gram**.

The *second*, the multiples of these units, represented by the following terms: **deca, hecto, kilo, myria**, which multiply the generic units by ten, one hundred, one thousand, ten thousand.

And finally the *third* category includes the three sub-multiples or divisions, which are expressed as **deci, centi, milli** to indicate the tenth, the hundredth or the thousandth part of the *metre*, the *are*, the *stere*, the *litre* or the *gram*.

B. — The manner of writing and speaking decimal weights and measures.

The multiples and sub-multiples of weights and measures follow, as can be seen from the table below, a numeric progression of ten, upwards or downwards, identical to the decimal system, that is, that the multiples go

TABULAR VIEW OF THE METRIC SYSTEM

	Metre,	measure	of length;
	Are,	——	of surface;
UNITS	**Stere,**	——	of volume or bulk;
	Litre,	——	of capacity;
	Gramme	——	of weight.

	MYRIA,	which means	10,000 times	
MULTIPLES	KILO,	——	1,000 times	larger than the unit.
	HECTO,	——	100 times	
	DECA,	——	10 times	

	DECI,	——	10 times	
SUB-DIVISIONS	CENTI,	——	100 times	smaller than the unit.
	MILLI,	——	1,000 times	

(NAMES OF UNITS)

from ten to ten times larger and the subdivisions go from ten to ten times smaller. When these values are written down, you should express them as a decimal calculation so that the basic unit, the metre, are, stere, litre or gram, is at the centre of the expression, with the multipliers on the left hand, each column representing an increase of ten times; and on the other side, to the right, you place the subdivisions, each column representing a figure ten times smaller than the last.

Here is that expression schematically expressed:

MYRIA.	KILO.	HECTO.	DECA.	PRINCIPAL	DECI.	CENTI.	MILLI.
o	o	o	o	O	o	o	o
Ten-thousand	Thousand	Hundred	Ten	UNIT	Tenth	Hundredth	Thousandth

You should write the name of the weight or measure **immediately** after the expression of whole units or before the expression of **fractions; if** there is no whole unit, you replace it with a zero and, when speaking, **you** enunciate the zero as if it were a whole number, giving the name **of the** subdivision at the end.

EXAMPLE:

1^{m},20 (one metre twenty centimetres).

0^{m},50 (zero metres fifty centimetres).

0^{m},05 (zero metres five centimetres).

There are different ways of expressing the decimal value of **weights and** measures, depending on which multiple or fraction you use as **the whole** unit.

Thus, if you take the number 15,332^{m},134, you can express this **either as** myriametres, or as kilometres, etc.

You would use one of the following expressions:

1	Myriametre,	5,332 metres,	134 millimetres.
15	Kilometres,	332 metres,	134 millimetres.
153	Hectometres,	32 metres,	134 millimetres.
1,533	Decametres,	2 metres,	134 millimetres.
15,332	Metres,		134 millimetres.
153, 321	Decimetres		34 millimetres, etc.

3. — Conversion of old measures to metric measures.

a. — Measures of line and distance.

CONVERSION OF MYRIAMETRES INTO LEAGUES AND LEAGUES INTO MYRIAMETRES

Myr.	Leagues	Myr.	Leagues	Leagues	Myr.	Leagues	Myr.
1	2.25	9	20.25	1	0.3898	9	3.5083
2	4.50	10	22.50	2	0.7796	10	3.8981
3	6.75	20	45.00	3	1.1694	20	7.9962
4	9.00	30	67.50	4	1.5595	30	11.9943
5	11.25	40	90.00	5	1.9490	40	15.9924
6	13.50	50	112.50	6	2.3388	50	19.9905
7	15.75	100	225.00	7	2.7287	100	39.9810
8	18.00	500	1125.00	8	3.1185	500	199.9050

CONVERSION OF FATHOMS, FEET, INCHES & LINES INTO METRES AND DECIMALS OF A METRE

Fathoms	Metres	Feet	Metres	Inches	Metres	Lines	Millimetres
1	1.9490	1	0.3248	1	0.0271	1	2.256
2	3.8981	2	0.6497	2	0.0541	2	4.512
3	5.8471	3	0.9745	3	0.0812	3	6.767
4	7.7961	4	1.2994	4	0.1083	4	9.023
5	9.7452	5	1.6242	5	0.1354	5	11.279
6	11.6942	6	1.9490	6	0.1624	6	13.535
7	13.6433	7	2.2739	7	0.1895	7	15.791
8	15.5923	8	2.5987	8	0.2166	8	18.047
9	17.5413	9	2.9236	9	0.2436	9	20.302
10	19.4904	10	3.2484	10	0.2707	10	22.558
20	38.9807	20	6.4968	20	0.5414	20	45.117
30	58.4711	30	9.7452	30	0.8120	30	67.675
40	77.9615	40	12.9936	40	1.0828	40	90.233
50	97.4518	50	16.2420	50	1.3535	50	112.792
100	194.9037	100	32.4839	100	2.7070	100	225.583

CONVERSION OF METRES INTO FEET, INCHES, LINES AND DECIMALS OF A LINE

Metres	Feet	Inches	Lines	Metres	Feet	Inches	Lines
1	3	0	11.296	60	184	8	5.76
2	6	1	10.593	70	215	5	10.72
3	9	2	9.888	80	246	3	3.68
4	12	3	9.184	90	277	0	8.64
5	15	4	8.480	100	307	10	1.60
6	18	5	7.776	200	615	8	3.20
7	21	6	7.072	300	923	6	4.80
8	24	7	6.368	400	1231	4	6.40
9	27	8	5.664	500	1539	2	8.00
10	30	9	4.960	600	1847	0	9.60
20	61	6	9.920	700	2154	10	11.20
30	92	4	2.880	800	2464	9	0.80
40	123	1	7.840	900	2770	7	2.40
50	153	11	0.800	1000	3078	5	4.00

[Note with reference to the tables relating to line and distance: The French league (*lieue*) was the league of Paris, defined in 1674 and in force until 1793. It contained 2000 fathoms (*toises*) and measured 3.898 kilometres (a mile is 1.609 km). The league was very variable depending on location in France (thus in Poitou it measured 4.630 km) but Madame Millet-Robinet has here adopted the Paris standard. A line (Fr. *ligne*) measures one-twelfth of an inch. The French fathom (*toise*) measures 6 English feet; the French foot (*pied*) 12.785 English inches; and the French inch (*pouce*), 1.066 English inches.]

b. — Agricultural measures.

CONVERSION OF ACRES TO HECTARES AND HECTARES TO ACRES

Acres of 100 perches square, the perch 18 feet long		Acres of 100 perches square, the perch 22 feet long		Conversion of hectares to acres of 18 ft perches		Conversion of hectares to acres of 22 ft perches	
Acres	Hectares	Acres	Hectares	Hectares	Acres	Hectares	Acres
1	0.3419	1	0.5107	1	2.925	1	1.958
2	0.6838	2	1.0214	2	5.830	2	3.916
3	1.0257	3	1.5422	3	8.775	3	5.874
4	1.3675	4	2.0329	4	11.700	4	7.832
5	1.7094	5	2.5536	5	14.625	5	9.790
6	2.0513	6	3.0643	6	17.520	6	11.748
7	2.3932	7	3.5750	7	20.475	7	13.709
8	2.7351	8	4.0858	8	23.399	8	15.664
9	3.0770	9	4.5965	9	26.324	9	17.622
10	3.4189	10	5.1072	10	29.249	10	19.580
20	6.8377	20	10.2144	20	58.499	20	39.160
30	10.2566	30	15.3216	30	87.748	30	58.740
40	13.6755	40	20.4288	40	116.998	40	78.320
50	17.0943	50	25.5360	50	136.247	50	97.900
60	20.5132	60	30.6432	60	175.497	60	117.480
70	23.9321	70	35.7504	70	204.746	70	137.060
80	27.3669	80	40.8576	80	253.995	80	156.640
90	30.7698	90	45.9648	90	263.245	90	176.220
100	34.1887	100	51.0720	100	292.494	100	195.800

c. — Measures of capacity for dry materials..

CONVERSION OF HECTOLITRES INTO SETIERS AND OF SETIERS INTO HECTOLITRES, THE
SETIER BEING 12 OLD BUSHELS, THE BUSHEL 13 LITRES

Hecto.	Setiers	Hecto.	Setiers	Setiers	Hecto.	Setiers	Hecto.
1	0.641	20	12.820	1	1.56	20	31.20
2	1.282	30	19.231	2	3.12	30	46.80
3	1.923	40	25.641	3	4.68	40	62.40
4	2.564	50	32.051	4	6.24	50	78.00
5	3.205	60	38.461	5	7.80	60	93.60
6	3.846	70	44.871	6	9.36	70	109.20
7	4.487	80	51.282	7	10.92	80	124.80
8	5.128	90	57.692	8	12.48	90	140.40
9	5.769	100	64.102	9	14.04	100	156.00
10	6.410	500	320.510	10	15.60	500	780.00

The average weight of a hectolitre of wheat is 75 kilograms.

[Note with reference to the table of capacity: The *setier* does not correspond exactly to an Imperial measure. In France its size was very variable (anything from 150 to 300 litres for measures of dry volume, much smaller when it was used as a liquid measure). Mme Millet-Robinet has opted for the Paris standard. Another large measure, the *muid*, was even more variable, depending on location and the commodity measured. It might be likened to the English cauldron. In England, there were 4 pecks to the bushel, 4 bushels to the coomb, 8 bushels to the quarter and 36 bushels to the cauldron.]

d. — Measures of volume.

CONVERSION OF FATHOMS, FEET, INCHES & LINES INTO CUBIC METRES AND DECIMALS OF
A CUBIC METRE

Cubic fathoms	Cubic metres	Cubic feet	Cubic decimetres	Cubic inches	Cubic centimetres	Cubic lines	Cubic millimetres
1	7.40	1	34.28	1	19.84	1	11.48
2	14.80	2	68.56	2	39.67	2	22.96
3	22.21	3	102.83	3	59.51	3	34.44
4	29.62	4	137.12	4	79.35	4	45.92

CONVERSION OF FATHOMS, FEET, INCHES & LINES INTO CUBIC METRES AND DECIMALS OF
A CUBIC METRE

Cubic fathoms	Cubic metres	Cubic feet	Cubic decimetres	Cubic inches	Cubic centimetres	Cubic lines	Cubic millimetres
5	37.02	5	171.39	5	99.18	5	57.40
6	44.42	6	205.66	6	119.02	6	68.88
7	51.85	7	239.94	7	138.86	7	80.36
8	59.23	8	274.22	8	158.69	8	91.84
9	66.64	9	308.50	9	178.53	9	103.32
10	74.04	10	342.77	10	198.40	10	114.80
20	148.08	20	685.55	20	396.80	20	229.60
30	222.12	30	1028.32	30	595.20	30	344.40
40	296.16	40	1371.09	40	793.60	40	459.20
50	370.20	50	1713.86	50	992.00	50	574.00
60	444.24	60	2056.64	60	1190.40	60	688.80
70	518.28	70	2399.41	70	1388.80	70	803.60
80	592.32	80	2742.18	80	1587.20	80	918.40
90	666.36	90	3084.95	90	1785.60	90	1033.20
100	740.40	100	3427.72	100	1984.00	100	1148.00

e. — Weights.

CONVERSION OF OLD WEIGHTS INTO NEW WEIGHTS

Grains	Grams . Decigr.	Oz.	Grams . Decigr.	Pounds	Kilogr . Grams
10	0.53	1	30.59	1	0.4895
20	1.05	2	61.19	2	0.9790
30	1.59	3	91.78	3	1.4685
40	2.12	4	122.38	4	1.9580
50	2.66	5	152.97	5	2.4475
60	3.19	6	183.56	6	2.9370
70	3.72	7	214.16	7	3.4265
Drachm		8	244.75	8	3.9160
1	3.82	9	275.35	9	4.4056
2	7.65	10	305.94	10	4.8961
3	11.47	11	336.53	20	9.7901

CONVERSION OF OLD WEIGHTS INTO NEW WEIGHTS

Drachm	Grams . Decigr.	Oz.	Grams . Decigr.	Pounds	Kilogr . Grams
4	15.30	12	367.14	30	14.6852
5	19.12	13	397.73	40	19.5802
6	22.94	14	428.33	50	24.4753
7	26.77	15	458.91	60	29.3704
8	30.59	16	489.51	70	34.2654
				80	39.1605
				90	44.0555
				100	48.9506

[Note concerning the table of weights: The measures current under the Ancien Régime were similar in principle to English measures but differed in detail. Their grain (*grain*) weighed 0.837 grains avoirdupois. I have translated their *gros* as drachm, it was one-eighth of their ounce. Their pound (*livre*) weighed 1.079 Imperial pounds.]

4. — Barometer.

The weather. — The earth is entirely surrounded by a layer of air which we call the atmosphere. It is about 72 kilometres thick. The air envelops all solid bodies and exerts a pressure on them which varies according to the weather and the location. The barometer indicates the variation of this pressure which, in a single location, will change according to a range of circumstances, such as the rise and fall of temperature, the accumulation of cloud cover, the wind direction, etc. These circumstances we commonly call the *weather*. The barometric record is therefore intimately wedded to the weather and will give strong indications that such and such a change in the weather will occur.

Stick barometer. — This is the most common type of barometer. It consists of a tube filled with mercury, 0^m,80 long. It is closed at the top and its open bottom sits in a reservoir, also open, of mercury. It is customary to write next to the highest mark to which the mercury rises the words *very dry*; then, 5 millimetres lower, *set fair*; then *fair, change, wind or rain, heavy rain* and finally *storm*, each at 5 millimetre intervals, because the widest range of movement in the column is six times 5 millimetres, that is 3 centimetres at any one location.

Wheel barometer. — This is made up of a tube filled with mercury which is curved like a syphon, with the long section closed and the shorter section open. This is enclosed in a circular frame and a needle is connected via a series of pulleys to a weight floating on the mercury in the shorter section of the syphon. The end of this pointer describes almost the full circle of the frame, on which are written the words I have already listed: *very dry, set fair,* etc. The float rises and falls as and when the mercury rises and falls in the long section of the syphon and its movement towards fair weather or towards stormy weather can be readily understood.

Reading the barometer. — Before reading the barometer, you should tap the frame or case lightly with your finger so that the mercury or the pointer runs free, unobstructed by any obstacle that might inhibit its rise and fall.

The mean height of the mercury in the barometer. — As the altitude above sea level of the location where you are taking the reading is the greater, so this mean height will be lower. Thus the mean height of the mercury in the barometer at 2,000 metres, such as at the hospice on Mount St Gotthard, is $0^m,60$, while in Paris atmospheric pressure will push the mercury to a mean of $0^m,76$ above the reservoir in a stick barometer, or above the level of the mercury in the short section of the syphon in a wheel barometer.

The uses of a barometer. — The changes in the height of the mercury indicate changes in the weather. In summer, the barometer can forecast the weather one or two days in advance; in wintertime, the forecast may only be good for the next few hours. We have already noted that when the weather is bad, the barometer falls, and when it rises, the weather improves. The barometer will often be a useful guide when deciding whether or not to embark on certain tasks about the farm.

5. — Thermometer.

Temperature. — The thermometer indicates the temperature of its location. We call *temperature* a set of calorific circumstances that affect the state and the dimensions of objects and which impose on our own senses the sensation of hot or cold.

The uses of a thermometer. — The growth of plants is intimately connected to the rise and fall of temperature. Hence the great value of the thermometer. It will inform you when best to protect or expose those plants which are sensitive to frost.

Where to place the thermometer. — So that the thermometer gives an accurate reading of the outside temperature, you should place it in a light housing on the north side of any obstruction, at least 1^m,50 above the ground. It should stand at least a metre clear of any walls. In a word, it should be isolated and protected from any outside influence.

The centigrade thermometer. — Standard thermometers are made of glass. They consist of a cylindrical or spherical reservoir surmounted by a very thin tube. The reservoir holds mercury which rises or falls in the tube.

When the temperature rises, the mercury expands much more than the glass and therefore rises in the tube. When the temperature falls, the mercury falls in the tube because it contracts much more than the glass. We call the levels to which the mercury rises or falls when immersed in boiling or freezing water the fixed points; but it is necessary that these immersions take place where the barometer is at 0^m,76, as it is in Paris, any seaport or other location close to sea-level. Then, the space between the fixed points may be divided into one hundred parts. Each of these parts we call a *degree centigrade*. The lower we call zero or freezing point, the upper we call one hundred, or boiling point. Below zero and above one hundred we mark as many degrees as the length of the tube can accommodate so as to have a thermometer capable of registering all normal temperatures.

Readings greater than zero (freezing point) are called degrees of warmth; these are indicate by the sign +, which means more than. Degrees below zero are called degrees freezing; these are preceded by the sign -, which indicates less than. Thus, when the mercury in the thermometer is at the tenth degree above zero, we say that the temperature is ten degrees of warmth and we write +10° (plus 10 degrees), i.e. 10° warmer than freezing point. When the mercury falls to five degrees below zero, we say that the temperature is five degrees of frost and we write -5° (minus 5 degrees), i.e. 5° less than freezing point.

It is customary to mark certain significant measures on the housing or mounting of the thermometer itself, which are the following in the centigrade scale:

+38° Heat in the shade in Senegal.
+26° Heat of the usual bath.
+20° Silkworms.

+15° Hothouses.

+11° Temperate.

+6° Orange trees (i.e. the temperature at which they should be brought into the orangery).

0° Ice.

-6° Freezing point of rivers.

In Paris, the lowest recorded temperature is -23°,5, on 25 January 1795; the highest was +40° on 16 August 1765.

Réaumur's thermometer. — Réaumur's thermometer only differs from a centigrade thermometer by its dividing the range between the highest and lowest fixed points into eighty degrees rather than one hundred. As a result, four degrees on a Réaumur thermometer are the equivalent of five degrees centigrade.

Alcohol thermometers. — Often the mercury is replaced by alcohol coloured with carmine. However, as alcohol boils at 74°, these thermometers are useless for reading high temperatures.

Minimum–maximum thermometers. — It is interesting to know the minimum and maximum temperatures reached each day. To do this you need a Six's thermometer, which registers the minimum and the maximum at once. It consists of a tube bent into two lengths. The mercury rises in the right-hand one as the temperature increases; and it rises in the left-hand arm when it gets colder. Little steel markers are pushed up by the mercury as it rises and remain where they are when it falls again. Thus the instrument records the highest and lowest temperatures reached, since the last reading. In this way you can find out every morning the highest and lowest temperatures achieved during the previous twenty-four hours. Once you have made your observation, you can move the markers with a magnet so they are once again in contact with the mercury.

CHAPTER VIII

THE LIBRARY

I do not pretend to treat thoroughly every topic that might interest my readers. My book does not save you the trouble of buying other books. On the contrary, as I am bound merely to touch upon a host of interesting subjects as this work progresses, so I will excite the curious among you to pursue these matters in more specialised studies.

Without going beyond this book's principal objects – all that relates to agriculture, the rural economy and horticulture – the *Maison rustique du 19ᵉ siècle* will satisfy the most exacting; the work treats thoroughly everything that might interest any grower or country proprietor, as too does the *Journal d'Agriculture pratique* which acts as its complement.[1]

The same is true of the cookery recipes I have given: the *Cuisinier impérial*, which gives the fullest treatment of cookery, suggests recipes for some dishes of such sophisticated luxury that I could not possibly mention them here without ignoring the constraints I have set myself.[2]

---

1. These two titles are to be found in the bibliography below. The *Maison rustique* was a large co-operative venture bearing the sub-title *Encyclopédie d'Agriculture pratique*, covering most aspects of agriculture, published from 1835 by the Bureau du Journal d'agriculture pratique.
2. *Le Cuisinier impérial* by Alexandre Viard was first published in 1806. As it progressed through several editions, and France in turn changed its regime, so the title mutated to *Le Cuisinier royal*, and later to *Le Cuisinier national*. It was one of the most important culinary manuals of the nineteenth century. Mme Millet-Robinet, as will become apparent when the recipes are reached at the end of this volume, depended on much less elaborate models for her dishes.

Finally, younger women could also profitably consult a book that I wrote particularly with them in mind, based on my own hard-won experience. Its title is *Conseils aux jeunes femmes sur l'éducation de la première enfance*.[1]

But women living in the country will not be satisfied with specialist technical literature alone. For that reason I have listed below such books as will feed anyone's legitimate curiosity. They include works of history, literature, travel, etc. Well-chosen books stretch the mind, improve the soul and banish the clouds of depression. The reader is happy, during the long hours of a winter night, to trace the wandering footsteps of an intrepid traveller, to lose herself in the dreams and fantasies of a well-loved poet, or to console herself with something uplifting, imbued with sound morals. A good book is sometimes the best of friends. It is always a wise counsellor. This is why I have taken such pains to make a list of the best-written and most thoughtful books, together with the best music.

It is not my suggestion that the mistress of a house should adopt this list in its entirety for her library, literary or musical. My only wish is to make an inventory of good books. She, of course, will choose from among them. If I have included titles that would not usually be found on a lady's bookshelf, it is because I have also considered the interests of her husband. I have also indicated the price of each book, because I know how difficult it is to establish this when living in the country, and yet it is something which a woman making a purchase should always consider before actually doing so.[2]

I need hardly add that the books I have recommended were chosen with the greatest prudence. It is a mother who made this list. Sufficient to say that while no mother should forget to lock the bookcase, she will run no risk if she does.

1.   The catalogue of the Bibliothèque nationale does not list a book under this exact title, but rather *Conseils aux jeunes femmes sur leur condition et leurs devoirs de mère, pendant l'allaitement*, by Mme Cora Millet, née Robinet, published in Paris and Poitiers in 1841. The title given here was first published in Paris in 1846 and there was a later edition of 1855.

2.   In later editions, the detailed list of books for the mistress's library was suppressed.

1. — Literary library.

AGRICULTURE AND HORTICULTURE.

Bibliothèque du Cultivateur, publiée avec le concours du Ministre de l'Agriculture. — 20 volumes in-12, 1 fr. 25 the volume, as follows :

Travaux des champs, by BORIE.	Races bovines, by DE DAMPIERRE.
Fermage, by DE GASPARIN.	L'Eleveur de bêtes bovines, by VILLEROY.
Métayage, by DE GASPARIN.	Médecine vétérinaire, by VERHEYEN.
Engrais et Amendements, by FOUQUET.	Choix du cheval, by MAGNE.
Fumiers de ferme et Composts.	Choix des Vaches laitières, by MAGNE.
Noir animal, by BOBIERRE.	Basse-Cour et Lapins, by Mme MILLET
Plantes racines, by LEDOCTE.	Économie domestique, —
Prairies, by DE MOOR.	Conservation des fruits,—
Houblon, by ERATH.	Le Jardin du Cultivateur, by NAUDIN.

Bibliothèque du Jardinier, publiée avec le concours du Ministre de l'Agriculture. — 10 volumes in-12, 1 fr. 25 the volume, as follows :

Arbres fruitiers, by PUVIS.	Dahlias, by PÉPIN.
Greffe, by NOISETTE.	Œillet, by de PONSORT.
Pépinières, by CARRIÈRE.	Pelargonium, by THIBAULT.
Asperge, by LOISEL.	Plantes bulbeuses, by LEMAIRE.
Melon, by LOISEL.	Chimie et Physique horticoles.

Bon Fermier, *aide-mémoire du cultivateur*, by BARRAL. 1 v. in-12. — 7 fr.

Bon Jardinier, by POITEAU ET VILMORIN. 1 vol. in-12. — 7 fr.

Chimie agricole, by le docteur SACC. 1 vol. in-12. — 3 fr. 50.

Cours d'Agriculture, by DE GASPARIN. 5 vol. in-8. — 37 fr. 50.

Culture des Cactées, by LABOURET. 1 vol. in-12. — 7 fr. 50.

Culture des Orchidées, by MOREL. 1 vol. in-8. — 5 fr.

Drainage, irrigations, engrais liquides, by BARRAL. 4 vol. in-12. — 20 fr.

Économie rurale de l'Angleterre, by LAVERGNE. 1 vol. in-12. — 3 fr. 50.

Flore des Jardins et des Champs, by LE MAOUT et DECAISNE. 2 vol. — 9 fr.

Journal d'Agriculture pratique (2 n^{os} a month, with engravings). — 1 yr., 16 fr.

Maison rustique du 19e siècle. 5 vol. in-4° et 2,500 gravures. — 39 fr.

Manuel de l'Éducateur de Vers à soie, by ROBINET. 1 vol. — 3 fr. 50.

Manuel de l'Éleveur de Chevaux, by VILLEROY. 2 vol. in-8. — 12 fr.

Manuel général des Plantes, Arbres et Arbustes, by JACQUES et DUCHARTRE.
    4 vol. petit in-8 in 2 columns. — 36 fr.

Manuel et Code de l'Irrigateur, by VILLEROY. 1 vol. in-8. — 5 fr.

Mémoires sur l'Industrie de la Soie, by ROBINET. Pamphlets in-8.

Poulailler (Le), by JACQUE. 1 vol. in-8. — 7 fr. 50.

Revue horticole (2 n^os a month, with engravings). — one yr., 9 fr.

FINE ARTS.

Histoire des peintres, by VASARI. 10 vol. in-18. — 40 fr.

Catalogue du Musée du Louvre, by FRÉDÉRIC VILLOT. 3 vol. in-8. — 3 f.

DOMESTIC ECONOMY AND MEDICINE.

Maison rustique des Dames, by madame MILLET-ROBINET. 2 vol. — 7 fr. 50.

Le Cuisinier impérial. 1 vol. in-8. — 4 fr.

La Physiologie du Goût, by BRILLAT-SAVARIN. 1 vol. in-18. — 1 fr.

POLITICAL ECONOMY.

BAUDRILLART. Manuel d'Économie politique. 1 vol. in-18. — 3 fr. 50.

BASTIAT. Œuvres économiques. 6 vol. in-18. — 21 fr.

FRANKLIN. Science du bonhomme Richard. 1 vol. in-18. — 3 fr. 50.

HENRIETTE MARTINEAU. Contes sur l'Économie politique. 8 vol. in-8. — 20 fr

EDUCATION.

Conseils aux jeunes femmes sur l'éducation de la première enfance, by madame MILLET-ROBINET. 1 vol. in-18. — 3 fr.

BERQUIN (Œuvres complètes). 4 vol. in-18. — 12 fr.

Magasin des Enfants, by Mme LEPRINCE DE BEAUMONT. 1 vol. in-8. — 9 fr.

Télémaque, by FÉNELON. 1 vol. in-12. — 1 fr.

Éducation familière, by miss EDGEWORTH, trans. BELLOC. 12 vol. — 18 fr.

Éducation des Filles, by FÉNELON. 1 vol. in-18. — 3 fr. 50.

Éducation des Filles, by madame de MAINTENON. 1 vol. in-18. — 3 fr. 50.

Éducation pour les Filles (cours complet d'), by THÉRY.

   1re partie, Éducation élémentaire de 4 à 10 ans. 1 vol. in-8. — 10 fr.

   2e   —   —   moyenne, de 10 à 16 ans. 8 vol. — 63 fr.

   3e   —   —   supérieure, de 16 à 20 ans. 7 vol. — 57 fr.

Éducation maternelle, by madame TASTU. 1 vol. in-8. — 15 fr.

Cahiers d'une élève de Saint-Denis. 13 vol. in-12. — 44 fr.

Éducation progressive, by madame NECKER DE SAUSSURE. 2 vol. — 7 fr.

Dictionnaire de l'Académie française. 2 vol. in-4. — 36 fr.

Dictionnaire d'Histoire et de Géographie, by BOUILLET. 1 vol. — 21 fr.

Dictionnaire des Sciences, Lettres et Arts, by BOUILLET. 1 vol. — 21 fr.

HISTORY.

UNIVERSAL.

> Histoire universelle, by BOSSUET. 1 vol. in-18. — 3 fr.
>
> Histoire ancienne, by GUILLEMIN. 1 vol. in-18. — 4 fr.
>
> Précis d'histoire moderne, by MICHELET. 1 vol. in-8. — 4 fr. 50.
>
> Histoire de cent ans, 1750 à 1850, by CANTU. 4 vol. — 14 fr.

GERMANY.

> Guerre de Trente Ans, by SCHILLER. 1 vol. — 3 fr. 50.

AMERICA.

> Histoire de l'Amérique, by ROBERTSON. 1 vol — 3 fr. 50.
>
> Histoire de Washington, by W. IRVING. 1 vol. in-8. — 7 fr.

ENGLAND.

> Conquête de l'Angleterre, by A. THIERRY. 4 vol. in-18. — 14 fr.
>
> Histoire d'Angleterre, by HUME. 13 vol. in-8. — 35 fr.
>
> Histoire d'Écosse, by ROBERTSON. 1 vol. in-8. — 5 fr.
>
> Marie Stuart, by MIGNET. 2 vol. in-12. — 7 fr.
>
> Révolution anglaise de 1688, by MACAULAY. 2 vol. in-12. — 7 fr.
>
> Guillaume III, by MACAULAY. 3 vol. in-12. — 10 fr. 50.

SPAIN.

> Histoire d'Espagne, by ROSSEUW SAINT-HILAIRE, 8 vol. — 40 fr.
>
> Histoire de Charles-Quint, by ROBERTSON. 1 vol. in-8. — 5 fr.
>
> Antonio Perez et Philippe II, by MIGNET. 1 vol. in-12. — 3 fr. 50.

FRANCE.

> Récits des temps mérovingiens, by AUGUSTIN THIERRY. 2 vol. — 7 fr.
>
> Essais sur l'histoire du Tiers-État. —   2 vol. in-18. — 7 fr.
>
> Lettres sur l'histoire de France.   —   1 vol. in-18 — 3 fr. 50.
>
> Dix ans d'études historiques.   —   1 vol. in-18 — 3 fr. 50.
>
> France (Histoire de), by HENRI MARTIN. 16 vol. in-8. — 81 fr.
>
> ————— by CHARTON ET BORDIER. 2 vol. in-8. 15 fr.
>
> ————— (Essais sur l'), by GUIZOT. 1 vol. in-12. — 3 f. 50.
>
> Siècle de Louis XIV, by VOLTAIRE. 1 vol. in-18. — 3 fr. 50.

Réfugiés protestants de France, by WEISS. 2 vol. in-12. — 7 fr.
Siècle de Louis XV, by VOLTAIRE. 1 vol. in-18. — 3 fr. 50.
Révolution française, by MIGNET. 2 vol. in-12. — 7 fr.
Histoire des Girondins, by LAMARTINE. 8 vol. — 40 fr.
Révolution française, by THIERS, 10 vol. in-8. — 50 fr.
Consulat et Empire, by THIERS. 15 vol. in-8. — 75 fr.
Deux Restaurations, by VAULABELLE. 5 vol. in-8. — 25 fr.

GREECE.

Vie des hommes illustres, by PLUTARQUE. 4 vol. in-18. — 14 fr.
HÉRODOTE. Histoire, trans. by LARCHER. 2 vol. in-12. — 7 fr.
THUCYDIDE, — trans. by ZEVORT. 2 vol. in-12. — 7 fr.

ITALY.

Italie, — by GUICCIARDINI. 10 vol. in-8. — 50 fr.
Florence, — by MACHIAVEL, trans. PÉRIÈS. 1 vol. in-18. — 3 fr. 50.
Abrégé de l'histoire d'Italie, by SFORZOSI. 1 vol. in-8. — 3 fr.
Naples (Histoire de), by le général COLETTA. 4 vol. — 12 fr.
Républiques italiennes, by SISMONDI. 10 vol. in-8. — 40 fr.

ROMAN EMPIRE.

Études sur l'histoire romaine, by MÉRIMÉE. 1 vol. — 3 fr.
L'histoire romaine à Rome, by AMPÈRE. 2 vol in-8. — 15 fr.
Grandeur et Décadence des Romains, by MONTESQUIEU. 1 vol. — 2 fr.
Guerre des Gaules, by CÉSAR, trans. LOUANDRE. 1 vol. — 3 fr. 50.
Histoire romaine, by MICHELET. 2 vol. in-8. — 6 fr.
TACITE. Œuvres, trans. by LOUANDRE. 2 vol. in-12. — 7 fr.
TITE-LIVE. Œuvres, trans. by BOUTMY. 1 vol. in-12. — 3 fr.

RUSSIA.

Pierre le Grand, by VOLTAIRE. 1 vol. in-18. — 3 fr. 50.
Russie (Épisodes de l'histoire de), by MÉRIMÉE. 1 vol. — 3 fr.

SWEDEN.

Charles XII, by VOLTAIRE. 1 vol. in-18. — 3 fr. 50.

JOURNALS.

Illustration (1 n° per week). — 1 year, 36 fr.
Journal d'Agriculture pratique (2 n°s per month). — 1 year, 16 fr.
Magasin pittoresque (1 n° per week). — 1 year, 6 fr.
Revue britannique (1 n° per month). — 1 year, 40 fr.
Revue des Deux Mondes (2 n°s per month). — 1 year, 56 fr.

Revue horticole (2 n^{os} per month). — 1 year, 9 fr.

Poets.

BOILEAU. Œuvres poétiques. 1 vol. in-12. — 3 fr. 50.

BRIZEUX. Marie. 1 vol. in-18. — 3 fr. 50.

BYRON. Child-Harold, Mazeppa. 1 vol. in-12. —3 fr. 50.

CHÉNIER (André). Poésies complètes. 1 vol. in-18. — 3 fr. 50.

DANTE. Divine Comédie, trans. by BRIZEUX. 1 vol. in-18. — 3 fr. 50.

FLORIAN. Fables. 1 vol. in-18. — 1 fr.

GŒTHE. Poésies, trans. by BLAZE. 1 vol. in-12. — 3 fr. 50.

HOMÈRE. Iliade, trans. by DACIER. 1 vol. in-12. — 3 fr. 50.

— Odyssée. — — — 3 fr. 50.

HORACE. Épitres et Art poétique, trans. by PATIN. 1 vol. — 3 fr. 50.

LA FONTAINE. Fables. 1 vol. in-18. — 1 fr.

LAMARTINE. Méditations. 2 vol. in-12. — 7 fr.

— Harmonies. 1 vol. in-18. — 3 fr. 50.

MILTON. Paradis perdu. 1 vol. in-18. — 3 fr. 50.

SCHILLER. Poésies, trans. by MARMIER. 1 vol. in-18. — 3 fr. 50.

TASSE. Jérusalem délivrée, trans. by DESPLANS. 1 vol. in-18. — 3 fr. 50.

VICTOR HUGO. Les Orientales. 1 vol. in-18. — 3 fr. 50.

— Les Feuilles d'automne. 1 vol. in-18 — 3 fr. 50.

VIRGILE. Énéide, trans. by PESSONNEAUX. 2 vol. in-18. — 7 fr.

— Géorgiques, trans. by DELILLE. — 2 fr.

Writers of prose.

BOSSUET. Oraisons funèbres. 1 vol. in-12. — 2 fr.

LA BRUYÈRE. Caractères. 1 vol. in-12. — 3 fr. 50.

LAMARTINE. Lectures pour tous. 1 vol. in-8. — 3 fr.

MONTAIGNE. Essais et Lettres. 4 vol. in-12. — 14 fr.

LA ROCHEFOUCAULD. Maximes. 1 vol. in-18. — 3 fr.

NOEL ET LAPLACE. Leçons de Littérature. 2 vol. in-8. — 10 fr.

PASCAL. Pensées. 1 vol. in-12. — 3 fr. 50.

— Provinciales. 1 vol. in-12. — 3 fr. 50.

PLINE LE JEUNE. Lettres. 3 vol. in-18. — 10 fr. 50.

SÉVIGNÉ (Madame de). Lettres. 6 vol. in-12. — 18 fr.

VAUVENARGUES. Maximes. 1 vol. in-18. — 3 fr.

VINET. Chrestomathie française. 3 vol. — 9 fr.

MEMOIRS.

Of Alfieri. 1 vol. in-12. — 3 fr. 50.

Of Franklin. 3 vol. in-8 — 4 fr.

Of Gœthe. 2 vol in 18. — 7 fr.

Of Montanelli, trans. by ARNAUD (de l'Ariége). 2 vol. in-8. — 7 fr.

Of Napoléon. 9 vol. in-8. — 40 fr.

Of madame de la Rochejaquelein sur la Vendée. 1 vol. in-8. — 4 fr.

Of madame Roland. 1 vol. in-12. — 3 fr.

Of cardinal de Retz. 1 vol. in-12. — 3 fr.

Of Saint-Simon. 20 vol. in-8. — 80 fr.

Of Silvio Pellico, Mes Prisons, trans. by LATOUR. 1 vol. — 3 fr. 50.

D'un Conspirateur, by RUFINI. 1 vol. in-18. — 1 fr.

PHILOSOPHY.

CICÉRON. Morale et Politique, etc. 1 vol. in-18. — 2 fr.

DESCARTES, BACON, LEIBNITZ. Œuvres. 1 vol. in-12. — 3 fr. 50.

FRANK. Dictionnaire des Sciences morales et politiques. 6 vol. — 55 fr.

LAROMIGUIÈRE. Leçons de Philosophie. 2 vol. in-12. — 8 fr.

NICOLE. Œuvres philosophiques et morales. 1 vol. in-12. — 3 fr.

Socrate, Épictète, Pythagore. 1 vol. — 3 fr. 50.

RELIGION.

Bible. — 2 fr.

Imitation de Jésus-Christ. 1 vol. in-18. — 2 fr.

Dieu est l'amour le plus pur. 1 vol. in-18. — 2 fr.

Confessions de saint AUGUSTIN, trans. by SAINT-VICTOR. 1 vol. — 3 fr . 50.

Méditations sur les Évangiles, by BOSSUET. 1 vol. in-12. — 3 fr. 50.

Connaissance de Dieu et de soi-même. — 1 vol. in-12. — 3 fr. 50.

Élévations sur les Mystères. — 1 vol. in-12. — 3 fr. 50.

Sermons Choisis. — 1 vol. in-12. — 3 fr.

Existence de Dieu, by FÉNELON. 1 vol. in-12. — 3 fr. 50.

Le Christianisme présenté aux hommes du monde. 6 vol. in-18. — 6 fr.

Petit Carème et Sermons de MASSILLON. 1 vol. in-18. — 3 fr.

Introduction à la vie dévote, by saint FRANÇOIS DE SALES. 1 vol. — 2 fr.

GERMAN TALES AND NOVELS.

FREYTAG. — Doit et avoir. 2 vol. in-12. — 4 fr.

GŒTHE. Wilhelm meister. 1 vol. in-12. — 3 fr. 50.

HOFFMAN. Contes, trans. by LOÈVE-VEIMARS. 2 vol. in-12. — 7 fr.

ZSCHOOKE. Mémoires d'un vicaire du Wickshire [*recte* ZSCHOKKE. Journal d'un pauvre vicaire de Wiltshire]. 1 vol. in-18. — 2 fr.

CHAMISSO, TIECK, etc. Nouvelles trans. by MARMIER. 1 vol. in-12. — 3 fr.

AMERICAN NOVELS.

COOPER. Œuvres complètes. 30 vol. in-8. — 120 fr.

MISTRESS STOWE. Cabane de l'oncle Tom. 1 vol. in-18. — 2 fr. 50.

MISS WETHERELL. Le Vaste Monde. 2 vol. in-18. — 7 fr.

CUMMINS. L'Allumeur de réverbères. 1 vol. in-12. — 2 fr.

ENGLISH NOVELS.

MISS BRONTÈ. Jane Eyre. 1 vol. in-12. — 2 fr.

BULWER. Paul Clifford. 1 vol. in-12. — 2 fr.

PISISTRATE CAXTON. 1 vol. in-18. — 2 fr.

DICKENS. Nicolas Nickleby. 2 vol. in-12. — 4 fr.

—   Dombey et fils. 2 vol. in-12. — 4 fr.

—   David Copperfield. 2 vol. in-12. — 4 fr.

—   Contes de Noël. 1 vol. in-12. — 2 fr.

—   Olivier Twist. 1 vol. in-12. — 2 fr.

—   Martin Chuzzelewit. 2 vol. in-12. — 4 fr.

—   La Petite Dorrit. 3 vol. in-12. — 6 fr.

FIELDING. Tom Jones, trans. WAILLY. 2 vol. in-12. — 7 fr.

FOE. Robinson Crusoé. 2 vol. in-12. — 2 fr.

GOLDSMITH. Vicaire de Wackefield [*recte* Wakefield], trans. BELLOC. 1 vol. — 3 fr. 50.

SMOLETT. Roderick Random. 1 vol. in-12. — 2 fr.

SWIFT. Voyages de Gulliver. 1 vol. in-18. — 1 fr.

WALTER SCOTT. Œuvres complètes. 25 vol. in-8. — 100 fr.

ARAB TALES.

Les Mille et une Nuits. 2 vol. in-12. — 7 fr.

SPANISH NOVELS.

CERVANTES. Don Quichotte, trans. by HINARD. 2 vol. in-18. — 7 fr.

—   Nouvelles. 1 vol. in-18. — 1 fr.

ITALIAN NOVELS.

BALBO. Toniotto et Maria. 1 vol. in-18. — 3 fr. 50.
MANZONI. Les Fiancés. 1 vol. in-18. — 3 fr. 50.
RUFFINI. Le docteur Antonio. 1 vol. in-12. — 3 fr.

FRENCH NOVELS.

BALZAC. Médecin de campagne. 1 vol. in-18. — 1 fr.
— Curé de campagne. 1 vol. in-18. — 1 fr.
— Curé de Tours. 1 vol. in-12. — 1 fr.
— Eugénie Grandet, 1 vol. in-18. — 1 fr.
— Recherche de l'absolu. 1 vol. in-18. — 1 fr.
— Ursule Mirouet. 1 vol. in-18. — 1 fr.
BERNARDIN DE SAINT-PIERRE. Paul et Virginie. 1 vol. in-18. — 1 fr.
— — La Chaumière indienne. 1 vol. in-18. — 1 fr.
BEYLE. La Chartreuse de Parme. 1 vol. in-18. — 1 fr.
DUMAS (Alexandre). Conscience. 1 vol. in-18. — 1 fr.
— Monte-Christo. 3 vol. in-18. — 6 fr. 50.
LE SAGE. Gil Blas. 1 vol. in-18. — 3 fr. 50.
MAISTRE (Xavier DE). Œuvres complètes. 1 vol. in-18. — 3 fr. 50.
MÉRIMÉE. Colomba. 1 vol. in-18. — 3 fr. 50.
NODIER. Contes de la veillée. 1 vol. in-18. — 3 fr. 50.
MADAME REYBAUD. Le Cadet de Colobrière. 1 vol. in-18. — 1 fr.
— Misé Brun. 1 vol. in-18. — 1 fr.
— Le Moine de Chailly. 1 vol. in-18. — 1 fr.
SAND (George). La Petite Fadette. 1 vol. in-18. — 1 fr.
— La Mare au Diable. 1 vol. in-18. — 1 fr.
— François le Champi. 1 vol. in-18. — 1 fr.
— Mauprat. 2 vol. — 2 fr.
SANDEAU (Jules). Catherine. 1 vol. in-18. — 1 fr.
— Madeleine. 1 vol. in-18. — 1 fr.
— Mademoiselle de la Seiglière. 1 vol. in-18. — 1 fr.
— La Maison de Penarvan. 1 vol. in-18. — 1 fr.
— Vaillance. 1 vol. in-18. — 1 fr.
MADAME DE SOUZA. Adèle de Sénange. 1 vol. in-18. — 1 fr.
SOUVESTRE. Le philosophe sous les toits. 1 vol. in-18. — 1 fr.
— Au coin du feu. 1 vol. in-18. — 1 fr.

—   Le Foyer breton. 2 vol. in-18. — 2 fr.

—   Souvenirs d'un Vieillard. 1 vol. in-18. — 1 fr.

TOPFFER. Nouvelles genevoises. 1 vol. in-18. — 3 fr. 50.

—   Le Presbytère. 1 vol. in-18. — 3 fr.

VIGNY(DE). Servitude et Grandeur militaires. 1 vol. in-18. — 3 fr. 50.

—   Chatterton et André Chénier. 1 vol. in-12. — 3 fr. 50.

—   Cinq-Mars. 1 vol. in-12. — 3 fr. 50.

RUSSIAN NOVELS.

POUCHKINE. La Fille du capitaine. 1 vol. in-18. — 1 fr. 50.

GOGOL. Mémoires d'un fou. Un ménage d'autrefois. Tarass Boulba. — 1 fr.

TOURGUENIEFF. Récits d'un chasseur. 1 vol. in-12. — 3 fr.

SWEDISH NOVELS.

MADEMOISELLE BREMER. Les Voisins, 1 vol. in-12. — 3 fr. 50.

—   —   Les filles du président. 1 vol. in-12 — 3 fr.

—   —   Le Foyer domestique. 1 vol. in-12. — 3 fr.

SCIENCES.

Animaux (Les), by BUFFON. 1 vol. in-18. — 3 fr.

Astronomie populaire, by ARAGO. 4 vol. in-8. — 20 fr.

Botanique, by JUSSIEU. 1 vol. in-18. — 6 fr.

Chimie, by REGNAULT. 4 vol. in-18. — 20 fr.

Chimie (Notions de), by PELOUZE & FREMY. 1 vol. in-8. — 5 fr.

Découvertes scientifiques, by FIGUIER. 4 vol. in-18. — 9 fr.

Époques de la Nature, by BUFFON. 1 vol. in-18. — 3 fr.

Flore des Jardins et des Champs, by LE MAOUT & DECAISNE. 2 vol. — 9 fr.

Géologie, by LYELL. 2 vol. in-12. — 7 fr.

Globe (Discours sur les Révolutions du), by CUVIER. 1 vol. in-12. — 3 fr.

Globe (Lettres sur les révolutions du), by Alex. BERTRAND. 1 vol. — 5 fr.

Minéralogie by BEUDANT. 1 vol. in-18. — 6 fr.

Physique (Lettres sur la), by Alex. BERTRAND. 1 vol. in-8. — 5 fr.

Physique et Chimie (Lettres sur la), by EULER. 1 vol. in-12. — 3 fr. 50.

Tableaux de la Nature, by HUMBOLDT. 2 vol. in-12. — 9 fr.

Zoologie, by MILNE EDWARDS. 1 vol. in-18. — 6 fr.

THEATRE.

CORNEILLE	(Théâtre). 2 vol. in-12. — 7 fr.	
CALDÉRON	—	trans. Dumas-Hinard. 3 vol. in-12, — 10 fr. 50.
GŒTHE	—	trans. by MARMIER. 1 vol. in-12. — 3 fr. 50.
MOLIÈRE	—	3 vol. in-12. — 10 fr. 50.
RACINE	—	1 vol. in-12. — 3 fr. 50.
REGNARD	—	1 vol. in-18. — 3 fr.
SCHILLER	—	trans. by MARMIER. 3 vol. in-18. — 10 fr.
VOLTAIRE	—	1 vol. in-18. — 3 fr.
SHAKSPEARE	—	1 vol. in-18. — 5 fr. 50.

BEAUMARCHAIS. Le Barbier de Séville. Le mariage de Figaro. — 2 fr.

AUGIER. La Ciguë. Philiberte, Gabrielle. In-18. — 1 fr. ch.

DELAVIGNE. L'École des Vieillards. Les Enfants d'Édouard. In-18.

DUMAS (Alexandre). Christine à Fontainebleau. Charles VII. In-18. — 1 fr.

FEUILLET (Oct.). Le Village. La Partie de Dames. In-18. — 1 fr. ch.

HUGO. Ruy-Blas. Hernani. — 1 fr. ch.

MUSSET (A. DE). Il faut qu'une porte soit ouverte ou fermée. Un Caprice.

PONSARD. Charlotte Corday. Lucrèce. In-18. — 1 fr. ch.

SCRIBE. Le Verre d'eau. La Demoiselle à marier. — 1 fr. ch.

TRAVEL.

Aventures en Chine, by FORTUNE. 1 vol. in-18. — 1 fr.

Voyage dans la Tartarie et le Tibet, by le P. HUC. 2 vol. in-12. — 7 fr.

L'Empire chinois, by le P. HUC. 2 vol. in-12. — 7 fr.

Grèce contemporaine, by ABOUT. 1 vol. in-18. — 3 fr.

Itinéraire de Paris à Jérusalem, by CHATEAUBRIAND. 2 vol. in-18. — 6 fr.

Lettres édifiantes et curieuses. 8 vol. in-12. — 8 fr.

Lettres sur l'Inde, by JACQUEMONT. 2 vol. in-12. — 7 fr.

Promenades en Amérique, by AMPÈRE. 2 vol. in-8. — 12 fr.

Rome au Siècle d'Auguste, by DEZOBRY. 4 vol. in-8 — 30 fr.

Voyages du jeune Anacharsis en Grèce, by BARTHÉLEMY. 4 vol. — 9 fr.

Voyage d'une femme au Spitzberg by Mme d'Aunet. 1 vol. in-12. — 2 fr.

Voyageurs anciens at modernes, by CHARTON. 4 vol. in-8. — 24 fr.

Christophe Colomb, by WASHINGTON IRVING.

Voyages de MARMIER.

Voyages autour du monde, by DUMONT-d'URVILLE. 2 vol. — 30 fr.

2. — Musical library.

METHODS.

Solfége of RODOLPHE. — 4 fr. 50.
Solféges du Conservatoire de musique. — 25 fr.
L'Art du chant, by DUPREZ. — 15 fr.
L'Art de jouer du piano, by VIGUERIE.
Méthode de piano pour les enfants, by LECARPENTIER. — 12 fr.
——————, by ADAM, by CZERNY, by KALKBREENNER, by ZIMMERMANN.

PIANO.

Études of BERTINI, CHOPIN, CRAMER, MOSCHELÈS.
Exercices of CZERNI. — 12 fr.
Gradus of CLÉMENTI.
Art de phraser of STEPHEN HELLER.
SONATES (for solo piano) of CLEMENTI, BEETHOVEN, HAYDN, MOZART, WEBER.
Échos d'Italie by ROSSINI, MERCADANTE, etc. 1 vol. in-4. — 5 fr.
Préludes et Fugues of SÉBASTIEN BACH.
Les bonnes traditions du pianiste, by HÆNDEL, HUMMEL. etc. 3 vol. — 21 fr.
PARTITIONS rescored for solo piano. A choice to make from the operas of MOZART, ROSSINI, BELLINI, etc. (See the list of operas on the following page.)
CONCERTOS de BEETHOVEN arranged for solo piano, by MOSCHELÈS.
FANTAISIES.

> MOZART. Rondos. Gigue. La Fantaisie.
> BEETHOVEN. Valses. Bagatelles.
> CZERNI, MUSARD, TOLBECQUE. Quadrilles.
> CHOPPIN. Valses. Mazurkas. Nocturnes.

FANTAISIES.

> MENDELSSOHN. Romances sans paroles. Caprice op. 3 Rondo 14.
> RAMEAU. COUPERIN. Morceaux caractéristiques.
> ROBERTI (Giulio). La Sérénade. — 1 fr.
> SCHUBERT. Valses et Marches.
> SCHUBERT. Mélodies arrangées by STÉPHEN HELLER.
> SCHUMANN. Scènes d'enfants.
> STÉPHEN HELLER. Promenades d'un solitaire. Nuits blanches.

J. Strauss de Vienne, Lanner. Labitzky. Valses. Galops. Polkas.
X. La Romanesca. — 1 fr.
Weber. Invitation à la valse. Dernière pensée.

Music for four hands.

Overtures, by Gluck, Mozart, Beethoven, Rossini, Auber.

Symphonies arranged for piano, by Haydn, Mozart, Beethoven,

Duos (piano et violon), of Beethoven, Haydn, Mozart.

Trios (piano, violon et violoncelle), of Beethoven, Haydn, Mozart.

Quatuors (piano, violon, alto, violoncelle) of Beethoven, Moschelès.

Auber, La Muette. Le Domino noir. Fra Diavolo. — 12 fr. each.

Bellini, La Somnambule. Norma. Les Puritains. — 7 fr. each.

Berton, Montano et Stéphanie. Aline. — 8 fr. each.

Beethoven, Fidelio. — 10 fr.

Boïeldieu, La Dame blanche. Le Petit Chaperon rouge. — 8 fr. each.

Cherubini, Les Deux Journées. Médée. — 8 fr. each.

Cimarosa, Le Mariage secret. Les Horaces. L'Impresario. — 8 fr. each.

Dalayrac, Gulistan. Camille. — 10 fr. each.

Donizetti, Lucie de Lammermoor. Don Pasquale. La Favorite. — 10 fr.
each.

Gluck, Armide. Iphigénie. Alceste. — 7 fr. each.

Grétry, Richard Cœur-de-Lion. Le Tableau parlant. L'Épreuve. — 7 fr.
each.

Halévy, La Juive L'Éclair. Guido et Ginevra. — 20 fr. each.

Hérold, Zampa. Le Pré aux clercs. — 12 fr. each.

Méhul, Joseph. L'Irato. — 8 fr. each.

Meverbeer, Robert le Diable. Les Hugenots. — 20 fr. each.

Monsigny, Le Déserteur. — 8 fr.

Mozart, Don Juan. Les Noces de Figaro. La Flute enchantée. — 7 fr.
each.

N. Isoard, Joconde. Jeannot et Colin. — 8 fr. each.

Paesiello, Nina. Tulipano. Le roi Théodore. — 7 fr. each.

Rossini, Le Barbier de Séville. Cendrillon. Le comte Ory. La Pie voleuse.
——, Sémiramis. Moïse. Otello. Guillaume Tell. — 7 fr. each.

Spontini, La Vestale. Fernand Cortes. — 40 fr. each.
Weber, Oberon. Euryanthe. Robin des Bois. — 8 fr. each.

ORATORIOS.

Bach, Passion de saint Matthieu.
Fél. David, Le Désert. — 8 fr.
Haendel, Samson. Le Messie. Judas Machabée.
Haydn, La Création. Les Saisons. — 7 fr. each.
Mendelssohn, Paulus. Élie.
Pergolèse, Stabat mater. — 7 fr.
Rossini, Stabat mater. — 7 fr.

MELODIES.

For one or more voices.
Rossini, Soirées musicales. — 12 fr.
Schubert, Mélodies. — 8 fr.

SONG COLLECTIONS.

Gordigiani, Vaccai, etc., Échos d'Italie. Rom., mélod. – 4 v in-4°. — 18 fr.
Lulli, Rameau, etc., Échos de France. — 1 v. in-4°. — 7 fr.
Spohr, Mendelsshon, etc., Échos d'Allemagne. — 2 v. in-4°. — 14 fr.
Thibaut, Luther, etc., Échos du temps passé. — 2 v. in-4°. — 14 fr.
Palestrina, Haendel, etc., Échos du monde religieux. — 1 v. in-4°. — 7 fr.
Delsarte, Archives du chant.

CHAPTER IX

THE ARRANGEMENT AND FURNISHING OF THE HOUSE

1. — General arrangement.

I do not pretend to offer plans for a house in the country; if you want to build a house, it's not me you should consult, but a good architect. I shall only tell you what I think necessary for comfort and convenience.

Ground floor. — This is where you should locate the kitchen and pantry and the laundry with large cupboards; the dining-room; the drawing-room, which is where the mistress will usually be found and which should be encumbered with no other function; a little room to one side of that, serving as a library and office, which is where the account books should be kept and where you can work without interruption, or receive people on business. You can put a divan in this room, to act as a day-bed in case of indisposition or convalescence.

First floor. — Here are the bedrooms, with their own dressing-rooms equipped with wardrobes or cupboards. A small, lockable room for household supplies should be on this floor or the one below.

Top floor. — This is shared by the servants' rooms and attics.

Layout. — To achieve the accommodation I have described, the house needs to be two bays deep, in other words have two facades with well-lit rooms. The best plan is a wing *set at right angles.*[1] If the house is sited

1. In French, *en retour d'équerre*. Where a farmhouse was attached to a barn and jutted out at right angles from one end of that barn, it was termed *la ferme en retour d'équerre*. Where there was a central *corps de logis* with wings at each end set at right angles, forming a courtyard in the middle, these wings were said to be set *en retour d'équerre*.

between the garden and the yard, then the dining-room and sitting-room should look on to the garden, while the kitchen, pantry and office look on to the yard. The staircase can either be put in the middle of the house, leading out of a hallway between the drawing-room and the dining-room, or at one end of the building, near the dining-room. If the house is so small that this arrangement is impossible, I would give up the drawing-room on the ground floor and furnish the office with a little more elegance. This I would then occupy for everyday, rather than having a drawing-room on the first floor. It would inevitably require frequent sorties from the upstairs drawing-room to keep the house running smoothly; as it is tiring to go up and down stairs constantly, one would be reluctant to do it and the supervision of the household would suffer accordingly.

The size of rooms. — The drawing-room ought to be spacious. It will be a refuge for the children in bad weather, and it costs little to heat. Wood is never expensive in the country and supplies are plentiful. On the other hand, in the summer a large drawing-room is much cooler and so much more pleasant than a small one. This is not the case with bedrooms, which are only occupied at night. They are both warmer and more appropriate if they are relatively small. The dining-room should be large because one often receives many guests in the country.

Bakehouse, wash-house. — A large bakehouse in the yard is an essential. It should have a large oven for the farm and a smaller one for the family. The laundry should be next to it.

2. — Drawing-room.

The drawing-room is for company. It should be seemly and elegant, without ostentation. Cleanliness and order should be its first qualities.

Parquet. — A parquet floor is the best. But in the country, a waxed surface on the ground floor can be inappropriate where there is a large family. It's almost impossible to keep it polished, and it will be a burden and a trial to the servant responsible for its upkeep when she has so much else to do. In that case you will probably have to resign yourself to it being always dirty, unless you make it the sole task of a single maid, which entails much extra cost. There is no doubt, however, that a parquet is both healthier and warmer than flagstones. The best thing is to give up all thought of waxing it and wash it frequently instead. For myself, I find the thought of the heavy labour involved in waxing a parquet in a farming household too much to bear. It will be the despair of a mistress to see muddy boots soiling her floor, and yet this will happen all the time. Even a dog with filthy paws will undo in an instant the hard work of a morning's polishing. One remedy is to put down one or two oilcloths, painted to look like wood. This way, the parquet can be washed with plenty of water every time it needs it. This is how they do it in Belgium.

If you wish to put down a parquet in the drawing-room, a floor made up of small tongued and grooved staves measuring 2 metres long and 0^m,10 or 0^m,12 wide is both cheaper and easier than a real parquet. If you need to proof it against rising damp, then the parquet backed with bitumen invented by M. Gourguechon of Paris is the cheapest and most suitable.[1] This system does not need to sit on a subframe and the wood used, which is extremely dense, does not require a tongued and grooved joint.

Tiles. — The unwelcome chill that comes from tiling is less noticeable in the country than in town because, come the winter, everyone wears heavy boots or even clogs. A tiled floor is easy to wash and looks smarter than neglected parquet; however, it doesn't wear well and creates a lot of dust.

Wallpaper. — A plain wallpaper, or something with a small and neat design, in a light and unbroken colour, seems to me preferable to those busy floral designs which quickly go out of fashion. Added to which they fade rapidly and so need frequent replacement, and there are better and more agreeable ways to spend your money..

The fireplace. — A mirror goes over the fireplace; at either end of the mantelpiece you should put a couple of statuettes or vases full of garden flowers; in the middle you should have a clock (not too showy), with candlesticks to each side, ready for lighting. Every hearth should be equipped with ash, a shovel, some tongs, firedogs for the logs and an iron curb to stop the logs rolling out. Often, the fire is built on a briquette of compressed coal dust, or of cast iron. To one side of the fireplace, if it's marble, is fixed a little row of hooks on which you can hang the bellows

---

1.   In 1844, Louis-Norbert Gourguechou or Gourguechon of rue du Ponceau, Châtillon-sur-Seine obtained a patent of 15 years for his system of parquet flooring.

and a small brush to sweep the hearth and tidy up any ash spilled when lighting the fire.[1]

The fireguard. — As well as the fender that keeps the cinders in the hearth itself, you should also have a fireguard made of wire netting to place before the fireplace. Originally this was needed to stop the sparks ejected by certain sorts of logs, setting fire to the room; today its purpose is more to save us from those all-too-common accidents caused by the ridiculous fashion for monstrous crinolines. How many young women have been injured by, or even succumbed to, terrible burns which a fireguard would have prevented?

In front of the fireguard you should put a small rug.

The log chest. — In the drawing-room and any other room occupied from day to day you should make space near the fireplace for a chest upholstered in tapestry or velvet, edged with braid fixed with copper-headed nails. It will be a store for logs, thus saving the needless interruption of the servants in their other work. If you burn coke or coal in place of wood, then the chest should be replaced by a sheet-metal scuttle.

Ornaments. — On the walls you should hang family portraits or good prints. You must ruthlessly set your face against those awful lithographs that you often find, even in town drawing-rooms. In my view, there is nothing in worse taste.

A few bronze or plaster statuettes, small reproductions of classical sculpture, mounted either on consoles in the corner of the room or on plinths, will give the drawing-room a lived-in feel as well as being an ornament. I have put two short columns measuring $1^m,33$ high and $0^m,33$ across in the corners of my own drawing-room. Their plinths are square and, to protect them from knocks from the broom, surrounded by a skirting-board to match the room's. I have put two family busts on these columns, but you could equally well mount one of those admirable miniature reproductions of classical pieces for which we are indebted to the

---

1. The briquettes of coal dust referred to in this paragraph were called *bûches économiques* (economical logs) and are more usually made today of compressed wood chip or sawdust. The *bûche économique* in cast iron to which Mme Millet-Robinet refers here was a device to increase the heat from an open hearth. It often took the form of a tube, to promote the circulation of air and, once heated by the burning coals or logs, it continued to emit warmth as the fire died down.

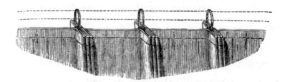

Figure 6. Hanging curtains.

Collas technique. For example, the Venus de Milo, the Belvedere Apollo, the Gladiator, the Diana of Gabii, the Bologna Mercury, or Michelangelo's Penseroso or Moses. These plaster statuettes look good and cost little. I can hardly bear to mention the abominable taste of those who insist on buying those plaster 'characters' – as horrid for the subjects they depict as for the quality of their execution – which cost just as much as the lovely statuettes I have described.[1]

Curtains. — They should be made so that they open and close easily; in the country, windows are often open. The best arrangement is for three gathered pleats, repeating every ten centimetres, attached to large rings running on a rod. Drapes are not suitable unless kept very simple. Summer curtains should be white (a figured muslin with a fringe is appropriate); it is easy to keep them looking fresh. In the country, coloured curtains will fade quickly in the sun. In winter, the muslin can be replaced with coloured calico or chintz (figure 6).

Usually, the curtain rings are sewn onto the curtains themselves. This can have several disadvantages. Every time you need to wash the curtain, the rings have to be unpicked and then sewn on again when you come to rehanging. What's more, the countless holes made with the needle when attaching or detaching the rings will weaken the fabric and cause it to tear. This can all be avoided by means of a series of buttons which can be undone or refastened in an instant. Fold a piece of tape in two, to form a loop, and sew the ends of this loop on the curtain where you would

1.   Achille Collas (1795–1859), engineer and inventor, developed a method of reproducing sculptures in miniature by means of a pantograph-like machine. He entered into partnership with the artist Ferdinand Barbedienne after patenting his method in 1836. Success came to the enterprise after they showed their products at the Great Exhibition of 1851 and the Exposition Universelle of 1855. They were able to produce sculptures in bronze and plaster.

otherwise have sewn the ring. At the same time you sew a button on the ends of this loop, just where they are attached to the curtain. To hang the curtain, you deal with the rings as follows. You pass the loop of tape through the ring and bring it round to the button, which you fasten as if it were a buttonhole. The length of each loop should be no more than what is needed to keep the ring touching the top of the curtain had it been sewn.

The table. — A table in the middle of the drawing-room is even more useful in the country than in the town, if only because you are for ever offering refreshments to visitors. It really should not be, as it so often is, covered with a liqueur-stand or a host of pretty little ornaments in porcelain or bronze, which are bound to require painstaking cleaning. They only get in the way of its proper employment. If the table has a marble top, it is simple to clean. Solid yet elegant tables are available at moderate cost.

The sofa. — A sofa or day-bed is essential for the drawing-room. In the first place it can serve as a proper bed; and otherwise, at those moments of indisposition or fatigue, it is useful to have somewhere to rest without being too far away from family or servants – important for the mistress of the house.

Chairs and armchairs. — Chairs and armchairs should be constructed from mahogany or walnut in preference to cherrywood. They should be solidly made and covered in horsehair or leather. Horsehair is rather sombre to look at but never wears out.[1] All other fabrics will soon soil or be consumed by worm. Utrecht velvet is appropriate, but hardly has the durability of horsehair and, in the country, the furnishings of rooms bearing heavy traffic are liable to fruit stains and having to cope with wet clothing, etc. Such stains are more easily lifted off horsehair. They leave no trace with a quick wipe and a wash.

At Chiavari, a small town near Genoa,[2] they make maplewood chairs which are nowadays fashionable throughout Europe. They are incomparably

1. In French, *étoffe de crin*, hence crinoline, the name referring to the horsehair fabric which was used to make the spreading, framed petticoats that supported the overskirts. Horsehair was used from the tails of horses. It formed the weft on a cotton warp.
2. The chairs manufactured at Chiavari and neighbouring towns in Liguria were designed by Giuseppe Gaetano Descalzi in 1807 during a period when the town was the capital of the Apennins Department of Napoleon's France, after he had annexed the Ligurian Republic.

light, robust and elegant. Unfortunately, transport costs mean that each chair delivered to Paris comes in at 18 francs.

Stools. — A few straw footstools are required. In the country you always have to deal with dirty feet, which are nigh-on impossible to keep out of the drawing-room.

The piano. — An upright piano, which has the advantage of taking less room than a long or square one, is both useful and delightful, even where the mistress herself is not musical.

Polishing furniture. — Furniture in the country should not be French polished: the winter damp alters their properties. Wax polish is much more suitable because it is easy to maintain.

When a piece of marble has lost its shine for any reason, it can be restored by rubbing with another small piece of polished stone or by giving it a coat of clear beeswax as if it were wood. The marble will never lose its gloss.

Flowers and foliage. — In high season, anyone wanting to make her house bright and cheerful will make sure to deck the mantelpiece and side tables in the drawing-room and the dining-room with plenty of cut flowers and foliage. In the winter, these can be replaced with ivy and pot plants which you have brought on in the conservatory.

These days they manufacture a host of inexpensive vases to make your rooms look nice. You can fill them with damp fine sand and then poke in short-stemmed flowers from which you strip almost all the leaves. You can do the same thing with wicker or wire baskets. In this case you line the basket with a fitted tin vase which you also fill with damp sand and stick with flowers. These keep well and fade very slowly.

They make wicker or wire vases and jardinières of all shapes and sizes. Some are large enough to take flower pots, which you can cover with moss; and others, like that illustrated here, can be lined with a tin vessel filled with water for cut flowers (figure 7).

They also make, at very low prices, charming pottery or wire vases which can be hung with light chains from the drawing-room ceiling, or in the hall or conservatory, etc. You insert flower pots filled with climbers which, because they have nothing to climb up, will cascade delightfully over the edge of the hanging basket. I list some that are suitable: snake cactus, creeping saxifrage, *Crassula perfoliata* or red crassula, trailing lobelia, ivy-leaved pelargonium, bristly-stalked mesembryanthemum, the fern *Lycopodium brasilianum,*[1] Siebold's sedum, Indian strawberry,[2] *Torenia asiatica* or wishbone flower, etc. The last plant here comes from the hothouse, it needs more heat than the others, all of which are very easy to grow (figure 8). If the vase is large enough, you can fill it with something handsome with a horizontal habit, for example a dragon-tree[3] or an aloe, and surround that with the plants I have mentioned. You can replace these quite ambitious plants with ivy.

Figure 7. Wire jardinière.

The aquarium. — Nowadays, you sometimes come across drawing-rooms, but more often conservatories, graced with an aquarium for fish, zoophytes, molluscs or coral, etc. These transparent containers are filled with living creatures swimming between mossy rocks, sand, pebbles, wrack and weed. There is infinite variety of form and colour. Water plants keep well and, while keeping the water in good condition, their waving foliage and thick tufts of growth afford places for the fish to shelter.

1.   Now *Huperzia pulcherrima.*
2.   *Duchesnea indica*, also known as mock strawberry.
3.   *Dracaena marginata.*

Figure 8. Hanging vase.

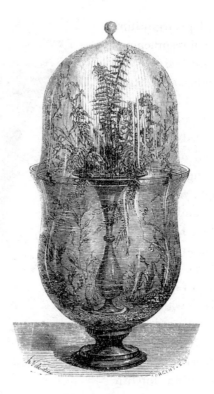

Figure 9. Aquarium.

These aquariums are the inspiration for the miniature version, like the illustration, that you can come across in even the smallest parlour (figure 9).

These fitments only cost six francs and are made of two bell-glasses, one measuring $0^m,25$ across, the other $0^m,30$. You invert the larger one and sit it on either a turned wooden base or a wooden bowl filled with sand. You put 5 centimetres of well-washed sand in the bottom of the jar, you fill it water and you introduce some goldfish. A narrow vase placed on this sandy bottom can then serve as a pedestal for a deep saucer filled with earth. In this you can plant ferns. Obviously the saucer has to be higher than the water.

Then you cut three pieces of zinc and fold them in an S-shape. These you hang on the top edge of the bell-glass. You then cover the whole with the smaller bell-glass, which rests on the metal hooks. They leave enough space for the air to circulate.

An indoor greenhouse. — This miniature hothouse is made out of oak or any other wood which matches the drawing-room itself (figure 10). It consists of a container measuring 35 to 40 centimetres tall and wide, folded out of a piece of zinc. The bottom, rather than being flat, should be shaped like a gutter. You make a hole at the lowest point and insert a spigot which can be opened when necessary. Into this you put a layer of coarse gravel 10 centimetres deep and then top it off with earth for planting. Any water you give the plants will filter through the earth and gravel and can be drained via the spigot, so that the roots don't rot. This container is covered by a glass frame made out of wood or metal, grooved to receive the panes. One of the panes is hinged like a skylight. You can open it to give circulation to the air, or to put your hand in when the plants need attention without having to lift the whole frame off.

Figure 10. Indoor greenhouse.

3. — Office.

Placement. — The office should open off the drawing-room or the dining-room and should have a door out into the yard to reduce the traffic in the house.

Furnishings. — Office furniture should not be elaborate: a bookcase or shelves for books; a simple but substantial table or desk, with lockable drawers where you can keep petty cash; a fireplace; a few chairs, and a plain carpet or mat are all that's needed for an office. On the table, an oilcloth blotting pad (which costs two francs), an inkpot, pens, paper, gummed envelopes, sealing wax, a seal, a little candlestick, a diary, a pair of long scissors, a paper knife, account books, a box file or folders for papers, each with a label denoting their contents.

A good barometer and thermometer are essential for the country. The place for the barometer is the office itself, while the thermometer needs to be outside in the fresh air.

4. — Dining-room.

Arrangement. — The dining-room, as I have already mentioned, should be large. You should install a slow-combustion heater or a fireplace *à la prussienne*,[1] which will be preferable to a stove because it is so often necessary to dry the feet or clothing and the open fire is so pleasing to the eye. Such a grate comes with a small oven, which is very useful for warming plates or keeping food hot. The dining-room should be tiled or parquet-floored, but never waxed, so that it can be readily washed. There should be cupboards aplenty, to hold crockery and everything necessary for service at table.

Hatch.[2] — If the dining-room is next to the kitchen, an opening that we call a *hatch* should be made in the dividing wall. This allows prepared dishes to be passed through and is an appropriate spot for plates and serving dishes. This opening, at chest height, is furnished with a small door which is only opened when crockery or dishes are ready to be passed and which, when closed, entirely separates the kitchen from the dining-room.

Furnishings. — The furniture should be very simple; this is what I would suggest: some suitable, substantial chairs with seats of straw, horsehair or rush; a round extending table which allows the number of diners to

---

1. A *cheminée à la prussienne* was a cast iron fireplace set into the chimney breast, as were many Victorian coal-burning grates, but with the addition of a heated cabinet or warming oven above the fire, and vents above that which promoted the convection of warm air into the room.
2. In French, *tour*.

Figure 11. Dumb waiter.   Figure 12. Hanging lamp.

increase without inconvenience; a simple sideboard, in mahogany, oak or walnut, with a marble top and a dresser above (figure 13); in default of direct communication with the kitchen, dirty dishes and anything cleared from the table can be stacked here during the meal; a little sideboard on wheels called a dumb waiter[1] which can be brought close to the table and serve as a repository for bread and for plates when only the family is dining, or even used to save on having servants in attendance (figure 11); and finally curtains in chintz or white calico hung in the same simple fashion as I have described for the drawing-room.

Custom permits that you dine without a tablecloth, but in this case the table must be waxed, and if you have an extra leaf or leaves installed they must be waxed too and perfectly clean; an alternative is to have an oilcloth, patterned to look like wood, on the table and the dresser; this is very easy to clean after any meal, using a wet sponge or a cloth soaked in alcohol or a few drops of lily oil.[2]

1. In French, *servante*.
2. Lily oil was more often located in the medicine cupboard, its properties were moisturizing when used on the skin or on wounds.

The dining-room is lit by a lamp hanging over the table, on a counterweight system, as in the figure (figure 12).

Figure 13. Sideboard with dresser.

5. — Bedrooms.

Figure 14. Washstand, open.

Furniture. — A lady's bedroom should be a refuge from disturbance, a place of rest and recuperation respected even by the family; in keeping with this, the furniture ought to be of useful simplicity, cleanliness its only ornament. It should include a bed, a mirrored wardrobe or a chest of drawers, a *secrétaire* or small desk, a wooden chest, a comfortable armchair, some more chairs, a stool and a carpet.

Washstand with a folding top. — If there is no dressing-room, or if that room is too small to accommodate a washstand, a washstand with a folding top can be put in the bedroom itself. Figure 14 shows it open and figure 15 shows it closed. When the lid is raised, the inner compartment, all lined in white marble, rolls forward. It contains a basin, a water jug, a glass, some bottles of toilet water and little pots for soap, dentifrice, toothbrushes, nailbrushes, and sponges with their oilcloth or net bags. The top drawer of the washstand is usually reserved for hairbrushes, combs and the innumerable items of personal care that would otherwise clutter up the marble washing compartment. The other drawers are used just as in a normal chest of drawers. In some of these folding or portmanteau washstands, the lower drawers are replaced by a small double-doored cupboard. This is divided into two compartments. One contains a bidet, while dirty linen is stored in the other, whence a servant can remove it every day.

Fireplace. — The mantelpiece should be marble with a mirror, a

Figure 15. Washstand, closed.

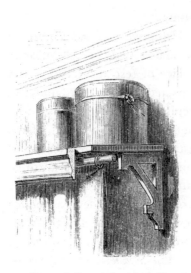

Figure 16. Coat rack with shelf.

clock, a ring dish, candlesticks with candles, matches, and fresh flowers in vases on the shelf.

6. — Closet.

A dressing-room next to the bedroom is indispensable; it is equipped with cupboards and wardrobes or coat racks.

Coat racks. — These should be enclosed behind doors as in a wardrobe, or else be crowned by a shelf on which hatboxes and shoes can be stored; at the fore edge of this shelf is hung a floor-length curtain. The curtain is hung on a rod fixed to the front edge of the shelf and any dust is barred from entry by a moulding fixed in front of this rod and below the shelf itself (figure 16).

Washstand. — The most important piece of furniture in the dressing-room is the washstand or dressing-table, with a drawer containing combs and hairbrushes (figure 17); it has a marble top and comes with all those objects itemized above; it also has a small mirror. These dressing-tables have largely replaced the old washstand[1] and are a vast improvement. If the dressing-room is not large enough to hold a full-sized washstand, then at least a basin or a small table with a washing bowl and water jug should be provided.

Towel horse, accessories. — Next to the washstand there ought to be a horse to dry the towels (figure 18), and under the table you can put a bidet, a copper for hot water, a zinc ewer with a lid, full of cold water (figure 19), and a stoneware jug with a zinc lid. To better hide these receptacles, you can have curtains running on rods set round the table.

Slop pail with inlet valve. — To one side of the washstand is placed a zinc slop pail with a sprung inlet valve into which you can pour the waste water that has been used for washing (figure 21). The figure shows the pail closed and full, such as it will be when the water has been poured into

1.   *Lavabos*, three-legged washstands with just a basin and ewer.

Figure 17. Dressing-table.

it; the other figure shows the concave lid with its spring valve (figure 22). When water is poured onto the lid, its force causes the valve to open; the water falls into the pail, and the valve springs shut immediately, saving sight and smell from any offence.

Parquet. — The parquet should be covered with an oilcloth patterned to look like wood, or by a carpet. In the latter case, it will be necessary to set the washstand and its accessories on a large piece of oilcloth, stretching far beyond its perimeter so that any splashes from your ablutions fall on it and do not spoil the carpet.

7. — Guest bedrooms.

It is essential in the country that you should have one or more bedrooms available for guests. Whether their visit is planned or unexpected, their room should be prepared before they

Figure 18. Towel horse.

Figure 19. Zinc ewer.

Figure 20. Stoneware jug.

are shown to it and nothing should be omitted to ensure their comfort. The candlesticks should have candles, the ewer full of water, the washstand perfectly clean and provided with soap, *eau de Cologne*, almond paste,[1] pincushion, etc.; three or four towels should be arranged to one side, and these should be frequently replaced so the guests do not have to ask for fresh ones. You should also place in the room the necessary for writing, a nightlight, some matches, a sugar caster and a glass and a teaspoon.

1.   Used for skincare.

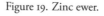

Figure 22. Spring-loaded lid to slop pail.

Figure 21. Zinc slop pail.

8. — Beds for the family.

Wooden and iron bedsteads. — One can buy excellent iron bedsteads very cheaply; in most cases they are the best choice. Although they may be less elegant than a mahogany frame, they have the serious advantage of not harbouring bedbugs, and they are very substantial. In any case, you can make them look more attractive by enveloping them in valances like curtains.

Runners. — The bed castors should run in wooden grooved rails, both to avoid damage to the parquet or carpet and so as not to tire the servants.

Bedding. — Bedding might consist of: (1) a palliasse of maize straw, which is perfectly clean, substantial, elastic, long-lasting, and does not suffer from breaking up or dissolution into dust, as might wheat or rye straw; (2) two mattresses, one bolster and a pillow. Some people also add a feather mattress but I do not advise this. If a person is very sensitive to the cold, an eiderdown may be procured quite inexpensively, and filled with goose or duck down then covered with cotton or a light silk.

Box mattress. — Straw mattresses are often replaced by flexible bed bases. These last a long time and make the bed very soft. They do not have to be turned when the bed is made, which simplifies matters. They consist of thick copper wires twisted into spirals which are fixed upright to cross-pieces of wood. Horsehair stuffed between two lengths of cloth is laid on top of the spirals. However, after long usage, or if the weight supported by the base is too great, it will lose its elasticity. Furthermore, if but one spring sags, the whole base is useless.

Tucker's Spring Beds. — This new bed base is more comfortable, simpler, and resists heavy loads better than ordinary spring beds.[1] It consists of

---

1. The Tucker Manufacturing Company of Boston, Massachusetts, USA patented the spring bed here described in 1855. In the *Illinois State Journal* of 5 November 1856, it was rhapsodically announced in an advertisement quoting the *Boston Ledger* of June 1856: 'The ne plus ultra seems to be attained in this bed—it combining simplicity of construction, comfort and durability. It is formed of slats running lengthwise, each connected with a spring which gives an equal vibration, making all parts of the bed alike luxurious to the occupant. There is no possibility of these springs getting out of order by losing any of their elasticity, as the strain is so light from each one bearing an equal proportion of the weight. It can be put together and taken apart in very few minutes, and may be rolled into a very compact shape for transportation. In fact, nothing has been lost sight of in this Bed that could add comfort, and restore nature in a more balmy sleep.' After suffering difficulties with regard to protecting his design, Mr Tucker transferred his attention to Europe in 1858, setting up a factory in Paris.

flexible wooden laths laid lengthwise and joined together in a single grid which is fixed at each end by elastic fastenings [coiled springs]. Each part is but *placed* [not fixed] where it should be, hence disassembly and reassembly are very easy. You only have to dust it to maintain it in a clean condition. The price varies between 12 and 30 francs. The essential difference between the two sorts of base is that the Tucker uses the metal springs in tension while the standard sprung base uses them vertically, in compression.

Figure 23. Bed for use by the family.

Coverlet. — A quilted coverlet in cotton or, better, in silk that has been combed like lint then carded before covering in chintz or silk, is light and warm, and really useful because it can be drawn up or cast off when necessary without unmaking the bed.

Curtains. — The bed should be hung with white or chintz curtains from a rod that runs the length of the bed, *not across it*, which is held up by two iron rods fixed into the ceiling joists (figure 23). The curtains, in wide pleats gathered at the head, are hung from gilded copper or wooden rings. The head of the curtains can be improved with fabric swags curving elegantly down from the ends of the rod. These swags may be replaced by a pelmet, more fashionable nowadays.

How to keep the feet warm. — When your feet are cold, just as you go to bed, you can warm them up either by putting in a warming pan or by filling a stoneware water bottle with boiling water – well stoppered and wrapped in a napkin. This bottle, placed between the sheets at the foot of the bed, gives off a pleasing warmth to your feet the whole night through. You can also wear knitted woollen bootees or put your feet in a felted woollen bag.

9. — Children's beds.

Bedding. — Children's beds should not be as well upholstered as adults'; it is good, for their health and to encourage their growth, to make children sleep on a hard, flat bed; I would never allow feather of any sort, even for the bolster, which should be horsehair.. A child's bed should have a maize palliasse and a mattress. In the South, almost everyone sleeps on maize in the summer, which is much cooler than wool or feathers. It's not good, in any case, to accustom the children to cosset themselves, and their sleep is so deep that anywhere is a good *bunk* to them.

10. — Servants' beds.

Curtains. — Servants' beds, like those of the master, are kept as clean as humanly possible. Curtains, hung from a rod that goes across the bed, are indispensable because the servants' quarters are usually cold.

Bedding. — As with children's beds, the servants' should be provided with a palliasse, a good mattress and a bolster. I make this appeal on behalf of the servants, because a good mistress should never forget that it is the hard necessity of social inequality that has made people like herself become her servitors.. If she wishes to earn their affection and devotion, she should discover in herself something of the maternal instinct, the only intimate connection between a mistress and her servants. What must go through the mind of a poor servant in a hard and unforgiving bed, and one that's freezing cold, as she thinks back to the soft luxury of the beds she made up that very morning for her employers! Every effort must be made to avoid provoking such thoughts that are fatal to social harmony.

11. — Loose covers for furniture.

If you need to cover upholstery because you fear it will be soiled or because it has suffered too much wear, you can make loose covers out of holland, cotton drill or, which is jollier, chintz – there are some charming ones at reasonable prices. Generally, it is better to cover just the upholstery, leaving the wood in full view. Here is a simple pattern. It doesn't cost much, it's easy to make and quick to put on or take off.

You make a pattern from paper or a piece of old fabric that exactly matches the shape of the piece you are covering. If it's a chair or armchair, you hem or edge the cover for the seat on three sides (figure 24), fixing the fourth at the back near the legs with stout pins. The hem at the front edge should be turned over a cord because the front of the seat is slightly curved. You wrap the cover over the front, pulling it tight underneath and tying the ends of the cord with a bow. If the cover stretches with use, you can retie the strings to pull it tight again. The cover for the back should be long enough to almost meet on the reverse side. It is held in place by three cords, as illustrated (figure 25).

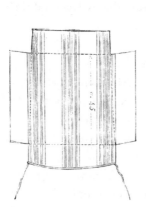

Figure 24. Seat cover.

Figure 25. Back cover.

12. — Bathrooms. — The bath and warming the linen.

The bathroom. — A bathroom is essential. If you have the room for it, its arrangement is not too costly. If you don't wish to install a copper and a cold tank, you must at least make a place for the bath and its accessories.

However, if the house, or your finances, does not lend itself to this, you should at least have a portable bathtub and a heating cylinder. So that you don't have to suffer the drudgery of heating and carrying sufficient water, the bathtub should be deep and narrow at the bottom. In a deep bathtub you can sit down and still be covered entirely by water. This will also mean the tub need not be so long. However, in this case, you will need supplies of hot water to keep the bath warm as the less water the bathtub holds, the faster it cools.

Bathtub. — This should be either of zinc or tinned copper. It should have three casters, one at the feet, and two at the end where your shoulders are. Copper tubs are without doubt the best. You can also take a bath in the washtub. If you are to bathe in sulphur waters or water from Barèges you will need a wooden tub, or a zinc one, because the potash of sulphur in these waters affects every metal save zinc.[1]

A child's bathtub. — A child's bathtub is essential because baths are even more necessary for children than they are for adults. It can be made of zinc. The water for this small tub can be easily heated in a copper.

Cylinder. — If you haven't installed the means to heat water in a copper, then almost the only way to heat the bathwater is a cylinder. But you will still need a cauldron on the fire to heat the water added later to keep the bath warm. A cylinder is heated with charcoal. When you are going to heat the water with this instrument, you must first tip it upside down to get rid of any ash which might clog the fire plate, impeding the circulation of air and stopping the charcoal from burning brightly. Then you lay down a shovelful of embers, topped with fresh charcoal, but leaving space for the addition of live coals on the top. The fire will catch more quickly than if you put the live coals on the bottom. Then you plunge the cylinder into the bath, making sure its top stays higher than the water. After an hour of this immersion, the bath should be warm enough. Five minutes before you take the cylinder out, you seal it close so the fire goes out. If you omit to do this, once out of the water, the cylinder will be damaged because it will continue to be heated by the charcoal without the heat being absorbed by the water.

1. Barèges is a spa in the Pyrenees, south of Lourdes, high on the Col du Tourmalet. Although the first road for wheeled traffic from Lourdes was not constructed until 1744, it was famous for its waters from the seventeenth century. It was made more famous and popularized by Napoleon III and his wife from 1859.

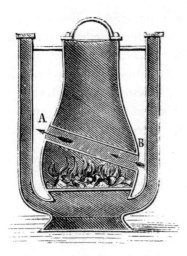

Figure 26. Cylinder with tubes.

A cylinder with tubes. — The cylinder can be greatly improved, as figure 26, showing the cylinder in section, demonstrates. The improvement consists of one or two pipes (A–B), each $0^m,04$ diameter, running across the cylinder just above the grate. These pipes are on an incline and are open at both ends. When the cylinder is plunged into the water, it enters the pipes, it heats and, being then lighter, rises to escape through the higher end of the pipes (A). This circulation results in the water heating much more quickly. These pipes should be copper. Any standard cylinder can be adapted to take two pipes.

The dangers of coal gas. — I cannot stress highly enough the need to take every imaginable precaution against any accident arising from the fumes given out by the burning charcoal. You must keep the door, or even the window, of the room where you install your bath wide open and not shut it until you have removed the cylinder from the water and taken it outside. If an accident still occurs despite these precautions, follow the instructions laid out in the chapter on asphyxia in volume II, below.

A bath thermometer. — This is not a costly instrument, yet it is really useful. It is very difficult to gauge the temperature of the water with the hand: if the hand is warm, the water seems cool; if the hand is cold, the water seems hot. One is nearly always mistaken as to its real temperature, which can be a nuisance. Bathwater should never be more than 30°. A thermometer fitted with a piece of cork to allow it to float on the surface of the water (figure 27) will cost 1 franc 25 to 2 francs.

Board, lectern. — It's simple to put a board across the bath to serve as a table. If you want

Figure 27. Bath thermometer.

to eat, it will take a bowl or plate; if you want to read, it will support a lectern.

Linen warming baskets. — There is a perfect method of warming bathroom linen. In Limoges, they make twisted-straw baskets bound with strips of chestnut (figure 28), much like they make bee-skeps in many districts. These baskets are broad at the top, with a large opening (A) and a straw lid that sits in the basket. The base is narrow, and there is no bottom. At the widest part (B) there is a wooden grid on which to place the linen you wish to warm. Once the lid is on, it is wholly enclosed within the basket. On the floor you put a small charcoal brazier filled with burning coals

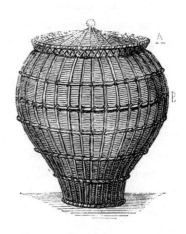

Figure 28. Linen warming basket.

or very hot embers and you place the basket over it. This brazier beneath the linen will warm it to perfection, and quickly too. The first thing on the wooden grid should be an unwanted scrap of fabric as it is bound to be scorched by the flames; in this way you will protect your bath linen from the effects of too fierce a fire.

Figure 29. Linen warming cabinet.

A linen warming cabinet. — If you can't find one of these baskets, you can replace it by a wooden box as I have illustrated at figure 29, a cutaway without its front panel so that you can better understand its internal arrangement which is just the same as in figure 28. The cabinet is square or tapered; it has no bottom, and its lid fits snugly in the top. Again, you put a grill or grid across the middle of the box and a brazier in the bottom. A cabinet like this is not quite so suitable as a basket but it is still preferable to any other method of warming the bath-linen.

Hip-bath, foot-bath. — It is also necessary to have a zinc hip-bath for bathing sitting down. The tub should be round and high backed. A zinc or china bowl is also required for bathing the feet.

13. — Attics.

Furniture store. — It is not as easy in the country as in town to do without attics. One part should be kept as a furniture store, under lock and key. You can use it for redundant furniture, or for the host of things you only need occasionally but which are really useful to have to hand. If you keep it well organized, you will be able to find anything you put away when you need it. Above all, you should not let things lose condition just because you piled them up anyhow. Better then to sell them or give them away.

Wooden hanging rails. — In one of the other attics you should fix hanging rails from one rafter to the other, supported by a couple of uprights. Or you can suspend them on wires, or rest them on freestanding uprights set in a heavy base or steadied by a cross-piece at the foot. You use these for dirty linen. On one you put kitchen linen, on the others bed linen and table linen. It is vital to keep the mice away from the linen and to avoid storing it in any attic where it may get damp and then rot, especially in winter.

Clothes lines. — You should install taut lines, nicely spaced, for drying linen on wet days. They are useful too when the sun shines so strongly that it lifts the blue and the laundry loses that brightness it gets from the tint.

Chest for dirty linen. — You also place in the attic a chest for dirty clothes and underwear. It can be divided into three compartments. One for coloureds, one for whites and one for delicates which should not be mixed with heavier things. The lid for this should be constructed as a frame with a couple of braces arranged lengthways which you cover with wire gauze so that the air can circulate. If dirty linen is shut away for too long, it will develop a most unpleasant odour — this lid will solve the problem.

If this linen is not going to be washed for a while, it should be rinsed as a precaution. This is called the *pre-wash*.

14. — Kitchen. — Kitchen equipment. — Accessories.

I have much to say about furnishing the kitchen. Not all my remarks conform to received notions, and my readers may take note only of those opinions they endorse. But I would claim that all my advice is founded on experience and that its only goal is economy.

Brick stove. — A kitchen should be large and full of light. It should contain a tiled stove built near a window. The wall on which it abuts should also be tiled, to at least $0^m,30$ to $0^m,40$ above the top of the stove; in some districts it is the custom to build these stoves out of brick and to paint them red every so often, never actually washing them; this apparent cleanliness is quite the opposite of true hygiene.

Cast iron stove. — For some years now, large cast iron ranges – provided with apertures in the top to take the cooking pots – have gained ground. Such ranges are economical and convenient; they combine in a single item the open hearth, the stove and the small oven, and they can heat a certain amount of water at all times. They are heated by coal or coke.

Figure 30. Range heated by coke.

The kitchener illustrated in figure 30 is designed to run on coke. It has two bottom warming ovens, separated by the ash box, which are useful for heating dishes just before they are loaded with food, and for keeping the prepared food warm until you want to serve it up. There are two ovens above these in which you can roast meats, bake pastry, etc. One side of the stove contains a water tank which you fill from the top (you can see the lid on the right hand side of the solid top in the illustration). When the stove is hot, so too is the water; you must only ensure that it is topped up when it loses water through evaporation. A tap dispenses the water. The solid top of the stove is made of cast iron and is pierced by an opening which gives onto the hearth. This hole is closed by means of concentric rings which you manoeuvre in place with a hook; they allow the orifice to be larger, smaller or completely closed. A particular advantage of this stove is that you can cover the solid top with saucepans and cook more or less rapidly depending on the proximity or otherwise of the pan to the hottest part of the top. Another advantage is that the temperature of the ovens may be regulated by means of a catch which keeps the doors ajar. To light this stove, you lift out the concentric rings in the top and introduce some embers or shavings and kindling; on top of these you place some *small* lumps of coke (and no dust); you set the fire alight and replace all the concentric rings. Once the coke is well lit, you add just as much as you require for the heat you need. You regulate the fire by means of the damper in the flue and the small door to the ash box – this can be left open or closed at will.

The interior of the hearth is lined with fire cement; this arrangement retains the heat and allows you, should the fire be extinguished, to relight it with ease. Cast iron hearths do not offer the same advantage.

The stove illustrated in figure 30 costs 250 francs in Paris; it consumes 10 centimes of coke in an hour. Identical stoves, but omitting one oven and one warming cupboard, cost 140 francs.

Coal-burning stoves are also manufactured; but the price of coal is higher than that of coke and the fuel gives off a black dust which soon clogs the flues.

Fireplace. — The hearth should be at least $0^m,10$ higher than the floor; enough to hinder the servants treading ash through the house. This slight elevation will never impede service and lets the servants warm their legs and feet just as well as one at floor level. In addition, it does not have the drawbacks of a really high hearth which make lifting off heavy saucepans or pots full of water quite difficult and which burn the servants' top halves while leaving the rest of their bodies freezing. This small plinth can be made with bricks. In the centre of the hearth there should be a cast iron disc, with a void beneath it. This is really useful in the winter for holding a hot dish before service; but you need to be able to shut this form of small oven.

The mantel of an open hearth in the kitchen needs to be at least o^m,50 higher than other fireplaces, and o^m,30 wider. You need to insert a hooked nail or a peg in the centre of the mantel and attach to it a cord a metre and a half in length and strong enough to take a lead weight of approximately 250 grams; you can use a fishing line weight for this, but it needs a small loop so the cord can run up and down. This cord, wound two or three times round a pot handle, will serve to stabilize it when it sits on a trivet or stand. The cook is then free to move around while the pot is on the fire, without risk of catching it and knocking it off, something that happens all too often when the pan handle is kept steady by the back of a chair.

Movable trammels. — The open hearth should be provided with two movable trammels [pot hooks], that is to say two trammels with rings at their tops which slide along a transverse bar fixed into the chimney by two pegs, securing the bar by hooks passed through a ring at each end. This means that you can move the trammels, or remove them, easily.

Movable trammel on a crane. — A movable trammel can also be mounted on a gallows or crane (figure 31) the upright of which is fixed by two pegs to the wall; sometimes the lower peg is replaced by a socket in the floor, similar to the arrangement of the lower hinge of many coach-house doors.

When the cook pulls the horizontal part of the crane towards her, it describes a quarter-circle

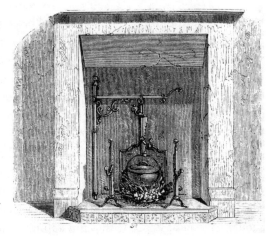

Figure 31. Movable trammel on a crane.

179

to bring the pot hook, and the pot hanging from it, outside the hearth, thus permitting her to undertake all those operations that precede or succeed the cooking without exposing her to the heat of the fire. Clearly, the longer the horizontal bar of the crane, the further away the pot will be from the fire.

Kettle. — One of the pot hooks will invariably carry a copper or sheet iron kettle (figure 32) with a capacity of 6 to 9 litres, with a lid. Some kettles have a long pipe extension, $0^m,04$ from the bottom of the vessel and $0^m,40$ long, with a tap on the end. This is so far from the hearth that it can be turned without needing to move the kettle and without burning the fingers. Thanks to this kettle, you will have hot water for every kitchen operation – something which facilitates service, ensures cleanliness and economizes on fuel. You should always make sure there is water in the kettle, otherwise it will boil dry; from time to time it should be emptied and cleaned because impurities will always accumulate in the bottom, which will affect the water. Although this kettle will never be in the centre of the fire, if it gets in the way of hanging a cauldron or similar object, it can be pushed right to the back of the hearth and still keep the water hot.

Figure 32. Kettle.

I cannot recommend this convenient and inexpensive arrangement highly enough.

Sink. — The washing stone, or sink, should be white so that any dirt is visible and you can remove it immediately. This stone should be set securely into the wall and be either in front of, or near to, a window; in the latter case the wall should be tiled for 40 centimetres above the sink; the stone should have some depth with a rim approximately 5 centimetres high. At the bottom of its slope it should be pierced by a drain which corresponds to a channel down which flows the water which is constantly thrown into the sink.

Nowadays sinks are made in enamelled metal: they are light, sturdy and only cost 15 francs. It is easy to keep them perfectly clean with a damp sponge.

Scullery. — It is more seemly to have the sink in a scullery next to the kitchen, acting as a sort of clearing house. You can place in this closet pots, pans and anything else which may otherwise render the kitchen cluttered and untidy and deprive it of its necessary order and cleanliness.

Draining basket. — Next to the sink you place a basket to receive and drain all the dishes which you place therein as and when they have been washed. No words are too harsh for the custom in some districts of putting dishes to drain on the floor; this habit is disgusting and inefficient.

Dish rack. (figure 33) — Rather than a basket for the dishes which, in a small kitchen, is somewhat bulky, you can have a rack fixed to the wall above the sink into which you place any dishes that need draining. The drips fall into the sink, whereas any drips from the basket will fall to the floor which only makes the kitchen dirty.

Drain. — The tiled floor ought to be designed with a slight slope towards a small opening in the wall at the same level as the tiles through which you can direct the water when washing the kitchen floor, rather than mopping it up. This opening can be stopped with a wooden bung that you can insert or extract with ease.

Figure 33. Dish rack.

Table. — Usually you place the table in the middle of the kitchen; it should be rectangular, 0^m,80 wide by 2 metres or more in length, and 0^m,10 thick. It should have drawers which can be pulled from either side of the table. Beech is the best wood for kitchen tables because it does not darken and you can wash it with impunity.

Chopping block. — A three-legged block should be placed at one end of the table or in a corner of the kitchen; it should be made from a single piece of wood, showing the endgrain, o^m,75 thick. A flat plank is not what is needed; it will chip and break up when used for cutting or chopping. It can be of the same wood as the table, or of elm.

Shelves. — To hang saucepans in the kitchen, you can fix to the wall (1^m,30 off the floor and somewhere bright and obvious to everyone) a flat piece of wood measuring o^m,02 thick, o^m,30 wide and of indeterminate length. Give it a coat of oil paint, in a different colour to the kitchen walls. o^m,10 above this, fix a crossbar the same length as the plank, measuring o^m,12 high by o^m,04 thick. On hooks nailed into this crossbar, hang your pots and other pans with handles, their edges resting on the flat plank below. 1^m,80 off the floor, you can erect shelves on brackets to accommodate pots, the spit, coffee pots, and other equipment that cannot be suspended as described.

Saucepans. — It is usual in Paris to use copper pans in the kitchen; in some regions copper is little employed, unless it be in larger households or catering establishments. Normally, the high cost of the metal and the risk of poisoning inhibit its adoption. I do not think these reasons well founded. Although copper equipment is costly, its durability is such that long before it has worn out you will have broken or disposed of terracotta pots vastly in excess of the cost you would otherwise have expended. As far as risk is concerned, it is very real if the pots are not properly tinned; but a diligent housewife is never exposed to such dangers because she will keep an eye on her saucepans herself.

There is nothing at present that rivals copper for good cookery; all iron pots and pans, however they are made, suffer from catching too readily; and in any case, once they have lost their first shine, even scouring will not recover it. Not only does copper cook better, it has a clean and handsome look to it that embellishes a well-run kitchen. Wrought iron pots can be used for foods that only need reheating or which do not require leaving on the fire for any length of time.

Cast iron pots are acceptable in default of copper; a low flame is enough to heat them; and I also recommend cast iron or wrought iron pots that have been enamelled. They are good to use and easy to maintain; but if the cook is careless, the enamel will flake only too easily and then they are

Figure 34. Necromancer.

useless. You should also have a small pan, in bell metal or in yellow porcelain, which is exclusively for heating milk.

Necromancer. [1] — This pan is hinged exactly between its top and bottom halves; they fit so tightly that the pan is hermetically sealed.

Heating this pan with a sheet of paper no larger than one of our daily newspapers, we can cook cutlets in two or three minutes, or fried eggs in a minute. The half-open pan is shown in figure 34.

Cutlets cooked in this manner are not quite as good as grilled cutlets, but they are very toothsome; eggs so cooked are also excellent, and in sum this pan is of great utility on journeys or in a small household.

Fish kettle. — Copper is preferable to wrought iron for fish kettles, as for other pans. Your kitchen should have kettles of various shapes and sizes; those of greatest utility are a long oval; but it is helpful to have some which are flat and lozenge-shaped, for cooking brill, turbot, sole, etc. Fish kettles need to be thoroughly tinned and come with a removable inner slip, pierced with holes and with handles at each end so that you can lift it out easily with the fish you have cooked thereupon.

Roaster, spit. — I prefer a roaster [or Dutch oven], as illustrated in figure 35, to a spit, even though the latter is in use in many households; meat cooks better and more quickly in a roaster; furthermore, you can expose the fleshy parts of a joint to the fire for longer, without drying out the leaner bits.

In some kitchens I have seen a niche fashioned in the kitchen wall that takes the form of a roaster. This has a little iron grill fixed to its bottom half which is then filled with coal; you hook the Dutch oven onto the front of this niche. When this grate is portable, it is called a shell [*coquille*]. This method of cooking is convenient, quick and economical; and, as you can place the grate wherever you want, it keeps the hearth clear. However, in

1. In French, *casserole à la minute*. This was also called a 'conjurer', for example in Eliza Acton, and is the subject of an entry in the *Oxford Companion to Food*.

Figure 35. Roaster.

country districts where there is plenty of wood but coal is always fairly dear, using a roaster like this is no longer an economy. You can roast the meat before the hearth which serves at the same time to cook the rest of the dinner.

Stewpans in cast iron. — Before I lived in Poitou I always used earthenware pots to make soup and even to cook vegetables. But here I found they used cast iron stewpans for many purposes and that they were very suitable because the water boils so much more easily; they can also be hung from pot hooks and thus disembarrass the front of the hearth. Certain vegetables oxidize and blacken, so you cannot give up earthenware entirely. But you can make an excellent stock-based soup in cast iron stewpans. Their price is never excessive and they last, so to speak, for an eternity, unless they are broken by some tremendous shock – but in fact there are craftsmen that will repair them. You will need an iron hook or handle to place them on the fire, and especially to lift off cauldrons or pans. This hook consists of a round iron bar that is fatter in the centre and hooked at each end (figure 36).

Figure 36. Hook.

If the purchase price of cast iron is higher than earthenware, you will soon make up the difference by dint of its lasting longer. Even if you avoid breaking earthenware, it is readily destroyed by the heat of the fire and soon taints from burnt fat which spoils anything cooked in it.

Cauldrons. — Two cauldrons, of different sizes, are also very useful for cooking green vegetables, for boiling soiled linen and a host of other purposes. They should be of copper lined with tin; cast iron is no substitute.

Preserving pan. — To make jam you should have a small pan or preserving pan in untinned copper. This may be used for other purposes:

because it is wide and flat, you can use it for cooking big flatfish such as brill, turbot, etc. Such a pan is quite dear but, as it is used infrequently, it lasts a long time.

Grills, frying-pans, bakers or camp ovens, extinguisher. — Other things which are necessary are iron trivets; two grills of different sizes which are scoured clean and shining; two or three convex lids in sheet metal, provided with a ridge on the circumference so that they can be piled with hot ash and embers; a baker or camp oven that can be placed over dishes that are going to rise in the cooking; an extinguisher in thick sheet metal that can douse any superfluous embers or the coal which remains in the stove after cooking is completed. A large cast iron stewpan could well serve as a damper, with a decent lid, as it is capable of long withstanding the heat of the fire. You will also need some frying-pans and a pot stand.

Sloping grill. — Figure 37 shows a new design of grill in two parts: a firebox in sheet metal, and a grill arranged in such a fashion that there is no chance of the stink of burnt fat. Once the firebox is filled with lighted embers, you place the grill on top already laden with the meats or fish that you wish to cook. Because the grill is sloping, the juices and the fat do not drip

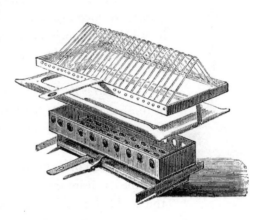

Figure 37. Sloping grill.

onto the coals, as in a normal grill, but flow into a small dripping-pan which surrounds the grill and is fixed to it.

For clarity's sake, figure 37 shows the grill in its constituent parts, at some distance from each other, as they would be when you lift the grill off the firebox. In normal circumstances the grill rests on the two transverse metal bars at each end of the firebox.

Colanders. — It is useful to have colanders of different sizes, with larger or smaller holes, according to the use you put them. They can be in tinplate, copper or enamelled metal. Colanders with large holes, for making purées, need to be on a wooden stand (as in figure 38) — with a large hole in its centre, the colander being supported by its flange — which will make the work easier. A plate under the stand will receive whatever is pressed through. With this in place, you can make the thickest purées, especially if you use a wooden pestle shaped like a mushroom, as in figure 39.

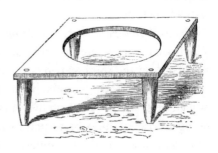

Figure 38. Stand for a colander.

Sieves. — Nowadays sieves are made out of tinplate or metal gauze, better for most purposes than horsehair, and much longer lasting. Horsehair sieves are nonetheless essential for passing stock and certain sauces, etc.

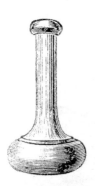

Figure 39. Pestle for purées.

Mortar. — Marble mortars are preferable to stone or those made with a hard wood such as service wood. The pestle is in box or service wood.

Pottery. — I have long since replaced my earthenware coffee pots with porcelain coffee pots described as from the Levant,[1] which are far preferable. You could also have a series of little porcelain or good earthenware pots. They are manufactured in sizes from a decilitre to a half-litre or more; milks heats up well in them and keeps hot a fair time. A few dishes in glazed porcelain or china from Sarreguemines[2] are quite useful for cooking eggs or warming up a dish, and they can be brought straight to table when it's the family at home.

Plates. — A kitchen should have plates reserved exclusively for the use of the domestic staff. They can be glazed pottery or 'opaque porcelain' – a

1. *Cafetière du Levant* is a term used for china or porcelain filter coffee pots.
2. Sarreguemines is a town in north-east France in the department of Moselle. Its porcelain manufacture began in 1790 and it was a favourite of Napoleon I. Production has now ceased.

rather pompous name for pipe-clay pottery – which is sturdy and cheap. It should also have some dishes, a salad bowl and a soup tureen. If you can buy these things in porcelain, as seconds – in which case they will be much the same price as pipe-clay – that would be a great improvement.

Cutlery. — For pots and pans, spoons must be wooden, not metal; but a few sets of cutlery for the servants and other purposes are required.

Knives, cleavers, etc. — The cutting instruments in the kitchen are: two knives, one tapered and pointed for peeling vegetables, gutting chickens, etc.; the other $0^m,40$ long, with a flexible blade, thick at the base and very pointed at the end, to cut meats, slice lardons, and chop herbs; a chopper consisting simply of a large blade mounted on a single handle (the best choppers are made with several half-moon blades fixed into handles at each end); and finally a cleaver for cutting large joints of meat, bones, separating cutlets, etc.; it should be heavy, so that its action is more certain and predictable. There is no point in economizing when buying this equipment: it is for the long term and greatly eases cook's labour when of good quality. A pair of scissors is indispensable.

Knife board. — A board on which you can polish your knives is the only way to keep them clean at all times. The board is $0^m,10$ wide by $0^m,80$ long and a length of buffalo hide $0^m,30$ to $0^m,40$ long is stuck to it. At one end of the board is a small box or pocket to house the polishing brick. This is the same as that used by soldiers for cleaning their weapons. With the back of the knife, grate some dust off the brick onto the buffalo hide and then rub all of the blade over the hide, now covered with brick dust, keeping the knife at right-angles to the board. In a short time the blade is brilliant and slightly sharpened.

Coffee roaster. — For coffee, it is essential to have a sheet metal stove and roaster; they cost little and last for ever. Coffee roasted in any other way loses much of its quality, especially as it will not be uniformly roasted, essential if it is to be good. You will also need a box for the roasted coffee beans, and one for ground coffee. These boxes are made from tinplate but I believe it preferable, to better preserve the aroma, to have tight-lidded glass or porcelain jars.

Milk saver. — A milk saver (figure 40) is a small tinplate gadget that you place in the milk pan to stop it boiling over. It takes the form of a funnel with the spout cut off, and what would be its top is so shaped that

187

Figure 40. Milk saver.

the milk can enter when it boils. Around its shortened spout there is a flange, making the whole thing mushroom-shaped. When the milk boils, it rises in the interior of the funnel, emerges through the spout and falls back onto the flange as illustrated in figure 41, showing the milk saver in a saucepan

The milk saver costs 1 franc: it is equally useful in preventing melting butter from boiling over the rim of the saucepan.

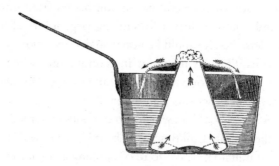

Figure 41. Section showing the milk saver placed in the saucepan.

Pastry rolling pin. — A country kitchen also needs a board and pin for pastry work; this allows the mistress to produce plenty of simple yet excellent pastries of her own for friends and family. The board should be soft wood and measure $0^m,80$ by $0^m,60$. There should be a five- or six-centimetre ledge on two sides. The rolling pin should be a hardwood, like service, box or ash.

Salt box. — A wooden box with a hinged lid is dedicated to holding a small supply of sea salt, or kitchen salt, for every day use. This box is hung by the stove.

Pepper box and mill. — A tin is very useful for pepper – it can be a round one, but its lid must fit tightly. This way you don't risk spilling the pepper and it keeps better in this than any other container.

They make small pepper mills that are no more than scaled-down versions of coffee grinders. You can buy whole peppercorns and grind them as needed. This gets round having to buy ready-ground pepper, invariably adulterated.

Storage boxes for flour, rice, etc. — I also have in my kitchen several tin-plate boxes with hinged lids in which I keep flour for immediate use in the kitchen, dried breadcrumbs, rice, semolina, etc. These containers are square and about $0^m,15$ high. They cost little and they can be easily stacked in a cupboard or on a shelf. Whatever they contain is proof against humidity, dust and infestation. Containers like these are thus infinitely better than the paper sacks in which the provisions I have mentioned are normally stored.

Bowls, tubs. — It is best to avoid washing up in earthenware bowls; crockery chips too easily, and flatware deteriorates and scratches. Large wooden bowls are found almost everywhere and are sturdy and convenient, but because they soak up any grease, they need regular care and attention. They can be cleaned with a little black soap, grit and a scrubbing brush. Generally, I prefer a sort of straight-sided bowl in zinc: it lasts a long time, is inexpensive and easy to maintain.

Brushes, brooms, ceiling brush. — Scrubbing brushes are useful for washing tables, the sink, the stove, etc. Horsehair brushes are no substitute: they are too soft and too dense; grease and other residue clog up horsehair and such brushes soon become unhygienic. Scrubbing brushes suffer from none of this.

Brooms to sweep tiled floors are either heather or horsehair. When you wash tiles, you can also scrub them with a parquet brush with a metre-long handle set at an angle.

You can dislodge spiders' webs with the aid of a ceiling brush, convex in shape, with horsehair bristle stuck on the end of a long handle.

Sponges. — Sponges serve a host of functions such as washing the stove or the table, mopping up spills on the floor, etc. It's best to insert a loop of string by which to hang them after you have pressed them dry; be sure not to wring them out as you will tear them.

Jugs, pitchers. — One or two zinc cans are very useful, and better than stoneware jugs, which cost almost as much and are very fragile. What's more, a zinc one is light and an appropriate shape.

Parsley pot. — You can have fresh parsley through the winter months by virtue of a terracotta pot (figures 42 and 43) in the shape of a truncated

Figure 42. Pottery vase to cultivate parsley in winter.

Figure 43. Pottery vase to cultivate parsley in winter.

cone – solid at the bottom, with a hole at the top – 50 centimetres tall and pierced by a multitude of holes. In September you fill it with soil and through each of these holes you introduce two parsley roots. You place the pot somewhere in the kitchen light enough so that the growth does not become leggy and etiolated, and every time the cook needs some parsley she cuts a bit off. After a few weeks it will sprout new growth.

Candlesticks. — The kitchen needs to have candlesticks and candle-holders, in copper or iron, with ejectors, and having a hook on the candle-drip. The ejector ensures that you raise the flame as the candle melts, and the hook means you can hang the candle-holder in places where you cannot put it down. Candlesticks need scouring with care otherwise they tarnish quickly. If you tin them every so often – it will only cost 30 centimes – they will be much easier to clean and you won't have the smell of copper on your hands.

Snuffers. — Snuffers are indispensable in a kitchen; there is nothing more disgusting than seeing a cook snuff out a candle with her fingers or with the kitchen scissors.

Extinguisher. — A [conical] extinguisher is no less essential for any rooms where tallow candles are introduced. When you blow a candle out, it spreads the very disagreeable smell of fat everywhere; although the flame is extinguished, the wick will smoulder down to the fat and then, when relighting it, you will have to melt the fat wastefully to expose the wick.

Cleaning the furniture. — The kitchen table, stove, washing stone, chopping block, and the basket for dirty dishes should all be frequently scrubbed with hot soapy water, or water prepared for the laundry [with wood ash], then rinsed with clean water.

For cleaning iron equipment, glass paper is better than sand, the grains of which are too coarse.

Scales. — You need scales to check the weight of foods sent by suppliers, as well as weighing out ingredients in their correct proportions for some confections, such as jam, pastries, etc.

Clock. — No kitchen should be without a clock; it is the only means of ensuring regularity and exactitude from the servants; what's more it saves them the bother, or removes the pretext, of going into reception rooms to check the time.

Advantages of good equipment. — It might be objected that the cost of furnishing a kitchen in the manner described is too high and that not every budget can extend to it. To this I reply that if your budget for kitchen furniture is so modest that you cannot afford sturdy, durable equipment, it's far better to only buy some of the things, hold back, and wait until you can afford it to buy the rest. I am convinced that if you were to make a careful calculation, and compare the costs over a period of ten years (short enough when you think how long copper and cast iron lasts) the balance would be in favour of the dearer equipment even though the initial outlay is so much greater.

15. — Pantry. — Meat safe.

Arrangement of the pantry. — The pantry is generally provided with shelves with a little beading round their edge to hold the fruit placed on them. But not every shelf should have this edge because it makes them more difficult to wash, something absolutely necessary if they are used to take the remains of the last meal or the infinity of other objects that may be placed there. If there is a window in the pantry, it should be provided with a thick metal grille covered with wire mesh to proof it from rats, cats, and even flies, as the window needs to be open all the time, except during heatwaves when it should be shut in the morning and opened in the evening to admit the cool night air. The room needs good ventilation; if the sun comes through the window, it should have a thick white curtain.

Tiling. — The pantry should be tiled and frequently washed. When it is on the ground floor, then a small hole can be made through the outside wall at floor-level. This makes the washing more straightforward as the water can be brushed through this drain.

A means to destroy mice. — You should look carefully for any points of entry for mice and stop these holes with either crushed glass coated with plaster or hemp mixed with tempered plaster.

Figure 44. Meat safe.

Meat safe. — The pantry should contain a meat safe, unless you can place this item somewhere cooler. The meat safe should be rectangular rather than round. Its side walls are made of wire mesh, of a gauge fine enough to keep out flies, and the top and bottom of wood or sheet metal to keep out dust. A horizontal wheel should be installed in the upper part of the safe, its axle going through the roof and fixed by a pin (figure 44). This means that the wheel will turn, and you can put hooks and nails round the circumference to take meat and poultry. You can also put a batten across the side walls, with nails for the same purpose. A certain way up the meat safe, you should insert a shelf, both to give you more room to accommodate different dishes and to have somewhere where they can be stored without coming into contact with raw meat.

The meat safe should be in a well ventilated and shady spot; but only in a cellar if it is really well ventilated, because without a draught meat taints and even spoils very quickly. The safe should be hung. Fix four short, strong cords to the corners and gather them in a knot over the central axle of the meat-wheel. Then attach a rope which passes through a pulley fixed to a joist where you want to suspend the safe. This rope has loops knotted at various points which may be hooked onto a cleat fixed on the wall. Thus you can bring the safe down whenever you want to take something out, and raise it up again afterwards.

Rack. — You can hang from the centre of the pantry what we call a rack.[1] This is made up of four vertical wooden battens nailed to the ceiling joists and reaching down to 2 metres from the floor. At the bottom of these risers you fix crosspieces from one to another. A rack like this, well away from any surface, is very appropriate for bread and anything else that would be better placed there than on shelves.

Exterior shelf. — The pantry door should close really tightly, so that no insect or animal can pass through. To one side of the door, on the outside wall, you should erect a shelf, about $1^m,10$ off the floor, on which you can place things while you open or shut the door itself. This is a great help and sidesteps a host of inconveniences such as leaving the door open because you don't have your hands free, or spilling something while attempting to open the door.

16. — Bakehouse.

We call the place where we make the bread the bakery or bakehouse. It should always be on the ground floor and in the backyard of the dwelling – from which is should always be detached. It ought to be clean, well ventilated and proof against any damp. It should have two ovens, a dough trough, a copper boiler, baker's linen and all the equipment necessary for making bread. It ought to have shelves laden with baskets. (See, for more details, the section *Making bread.*)

17. — Laundry.

The laundry is where we do the washing. It answers to the same requirements as the bakehouse, which it abuts in almost every farmhouse. It needs a copper boiler or a fireplace, cauldrons, several tubs, and all the equipment required to do the washing. (See, for more details, the section *Laundry.*)

---

1.   In French, *tenailler.*

18. — Water, cistern, filter.

Water quality. — Good water is clear, limpid, colourless, odourless and with a fresh taste to it; it dissolves soap easily; it cooks vegetables and meat well.

Save in exceptional circumstances, the best water is:

1   Springwater;
2   Water from large rivers flowing to the sea;[1]
3   Water from smaller rivers or tributaries;[2]
4   Water from streams;
5   Rainwater;
6   Water from artesian wells.

In a word, the best water, after springwater, is that which has flowed a long way, and in consequence has had long contact with the atmosphere which allows it to take up lots of oxygen from the air. Pondwater, water from most wells and any stagnant water are inadequate from the point of view of health and for most other purposes.

Filter. — The equipment we use to clarify water is called a filter. As the best water is often full of impurities, a filter is essential. This is not expensive. If such a thing cannot be found, it suffices to put well-washed and pounded charcoal mixed with gravel in the bottom of a stoneware cistern and place over this the false bottom that these cisterns usually come with. The water will soon run clear.

Cistern for handwashing. — A cistern for handwashing is no less requisite. It can be sheet metal, copper, zinc or ceramic, although copper is the longest lasting – it can be tinned inside. To one side of the cistern you should hang a handtowel. Keep the cistern and basin perfectly clean.

19. — Crockery, — Cutlery. — Plate warmers. — Glassware. — Coffee pot, etc.

Inventory. — The crockery falls into the realm of the pantry; it is a significant item for any household, and its upkeep can be costly if the servants are careless. It is therefore useful to make an inventory of all the china and glassware and check it every three months. Breakages should

1.   In French, *fleuves*.
2.   In French, *rivières*.

be replaced. If you omit to do this you only encourage carelessness and disorder, and the subsequent cost will only be greater. In the meantime, the household lacks what's needed and you will be caught out at a moment of crisis. What's more, this quarterly review acts as motivation to the servants, who will take more care and break less in the knowledge that they will be discovered. On the other hand, I do not think it fair that servants should be charged for breakages that were the result of accidents beyond their control.

China. — China costs so little today that you should prefer it to all other sorts of crockery. It is more hygienic and supports far greater shocks without breaking than any other pottery. You cannot scratch it and the surface is hard enough to last for several years. I am therefore convinced that the true economy is to use porcelain, even in the humblest households. If your means are indeed straitened, rather than buying perfect examples, look out factory seconds. Among the rejects you will often be able to find pieces where the actual blemishes are hidden from view and the result will be very presentable for family use.

The principal manufacture of porcelain is at Limoges. China made at Vierzon, in the Department of the Cher,[1] is most attractive, and may even be finer or more transparent that Limoges, but is far from having the strength. Boiling water will shatter it, the slightest knock will break it, while Limoges is even fireproof. I urge my readers to pay the extra, if necessary, for Limoges rather than buying Vierzon for a lower price. They will find this a great saving in the long run.

Fruit bowls and baskets. — The cost of porcelain is so reasonable that you can contemplate having some ornamental items for the table such as mounted fruit bowls, creamers, fruit baskets and flower baskets.

Tea and coffee service. — A modest coffee service, and another for tea are also virtually indispensable – especially today when we take these beverages as a matter of course. White cups with a narrow fillet in a colour or gold are always up-to-the-minute and, most important, in good taste.

---

1.   Vierzon, between the Sologne and Berry, north-west of Bourges, developed as a centre for china and porcelain after 1816, largely thanks to the existence of a refractory clay and kaolin in the district. The manufacturer Pillivuyt was also established at the Château de Foëcy nearby. While enjoying much success through the nineteenth century, there were multiple problems after the Second World War and the last Vierzon manufacturer closed its doors at the end of the twentieth century.

These sets should not be left in the parlour, as you often see; they run too great a risk of being broken, especially when there are children about – why give yourself an occasion to scold them for clumsiness when you can avoid the issue? In the country, children are always running into the parlour with their toys – bats, balls, balloons – and *an accident soon happens.*

The number of plates necessary for service at table. — For a formal dinner, you will need twelve plates, two spoons and six forks for every guest. It is possible to do it with fewer plates and covers but it will be necessary to wash some of the dishes in the course of the meal for their reuse towards the end. Be mindful, more than ever, that when you have washed them in hot water, you will have to plunge them in clean, cold water to rinse and chill them (I will touch on this later), as a warm plate is not acceptable later in the meal and it is not pleasing to eat some cold sweet dishes or dessert on them. It's best to have smaller plates for the dessert, piled separately – you are wise not to mix them with the other plates as they are easily broken in mixed piles. Hot plates should be kept for hot dishes.

Plate warmer. — You can warm plates by means of a sort of small stove with double doors, like a wardrobe, which is called a plate warmer (figure 45). During the meal you place it on top of either a room heater,

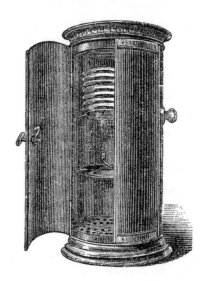

Figure 45. Plate warmer.

a stove, a cooker or on embers. Inside, it is divided by shelves into three compartments. The bottom is pierced with holes so that the heat can penetrate. You can put plates on the bottom as well as on the shelves. In default of a plate warmer, you can put plates to warm on a stove, or rinse them in hot water at the moment of service. Nothing takes less time than drying a hot plate.

Cutlery. — Cutlery or flatware, whether plain or beaded, is usually made of silver. The price of each place-setting in silver is from 40 to 45 francs. In most of France, and especially in Paris, the preference is for electroplated flatware, made by Christofle according to the Elkington process.[1] This only costs 6 francs per setting and both looks like and is often confused with solid silver. It will withstand five or six years of constant use without deterioration and can be replated in whole or in part very cheaply.

Food warmers for the table. — You should have several lamps in copper-bronze or electroplate (by the Elkington process); old-fashioned silver plate rapidly loses its condition and has been superseded. In winter, a lamp is the only way of keeping dishes hot at table. When there are guests, a handsome lamp is an ornament, and is not too dear. The ones in which you simply place hot embers, or which are heated by hot water (kept that way by a candle), are the most appropriate. Those heated by oil often give off a strong odour and sometimes boil the food. Lamps fuelled with alcohol are at least clean, but they too can produce too high a heat.

Glasses, decanters. — Glassware should be crystal. Ordinary [lead-free] glass costs less but is much more fragile, it is therefore a false economy. Glasses and carafes in plain or lightly cut crystal are nowadays quite cheap. Much crystal is not really clear, but has an unattractive violet or greenish tint which makes them look dirty. You should beware buying these as they cost just as much as the sparkling uncoloured crystal. Moulded crystal is sometimes quite attractive, but the mouldings are usually too deep and attract grime, which is difficult to clean. It is easy to tell moulded from cut glass. In the first, the angles are rounded, while the second has sharp edges. Given that for the same price as cut glass you can buy extravagantly ornate moulded crystal, I would always plump for something cut simply, or even plain – they are just in better taste. When moulded glassware needs cleaning, you should scrub the decoration with a brush and soap. It's the only way to get to the bottom of the mouldings and give them a bit of sparkle.

You can drink fine wines from stemmed glasses, and even wine and water mixed: this style lends elegance. But such choice glassware should be reserved for when you have company. When it's just the family, I would advise ordinary glasses; they are easier to wash and consequently fewer are broken. A few crystal decanters for everyday wine are an ornament to the table, but fine wines are better not decanted.

1.   The inventor of electroplating was George Richards Elkington (1801–1865) of Birmingham.

Corks. — It is often difficult to put a pulled cork back in the bottle, in which case the wine will be badly stoppered. Silver plated corks with a ring-pull on top are clean and suitable.

Oil cruet. — A neat oil cruet, whether in wood or silver plate, is desirable, but it is better that it should be simple and well made than elegant yet badly designed. Sturdy, durable objects are always to be preferred to those which do no more than flatter the eye – giving you a short-lived pleasure betrayed by lack of substance. Simple, serviceable things are so much better than a flashy show.

Cabaret or tantalus. — Something to bring liqueurs to table, whether on a stand or in a box, is quite an expensive piece but is as useful as it is attractive.

Figure 46. Basket.

Figure 47. Egg-basket.

Egg-basket. — A wire basket (figure 46) or a wire egg-basket (figure 47), or one made in japanned tinplate are the most reliable and simplest way of boiling eggs precisely.

English teapot. — If you take tea frequently, you will need to secure for your use a Russian samovar and an English metal teapot which both preserves the leaf's aroma and has in addition the advantage of serviceability and cleanliness (figure 48).

The *Samovar* [1] (figure 49) is very useful; it is clean, elegant, and avoids the use of alcohol [for a lamp to heat it] and all the attendant bother. Figure 50, which is a section through the samovar, shows the flue A, running vertically through the centre of the kettle and provided with burning

1.   In French, *bouilloire russe.*

Figure 48. English teapot.

charcoal. Two rings of holes at the bottom and the top of the samovar itself (figure 50) allow a passage of air sufficient to keep the coals alight. This flue is closed with its own lid (B) which is lifted or left in place depending whether you wish to let burn or extinguish the fire. Another lid (C) closes the samovar itself.

When you wish to use the samovar, you take off both lids. You pour water into the body of the kettle. The water can be cold, as the flue, half-filled with burning coals, will soon boil it. If you need it more immediately, you can start with hot water. You put the lid C on the kettle and place red hot coals at the bottom of the flue – on a grill so that they get complete combustion. The tap D allows you to obtain hot water. The only precaution you must always take is to keep the kettle provided with water whenever there are burning embers in the flue. Failing this, the heat of the fire will dissolve some part of the samovar.

When you have done, you put on the lid B to extinguish the fire, you empty the water out via the tap, and you turn the whole thing upside

Figure 49. Samovar.

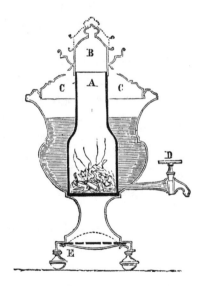

Figure 50. Section through samovar.

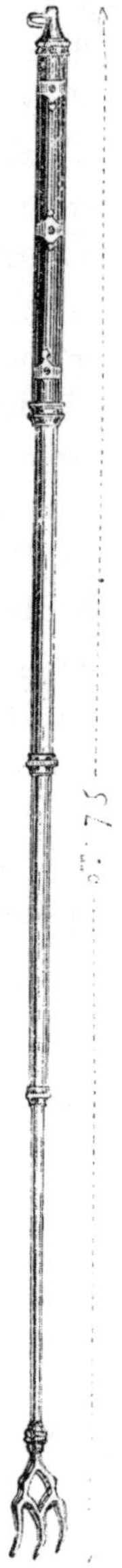

down to shake out the coals. The cinders that fall while the fire is burning are held by a hinged flap (E) which opens at the bottom of the samovar. To empty these out, you have but to open the flap and knock the bottom of the samovar a couple of times with your hand to dislodge them.

Coffee pots. — For coffee pots you are best with porcelain or earthenware with a hard glaze. The filter should be pewter.

Toasting fork. — The length of this fork, illustrated at full extension in figure 51, and closed like the telescopic handle of a lorgnette in figure 52, means that you can toast bread without burning your fingers.

Figure 52. Toasting fork, retracted into its handle.

English corkscrew. [1] — By means of a simple yet ingenious mechanism, this corkscrew, illustrated by figure 53, inserts the screw into the cork and permits its removal without noise or effort, thereby leaving the wine undisturbed.

Soda syphon. — This allows you to make soda water for very little. It consists of two thick glass spheres of different sizes superposed one on the other and enclosed within a rush or brass wire net. (See the detailed description in the section, *Making Seltzer water.*)

Figure 53. English corkscrew.

20. — Flower vases.

Some vases in cut or moulded crystal are charming

Figure 51. Toasting fork, extended.

1.   The corkscrew illustrated is related to or derived from the design patented by Edward Thomason of Birmingham in 1802.

decoration for a room, especially if you make the effort to have fresh flowers. Nowadays you can find stoneware vases of graceful design which do not cost too much; they are far better than porcelain vases that are nearly always clumsily gilded, badly painted, in poor taste and very costly.

21. — Warming pan, brooms, brushes, sponges.

Warming pan. — You ought to have a good copper warming pan. When you want to use it, you should ensure that you fill it with a fair quantity of embers (making sure they are still glowing) and that you leave it to warm up thoroughly before actually inserting it because at that point the fire will be promptly snuffed out and the bed will not be warmed well enough. You will need to move the pan around in the bed, otherwise the sheets will scorch. A stoneware hot water bottle, such as I mentioned on page 171, can serve the purpose of a warming pan.

Brooms. — A household also needs good brooms; but you should watch the quality of horsehair brooms: generally, those with reddened wood are poor. Horsehair bristles show their quality when they resist the pressure of the hand, and spring back when the hand is removed. They have found a way of replacing horsehair with very finely split whalebone; it looks the same, but is far from having the same qualities. For courtyards, the kitchen, etc., you can use birch or heather brooms.

Brushes. — With brushes, as with brooms, horsehair is the preference, but it is now difficult to spot the whalebone mixed in with the horsehair, so much do they look alike.

Sponges, etc. — A horsehair bottle brush, a horsehair brush, some sponges, some corks with chains attached to wash bottles are all very useful for keeping crockery and glassware as it should be.

Feather dusters. — Dusters with cocks' feathers are more durable than any others; their flexibility means they do not break. A provident housewife can obtain her own in the country and, with a modicum of intelligence – studying how the feathers are attached to the handle – she can also revive her worn-out feather duster. A good duster costs enough to encourage her to set aside any feathers from the cocks or capons served at table. In districts where geese are raised, they often use the last two wing joints of these birds as dusters, and find them very serviceable. After they are killed, they cut them off before they pluck the rest. This small duster is called a *plumail* in some districts, and is used for dusting. Its form permits it to deal with a host of small corners where a large duster would never penetrate.

22. — Storage cabinet.

In the room where you keep provisions, it is very useful to install a chest for dry goods (figure 54) in which you can store dried vegetables, rice, the various pasta in common use, as well as coffee and sugar. This chest is split into compartments and drawers. At the bottom there should be large bins (A) with sloping lids, with shallower drawers (B) above. Grocers have very similar fitments in their shops. In the large bins (A) you put those dried vegetables that you use in larger quantities such as beans, lentils, peas, etc. If necessary, you can divide each bin in two, still accessed by the one lid. At the bottom of each bin there should be a small trap, a sliding door (C), by which you can clean out the bottoms of the bins. The chest can also be used to store the seed for garden vegetables.

In the upper drawers (B) you can put rice, semolina, coffee, the sugar loaf in use, etc., etc.

The chest ensures that all provisions are proof against all those animals and insects that otherwise attack them. They are also protected against the damp, and you are sure that anything stored there will be neither wasted, suffered to lose condition, nor given into the hands of those who would misuse them or not take pains to use them as they should be used.

I recommend this useful fitting, which can be made in pine.

23. — Tools necessary for the country.

Although this book is directed at womenfolk, they may not take it amiss that I treat of some questions that are usually a male preserve.

These matters might doubtless seem fairly alien to a woman living in town, but they will certainly concern a farmer's wife, who is sometimes called on to replace her husband in supervising the whole affair. And who knows whether the husband himself might not sometimes find useful tips within these covers?

It is essential in the country to have a variety of tools. At any moment, there may be occasion to undertake a light repair and a suitable workman is nowhere to be found. And at other times, you may not wish to call someone in because the job is too insignificant. However, without constant

Figure 54. Storage cabinet.

attention, a host of useful objects within the house will not survive. And an urgent project may have to be abandoned simply because you don't have the tool necessary to repair a ploughing implement. In fact, these tools will be needed at every turn. Here is a list of those most in demand:

A workbench, to start with. It is really useful for the staff and, because it is difficult to carry about – and yet is essential for any carpenter or joiner – it is best to have him come to the farm unless he can travel with his own bench. This bench should contain:

A screw clamp,
A comb,
A bench clamp,
A mallet,
A plane,
A jack-plane,
A jointer plane,
A drawing knife,
A hatchet,
A large and a small hammer,
A small and a large pair of pincers,
A selection of gimlets,
A screwdriver,
An awl,
An axe,
Some scissors,
An adjustable spanner,
A square,
A ruler,
Wedges to split wood,
A sawhorse,
A selection of nails,
A selection of brads,
Glass paper,
A pot of strong glue,
Two or three paintbrushes,

A selection of screws,
A large and a small saw,
A bow saw for firewood,
A small anvil,
A vice,
A bit-brace,
A selection of drill bits,

A knife to cut leather,
A punch to make holes in
    straps,
Well-seasoned timber such
    as oak, ash, elm, walnut,
    pine and poplar.

Thus equipped, a workman is never at a loss when making a repair and, as necessity is the mother of invention, it is rare that there is no one among the farm employees intelligent enough to take advantage of the tools at his disposal.

24. — Heating equipment.

A. — Chimney construction and how to stop it smoking.

Hearth. — In the country the hearth should be large, because one often burns tree-stumps or other extravagantly shaped pieces of wood. You leave the embers in place because that is a way of getting the most heat while consuming the least fuel. A grate lined with tiles is both cleaner and reflects lots of heat into the room.

How to stop chimneys smoking. — It is very important when building chimneys to stop them from smoking – a point often ignored in houses designed by architects who have not studied the matter. Chimneys that follow the proper rules never smoke.

A chimney that has been badly designed from the start will often resist all attempts by experts to improve its draw. These efforts may either be costly, or have grave consequences: they include trying to introduce a flow of fresh air at the front of the hearth or pushing the hearth so far back behind the chimney breast that you lose much of the heat. Sometimes you can stop a chimney smoking by nothing more than a sheet of zinc, or brickwork, running from the outer frame of the fireplace back at an angle into the hearth (figures 55 and 56). With kitchen fireplaces, where any reduction of the size of the hearth would be inappropriate, it is sometimes enough just to raise the level of the hearth by means of a small platform 15 centimetres high. The essence is that you must constrict the draught in such a way that it is forced to rise as fast as possible.

Brick-lined chimney. — If these simple measures are insufficient, you may have recourse to something which does not cost too much and is

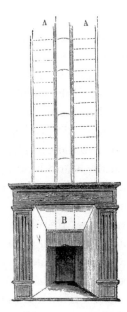

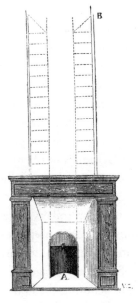

Figure 55. Fireplace lined with brick.   Figure 56. A Fourcroy fireplace.

nearly always successful, unlike those attempts I described earlier.

The interior of the chimney should not be rectangular (figure 55); the back corners should be filled with either dressed stone, plastered brickwork or cast iron plates. This infill should rise to point B in the interior of the fireplace. On top of this construction, you build a sort of truncated pyramid (AA), also in plastered brickwork, that fills almost the entirety of the flue, just leaving an aperture sufficient to admit a metal flue such as you use for a stove. This extends two or three metres up the chimney. This flue is fixed to the wall at the back of the chimney breast by means of straps and wire before you build its housing. You must not allow any air to pass between the metal flue and its seating. The draught will thus be closely confined and the chimney will draw just like a stove's. It will hardly ever smoke.

Sweeping. — To sweep this flue, which will quite quickly clog with soot, you have but to use a long flexible rod, at the end of which is fixed a small broom. Above the flue, the chimney itself rarely needs sweeping. When that becomes necessary, the same method is used as for stoves: you remove the chimney cowl and sweep from above.

I have often done this and it always works.

Fourcroy fireplaces. — There is another method, no less effective and based on almost the same principles, recommended by the celebrated Fourcroy.[1] It consists of a great reduction in the fireplace itself (figure 56). It achieves this by closing off with brickwork almost all the mouth of the chimney, leaving a niche such as might accommodate a stove (A) with, at the rear, a narrow passage for the smoke. This constriction is continued for the first two metres of the flue by means of two slabs in plaster or brick (B). The result of this arrangement is that the hearth is pushed to the front, almost beyond the chimney breast. When this is the case, it is necessary to surround the hearth with a wire fireguard to avoid those accidents which today's extreme developments of ladies' dress have made so common. These fireplaces never smoke, and a very small amount of wood maintains a gentle warmth throughout the room. The design offers almost all the advantages of a stove, without any of its drawbacks. I have seen it in action in the home of the sainted chemist's widow and in those of her friends; I have myself installed it with complete success. The savings in wood are considerable.

Sweeping. — You sweep these chimneys like those I first discussed. You can make an opening in the upper part of the flue, at attic level, so that you can introduce the brushes without climbing onto the roof above, or demolishing the brickwork to access the flue from the bottom. The narrowest part of the flue can be cleaned with an old cobweb brush attached to a stick or with a rope that you drop down from the opening in the attic.

Upper chimney and pot. — The upper part of the flue, in clay, stone or brick, that rises above the roof is also called a chimney.[2] The top of the chimney must be higher than any neighbouring building to avoid gusts of wind bouncing off walls and pushing the smoke back down the chimney.

---

1. Antoine François, comte de Fourcroy (1755–1809), chemist, entomologist, medical scientist and revolutionary politician. His wife, referred to here by Mme Millet-Robinet, was Mme Adélaïde-Flore de Wailly (1765–1838), her first husband being Charles de Wailly, architect to Louis XVI. It was thanks to the patronage of the comtesse de Fourcroy that Mme Millet-Robinet's brother, Stéphane, gained his entry to the laboratory of Louis Nicolas Vauquelin at the outset of his scientific career in 1812.
2. In French, *cheminée* may refer to either the fireplace, the flue or the chimney.

The smoke will disperse more readily and the draw will be that much stronger if the chimney rises above everything that surrounds it. If that is not possible, then you must extend the chimney with pots such as I discuss below.

T-shaped chimney pot. — A clay pot narrowing towards the top in the form of a mitre, or a stove-pipe placed on the top of the chimney stack, inhibits the large draughts that push the smoke back down the flue and thus into the room below. If the chimney smokes when the wind is in a particular direction, you can install a metal cowl in the form of a T, with the transverse of the T at right-angles to the wind in question. That is, you position it to run north to south if the chimney smokes when the wind is in the west or east, while in the opposite case you position it west to east if the chimney smokes when the wind blows from the north or south. However, if the chimney's smoking is down to lack of draw, this will have no effect whatsoever and you will have to resort to one of the remedies I have already discussed.

Chimney cowl. — You can also prevent the wind making the chimney smoke, as well as keeping the rain out of the flue, by covering the opening with a metal cap or cowl (figure 57). This cowl is always wider than the chimney pot and fits so that its edge is a little lower than the top of the chimney. It is held in place by metal straps pinned at their ends to the flue. The smoke escapes through the open ring between the flue and the cowl.

Weather-vane chimney cowl. — Another fitting which serves the same purpose is a sort of weather-vane (figure 58) which is made up of an

Figures 57 & 58. Chimney cowl (left) and weather-vane chimney cowl (right).

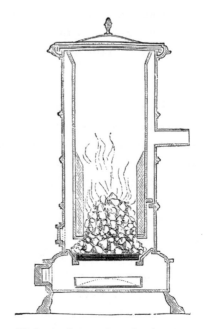

Figure 59. Coke stove.

Figure 60. Section through coke stove.

elongated cone (wider than the pot) which pivots on a metal rod fixed inside. This cone has a horizontal duct extending about 8 or 9 centimetres, and open at the end to allow the smoke to escape. The slightest puff of wind will make the cowl turn so that the issue is always away from the current of air.

B. — Coke-burning devices.

When you live near a plant that produces coke, there are great economies to be had by employing devices which burn this fuel for your heating.

Coke stove. — Coke stoves as illustrated by figure 59, shown in section in figure 60, are manufactured by M. Muel.[1] They cost between 40 and 60 francs and are truly a slow-combustion stove. They stand between $0^m,90$ and $1^m,30$ and do not consume more that one or two litres of coke per hour, that is to say, from 2 to 4 centimes at Paris prices.

1. In 1832 Pierre Adolphe Muel instigated a foundry famed for artistic productions and sculptures at Tusey in the Meuse. Early instances of its work are the cast iron fountains, columns and candelabra in the place de la Concorde in Paris (1838–9).

The stove consists of an outer cylinder made of cast or sheet iron and an inner cast iron cylinder, the inside lined up to half its height with fire cement. Each cylinder is closed by a lid. The inner vessel has no bottom, and is separated from the fire grate by a gap of around 10 centimetres, the ash falling through the grate to the tray below. A flue sits halfway up the outer cylinder.

When you wish to light the stove, you insert kindling, shavings or embers through the small door situated just above the ash tray (figure 60) into the space between the grate and the inner cylinder. You lift the lids of the cylinders themselves and put as much coke as you want the fire to last into the inner vessel. Replacing the lids, you light the shavings and the flames spread to that layer of coke in contact with the kindling but does not extend to the coke that sits above the refractory lining. This is because the lid to the inner cylinder is sealed with sand and is wholly airtight. The fire can only be fed by the draught which passes from the opening of the ash compartment and onwards horizontally through the coke on the grate to vent through the flue. The gases released by the combustion will rise through the whole mass of fuel but, finding no escape through the top lid, will fall again onto the burning coals, which will consume them almost in their entirety.

Until the coke is thoroughly alight, you should leave the half-moon door in the ash tray fully open. But if you leave it open all the time, the draught will be too great and too much coke will be consumed. You control the rate of burn by opening and closing that small door. You can even close it completely if the fire is too intense. In that way, the fuel and the heat will last a very long time, and even longer if you riddle the cinders every so often by means of a bent iron rod which you insert between the gaps of the grate via the ash compartment.

When a stove like this is properly tended you can run it virtually indefinitely, just adding fuel morning and evening so the inner cylinder is kept full.

When you wish to clear the hearth of the clinkers which sometimes accumulate on the grate and obstruct the draught, you open the [upper] hearth door and you poke the burning coke with the riddle. When clinker is exposed to the air, it blackens quickly and, once seen, you can pull it out.

If you wish to clean the firebox comprehensively, when the stove is completely cold you remove the ash tray, put your hand into the now-vacant space and, grasping a lug attached to the grate, lift and turn it then pull it out. You clean it, then replace it by inserting it upside down and, by twisting it, put it on the three brackets that hold it up – make sure that the bars of the grate are in line with the ash compartment door so that you can readily manipulate the poker.

Coke-burning fireplaces. — A disadvantage of a stove is that you cannot see the fire. To rectify this omission, coke-burning fireplaces have been developed (figure 61). These fireplaces are either sheet or cast iron, although the grate itself is always cast. The fire basket is located towards the bottom and at the front of the fireplace. It is distinct from the ash tray, leaving

Figure 61. Coke-burning fireplace, in sheet or cast iron.

sufficient space to introduce the poker to riddle the cinders and promote combustion. This fire is lit in the same way as the stove and the range, with shavings and kindling. The only difference is that in order to light it more easily, you increase the draught by placing over the upper part of the hearth a sort of hood of metal sheet or mesh which you can lift on or off at will.

Economic stove. — This small stove (figure 62) is constructed from thick sheet metal; it is lined with fire cement. It costs 17 francs in Paris and only consumes 30 centimes of coke in twelve hours. It is extremely economical for a small household because it is at once a room heater and a kitchen stove. The firebox is at the opposite end to the flue; you put kindling and coke into the aperture that you can identify on the right hand side of the stove top; then you close the hole by means of concentric cast iron rings

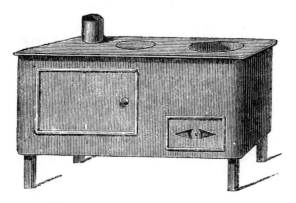

Figure 62. Economic stove in sheet metal.

such as are illustrated in figure 30. You open the small door that you can see on the right hand side, and you light the kindling. If you wish to cook food, you can either place a saucepan on the solid top without removing any of the rings, or you can take out one or two rings, depending on the size of the saucepan or stewpan you wish to place there. You can even have saucepans all over the top; the speed at which the food they contain will be cooked will depend on their proximity to the firebox. On the left of the stove there is an oven in which you can cook a joint, pastries, chestnuts, etc.

C. — Coal-burning devices.

These devices do not differ radically from those which burn coke, and their price is pretty much the same. It is only that coal has the disadvantage of producing a black smoke and an unpleasant smell as well as quickly clogging up the flues and chimneys. In addition, coal smoke deposits a great quantity of soot particles on anything close to the hearth. I must admit however that the Dutch, whose standards of cleanliness are legendary, have found means of minimizing the defects I have just listed.

CHAPTER X

THE UPKEEP OF THE HOUSE AND FURNITURE

I. — Cleaning, maintenance and repair of wooden furniture.

French-polished furniture. — French-polished furniture is less suitable than wax polished pieces because the finish suffers from winter damp, always a problem in the countryside. When a French-polished piece has been soiled for one reason or another, it only needs washing with a slightly damp fine sponge, then rubbing with a soft cloth. When the finish has been spoiled in some place, you can rub it lightly with a sponge moistened with a small drop of oil. You won't repair the damage, but it will restore a shine to the part in question. If the damage is extensive, you have to use polish, which will, by small steps, convert your French-polished furniture into something wax polished. You should never wipe French-polished furniture with a woollen cloth.

Polished furniture. — Furniture that is polished with wax or oil keeps well, or at least you can maintain it with a finish as bright as the day it was bought if you rub it every day with a coarse woollen cloth, like serge. If they have been neglected, water-stained, or even mud-stained, as can often happen with the lower extremities of chairs or other pieces, you first rub them with a woollen cloth impregnated with olive oil or drying oil,[1] then with a dry woollen cloth, and a little wax if necessary. After that, rub them again with a cloth. The oil will get rid of water marks and preserve the wood.

---

1.   Drying oil (*huile grasse*) is a vegetable oil (from e.g. linseed, poppy seed, perilla, walnut) that hardens to a solid film when exposed to the air.

Dining-table. — The dining-table requires particular attention if you dine without a tablecloth. Whether it be made from walnut or mahogany, you should clean it with a woollen cloth that has been wetted with really hot milk. This will remove any stains that result from meals. Then you rub it with a woollen cloth that has been lightly dipped in olive oil. The milk gives a shine to the wood, and an attractive colour. You can also use wax.

Table covers. — An oilcloth table cover, the same colour as wood, has been widely adopted. These cloths are neat and easy to maintain, but much less attractive than lustrous wood.

Repairs. — For the proper upkeep of your furniture, it is important to repair it as soon as possible. The slightest damage only gets worse if you do not repair it immediately; for want of a pittance, you will need to spend much more. It may be a nuisance to be bothered with these minutiae, but it is essential. Once a year, you should call in a capable craftsman and get him to check and repair all the furniture. The same level of attention should be given to the upholstery of armchairs, cane seating, and the upkeep and cleaning of covers. The effort expended will be repaid by the good order and economy of the household.

2. — Cleaning the kitchen table, the draining basket, the block, the washing-stone, etc.

The kitchen table should be washed frequently, not scraped as in many households. First you scrub it dry, with white or black soap. Then you throw a little boiling water over it and scrub once more with a scrubbing brush. If the table is really dirty, you can scrub it with a little grit or fine sand. Then rinse it with a sponge and clean water. A table treated thus will be utterly cleansed.

The same methods are used to maintain the sink, the draining basket for the washing up, the chopping block and the range. These kitchen fitments need to be spotless. You may use lye, prepared by boiling a little wood ash in water for an hour. Afterwards, you let it stand and then filter it. This lye should be used hot. If the table is ash or beech, and therefore naturally white, you keep it white by sprinkling it with a little bleach after you have washed it.

3. — Cleaning glasses and crockery.

Glasses. — Glasses should be rinsed in a bowl filled with freshly drawn water and not by pouring water from one glass to another as is too often the case. After this, they must be polished with a towel reserved exclusively for this function. You put them *upside down* in the glass basket. This is one way to stop dust and flies staining the glasses and helps you distinguish the clean from the used when you wish to take a drink between meals. The glass cloth ought to be hung from its own hook in the pantry so that it can dry out after use; it must not be employed for anything else.

Dishes. — Dishes should be washed in very hot water, with great care. Nothing puts people off more than being served crockery that is anything less than spotless and shining. The washer-up must first put the dishes in order, that is, pile them up after scraping all the leavings into a bowl (these scraps are excellent food for the pigs). Without this precaution, the water will be dirty from the outset. After this, the washer-up should range everything around the bowl filled with hot water, so that nothing is forgotten. First she washes what is not greasy, such as dessert plates, bowls, coffee cups, etc., and she finishes with the saucepans, stewpans, etc. To wash these last things really well it is almost inevitable that she will have to reheat the water. To do the washing-up, you should use a large, somewhat coarse cloth, called a dishcloth, and hold it in your hand. If you have it fixed to a wooden handle, it will not scrub the dishes so well. Next to the sink of hot water, you should have another bowl of cold or lukewarm water into which you can plunge the dishes as and when they have been washed. After that, you put them to drain in the basket or on the dish-rack, then dry them vigorously on every side. If you have two maids, one should wash and the other dry immediately. The work is easier and the results better.

Without these measures, your crockery will never be properly clean because the glaze will retain a thin layer of grease which will make it dull. After washing, the china should be as lustrous as when it was bought.

You must never, as is all too often the case, allow the dishes to be washed in a cast iron cauldron. Such a receptacle soon gets soiled – in the most unpleasant manner. It is very difficult to clean, and it blackens everything that comes near it. It is even more insufferable if this cauldron, like the washing-up, is left on the floor after washing is done.

I have already discussed in the section on *Kitchen equipment* wooden bowls and zinc tubs that are very convenient for doing the washing-up, as well as touching on the crockery basket. I will not rehearse this again.

I must repeat that the mistress cannot insist strongly enough on the closest attention to the washing-up on the part of her servants. The first essential of good dining is complete cleanliness. To ensure that it is so, each time a maid presents a plate, glass, etc., that is not up to the mark, you must give it back to them and gently point out its deficiencies. The shame that this will elicit, especially when strangers are present, will be an excellent lesson. The maid who serves at table, therefore, should be charged with drying the dishes, or making sure before every meal that they have been polished with due care and attention.

4. — Cleaning windows, mirrors, lamp glasses and crystal.

Windows. — Put whiting in a small bowl;[1] cover it with water; soon it will dissolve and form a sort of milk. Dip a small cloth, then fold it into a pad and rub the window you wish to clean. Wipe it immediately with a perfectly dry cloth; then finish cleaning with another soft cloth, also dry, not omitting the corners – which you can get into by wrapping the cloth round a small piece of wood.

You should watch that you don't cover all the window panes with a layer of whiting before you start wiping it off. The whiting will dry and then it is extremely hard to remove. You should always do one pane at a time.

Lye and alcohol also clean windows well enough, but it is more difficult to dry them once they have been washed, as well as to remove the whiting, and the job is not so thorough.

Mirrors. — Clean large mirrors in sections, because if you cover the whole surface with whiting, it will dry and be difficult to remove. Do not put whiting on to the gilt fillet that runs round the mirror, it will damage the gilding. Alcohol is more suitable for cleaning mirrors than whiting, although you still have to avoid touching the gilding. When gilding of this sort has been spoiled by any stain whatever, it is not easy to remedy because the gilding is usually so light that it disappears with the slightest friction. However, you can try to get rid of any mark by light strokes of a very fine, well-wetted sponge.

1.   Whiting (calcium carbonate), in French, is *blanc de Meudon*, *blanc de Toulouse*, or *blanc d'Espagne*. Meudon is a quarry near Paris where the chalk was obtained.

Lamp glasses. — These you clean with a bottle brush, or a stick wrapped in a cloth so that you can rub the insides of the chimney hard enough to lift the traces of soot deposited there. If the glass is marked by splashes of oil which have then burned and left a hard deposit, you can clean them with a damp cloth and a little fine ash. Before you expose a damp glass to the heat of the flame, it is wise to heat them very gently, otherwise they often shatter. All lamp glasses will readily shatter if subjected to rapid shifts from cool to hot; it is therefore sensible, immediately after lighting it, to keep the wick quite low for a minute or so to give the glass a chance to warm up.

Decanters and crystal. — Pour a little water into the carafe and then add some pellitory or lichwort (a plant that grows at the foot of walls almost everywhere),[1] or Jerusalem artichoke leaves, or egg shell, or brown paper or very fine sand. Shake vigorously; dust, stains and encrustations will soon lift off.

5. — Cleaning porcelain or glazed ceramic vases.

If a porcelain or glazed ceramic vase is dirty, you rub it with damp ash and a pad of paper. Afterwards, rinse it. You will get the same result with lye or potash.

6. — Cleaning silverware and copper gilt.

Silverware. — Silver is cleaned with whiting which has been dissolved in a little water. When it makes a sort of light paste, you dip a fine cloth in it and then rub the silver. Leave it to dry a little, then wipe it off with a worn cloth or a piece of soft leather such as very thin buffalo or sheepskin. If the silver has a beaded pattern, you need to use a brush to get into the corrugations.

It is best not to use whiting too often, it will cause the silver to wear. You can wash it with a sponge and some soap, or with lye, but these clean less thoroughly than whiting.

Copper gilt. — Sconces and other small objects in copper gilt should be cleaned with a sponge, soap and warm water. Pass the sponge across the soap, rub the object you wish to clean, then rinse and wipe dry.

---

1. *Parietaria officinalis.*

7. — Scouring copper, iron and tin.

Copper. — To scour copper, you should have recourse to a mixture that makes the task run smoothly and gives a perfect finish. You mix a quantity of [powdered] sandstone or fine sand with a tenth of its weight in flour and moisten it with vinegar. Apply this mixture with your fingers, then rub it with a little rotten stone.[1] It is much quicker and much better this way than if you use a pad of cloth, straw, hay or sorrel. Once the pot is shining, plunge it in cool, clean water and dry it carefully forthwith. After that you should place it close to the fire or in the sun so that it dries completely. Without this step, it tarnishes and loses its brilliance. Copper pans thus cleaned are as dazzling as gold.

To achieve a perfect polish, the best way is to rub the pot with a mixture of rotten stone and olive oil, followed by rotten stone alone.

Burnt saucepans. — If a saucepan is burnt, or the tinning has blackened, you put in ash and water and boil it for two hours; then you scrub the inside with a stiff brush and it should clean up perfectly. Never try to remove the burnt food with a sharp implement: you run the risk of damaging the tinning. The insides of saucepans should never be scoured; the most you can do is scrub them with a little ash.

Candlesticks. — To clean copper candlesticks, you should first place them near the fire to melt off any tallow stuck to them, and then dry them off with an old duster reserved especially for the job. You can then clean them as if they were saucepans, but, as they are never as tarnished as saucepans and other copper that is put directly on the fire, you can manage with just rotten stone. This you first moisten with olive oil or drying oil, then use dry.

Iron. — You scour iron as you would copper. You can rub it up with glass paper.

Kitchen equipment that you do not use every day, you should clean once a week, or at the least every fortnight.

8. — Plating old candlesticks.

When your old candlesticks have lost their gilt or silver plate so that

---

1.   Rotten stone is powdered sandstone, sometimes, though erroneously, called Tripoli powder. Tripoli is in fact another sandstone, named for its resemblance to a diatomite from Tripoli in Libya. Tripoli was also used as a cleaning or scouring agent.

you can see the copper beneath, you should either have them made as good as new by electroplating by the Christofle and Elkington method, or you should tin them. If the latter, they will not be as bright as if they were plated, but they will be quite serviceable. Rubbing more or less vigorously with a soft cloth will maintain their shine. The same effect will be obtained using whiting as I have described with respect to silverware.

9. — Lighting. Maintaining and cleaning lamps.

Lighting is rarely a matter of great expense in the country because usually one does not stay up very late. Mostly, tallow candles are used, which hardly cost any less than the oil burnt in a small yet good lamp.

Candles. — I advise the mistress of the house to choose stearin candles for her own use. They cost only twice as much as tallow candles, but last much longer and are much more agreeable. The greater cost is negligible, especially in the summer, when tallow melts so quickly. When the dark nights set in and you stay up betimes, there is nothing better than a good lamp.

Tallow candles. — The tallow candle, which you have to snuff at every turn, which smells foul, and the use of which squares ill with proper cleanliness, is still today the most usual method of lighting for servants and small households. This is despite the fact that tallow is perhaps the most expensive lighting in the summer, because it gets soft and melts more quickly.

You should guard against leaving candlesticks with tallow candles on the kitchen mantelpiece. They don't look attractive and they can melt. On a summer's day, they should be left in the coolest part of the house.

A box for tallow candles. — You need a box with a sliding lid for tallow candles, large enough to hold a whole packet. The tallow is then proof against insects.

Carcel lamps. — There are many sorts of good [oil] lamps. There is no doubt that the best are Carcel lamps,[1] where the oil is lifted from below

---

1. Named for their inventor, the Parisian watchmaker Bernard Carcel (1750–1818) who patented a lamp in 1800. At that date, lamps were fuelled by a thick oil such as colza which needed to be gravity-fed, meaning that their reservoirs were to one side of or above the wick, impeding their efficiency as a light-source. Carcel proposed a clockwork motor powering a small pump which lifted the oil from a reservoir below

up to the wick by a clockwork movement, but they are expensive and they consume a lot of oil. Some of them have a small burner and consume less. However, there is one grave drawback with Carcel lamps: when the movement breaks, you will find no one in the country able to repair it and you will have to send it to Paris or a large town. The cost of repair will be high and you are left without a lamp for a long while.

Moderator lamps. — I cannot recommend the spring lamps, called *moderator* lamps, highly enough (figure 63). They are both extremely simple and extremely ingenious.[1] They have all the advantages of the clockwork lamps but at much less cost. There are models with small burners which only consume 2 centimes-worth of oil per hour and which, when the shade is in place, give sufficient light for four or five people working around

Figure 63. Moderator lamp.   Figure 64. Wick burning white.

the lamp itself to the wick. When fully wound and fuelled, they could burn for up to sixteen hours.

1.   Moderator lamps were invented by a M. Franchot in about 1836. Like the Carcel lamp, they allowed the colza oil reservoir to be below the burner, but they pushed the viscous oil towards the wick by means of a coil spring and piston which were primed by a simple pressure device.

them. These lamps are even capable of lighting a round table of $1^m,15$ diameter for a meal. They are very easy to clean and so easy to turn down that you can use them as nightlights and they will hardly use any more oil than standard nightlights. If you need more light suddenly, all you have to do is turn up the wick and lift the glass and it will burn brightly. Generally speaking, the best are those where you can turn up the wick without it burning all the way down to the copper and where you can increase the strength and brightness of the flame by raising or lowering the glass. This is called *burning white.* When these lamps have been well designed and are well adjusted, you can see at least 3 centimetres of white [unburnt] wick (A) between the copper (B) and the part of the wick that is alight (C, figure 64).

Self-levelling lamps. — There are also copper or tin lamps where the reservoir is mounted in such a way that it will not spill when carried about. They can be used in place of candleholders (figure 65) and have a hook so that you can hang them off the wall (figure 66). They are extremely useful and cost little.

Maintaining the lamps. — You should not leave the care of lamps to the servants: it is exceedingly unusual to find one sufficiently responsible and intelligent enough to look after this particular task. This daily chore falls to the mistress. She should get herself a box for all her equipment: wicks, a cloth to clean the lamps, and also an oilcan with a nozzle or burette. It will take but a moment to assemble them.

Figure 65. Self-levelling lamp, set down.   Figure 66. Self-levelling lamp, hung up.

The factors essential to a light giving as much illumination as its dimensions merit are that the fuel should be pure and of good quality, and that the wick should be cut straight. For that, special scissors are required. Lower the wick so that only what needs trimming shows above the burner and cut it flush. Take extra care that no snuff from the trimming falls into the interior of the lamp, especially if it is a Carcel lamp. The clockwork machinery can be obstructed. When you trim the wick, do not cut off all the black, burnt parts. You will find that it lights more readily, burns brighter and the wick smokes less.

If you have two lamps, make sure you use them alternately. Otherwise one will wear out before the other and the pair will be incomplete. At the same time, the lamp that is not used so much will get very dirty and will need to go to the lampman's for cleaning.

Cleaning lamps. — All the lamps need cleaning at least once a year, at the beginning of winter, and at any time that a lamp starts burning unsatisfactorily. If the lamp is copper or tin, you should empty and drain the reservoir. Then dissolve 25 grams of red potash (sometimes called American potash) in a litre of water and boil it.[1] You wash the insides of the lamp several times with this hot water, not boiling, watching that it has no contact with any of the lamp's painted surfaces because it will both yellow and flake the varnish. Once the lamp is clean enough, rinse it several times with hot water then drain it for as long as possible. You don't need to clean the lamps until just before they are refuelled for lighting. This is a sure-fire way of avoiding the rust which will quickly eat away the metal, causing holes and consequential leaks.

If you do not plan using any moderator and clockwork lamps for some time, you should empty and drain them over several days. Then you fill them with olive oil and wind them up every fortnight until the nights grow short again. Olive oil does not thicken like colza oil so it does not clog the pipes when it's used. Make sure you cover with paper any apertures by which dust can enter the lamp.

---

1.   The normal form of potash then commercially available was called either American or Montreal potash. Its red colour was as it came out of the mine. White potash is red potash which has undergone a process of dissolution and recrystallization, giving it a slightly higher level of potassium chloride.

All the copper on any lamp can be perfectly cleaned with a cloth soaked in oil with very fine Tripoli or rotten stone. After that, rub them with a very dry cloth and some whiting. Some use copper water for faster results but, although the shine is intensified by the acids, it does not last as long, nor is it as good-looking as that produced by an oil-based material.[1]

Lampshade. — The insides of a tin lampshade that have been painted white should be cleaned with a cloth impregnated with oil and whiting.

Wicks. — If you don't wrap [stored] wicks carefully, they will soon lose condition on exposure to the air and when you light them, they will smoke and burn red.

Lamp glasses. — I counsel a selection of lamp glasses: too low a throat reduces the light's intensity; too high a throat produces a red flame and draws it upwards. I have already talked about cleaning lamp glasses on page 216.

10. — Polishing tortoiseshell and horn.

Tortoiseshell. — After more or less use, tortoiseshell loses its subtle transparency and dulls, thus sacrificing its principal attractions. You can restore its original lustre with a soft cloth and some *rotten stone* moistened with olive oil. You should rub until you see the sheen reappear. Then wipe it clean and rub lightly with a thin cloth and just some rotten stone. Finally you give it a final buffing-up by rubbing for a certain time with the palm of your hand or with a piece of buffalo leather.

Should a piece of tortoiseshell, especially a comb, become bent out of shape, that is to say, have lost its original form, or should you wish to bend it to a different shape, hold it close to the fire and turn it one way and the other (always watching it does not scorch) until the tortoiseshell is hot. At that point it will soften and you can return it to its original shape or give it a new one by gentle pressure over a fair length of time. As it cools, the shell will keep the form you last impressed on it. It will cool quite quickly.

Horn. — You clean and treat horn in the same manner.

---

1.   Copper water (*l'eau de cuivre*) is a traditional recipe for a dip to restore the shine. Its ingredients range between bleach; sorrel salts or oxalic acid; hydrochloric acid; household soda.

11. — Washing tiled rooms.

When you want to wash a room with a tiled floor, don't start off by throwing streams of water all over it, proceed instead with order. Once you have removed all the furniture, or at least concentrated it in one particular spot, provide yourself with a pitcher of water. Pour three or four litres over the tiles and scrub it well with a broom or a brush. Push this water from one section to the next, and rinse that part you have just scrubbed with some clean. Push this clean water to yet another section and use it to scrub the new part. Rinse this as you did the last and continue in this manner until the whole floor is clean. There is no advantage in flooding the entire surface at once. When the floor is well scrubbed, take off with a sponge any water that might otherwise soak through between the tiles.

If you undertake this task in a different fashion, damp will penetrate the underfloor via the gaps between the tiles. You need to avoid this as it will take a long time to disperse.

12. — Making up and carding mattresses.

Carding. — The point of carding is to give the wool elasticity. Carding is when you tease apart with carders the balls of wool that form in a mattress after long use.

A card is an instrument similar in shape to a currycomb for grooming horses, with fine metal teeth all over its surface which catch the wool you place upon it as you stroke one card across another.

Some people do not hold with carding the wool in mattresses on the grounds that it breaks the fibres and the wool has a shorter life. It's true that if it is done badly or too often carding may have these drawbacks, but if the carders are not too fine and you don't overwork the fibres, the wool does not suffer much at all, and well-carded mattresses will last indefinitely. It is impossible to have good mattresses without carding. The only benefit of beating is to get the dust out of the wool; but the clumps of wool do not readily untangle and only two or three days after beating, mattresses are just as hard and flat as they were before. If you really do not want to card them, the only alternative is to *tease* the wool by hand, that is to say, to divide each clump with the fingers. This exceptionally long and costly process is much less appropriate than carding, which achieves the same result and, in addition, rids the wool of any dust. One thing you can do is to beat the wool on a riddle before carding; subsequent work will be greatly hastened.

It is simple to card mattresses at home. In districts where this is not usually undertaken, you will have to obtain cards designed for mattresses. These are less fine and less dense than those intended for wool for spinning. They cost 7 francs the pair in Paris. They should last indefinitely in a private house, where they will only be used occasionally. Any woman can card: you have merely to show her what to do and she will soon have the hang of this simple task.

The worker sits down; she holds one card in her left hand, which she places on her left thigh while turning the handle downwards, thus lifting the implement chest high and resting it on her upper arm. She loads the whole of this card with a layer of wool, about the thickness of a finger; then, with the other card, which she holds in her right hand, she strokes across the wool, without pressing too hard. Some of the wool will adhere to the second card. By repeating this movement several times, the wool is combed between the two cards and will be distributed equally between them. To detach it, you rub the two cards together, alternately one on the other, in the *reverse direction* to that which you have just done when carding. The wool is gathered into a sort of sheet which can be easily lifted off. The worker puts this in a pile next to her until the whole job is complete. There are several other small practical details which are difficult to describe but which the worker will soon understand.

The worker should wear a canvas apron to protect her own clothing; there will be a great deal of dust from the wool and friction from the backs of the cards will cause wear. My advice is to press the cards together as little as possible, but to make the action of carding one of lifting rather than pressing down. Mattress wool is carded more coarsely than wool for spinning.

Reassembly of mattresses. — To make mattresses up again, you use a loom (figure 67) consisting of four wooden beams fitted with hooks at ten-centimetre intervals. The hooks are bent like a parrot's beak (figure 68) and are rounded so as not to tear the fabric attached to them. Two of the beams are $1^m,70$ long, and the two others 2^m. They are $0^m,08$ wide and $0^m,03$ thick. The hooks are fixed in a rebate, that is a notch cut into one side of the beam, so that they just protrude beyond its edge. The four beams are

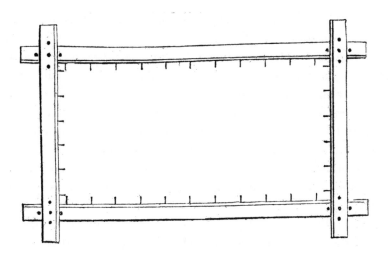

Figure 67. Mattress loom.

drilled at each end with holes large enough to accept a bolt. Tie the shorter beams, flat, to the backs of chairs, each positioned so that the hooks are on the topside and are exactly facing the hooks of the other beam. Then, using the bolts to secure them, you place the long beams *on top* of the beams tied to the chairbacks (not *beneath* as shown in figure 67). The hooks are also uppermost and are now are placed half the length of the mattress ticking, and the whole of its width, apart. Stretch [half] the ticking by hooking it to each side. Once fixed, spread the wool evenly, ensuring that it fills the corners and putting a little more towards the centre. Once all the wool has been distributed, lift the other half of the ticking over and stretch this too onto the hooks. The wool is now sandwiched by the ticking. At this point the mattress must be *pricked*. The object of this is to stop the wool shifting about the mattress, bunching up in one place and leaving other parts

Figure 68.
Hook.

unstuffed. To avoid this defect, the wool is secured here and there in the following manner. Take a large iron needle, about 60 centimetres long, with an eye large enough to thread a thin piece of packthread. Make a knot at one end of this thread and push the needle vertically all the way down through the mattress, pulling it from the bottom. Push the needle back up, just to one side, and it should appear next to where you made the first prick. Make a rosette of a small tuft of wool, which you insert into the loop formed by the twine as you changed direction: this stops the twine tearing the fabric. You do the same on the topside, looping the knotted end of the twine round the thread at the needle-end, and by pulling on the twine adjust the thickness of the mattress to what it should be, then tying it off. The rosettes will sit in little hollows. Before you take the mattress to bits, you should check the location of the rosettes so as to reconstitute them as they were. There are usually three rows of rosettes, arranged in quincunx formation. After this, oversew the outside of the mattress, using a strong thread. As you sew, progressively unhook the edges of the fabric and use a couple of chairs to support the mattress while you do this.

It is sensible to put a layer of horsehair between every two layers of wool in the centre of the mattress. Horsehair doesn't compact as easily as wool and reinforces the mattress. When the mattress is taken apart, it is easy to separate the horsehair from the wool. It does not need carding, just untangling with the fingers. Take advantage of this remaking of the mattress to wash the ticking in lye.

13. — Eradication of bed bugs, fleas and lice.

Bed bugs. — In a new house, where there are few or no cracks at all, a little attention and perseverance will ensure you will be rid of bed bugs. In an old house, full of cracks or rotten woodwork, or where wallpapers are hung one on top of the other, killing bed bugs is much more difficult. This is the best way of destroying them.

Get your pharmacist to prepare a bottle of water to which he adds 20 grams of mercuric chloride[1] dissolved in alcohol. Keep this liquor in a locked cupboard and label it carefully. Its use has its risks and you cannot take too many precautions against its misuse.

In spring, before the bed bugs hatch, strip all the wallpaper out of the room you think infested.

Then, use a paintbrush to go round carefully treating with the liquor all the cracks, cavities and such like in the woodwork, furniture and walls.

You do the same for the beds, where all the mortises and joints are carefully soaked with the liquor, again with a paintbrush. The fluid will not damage anything it comes in contact with, unless it be metal.

1.	In French, *sublimé corrosif.* Highly toxic; formerly used to treat syphilis.

Then line the walls with brown paper, making sure that each bucket of paste mixed by the decorator contains about half a litre of the liquor you have obtained. If the paper is carefully pasted, it will prove deadly for some time to any bugs that might have survived in holes or cracks in the wall.

I can guarantee the effectiveness of these measures, provided they are undertaken with care and intelligence.

Fleas. — Sometimes, one can be infested by myriads of fleas in spring or autumn. Even exceptional cleanliness will not be proof against them. In any case, they are brought in by dogs and cats, and often enough even by yourself from less nicely maintained houses that you are obliged to visit. To get rid of them, you must place a dish full of water with a layer of oil floated over the top close to the bed subject to an infestation. Put a lighted night light in it. The fleas jump into the dish and almost all perish.

Lice. — Children who are properly cared for, and whose hair is combed with a fine comb every day, do not have lice. If, however, in spite of your attentions, a child is infested with lice, you can have recourse to insecticidal powders. Harmless to man or beast, these can be quite properly and successfully applied to a child's head. You repeat the process a few days later, when the eggs have hatched. Oxen and cows are sometimes cruelly tormented by lice. You can relieve them by lightly powdering their heads, necks and backs – which is where they are most likely affected. To eradicate this pest from fowl, pick the bird that you wish to disinfect by the feet and, holding it upside down so the feathers spread, dispense the powder by means of a small puffer. Dogs and cats are kept free of lice by the same powders.

Insecticidal powders. — Insecticidal powders are also a very effective way of destroying bed bugs, fleas, ants, aphids, etc. Almost every town has a stockist of these powders. I will cite the one that I have had complete success with: Dessille powder, 8 rue Poissonnière, Paris.[1] With a little puffer that has been made for the purpose, you can blow this powder anywhere that might harbour bed bugs, who will die in the space of a day. Equally successful results can be had in hen coops, dovecotes, etc., where lice are sometimes fatal to poultry. Most of these powders are made from

---

1. A patent for an insecticidal powder, *le poudre Désille*, was obtained in 1852 by François-Adolphe Desille or Désille, a hairdresser. The most successful powder was manufactured by Joseph-Henri Vicat, a former teacher from Lyon.

pulverized pyrethrum leaves and the powdered dried fruit of the pepper tree, commonly known as Cayenne pepper.[1]

Boxes of insecticidal powder should be kept in a dry place; it is difficult to dispense when it is damp.

14. — Disinfection of rooms.

The best way to disinfect rooms is to ventilate them really well by leaving doors and windows open over several days and nights in succession. If either circumstances or the rigours of the season do not permit this course of action, you should light roaring fires in the grate to promote plenty of air circulation. You should have at least one door open during this whole process to admit fresh air. This simple stratagem should be employed on even the hottest of days. If it is impossible to light a fire, then evaporate some vinegar on a red-hot shovel.

If it is a question of disinfecting the atmosphere, and even the walls, furniture and curtains of a room which has housed a sick person, you start by removing any silver or gilt items. Then you spread out the blankets and mattresses over the backs of chairs and introduce some fresh air by opening the windows. Carefully close all the doors and windows and burn a few pinches of sulphur on a portable stove, making sure you leave the room as soon as possible to minimize the consequences of the suffocating fumes given off by burning sulphur. You can also put a handful of chlorinated lime [bleaching powder] which you have mixed with water, in some plates dotted about the floor. So long as you can smell the chlorine, the job is done.

15. — Privies and emptying cesspits.

Construction. — Privies should be built in the English style [i.e. a water closet] and so situated that a person can go to them without passing through any occupied room. They should really be as far away as possible while still being within the confines of the house itself. I am not in favour of their being either in the garden or the yard, as this means they cannot be reached in bad weather, or puts them most inappropriately in full view. They should be spacious, well lit, well ventilated and kept scrupulously

---

1.   In French, *piment enragé.*

clean. If they are to be presented as they should be, you should equip them with a little basin for washing hands, towels, zinc jugs or pottery pitchers full of water, a box full of paper, a couple of chamber pots on a shelf, a stiff broom for cleaning, and finally some large bunches of lavender, the pleasing yet penetrating smell of which will mask any other. I think too that in the country, flushing is better done with pitchers of water than a mechanical cistern, as the village tradesmen will find them difficult to repair.

Emptying the cesspit. — When you wish to empty the cesspit you should first disinfect its contents with zinc sulphate. A kilogram of this salt, dissolved in a bucket of water with 50 grams of lime, is enough to disinfect a pit of eight cubic metres. Twelve hours before you empty the pit, pour in this liquid and stir it around with a pole. If the first solids you extract are still stinking, increase the dose of zinc sulphate. Ferrous sulphate can be used instead of zinc, although it is less effective and you have to double the dose.

Using zinc or ferrous sulphates does not affect the quality of the manure you obtain from this source.

Utilization of sewage. — The solid matter is deposited in a manure pit and mixed with an approximately equal amount of siliceous clay [1] which will absorb the fertilizing vapours of the manure and stop their leaking away. After a few months, this material can be dug out of the pit and mixed with farmyard manure, or it can be used on its own as a fertilizer, at the same rate as sheep manure. It is particularly effective for cultivated crops [potatoes, maize, beetroot, etc.], forage roots and sown grassland.

The liquid from the cesspit is added to the dungheap or watered on dry ground to be absorbed. It can also be carried out to the fields under cultivation, or to permanent pasture or sown grassland when growth has only just begun.

Care should be taken that what is brought out of the cesspit is not exposed to the rain; this would deprive it of much of its utility as a fertilizer.

---

1. i.e., clay containing silica. Flint is a silica; other clays contain predominantly lime-stone.

CHAPTER XI

LINEN. —
WOOL AND SILK FABRICS. — FURS.

1. — Linen.
A. — Supply and maintenance of linen.

Linen is one of the most important household articles. A farmer's wife should ensure a proper supply of linen and devote much care to making it up, its maintenance and repair. Once she has enough linen in her possession to ensure the household's smooth running, she should buy a small amount each year just to replace any that is worn out. It is easier to lay out a modicum each year than a larger amount more infrequently – replacing a great deal of linen at one time will not only cost a lot, but will be less convenient in terms of household management. That said, it may be advantageous to buy a single large lot of fine sheets and napkins because you can get a discount when bought like this.

Linen for the master's house and linen for the farm ought never be confused, but servants' sheets can be treated as one with the farm's sheets.

I am not of the opinion that it is a good thing to have enormous quantities of linen, as seen in some households, and even in some regions where they seem fixated by it. In the first place, it's good money that pays no dividend; then, it's a tremendous bother putting all this linen in proper order and storing it; finally, it yellows and loses condition just resting in cupboards. I see no cause for rejoicing in exhibiting, as do so many women, presses filled with linen that is almost never used, nor in having only six-monthly or twelve-monthly washes. A wash-day like that becomes a dreadful event in the life of a household and an extremely tiring undertaking for both mistress and servants. It is a lengthy distraction from other responsibilities. If bad weather coincides with this fuss and bother, the wash-day will be almost interminable.

On the other hand, I cannot be too critical of those women who spend their money on luxuries or fripperies while failing to provide the household with a proper supply of linen, an element of the first importance, as indispensable to health as to well-being, and which a true housewife cannot possibly ignore.

The quality of linen will vary according to region. Where flax is grown, it will usually be more handsome than in districts which grow hemp. It is appropriate to conform to the customs of the locality, particularly when buying for the wider household. But you may make an exception for your own lingerie and get the fabric you have always been familiar with.

B. — Bed sheets.

Choosing the fabric and the size. — Sheets for large beds[1] must be generous and long. A bed is not well made unless the sheets tuck into all sides of the mattress. It is not necessary, however, for the top sheet to turn over the blanket all the way to the end of the bed, as I have seen nearly everywhere in Paris. It's enough that, tucking into the mattress all round, the sheet turns over two-thirds of the coverlet. Sheets that meet these conditions perfectly can be made from fabric 1^m,20 wide, using 16 to 17 metres for a pair. Cut the fabric into four equal parts, and join two widths with an overcast seam on two selvedges. Each sheet will then measure 4 metres to 4 metres 25 centimetres wide. This will fit a bed that is 1^m,40 wide. For a narrower bed, you can use fabric 90 centimetres wide, but the same length as before. However, for young people's beds, 14 metres of fabric is enough.

Calico sheets. — They make calico expressly for sheets; it is strong, durable, and costs a third less than linen. These sheets are very welcome in winter. You should beware using ordinary calico: not only will it not last very long, but it is nearly always crumpled, which makes it unpleasant to use.

Sheets in unbleached cotton. — There is another sort of heavy cotton, usually sold unbleached, but whitening quickly in the wash. It comes in two widths: one of 1^m,10, the other 80 centimetres. It is made from fairly low-grade cotton, so is somewhat coarse; its weave is uneven, sometimes with little slubs; nevertheless it is much nicer to use than coarse linen and

1.   In French, *draps de maître.*

costs less. You can make very good sheets for children and young people.

Linen sheets. — In most regions of France linen is woven, 1^m,20 wide. There is an economy in this dimension as the manufacture of this width of fabric costs very little more than something narrower. And as manufacture constitutes at least a quarter of the value, this represents a considerable saving. However, this measure is often a nuisance if you want to make sheets for a narrow bed.

Sheets for children. — You make small sheets for children with one width of fabric of 1^m,20, or two widths of narrower linen. If you need to turn sheets that are made out of only one width you whip together the two selvedges and split the sheet down the middle.

Servants' sheets. — Country people make up servants' sheets crosswise: they make up two widths together and have the two other selvedges at the foot and the head [of the bed]. This means their sheets are only 2^m,40 long. In consequence the bottom sheet is not long enough to wrap round the bolster, and the top one will not be sufficient to turn over the coverlet. The arrangement may be economical, but is evidently grubby. The sheets neither wrap the bolster nor cover the blanket and are thus easily rumpled; and the naked face will come in contact with both bolster and blanket. For servants' sheets, I have adopted a different way of doing things which uses no more fabric, but provides extra length. For a pair of sheets I allow 10 metres of fabric which I cut into three. I cut one of these three parts in half lengthwise and thus make up each sheet with a width and a half. The sheets are long enough to roll completely round the bolster and to generously cover the blanket. And they are wide enough for a one-metre bed. They would be a little narrow for a bed of 1^m,33, but servants' beds are rarely this size. If you want two girls to share a bed, 1^m,16 is large enough.

Shrinkage of linen. — Unbleached linen sheeting will whiten during use, therefore I think it pointless to bleach it before making up sheets for the servants; bleaching always weakens the fabric. It is enough to wash it once before use, just to ensure there is no mistake when cutting it up for sheets – it will shrink somewhat in the first wash. When you buy the fabric you should bear in mind that it will lose a twentieth of its size, i.e. 5 in 100. Before you put fabric that you have got straight from the dealer in the wash, you should soak it in water for twenty-four hours otherwise the lye will not penetrate properly.

Numbering. — Sheets should be numbered in pairs, that is, two similar sheets should bear the same number. It is the only means of keeping them together, of using each pair in rotation, and of keeping a proper count. What's more, by matching them, they will wear evenly.

When you arrange sheets in the press, you should hang a small card on a ribbon off each pair. The card identifies the sheets and you won't have to unfold them to discover their number.

Mending. — When sheets wear out in the centre, you have to turn them, which means unpicking the seam uniting the two selvedges and resewing it to join the two other, outer, selvedges. There's no need to wait until the sheets have actual holes in them but just when they wear thin. Change the mark as well, otherwise it will be in the middle of the sheet and this will be tiresome when you want to know its number. Do this and you will even out the wear and sheets will last longer. If a sheet is only a width and a half, then you unpick the half-width and sew it to the selvedge on the other side.

You should avoid patching sheets: it's unsightly; the general rule, whenever possible, is to darn them. If it is absolutely necessary to patch sheets that still have some life in them, you should cut out the damaged portion and match it with one of exactly the same fabric and exactly the same size. Join them together with a really appropriate and strong stitch that entails sewing a certain width of the sheet, without turning it, and the same width of the patch and then matching the stitches exactly and sewing them together. I call this stitch a *here and there* (figure 69) and I often use it when I don't want to darn something, or to patch with an overstitch. When this stitch is done accurately, it is really neat and absolutely flat. If you turn and overstitch a patch it never looks good.

C. — *Pillowcases.*

Choosing the fabric. — Because it has a nap to it and doesn't feel right on the face, calico is not used for pillowcases. Usually they are made from linen 90 centimetres wide; Breton linen is most suitable because it's soft and white.

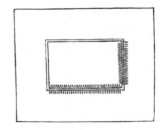

Figure 69. Patched sheet.

Pillowcases with buttonholes. — Pillowcases closed with buttons are far better than those closed with string-ties. When you make these up you allow the fabric a little more length than you would to form a square and, in sewing it, you let one side extend further than the other. On the shortest side, turn a fairly large hem and sew buttons on it; make a similar hem in the longer side and insert buttonholes. This second hem will be long enough to turn over the first and reach the buttons, leaving the pillowcase a perfect square. The two wide hems, therefore, are doubled on each other. Make the buttonholes crosswise, not parallel to the hem; otherwise the buttons will not stay in the buttonholes.

Pillowcases with eyelets. — You can replace buttons and buttonholes with two rows of eyelets through which you pass a lace knotted at each end. This is not without its merits.

D. — Napkins.

Size. — The dimensions of napkins, and particularly the sort of fabric used to make them, varies according to the region. One should, as far as possible, keep their size within sensible limits. Napkins less than 90 centimetres long are too small, will be inadequate for their intended purpose, and look penny-pinching; those which are more than a metre long are too large and can become an embarrassment. Ninety centimetres is the most seemly.

Choice of fabric. — I would not advise a farmer's wife to have delicate napkins: a lot of fruit is eaten in the country; napkins are often stained; delicate fabrics will not stand the strong washes or the scrubbing required to get rid of the stains.

Diaper napkins. — When buying an assortment of table linen, it is best to choose diaper, which looks good even when of not very high quality. This sort of linen is sold by the metre, not by the napkin, so it is simple to make your napkins the length you prefer. Linen diaper is very attractive and although it costs a little more than plain linen, its greater durability means that in the final analysis the money is well spent. You can even buy it unbleached; it whitens quickly because it is woven from fine linen.

Banded or striped napkins. — Another sort of linen is made in Brittany which seems to me most suitable for the country: napkins and tablecloths are made with broad bands or stripes in pink or violet. The linen is very decent, inexpensive and of a beautiful white colour. I much prefer it to Norman or Flemish fabrics which are hardly suitable for country dwellers.

Cotton napkins. — Cotton is widely used nowadays for the table, but I do not advise its adoption: it's fine when it's new, but once it has been in use for some time, it becomes soft and fluffy. You must iron it damp, and never on the underside. To keep it for a long time, and to ensure it's nice to use, it's best to have a rotary iron, not easy in the country.

Numbering. — Napkins should be numbered in groups of ten, that's to say that each napkin of a group of ten should bear the same number. This is the best means of checking their number and ensuring that they are used in rotation. To store them, wrap each group of ten in one of their number, fixing it with three pins. Hang a small label – such as you used for sheets – off each packet, writing on it the number of the group.

Mending. — Napkins should be mended, as far as possible, by darning. If it is necessary to patch them, use the same method of sewing that I described for sheets.

E. — *Tablecloths.*

Tablecloths should match the napkins. However, if you don't have sufficient matching fabric you can have some tablecloths in a different fabric or in a cotton damask, which you can use when necessary with linen napkins.

You mend tablecloths in the same manner as you do napkins.

F. — *Kitchen cloths.*

Choice of fabric. — Sometimes kitchen cloths are made from a coarse, loosely woven cloth so that they may be put to use immediately in drying the washing-up, because new cloths made from a more densely woven fabric can't be used in this way. However, as soon as such cloths begin to wear, they become soft and frayed, leave fluff on the china, and tear much too easily; in such a way that the economy that you thought to pursue by investing in coarse fabric is in fact an illusion. It is therefore most economical to have a good fabric, of a convenient width, not too loosely woven, but properly dense, with good selvedges. At the outset, sew some strings onto the cloths and they can serve as kitchen aprons: after they have been washed a few times, remove the strings and the cloths can be employed as they were first intended.

The fabric used for kitchen cloths should be what they call *square*, that is to say that the warp and the weft should be almost the same size and made with a round thread, not flat as is so often the case.

The size of kitchen cloths. — In Paris, kitchen cloths are made from a fabric that measures roughly 70 centimetres wide, and each cloth is cut 90 centimetres long; this is the most convenient size for service. In many regions, a fabric of 1 metre 20 width is cut *in two*, and then into pieces much longer than they are wide, or they are cut in strips across the width of the fabric, which gives the same result. This shape is not suitable for grasping a plate and drying it, or for wrapping anything; it is too long and too narrow and, if a decent width is allowed for, then it is too large. I find the width of fabric used in Paris is far handier.

If you have to use fabric 1 metre 20 wide, you should use two-thirds of its width to make one kitchen cloth, which should be 90 centimetres long, and join the other two-thirds with a whipped seam. This will make a cloth the same size as the two others, but made of two parts. This central seam, on the selvedges, is not too troublesome; a third of your cloths will have it.

Numbering. — Kitchen cloths, like napkins, should be numbered by the dozen; it is wise to buy a certain number every year to keep the stock in rotation. Three or four dozen annually will be enough for a sizeable household.

Supervision. — The mistress should be aware of how kitchen cloths are being used. If she limits their weekly issue to excess, she risks her dishes being dried with dirty cloths; if she leaves the servants to help themselves to clean cloths when they wish, they will take liberties and not take care of them. She should therefore ensure herself that they are properly used; when the servants know their mistress keeps an eye on them, they will use their cloths as they should.

You ought to insist that good cloths are not used for the dirtiest jobs, which will only ruin them.

G. — *Aprons.*

Kitchen aprons. — As well as kitchen cloths, the kitchen needs linen aprons. It was once usual, and still is in some towns, for cooks always to have white linen aprons; however, their maintenance is quite costly as they are quickly soiled, and you need a lot of fabric to make an apron. Now that cotton goods are so cheap, cooks are often supplied with coloured cotton aprons. This is economical but, it must be admitted, not nearly so clean.

Kitchen cloth-aprons. — In Paris, where laundry is so dear and where none the less they insist that cooks should have scrupulously clean clothing, they have adopted the style of kitchen cloths with string-ties. These cloths are 4 or 5 centimetres larger all round than usual; 10 centimetres from the selvedge on each side, you sew a ribbon to the hem that is long enough to cross over at the back and tie at the front. This form of apron is preferable to any other: it costs little to buy or to launder and, the moment the cook starts working at the stove, she can tie it on over her white apron. She can change it often without incurring the high cost in fabric or laundry of white linen. The other servants can also use these kitchen-cloth aprons when they are cleaning the rooms.

Calico aprons. — In the normal course of events, servants in a modest household such as that of a farmer's wife should wear coloured aprons; but I advise the purchase of white calico aprons for servants to wear when either serving at table or out with their mistress or her children; they are much smarter and more appropriate.

H. — Hand-towels.

A household also requires hand-towels for the family and the servants. Those for the family should be of fine white linen; those for the servants of the same stuff as the dishcloth aprons. A hand-towel should be hung to one side of the handwash basin. Sew small tape loops on two corners of the towels so they may be hung on a nail by one of them.

2. — Silks and woollens.
A. — Cleaning silks and fine woollens.

It is easy to clean silks and fine woollens, such as merino or light fabric, etc. If the silk you wish to clean is properly dyed, then it will preserve its original colour and suppleness; the better the quality, the less it deteriorates when cleaned. Cleaning, therefore, is a valuable resource, particularly for black silk neckties, aprons – which are so often stained – taffetas, heavy silk gros-grains of Naples[1] – either of a single colour or plaid – Levantine silk,[2] satins *à la reine*,[3] scarves, etc.

Having removed the lining to the silk you wish to clean, and unthreaded the seams, you place 125 grams of honey, 100 grams of black soap, and half a litre of alcohol [surgical spirit, brandy, gin] into a shallow fireproof bowl and melt everything over a gentle flame, stirring to mix. The quantities I have given will be plenty to clean a whole gown, and all ingredients together cost no more than 1 franc.

Spread the piece of fabric on a nice clean table and then, without pressing too hard or creasing it, scrub it with a horsehair brush dipped in the solution (which is left on a low heat during this operation). Both sides of the garment are cleaned in this manner, using plenty of the solution so that the fabric is fully impregnated. Another person then holds the fabric by one side and dips it several times in a large bowl filled with water, but *never rubbing or scrubbing it.* Most of the solution will come out in the water. It is then dipped in a second bowl of water, and then in a third; so that any water running out is entirely clear. Then the fabric is put on a line to drain, *without wringing it out.* The rinse is more effective if you have running water – a river or stream. While this is going on, you continue to clean further pieces of fabric.

Once the first piece is drained, but still damp, you proceed to iron it. If some of the stuff is still too wet, you can wipe them lightly with a soft dry cloth and then spread them out carefully on a woollen blanket. You should iron the inside of the fabric. The iron should be fairly hot, because the fabric is damp; but it must not be so hot that you scorch it. Iron it slowly, following the grain of the fabric, taking great care not to create false pleats.

A piece of silk cleaned in this manner is almost as good as new; the colours will glow, and have a finish that never detracts from its suppleness.

1.   In French, *gros de Naples*: 'a plain weave silk fabric of Italian origin made with organzine or ply-warp and heavier two-ply filling, producing a pronounced grain.' (*The Fairchild Books Dictionary of Textiles*, 2013)

2.   A strong, twilled silk.

3.   'A closely woven silk fabric made with a double warp in a six-harness satin-type weave, with six picks in a repeat.' (*The Fairchild Books Dictionary of Textiles*, 2013)

You need not unthread the waistbands or pockets in aprons, but you will have to dismantle a dress, where the cut and construction of the bodice and sleeves will impede the access of both the brush and the iron. However, the work is well rewarded by your having a gown as good as new in place of one that was dirty and stained.

B. — Cleaning flannel and coarser woollens.

To clean woollens, you proceed in exactly the same way as for silk, save you do not add honey to the solution.

To clean woollen vests and pants, you wash them in very soapy hot water, scrubbing them *with a brush* on a washboard. You add extra soap to the most soiled parts, then you proceed to a second soapy wash and a rinse. Do not use indigo [blue]. Iron woollens when they are still damp. If you scrub the fabric between your hands, you will crush the fibres and cause the clothes to shrink a lot.

It often happens that the soap is not powerful enough and the wool seems to retain a certain amount of grease so that, once ironed, it is stiff, hard and uncomfortable to wear. To get over this, you should dissolve potash [lye] in hot water, say 100 grams of potash to every ten or twelve litres of water, and scrub with a brush, as I have already instructed. Soda crystals will do as well as potash, but you will need a bit more of them.

C. — How to rid trousers of knee indentations.

When cloth trousers have been worn for some time, they take on the shape of the knee so that, when you are standing up, there is a certain unsightly looseness at knee height. You can get rid of this by dampening the cloth and ironing the underside with an iron hot enough to dry out the fabric. This should not affect the cloth.

3. — Summer storage of furs and woollens.

Once the season for furs and woollen garments has passed, you should shake them out very carefully; you may even lightly beat them; and then you put them into a thoroughly air-tight box or carton. So that no insect can gain entry through a hole or joint, it is best to line it with paper that you paste with every care. Once you have deposited everything you intend to store, cover it with a towel that extends to all the edges, which should be thick enough so that you can only close the lid with a certain difficulty – or else you should stick a strip of paper all round the edge of the lid. This precaution in place, try not to look at the furs or woollens in the course of the summer, or expose them to the air, as is often the case, because the moth will deposit their eggs. It will not be necessary to put any camphor or other strong-smelling substance into boxes which have been stopped up in this fashion.

If you find that insects have got into any of your furs or woollens, you can guarantee their destruction with the bedbug powder already described.

CHAPTER XII

LAUNDRY AND IRONING

The object of the wash is to clean a large quantity of linen all at once, and at small cost. To do a wash, you must have:

A bucking tub,[1]	A support for the cauldron,
A bucket,	A saucepan with a handle,
A cauldron or copper full of water,	Some good wood ash.

The principal operations of a wash consist of:

1. The pre-wash,	6. Soaping,
2. Arranging the linen,	7. Putting in blue,
3. Putting in the wood ash,	8. Drying,
4. Running the water,	9. Folding,
5. Lifting out the linen,	10. Ironing.

The wash is an important task in the country, and the farmer's wife should know exactly how to ensure its success. The cost of a good or a bad wash is much the same, but the results are very different; I will thus describe in their proper order, and in detail, the successive stages of the wash because I have seen them so ill-performed in many districts, despite their being very well known, that I think it would be useful to record here which methods have always worked for me in my long career.[2]

1. — The wash-house.

We call the room exclusively devoted to laundry the wash-house.

1. The French word is *cuvier* (*cuve* is a vat) and can be translated as wash tub or, in specific laundry parlance (when using, as here, lye), 'bucking tub' (buck is lye, *OED*).
2. Readers keen on laundry must refer to Thuillier, *Pour une histoire du quotidien au XIXe siècle en Nivernais* (1977) for more enlightenment.

Figure 70. A copper fixed on a boiler.

Boiler. — So as to have a well-organized wash-house, you should fix a copper on a boiler (figure 70). The boiler's front aperture should only be large enough to take wood, and on the other side of the firebox there should be a chimney-pipe for the smoke. This flue can be sunk into a cross-wall. I don't give construction details here, although they are very simple, because they are known to any workman used to building them.

Platforms. — Either side of the boiler you should build two platforms, the same height as the boiler, and of a size to accommodate the bucking tubs which they are to support. These platforms should be of brick or masonry. The resulting saving in fuel will repay the cost of their construction.

These platforms are a useful and secure location for the bucking tubs; if you wish to improve them still further, then fashion a declivity in the top to house the lower rim of each bucking tub, so the bottom sits flat on the platform.

Cauldron. — It is in the cauldron that you will heat the water for the wash. This cauldron can be copper or cast iron but it must have a flat rim or flange about 8 or 10 centimetres wide around its top circumference which will sit onto the boiler and will also act as a support. The copper needs to be moveable and capable of easy removal from the boiler for cleaning. A cast iron cauldron without such a flange is very difficult to get out of its seating in the boiler, because there is nothing to grip. Anyway, the flange is indispensable for other purposes.

Bucking tub. — What we call a bucking tub is a sort of barrel, entirely open at the top. In this we place any linen to be washed. Bucking tubs can be made in pine, in dressed stone, or in pottery, as they are in Poitou, and as seen in figure 74. If they are made of wood, you should take care that, once the wash is finished, they are put somewhere quite cool so that the bands don't expand and drop down. The day before the wash, you should bring the bucking tubs out of the wash-house, put them upside down in the fresh air, fill their bottoms with water and tap back in place any bands that seem to have dropped. A bucking tub banded with iron is better than one banded with wood; in any case, it needs at least two metal bands. Stone or pottery bucking tubs need nothing more than cleaning. It is more convenient to have a large and a small tub rather than two of the same size.

2. — In place of a wash-house.

If you should not have a wash-house organized along these lines, then you will need to heat the water for the wash in a cauldron on a tripod in the kitchen fireplace. In this case, the bucking tub should be supported on its own very low table with very stout legs canted slightly outwards, as in figure 74, to give it greater stability.

3. — Preliminary processes before the wash.
A. — *The pre-wash.*

How to wet linen.[1] — I have already said, in the sections relating to *Attics* and *Chest for dirty linen* (p. 176 above), that it is good practice to avoid putting linen that is going to the wash into the dirty-linen chest without first putting it through a preliminary wash which we call *wetting*. I will describe it. If it was not possible to pre-wash the linen at the very moment it was declared dirty, it is none the less necessary that it should be wetted before being washed.

To pre-wash linen, it must be taken somewhere with abundant water, soaped, rubbed between the hands, or brushed where it is stained or most

1. The French word used here is *essanger* (vt., the n. being *essangeage*). This may be translated in modern dictionaries as 'to soak', but in fact is the preliminary wash, with soap, before the soiled linen is put into the bucking tub with lye. Cotgrave translated the word as 'to wet linnen, before it be layed in the bucking tub.' A modern version of the process is 'to pre-wash', which shares attributes of washing and of soaking.

Figure 71. Washerwoman pre-washing the linen.

soiled, and beaten with a wooden beater (which is not too heavy). You can restrict yourself to merely working on the dirtiest parts of the linen in a bucket of hot water, or even just leaving it to soak for a few hours.

Pre-washing kitchen cloths. — The day before the wash, kitchen cloths should be soaked in hot water. Cover the bucking tub or bucket, then carefully rub them while adding some soap: a brush is very useful for pre-washing kitchen cloths.

The position to take for the pre-wash. — Some washerwomen stand up for the pre-wash: this results in much lost time; but you can't make them give up the practice. Generally speaking, women who wash standing up don't reckon on rubbing the linen on their *saddle* or four-legged washing-stock (figure 73), instead beating the life out of it with a beetle, which wears out the linen. It is far preferable to wash on your knees (figures 71 and 73) as you are closer to the water and better placed to rub the linen on a board or stone placed exactly in front of the washerwoman.

Washerwoman's pulpit. — To undertake the work on her knees, the washerwoman needs a *pulpit* (figure 72); the laundress should put down some straw on which to kneel; and on one side of the pulpit is a little box for the soap. In front of the pulpit, in the water, she has a battling-block or beetle-stone, which she may cover with a cloth. The laundress places the piece of linen she is washing on the block to rub it with soap or with her hands. A laundress working on her knees (figures 71 and 73) washes a third more linen than were she to wash it standing and as she is near the water it is better washed, and above all, better *rinsed*.

Figure 72. Pulpit.

Scrubbing. — In some districts, the linen is scrubbed (with a brush) not rubbed. If the brushes used are not too stiff, I do not think their employment more destructive of the linen than a lengthy rub between the hands, and the work may be quicker; but you will need women who both wish and know how to use the brush because, in most districts, washerwomen usually set great store by their expertise and it will be difficult to persuade them to a new way of working. However, if you manage to introduce brushes, giving them perhaps to younger, more accommodating girls, and you find there is a real advantage to be gained, you will often succeed in overcoming the prejudices of the senior washerwomen because they are loath to be outperformed by their juniors.

Drying.— When the pre-wash has been completed, the linen must be carefully dried, repaired, then placed in the dirty-linen chest. If it is not

Figure 73. Washerwoman working on her knees.

properly dried, it will moulder. Drying is unnecessary if the pre-wash is immediately followed by the wash itself.

B. — *Removing stains from linen.*

Neither the pre-wash nor the wash itself will remove certain stains, for example from acid fruits, ink, rust, grease, etc. You must therefore, if at all possible, lift these types of stains as soon as they are made or at least before the pre-wash or the wash itself. Here are a few means to that end.

Fruit stains. — You lift red fruit stains with sulphur. Moisten the stain and an area around it. Two people stretch the fabric tight while one of them takes a number of well-sulphured matches in one hand and lights them *below* the wet surface. You can put some sulphur in a bowl instead of the matches, or use a strongly sulphurated wick. The fumes, passing through the damp cloth, will cause the stain to disappear. The process can be repeated several times, if necessary. Sometimes the fruit pulp leaves a yellowish stain. You should try to get rid of it with soap. If this does not work, then use bleach as follows: pour a certain quantity into a bowl and add a like amount of water. Rub the stained part of the linen in this mixture. If, after one or two minutes, the stain has not vanished, it may be that the bleach is not strong enough. Try again, with bleach alone. If the stain persists, it means the bleach has no effect. I must impress on you that anything washed in bleach must be well rinsed; without this precaution, they will be burned and after a little while they will fall away in tatters. Bleach has a strong smell, but it doesn't last.

Ink and rust stains. — You remove ink and rust stains with salts of sorrel.[1] To effect this, you damp the stain with water and sprinkle a thin layer of powdered salts of sorrel over the top. Then you put a few pieces of burning charcoal in a spoon and rub the back of the spoon, which will be very hot, over the salts, which you moisten once more. As the heat of the spoon evaporates the water, the stain disappears under the influence of the salts, which the water has dissolved and which evaporates with the heat. Once the stain is gone, any of the cloth in contact with the salts (and sometimes more than that) must be washed in plenty of fresh water, then rinsed thoroughly. Instead of the spoon, you could use a hot smoothing iron.

---

1.   Salts of sorrel will give the housewife oxalic acid. In England they used 'sorrel juice'.

If the stain is on a piece of coloured cloth, there is a risk that the sorrel salts will alter the colour. It is prudent, therefore, to make a test application on a piece of the same cloth, so that a small stain does not end up an enormous one. There is no point in trying this with something green or rust-coloured. These tints will be invariably affected by the salts.

Keep the salts of sorrel in a small glass phial the top of which is large enough to admit a finger, which you moisten before dipping it into the phial. The salts will adhere to the damp fingertip and you can then spread them on the stain.

Stains from grease or resin. — When a stain has proved impervious to burnt sulphur, sorrel salts or bleach, I consider it pointless to try other methods unless the stain is caused by grease or resin. In this case, use some ether, oil of turpentine, lemon juice, or, better still, *benzine*, which is infallible for all grease stains.[1]

Grease sludge stains. — With the blade of a knife, take off any surplus sludge that has not got into the fabric, and then lift the stain by washing it in benzine, and then in soap.

Paint marks. — Remove these with turpentine.

4. — Laundry with wood ash.
A. — The choice and proportions of wood ash and potash.

Quality and sorts of wood ash. — Wood ash is indispensable to the wash. You can undertake a wash with ash from all sorts of timbers: ash from fruit trees, oak, elm, ash and hornbeam is best; white woods are in the second rank, with the exception of fir which is perhaps of the first. I use fir faggots to heat my oven and I have had excellent results with its ash. Ash from chestnut stains the linen: you will need to wash it before use – this you do by putting it in a bucket of water for four hours, changing the water several times. Even then, this ash is less effective than others. Ash from alder will give you a black lye which stains, while that from thorn or gorse is very bad. Ash from live vegetation in general or the leafy tops of root crops, as well as from vine clippings, is very active. Twice-burnt ash (from the bottom of the fire) is better than new ash because it will contain less charcoal and fewer foreign bodies.

---

1. Ether is now usually called diethyl ether (and was once called sweet oil of vitriol); benzine is petroleum ether.

Sifting the ash. — Before you use the ash, it is absolutely necessary to pass it through a fine riddle or a coarse sieve. This will remove the charcoal which is always present. This charcoal is in the first instance useless and secondly may confuse your measuring the ash because you cannot tell how much charcoal is contained therein. Sieving also removes any foreign bodies that may stain the linen.

You should avoid storing ash destined for the wash in a damp place. It will deteriorate.

Proportions of wood ash and potash. — Ten litres of good wood ash are sufficient for a hectolitre of wet linen. If you are washing delicates that are not very dirty, then less ash is needed. If you do not have sufficient ash, or if it is not strong enough, you can add half a kilo of potash or 1500 grams of soda crystals to 2 hectolitres of household laundry, or 800 grams if washing more delicate linen. These crystals are only soluble in hot water. It is important to watch the quantity of ash used in a wash because, if you use too much, the caustic salts it contains, being in too great a concentration for the amount of laundry you are dealing with, may damage the linen. If, however, you use too little ash, the salts will be too weak and your linen will not be well washed.

B. — How to arrange the laundry and the ash in the bucking tub.

Counting the laundry. — When embarking on a wash, you should begin by gathering together all the linen to be washed. You sort it, that is to say you group each type of linen: table linen, bed linen, clothing, kitchen cloths, etc.; then you count it and note the result.

Arranging the laundry in the bucking tub. — Usually you do this the evening before. Whichever sort of bucking tub you are using, close the tap or stop up the drain at the bottom, so that any water added does not leak out. Then line the bucking tub with a large sheet or, better, some canvas made for the job. Then you place: 1) sheets, but keep back a few; 2) delicate linen; 3) bed linen; 4) table linen; 5) those sheets you have kept back. All this linen should be put in piece by piece, spread out carefully and kept in flat layers. Take the sheets by their selvedge and place them one after the other in the tub, in such a manner that they are easy to take out at the end of the wash. This is a wise precaution because otherwise they may tear. The same is true with the other sorts of linen. Each time you have a complete layer in the tub, wet it with cold water, which will cause it to pack down firmly. Make sure as you go that the laundry is arranged flat and that the lye will get to all parts evenly, not just to one section at the expense of the others. If you wait until you have put in all the laundry before dampening it, the water will not penetrate, and it will not pack down as it should. Once all the laundry is in the tub, fold the canvas lining the tub over the top. Then pour in enough water so that this canvas is covered. Then leave it to soak overnight.

Placing the ash on the bucking tub. — The next morning, spread over the top of the bucking tub a canvas larger than the tub itself, called the bucking-cloth.[1] Spread over all of it an even layer of ash which has already been wetted or, better, that you wet once it is in place. Then fold over the excess canvas. If you are using two bucking tubs, then it is best to put the general laundry in one and the delicates in the other: always topping the delicates with something coarser, however, immediately beneath the bucking-cloth, so it doesn't come in contact with the delicates and turn them yellow, especially if they are cotton.

C. — Reprehensible ways of ordering the ash and the linen in the bucking tub.

There are other ways of preparing a wash with lye; but they all have disadvantages which I will detail. I may be criticized for calling these methods reprehensible but, in a matter so important to domestic economy, I consider it a duty to warn my readers against defective methods, even though they may be so sanctified by custom in various districts that it never occurs to them to change their ways.

Buck-washing with the ash at the bottom of the tub. — In this case, you put the ash at the bottom of the tub and you lift the linen high above it by wrapping it in sheets to keep it contained.

This procedure has many serious disadvantages: the ash is not wetted until the water has run through all the linen, and you will run the lye for a very long time before all the caustic salts are dissolved by water that is sufficiently hot. This method of *running* the lye requires much more ash, and much more time to achieve a good result, than the system of having

1. The French word is *charrier*, i.e. a cloth for the *charrée*, the wood ash that produces the lye. So far, the author has only referred to this ash as *cendre*.

the ash at the top of the tub. It may be suitable for delicate clothing that is not very soiled because it avoids the risk of staining the fabric from close contact with the ash; but it does not suit very dirty and coarser laundry. By putting the ash at the top of the tub, you achieve a strong lye with less ash, less heat and less time, whatever women who espouse the other method may say.

Buck-washing with two layers of ash. — In some districts they lay two layers of ash, one in the middle and one at the top. This procedure has the disadvantage of staining the linen.

Buck-washing with the ash in a heap. — In other districts, they place the ash on a bucking-cloth, as usual, but then they gather up the four corners of the cloth and pass them through a hoop. Then they turn the corners back on themselves to form a large roll. The water is then run through this sort of funnel. This is a detestable procedure: the ash is piled in the middle of the tub, the water will barely penetrate it and will be unable to dissolve out all the caustic salts. And frequently, as if to make a bad procedure worse, small sticks are placed upright all round the inside edge of the tub to accelerate the running of the lye water. The consequence is that the water flows almost exclusively down these conductors, and not through the laundry itself. This method of working, which is too absurd to need debunking, is the most popular system employed in the Touraine.

D. — *Running the lye.*

The preliminaries of the wash completed, it now remains to *run* the lye.

To run the lye means to let flow through the laundry, repeatedly, the hot water which is a solution of the active elements of wood ash.

The generally accepted method of running the lye. — There are several ways of running the lye. Some people remove the plug from the drain hole at the bottom of the tub and the water flows into a bucket placed to receive it (figure 74). When it is full, the plug is replaced and the bucket emptied into either the copper described in the article 'Wash-house', or into a cauldron on a fire. When this water is hot enough, it is poured over the bucking-cloth, it dissolves the active elements in the wood ash, and carries them successively to all the layers of washing. The bucket is put back in position below the bucking tub; the plug is replaced by some straw, about 0^m,30 long, loosely gathered into a neat bundle, down which the lye will trickle into the bucket. Thereafter, using a long-handled saucepan (figure 78), the lye is taken out of the bucket and poured into the cauldron to be reheated. Once it is hot, it is run over the bucking-cloth once more. This process is repeated until it is considered sufficient.

Figure 74. Bucking tub and bucket for running the lye.

I have described this procedure because it is the one most often followed, but it requires much more time, more wood and more trouble than the one I am going to describe, mostly because the lye cools down too much in the bucket, and needs more fuel to reheat it, and one loses time drawing the water from the bucket to pour into the copper.

Preferable method of running the lye. — Here is another method, which I have used for twenty years with great success.

You put the bucking tub on a pedestal high enough to raise the bottom of the tub above the lip of the copper in which the water will be heated,

Figure 75. Running the lye.

and near enough so that you can run a metal or wooden pipe from the drain hole in the bottom of the tub directly to the copper, down which the lye will run of its own accord (figure 75). You should place a little piece of curved tile, or a plate, on the inside of the bucking tub, just where it drains, to stop the linen blocking the mouth of the pipe. It will be seen that this arrangement allows the lye water to flow without hindrance into the copper, that it has no time to cool down, and very little fuel is required to get it back to boiling point. And all that needs be done is to take it out of the copper and pour it over the bucking tub.

If you wish to stop running the lye, you plug the bucking tub drain. This procedure is vastly preferable in every way to the preceding method and very easy to set up. To fix the pipe in the drain hole in a watertight manner, wrap the end of the pipe in hemp or linen. The pipe should extend three or four centimetres inside the tub. Should it be inserted more than this, it would be difficult to place a tile over its end to impede the linen from blocking it up.

Wooden pipes for this are not usually completely enclosed for more than about 15 centimetres (figure 76), after that they are open gutters (figure 77) which take the lye to the copper; it would be too complicated to drill a hole through the whole length of a thin piece of wood – and would even be superfluous. Metal pipes can be easily replaced by old gun barrels.

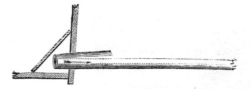

Figure 76. Pipe connecting the tub to the copper.

Figure 77. Bird's-eye view of the same pipe.

Figure 78. Saucepan with long handle for transferring water.

Saucepan with handle for transferring water. — The container best suited to transfer the lye, that is to say to take it out of the copper and pour it over the bucking tub, is a tin-plated pot holding about 2 litres, with a handle about 70 or 80 centimetres long.

Quantity and heat of water. — Calculate the quantity of water to pour over the bucking-cloth in this manner: when the bucking tub is full of water, i.e. when you have transferred enough water from the copper to cover the laundry entirely, the copper (always reckoning that it is the right size for your bucking tub) should still be half full. At the end of running the lye, that level will be greatly reduced by evaporation.

At the outset, the heat should be gentle, building the fire up gradually. If the water is boiling before you have run the lye for seven or eight hours, you risk *scalding* the wash, that is to say you 'seize' the wood ash which means either that the lye is expressed too quickly and stains the laundry, or that the dirt is fixed too quickly and does not dissolve. The heat should be kept very regular and only increased little by little. A buck-wash's success depends in large part on how it is heated. The copper should always be placed towards the rear of the fire, so that the column of hot air which rises towards the chimney is in permanent contact with the copper, thus heating it far more than if the copper is near the front.

The duration of the running. — The running of the lye should continue over at least twelve or fifteen hours if the wash contains table linen, bed linen and kitchen cloths; seven or eight hours is enough for delicates.

If, at the beginning, the flow of lye is slow, do not worry. Above all, do not introduce small pieces of wood between the linen and the edge of the tub to accelerate the flow, as is so often done, because if the flow does quicken thanks to this, it is of no help to the linen itself, which won't come into contact with the water.

Ending the running of the lye. — When you wish to finish the running, you stop heating the water and cease transferring the water from the copper to the tub. Instead you empty the copper of any lye flowing into it from the tub. Once the flow is reduced to drops, you leave it to its own devices and let the tub drain overnight. The linen will retain just enough water for the washing that is in store for the next day.

Cleaning various items. — Lye is used for cleaning various household articles such as silverware, coffee pots, or pottery or tinplate chamber pots. They are dipped into the lye and left for a while, then buffed with a hand brush or a scrubbing brush. This procedure is simple and perfect. But you should beware putting the chamber pots at the top of the bucking tub before the running of the lye is completed, as is done is some districts. On the one hand you complicate the procedure, on the other you don't clean the pots as well and you risk imparting a nasty smell to the linen.

Coloured linen. — If you have a few items of laundry which you wish to add to the wash, or coloured linen which will not run if left for a while, add it *on the heat*, that is to say, when the lye is really hot you should put them on the bucking-cloth, where they can remain for a couple of hours. They will be perfectly cleaned. Anything coloured should be washed immediately because, no matter how fast the dye, if they sit in lye until the next day, the colour will be affected.

Kitchen cloths. — When you have really dirty cloths which in consequence you do not want to include in the buck-wash, put them in the copper boiler (figure 70) once you have completed the running and leave them to the next day. The heat of the fire will be enough to keep the lye nicely warm all night. It is good to soak them for at least twelve hours in water and scrub them with a brush and some soap before you add them to the lye. Without this they will not be clean.

E. — Emptying the bucking-tub. Using the ash and the water.

Emptying the bucking-tub. — Ten or twelve hours after the running of the lye has finished, you should then lift out the laundry, and transport it to wherever it is to be washed. The most convenient method of doing this, which keeps the laundry wet and warm, are some bags to carry it, and from which you take the linen as and when you wash it. After it has been washed, if you don't dry it where you wash it, you can carry it back to the house in these same bags.

Using the ash and the lye. — The ash which produced the lye should be kept and deposited somewhere for re-use. It is often used to condition certain soils. The lye water should also be gathered up and thrown on the dung heap. Nothing that might improve the quality of manure can be lightly ignored in the country.

F. — Soaping.

If the lye was satisfactory, which will be apparent if the copper is covered with suds towards the end of the running of the lye, you will not need much soap to wash the linen; none the less a small quantity of soap will be necessary to lift any stains which are still visible.

The linen should be beaten with a wooden bat or beetle to encourage the dispersal of any dirt or foreign bodies left by the lye; but supervision of the beetle's use is essential as many laundrywomen invariably rely on it to avoid having to rub the linen with their hands. Once the linen has been properly washed, it should be left soaking in the water for some time; then it should be left to drip for as long as possible before wringing it out and spreading it to dry. First, however, the linen that needs blue should be separated.

G. — Blueing.

To blue linen is to plunge it into water that contains indigo. The balls of indigo that you dissolve should be wrapped in a scrap of cloth so that the indigo can be easily removed from the water once it seems blue enough.

Well water is much better than river water for blueing because it contains various calcareous salts which fix the blue in the linen. You should immediately wring out and stretch to dry linen once it has been blued otherwise, as it drips, the blue will form darker stripes on some parts and not others, which will be unsightly. Any underwear should be turned inside out for washing: this ensures that the *right* side is the whiter because sometimes, while the linen is drying, it picks up little marks which are less trouble on the inside, which is never seen, than on the outside, which is always apparent.

H. — Drying, folding, etc.

Drying. — You should not dry the linen too much the first time it is hung out; it is better to take it off the line damp, and then to *table* it, as I will explain, either for ironing or for stacking, so that it is crease-free and crisply folded.

Any linen for ironing that cannot be ironed immediately should be left to dry completely, taken off the line and carefully wrapped up so that it doesn't yellow.

How to table and prepare the linen for ironing. — Sheets should be stretched in line with the hem and folded by the selvedge; towels should also be stretched and folded in three by the selvedge. All underwear should be folded inside out. For stacking, you should not fold it completely, as if for putting away in a wardrobe. You lay it out on a table and press it beneath a board with weights on top. This is what we call *to table*. Leave it thus for ten to fifteen hours after which, without unfolding it, lay it out again to dry completely. It will be as smooth and firm as if it had been ironed.

Linen that has been through a good buck-wash will be well rid of any stains, grime and impurities that it might have had; it will smell wholesome; it is firm, without creases, a beautiful white.

Some hours before you wish to iron it, *table* it, as I have just discussed, sprinkle it with water, then stack it up so that the moisture penetrates evenly. If it is not dampened and *tabled* with care, it will be more difficult to iron, and the maid will waste time stretching out and dampening each piece, while the irons are heating to no purpose.

Each sort of linen should be grouped with its own kind before ironing begins so that it is possible to iron everything of one type one after the other. The hand gets used to a certain type of work, and much time is gained.

Inspection and mending of linen. — As soon as the linen is put to the pre-wash, it should be looked over and mended. If there is no time to mend it then, it should certainly be done before ironing, or at least before putting away. Careful upkeep is the best way of prolonging the life of your linen.

5. — Small washes.

It often happens that in the interval between two general washes the supply of either undergarments or kitchen cloths is exhausted. It is convenient, in this case, to have a small bucking-tub of perhaps 80 to 100 litres, on a tripod, in which – in only six or seven hours, or even less if fine linen is being dealt with – one can run a little lye using a cauldron set on the kitchen fire. It's less expensive than washing with soap, and the linen will be whiter. You proceed exactly as for the more general wash.

6. — Buck-washing kitchen cloths.

It sometimes happens that you don't have enough kitchen cloths to get you through to the next wash. In this case you pre-wash them and then put them in the copper with water and wood ash and heat it steadily to boiling. You continue to boil for two hours, after which you take them out and let them drain for a minute or two. Then you wash them in water just like the usual buck-wash.

This simple, but somewhat crude buck-wash is not suitable for any linen save kitchen cloths. It can be undertaken once between general washes.

7. — Bleaching or washing with soap between washing in lye.

When washing with soap can replace buck-washing. — It is not invariable that underwear needs to be buck-washed every time it needs washing. Many people labour under the illusion that linen that has not been treated with lye is unhealthy. What is unhealthy is to wear linen that has not been properly whitened and badly dried. Lye yellows cotton, unless it be very weak and let run for a short time: in which case the linen will be well bleached. However, a good soaping, undertaken in the manner I will set out, can serve the same purpose. I do advise you not to put into a general buck-wash small garments made of delicate fabrics such as babies' underwear, scarves, white dresses, bonnets, etc. A good soaping or a small wash (5, above) will whiten them perfectly. Here is how you should proceed.

Equipment necessary for soap-washing. — Provide yourself with a large copper cauldron and two white-wood buckets or tubs. New oak stains the clothes: oak tubs, therefore, should be made with well-seasoned wood and, before use, they should go through two soakings with lye.

How to wash with soap. — You should sort out the cleanest and most delicate linen to be washed separately. In the evening, heat the water in the copper, but do not boil it, and pour this water into the tubs. Take care to put the dirtiest linen in one of the tubs and begin the whole process with absolutely the dirtiest items which you place at the bottom of this tub. You put each item of linen into the water, you rub the most soiled parts with soap – the cuffs, the casings, the hems, etc. – you rub them again between your hands, then you roll them up and stick them at the bottom of the tub. You carry on in this way for every piece. The rest of the linen is put in the second tub. The tub should not be filled to the brim; in fact, not even half filled. You should cover the tub with a cloth and leave the linen to soak until the next day. Then you add some water to the tub, or you heat up the surplus water that is already in there. Then you progress to the *cleansing*.

First you rub between the hands all those parts which were soaped, and then the rest of the item, adding a little more soap. You rub it once more, on a well-polished board that has one end in the tub, the other wedged against the person doing the soaping. It is the care with which this *cleansing* is undertaken that determines the whiteness of the linen. But I should remark that linen that has soaked for fifteen to twenty hours is much more easily washed. None the less, I counsel that a mistress should supervise this work closely, unless she has a washerwoman of sufficient intelligence and enthusiasm to work without supervision, which is rare enough.

Before the cleansing is finished, put the copper half filled with clean water back on the fire. When the water is a little more than lukewarm, add some small slices of soap cut very thin – enough to make a nicely soapy water which you whisk with a spoon or wooden spoon so as to dissolve the soap. Put the cleansed linen into this water, beginning with the most delicate, and boil it for about twenty minutes. You should remove it piece by piece, holding it up with a spoon to drain back into the cauldron; then you put each item into an empty tub. When you have emptied it once, you put more linen into the copper, taking care to add a little more soap and water if there is not enough to cover the linen completely. You can press the linen down lightly in the copper, but there must be enough water so that there are no problems when it is left to boil. If there is not enough water, the linen in contact with the copper itself may scorch.

When you have boiled all the linen in turn, leave it in fresh water until the next day, which is a much better way of doing things than washing it immediately. You may rub up the linen in this water, checking carefully if there are any bits that still need soaping, which they won't if the cleansing was properly performed. They only need rinsing after this.

If you live near a river or spring, it is best to take the linen there to rinse in plenty of water. If not, rinse carefully in a change of waters, successively, and put in the blue, as described on page 255, above.

I can assure you that linen washed in this fashion is perfectly white and perfectly healthy; what is more, it will not have run the risk of staining as it might otherwise have done if the lye was too strong.

Soaping coloureds. — The water that was used to boil the white linen would be fine to wash coloureds. You can also let it boil for an instant, unless it is not *well dyed*.

The position of the washerwoman. — To ease the work of soaping, if the tub is not raised up on legs, place it on two chairs. The laundress stands in front of the tub and is thus best placed to rub with speed and force.

Using bleach. — Some people are accustomed to add a certain amount of bleach to the wash-water after the *boiling*, i.e. after the linen has been boiled. This gives a startling whiteness to the linen. This is not a bad idea if undertaken from time to time and with discretion. But it is essential that each piece is immersed in the bleach and water and that each piece, as it is lifted out, is very carefully rinsed. If this is neglected, any linen that comes in contact with the air may be scorched by the bleach, which is very caustic. It is, above all, the action of the air which makes bleach so dangerous. I therefore only use it with the greatest trepidation. If you do use it, you must not add more than half a litre of bleach to a tub containing fifty litres of water. You should mix this up before putting the linen in the water.

8. — Steam washing. — The Charles machines.

Chaptal and Berthollet were the first people to pronounce that, for linen as well as for fabrics and calicoes, washing with free steam – i.e. not under pressure – was the healthiest system, the most economical, and the one which had the least effect on the fabrics, all the while giving the best, the speediest and the cheapest results.[1]

At the same time, Messrs. Curaudau and Cadet de Vaux, and since them M. Bourgnon de Layre, have attempted to put these ideas into practice. However, with their equipment the wash still lasted eight hours and, in fact, steam washing made little progress, owing to the lack of a

---

1.   Jean-Antoine-Claude Chaptal (1756–1832), whose name is remembered in the word 'chaptalization' (and his work was the foundation of modern viticulture) was a French chemist and politician who developed the application of steam to bleaching. His *Essai sur le blanchiment* was published in 1801. Claude Louis Berthollet (1748–1822) was a significant French chemist and politician (vice-president of the Senate in 1804). He was 'the first to demonstrate the bleaching action of chlorine gas and to develop a solution of sodium hypochlorite as a bleaching agent.'

simple, straightforward machine, until the *Société d'Encouragement pour l'Industrie nationale* announced a competition to make improvements, not in laundry in general, but in steam laundry, the only avenue deemed worthy of encouragement.[1]

In these competitions, it was judged that the *Charles* machines had succeeded in offering the domestic economist a chance to embrace steam washing, hitherto recommended in vain.[2] In fact, since their invention, these steam washers are more and more sought after and have replaced other systems of buck-washing in Paris hospitals, and in many hotels, public establishments and private houses.

This equipment's simplicity (figure 79) – which, when a medium-sized model is installed, can double as a bath – makes it simple to operate and maintain, and at little cost. The steam works without pressure and there are no valves or other complex mechanicals. The installation, the size of which varies according to requirements, is made of galvanized sheet iron which is wholly rustproof and does not need tinning. The largest installations are only 1^m,20 high and are easy to access. All are moveable and portable. They are sent out everywhere and there are no building works necessary to install them; they can be placed in the smallest of locations and can be heated in any way you choose.

As to working them, nothing could be easier. You pour into a tub as many litres of water as the machine will hold, in kilograms, of dry laundry. In this you dissolve 1 kilogram of soda crystals or half a kilogram of soda salts for every 25 litres of water. If you want to use wood ash, you dissolve it in the water and should look for a strength of 2 to 3 degrees on a hydrometer. Now you put the linen into this solution (it is pointless doing

1.   François-René Curaudau (1765–1813) was a French chemist and pharmacist who wrote *Traité du blanchissage par la vapeur* in 1806. He also developed an artificial alum which was very suitable for dyeing. Antoine-Alexis Cadet de Vaux (1743–1828) was a French chemist who wrote on the application of steam to laundry. Antonin Bourgnon de Layre (d. 1855) wrote *Traité pratique du lessivage du linge à la vapeur d'eau* in 1837. This was published in Paris, but many of his other works first appeared in Poitiers, where he resided. A survey of many of the improvements in the laundry business at this time is contained in *La naissance de l'industrie à Paris: entre sueurs et vapeurs, 1780–1830*, by André Guillerme (Champ Vallon, 2007).

2.   A patent was granted in 1847 to M. S. Charles et Cie for an *Appareil de lessivage à la vapeur perfectionné*.

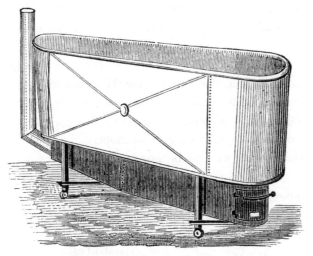

Figure 79. Charles steam laundry tub.

a pre-wash with soap as you have been used to do) and, having briefly
wrung it out or left it to drip a little, you put it into the machine (after
adding a little water to it). This soak can be undertaken in the tub, thus
avoiding any handling of the laundry at all.

You replace the lid, for which nothing is simpler than fashioning a knob
so that handling is easier. All that you need do now is to light the fire in
the hearth and keep it going until puffs of steam emerge from the sides of
the lid, a certain indication that the wash is perfect and complete because
the mass of laundry has got to boiling point – something that usually takes
two hours if the fire is properly maintained.

Considering that all the other ways of undertaking a buck-wash require
twelve or fifteen hours of running the lye, consuming enormous amounts
of labour and fuel, this machine does it all in two hours, without any work
or worry as all you need do is keep the fire in.

When you do a wash with this equipment, you put the dirtiest linen at
the bottom of the tub and, because it is only clean water (the result of the
condensing of the steam) which penetrates the linen itself, there is nothing
to stop you mixing the coarsest and dirtiest linen with the most delicate.

When you take the linen out of the machine, all the dirt is so well
dissolved by the action of the soda and the heat of the condensed steam
that it has in effect been soaped and all it needs is a simple rinse or paddling

and wringing out to rid it of all filth. The wash is much quicker and easier and the cost of labour is claimed to be a quarter of that for a traditional buck-wash.

One result, therefore, is that soap is no longer needed except to tackle the most stubborn stains that have resisted the wash itself.

The advantages of this system have been witnessed by many public and private establishments. We would urge serious thought before taking any decisions about what laundry system you adopt.

The *Charles* laundry tubs can be found at 16 quai de l'École, Paris. Their cost is:

For 10 kilograms of dry laundry			50 fr.
— 20	....		80 —
— 30	....		100 —
— 45	....	(standard capacity)	125 —
— 60	....	(standard capacity)	150 —
— 80	....	(large capacity)	200 —
— 100	....	(large capacity)	220 —
— 150	....		300 —
— 200	....		400 —
— 300 to 600	......		600 to 1,200 —

9. — Starching.

Starching with starch. — You can starch men's shirts and petticoats with raw starch; but it is essential that you cook any starch to be used on muslins. Far from seeking to economize on the cost of starch, you should seek out the whitest, no matter what its cost. You should also watch closely that the person applying the starch has the cleanest hands: without this precaution, when the linen is wrung out after it has been starched, the hands will leave grey shadows which will dim its brilliance. If cooked starch is used, then the garments that are beaten with the hands after starching will be even whiter when they are ironed.

Starching with starch and borax. — Since fashion has decreed that petticoats should be starched, the world has taken to mixing starch with a salt called *borax*, which gives the linen a firmness and brilliance it would not get from starch alone. First the petticoats are starched with cooked starch; while they are drying, you melt four borax stones in half a litre of water (for every two petticoats) over the fire. Once it is all melted, add a little raw starch, a little blue and enough water to thoroughly wet the two petticoats. Dip them into this preparation, wring them out and fold them into a dry white sheet, from whence you take them still damp for ironing.

You can deal with the fronts, cuffs and collars of men's shirts in the same way, as well as women's collars and cuffs. However, rather than using cooked starch, you are better using raw.

If you don't use all your borax solution, leave it in a cool place where it will keep in good condition for eight to ten days.

10. — Ironing.

A.— *Preliminaries.*

Any linen destined to be ironed should remain well wrapped until the moment it is dampened. You sprinkle water over it by hand or use a horsehair sprinkler, then table it (see page 256, above) and leave it to moisten before ironing. Everything that was turned inside out for washing should be turned to the *right* side, because it will press less well if it's inside out and, once ironed, you cannot turn it out to the right side without crumpling it. Everything that is going to be pleated should be put to one side, likewise everything that is to be starched. For plain linen, the ironing lady should choose the moment when the fire is burning at its brightest and the iron is hottest; once the fire has died down a little, she can iron the small items and the pleats.

The mistress should ensure that the general linen is ironed by the housemaids and that hired ironing ladies are only employed on pleated and starched objects.

Sorting the linen. — They should iron one sort of laundry at a time, because the hand gets accustomed to one sort of work and therefore does it more rapidly. It is not moving the iron at speed that makes for fast work, but directing the iron in such a way that you never go over work already done.

Folding. — You should adopt a method for folding each piece of linen to be ironed, and you should fold it *on the spot* and always in the same way. You should not fold it too large or too small; if too large it is difficult to put away in the wardrobe, if too small, you won't be able to stack it in piles.

B. — Irons and stoves.

Heating the irons. — Many households are accustomed to put the irons at front of the kitchen hearth to heat. In the first place you will have to burn a lot of wood, and wood of the best quality, to ensure a fire sufficient to heat the irons; and in the second, they will invariably be covered with ash, which means the ironing lady will risk soiling the linen. The slightest smoke will mark the irons and detract from their polish and mean they will not slide so easily over the linen; this soot will be difficult to remove and may mark the linen; finally, the irons will warm up slowly and unevenly.

Stoves. — Charcoal, in a stove designed for its use, seems to me preferable and much less costly. With a stove like this, you can regulate the fire according to the needs of the ironing lady, even let it out and relight it with ease; the irons are never marked or soiled, and they heat evenly, though not the handle.

Harel stoves are very suitable;[1] they are made from sheet iron with firebricks inside; they have doors which open and close at will, and have a lid on the top with slots for the irons, which are placed on a grill. The smallest fire will heat the irons and keep them at a proper temperature without them coming into any contact with the charcoal. You can control the fire by means of the doors, which all you have to do is open more or less.

Most towns have cast iron stoves for sale which, if they do not have all the advantages of Harel stoves, are none the less perfectly suitable and at an even lower price. They have neither doors nor a lid, but they are quite long and wide enough for a decent fire. They stand on four legs and have a small vent at the bottom to supply the current of air that feeds the flames. I advise my readers at least to have one of these cast iron stoves. There are some made out of ceramic to the same pattern, but they are fragile.

Irons. — Irons have been perfected for a number of years. Those made in polished cast iron seem to me preferable to those made with sheet iron. I realize that sometimes the handle breaks or comes away, which means they are no longer viable, something which does not happen with sheet

---

1. Harel was a Parisian inventor and manufacturer of small stoves and heating appliances in the first half of the nineteenth century, with showrooms at rue de l'Arbre sec in the first arrondissement of Paris. It is now bisected by the rue de Rivoli. His speciality was appliances suitable for use in smaller households, particularly in towns: chafing dishes and necromancers were also part of his range.

iron ones which can always be mended; but despite these small drawbacks, I prefer cast iron, because they smooth better and their polish is more durable. If an iron is not sliding smoothly, you can rub it with some wax wrapped in paper.

They manufacture irons in two sizes. I prefer the larger one: it maintains its heat better and will do everything that a smaller iron can do. The best I have used are cast iron, and bear the initials J. B. 4; they are a very convenient shape and have an iron handle fixed with a screw; they cost 1 fr. 40 cent.

Hollow irons. — In some districts they use hollow irons with charcoal inside. I do not reckon this method sound. In the first place, the ironing lady continually breathes in the charcoal fumes, which can make her ill; furthermore, these irons are very heavy and difficult to handle; and finally, they require a special talent to keep the fire going at a satisfactory heat.

Box irons. — In other regions, they use iron boxes into which they introduce bars of cast iron that have been heated to red-hot in the fire. This is not bad as a method, particularly for delicates and starched linen, but less successful with normal laundry. This box iron is most used in districts where wood fuel is cheap, or where coal is most used. It saves recourse to charcoal, which is sometimes costly, and the use of which has its own drawbacks, for example where the ironing takes place in a poorly ventilated room. With these box irons, there is little risk of marking the linen and little danger of scorching it.

Iron stands. — It is wise to have a small six-footed iron grill on which to stand the irons on the board (figure 80).

Irons for trimmings. — You should also have a small iron capable of easy treatment of the frills of bonnets and able to get between two frills or between pleats, under the arms of bodices, or into a bodice that has been gathered from top to bottom. The iron should be made of thick metal, rounded at the heel and like a normal smoothing iron at its pointed end. It should be 0^m,10 long and 0^m,06 wide. You should also equip yourself with some little goffering

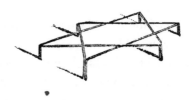

Figure 80. Iron stand.

irons with two blades [like scissors], of different thicknesses, to press the pleats of any furbelows.

C.— *Ironing table, padded shapes, flat-iron gloves.*

Ironing board. — An ironing board is extremely useful, particularly since dresses have had such full skirts that it is almost impossible to get the iron into the pleats. This board can be made from poplar, with end pieces of oak. It should be about 1 metre 60 long, 40 centimetres wide at one end and 60 centimetres at the other. You should lay on it a piece of old tapestry, or some blanket, itself covered with a green serge. And over the whole you should lay a very clean cloth. If the board is not covered as I have described, wrap it, when putting it to use, with an ironing blanket, well fastened on the underside. You cover this with the cloth, which I will speak about later.

To use this board, put one end on a table and the other on a chair-back or other piece of furniture the same height as the table. When you have ironed the bodice of a dress in the usual manner, slide the ironing board through the skirt and it will be much easier to press because that's all you have to deal with. Because it hangs down from the board and may therefore be soiled by contact with the floor, lay a clean cloth beneath it. As the ironing progresses, so you turn the skirt.

Table. — It is convenient to have a table, in addition to the ironing board, devoted solely to the task of pressing clothes. This table should be large enough for two people to work at and should be made of white wood, with oak end pieces. It stands on trestles and, once the work is done, it is lifted off and leant against a wall so that it doesn't take up too much space. If, however, you have a room devoted to nothing but ironing, it can stay on its trestles. When ironing is to start, lay on the table an old woollen blanket that is used for nothing else. Then lay on top of that an *ironing-cloth*, that is, a piece of cloth finely woven enough so it doesn't leave any marks on the ironing. You should stretch the ironing-cloth and the blanket with strings under the table which are then tacked to the ironing-cloth along the edge of the table, a bit like lacing a corset. These strings will keep the cloth and blanket nicely taut which will greatly ease the work.

Padded shapes. — For a whole host of garments that cannot be ironed flat on a table, it is essential to have small padded shapes, covered in serge and mounted on a foot. You introduce these shapes into whatever is to be ironed, such as puffed sleeves, etc.

Gloves. — Finally, so that you can handle the irons without burning yourself, you need ironing *gloves.* The best are made from old linen; but you can find them in felt, covered with leather stitched round the edge, which are quite convenient.

You should not let the ironing women use good kitchen cloths to clean the irons; old linen is all that is needed as inevitably it will be burnt.

CHAPTER XIII

CELLARS AND KEEPING WINES

1. — The characteristics of a good cellar.

We call the cellar that underground, vaulted location where we store wine. The best cellars are excavated deep into the rock or soundly built with lime and sand, well ventilated, where it remains cool and dry all through the year. A cellar that is sometimes dry, sometimes damp, is not good. To avoid variations in temperature, you should take care to close the cellar windows in cold snaps and open them in heatwaves. If, despite this precaution, the temperature rises too much in the summer, you will have to water the cellar freely.

Cellar floors. — Cellar floors should be clean, without cracks, and covered with river sand if possible. You should avoid scattering water about willy-nilly, and there must be no filth, the smell of which will affect the wine to its detriment.

Division of cellars into bins. — Cellars should be provided with bins along their length. These bins are made either with small brick or stone retaining walls, or out of planks. These walls should be about a metre high, and project about $0^m,60$, i.e. the length of two bottles. They should be a metre apart. You stack the bottles in these compartments. I will describe later how to stack the bottles.

Drawbacks of placing shelves above the bottles. — In some cellars, shelves are placed across the bin walls and they are loaded with encumbrances. This is a dangerous habit, as anything may provoke these objects to fall thus breaking many bottles.

Drawbacks of burying bottles. — There are also drawbacks in burying bottles in heaps of sand, as is done in several regions. They take up much room; the corks perish; you cannot count the number of bottles; the slightest accident will break a large proportion, and the moment when the wine achieves its greatest bouquet is delayed.

Bottle racks. — You usually install along the walls of the anteroom of the cellar or, if you don't have an anteroom, then of the cellar housing *vin ordinaire*, boards pierced with holes. These accommodate empty bottles, which you put in upside down so that they drain well.

Dividing the cellar into two parts. — It is most convenient to split the cellar into two, one part for fine wines, the other for *vins ordinaires*, equipment, and other bulky objects that may be stored in the cellar. The two parts should be locked, for wine is too great a temptation for the servants to be allowed access, except in exceptional circumstances.

2. — The care of barrels.

Barrel rack. — You must create a *barrel rack* in the cellar, that is to say two large level and parallel beams 50 centimetres apart on which you arrange the barrels so as to avoid any rot that may eventuate from contact with the damp floor. The beam which supports the back of the barrels should be 10 centimetres higher than that at the front so that you can extract all the wine without tipping the barrel, which will disturb the wine.

If the beams are not of sufficient height so that you can put a bottle under the spigot of the barrel when you want to draw some wine, you should raise them up with chocks of wood or stone. When arranged thus, the barrels will be much better preserved.

Mallet. — In order to broach the barrels you need a mallet, smaller than a bat for corking bottles, and fixed to a long, slender, flexible handle. You tap each side of the bung to get it out. With this mallet you don't risk damaging the staves because its elasticity reduces any rude shocks.

Chain and iron hoop. — It is useful to have a chain or an iron hoop pierced with holes in your cellar which can be adapted quickly and easily, before the cooper gets there, to any barrel whose hoops may by chance have burst. By doing this you will avoid considerable loss.

Visits to the cellar. — A mistress should often visit her cellar, examine the barrels, taste the wines, check that the bins of bottles are stable, and that the corks are not crumbling.

Labelling the bins of bottles and the barrels. — In a properly run cellar all the bins should be labelled. This can be easily done with square tiles or roof tiles on which you write the name of the wines in chalk. Barrels should likewise be labelled, and the vintage of the wine they contain noted.

Demijohns. — When you have insufficient wine to fill a barrel to the top, you can put it up in large earthenware bottles called *demijohns*, which you can find everywhere at a low price. You should take care to cork them so that no air can pass.

3. — How to arrange full bottles.

Stacking. — You stack the bottles between the short walls that divide the cellar into bins. You should always stack bottles of the same shape together, otherwise the stack will not be stable and will collapse, breaking all the bottles.

First row. — Before arranging the bottles, make sure that the cellar floor is smooth and even, and cover it with a layer of sand which is given a slope towards the centre of the cellar. Then you put down a first row of bottles, horizontal, not touching, with their necks to the wall. You should support these necks with a lath, or two laths one on top of the other, making sure that they are always a little higher than the bottoms, which should rest directly on the floor. This first layer should be constructed with the greatest care, because the whole stack will depend on its stability.

Second row. — How the second row is arranged will depend on the shape of the bottles you are stacking. If you are dealing with bottles said to be Champagne or bottles said to be Bordeaux, you place the bottom of each bottle of the second row between the necks of the bottles of the first row, making sure the bottoms are about 9 centimetres beyond the ends of the necks, so that they can rest on the laths which support the necks of the first row.

Third row. — To arrange the third row, you put a lath on the necks of the second row and you place exactly, with equal deliberation the bottoms of the third row on top of the bottoms of the first row.

Fourth row. — You arrange the fourth row exactly as you did the second, you check that the levels are such that they ensure the stability of the whole stack, and you continue as before.

The advantages of stacking. — When the bottles are thus solidly stacked, it simple to count them, the air circulates between them – which aids the

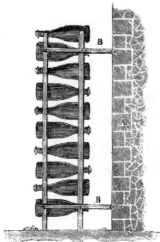

Figure 81. Iron bottle rack.

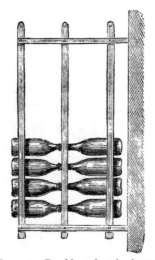

Figure 82. Double rack, side elevation.

conservation of the corks – they take up very little room, and they present a picture of order and tidiness which is a pleasure to behold.

Bottle racks. — They now sell metal bottle racks suitable for empty or full bottles. I recommend their use.

Bottle rack for 100 bottles. — The metal rack (figure 81) measures 90 centimetres high by 1^m wide. It accommodates 100 bottles and costs 15 fr. To install this rack properly, you must ensure that the floor is level. If the floor is neither level nor of a single piece, then put a piece of floor or roof tile under each of the legs. If the rack is well wedged, you need not fear it falling over. To guarantee no possible accident, you can fix the rack to the wall in the following manner: place the rack near wall A; you will thus be absolutely sure where the cross struts BB should be fixed. These struts are pierced to accommodate nails or screws which will fix the rack to the wall. You mark the wall with the position of the holes; you pull back the rack, and drill holes 6 centimetres deep and 15 millimetres wide with a bit and brace. Into these holes you place wooden plugs. You replace the rack and drive nails into these plugs through the holes in the cross struts, using a piece of metal, which is what you strike with the hammer, as a punch. Alternatively, instead of nails, you can put in screws with a screwdriver.

Double rack. — This rack can be double, as figure 82 shows in side elevation and figure 83 shows from the front. This will contain 200 bottles

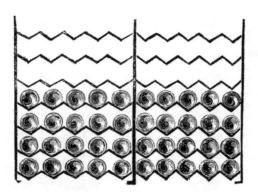

Figure 83. Double rack, front elevation.

and costs 25 francs. The depth of the rack assures its stability and rather than fixing it to the wall as in figure 82, you stand it free of all support so that you can arrange several such racks through the cellar, leaving space to move around between each rack. With this arrangement, the racks don't need cross struts, which would simply snag you as you pass.

Locked rack. — They also make lockable racks, as in figure 84. You fix these to the wall as I have described. They cost 25 francs for 100 bottles.

The advantages of metal racks. — All these racks are manufactured by M. Barbou, 41 rue Montmartre.[1] Their superiority over other ways of storing

Figure 84. Lockable bottle rack.

bottles is incontestable. They last indefinitely because their paint stops any oxidization; you can deposit and withdraw bottles with the utmost ease because each is supported independently of the others and thus you risk no breakages; the bottles can be different sizes without vitiating the stacking; you can take out any bottle irrespective of where it is in the stack, and in consequence store several different sorts of wine; you can replace full bottles with empty bottles; and finally, as the bottles are stored in rows of a dozen, you can count them easily.

4. — The care of empty bottles.

Usually, the servants take no care of empty bottles and, through fecklessness, break many of them, as if they have no value. You should therefore often urge them to handle them carefully, and be ready to complain when they carelessly break one; because the result will be a large expense when you put all your wine in bottles. The servants' negligence stems from two factors: the first is that the value they attach to the wine leads them to dismiss the bottle when empty; the second is that they see so many bottles around that it is incomprehensible to them that they have any value. They take great pains with a bowl that costs 10 centimes, but break with not the slightest regret a bottle that costs 25 centimes.

Bottle crate. — A bottle crate, divided into compartments, is essential for carrying bottles around, full or empty. It is a wise purchase that avoids many accidents. Figure 85 shows one of these metal crates, holding six bottles. It costs 12 francs.

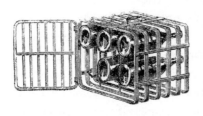

Figure 85. Bottle crate.

Washing bottles. — You will wash bottles best with a chain fixed to a cork, and made for the purpose, rather than lead pellets, which don't clean as well and some of which are often left in the bottom of the bottles. You can find these chains in every ironmonger and their cost is not high.

---

1.   The firm of Barbou et fils in rue Montmartre displayed a bottle rack and bottle corking machine at the Exposition Universelle in Paris in 1867.

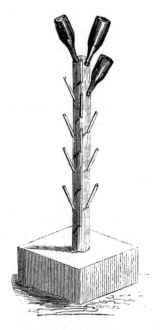

Figure 86. Stand for draining bottles.

Bottles should be washed as soon as they are emptied. This means they are always clean when the time comes to draw off a barrel of wine and you avoid the lees drying out inside.

Stand for draining bottles. — A stand for draining bottles is a useful item to take any bottles as you wash them so that they dry before being stacked or filled again. It is made from a block of hardwood, about 40 centimetres diameter and 20 centimetres thick, in the middle of which is fixed (with a mortise) a large round post, in oak or something similarly solid, of 10 to 12 centimetres diameter and $1^m,50$ height (figure 86). Round this post, from top to bottom, you drill $0^m,01$ holes at $0^m,10$ intervals. These holes should be drilled almost vertical, with only a slight outward angle. Insert oak pegs of 15 to 16 centimetres, or you could substitute 5-millimetre metal rods, the whole then resembling a tree with branches from top to bottom. When you wash a bottle, you put the neck over one of these pegs and it will drain perfectly. Once sufficiently drained, you replace it with another bottle.

5. — How to cork bottles.

To cork a bottle properly you should not soak the corks in advance but, rather, moisten them slightly after you have tried them in the neck of the bottle to ensure they are the right size. Once the cork is placed in the neck, the operator seizes the bottle in his left hand, puts it on his left thigh and then, with his right hand, strikes the cork with some force with a heavy, thick, wooden mallet shaped like a racquet. If you are corking up *vin ordinaire*, the cork enters the neck with some difficulty and should only be driven in two-thirds of its length so that the part sticking out offers sufficient *purchase* for you to extract it without a corkscrew – which will allow you to recork the bottle and serve it at table again should it not be completely emptied. For fine wines, which are to be kept and which are opened with a corkscrew, the cork should not protrude from the neck more than a centimetre at most.

6. — Keeping wines.

The first condition for keeping wines in good condition is to take great care of them and hold them in a good cellar.

When to put wines in bottle. — You should bottle wine at least three to six months in advance, the time necessary for a *vin ordinaire* to improve in quality. So far as fine wines are concerned, they should always be bottled.

Keeping wine in small barrels.[1] — If you wish to avoid buying bottles and corks, and to draw the wine from the barrel as and when you need it, you should, as far as possible, split the wine between small barrels of 60 to 80 litres so that it spends less time broached.

Drawing the wine. — If, when you wish to draw wine from a barrel, you have to open the tap at the bottom of the barrel, the air pressure acting on the mouth of the tap may stop the wine from flowing out, because this air pressure is stronger than the force exerted by the column of wine above the level of the tap. It is necessary, in order that the wine will flow, for the column of wine to be 12 metres high because the weight of the column of air (see the article *Barometer*, page 133 above) is equal to the weight of a column of wine of about 12 metres.

To ensure a free flow, you have to allow air to press down on the wine in the barrel as you open the tap. To achieve this you could take out the bung stopping the upper hole, through which the barrel was filled; but the wine would lose quality because too much of its surface area would be in contact with air. Usually, a small hole is made in the top of the barrel which you stop with a dowel. You take out this dowel each time you want to draw off wine, and you replace it as soon as it's drawn.

A way of preserving broached wine from the action of air. — In years of good harvests, proprietors who do not have enough barrels to accommodate the wine are forced to sell at a derisory price. Here is how M. Gourdon, of Beaune, avoided this dilemma. You leave the wine in the vat and, after

1.　　The French word is *feuillette*. This, according to the *Oxford Companion to Wine*, is the traditional Chablis barrel of 132 litres. A *tonneau* (the word for barrel used by the author) was, when used as a term of measure, a barrel in the Bordelais of about 900 litres.

fermentation, you slowly pour over the wine 12 litres of very pure oil (for a vat of 2 metres diameter). You cover the vat with boards or canvas to protect the oil from dust.

When you wish to draw off the wine, you take it through the tap until the oil is level with the tap; then, so that you can recover the oil without mixing it, you draw the rest of the contents of the vat into a narrow vessel with a tap at its base. M. Gourdon's workings show that you will only lose 2 litres of oil from the 12 litres which allowed your wine some shelter from the air. As the price of oil can be calculated at 2 francs the kilogram, the cost is therefore only 4 francs.

You can follow the same method to preserve wine from contact with the air if it is in a barrel that must remain broached for a long time. But the amount of oil should be infinitely less, and always proportionate to the size of the barrel.

The care of wines in barrels. — Wines in barrels that are not to be consumed merit some attention.

You should check the hoops from time to time, to see if they are in good condition and that none has come off. Every month, you take out the bungs and *completely* fill, with wine of the same quality, any barrel with a gap at the top. Then you replace the bung carefully. If the wines are new, you should give them some air every so often, usually through holes in the bung sealed with small conical wooden stoppers.[1] If you don't take this precautionary measure, it can happen that the gas produced by the fermentation builds up too much pressure and bursts the barrel.

When you want to keep wines in barrel for several years you should rack them twice a year, in March[2] or June when the vines are flowering, and in September or October at the harvest. If you are not accustomed to undertake this operation, you should get it done by a good cooper, and stay and watch yourself.

Fining. — When you wish to bottle the wine, you fine it eight or ten days beforehand. To do this you first must broach the barrel by introducing a tap from which you draw 3 or 4 litres, just to make a gap at the top. Next you beat egg whites in a bowl with a little water; the proportion is one white to fine 25 litres of wine; however the quantity of egg whites should

1. The word here is *fossets*, a coopering term.
2. *Recte* May?

be increased in relation to whether the wine is darker or lighter and to its level of alcohol. You pour this mixture into the barrel and stir it long and vigorously with a white-wood stick that has been split into four at one end. The four twigs spread out in the barrel and aid the liquid's agitation.

A fining of egg whites is only good for red wines; white wines should be clarified with isinglass. To effect this, you obtain 10 or 12 grams of isinglass for a barrel of 260 litres of wine; you beat the isinglass vigorously on a paving slab with a hammer so that it divides into little leaves; and then you soak it in a glass of cold water. When it is softened, you break it up still more by hand, you add a litre of water and you pass it through a muslin. You pour it into the barrel and stir vigorously.

7. — Defects in wines.

Sourness. — When a wine becomes sour there is no other remedy than to drink it as soon as possible if you are not going to lose everything. There is no cure for sourness, it can only increase.

Bitterness. — It sometimes happens that old wines become bitter. To lessen this bitterness, for it is not possible to banish it altogether, you can mix the bitter wine with an equal volume of similar wine, but less aged. You should fine it and bottle it. This wine should then be drunk forthwith.

Fat [ropiness]. — They say that wines turn to fat when they become too viscous; in fact they become quite unsuitable to serve as drink. When you see that a wine is turning to fat, you may be able to save it with the following: begin by racking it off, that is to say decant it from one barrel to another, preferably one you have fumigated or strongly sulphurated. You take the fruits of the service tree, just before they are completely ripe – 500 grams will be enough for a barrel of 260 litres – crush them in a mortar, throw them in the barrel and mix well in. Leave them to rest for a day or two; fine the wine in the normal manner, and then bottle it. You may obtain the same result with grape pips, and even more with well-crushed grape stalks. It is also sensible, in this case, to add a bit of alcohol to the wine; the proportion is usually 5 litres of alcohol to the barrel.

Sprouting. — This name[1] is given to a disease which strikes wines in the summer heat; it appears as if it is fermenting. You can get around it by racking the wines in spring, before the cellar temperature rises. When

1.   The French word is *pousse*.

you notice that a wine is 'sprouting', you should immediately take out the bung, sulphur another barrel (that is, burn a 4-millimetre sulphur wick) and then rack the defective wine. Adding 250 grams of mustard to the wine is also good. You should fine the wine immediately after racking. It is prudent, in any case, to start putting any wines that have begun 'sprouting' into circulation.

CHAPTER XIV

BAKING

Making bread at home has not lost its importance in the wake of the great spread of commercial bakeries. In fact, there are scarcely any bakeries outside towns of a certain size, and it is always in the interests of people living in the country to be able to make good bread quickly and economically.

A. — Choice of flour.

In country districts, the mistress will rarely make any bread with flour other than from grain harvested on her own farm: she knows from experience the quality of the grain and flour, as well as the flour's yield in bread.

Wheat flour. — When you wish to buy flour to make household bread, you should pay attention to its tint and smell. Freshly ground wheat flour of the first quality should be white with a very slight hint of light yellow; if you plunge your fingers into it, it should adhere to the skin, and if you take a little into the palm of your hand and press it hard, it should pack together rather than dissolve into dust.

Wheat flour of the second quality will be white and shaded a slightly darker yellow; pressed in the palm of the hand, it will turn merely to dust. Finally, in flour that is wholly inferior, you will see a multitude of grey particles: this, the millers say, is *spotted flour.*

Rye flour. — Good quality, freshly ground rye flour has a particular smell, most likened to violets. It loses this smell in aging. Thus any rye flour that doesn't smell of violets is either old or of inferior quality.

Barley flour. — It is a dull white and perceptibly coarser, less soft to the touch than wheat or rye flour.

The proportions of flours to use. — You make household bread with wheat flour, either on its own or with a quarter or even a third of its weight in rye flour. This mixture, far from making household bread less good, improves its quality greatly. A moderate dose of rye flour in the bread makes it more refreshing and at the same time less liable to dry out during hot spells. It is better, from the point of view of making bread, to grind the wheat and rye separately rather than put them through the mill at the same time; bread made with flours ground separately rises better and has a better flavour.

B. — Leaven.

Preparation of leaven. — Leaven is a morsel of dough kept back from the last batch. It usually consists of the scrapings of the dough trough with the addition of a little cold water and a little flour. The proportion of leaven cannot be determined with precision; the most usual is 5 or 6 per 100 of the total weight of dough to be kneaded. The leaven, worked into a very stiff dough, is wrapped in a cloth and kept in the cool until it is needed. The day before you bake bread, the leaven is moistened with cold water in summer, warm in winter, and left overnight, covered by flour in a corner of the trough. In the summer, you put in a third of the flour required for the whole batch; in winter, a half. When you are working in cold weather, you encourage the leaven's fermentation by using warm water and wrapping it in a woollen blanket; when you are working in the summer, you slow down the fermentation by using cold water and leaving it open to the air.

Leaven which has reached its peak of fermentation should have risen to double its volume after a few hours and have a rounded shape; it should smell agreeably like wine; and if you throw a morsel into water, it should float.

C. — The dough trough and kneading.

The dough trough. — The dough trough or bin is made of hardwood; it has the form of a trough, wider at the top than at the bottom; it is usually 2 to 3 metres long by $0^m,50$ wide at the top and $0^m,30$ wide at the bottom; it comes with two or three planks which form moveable partitions and which can form two or three compartments; one will contain the rising doughs, the other will be used for kneading.

Kneading the dough. — As soon as you have poured the flour into the trough, you make a well in it and introduce the leaven. First you mix it with half the water the dough will need to absorb, taking care that no lumps remain; once it is well mixed, you add the rest of the water. Then you add the rest of the flour and you start to work it, first by punching holes in it with your closed fist and turning it vigorously. Now is the moment to add salt: the amount varies according to local usage, from 5 grams to 10 or 12 grams per kilogram of dough. The dough is then stretched, folded on itself, beaten, and pressed, then once more stretched, folded, etc., until it is smooth. The more it is worked, the better the bread. Kneading, to be well done, should be neither slow nor hasty; you must proceed steadily, with regularity, with a continuous and uniform action. The slightest interruption of the kneading will detract from the quality of the bread.

Dividing the dough. — Once made up, in winter the dough should rest somewhere warm on a table; in the summer it can be divided immediately into pieces, according to the weights the loaves should have. The dough is usually weighed on the basis that you will lose by evaporation of water in the cooking 600 grams to every round loaf of 6 kilograms, i.e. 100 grams per kilogram. With smaller loaves, the weight loss in cooking is a little greater; it works out at an average of 125 grams per kilogram for loaves weighing 1 or 2 kilograms.

It is very important that as soon as the dough has been cut and weighed it is formed into balls[1] without the slightest delay, then stretched to the shape you desire, whether to obtain split loaves (figure 87), round loaves (figures 88 and 89) or rings (figure 90). The dough is then put into wicker

1.   The French is *boules*, and the author remarks that hence come the words *boulanger* and *boulangerie*.

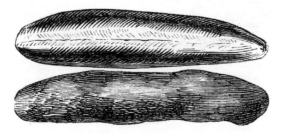

Figure 87. Split loaves.

Figures 88–90. Round and ring loaves.

baskets (figures 91 and 92) lined with coarse linen, on which you sprinkle a little fine bran. Baskets are much to be preferred for this purpose than the wooden bowls that are still used in many departments.

How long the dough should prove, that is to say ferment, in these baskets cannot be stated with precision. In winter, the dough rises under the protection of a woollen blanket, near the mouth of the oven; in summer, by contrast, you leave the dough to rise with no covering. Only experience will tell you when to put the bread in the oven.

Figures 91–92. Proving baskets.

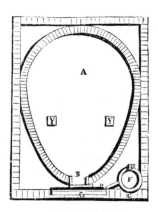

Figure 93. Oven.

D. — Oven.

Construction. — The oven's dimensions will depend on the quantity of bread you wish to bake. Generally, a household oven is 2 metres wide by 40 centimetres tall, and about 3 metres deep. The best shape to conserve, concentrate and distribute the heat is a flattened hollow hemisphere (figure 93). It consists of several elements, which I will describe.

Sole. — The *sole* or floor of the oven is paved with tiles. It is $0^m,04$ higher at the back than at the mouth of the oven.

Vault. — The vault should be close to the sole. The nearer it is to the sole, the easier it is to heat. A distance of $0^m,40$ at the centre is the most suitable.

Flues.[1] — These vents are flues built over the oven vault and issue into the chimney above and to each side of the mouth. There are three flues: two from the back of the oven along the sides and the third running across the centre of the vault. When the wood is lit, you close the chimney above the issue of these flues with a damper. The flame and the smoke is thus forced to use these flues to vent and the draught is thus much energized.

The mouth. — The size of the oven mouth B (figure 93) will depend on the size of the loaves; it is equipped with a door of heavy cast iron which closes it hermetically and inhibits the evaporation of the steam or moisture which is produced by the cooking. This steam falls back onto the loaves, giving them an agreeable colour and taste, and it also reduces any weight loss due to evaporation.

The altar. — When the oven is open, the door is placed on a slab of dressed stone which is called the *altar*.

Above the oven. — The space above the oven is almost always wasted when it could be used to heat the water or dry the wood.

Below the oven. — The space below the oven should be solid. I have renounced the opportunity for an excavation, recognizing that it would cause a great loss of heat.

1. The French is *oura(s)*, a word used only in *boulangerie*.

Cauldron. — There is a tinned copper cauldron to heat the water for the dough. It is usually located within the body of the oven at a convenient height for drawing water through a tap into jugs or basins to carry to the trough. In this manner you have hot water at no cost.

E. — Baking bread.

Heating the oven. — The oven should be heated while the dough is being prepared. The oven must *wait for the dough*; bread is never so good when the dough is prepared before the oven is hot. In reality, once the oven is hot, a few logs or armfuls of twigs are enough to make sure the heat is kept up. You should only use really dry wood to heat the oven, which will give plenty of flame and very little smoke; practice will provide the knowledge of how much wood is needed to heat an oven. You encourage combustion with the aid of rakes (figures 94 and 95). These are long poles with a iron blade bent at the end which allow you to stir up the wood and the cinders and push them to various parts of the oven.

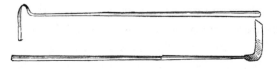

Figures 94–95. Rakes.

Charging and unloading the oven. — To charge the oven, you turn the baskets containing the loaves out onto peels that you have dusted with flour (figures 96, 97, and 98). If the loaves are of different sizes, you place the largest at the back and the smallest at the front. They should touch, but not crowd so as to avoid deformation during the baking. As a general

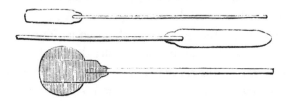

Figures 96–98. Peels.

rule, it is not wise to make loaves weighing more than 6 kilograms; it they are heavier, they bake badly.

Once all the bread is in the oven, you close the mouth of the oven. After twenty minutes you open it to check the progress of the baking, which will last between half an hour and three-quarters, according to the size of the loaves and the consistency of the dough. Any bread taken out of the oven should sit without any covering on a table until it has cooled completely.

In smaller households, where only a little bread is made, a small portable sheet-metal oven is very useful. The advantage of an oven like this is that the fuel is never in contact with the bread, which means you can use coal, coke, or even peat, which makes baking very economical in districts where wood is expensive.

F. — Making bread according to the Eeckmann system.

In something as important as bread-making, all improvements are a boon. This is why we give here a description of the kneading-machine and family oven of M. Eeckmann-Lecroart of Lille.[1] These machines were given a prize at the Regional Competition at Melun in 1857.

1.   M. Eeckman-Lecroart (he spelled his name with a single 'n') wrote a pamphlet, *Boulangerie des familles. Faire le pain chez soi*, first published by A. Goin in Lille in 1856; a second, larger edition was published by E. Reboux in Lille in 1857.

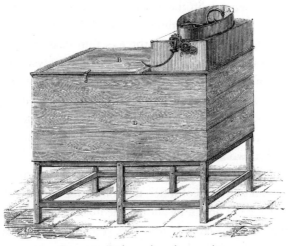

Figure 99. Eeckman kneading machine.

The kneading-machine (figure 99) consists of a half-cylinder in tinned sheet-metal which sits in a bain-marie. The body of the machine D is a wooden box closed by the lid B; this box serves as the base for the dough trough and a table to shape the bread. The dough mixer A is in tinned metal and is in the shape of hooked fingers. A cranked handle, connected to the gear wheel C, works the machine, which can be cleaned with the

Figure 100. Eeckman bread oven.

Figure 101. Eeckman bread oven, open.

greatest of ease when you lift the lid B. Here is how you make bread using this machine. If this is the first time you have baked, and you do not have at your disposal a morsel of dough three or four days old, you will have to mix one-and-a-half litres of flour with half a litre of warm water twelve hours before you begin. Throw in one or two spoonfuls of brewer's yeast, mix everything, and make up a little ball of dough which you keep from the cold by putting it in the bottom of the trough. Two hours after this, you add the same quantities of flour and water and, once well mixed, form a double ball which, after two hours (if it has fermented well) will have increased in size by one-third. With this amount of leaven, you can make up twelve litres of flour and four litres of water, thus obtaining about 13 kilograms of dough. You make the dough by adding the flour and water one-third by one-third and, towards the end, make sure you salt it with the appropriate quantity. A few minutes is all that is needed. If you use hot water and you work in a room that is more than 20°C, the bread will rise in a very short time. While you are waiting for this, you can light the fire in the oven which is shown in perspective in figure 100, and which figure 101 shows open, and figure 102 shows in section. This oven is made up of revolving shelves one above the other, accessed through the doors A. These shelves turn on an axle turned by the crank E. The door to the firebox is at C and B is the door to a hot cupboard where you can cook pâtisserie or roast meats. The

Figure 102. Eeckman bread oven, section.

smoke vents through the flue F and thence to the outside. A thermometer G indicates the temperature needed for cooking (175° to 200°).

We will not go into further detail. It is enough to say that the kneading-machines cost from 60 to 200 francs, depending whether made for 13 to 100 kilograms of dough, and that the price of the ovens varies between 135 and 300 francs. M. Eeckmann-Lecroart gives full instructions for the use of his equipment, which has been successfully installed not only in private households, but also by the navy and various enterprises.

G. — *Making bread according to the Mège-Mouriès system.*[1]

I think it useful to give a succinct idea of a new system of panification which is both extremely rational in theory and of little practical complexity, but which may fall foul of the tyranny of habit for the simple reason its performance requires that you jettison all the equipment and all the manual

1. Hippolyte Mège-Mouriès (1817–1880), French chemist, invented margarine in 1869. This description of his discoveries in the field of panification is somewhat abbreviated, none the less, the fact was that Mège-Mouriès succeeded in accelerating the then very slow process of making bread with leaven and did manage to make white bread more economically than the usual method of using only bolted white flour. His use of sulphuric acid (or tartaric acid by some accounts) generates carbon dioxide which raises the dough. It anticipates the aerated bread pioneered by Dr John Dauglish in the early 1860s in London.

routines of making household bread that have been embraced since time immemorial. This is what M. Mège-Mouriès proposed in 1854. Grain is milled to deliver the bran separately, then flour of the first quality, then what the inventor has called *mixed grist*. This grist, wetted with four times its weight of water and lightly acidulated with a few drops of sulphuric acid, ferments at a low temperature and yields to the water all its active principles. The solution is then strained and used to make a dough, with no further assistance from any other leaven. The dough rises perfectly, and the yield of bread from the flour is increased by twenty per cent. This innovation has to be seen to be believed and could be of great service in times of poor harvests.

H. — Rice bread, oaten bread, potato bread.

I only mention breads made with rice, buckwheat, oats, maize, and potatoes to remind you that all these classes of foodstuffs lend themselves poorly to bread, and that any bread obtained from them has little nutritive value and almost always an inferior taste. It is better, even when cereals are scarce and expensive, to consume rice, potatoes, oats, etc., in any other form than bread.

CHAPTER XV

CONCERNING PROVISIONS

In a properly conducted household it is provident to lay in, among all those items which can be stored, anything that is cheaper to buy in large quantities or which costs less at one season than another. A large proportion of stores can be prepared by the mistress herself. If she takes on board these details she will be able to provide her household with a host of good things, at very little cost and with only a little work, which would otherwise be denied it had they to be purchased. The pleasure she derives from offering them, as well as the savings she will make, is ample recompense for her trouble. But she should beware that abundance does not lead to over-supply and waste. To avoid these pitfalls, it is essential that she alone controls the provisions and that she determines upon a room or a cupboard to serve as a store to which she alone holds the key. If she passes this key to the servants, it is almost inevitable that they will abuse it.

SECTION I. — PURCHASED STORES.
1. — Firewood.

Supply. — Firewood is a significant item of expenditure in most households, especially on a farm where a great deal is consumed. The mistress should therefore make plans in advance concerning its supply and supervise its consumption and storage with great solicitude.

It is wise to lay in two years' supply of firewood so that you always have fuel at your disposal that is at least one year old and therefore dry.

Wood-shed. — Firewood should always be stored under cover in what we call a wood-shed, because bad weather will soon cause it to deteriorate. If you do not have one, you should quickly construct a shelter or lean-to which can be covered simply with straw or straw matting, which costs little.

Division of timber into logs. — Timber should first be sawn into convenient lengths, rather short than long; that will be more economical. The wood should then be split into logs, so that what is needed at any time can be seized without hesitation.

Properties of different species of timber. — Firewood may be of different species, depending on the region; oak is most widely used, and the best.

Oak. — *Black oak*, so-called because of its bark, is preferable to white oak; either one is better if grown in dry ground. Wood from the trunk is better than from the boughs. Split wood loses a lot of its quality; it is best to burn large pieces.

Beech, elm, ash. — These species also have many qualities, although they burn faster than oak; beech, elm and ash burn very well and form plenty of large embers which give out a lot of heat and make a fine fire.

Chestnut, pine. — Both chestnut and pine spit in a fire, sometimes to such an extent that you must mind where the little sparks are propelled if you wish to avoid the accidents they can provoke; pine bark is especially susceptible.

Driftwood. — Driftwood has lost many of its properties; thus it is much cheaper than *new* wood, i.e. which has not been in the water. But it burns with the same ease as a faggot, which makes its employment sometimes to our liking.

Fruit trees. — Wood from fruit trees that have been chopped down or pruned is the best of all firewood, but it is so rare and so costly that it is seldom used. Its twists and turns make it sometimes difficult to accommodate in the fireplace, but it makes a fine blaze.

Using bad wood. — The worst wood should be kept for cooking vegetables to feed the animals. However, if the mistress is not on her toes, she can be sure it will be otherwise, because good wood burns so much more easily than bad and servants are always ready to save their own effort, even to the detriment of the general good.

Faggots. — Faggots should be kept under cover, like timber. If they take up so much room they cannot be housed, you should make a *bulls-eye*,[1] i.e. a stack piled slightly above ground level so that when it rains they do not sit in water.

---

1.   The French is *mouche*, which may mean a fly, beauty-spot or bulls-eye.

Heather and gorse. — In many parts, they use heather and gorse to heat ovens, this is both cheap and convenient. If you don't have this resource, you should use the worst faggots for the oven.

Fir cones. — I should not omit mentioning vine clippings, and pine or fir cones, which burn brightly and attractively, and catch alight as soon as you show them a lighted candle, or even a match. Whenever you can, I advise you to secure these resin-filled cones, currently in general use in Paris as kindling.

2. — Soap.

Supply. — Dry, hard soap is an infinitely wiser investment than when it is fresh and soft, because in the latter condition it dissolves too quickly in water. You need, therefore, to secure a proper supply. You should even buy it in bulk, buying a box of it for example, so great is the advantage of using it hard, not soft. It keeps for several years without losing condition; so you can buy it in advance without risk; and in any case, you will buy it at a lower price.

Figure 103. Soap wire.

How to cut soap. — Once the supply is laid in, you should cut the soap into pieces of a size that can be handled with ease. It is always prudent to issue servants a little at a time. Use a thin wire to cut it, attached at each end to a small wooden handle to form a loop large enough to accept a whole block (figure 103). If you use a knife to cut it, even a sharp one, the soap will crumble, whereas the wire will cut it perfectly cleanly and easily.

Keeping soap. — Once the blocks are cut, store them one on top of the other in a well-ventilated spot, leaving between each one a little gap for the air to pass. Once they have dried, you can put them in a cupboard, so long as it is not damp.

There are two sorts of soap, white soap and marbled soap.

White soap.[1] — White soap is more expensive than marbled, but its action is more potent. When you have experienced laundresses, who know how to handle soap, it is more economical to use white soap. There is a type of white soap that is more mordant, and is cheaper than the two soaps I describe here; it is suitable for coarse linen, but it changes the colour of cottons, chintzes, etc.

Marbled soap.[2] — If it is good marbled soap, its white parts are a pure white, without yellow shading, and its blue parts a clear blue, and nicely contrasted, like a good marble; its texture is fine, smooth, with holes or *eyes* like Gruyère cheese. It does not break up into round crumbs but rather into leaves, and it has a pleasant smell, which disappears once the laundry is rinsed. Any soap without these characteristics is of poor quality.

Black or green soap. — There is one other type of soap, called *black* or *green*. It is much more powerful than the others and leaves a somewhat disagreeable smell. In some regions, no other soap is used. I do not advise general use of this soap, but it is very useful for washing wool, very dirty linen, and kitchen furniture. It costs less than the others and because it is runny, you buy it in pots.

3. — Sorrel salt, bleach, indigo, starch.

Sorrel salt. — It should be nicely crystallized, transparent and white. Before use, pulverize it with a wooden rolling-pin, a bottle or a glass. You should try not to let it fall onto marble or limestone because it will cut into it and destroy the polish. To keep it, put into a small phial with a large neck, cork well, label, and place in the dry.

Bleach. — Good bleach should have no colour or else a slight pink, a strong smell and sting the skin when you dip the fingers into it, especially if they are at all scratched. Keep bleach in a labelled bottle, well corked,

---

1. Castile soap is often thought of as the original white soap. However, *savon blanc* in France was a standard description of white toilet soap from Switzerland, and the soapmakers of Marseille also made a white soap. The distinction between this and *savon noir* was that white soaps were made on a base of sodium hydroxide and black soaps were potassium hydroxide-based, stronger and more liquid.
2. This survives today in Portugal, where it is known as *azul e branco*. It is stronger than the usual cosmetic soaps and is used for cleaning carpets and furnishings as well as for antiseptic purposes.

which should be of either *black glass* or stoneware, because light will break down the bleach little by little.

The need to label stores. — I cannot recommend you strongly enough to label everything kept in the storeroom; it is an essential precaution.

Indigo or blue. — Blue or indigo, which serves to give a slight tint of blue to the linen, is very often adulterated by retailers. It is extremely difficult to find the genuine article. The solid blue of M. Bergeron, 9 rue Sainte-Croix-de-la-Bretonnerie in Paris,[1] is excellent; it is clean and brilliant and gives the most attractive tint to the linen; but it must be used circumspectly because, if abused, the linen will be too blue and it will have to be soaped again, or even boiled and put through lye to lift the colour it has taken, just as you may have to wash the stains caused by some blue escaping from the envelope that wrapped it before being added to the water in which you wish to mix it. This envelope should be made from a closely woven piece of new fabric; a piece of flannel, doubled, serves even better. If you find yourself forced to use sub-standard blue, you must use more of it in the water. When the linen has been blued, i.e. plunged into the water in which you have dissolved the blue, you should wring it out carefully and spread it to dry somewhere shady, avoiding too great a heat. As soon as you have taken out the scrap of cloth containing the indigo, you should hang it up somewhere so it will not get dirty. Once all the blue in the envelope has been used, you replace it without changing the envelope.

It is most economical to buy blue in bulk, 250 grams each time; it will keep several years without change.

Starch. — It is a false economy to buy common-or-garden starch. Good starch, which is sold under the name Paris starch, is perfectly white; it costs 30 centimes per kilogram more than starch of an inferior quality, but there is so great a difference in the whiteness of the starched linen that you must not hesitate to buy the best.

4. — Matches.

I only comment on matches to offer some prudent advice.

Since the invention of matches that light by simply being rubbed,

1.   L.-E. Bergeron is listed in the catalogue of the Exposition Universelle in Paris in 1855 as trading from number 7 rue Sainte-Croix-de-la-Bretonnerie in chemicals, laundry blue, stationery and printing requirements.

accidents of the most diverse nature have multiplied to infinity. These may be complete conflagrations, or more limited fires – often of clothes or bedding – which have cost the lives of children, the old or the infirm. We have also seen the occasional case of poisoning due to ingestion of the flammable matter on matches.

I do not know how to recommend strongly enough that the mistress should *insist* that sulphur matches should be kept tightly enclosed in a tin box, and that this box has just one location, out of reach of children. She should ensure that it is not left about willy-nilly in the house and, above all, in the yard, the stables, the attics or barns. On a subject such as this, one can never be too severe.[1]

5. — Tallow candles.

Supply. — Candles are not the same quality all the year round; the moment of purchase is therefore germane. Generally, tallow is cheaper and better in the summer and autumn than the winter and spring; hence you should buy in the summer and autumn. If exposed to the air, it hardens and whitens as it ages, two qualities that contribute to it lasting longer and looking nicer. You cannot keep tallow longer than a year. It is most economical to buy it all at once.

Keeping. — The packets should be stacked in the storeroom. However, it is better to unpack them and put all the candles into a box specially for them. It is essential then to have a smaller box, with a sliding lid, for the candles needed for the day's use, because it is difficult not to supply the servants with a certain number. In this box, the tallow is protected from mice and other pests who love to eat it. It should be kept somewhere cool, especially in the summer, because heat softens the candles and they break easily.

Number six candles. — A candle called *six* to the half-kilogram, weighing therefore 80 grams, seems to me the best suited to everyday use. It burns for seven hours.

1. An excellent summary of matches and fire-lighting in the nineteenth century is available in Suzanne Tardieu's *La vie domestique dans le Mâconnais rural préindustriel* (1964). The first chemical matches were self-igniting, invented in France in 1805. The flame was achieved by dipping the tip in a small bottle of sulphuric acid. The first friction match was invented in England in 1826, but the modern phosphorus match was first developed in France by Charles Sauria in 1830.

Number eight candles. — The candle called *eight*, i.e. weighing 62 grams, has a wick as large as the sixes. As a result it burns much faster and melts more easily because the wick consumes the little tallow that surrounds it.

Improved candle. — The candle called *improved* is much preferable to the ordinary candle. Although more expensive, it is cheaper to run because it melts less.

How to insert a candle in a candlestick. — To insert a tallow or wax candle into a candlestick firmly, you cut a 5- or 6-centimetre disc or square of soft paper and place it on the candleholder and then press the paper and candle together into the holder. This simple method is much easier than wrapping a piece of paper of varying length around the candle itself. If one piece of paper is not enough, use two or three. By using alternate colours you will have yourself a pretty trimming at the bottom of the candle.

A burn-all. — You should have at least one candlestick with a holder called *burn-all* or *burn-end* [1] which has one, two or three spikes on which you can stick the little wax or tallow candle-ends when they are too short to work in a regular holder. You want to make sure that these ends are all used, and keep a little box for them. Those which can be burnt no more should be kept back and saved, because tallow is often useful around the house, particularly on a farm. These are doubtless small economies, but you cannot have too many of them in a country establishment. It is not uncommon to see people who have mocked cheeseparing economies themselves staring ruin in the face a few years down the road.

6. — Wax candles.

Stearin candles. — Candles give much less light than lamps; it is lighting most suitable for card tables, to carry from one place to another, etc. Since *stearin candles* have been invented, they have replaced tallow candles in even modest households, for these latter are dirtier, nearly as expensive, and have the great disadvantage of smelling unpleasant, smoking, and needing to be trimmed at any moment. [2]

---

1. In contemporary English usage these devices were called save-alls. They are made of porcelain, the same diameter as a candle, and fit snugly into a candle holder, thus lifting the end above the metal cup and allowing it to burn to the end of its wick.

2. The French for a candle snuffer, used here, was *mouchette*. In the twentieth century, the meaning of the term shifted to mean candle extinguisher. A snuffer originally trimmed the wick (i.e. removed the snuff), it did not necessarily put it out.

Wax candles. — A *wax* candle is much dearer than a stearin candle. It should be white, hard, shiny, and have a hollow sound when tapped. It should leave no stench of tallow on the fingers, even when rubbed. As wax yellows with age, it is best to buy them when you need them.

7. — Lamp oil.

The longer that lamp oil is stored, the better, because all the impurities sink to the bottom of the container. It is thus worth buying in a lot of it, which can be put in large stoneware crocks, well corked, or in a little barrel, or better still in tin drums which do not suffer from the leaks that arise from wooden barrels where the oil never delays soaking in and leaking out. Oil is better stored in the cellar than elsewhere because heat thickens it. If you don't buy a large amount, you can use purpose-made tin containers with a spout. An oil can is indispensable for the day-to-day maintenance of the lamps.

8. — Edible oils.

Olive oil. — Olive oil should be neutral in flavour. There are oils, however, that smell and taste of the fruit; some people prefer these, when the taste is pleasing and not acrid. It is very difficult to procure good olive oil from retailers; it is almost always adulterated. The best thing to do is to lay in a supply from the south of France that will last you the year. If you are not confident of the purity of the product, at least discover an owner who will send you oil he has harvested himself.

Adulterations. — The high price of olive oil excites the greed of the dealers. For a long time now, the north has exported poppy seed oil to the south, and this is much less expensive than olive oil. The adulteration is undertaken in the south, and the mixture is sent out to consumers, who are deceived by its origin into thinking it the genuine article.

A certain method of recognizing olive oil is to pour it quite quickly from one vessel to another. If it is olive oil thus decanted, it will not produce any foam or scum whereas all other oils froth and scum a great deal.

Storage. — You should keep olive oil in the cellar in glass bottles or glazed stoneware, filled to the brim. It is a fallacy that oil that freezes readily is good oil. This rapid freezing certainly indicates it is olive oil because olive oil congeals more quickly than any other; however, a poor-quality, even rancid oil freezes just as quickly.

Poppy seed oil, walnut oil, almond oil, etc. — Good, fresh poppy seed oil is very pleasant; and so is walnut oil and sweet almond oil, which are even better when they are cold-pressed. They are sometimes good enough to delude the most refined palate, but they become rancid very quickly and then lose almost all their qualities.

Keeping walnut oil. — Walnut oil can only be kept if it is well heated. To have it at its best, leave it to rest for a certain interval; it will throw a deposit which can be used in the farm kitchen and servants' hall.

Huile blanche or poppy seed oil — Poppy seed oil, called *huile blanche* [white oil] in commerce, while not replacement for olive oil, can be used in its stead when necessary. It costs much less. It does not taste unpleasant when freshly made, so is best purchased from a merchant with a large trade.

9. — Vinegar.

Wood vinegar. — Wood vinegar (pyroligneous acid) has none of the pleasing taste or aroma of wine vinegar and has the added drawback of being much more corrosive.

Making wine vinegar. — To be sure that you are not buying pyroligneous acid instead of wine vinegar, you can have a vinegar barrel[1] in your own home, especially if you are in wine country.

Vinegar barrel. — It is a barrel of about 30 litres' capacity which should be located in a loft and mounted on a frame so that you can draw off the vinegar easily. The tap should be wood; were it copper, it would soon be covered in verdures; were it lead, it would oxidize so much that it would be quickly unusable. Don't locate the tap at the bottom of the barrel, because there will be sediment there. The bung should not be too tight a fit. You keep the vinegar going with wines that have lost condition, the last bits of the barrels – which you strain through a woollen straining bag[2] before putting into the vinegar – and stale wines.

Vinegar mother. — To make vinegar you need first to put in a *vinegar mother* which will serve as a leaven. You make one thus: you begin by pouring into the barrel 1 litre of the best vinegar you can obtain, *boiling*;

---

1. In French, *vinaigrier*, i.e. a barrel in which you keep a vinegar mother and make your own vinegar.
2. This is the *chausson*, used in wine-making. A domestic equivalent, although not made from wool, would be a jelly bag.

you stop the barrel and shake it about in all directions so that the vinegar makes contact with every part of it. The next day, you should add the lees of a barrel of wine and 30 grams of powdered wine tartrate; it is simple to obtain this tartrate when you break up a *barrique* that has been used for a number of years. You leave this composition to ferment in the barrel, without stopping it. Eight or ten days later, you add some wine and after twenty days it will have turned to vinegar, which you can begin to consume. To keep it going, you only need to add wine to replace the vinegar you have drawn off.

You can also obtain a good mother by souring an open barrel of cider or red wine by leaving it in a warm place such as a loft, especially if the roof is tiled. You add wine to it once you are absolutely certain that the contents have completely soured; but you should only add the wine little by little, adding some strong vinegar at the same time.

A vinegar mother resembles soft skin without any hair [e.g. a chamois leather]. Sometimes it grows too large and the vinegar is affected. In that case, you break the barrel open, take out whichever part of the mother appears less healthy, leave the remainder and reseal the barrel, add some vinegar then, a fortnight later, some wine.

White vinegar. — If you wish the vinegar to be white, you use the lees and tartrate from a white wine.

Red vinegar. — If you put red wine on a white mother, the vinegar will be red. If you pour white wine onto a red mother, the vinegar will be a lighter colour than if you used red wine, but it will never be white.

White vinegar has a better, more pleasing taste than red. If you are only able to make red vinegar in your own home, then it should be left to the servants and the farm and you should buy good white vinegar for the family table.

How to flavour vinegar. — You can flavour vinegar in the following manner: in a crock of 10 litres, you add to the vinegar two cloves of garlic, six small onions, 60 grams of half-dried elderflower, half a handful of fragrant rose petals, half a handful of nasturtium flowers, two small branches of thyme, three bay leaves, two handfuls of young stalks of tarragon, fifty peppercorns, ten cloves and 60 grams of kitchen salt.

Cover the crock with a cloth and leave it somewhere exposed to the sun. Three weeks later, decant it; then you filter the vinegar through a glass or gutta-percha funnel fitted with a filter paper. This vinegar is excellent. Pour it into well-stoppered bottles.

Effect of boiling vinegar. — You can boil vinegar before adding aromatics. The boiling gives it greater strength. You leave it to rest, decant it or filter it, then add the herbs when it's cold. If the vinegar is less strong after you have added the herbs, you can, once you have taken them out, expose it to the sunlight again in a crock covered with a tile. But this exposure will lessen the finesse of the aroma.

Effect of freezing. — Freezing also has an excellent effect on vinegar. It makes it much stronger because it gets rid of some of its water. To achieve this result, you should expose the vinegar to the cold in a pottery vessel and you lift the ice that forms on its surface, so that you get rid of a tenth of its volume. It is simple to work out how much you have lifted by melting the ice and measuring the meltwater in a jug. In effect, it is only the water which freezes in the vinegar and which you remove. This is a much better procedure than boiling because you change nothing of the aroma the vinegar has inherited from the wine which was used to prepare it.

10. — Mustard.

To make good mustard, you ought to obtain good mustard seed free of all foreign bodies. If not well cleaned, then put it through a fine sieve, winnow it by pouring it from one bowl to another in some place exposed to a draught, even wash it and then dry it. After that, grind it in a marble mortar with a wooden pestle. Once it has been perfectly ground, sieve it so that you have only the finest particles. Generally, this powder is mixed with tarragon vinegar, to which you add a little salt and some good red wine – but that is not essential. A good mustard mixed with water tastes very strong and has a piquant aroma, even if less attractive than a mustard mixed with flavoured vinegar.

You can keep mustard a long time if it is potted up into containers that are well stopped. If you ignore this precaution, it will dry out, although it will not rot.

11. — Pasta, rice.

Pasta. — You should lay in vermicelli, semolina, macaroni and other pasta; but you should not buy in too much, because grubs attack all sorts of pasta and by the same token it takes on a dusty taste as it ages — very disagreeable. Italian pasta is best; there are warehouses in Paris. The granulated gluten of Poitiers[1] and the potato rice called *Touraine rice*[2] are excellent and very nourishing.

Rice. — Rice is harvested twice a year. As it is infinitely better when it is fresh, enough should only be purchased at one time to last six months. It should be transparent, unbroken, large, not smell dusty, with no trace of a musky smell which it often carries. Piedmont rice is easier to crush and swells more than Carolina rice, which is longer and generally better. Florida rice is very cheap. We will see, when we get to the relevant topics, that it can be used to advantage in soup or in bread, when bread-corn is expensive.

12. — Sugar.

Qualities of good sugar. — Good sugar should be bright, sound resonant when you tap it with your finger, break cleanly without crumbling, not make the water in which it is dissolved cloudy, and above all should dissolve completely therein; water should spread to all parts without any segment turning a flat white colour. It should have a clear taste, and smell of neither dust nor butter, which sometimes may happen.

Supply. — Sugar is a significant item of consumption in a household, especially since it reduced in price. Unless you are going to a refinery in the neighbourhood, there is no great saving in buying by the 100 kilograms as opposed to buying in loaves. The weight of the paper which grocers add to it when selling it retail is for them a significant margin; by buying it in loaves, the saving is in your favour; if you buy it wholesale by the 100 kilograms from a grocer, you will gain about 10 centimes the kilogram. The

1. Granulated gluten was developed by the firm of Veron, manufacturers of starch in Poitiers, in the first half of the nineteenth century. Having extracted and broken up the gluten, they mixed it with twice its weight of flour and then turned it into pellets of varying sizes which were dried. It could then be used, for example, as a soup pasta.
2. Touraine rice or potato rice was the product of a Madame Chauveau in Tours who developed and patented a process for making various forms of dried pasta using potato flour in the first decade of the nineteenth century. The potato was cooked, broken up, rebaked, then broken once more into varying sizes, to make a 'sago', semolina', 'rice', etc.

loaves called *four lumps* [1] which weigh approximately 7 or 8 kilograms, seem to me to be the best quality for tea, coffee and making sugared water.

Coarser sugar can be used for cooking, that which they call *cassonade* [Demerara] [2] or *lumps*:[3] these loaves weigh from 12 to 15 kilograms. There is not much difference in the price but *cassonade* sweetens more than white sugar and tempts the servants less; it gives dishes, particularly those made with milk, a slightly individual flavour which is not unpleasant.

Royal sugar.[4] — It is very hard and very handsome; you might use it when you have visitors to the house, but its hardness and the time it takes to dissolve doesn't make it entirely suitable for general use. However, if you want to make a syrup of absolute transparency, this is the sugar to use. It is slightly dearer than other sugars.

White cassonade. — White *cassonade* is not as good as refined sugar or even raw sugar, because generally it is made up of *fallen* [5] sugar, that is to say sugars which have not crystallized satisfactorily or which have gone stale in the warehouse, and therefore, in consequence, do not have the properties of good sugar.

Storage. — To keep sugar, it must be well wrapped and put somewhere utterly proof from the damp and free of any strange smells, for those it will quickly absorb. For everyday use, it is easier to break up the sugar in advance than to break it as and when required. You would be well advised to have a light box with a cover in which you can put a certain amount of broken sugar. Sugar will keep in perfect condition for a year. After than, it can *fall* [out of condition] [6] and lose many of its qualities.

How to break up sugar. — To break up a sugar loaf you need a thick-bladed knife specifically for this purpose, and a wooden mallet.

Pulverizing sugar and grating it. — To reduce sugar to a powder you

1. The French is *quatres cassons*; *casson* is a large lump of sugar.
2. *Cassonade* is not much different from loaf sugar save that it has not been so refined and purified by the clay treatment. It might resemble golden caster sugar in some modern parlance. Such sugars could be further purified and fined at home.
3. This English term was adopted by the French, as here, to indicate a sugar of inferior quality.
4. Royal sugar – *sucre royal* – was more refined and ground more finely than normal loaf sugar.
5. Cf. the use of *tomber* (fall) in the next paragraph.
6. The French is simply *tomber*.

can pound it or grate it. It is quickest to pound it in a marble mortar with a wooden pestle, but it does take on a particular, not very pleasant taste, which will be detectable in water but in no other mixtures.[1]

13. — Coffee.

One of the essential conditions for coffee to be good is that it be old. When new, it is acrid and over-stimulating; as it ages, it loses these defects, and in this respect can be compared to wine. The inexperienced give their preference to green beans of rounded shape; good coffees, by contrast, should have a flat bean, yellow, and often broken. Mocha coffee is the best of all. It is rarely found, even in the largest groceries. But you will find there good, old Bourbon coffee that has nearly the same aroma as mocha.[2] Martinique coffee is stronger and more stimulating than either of these varieties; and it too needs to be aged before it achieves its full aroma.

You should therefore lay in ample supplies of coffee, shut it up in a dry place and let it mature. It is good to make a blend of half mocha or Bourbon coffee and half from Martinique or Haiti.

So that the coffee should be pleasant, it should be somewhat burnt: it should not be black, but reddish-brown.[3] Once it has been roasted, shut it up carefully in a well-sealed glass container and only grind as much as you need at the moment you are to drink it.

You should not store it in a box that carries the slightest smell, or next to anything which smells at all strongly. It will take on this smell quite quickly, which will detract greatly from its quality.

There are nowadays merchants that undertake nothing but the coffee business. They have machines for roasting it that conserve the aroma far better than the devices employed by inexperienced cooks. I have had coffee which is sold in tin boxes at Plaisance at 53 rue Constantine in Paris.[4]

1. See the long note about pounded or grated sugar on page 452, below, in the chapter on hors-d'oeuvre.
2. Mocha coffee originated in the Yemen; Bourbon coffee came from the island of Réunion in the Indian Ocean where it was first planted by the French in the early eighteenth century, it eventually spread to Brazil and El Salvador in Latin America.
3. In French, *roux*.
4. Plaisance is a district in the 14th arrondissement of Paris; rue Constantine is now called rue Vercingetorix. The coffee to which she refers is described in more detail on page 640, below.

This coffee is excellent and costs no more than the coffee that is roasted by householders themselves. But with reason, gourmets prefer coffee that is roasted and ground the moment they wish to drink it over any that is ground in advance.

14. — Tea.

It is uncommon to find good tea in grocery shops; now that its consumption has spread all through France, every large town has a specialist shop selling tea. You would be wise to take your supplies from one of these; otherwise you risk buying a substance which shares but its name with the genuine article.

Green tea, which is almost the only variety that you find everywhere, is the less healthy and the less good. It has little flavour and is very stimulating. Black tea, by contrast, is gentle and flavorous. To make a truly pleasant tea, you should make a blend which, if properly composed, offers great quality. I describe in the *Kitchen Manual* (below) how to achieve this.

You can keep tea for a very long time provided it is in a firmly closed container in a dry place. If you do not have a tea caddy, put it in a glass jar with a tight cork. You should ensure that it is kept away from any strong smells.

15. — Chocolate.

It is almost impossible to find good, properly made chocolate at less than 4 francs the kilogram. To have something of guaranteed quality, you will have to pay 5 or 6 francs and buy it from a house in which you have confidence, such as Devinck,[1] Peron, or Marquis[2] in Paris. All chocolate sold at lower prices than these is adulterated, or else the cocoa used in its manufacture is of poor quality. The things that are added to cocoa to bring down the price of chocolate are not harmful in themselves; they only detract from the taste. Chocolate soon loses its quality; the oils go rancid, the flavour vanishes. You should not store it for longer than a year.

1. François Jules Devinck (1802–1878) was a successful chocolate-maker whose posters and ephemera can still be bought today. In 1831, he patented an apparatus for roasting coffee and cocoa by steam.
2. The house of François Marquis was founded in 1818 at the passage des Panoramas in Paris. It sold chocolate and confectionery, tea and coffee. The original premises are now occupied by the restaurant L'Arbre à Cannelle.

Spanish chocolate, like chocolate from Bayonne, is much less worked and less sweet than Paris chocolate. It is not so good for creams, but is nicer to eat on its own. When chocolate is cooked with water or milk it should have globules all over its surface like the globules of fat on a stock.

SECTION II. — VINEGAR PICKLES.
1. — Gherkins.

Gherkins pickled in vinegar are a very pleasing and inexpensive hors-d'oeuvre. You can also pickle the tender young sprouts of various plants and young fruits in vinegar; they lose their own taste and take on that of the vinegar and whatever flavourings you introduce.

Gherkins are young cucumbers; all cucumbers can provide gherkins, the Dutch yellow[1] and the snake cucumber[2] are the two varieties usually preferred. You should choose those which are nicely shaped, about as long as your little finger and properly green. You should take off the stalk, and rub them with a coarse cloth to remove the small surface nodules which cover them. You may prepare gherkins in two ways.

First method. — You put cold vinegar into a well-scoured, pure copper[3] cauldron that is not tinned on the inside: this is the *essential precondition* to obtaining green gherkins. Salt the vinegar and throw in the gherkins with some whole peppercorns, cloves, thyme, bay leaves, green chillies, peeled small onions and two or three cloves of garlic. In a word, the seasoning should be of the strongest. Liven up the fire to get it boiling quickly and vigorously. You need to stir the gherkins around so they cook evenly and remain as green as possible. They should be well covered by the vinegar. To begin they will turn yellow, but soon after they turn green again. Once they have taken an attractive green hue, take them off the fire and pour them into a pottery or china bowl to cool. Then put them into glass or stoneware jars suitable for the job and layer them with young sprigs of tarragon or samphire, a few nasturtium flowers and even a few rose petals. It is best to replace the hot vinegar with cold before you add the aromatics. The vinegar used in the cooking can be consumed by the servants, who will find it

---

1.   Dutch yellow cucumber is a true cucumber, called in Holland 'the ancient race'.
2.   Snake cucumber is the Armenian cucumber, *Cucumis melo.*
3.   The French is *cuivre rouge* which is a term sometimes used to distinguish it from *cuivre jaune*, an alloy of copper and zinc.

excellent because it is more acid. You can also use it for scouring copper. In general, people are not generous enough with the vinegar when preparing gherkins and this detracts from their success.

Second method. — Put the gherkins you want to pickle into a large bowl. Pour on boiling vinegar and leave the bowl covered. Leave them in this infusion for twenty-four hours, when they will turn yellow. Then you put everything into an untinned copper pan and add pepper, thyme, bay, cloves, chillies, onions, etc. Get the fire going; when the vinegar is at the rolling boil, stir the pan. Soon the gherkins will turn green. Take them off the fire and put them in cold vinegar with the aromatics described for the first method, above: tarragon, samphire, etc. You can, for economy's sake, omit the change of vinegars; but the gherkins will not be as green.

Eight days after the gherkins have been prepared by either of these methods, they are ready for consumption.

2. — Pickled corn cobs.

When the ears of maize have begun to develop and they are no bigger than your little finger once stripped of their husks, you pick off those nearest the bottom of the plant, which will not achieve full maturity. You can also harvest those cobs which are growing on maize destined for animal fodder. Take off the leaves and the silk which envelope them; peel the small stalk; add a certain quantity of small onions and one or two cloves of garlic, according to how much corn you have. Put some vinegar in a tinned copper pan, not an earthenware pot which will give the corn a dirty white colour. Put the pan on a clear, hot fire; when the vinegar is boiling, salt it and add the same ingredients as for gherkins. Then add the corn and pour the whole into an unglazed pottery terrine to let cool. Afterwards you put the corn in jars, adding tarragon, samphire and rose petals. Ears of maize prepared like this are an hors-d'oeuvre as attractive to eat as to look at.

If there are not enough cobs, you can choose the tenderest parts of the husks, cut them in strips of $0^m,05$ and add them to the corn you have. They are both pleasing and tender and give the corn a look that is at once bizarre and graceful.

3. — Pickled cabbage.

In the wintertime, if you have no gherkins, you can replace them with pickled cabbage. Choose a handsome white cabbage, tender and fresh; cut it into quarters; take out the heart and the largest ribs; then throw it into boiling water and leave it for a few seconds, and separate out the leaves one from the other. Put to boil with the vinegar some salt and pepper, a few small onions, cloves, a clove of garlic and if possible some tarragon. When the vinegar is boiling, add the cabbage leaves, leave them a few minutes then take them off the heat and put them in the pots in which you are going to store them.

4. — Pickled French beans.

Put some tender and nicely green beans in a terrine, pour on some well-salted boiling water, and cover. Flavour the vinegar as if you were pickling gherkins and then add the beans. You may add some small onions.

5.— Pickled onions.

Very small onions, nicely peeled, which are given a short simmer in a well-flavoured vinegar, are as good as might be imagined in place of gherkins.

6. — Pickled nasturtiums.

The seed pods of nasturtiums prepared as if they were capers can replace the real thing. If the vinegar in which they are pickled is well flavoured, they are almost as good.

Put some good white vinegar into a jar. Add some young sprigs of tarragon, samphire, elderflower, cloves, peppercorns, salt and a little garlic. Every couple of days go and look at the nasturtiums. When they are in flower, harvest the seed pods that have scarcely formed and add them to the jar, which you take care to seal well and leave exposed to the sun.

7. — Piccalilli.[1]

Infuse 15 grams of turmeric[2] for three days in three litres of good white wine vinegar; add a handful of young tarragon sprigs; strain through a sieve and pour into a stoneware jar; add three cloves of garlic, and a score

1.   The word used here is *aschard* which was a generic term for anything pickled. See the note on page 655 below on its use in Mme Millet-Robinet's menus.
2.   The words used are *curcuma ou safran des Indes*. Turmeric is *Curcuma longa*.

of peeled small onions, 50 grams of red chillies, 2 soup spoons of fine salt, fifteen cloves and leave to infuse for three weeks. Prepare a head of cauliflower and cut it into little branches, cut the heads off a bunch of asparagus, extract the heart from a Savoy cabbage and slice it up, some French beans, some unripe cherries, some little carrots, some unripe gooseberries, etc.; put all these fruits and vegetables into salted boiling water. Take them off the fire after the water has bubbled up twice. Drain them and put them into the vinegar you have already flavoured. When the maize has grown enough, take some very small ears, remove their wrappings, take the tenderest part of these leaves and also mix in some young French beans. Blanch these like the other vegetables and add them to the first pickle you made. You can start eating this two months later; it will keep easily for a year with no loss of quality.

SECTION III. — CONSERVES OF FRESH VEGETABLES.
1. — The Masson method.

Some years since, Messrs Chollet and Morel-Fatio have managed, by following a procedure invented by M. Masson,[1] to compress and dehydrate vegetables into very small blocks, each containing the wherewithal to prepare a platter of vegetables for several persons. These preparations are very well executed, very convenient, and of so low a price that today it is quite possible for even the most modest of households to eat vegetables the whole year round.

2. — The Appert method.

By taking advantage of the Appert method,[2] you can preserve several sorts of vegetables for winter consumption that taste little different from when they were harvested. Young peas are the easiest of vegetables to preserve in this manner. You pod them the very moment you wish to prepare them; you put them into a litre jar with 75 grams of ground sugar, and you cook them in a bain-marie for at least an hour. When you open the jar for use, they sometimes give off a slightly displeasing smell; so you

---

1. Masson was gardener to the Horticultural Society of Paris and developed and patented a method of drying and preserving fresh vegetables in the 1840s. His patent was bought and then developed industrially by the firm headed by Chollet.
2. Nicolas Appert (1749–1841), the pioneer of bottling and canning.

wash them two or three times in cold water, then you season them with fresh butter (see the *Kitchen Manual*, below). Some people preserve them without sugar; others, by contrast, season them exactly as they would were they going to eat them, and then bottle them. It is then sufficient only to boil them for ten or fifteen minutes before eating them. I think this last method preferable; it is the method adopted for conserves for the navy.

You can treat little broad beans,[1] asparagus tips and French beans in the same way. You don't add sugar to French beans; it is better to cook them and season them before bottling.

You should avoid overfilling the jars because they may burst while they are being boiled.

These preserves are certainly good as long as they are properly sealed, so as not to deteriorate; the essential precondition of their conservation is their being *deprived of all contact with the air*. But because one is accustomed in the country to enjoy nature's bounty without gluts, to wait for each crop to mature in its own time, I consider that one should limit the supply of preserved food to a small number of vegetables.

3. — Tomatoes.

Tomato sauce is a great standby for a household; you should lay in a generous supply; whatever you do, this sauce when bottled is never so good as when it is made with fresh tomatoes.

Towards August, when the tomatoes are at their most abundant, you pick a quantity. Wipe them carefully, pick off the stalks and break them into several pieces. Then put them in a large pan on a bright fire. Stir them to begin with, so that they do not burn before they have softened; leave them on the heat until they are sufficiently cooked to be easily crushed; then, to separate out the skins and the pips, pass the juice and the pulp through a horsehair sieve, helping it through with a sieving mushroom.[2] Fill up half-bottles, or whole bottles if the family is large enough to get through a whole bottle at one meal – because these preserves lose condition quickly in an opened bottle. When bottling, you should be sure to stir the

1.   The French is *fèves de marais*.
2.   In French, *pilon à purée*, which may now be understood as a *champignon à passer* or sieving mushroom. Today, a *pilon à purée* is a potato masher. A *pilon à passoire* is illustrated on p. 186, above.

sauce at the bottom of the pan, as the pulp will settle and it needs to be distributed evenly through all the bottles. Proceed thereafter as for currant juice, i.e. cork it, tie it down, then cook it in the bain-marie and seal it.

You use this bottled sauce as you would use fresh tomatoes. It can be heated up as and when needed.

This way of preserving tomatoes is infinitely preferable to the one which consists of cooking them for a very long time to make a sort of paste by evaporating all their liquid content.

4. — Sauerkraut.

A supply of sauerkraut is very useful for a small household. In those regions not accustomed to this excellent foodstuff, the servants may at first make something of a fuss about eating it, but they will soon be reconciled for it is both tasty and good for you, and they will take to it the faster if they see their masters eating it too. Sauerkraut is much more digestible than cabbage that has not been treated in this manner thanks to the preliminary fermentation that it undergoes. Furthermore, it is simple to prepare, costs very little, and keeps a long time.

The mistress should have a mind in spring to sow the right sort of cabbage to make sauerkraut. This is any hearted cabbage with uncrinkled leaves, but above all the white cabbage of Nantes and the quintal d'Alsace are the ones to choose.

Find yourself a small and straight barrel, one with iron bands is better. Close it at one end only and provide yourself with a lid (with a wooden handle) that fits inside the barrel. If the barrel is oak, which is better, and the wood is new, you should take care to fill it with water some time in advance and leave it for at least a fortnight. The water will take out any colour in the wood that might stain the cabbage. You should drain and replace the water until it runs clear.

In those districts where sauerkraut is most popular, everyone has a tool for cutting up cabbages in his house. This item may cost 20 to 25 francs; it is very similar to that used by coopers to shape their barrel staves which is called a jointer; the difference is that it has several blades, whereas the jointer has but one. Using this tool is far preferable to any other method of slicing cabbages for sauerkraut. However, households which don't make a great deal of sauerkraut may well not have one of these; they may use instead a well-sharpened chaff cutter or a long, thin and very sharp knife. The cabbages will be sliced less evenly than with the instrument I have mentioned, and the slices will be thicker, but in spite of that the sauerkraut can still be excellent.[1]

Cabbages intended for sauerkraut should be picked and brought to the house in times of fine weather. Clean each cabbage and take off the green leaves as well as any that may not be perfectly white but can serve some other purpose. While one person prepares the heads of cabbage, another slices them. If provided with the tool I have described, he first cuts the head into two halves; then he takes one half and draws it down the tool, just the same way as coopers do their staves. The cut cabbage falls onto a cloth placed to receive it. From time to time, the blades are cleared, as the cabbage shavings often obstruct them. If you are using a knife, then you place the two halves of cabbage on a clean table and cut them into very thin slices.

Once a certain amount of cabbage has been sliced, you should put a little layer of salt about 5 millimetres deep at the bottom of the barrel; then you put in a layer of cabbage, scattering some peppercorns, juniper berries and bay leaves. This layer can be 10 millimetres deep. Using a pusher in the form of a flat-bottomed club, you compact the cabbage, without hitting it, so as to reduce the thickness by about half, without however crushing the cabbage. Add another layer of salt, but much less than the first; then some more cabbage seasoned as I have described; press again, and continue in like manner until the barrel is three-quarters full. In a 120-litre barrel, you should be adding about 2 kilograms and 500 grams of salt, 125 grams of peppercorns, at least as many juniper berries, and thirty bay leaves. Then you put the barrel in the cellar or somewhere cool. To finish the job, you cut out a circle, a little larger than the barrel, of new, clean coarse cloth; you place it on the cabbage, which should have a small top layer of salt; and you put the lid on the cloth. Then you weigh it down with 40 or 50 kilograms of well-washed stones.

---

1.   The French for this specialized instrument is *colombe*, a word also used by anglophone coopers. A jointer 'is a long plane, held fast, which does not move, and with the cutting blade uppermost, over which the stave moves.' In culinary terms it might be a reversed mandoline standing on legs.

In a short while, fermentation gets under way, water comes out, the lid sinks down. Some of the water should be removed, although not so much as to leave the lid dry. After one month of fermentation, you may start to eat the sauerkraut, although it will not, as a general rule, arrive at perfection for two months.

When you wish to take out some sauerkraut to cook, you lift off the stones and the lid and any surplus water; once you have removed what you want, you rinse the cloth and lid, then replace them as before. Then you add enough cold water to come over the top of the lid, which you load up with stones again. These attentions *are indispensable* each time you extract some sauerkraut.

You should not be alarmed by the unpleasant smell that emanates from the sauerkraut when you take the lid off the barrel and stir it about. This odour is the result of fermentation; it will disappear when you come to wash the sauerkraut before you cook it. (See the *Kitchen Manual*.)

5. — Cooked sorrel.

You can preserve cooked sorrel without it losing its properties; you prepare it from the end of September to the end of October. You will have had the foresight to cut back the sorrel plants in August so that you use only young leaves, and you don't wait for the frosts before preparing them. Cut an ample supply at a time, pick it over carefully and take off the stalks and the ribs; wash it and throw it in a large pan of boiling water. It must cook in plenty of water. When it has boiled a little, take it off the heat and drain it; then put it back on the heat in a tinned copper cauldron or a saucepan – depending on the quantity you are dealing with – and finish cooking by stirring it often, so that it does not stick to the bottom of the pan, until it becomes a purée. Once it arrives at a certain consistency, like a thick porridge, put it into stoneware pots and leave it to cool. Then cover it with a certain amount of melted butter, which you pour over the pots while still hot so as to exclude the air completely. You can replace the melted butter with olive oil, something I think preferable. You should watch against keeping cooked sorrel in glazed pottery vessels as the acid in the sorrel will attack the enamel, which almost always contains lead oxide, and degrade it. This oxide, even in small doses, will result in certain poisoning.

When you want to take some sorrel from the pots, lift off the butter or oil, take the sorrel, level the surface with care, and replace the melted butter or oil. It is wise to make up small pots because once a pot is broached it is very difficult to exclude the air completely and the air will make it go mouldy at the drop of a hat.

6. — Burnt onions, onion balls, caramel to colour sauces and stock.

Burnt onions. — Burn only large and fine onions, the larger the better. Remove those layers of skin which come away easily, but not those which seem attached to the flesh. Immediately after the bread has come out of the oven, put in the onions you have prepared, on a dish; after quarter or half an hour, depending on the heat of the oven, take the onions out, turn them over, and put them back in; the next day, heat the oven again, but not as much as you would for bread, and put in the onions on a wicker fruit tray,[1] after you have pressed them flat. You should watch that they do not burn, which may be a problem if the first baking dried them out too much. The contrary is sometimes the case, and they will have given out a bit of juice on the dish while cooking. Dip them in this before putting them on the wicker tray. After an hour, turn them over and leave them in the oven until the next day. If they have not darkened, you can put them back in the oven for a third time; but it is not essential that they should be as black as commercial onions to do the job of colouring a stock nicely and be at the same time appetizing.

Onion balls. — You can buy onion balls, either in tins or in small bottles.[2] Half a ball suffices for a normal *pot-au-feu*. You will learn by practice how much is needed to colour a stock.

Caramel. — To make caramel, you should plunge four or five large pieces of sugar into cold water, then take them out immediately and put them in a small saucepan where they will dissolve without exposure to a

1. The French is *claie* and may denote a flat wicker hurdle on which you lay out fruit – grapes, plums, etc. – to dry.
2. *Boules d'oignons* were also called *boules colorantes* and were compressed, caramelized onions. As with each of the three items in this section, their use was to give colour to a stock. Jules Gouffé, in his *Livre de cuisine* (1867) advocated using only caramel for this purpose. He wrote, 'burnt onions, burnt carrots, *les boules colorantes* and other ingredients can only give a sour flavour to the stock.'

very high heat. As soon as they form a dark caramel, without being black – you must watch the cooking very carefully – be ready to pour in some hot water before the caramel burns, i.e. blackens and becomes bitter, something which will happen quite suddenly unless you take this precaution. Let it boil until all the caramel has melted and it looks like a syrup. Let it cool down somewhat and then pour it into a small bottle, which you leave uncorked until it has cooled completely. A few drops are enough to colour a sauce; a spoonful is enough for a *pot-au-feu* of 2 kilograms of meat. This caramel doesn't cost any more than onion balls and is just as convenient. You can keep it for a fortnight in the winter.

SECTION IV. — DRIED VEGETABLES.
1. — Peas, lentils, beans.

Peas. — Split green peas will keep for a whole year; you should not buy them until the month of December. If you wish to be sure that you are buying this year's harvest, they should be very green, not broken at all, and well podded. Most other varieties of peas are yellow when dried and cook poorly; they are hardly good enough for anything except stock.

Beans.[1] — Beans should be plump, shining, a nice white, black or red, etc., whichever colour is that of their variety, but without yellowish or blackish marks; these marks indicate the start of a deterioration which will impart a most unpleasant flavour. If they have been damaged by maggots, which happens to a lot of beans when they are still fresh, they are still good to eat, but they will not be any good as seed stock. This year's beans are always preferable to two-year-old ones. Before you buy them in, if you are not harvesting your own, it is best to try them, that is, to cook a few to make sure they don't have tough skins and that they cook well; for beans are harder or softer depending on where they are grown. White varieties are to be preferred over red for large-scale purchases. After a year, all white beans change their colour; you can always recognize old white beans mixed with those from this year's harvest; it is more difficult to recognize this difference in red beans because their colour does not change as they age.

Lentils. — Lentils should be plump and a good colour; they sometimes have little green veins which mar their appearance but do not affect their quality. There are several varieties, larger or smaller; I do not find much

1.   In French, *haricots*.

difference in their flavour. In the south, they harvest a variety that is a marbled dark green which is very delicate.

2. — Artichoke bottoms.

Drying in the open air. — Dried artichoke bottoms are a useful resource for winter cookery; they are excellent in all ragouts, above all in fricassees. When you wish to preserve artichoke bottoms, you gather in the artichokes and split them into four. Cut the leaves flush with the bottom and take out the choke; then put the bottoms into water acidulated with a little vinegar. Heat some river or spring water in a pot or copper pan, because iron will blacken the artichokes. When the water boils, throw in the artichokes, and blanch them; then take them out of the water and place them on a sieve or a wicker fruit tray to drain and cool. Once well drained, thread them with a bodkin and make strings to hang up somewhere dry and airy, away from the sun. The string should be almost stretched tight so that the bottoms do not slip down together, which will hinder their drying; you must in fact arrange them so that they do not touch and the air can circulate between them. They dry quite quickly and they can be kept quite easily if you place them somewhere dry. When you want to eat them, all you need do is put them to cook in the ragout for which they are intended.

Drying in the oven. — You can also dry artichoke bottoms in the oven. This method is preferable when the weather is wet, air-drying will be very slow and they may go mouldy. But the oven should only be moderately warmed, otherwise they become tough and inedible.

3. — French beans, broad beans.

French beans. — You can prepare these like the artichokes; choose very young and tender ones, but they do take on a slight taste of hay, which is not disagreeable, no matter what you do. You need not thread the beans, but spread them out on wicker fruit trays of very open construction, or on frame sieves arranged so that the circulation of the air is not impeded. I think it better to dry them in the oven.

In Belgium, they dry young peas and small broad beans, even parsley, by the same method; but I do not think it answers for these vegetables as well as for French beans and artichokes. I have not done it myself, I prefer to preserve vegetables by the Masson method.

Broad beans. — Large broad beans can be successfully preserved. You skin them when raw and split them in two; you then dry them. They cook perfectly well and are excellent, especially as a purée.

SECTION V. — FLOURS AND CEREALS.
1. — Maize flour or *Gaudes.*

Harvest the maize when it is almost ripe but not yet quite dry. Strip the cobs of their husks, then put them in the oven after the bread has been taken out. This will give them an excellent flavour: the oven should be hot enough to turn the cobs a light brown. You strip the grains off as you take them out of the oven by rubbing them against a pan handle (the person shelling the grains holds the pan between his knees while seated). If there is trouble getting the first grains to come away, the sheller can pass a small pointed stick between the first two rows. Once the first row is off, the cob will be easily stripped. In those districts where maize is part of their everyday diet, they shell the ears by rubbing them across the blunted blade of a scythe or old sabre mounted across an open barrel. Once the ears are all shelled, put the grain back in the oven, which should be cooler than it was the first time. A few hours later the grain is riddled or, better, is put through a winnowing machine to separate the skins which come off at the foot of the kernel. Then it is sent to the mill. Maize flour is bolted in the same way as ordinary flour. Too much maize should not be ground at a time; the flour spoils very easily.

The bran, which retains a lot of flour, is good for livestock. The middlings make an excellent sort of semolina. Flour prepared in this manner is far better than from ears of corn that have dried on the plant, and which are not passed through the oven. Properly prepared maize flour is eaten as a pottage, either with a meat stock or vegetable-based;[1] these are the pottages that are called *gaudes* in several departments in the east;[2] various cakes are also made with it. This flour is not suitable for making bread.

---

1. i.e. *gras ou maigre*, the constant culinary distinction between dishes suitable for eating on fast-days or days of abstinence and those with animal products that might be eaten on all other days, as prescribed by the Catholic Church.
2. *Gaudes* is described by *Larousse gastronomique* as a *bouillie* (i.e. a thickish porridge, which is why I have translated Mme Millet-Robinet's *potage* as pottage rather than soup which we tend to reckon to be liquid).

2. — Buckwheat flour.

When the buckwheat is reaped, it is stood in little stooks. If it is left on the ground, the lightest rainfall will make the grain sprout. Once it is dry enough, it is threshed, either with a flail or in the threshing machine, and then it is passed through the winnowing machine. The grain must not be heaped up until it is very dry, and you must have a care to stir it often otherwise it heats up and takes on a mouldy smell. Very little should be ground at once as the flour loses its quality as it ages.

SECTION VI. — DRIED FRUITS.

When the weather is suitable, you should dry certain fruits – at least those which will keep when dried. The costs of doing this are virtually nothing in a household and such a supply is very useful come the winter. In good years, most of the fruit will be lost if it is not dried. If only a little extra work is needed to secure her family something nice to eat, the good housewife will not hesitate.

1. — Pears, flattened and dried.

Flattened pears[1] are excellent as dessert; they can be eaten dry or in a compote.

You can prepare almost every good variety of pear in this fashion, so long as they are not acid. As the pears will lose a great deal of volume in the drying, they do not usually bother with the smaller sorts. The Doyenné, all the Beurrés, the Martin-sec, the Rousselet, the Messire-Jean, in fact all the autumn pears, are suitable for drying. I do not even exclude the woolly varieties, when sweet. Drying does not cause them to lose their qualities.

When the pears are ripe, peel them, but leave their stalk. Put them as tightly as possible into an earthenware pot. Fill it with water, cover it and put it before a bright fire. Once the pears are nicely cooked, which may take a certain time for even the most tender varieties need quite long to cook, remove them one by one from the pot and place them side by side

---

1. In French *poires tapées*. The process, described in the text, takes its name from the flattening of the drying fruit (from *taper*, to strike). Apples can be processed in the same manner. The method is a speciality of the Indre-et-Loire department. In England, the dried Norfolk Biffin is an apple treated in very similar fashion, although its skin is left on.

on a wicker fruit tray. If you have more pears than the pot could hold, put them into the same pot and juice that you have just cooked the first ones. Add water to cover. Once these are cooked, join them to the others. You can continue thus until you have done all your pears: the more that are cooked in the same liquor, the sweeter they will be because the last ones absorb all the sugar left in the liquor by the earlier batches. The wicker fruit trays laden with pears (I will describe these trays in more detail in the article *Prunes*, below) are put in the oven after the bread has been baked. The next day you take the trays out of the oven and reheat it (but only to the temperature it would be after baking the bread). Then you take the pears one by one and flatten them between the fingers and dip them into the liquor you have reserved – which you have previously made into a syrup by boiling it down – and then put them back onto the trays and into the oven until the next day. When your pears are small ones, after two goes in the oven on the trays, they are sometimes dry enough – something you will recognize from their being firm but not hard. But often you will have to put them back in the oven for a third time. Have a care not to overheat the oven the third time because the pears burn easily, or will dry out too much, which will deprive them of much of their quality. A slight warmth suffices.

The final time you put the pears in the oven, it is wise to look at them closely after they have been there a certain time because they can dry out too much. If the pears seem too dry at the very moment of taking them out of the oven for the last time, it is nothing to worry about, because given time they will soften. When they are cold and dry, arrange them in boxes lined with white paper and put them somewhere dry.

When you have a large number of pears to preserve you may, without any problem, wait six or eight days to prepare those which were first put into the oven, and not worry about them again until you have a decent quantity to dip into the liquor you have reduced to a syrup.

The nice flattened pears available commercially are prepared in a slightly different manner. They are not peeled at the start of the process;[1] the peeled pears are cooked *without water* in shallow round dishes where they are arranged in concentric circles of diminishing size in a way that gives each plate the look of a cone, with a single pear to finish it off. The peel is spread

1. The rest of her account would not appear to support this statement.

out over this cone; the small amount of juice that is expressed during the cooking gives the pears a pleasing flavour. The oven must only be heated to a moderate extent for the cooking and desiccation of flattened pears, and they should be returned to the oven as often as judged necessary. The rest of the operation proceeds as I have already described.

You can also dry whole, unpeeled pears in the oven if they are small ones. When you have taken the bread out of the oven and it remains hot, charge it with half a load of wood. Once it has burnt down, take out the embers and charge the oven with wicker trays loaded with pears. Close tightly all the vents and doors so that no heat is lost.

This first bake will half-cook the pears. After that you proceed as I will describe for prunes; the pears must be cooked for some time.

Pears preserved in this fashion will keep for a long time, they are excellent in compotes.

2. — Prunes.

Choice of plums. — Not all varieties of plums are suitable for making good prunes, even though you can dry any of them. Greengages, for instance, which are the best eaten raw, are dry and sour as prunes because they are too juicy. Plums which have the least juice, whose flesh is denser, and which seem characterless to eat, are the best for making into prunes: Agen plums or Robe de Sergent, and St Catherine damsons or plums, are the best varieties of plums for prunes.

Gathering. — You should not pick plums to make prunes. Rather, you should lightly shake the tree's branches and gather any fruit which falls, having a care to put to one side the maggoty or green ones – these will make very poor prunes.

Drying. — Then arrange the plums in a single layer on wicker fruit trays. Put the trays into the oven after you have baked the bread, and leave them until the following day. Then take them out. You should turn the plums over and push them closer together as they take up much less room than the day before, because the heat of the oven has caused them to lose some of the liquid they contain: for example, from three trays, you can now fill two. You put fresh plums onto any trays you have freed up. You reheat the oven to the temperature it would have had when taking out the bread and you replace the trays in the oven.

If two bakes do not suffice, you do them a third time. But take care that the oven is not too hot because the half-dried plums burn easily.

Dried prunes should be neither too hard nor too soft; if you find a softness around the stone when you open them, it may indicate that the prunes will not keep a long time. If they seem a bit hard when they come out of the oven, they will soon soften. When they have dried to your satisfaction, arrange them in a box which you put somewhere dry.

Wicker fruit trays. — The best trays to dry fruits on are those which we call *roundels*.[1] These trays are made with thick withies, with their bark still on, and measure about 70 or 80 centimetres in diameter, with a slightly raised edge. First off, you place one tray at the back of the oven. The second encroaches slightly on the border of the first, the third on the second, and so on until the whole sole of the oven is covered.

Stuffed prunes. — When you wish to have very good prunes indeed to eat as they are at dessert, after the first or second bake – according to whether the prunes are more or less dry, but while they are still soft – you should split them down the length of one side, open them and remove the stone. In its place you put a smaller prune, also stoned. Close the prune back up and return it to the oven. When the prunes are completely dry, you will be unable to discern the slit. These we call *stuffed prunes*.

3. — Dried cherries.

Cherries dried in the oven delight children; they taste pleasingly sharp when they are cooked in a compote like prunes with a little sugar.

Sour cherries with a firm flesh, like morellos and all Dutch and English varieties, are the only ones suitable for drying; the largest are the best. It is not necessary to gather them into bunches before putting them in the oven. Treat them as prunes except that, as they are small fruits, it will be enough to put them in the oven twice; and the second time, the oven should be very cool. You can even limit yourself to a single visit to the oven and finish them in the sun; they will only be better.

It is not obligatory that dried cherries should be very firm to be kept a long time; all that they require is to be put in a dry place.

---

1.   In French, *rondelles*.

4. — Dried grapes.

You can dry grapes in the oven in the same way, but they are not as good to eat as cherries. With the climate of Paris and central France, you cannot expect to get raisins such as come to us from Spain, Italy and Greece; it needs the fine weather of those countries to produce their excellent raisins, and their burning sun to dry them. The grape used to produce wine is not suitable for turning into good raisins; it is too juicy. However, our best grape, well ripened, may still be nice enough when dried in the oven; children like it a lot. In any event, you should dry those varieties with the least juice; others will shrink to skins adhering to pips; they are not edible.

5. — Dried apples.

Of all fruits, apples are the least suited to drying in hot air. You can, however, dry them whole, treating them like flattened pears; all you need do is peel them and put them in the oven two hours after you have taken out the bread. You get them to dry like pears, but they don't give off any juice so you cannot moisten them before putting them in the oven the second time. These dried apples may be a little hard but have a pleasing flavour; but there is no advantage to drying them and then using them in a compote as you can keep them fresh quite simply. None the less, it's worth observing that the apple crop is only abundant every other year, so that in a year when fresh apples are thin on the ground, dried apples cooked in a compote are a grand resource, particularly for convalescents.

You can also cut apples into slices in order to dry them; you do not peel them. If you put these dried slices into water to ferment, you can make a very pleasing light beverage.

6. — Apple cheese.[1]

Reinette apples, especially those from Canada, are the best for making apple cheese. For this, you peel them, take out the pips and put the apples in water. Cook them on a bright fire in a covered copper pan. They will be quickly cooked; once they are done, you stir vigorously to create a sort of thick purée which you pour into dishes to the depth of about six centimetres. Put these dishes in the oven as soon as the bread has been

1.   In French, *pâte de pommes.*

taken out. The next day lift the paste with a knife. The top will form a fairly dry skin, but the underside will still be soft. Place these cakes on a wicker tray for drying prunes, bottom upwards, adding any paste which may have remained in the dishes. Smooth over the surface of the cakes and put them in the oven at the same temperature. After this baking, you can keep the apple cheese as you would other dried fruits. If you add sugar and cinnamon when you first cook the apples, you will make them taste more delicate. Once the season for apples is over, you can make stewed apples with this preserve. You *tear* it into pieces and cook in plenty of water, taking care to stir from time to time.

SECTION VII. — JAMS.
I. — General principles.

Jams give variety to the daily fare of a household and, since sugar is so cheap, I can guarantee that this commodity will cost no more than most cheese; often it is no dearer than butter. It pleases children a great deal and suits their digestion; and a large number of adults are children in this respect. Jams have the added advantage that they keep indefinitely without the slightest care, so long as they are put somewhere dry, out of the light. There are plenty of types, and many varied flavours, but they are almost all very easy to make, although the contrary view is widely held. If you follow my instructions to the letter, I guarantee complete success. I will not discuss any jams that I have not always made in my own household; they are simple. I leave to the experts the task of demonstrating more complicated jams, though I doubt that they are any better.

It is almost always a false economy to skimp on the sugar in jams. There has to be at least the proportion of sugar necessary to preserve the fruit. If you save on the sugar, the cooking will take longer; then the jam will lose its pretty colour, take on an unpleasant *cooked* taste, and it will lose its flavour almost entirely. The questionable economy that you wished to realize will never compensate for these faults. Nor is there an advantage in using inferior sugar; it is truly a disadvantage to make jam with *cassonade*, which will change the taste completely giving it a flavour of molasses. What is more, jam made with *cassonade* or raw sugar is never transparent; it will never gel as well as that made with crystallized sugar, and you will lose a lot of volume in scum.

2. — Currant jelly.

A. — *The best ways to make currant jelly.*[1]

Currant preserve is the most health-giving of all preserves and the one of which one tires the least. It pleases both those in good health and the sick.

There are two ways of making currant jelly; the first is more expensive and more refined than the second, which is still very good. The two methods are none the less very simple.

In Bar[2] they follow a method that produces a jelly finer than the two other ways, but it is more difficult to make and to keep. I give its recipe also.

First method. — Choose fine currants, perfectly ripe, but not gone over. You can have a quarter white currants and three-quarters red; the preserve will be the brightest red. You strip the currants neatly and then weigh them, making sure you make allowance for the bowl. You either break the sugar into small lumps or you pound it coarsely; the weight of sugar should be equal to that of currants. You put everything into a pottery bowl and leave it to macerate for two hours. Then you pour it into a preserving pan (figure 104)[3] or a small untinned copper pan, which you first place on a low fire. Stir with a wooden spatula. It is important that the pan be not tinned; preserves made in tinned pans take on an unattractive purplish hue. As the currants melt down, you increase the heat, so that it soon comes to the boil. After it has boiled for ten minutes, the currants will be perfectly cooked; pour everything into a large horsehair sieve over a pottery bowl and let it drain for a few instants. Lift off the sieve and pour the preserve into dry pots. Each pot should hold no more than 500 grams. Preserves which you want to convert into jellies should not be put into large pots; they set less well and, if the pot is tinned, part of contents will turn to syrup.

If you wish to give an exquisite flavour to your preserve, add 1 kilogram of raspberries to 5 kilograms of currants. The proportion of sugar and the mode of working are the same as if you had not added any raspberries.

1. In this section the author uses two words *gelée* (jelly) and *confiture* (jam or preserve) although she is indubitably describing making a jelly. Sometimes she writes *confiture* where we might have expected *gelée*. I have translated each use of these words as jelly (*gelée*) or preserve (*confiture*).
2. Bar-le-Duc in the Meuse department in Lorraine in the east of France.
3. I have translated this as preserving pan, but the figure makes plain that the *bassine* has a different shape to our flat-bottomed pans.

Preserves made in this way have the best colour possible and keep the savour of the fruit better than if they are prepared in the method I am about to describe. They are also more transparent because all the elements that might make them cloudy remain in the solid residue. This is the best method.

Figure 104. Preserving pan.

Second method. — To make currant jelly slightly more economically, this is how to proceed.

Having stripped the currants, you join to them some raspberries, always in the proportion of a fifth or a sixth or thereabouts; put everything on the heat and carry on as before, but without adding sugar. When the fruit is cooked, tip them out into a sieve and leave them to drain for two or three hours. Some people then squeeze the pulp in a new cloth, which they have taken care to wet in advance; but you only extract a little juice by doing this, and it is very cloudy and will affect the transparency of the preserve. Once you have obtained the juice, you weigh it. Break an equal weight of sugar into pieces and add to the juice. Let the sugar dissolve for half an hour, stirring from time to time. Put everything into the preserving pan on a bright fire and let it boil for a little while, ten minutes at the most. Take off the heat, skim it and pour it into pots.

These preserves, although a little less fine that those obtained by the previous recipe, are still excellent and generally vastly superior to those which you buy.

Currant water. — A certain amount of sugar remains in the skins and pips; you can add water to this residue, leave it to steep for two or three hours, then strain it; you will thereby obtain a very pleasing currant water, which will need drinking quite quickly because it will start to ferment after three or four days.

B. — *White currant jelly.*

You make a white currant jelly exactly as you make one with redcurrants, except that you add a little lemon peel which gives it a nice flavour somewhat reminiscent of apple jelly. It is transparent and good to look at; it does not have the same flavour as redcurrant jelly.

If you wish to leave a few strips of lemon peel in the jelly, once you have cut them to the right shape and size you boil them in the water and when they are cooked you take them out to put into the preserve, either when it is still on the fire, or as you pot it up.

If you use raw sugar, *cassonade* [Demerara], or even just [white] sugar of inferior quality, you will have to clarify it in the manner I describe in the recipe for jelly as it is made in Bar.

C. — *Uncooked currant jelly.*

It is quite difficult to make an uncooked jelly successfully. You do it by stripping the currants and crushing them in an earthenware bowl with a wooden pestle, the sort I have described for a purée is the best.[1] You should press them without crushing the pips; if they are crushed, they make the juice cloudy. When you have pressed them enough, put them on a frame-sieve to express their first juice. Then you put them on a clean cloth, which you have taken care to wet previously, and by twisting and pressing you should extract more juice which you mix with the first. You weigh everything, because I am sure you have taken account of the weight of the bowl in which you have poured the juice. You add 2 kilograms of finely powdered sugar to 1 kilogram of juice and you mix together. To begin with, the sugar will dissolve with difficulty. Once it has completely dissolved, you carry this mixture to as cool a cellar as you can find. You leave it for twelve hours in its bowl, stirring from time to time. After that you put the preserve into pots of no more than 500 grams and leave them in the cellar. These preserves can only be brought out of their cool resting-place when there is no risk of hot weather. They taste extremely refreshing, but they are cloudy and sometimes they ferment despite all the care lavished on their conservation.

D. — *Preserves made with whole currants, or those made in Bar.*

Bar preserves, which have taken the name of the town where they have been made since time immemorial, require quite a different way of working than ordinary jellies. The currants must remain whole, only the finest ones chosen, and they should not be wholly ripe. It is enough that they have a nice colour if they are red, and transparent if they are white. You take *each*

1.   See under *Tomatoes*, above.

currant and, with the end of a *quill* toothpick, which you cut back on one side of the point and taper on the other, you pick out with the hook thus formed all the pips from the centre of the fruit, taking great care not to damage the pulp or the skin as far as you are able. If you wish the preserves to be as beautiful as possible, you don't pick a currant off its bunch, but that makes the task more difficult. When all the pips have been removed, weigh the currants. Then weigh out 750 grams of the finest sugar for each half-kilogram of currants. Break the sugar into large pieces and put it on the fire, adding half a litre of water to each kilogram of sugar. When it is completely dissolved, clarify it by throwing in (depending on how much sugar is used) one or two beaten egg whites, or adding them in a glass of water for every two eggs. Beat the syrup all ways, bring it to the boil, skim it carefully and let it cook to *soft ball*.[1] You can say that the syrup is cooked to soft ball if, when you plunge the skimmer into the syrup and blow vigorously through the holes, the syrup forms bubbles on the underside. Pour the currants carefully into the syrup and leave until it just boils, then take off the heat. This preserve is put into little glass pots containing about 125 grams. The currants, which collapse a little during the cooking, absorb a great deal of sugar, plump up as they cool, and can be seen bathing in a perfectly transparent jelly. Share the currants out evenly between all the pots then top up with the syrup.

Often the currants will rise to the surface as you pour in the syrup; a moment later you should press them down with the handle of a coffee spoon.

These preserves do not cost much more than the others, if you discount the time you must spend preparing the fruit. You will make about ten of the recommended pots with about 500 grams of currants. These preserves are the best of all those with currants as their chief ingredient. The pots should not be covered until ten to fourteen days after the preserve has been made.

E. — *Raspberry jelly.*

You make this in exactly the same way as currant jelly, but it sets less easily. You should cook it for five minutes longer.

1.   116°–118° C.

3. — Apricot preserves.
A. — Marmelade.[1]

You can make several sorts of preserves with apricots. *Marmelade* is the most common and the most convenient when there are children, because it spreads easily on bread. Choose ripe apricots; all varieties are satisfactory. Split them in two and remove the stones; then put them in an untinned preserving pan on the kitchen fire or the stove. When they are cooked enough for the skins to come away from the flesh, peel them. Put them into a horsehair sieve, two tablespoonfuls at a time, and press them through with the help of a mushroom-shaped pestle. When you have all the flesh, weigh it (the skin is only good for chickens), and add an equivalent amount of sugar – either coarsely crushed or broken into very small pieces. Leave to rest together for an hour, stirring from time to time. Then put the mixture on the fire, gentle at first but gradually increased, and let cook for ten minutes *at the most* once it has come to the boil. If you cook it for longer, the colour of the *marmelade* will be spoiled.

After this, put the *marmelade* into pots. As it will not have set, and only firms up as it cools, it can be put in large pots without any trouble.

You can also make this without detaching the skins. The *marmelade* is still enjoyable, but the presence of skins will inhibit the long-keeping of this sort of preserve. After taking out the stones, you weigh the raw fruit and add an equal amount of sugar. Then you mix the powdered sugar and the fruit and leave to macerate for three hours before putting on the fire. When they are on the heat, you stir constantly until the sugar has entirely dissolved. When it comes to the boil, you boil it for quarter of an hour. The apricots will remain in quite large pieces, which are difficult to crush, but they are excellent to eat.

You can break one-eighth of the stones, peel the kernels, let them boil an instant with the jam and then place them on the surface of the filled pots.

B. — Whole apricot preserves.

You can make a good jam with whole apricots. This is how to prepare it.

---

1. The French word *marmelade* describes a stewed and puréed fruit. A jam where the fruit is not identifiable in its original form.

Choose apricots that are not very ripe, with smooth skins. Split them only as much as needed to stone them. For this jam, you will need one and a quarter kilograms of the finest sugar to each kilogram of fruit, weighed after the stones have been removed. When you have broken up the sugar, put it in a preserving pan with half a litre of water per kilogram of sugar. When it has dissolved, clarify it, unless the sugar is good enough not to need clarification. If this is the case, add only one glass of water per kilogram of sugar. Cook this syrup to *hard ball*,[1] that is to say that when it is at soft ball (see *Preserves made in Bar*, above), you carry on cooking until when you blow hard on a skimmer that has just been dipped in the syrup, the bubbles which form on the underside break off and fly away like soap. Immediately place the apricots in this syrup, not all at once but only sufficient to cover the surface of the preserving pan; ginger up the fire, then after a few instants turn the fruit so that it cooks evenly on both sides. When they are cooked, but not collapsing, something which will be plain from the transparency of every part of the fruit, take the pan off the fire. Then lift out the apricots with a fork placed below them, one by one, and put them in sloping-sided glass pots of 250 gram capacity. Five apricots in each pot will be enough. Once you have taken out all the apricots, if the pan could not hold the whole batch, put the syrup back on the fire, heat it once more to hard ball, and continue the process as described above. Once all are cooked, drain back into the pan any juice that has come out of the fruits in the pots and put the syrup back on the fire. When it achieves hard ball once again, fill up the pots, having a care to strain the syrup through a small horsehair sieve. The apricots, which will by now seem flattened, will plump up. You lift the fruit from the bottom of the pots so that it floats in the syrup, which firms up as it cools and makes a superb transparent jelly. One can also add kernels prepared as those which were placed on the *marmelade*.

C. — *Apricot jelly.*

You proceed exactly as if you wanted to preserve whole apricots. You pour the flesh onto a sieve, you let it drain, then you pot up just the juice which comes through. This jelly is magnificent and delicious. The apricots

1.   121°–124° C.

which provided the juice can be eaten there and then as a compote or be preserved themselves in pots. These apricots, which may have dried out a little, resemble a conserve; they may harden as they age, but they are none the less excellent. If you place them in an oven on a little brass sieve or something similar, six or eight hours after the bread has been baked, they will dry out completely and become dried apricots which you can store in boxes.

4. — Cherry jam.

Cherry jam is delicious, even if not quite as delicate as that made from currants. Choose for it the sour cherries of Montmorency, morello cherries, or English cherries; they should be ripe, but not *spoilt*. Take out the stones and the stalks. Once all the cherries have been thus prepared, lay them on a horsehair sieve to drain for a few moments, discarding any juice that comes out of them; then weigh them and put them in a preserving pan with an equal weight of powdered sugar. When they have boiled for twenty minutes at the most, they can be put into pots. This jam does not set; that is why you discard the juice, because it will be too runny. You cook it over a high heat, stirring the pot until the cherries have exuded sufficient juice that you no longer fear they will stick to the bottom of the pan. By adding 1 kilogram of currant juice to 5 kilograms of cherries, this jam will set almost as well as a currant jelly; it will take on a fine colour and pleasing flavour.

If you do not add the currant juice, the disadvantage is that the cherry jam will crystallize on the top surface of the pots and will turn brown.

You can make this jam with one and a half kilograms of sugar to 2 kilograms of fruit; but you will have to leave it to cook for at least an hour and a half; you lose the value of the sugar you have saved by the evaporation of the jam; the jam is not so good, but is more like the dried cherry conserve.

When the cherry jam has cooled in its pots, you can also pour a layer of currant jelly no thicker than a five-franc piece over the top. This layer of jelly will inhibit the jam from crystallizing. It is infallible.

In Belgium, rather than straining out the cherry juice, they evaporate it over a gentle fire while cooking the cherries *without sugar* until they make a purée of the right texture; they weigh this purée and add fine white sugar, pound for pound. Once the sugar is dissolved, the jam is finished.

5. — Strawberry jam.

Choose fine pine strawberries, or Bargemont or Capron or any other similar variety.[1] Remove the stalk; weigh equal quantities of sugar and strawberries; put the broken sugar in the preserving pan with half a litre of water per kilogram of sugar; cook the syrup to hard ball (see *Whole apricot preserves*, above) and then add the strawberries. When they are cooked but not collapsing, i.e. after a short while, take out the strawberries with a skimmer and half-fill the pots. Put the syrup back on the fire and, when it has reached soft ball, fill up the pots. Have a mind to lift up the strawberries [in the pots] so the juice penetrates to every corner.

6. — Mirabelle plum jams.

Mirabelle plum jam is excellent; but its preparation demands a little extra time and care than other jams; it can be made as a *marmelade*, or with whole plums.

You make the *marmelade* exactly as the apricot *marmelade*.

To make jam with the whole fruit, you use as much sugar as fruit. They should not be very ripe. Split them down one side and take out the stone; put the sugar in the preserving pan with a half-litre of water per kilogram, and you clarify it, unless the sugar is of the first quality. You cook the syrup to soft ball (see *Preserves made in Bar*, above) and then add the mirabelles. After three or four walms,[2] take them off the fire. Pour this into a pottery bowl and leave to cool until the next day. Drain the syrup into the preserving pan and then put back on the fire to reduce to soft ball again. Put the mirabelles back into the syrup, and give it another three or four walms. Remove them from the fire and do exactly as the day before, unless you find on opening some of the mirabelles that they are perfectly cooked and infused with the sugar. In that case you can dispense with beginning a third boiling. Lift the out the plums with a skimmer and place them in pots, taking care to only fill them to half their height. Then you

1.　　The pine strawberry is a generic term for the garden strawberry, *Fragaria x ananassa*, the hybrid of American varieties first achieved in Britanny in the eighteenth century. The Bargemont strawberry is a variety of alpine strawberry, indigenous to Europe. The Capron strawberry is *Fragaria moschata* or hautbois strawberry, an indigenous European fruit.

2.　　Walm is an old English term corresponding to the French *bouillon* when it indicates the heaving motion of boiling water or liquid in the pan.

cook the syrup again to soft ball and fill up the pots. Gently lift the plums with a fork so that the syrup penetrates everywhere in the jars.

In some regions, the stones are left in the mirabelles; it keeps the fruit plump and imparts a nice flavour. But if this is what you do, you should prick the fruit with a needle in a few places which inhibits it from wrinkling and shedding its flesh.

7. — Greengage jams.
A. —*Marmelade.*

You make *marmelade* with very ripe plums. It doesn't keep well, at least when made with equal quantities of sugar to fruit; it needs to be very well cooked; it may take a brownish tint which is not pleasing to the eye; as it ages, it dries out and forms a sort of paste that can be eaten in the hand. You can make it with one kilogram or one and half kilograms of sugar to 2 kilograms of fruit, but it will need to cook for two or three hours. It is preferable to make it as you do *marmelade* of apricots.

B. — *Whole greengage jams.*

Greengages can be cooked whole in a jam; it's even a good jam and resembles a conserve. It is achieved by exactly the same method as followed for whole mirabelle plum jam, but it is unavoidable that the greengages will have to be put back into the syrup three times. You should choose not very ripe fruit and very smooth-skinned; do not stone them, cut off half the stalk, and prick them with a needle on all sides right to the stone. The syrup in which they cook will not set, but it thickens in time and sometimes crystallizes.

The plums should stay in the syrup for twenty-four hours. Put a weighted plate on top of them so that they remain entirely covered by the syrup; otherwise those that float to the top will brown in contact with the air.

8. — Marmelade of St Catherine plums.

This plum, very common in some provinces, is the one they use to make what are called Tours prunes.[1] You can make a good *marmelade* with

---

1.   St Catherine plums are large and yellow.

them. Choose very ripe fruit, which you sweat down, while stirring, in the preserving pan once you have stoned them. You sieve the flesh and add an equal weight of powdered sugar. Let the sugar steep while off the heat for a couple of hours, stirring from time to time. Put this back on the fire; after ten minutes of boiling, put it in large pots. It will not set.

9. — Pear jams.

Pear jam is excellent. It can replace all the summer jams. Choose English pears, or Beurré, or Coloquint, or Doyenné: in a word, a pear that is sweet and juicy, with no sharpness. The jams are either red or white, depending on the sort of pear you have chosen, because there are some pears which turn red in cooking.

Peel the pears carefully; cut them into quarters; take out the pips and any parts with stone cells in them;[1] weigh the fruit and put it in an earthenware bowl, a stoneware terrine for example, adding 3 kilograms of sugar to every 4 kilograms of fruit. Mix the sugar and the pears and leave in the cellar to macerate for six hours, stirring from time to time. When the sugar seems to have pretty much dissolved, put the mixture in a preserving pan over a gentle heat, and stir frequently to stop the jam sticking to the bottom of the pan. When the pears seem perfectly cooked, which is easy to see by their transparency, put the jam into pots. Cooking should take an hour. This jam keeps very well; it may crystallize towards the end of the jam season, but is only the better for that.

If you wish to make a jam that has an even more delicate flavour, put in a little vanilla cut into small pieces. One tires of these jams more quickly than the others which I have described earlier because they have very little acidity.

If you have small, sweet pears, whether soft or not, you can make a whole pear jam. In this case you peel them, and as soon as they are peeled you throw them into cold water acidulated with lemon juice to avoid their blackening. You leave half the stalk and you put the pears in a preserving pan with an equal weight of sugar and a half-litre of water per kilogram

---

1. The stone cells in pears are what make the flesh of pears appear gritty in the mouth. Sometimes they are more than grit and can be identified by eye and thus removed as advised by Mme Millet-Robinet.

of sugar. You cook them until the pears seem perfectly transparent. You then put the jam into pots. If the syrup seems too runny, boil it to soft ball before you pour it over the pears (see *Preserves made in Bar*, above).

10. — Apple jelly.

Apple and quince jellies are also late-autumn preserves. Apple jelly, justifiably sought after but often thought difficult to prepare, is as easy to make as other preserves. The Reinette franche [also known as the Reinette de Normandy], when in good condition, is to be preferred over other varieties. As the apples should not be too ripe, this jelly should be made in October at the latest. Fill the pan with clear water; wipe the apples, cut them in two without peeling, and take off the stalks; then, as each apple is peeled, throw it into the water, which should cover them and which should be acidulated with some lemon juice. Thirty medium-sized apples should, with the sugar you add to them, provide 6 kilograms of preserve. When all the apples have been prepared, pour off the water in which they were kept and replace it with clear water to cover completely. Put the preserving pan on a lively fire, cover it carefully and leave it to cook undisturbed.

When the apples are cooked, but not yet a purée – something which will not need more than a quarter of an hour's boiling – pour everything out onto a frame sieve. Let it drain through for a few moments only; weigh the juice by pouring it into a pan (which you have weighed beforehand) and then add one kilogram of the best sugar to each one and a quarter kilograms of juice. The sugar should be broken into very small pieces, or coarsely ground. Depending on the amount of preserve, you should squeeze the juice of one or two lemons into the pan, taking care to get rid of the pips. Put the pan on a very bright fire and leave it to *boil* for quarter of an hour at most. Take it off the heat and pour it into pots, as other jellies.

Usually we flavour an apple jelly with lemon zest. Peel the lemon, cut the skin into thin strips no wider than 2 millimetres and put them to cook on a lively fire in a little water. Add this water to the apple juice.. You put the little strips of lemon you have just cooked into the preserving pan with the sugar and the apple juice. You distribute them evenly between the pots. They take up the sugar in the jam and are good to eat.

You can make apple jelly in the same way as I have described for preserves made in Bar, that is to say, clarify the sugar, cook it to hard ball, pour the juice in, let cook for a short while, put into pots. You still add lemon juice and zest. This method is just as good as the other.

If you work quickly, the jelly will be perfectly white. If it is not as white as the apple jelly of Rouen, it will probably only be the better, because the Rouen confectioners only achieve a very pale jelly by using too few apples. The principal flavour is that of lemon juice and zest.

Apple jelly will not set immediately; it only firms up over time.

You cover it, like all other preserves, ten or twelve days after making it.

11. — Quince jelly.

You make quince jelly pretty much like apple jelly, except you cannot cook the pips with the fruit; they are coated with a mucilaginous substance which affects the quality of the jelly, if every single one is not removed. Having selected quinces that are fully ripe and blemish-free, wipe them carefully to get rid of the fluff on the skin; cut them in two, with a silver-bladed knife if possible, and take out the core. As you cut them up, put them in plenty of clear water. After this, you proceed exactly as for apple jelly, but omitting the addition of lemon, and adding an equal weight of sugar to juice. Quinces take much longer to cook than apples.

You can use the pulp to make quince paste, as I will describe later.

You can also make quince jelly by putting the whole quinces, after wiping them, in a cauldron with enough water to cover. Cook them over a bright fire until they are soft enough to have a piece of straw thrust through them. Take them off the heat and cut them into quarters with a wooden or ivory knife (a paper-knife is very suitable for this). Put them into a pottery bowl, cover them with cold water and leave to infuse for 12 hours. Pour them onto a frame sieve and let them drain for two hours. Then you proceed as for the other juice, either adding broken sugar to the juice or boiling a syrup to hard ball. All these simple methods give the same result. I have used them with complete success.

Quince or apple jelly is not more expensive than other preserves.

Using the quince pips. — Quince pips are used in ladies' hairdressing. You should dry them and sell them if you do not use them yourself. To employ them, soak them in water for a few hours; a clear jelly will form around them which, when spread under the hair, will fix it invisibly on the forehead.[1] This jelly is the basis for the *bandoline*.[2]

12. — Marrow, grape jams, etc.

You can make jams with several other fruits than those I have indicated. You prepare them by different methods, depending on the fruit. You make grape preserve with large muscat grapes, in the same way as Bar preserves; but you peel the grapes. You make marrow jam like pear jam, etc. (See my book entitled *Conservation des Fruits* [Fruit Conservation],[3] a specialized work in which I go into details which could not be included here.)

13. — Raisiné.[4]

Raisiné is the least delicate of all preserves, and also the least costly. It pleases children a great deal; it is most welcome to servants and the sick poor, because it is very health-giving, and seems as good as the most sophisticated preserves to those who are not used to dainty morsels. It is therefore sensible to produce an ample supply in those regions where grapes are good and plentiful.

Raisiné is made with grape juice and pears, quinces or other fruits; you can even incorporate pieces of carrot, squash or beetroot.

To make raisiné, some people simply take the grape must from the vat before it has fermented; but it is better to pick the best grapes in the vineyard, not rotten, perfectly ripe. Black grapes are preferable; however you can make raisiné with white. When you have picked some, take them off the bunch, and crush them with a pestle or a fruit press. Place them batch by batch on a frame sieve so that the juice can run. You can even squeeze them in a new cloth that you have first wetted. You can also put the uncrushed grapes in a cauldron on a gentle fire and stir them with a wooden spatula until they have produced enough juice so that they don't stick to the bottom of the pan; once they are cooked sufficiently to let

1. That is to say, a lady may ensure that her kiss-curl stays in place.
2. *Bandoline*: 'a gummy preparation for setting hair.'
3. *Conservation des fruits* was published by Dusacq, Librairie agricole de la Maison Rustique, rue Jacob, Paris, in 1854 as part of the series Bibliothèque du cultivateur, publiée avec le concours du Ministre de l'Agriculture.
4. There is no English word for this, so I have Anglicized it.

their juice down readily, you place them on a frame sieve in small batches. The *must* obtained by the first method is sweeter and clearer; the second is more plentiful and more coloured, it is also slightly sharper thanks to the cooking of the skin and pips. The solid residue can be put back in the vat if you don't want to make a drink out of it.

Once the must has been prepared, set aside a third of it. To the other two-thirds, add little by little some white marble ground to dust. A kilogram of this powder is enough for 60 litres of must. Stir it; it will bubble briskly, as if it were boiling, even though cold, or tepid at most. Once the effervescence has ceased, let the liquid rest, decant it, and pass it through a woollen straining-bag if you do not wish to lose the small amount of juice remaining mixed with the marble. (See the article *Boiled wine*, below, on how to use crushed marble.) If you do not have a draining-bag, it is enough to tack a scrap of thick woollen cloth on a hoop or a rough wooden frame, which you support by resting the edges on two chairs. The effect of the marble is to reduce the acidity of the must; it becomes extremely sweet, and would be unacceptably dull if you did not add back the third of the must that was set aside at the outset. This is enough to give the whole a pleasing acidity. Raisiné which is made without the chemical procedure I have described is usually so acid that you can scarcely eat it, unless the grapes used are excessively ripe and exceptionally sweet such as are harvested in southern departments.

Early the next morning, put the must in a cauldron and boil vigorously. When it begins to thicken, after eight or ten hours on the fire, and when it has reduced by about two-thirds, stir it and add the fruit that is to be preserved therein. Soft and sweet pears such as the Messire-Jean, the Doyenné, the Martin-sec, and other similar varieties are especially suitable. Peel them, take out the pips and any stone cells, cut them in quarters, add them to the grape juice. Quinces are also very good in raisiné, so long as not in too high a proportion; generally you should have 1 part quinces to 15 parts pears. The quantity of fruit in relation to the quantity of juice cannot be exactly forecast. Once the grape juice has reduced to a third of its original volume, you put in as much fruit as will fit; so long as the sections of quince and pears are fully immersed, you cannot add too many. In any case, the raisiné – with more or less fruit – will always keep, so long as it is sufficiently cooked.

When the pears begin to cook and the raisiné thickens, you must stir it unremittingly with the wooden spatula, particularly at the centre of the bottom of the pan, otherwise it will stick and take on a burnt taint. The pears are entirely cooked when you cut in two those segments not already collapsing into a purée and you find that their colour all the way to the centre is that of the grape juice, and that the juice itself does not split from the pears when you pour a small quantity onto a plate, but appears all bound together as a syrup: then the raisiné is cooked. You can pot it up, it will keep perfectly. You should fill the pots to the brim because the raisiné will shrink quite a lot as it cools. However, it will not set.

If you have no pears, you can add to the raisiné slices of squash, a sort of pumpkin known under the common name Turk's turban because of the strange form it takes. The alteration in flavour resulting from this substitution is barely perceptible. If instead of Turk's turban you put ordinary pumpkin into the raisiné, you will have to cook it in advance in a cauldron, having first peeled it and cut it into chunks. Put it on the heat with a little water; when it is cooked, drain it on a frame sieve, then put the pulp into the grape juice. Some people even add carrots cut into small pieces or beetroot. These latter may at first contribute an earthy taste, but it dissipates with time. Beetroot needs to cook longer than either carrots or Turk's turban; it will make the raisiné much sweeter. In some parts where apples are plentiful, they put them in the raisiné. This is bad practice; it must be refrained from. Apples are not at all suitable for this confection.

14. — How to cover jam pots.

About ten days after jams have been potted up, they must be covered. You cut discs of thin paper, ensuring you leave a little tongue at one point in the circumference with which to pull back the paper when starting the jam. You put some eau-de-vie in a plate and dip each disc before placing it on the surface of the pot and then pressing down. The paper should not be larger than the jam itself or overlap onto the sides of the pot. About an hour after installing this first piece of paper, you cover the whole pot with a second piece, on which you write the type of jam and the year it was made.

There are those who dismiss this use of thin paper to cover the jam: they are wrong. It often happens, above all in the country, that the jam will grow mould in the winter. When the paper is lifted off, the mould disappears because it grew on the paper. Had the paper not been there, it would have grown on the jam itself.

There are several ways of attaching the second paper. The first is to dip some stout adhesive paper into water for a second, then stretch it across the top of the pot and press it to stick, before tearing it gently with the fingers round the underside of the rim. As it dries, the paper tautens, hardens and its edges bond to the rim; however, it only needs a tap to release. This method of covering pots is the neatest.

You can also cover pots with papers tied round with a thin white or red string. This is the most secure. Finally, you can also roll the edges of the paper under the rim of the pot. This is the quickest and, when executed with skill, is clean enough.

You should always completely fill the pots because evaporation will always cause the jam to lose some of its volume.

You can always fit into a cupboard a great many more pots than appear to fit onto the surface area of the shelves by stacking layers of pots on a single shelf separated by a piece of thick glass or cardboard. You should take care that these pots are stacked tidily and are of the same height.

SECTION VIII. — FRUIT PASTES.
I. — Quince paste.

To make quince paste, you use either fresh quinces cooked in a covered vessel on a lively fire, or the fruit pulp that has already served in making jelly, which you sieve to take out the skins. After that you drain the pulp again because it will serve better the drier it is.

You incorporate into this quince purée as much sugar, grated or pounded into a very fine powder, as will give the paste the look of a bread dough before it has risen. Roll out this paste with a rolling-pin, scattering sugar onto the table or paper on which you are working; reduce the paste to a half-centimetre thickness; have a mind to sugar the top-side of the paste so that it doesn't stick to the rolling-pin. Cut this *sheet* of paste with a pastry-cutter or an inverted glass and place the pieces on sheets of paper dusted with sugar. Put them in a very cool oven – six hours, for example, after the bread has been baked – and leave them 12 hours. Afterwards, you can arrange the paste side by side in boxes, and then in layers separated by sheets of paper. This preserve is very dry when freshly made, but softens a little in time.

Another method I think preferable. Wipe the quinces to remove their fluff; top and tail them. Cook them in plenty of water on a bright fire. When you can pierce them through with a straw, take them off the heat. Swiftly peel the quinces while another person pushes them through a horsehair sieve with a mushroom-shaped pestle. Drain the paste on a frame sieve, then add an equal weight of grated sugar. Put back on the fire and stir it constantly until the liquid has all but evaporated. Ten or fifteen minutes boiling should suffice. Pour the paste onto plates, in layers about half a centimetre thick. When it has cooled, scatter sieved, grated sugar. Put the plates somewhere dry. After eight days, turn the paste over, sprinkle likewise with sugar, and cut into ribbons which you roll or bend to an S-shape. Or you can cut into rounds using an inverted liqueur glass. Dry once more somewhere airy and damp-free. Put in boxes between sheets of white paper.

2.— Apricot paste.

Apricot paste, like quince, is an inexpensive sweet. You make it in exactly the same way except that in order that the apricots should be able to receive the powdered sugar, you cook them after you have stoned them, and then pass them through a sieve. And then you cook them again, stirring constantly, until they have achieved a consistency much like the quince pulp. Towards the end of cooking, unless you reduce the heat greatly you will be unable to stop this purée from catching on the bottom of the pan. Let it cool completely before you add the sugar. This you will have to add quickly or else it will not dissolve.

It is impossible to forecast how much sugar to add in proportion to the fruit: that will depend on how runny the pulp is; but you can be sure that it will need at least three times the weight of the fruit.[1]

You can also cook the fruit with some of the sugar, so long as you stir it ceaselessly. Let it cool, then finish the paste by adding pounded sugar.

1.   No contemporary recipe by other authorities suggests this high proportion of sugar.

SECTION IX. — COMPOTES AND BOTTLED JUICES.
1. — **Compotes.**

Although the Appert method [of canning and preserving] is very well known, I think I had better describe it here. It is ideal for the conservation of various foods. Since his discoveries, sailors can have as well-supplied a table as if they were ashore, which contributes greatly to their health. The process has been perfected for some years, and its application has been widely developed.

For the navy, they produce conserves in soldered tin cans. In a household, where the process has fewer applications, use is made of litre or half-litre bottles, which is much simpler and cheaper. The mouth of these bottles should be 4 or 5 centimetres across. You should also procure first-rate corks. However, some substances may be preserved in ordinary bottles, but you should choose those with the widest and sturdiest necks possible.

A. — *Bottled cherries and apricots.*

The cherry is one of the fruits which bottles the best. You should choose fine sour cherries that are suitably ripe (the short-stem Montmorency is the best) or, better still, English cherries like the White Heart.[1] Reduce the length of the stalks by a half. When the bottles are filled, add 200 grams of crushed sugar and cork with care. Then you should tie down the cork with string. When all the bottles are ready, you wrap them in hay which you have twisted together like a rope, or you use coarse canvas such as is used for wrapping. Then you arrange them standing up in a cauldron in such a manner that they won't knock into each other when the water is boiling. Fill the cauldron with cold water to a level that stops short of the corks. Light a substantial fire. Keep the water boiling for twenty or twenty-five minutes, then extinguish the fire without touching any of the bottles, or lift the cauldron off the fire, and let it cool. Lift out the bottles and once the corks and the string are completely dry, pitch them neatly.[2] When they are thoroughly cold, take them down to the cellar and lay them down.

1. The variety named is *la nacrée* (mother of pearl). This may indicate a white-fleshed variety.
2. It was usual to coat the corks of bottles of fine wine with pitch to protect them from insect attack as well as the damp.

Once the fruit has been put into bottles, you can also fill them with syrup cooked to hard ball (see *Sugar syrup*, below). Cork them, and cook them. By this method, preferable to the first, the fruits keep their shape better, suspended in a transparent syrup.

Cherries conserved in this fashion are delicious compotes, which keep in perfect condition for two years and more if stored in a dry place where the corks will not spoil. They are very like a compote of fresh fruit.

Apricots are prepared in the same way. Choose small ones, without blemish, and split them to take out the stones. They will need boiling for three-quarters of an hour. The cooking will not alter their outward form.

B. — Bottled raspberries and strawberries.

You preserve raspberries by the same procedure: choose fruit in good condition, not too ripe, and boil them for only seven or eight minutes. Instead of preserving them in one-litre bottles, it is better to choose those of half-litre capacity, because once the bottle is uncorked you should consume the contents within twenty-four hours, or risk seeing them sour when in contact with the air.

You can also preserve strawberries like those of Bargemont, which are sweet and not too juicy.

C. — Bottled plums.

Mirabelle plums can also be preserved in bottles. You prepare them in exactly the same fashion as apricots, save that you do not stone them and you boil them for three-quarters of an hour. This fruit is very liable to ferment. Greengages turn yellow when cooked in a bain-marie and do not keep their shape.

2. — Bottled currant juice.

You prepare the currants as you would for making a conserve, that is, after having picked off the currants you sweat them in a pan on the fire; you put them to strain in a frame sieve, and you add one-eighth of the quantity of sour cherry juice.

Leave the juice in a cool place for eight or ten hours so that the gelatinous element may settle (otherwise the juice will ferment). It forms a clot which you break up with a fork or a whisk made of bare twigs. Strain it through a piece of linen or a sieve to obtain a clear juice. Put this juice in ordinary half-bottles. Cork them, as I described in the article *Cherries*, above, and then immerse the bottles in a bain-marie and boil them for five minutes. This juice will keep, without sugar, for several years if it is perfectly sealed and kept somewhere cool. To drink it, sugar a glass of water and add enough juice to flavour it.

This drink is very refreshing and is preferable to a currant syrup or cordial. You can flavour the juice with raspberries. Once the bottle is opened, it will not keep longer than a couple of days, unless the weather is very cold indeed. Hence the reason for using very small bottles. This currant juice is also most suitable for making ices.

You can flavour currant juice with raspberry juice. This last is preserved in the same fashion. Raspberry juice does not need clarifying with sour cherries.

You can wrap any bottle that you are using for these preserves in coarse fabric bags. They can well be boiled like this.

SECTION X. — CORDIALS.

Although it is easy to buy good cordials from confectioners or pharmacists, I will give a few recipes here because it is very economical to make your own cordial, and you will derive much pleasure in offering the fruits of your own handiwork to your friends.

1. — Sugar syrup and the different stages of cooking sugar.

I will start by giving the recipe for clarified sugar. You make it by dissolving 2 kilograms of crushed sugar in 1 kilogram of very clear water. Mix an egg white in water and add to the sugar then place on the heat and bring it to the boil. When the egg white is well cooked, let it rest a moment, then lift the scum with a skimmer. The syrup is cooked to *soft ball* [1] when, as you dip the skimmer into it and then blow vigorously across the holes, the syrup forms bubbles beneath these holes; it is cooked to *hard ball* when in doing the same, the bubbles detach and float away like soap

---

1. The terms for the degrees of sugar boiling change over time, and it is not always certain that each author is describing an identical temperature when they use the same names. For example, Mme Millet-Robinet's description of the physical identifiers of *petit boulé* or soft ball seem better to accord with *Larousse Gastronomique*'s large pearl or soufflé. She calls her third stage of sugar *à la nappe* (which here I have translated as feathered), whereas for many authorities *nappé* sugar is the earliest stage.

bubbles. The syrup is *feathered* when it flows from the skimmer in sheets which drop slowly; *crackling* when it forms threads when you put the sugar into cold water; *barley sugar* when it begins to turn golden; and finally *caramel* when it turns brown. If it remains for a few seconds more on the fire, it will burn.

2. — Currant cordial.

Redcurrants, picked off their stalks   4 kilograms
Sour cherries   500 grams

Once you have stoned and picked the stalks off the cherries, you should crush them with the currants in an earthenware bowl using a pestle for purées. Then squeeze the mixture in a new and wetted cloth. Leave the juice for twenty-four hours in the cellar, in an unglazed terrine. It will set. Beat it with a little wicker whisk, then pour it onto a piece of white woollen felt nailed onto a wooden frame, which is called a *strainer*, which forms a sort of frame sieve.[1] The juice thus obtained will be perfectly clear. Add 800 grams of fine crushed sugar for every 500 grams of juice thus prepared. Dissolve the sugar on a low fire; at the *first* sign of boiling, take it off the heat; decant into bottles and leave to cool. You only cork it when the syrup is completely cold. The bottles should be stored upright in a cool cellar.

You can replace 500 grams of the currants with a like quantity of raspberries. They will impart a nice flavour to the syrup.

Before you express the juice from the blanched currants, you can cook them over a low fire. The syrup will have more colour. Add the crushed cherries to the juice and then treat it as I have described.[2]

3. — Raspberry cordial.

Cook the fruit, while stirring, for a few moments, then put onto the frame sieve to strain the juice. You treat this exactly as you have the currant cordial with sour cherries.

4. — Strawberry cordial.

You make strawberry cordial in the same way as raspberry cordial, which is much more enjoyable. You should use large pine strawberries above all others.

1.   The French for this device is *blanchet*.
2.   Mme Millet-Robinet refers here to 'blanched currants' (*groseilles mondées*), but she hasn't blanched her currants in the earlier part of the recipe.

5. — Barberry cordial.

Using a pestle for purées, crush well-ripened barberries in an earthenware bowl. Sweat them on the fire; squeeze out the juice in a new wetted cloth and strain it through the woollen strainer. Add 800 grams of crushed sugar to 500 grams of juice. Dissolve the sugar in a bain-marie or on a very gentle heat, then put the syrup in bottles, before it has cooled entirely. This sharp syrup is very refreshing.

6. — Orange cordial.

Choose blemish-free oranges that are not too ripe. Take off the zest, which you should keep to perfume the syrup. Take off the rest of the peel and crush the pulp. Squeeze out the juice through a new wetted cloth. Use 800 grams of sugar for 500 grams of juice. To one side, you stretch over a wooden frame, much like the woollen strainer, a very clean and wetted cloth, on which you arrange the zests of one or two oranges, depending how much juice you want to perfume. As soon as the syrup has come to the boil, pour it over the zests, then bottle it.

7. — Lemon or lime cordial.

You prepare these like the orange cordial. However, as lemon juice is very acid, you can add an equal amount of water.

8. — Raspberry vinegar cordial.

Infuse for a fortnight 250 grams of ripe raspberries in a litre of vinegar. Strain it, then dissolve 900 grams of sugar in it.

9. — Orange flower cordial.

Double orange flower water [1]	500 grams
Crushed fine sugar	1 kilogram

Dissolve the sugar in the orange flower water and strain it through a grey filter paper. Do this in the cellar, to avoid evaporation.

---

1. Double orange flower water was an expression of the proportion of water to flowers, in this case two pounds of water to one pound of flowers. Triple was at the rate of 3:2; quadruple was 1:1; and simple was one part double water cut with one part plain water.

10. — Gum arabic syrup.

White crushed gum arabic	500 grams
Water	750 grams
Sugar	1 kilogram

First, wash the gum, then put it in the water in a copper or silver pan on a very gentle fire to dissolve. Strain the gummy solution through a cloth, add the sugar, which should be of the best and well crushed, and when it has completely dissolved, put it in bottles. You may add 30 to 32 grams of orange flower water.

11. — Marshmallow syrup.

Marshmallow root, very white and dry	125 grams
Water	1 kilogram
Sugar	2 kilograms

Infuse the marshmallow, cut into very small pieces, in the water for twenty-four hours. Strain the infusion. Add crushed sugar. Put the liquid on the fire, taking care to stir it. After boiling a very short while, take it off the fire and when it is half-cooled put it into bottles. Do not cork them until the next day.

This syrup does not taste very nice.[1] You can flavour it with about 30 grams of orange flower water added when it has cooled down.

12. — Barley water.

Sweet almonds	500 grams
Bitter almonds	80 grams
Orange flower water	32 grams
Pure water	1 kilogram
Sugar	1 kilogram

Blanch the almonds in boiling water. Pound them in a marble mortar with 500 grams of sugar and 150 grams of water added little by little. Divide this paste into six or eight and pound it again until it is extremely fine. Now add the water you have held in reserve and mix it with the paste; then squeeze it hard through a new wetted cloth. Dissolve the rest of the

---

1. Although not pleasing to swallow, its purpose was as a cough syrup, or to soothe a sore throat.

sugar in the almond milk you have thus created. Put it on a gentle fire and stir constantly. As soon as it comes to the boil, take it off the fire and add the orange flower water. The barley water will settle into two parts, the one cloudy, the other clear. You must shake the bottles well each time you pour from them.

SECTION XI. — LIQUEURS, BOILED WINE.[1]
1. — Choice of alcohol and general matters.

Alcohol (spirit of wine) should be without colour, and clear; it should register 33 degrees on the areometer [a hydrometer] and be free of any odour.[2] To be sure of it, pour a few drops into a glass of water and taste the mixture. If the spirit of wine has a particular taste or smell, you will identify it more readily by such a test. Spirit or alcohol distilled from beet, when properly rectified, is suitable for making liqueurs, and is much cheaper than spirit of wine.

When you take the trouble to make your own liqueurs, their cost is not great, and if you make sufficient to enjoy for many years after their production, they will improve as they age. However hard you try when making liqueurs, they are not usually very enjoyable when freshly concocted. Nothing can replace the benefits of aging. It is best, therefore, to lay in a supply to last several years and thereafter to produce in any one year no more than will be needed for a year's consumption. If you carefully label and date each bottle, you will always know which is the oldest and therefore the first to be drunk.

I am going to restrict myself here to giving recipes for home-made liqueurs that can be made without any distilling apparatus. In any event, liqueurs that are made by infusion are generally preferable to those that are

1. The French is *vin cuit*, 'cooked wine' or, so called by Cyrus Redding in *A History and Description of Modern Wines* (1833), 'boiled wine', i.e. 'wine which has undergone heating during maturation' (*OED*).

2. The clear white spirit she describes is available to people in the drinks trade, but less so to ordinary mortals, except in small quantities from pharmacies (in France). Its best substitute is vodka, rather than brandy which has taken colour from its casks and is more flavorous. In the *Dictionnaire de médecine et de chirurgie pratiques*, published by Gabon, etc., in Paris in 1829, it is explained that an eau-de-vie is usually 20–22 degrees Baumé, *eau-de-vie double* is 26–28 degrees Baumé, and a spirit or *esprit* is above 30 degrees. When Mme Millet-Robinet specifies eau-de-vie rather than spirit or alcohol, she is advising a weaker or less alcoholic ingredient.

distilled. They may have more colour than these last, but this slight defect matters little for consumption at home.

Every infusion will go cloudy the moment it is mixed with a sugar syrup; but they soon become clear.

It is advisable to filter all your liqueurs through a filter of good, plain white paper in a glass funnel; you should use care in pouring in case you displace the filter.

All liqueurs should be kept in a cupboard, not the cellar.

2. — Peach kernel liqueur.

Crack fifty peach stones and put the kernels and the shells into four litres of good eau-de-vie in a jar with a fairly narrow neck, so that it can be easily corked. Cover the cork with wet vellum, as I explain in the article *Fruits in eau-de-vie*, below. Leave this jar in full sunlight to infuse for two months. Elsewhere, dissolve 1,800 grams of sugar in a litre of water: you put less sugar in if you want a stronger liqueur. Strain the eau-de-vie through a fine sieve to separate the kernels and then mix it thoroughly with the syrup. Put this into bottles, or better into stoneware jars, and cork carefully. You may begin drinking this liqueur one or two months later. It is perilous to abuse this particular liqueur because it retains traces of cyanide [from the kernels].

3. — Apricot kernel liqueur.

Crack two hundred stones; take one hundred of the shells and leave the rest. Put everything [i.e. the kernels and the 100 shells] in 4 litres of good eau-de-vie. After that, proceed as for the peach kernel liqueur. This liqueur is very pleasant and greatly improves after some aging. It is best to make these liqueurs with thirty-six degrees of strength: it is stronger and dissolves the kernels' flavours better. Finally, you add an equal quantity of syrup made of 1 kilogram of sugar to 1 litre of water.

4. — Orange flower liqueur or cream.[1]

Pluck 250 grams of orange flowers, i.e. pick off the petals from the calices. Infuse them in 2 litres of spirit for half an hour. Dissolve 1,800

---

1.   When a liqueur or beverage is described as a *crème* (cream), it is not because it has cream but because it has the consistency of a syrup. It is also usually, but not invariably, less alcoholic than a liqueur.

grams of fine sugar in 2 litres of clear water, strain the infusion of flowers, mix with the syrup, and bottle it. This liqueur is very delicate.

5. — Anisette.

Wash the aniseed in plenty of water and dry it in the shade.

Pound 60 grams of green aniseed, put this to infuse for twenty minutes in two litres of very white spirit; then strain it. Dissolve 1 kilogram of finest sugar in 2 litres of very clear water and then mix it with the infusion. Put it in bottles or, better, stoneware jars. Two months later, this anisette may be drunk, but it improves greatly with aging.

Star anise is much to be preferred to green aniseed to make this anisette, but it is more expensive.

6. — Angelica cream.

Cut into small pieces 500 grams of very fresh angelica stalk. Infuse them for twenty-four hours in 2 litres of spirit. Shake or stir from time to time. Dissolve 1 kilogram of fine sugar in one and a half litres of clear water: strain the infusion and mix it with the syrup. Put it in bottles, but it is better in stoneware jars, which are kept like other liqueurs.

7. — Tea cream.

Infuse 125 grams of good tea, blended as I advise in the article *Tea* (below), for two hours in two litres of alcohol. Decant it or strain it. Add 1 kilogram of sugar to two litres of clear water and mix.

When the tea is really good, this produces a fine liqueur, which improves greatly with keeping.

8. — Coffee cream.

Put 250 grams of crushed *green* [unroasted] mocha coffee in a glass jar with two litres of alcohol. Leave to infuse for twenty-four hours, then strain. Dissolve 1 kilogram of fine sugar in two litres of clear water, mix with the infusion, etc.

You can make this liqueur with lightly roasted coffee; this is also very enjoyable.

9. — Vanilla cream.

Split two pods of good vanilla and cut them into very small pieces. Put them to infuse for two hours in 2 litres of alcohol. Dissolve 1 kilogram of sugar in two litres of water; decant the infusion and mix it with the sweetened water. This liqueur is exquisite.

10. — Ratafia of wild cherries or cherry brandy.[1]

Put 1 kilogram of well-ripened geans, picked off their stalks, in a glass jar or stoneware jug with four litres of strong eau-de-vie. Stop it up. Leave it in the sunlight for two months. Dissolve 1 kilogram of sugar in a very small quantity of water, if you wish to make a sweet ratafia; 500 grams if you want something stronger; the sugar should be just moistened. Strain the liqueur, add the sugar, and put it in bottles. This ratafia is only good to drink after being kept for two or three years.

11. — Ratafia of blackcurrants.

You make this the same way as you did the wild cherry ratafia, but you add 4 or 5 cloves, 12 to 15 blackcurrant leaves, and a few apricot stones, which you crack but don't shell.

12. — Ratafia of raspberries.

Make this as you made the wild cherry ratafia. Use very ripe raspberries. You can make this with alcohol, in which case you only leave it to infuse for twelve hours, and you dissolve the sugar in the same amount of water as you have alcohol.

13. — Quince ratafia.

Cook eight fine whole quinces, unpeeled, in enough water to cover them generously. While they are cooking, top up with boiling water to ensure the quinces remain covered. When they are cooked enough to be pierced by a straw, take them off the heat and cut them up with a wooden knife. Leave them to cool in their cooking water, then drain them on a frame sieve [and discard]. Dissolve 1800 grams of sugar in 2 litres of this

---

1. The French is *merises*: wild cherries or geans. Cherry brandy is called *guignolet* in French. *Eau-de-vie de merises* is, in fact, kirsch.

liquor, to which you add one and a half litres of alcohol. Finally, bottle it. This liqueur is almost colourless and very aromatic.

You can content yourself with just infusing quartered quinces in eau-de-vie for a month, and adding 500 grams of sugar per litre of liqueur, dissolved in a glass of water.

14. — Grape liqueur.

Cau,[1] an excellent black grape much cultivated in the centre of France, is the best variety for this liqueur. You can substitute any other good black grape, but you will have to add sugar.

You should pick the very best *cau* off their stalks and put them to cook on a gentle fire, stirring with a wooden spatula. When they have let down their juice, put them to strain on a horsehair sieve. When the juice has cooled, mix it with strong eau-de-vie at a ratio of 1:5. Put it into big bottles, or stoneware jugs with a narrow mouth after you have provided each bottle with a linen bag containing crushed cinnamon, cloves and coriander. Let the string tie for the bag hang out of the mouth of the bottle. Stop up and leave upright. After a month you can bottle it in ordinary bottles, which you cork carefully.

15. — General-purpose eau-de-vie made with beet spirit.

For the farm workers during heatwaves, and for various purposes in the household, you can make an eau-de-vie very similar to that generally sold by retailers.

To a good beet spirit of 36 degrees Baumé, add an equal quantity of either water or, which is better, a weak decoction of good black tea. Colour it with a pale caramel.

This eau-de-vie costs very little. Beet spirit purchased in 30–40 litre barrels comes out at 1 franc to 1 franc 25 centimes the litre, plus 50 centimes transfer tax.[2]

---

1. In later editions Mme Millet-Robinet spells this variety more conventionally as *Cot* (it can also be written as *Côt*). More generally, the variety is now known as Malbec or, in Cahors, as Auxerrois. The variety was introduced into the Touraine in the seventeenth century and it is there mostly known as Cot.
2. In French, *droit de mutation*. This is a tax usually levied on property transfers. It is not dissimilar to the English stamp duty.

16. — Boiled wine.

The cooked must of white wine,[1] if properly prepared, can be a most enjoyable sweet wine for family consumption – with no harm to the children because it is not very strong – so long as the land on which the grapes grew does not produce too heady a wine. Particularly during heatwaves, this drink (let down with water) is as healthy as it is refreshing for children, who can dip their bread in the beverage – which pleases them greatly as well as giving tone to bodies enfeebled by heat and perspiration.

In those districts where the wine is of good quality, the south of France for example, it is enough to boil off one-third of the must and then to put it in a small barrel to ferment. As the fermentation is slow, it is wise to provide the barrel with a pierced bung to which you fit a bent glass tube with one end in the bung and the other in a glass of water (figure 105).

By this means, there is no evaporation. Any gas created by the fermentation will only be vented by this tube. Lacking this, you can use a feather or a reed, though the end will not be immersed in the water, but this would still be better than leaving the bung-hole completely open. In fact, it is simple to bend a glass tube in the manner shown in figure 105. All you need do is to expose to a hot flame that part of the tube which needs bending and when it glows red, you take the tube at both ends and bend it as you wish.

In those districts where the wine is not so good, you should reduce the must by a half. Then you put to one side a third of this and add to the other two-thirds crushed marble or powdered limestone. When the marble or limestone has rid the must of excess acidity, you put it back with the remainder. The whole is then a delightful sweet wine.

This is how you reduce the must which you have allocated to making boiled wine, because it is not a given that your household will possess a container that is at once able to survive the heat of the fire and large enough to contain all the must that you wish to reduce by a half.

1.   Must (in French, *moût*) is defined in the *Oxford Companion to Wine* as the 'thick liquid that is neither grape juice nor wine but the intermediate, a mixture of grape juice, stem fragments, grape skins, seeds, and pulp that comes from the crusher-destemmer that smashes grapes at the start of the wine-making process.' It is defined in *Larousse gastronomique* as, 'grape juice that has not yet been fermented.' This latter is the more apposite definition here.

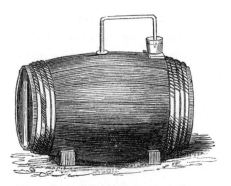

Figure 105. Barrel arranged for boiled wine.

I presume that you wish to deal with 50 litres, for example. You measure out 40 litres of must and you place on the fire 20 or 10, according to the capacity of the cauldron in which you are going to achieve the reduction. If the cauldron is large enough to accommodate half the must, it will be easier. Make a note of the level of the liquid when you commence the operation. Get the fire burning brightly, bring the liquid quickly to a rolling boil and strive to keep it there. Once the must has reduced a little, add one or two litres of that which you have kept in reserve – usually one litre rather than two because that quantity will not stop it boiling but merely slow it down for an instant. Once the must you held in reserve has been added in its entirety to that which is boiling, and the quantity in the cauldron is the same as when you started the operation, the reduction is complete. Now you remove the cauldron from the fire. Pour two-thirds of this boiled must into a large wooden container and put it through the crushed marble treatment. You should not add all the marble at once, but rather bit by bit, stirring vigorously the while. As and when the effervescence provoked by the marble slows down, so you add some more, until it no longer has any effect. Now you should let it settle, then decant it and strain it through the woollen strainer [*blanchet*]. Then you combine the two musts in the small barrel you have chosen for the fermentation, and you leave it to ferment as I have explained above. The marble produces the same effect here as it does in making raisiné: it neutralizes some of the acid in the grape. Without this precaution, boiled wine would be unacceptably acid.

Once fermentation is complete – which you will identify because there will be no gas coming out of the tube – you stop up the barrel and leave it for two months. After this you can bottle it. If you find the *vin cuit* insufficiently alcoholic, you can add a tenth of its volume of good eau-de-vie.

If the grapes you have used to make the *vin cuit* are of extremely high quality, it can happen that putting two-thirds of the must through the crushed marble treatment makes it too sugary. In this case you should limit yourself to reducing the acidity of just a half of the must. And in the opposite case of the must being very acid indeed, then you subject three-quarters of it to the action of the marble.

Now that marble is used so generally for furnishings and chimney-pieces, it is a simple matter to obtain broken pieces at monumental masons. These fragments can be crushed at little cost at a pharmacy, or grocer, anywhere indeed that has an iron pestle and mortar. You can also crush the marble on a hard [igneous] stone with a hammer. Afterwards, you pass the powder through a horsehair frame sieve or fine strainer. Five or six hundred grams of crushed marble will be enough for 20 to 25 litres of must; if the marble has not been ground to a very fine powder, you will need more. Once the process [of treating the must] is complete, wash repeatedly in plenty of water any marble that has settled in the bottom of the container. Once this powder has been dried, it can used once more for the same purpose so long as it is pounded in a mortar again, because it is only the finest grains which are dissolved. White marble is to be preferred, but it is not essential.

If marble is lacking, you can use limestone, but this does give an off-taste to the wine. Sometimes, too, limestone contains iron and this colours the wine. To test the effect, you can try it on a small quantity and taste the must.

You can also leave the must which you have reduced by evaporation to ferment for two months before subjecting it to the marble treatment. This can sometimes produce a better result than when you undertake it on unfermented must because a fermented wine often picks up less taint when mixed with the marble. This will depend in large part on the quality of marble used, as well as on the quality of the must. It is simple to test the two procedures.

The best must for making *vin cuit* is that which flows when you press the grapes to extract the juice which has not already been expressed of its own accord while you have been handling the grapes in the press. This must is clear, because free of any solids, and it is usually very sweet.

To decant the must that is clear of the marble sediment below, you can use a siphon. The glass tube that I proposed for the barrel-bung during fermentation can serve in this role. It is enough, when one of its ends is placed in the container with the must, to suck on the other until the wine arrives. Once it starts to flow, it will continue as long as the tube remains in the liquid. You should watch that the tube does not drop into the sediment or else the marble will be decanted with the wine and the whole process will have failed.

17. — Seltzer water and artificial sparkling wines.

The consumption of seltzer water has become so universal that I cannot possibly avoid discussing how it is made.

Seltzer water is prepared at home by two methods.

The first is by introducing into a bottle of water two small packets of a powder especially prepared for this purpose. One contains bicarbonate of soda, the other tartaric acid. The combination of these two substances in the water produces a gas which makes the water sparkling and acidulated. But whoever drinks this will simultaneously absorb a salt produced by the dissolution of the bicarbonate and the acid. This salt is tartrate of soda and mildly purgative. Delicate people, with irritable stomachs, will be unable to support the constant ingestion of this salt without occasional mishaps. In any event, this water absorbs an unpleasantly salty flavour.

There is another way of preparing sparkling water. The equipment necessary takes a variety of shapes and materials, although at the end of the day the principal of operation and the product are identical.

In the seltzogenes, gazogenes or other devices for the same purpose,[1] the mixing of the two substances, which produce the gas by their decomposition, is confined to a small, discrete reservoir. By this arrangement, only the gas

1. The seltzogene and gazogene were predecessors of the syphon with which we are familiar. They were of French origin. A famous manufacturer was D. Fèvre of Paris, but the illustration overleaf most closely resembles a machine designed and patented in 1847 by a mechanic and clockmaker, Jean-Claude Briet. His firm and patents were later taken over by Mondollot. He called his a *gazogène*. Fèvre's was called a seltzogene and had its outlet on the top, like later soda syphons. His firm was founded in Paris in 1835. There is an advertisement from the London *Pharmaceutical Journal and Transactions* for 1863 placed by E. Geraut, describing himself as 'Formerly Workman to De Fèvre and Briet', offering to repair devices made by either house.

Figure 106. Device for
making seltzer water.

combines with the water to be drunk, and the salt remains behind in the special reservoir. You have therefore, in this case, a sparkling water entirely free of salt and any purgatives. In addition, because it is impossible that the water thus prepared should ever be purgative, you can greatly increase the dosage [of bicarbonate and tartaric acid] to obtain a very fizzy water indeed.

The most popular device (figure 106) consists of two globes of very thick glass, of unequal size, one on top of the other and screwed together, covered with a wicker or wire mesh that will diminish the effects of an explosion, in the rare cases where it occurs.

To make seltzer water with such a device, you do the following. You ensure that the tap is firmly closed; you unscrew the larger globe, turn it over and fill it with water. You take out the tin tube that connects the two globes; you place a small funnel on the smaller globe and pour in a packet of each powder; take out the funnel; replace it with the connecting tube, which you make sure is nicely vertical; you then turn the smaller globe upside down, the tube serving as a stopper, and introduce this tube into the large globe filled with water. Screw them together carefully and invert the device back onto its base, that is, to the position illustrated in the engraving. As soon as the device is turned over, enough water to dissolve the powders descends via the tube into the smaller globe.

It is essential to let the machine work for at least a quarter of an hour, the time required to complete the solution of the powders, and to hasten this solution by shaking it several times, which you do by leaning it so that it is supported by just one part of its base and tapping the upper part of the machine with the palm of the hand. If you leave the device to work over a number of hours, the water will only become fizzier. Each time that you consume all the seltzer water thus created, you must carefully wash the whole machine, especially the lower globe.

You should buy the powders in packets of 1 kilogram from dealers in chemical substances, not from pharmacists, who charge a great deal. Then you divide each powder into little packets and, so that you never confuse them, you wrap the tartaric acid in coloured paper and the bicarbonate of soda in white paper. To make a litre of sparkling water, you need 18 grams of tartaric acid and 21 grams of bicarbonate of soda. A litre of seltzer water made in this manner will cost no more than 10 centimes. A device that makes a litre each time costs 12 francs. A two-litre machine costs 15 francs.

The powders should be kept somewhere dry, and any liquid that you wish to render sparkling should be kept as cool as possible; the colder it is, the better it will dissolve the gas.

With this device, you can also make any mineral water artificially such as Vichy water, etc.; all you need do is replace the powders used to make seltzer water with the formula of each mineral water.

You can also make sparkling wine with the help of this machine. It is enough to dissolve 30 to 50 grams of powdered candy sugar in the wine. Then you proceed in the same manner as if making seltzer water.

To make a sparkling lemonade, pour the lemon syrup that you wish to use into a glass and top it up with fizzy water.

SECTION XII. — FRUITS IN EAU-DE-VIE.
1. — Plums in eau-de-vie.

It is quite difficult, following the many and varied procedures detailed by manuals of domestic economy, to prepare fruits in eau-de-vie, and most especially plums, while keeping their colour.

None the less, here is a recipe that I have used with great success over a number of years.

Gather a hundred fine greengages when still hard and green, with a smooth skin and stalk. Once you have wiped them well, pierce them to the stone with a needle. Cut the stalk to half its length and throw the fruit in cold water. Meanwhile, dissolve 2 kilograms of fine sugar in 1 litre of water in an untinned preserving pan. When the syrup boils, pour it onto the plums now held in a pottery or porcelain bowl – a large soup tureen will answer perfectly for this – the plums will float. Place a plate or dish on the plums, weighed down with a well-washed pebble heavy enough to submerge the plums in the syrup; if they float and come into contact with the air, they will blacken. Cover the bowl and leave to infuse until the next day. Then strain the syrup and put it back in the pan on a bright fire. Once it has boiled for 15 or 20 minutes, pour it once more over the plums, which you will have had a care to keep covered and submerged. This is essential. Leave them to infuse for another twenty-four hours: the plums will turn yellow. Pour the plums and the syrup back into the preserving pan and put everything on a bright fire. At first the plums will sink, but soon they will return to the surface and turn green. You lift them out with a skimmer as and when they have turned a nice green, and leave them to drain on a horsehair sieve or a plate. Once they are all out of the syrup, you leave this to cook to soft ball. Then you arrange the plums in a jar and pour over the warm syrup. The next day, you stop it up.

After three or four days infusing, you add one and a half litres of clear eau-de-vie for every hundred plums and you should carefully stir it to blend. If you use 3/6[1] instead of eau-de-vie, three-quarters of a litre will be sufficient for a hundred plums. The jar must be hermetically sealed.

Another way. — After you have prepared the plums as I have already described, you add them to the boiling syrup and leave them only the time necessary for them to turn yellow. Pour them into a bowl with the syrup and make sure they remain submerged in the syrup by placing a weighted plate on them. The next day, put the syrup and the plums in the preserving pan on a bright fire; the plums will turn green again. Take them out with a skimmer and put them in a jar. Cook the syrup to soft ball, then pour it over the plums. Eight or ten days afterwards, pour clear eau-de-vie over the plums or, which is better, use clear spirit, and stir carefully to mix everything without damaging the plums. One litre of 3/6 will be ample for one hundred plums.

2. — Apricots in eau-de-vie.

You prepare these exactly as you do the plums. Choose apricots of middling size, not too ripe and with a smooth skin. Espaliered apricots are usually more suitable than those from orchard trees. The nectarine is not as suitable as the ordinary apricot: neither the syrup nor the eau-de-vie is sufficiently absorbed because the fruit is too large.

---

1.   Mme Millet-Robinet uses the term '3/6' to refer to a spirit or alcohol of 33 degrees Baumé, i.e. stronger than eau-de-vie.

3. — Cherries in eau-de-vie.

Sour cherries[1] are better than any other variety for preserving in eau-de-vie; however, you could use the fine Montmorency cherries. They do not have to be perfectly ripe, but they must be well coloured.

Cut the stalks and pierce the fruit from all directions. Then arrange them in a pottery bowl and treat them the same as plums, above; the only difference is that it is absolutely necessary to add the eau-de-vie to the syrup at the very moment that you pour it over the cherries, that is to say, after they have infused for twenty-four hours, after their second infusion in the syrup.

Some people do no more than put cherries in eau-de-vie to which they have added sugar. However, prepared like this, the cherries absorb all the alcohol from the eau-de-vie but go hard and do not take on any sweetness. They may perhaps look better than those prepared according to the previous method, but they are far from being as nice to eat.

You can also put into eau-de-vie cherries you have preserved by the Appert method, described above on page 307. For this, replace some of the syrup with 3/6 alcohol; seal the bottle hermetically; the cherries will absorb the eau-de-vie and can be immediately consumed. You can also add alcohol to the syrup you have strained out of the Appert bottle. You keep this mixture for pouring over the jar of cherries in eau-de-vie once you have eaten them all.

You can prepare apricots and mirabelle plums along the same lines.

4. — Pears in eau-de-vie.

Rousselet de Reims pears, and other varieties of the same size and flavour, are about the only ones that you should prepare with eau-de-vie. Choose well-shaped, medium-sized fruit before it is completely ripe. Carefully remove all the skin, even the stalk. As you go, throw them in water acidulated with lemon juice. Once they have rested there for quarter of an hour, transfer them to the preserving pan with enough fresh water to ensure they are completely covered. Add 200 grams of sugar for every 500 grams of pears, weighed before you peel them. When they are cooked enough for you to pierce them with a straw, take them off the fire, let them

---

1.   In French, *griottes*.

cool in the syrup, then arrange them in a jar. Add to the syrup a generous glass of white eau-de-vie to every 500 grams of pears, pour this mixture hot into the jar and stop it up carefully. You can also conserve the pears in the syrup and only add the eau-de-vie at the moment of eating.

Pears in eau-de-vie are perhaps the best of all fruits preserved in this manner; they have a most pleasing and strong taste of vanilla.

If you find the proportion of eau-de-vie I have suggested not strong enough, you can increase the dose. But I reckon this is the most suitable for fruits to be eaten at the family table, and therefore by women and children.

It is not necessary that you choose an old eau-de-vie of very high quality to infuse the fruits; because the particular taste which marks each sort of eau-de-vie is lost in mixing with the fruit syrup. A white beet spirit is quite suitable; and it is much less expensive.

The jars in which you conserve fruits in eau-de-vie should be stopped with a cork. To adjust this to the mouth of the jar, which is sometimes very wide, you should employ a smooth wood-rasp which will shave the cork effectively. Cover the cork with a scrap of parchment, which you will have taken care to soak in water to render it flexible.

When you have to stop up a fair number of jars, you can replace the parchment with a layer of gum. To this end, dissolve the crushed gum in some cold water so that you have a thick liquid. Paint the cork and the rim of the jar with a brush. When the first coat is dry, put on a second.

SECTION XIII. — SALTED MEATS.
I. — Pork.

Pork meat and pork fat are among the principal resources of a household in the country. One or more pigs, therefore, should be killed every year, depending on the needs of the household and local preferences. This supply should be common to the master's house and the farm, but if you wish to keep an exact account of each of their expenses, you should share out and weigh all the joints of pork before salting them.

Pork is most suitable for country folk, who otherwise live on almost nothing but grain and vegetables. Mankind needs to eat meat: it keeps him in good health. In any event, pork from a pig raised in the farmyard on leftovers at virtually no cost comes in at a very low price. And its lard can replace butter as well as giving relish to vegetables. And even this is economical as you need less lard than butter.

A. — How to kill and prepare the pig.

I am of the opinion that when you want to kill a pig it is always better to go to a man who knows the work than to have it done by someone without experience. How well or ill the pig is bled, and the address with which the meat is butchered, will in some degree affect its long-keeping. In some districts it's the butchers, in others, the pork butchers[1] who undertake this task. Their charge is usually fixed; you pay the going rate.

When you plan to kill a pig, you should starve it for thirty to forty hours. As far as possible, reckon to undertake the operation when the weather is cool and dry, certainly at a season when there are no large flies about who will, whatever measures you take, lay their eggs on the meat to turn to maggots a few hours later.

Some people scald the slaughtered pig with boiling water to remove all the bristles; this improves the quality of the rind, thus entirely free of bristles, but it softens and sometimes damages the meat. Other people burn the bristles off with straw; I consider this the better method. Once the pig has been properly singed, you wash it with cold water and scrape it with a tool made for the job, which takes some of the root as well as the burnt hair. You can also rub the skin with a tile until it is entirely clean. It is advisable not to leave this task to those who have been hired to slaughter the pig as there is nothing they would like more than to get it over with prematurely.

The blood is usually caught in a saucepan, but it should be immediately poured into a bowl and stirred with the hand to stop it coagulating. Whoever is stirring it should dispose of any clots that form on his hand. Leave the blood somewhere cool, out of the way of cats, mice and flies.

B. — Cleaning the intestines.

When the pig is split open, you need to wash the intestines. The first thing is to take out the fat which wraps round all those parts you will need to make puddings. This fat is put to one side and melted. It is used

---

1.   In French, *charcutiers*.

exclusively to grease axles. It is known vulgarly as *cart-grease*.[1] Then the intestines are taken somewhere where there is plenty of running water, such as a riverside or a stream. Straight away, you wash the outsides of the guts, then, using a small piece of wood, you turn them bit by bit to wash the insides. You should divide the guts into fairly long pieces; this will be better for making puddings.[2] To scrape out the insides, you use a small wooden knife – the best instrument for the job. It is essential that the intestine which will be used for puddings is completely rid of its internal membrane and there is nothing left but the skin, which should be transparent when you blow it up. You should then leave the guts to soak in a bowl filled with water until the moment they are to be used, i.e. when you have cut up the pig. The other parts of the intestines are thoroughly washed but not scraped; they are kept back for *andouilles*.[3]

C. — Using the pluck or haslet.

Some people think a delicacy that which we call the pluck or haslet, which consists of the lungs, the heart, the liver, the spleen and the kidneys. The only things which strike me as presentable at the master's table are the liver and the kidneys; the rest should be left to the farm workers.

D. — Butchery and salting.

The procedure most generally followed is to butcher the pig the day after it was killed: this is mistaken; meat that is kept for a few days will be more tender; you should not salt it, therefore, until three or four days have elapsed, if the weather is cold and dry. The delay is shorter if it is warm and wet. In the latter case, you must put the pork somewhere utterly dark to avoid flies laying their eggs; they flee the dark.

There are several ways of cutting up the pig for salting. Once you have split it down its length and taken out the internal fat which is only good for melting down as lard, you separate the hindquarters from the forequarters. It is now that you weigh the various parts of the pig to determine its

1.   In French, *oing*.
2.   In French, *boudins*. These puddings are our white or black puddings, not the ancestors of the sweet or savoury boiled bag-puddings.
3.   *Andouilles* are sausages made from the guts and stomach of a pig. They are a speciality of Vire in Normandy, but made throughout France.

weight. You should not include the pluck in this calculation because it will not keep. At this point you can either remove the lard in one piece from the forequarter which you then salt whole, or you cut it into joints, from which you also take the lard, to salt it as well, but in pieces. You should cut the meat into large or smaller joints depending on local preferences or the needs of the household, but I do think there is something to be gained from not having them too large. On the hindquarter you take off the hams, slicing them in a nice circular shape at the top; the skin should lap over the flesh rather than finishing just at its edge. It is important not to cut into the *molette*, which is the ball of the thigh bone which sits in the hip socket; this will otherwise detract from the keeping-qualities of the ham. You cut up the rest of the hindquarter in the same way that you cut up the forequarter.

Instead of splitting the backbone down through the middle, you can leave it whole and cut the two flanks, leaving a hand's breadth which you cut into pieces. These should be eaten first as the bone-marrow which they contain can quickly spoil and affect the neighbouring parts. It is also wise to keep them apart from the rest of the meat.

Once all the meat has been cut into joints, you go on to salt it. For this, you put salt on a table and then vigorously rub this salt into the whole surface of each joint, which you then arrange in the salt crock, at the bottom of which you have already put a small layer of salt. All the salt used in salting should be seasoned with whole peppercorns and crushed pepper. Put the pieces one by one into the crock, taking care to lay them close together so there are no voids between them. Once you have put in a layer of meat, sprinkle salt over it, seasoned with bay leaf, thyme and some juniper berries. Carry on like this until the end, keeping back – so that they can be laid at the top of the crock (because they will be eaten first) – those joints that keep the worst, such as those next to the neck, collar, head, front legs and those joints with a great deal of bone in them. You finish with a thick layer of salt, which should fill up any voids on the surface.

The pork butchers of Paris follow another routine which is equally simple to copy in private households. After cutting up the pig and laying the joints in the brine tub in alternating layers with salt seasoned with thyme, sage and a few bay leaves, they prepare a brine strong enough so an egg will float without falling to the bottom of the bowl. Then the barrel or covered tub which serves as the brine tub is place on a tripod, as is done with washtubs. The barrel has a drain hole in its lower half, stopped with a straw bung. Once the seasoned meat is installed, the brine is poured over it so that it completely covers the meat. As it flows out of the drain hole below, it is caught in a terrine and poured once more over the meat. After two days of this sort of buck-wash, the pork is salted, seasoned and has an excellent flavour; it will keep more reliably and longer than when the meat is salted by any other method.

E. — Backfat.[1]

Once the meat is salted, the backfat is salted in a separate crock. You can also melt it and add it to the internal fat or lard for kitchen use. In any case, you do this with any pieces of backfat that are too small to be salted conveniently. The pieces that are salted should be cut square; this the most suitable shape for their intended use. You put any offcuts with the flare from around the kidneys, which can only be kept by being melted.

When you wish to preserve the backfat whole, you will have to obtain a brine tub shaped like a trough, the same size as the leaves of fat and 35–40 centimetres deep. You put down a layer of salt and herbs on the bottom; you vigorously rub coarse salt into every part of the fat, then you place it in the tub, rind uppermost; you scatter salt over it again and then place the next leaf of backfat, and so on. You cover it all with salt, then you put a thick plank of wood on top, of such a size that it can sit just inside the

---

1.   English and French terms relating to pig fat are fraught with difficulty and liable to misunderstanding. I have almost invariably used the word 'backfat' to translate the French *lard*, even though some of that fat may come from the neck as well as the back. Our 'lard' – which is the rendered fat of the pig – is called by the French *saindoux*. Some fat melts more easily than the harder fat closer to the skin running along the pig's spine. It is this softer fat which the French use to make *saindoux*. The harder fat they do not melt, but use in cookery and, especially, to make *lardons* or *bardes*. This may be fat taken from the salted and cured pig, or fresh. Mme Millet-Robinet often advises to add a piece of the skin or rind of salt pork with its fat attached to the base preparation of some dish or other. The fat from the back of the pig is pure, there is no intermingling flesh. The fat in the belly part of the animal is layered with flesh. It too forms part of many base preparations, especially when taken from a salted and cured animal: Mme Millet-Robinet will then call for *poitrine de porc salé*. This fat is sometimes described as *lard maigre*. When cured in the English fashion, it may be streaky bacon.

tub. This board should be heavily weighed down, either with stones or with weights: you will need at least 50–60 kilograms. You leave the fat like this for a fortnight; after which you can take it out and hang it up somewhere dry and airy, taking care not to knock off the coating of salt. Otherwise, you can just leave it in the tub and take it when you need it.

Some people prefer backfat preserved like this, others like it better when it is cut into pieces, as I described earlier. Usually, I adopt the latter method; I find that the fat is not more salty and that it is slower to rust, especially in a hot climate, where flies are a great threat. However, in Lorraine, the district that cleaves to lard more than any other, they always preserve it in leaves.

F. — Brine tub.

Containers for preserving salt meat have different shapes and materials depending on their region. In the district where I live, they use large stoneware crocks called *jalles*[1] which have quite a narrow mouth and a generous girth. These *jalles* have a lid, which is also stoneware, some of which sits inside the opening, lined with a coarse cloth folded over on itself. This lid is weighed down, so that it cannot be tipped off by rodents and offers a closer seal. In other districts, they use wooden salting tubs, looking like washtubs, which are just as suitable. They are stopped with a lid which is also lined underneath with a cloth. I have used both these types and I find them equally satisfactory. I do think, however, that there is no inconvenience in conforming to the usage of the district in which you are living. The one particular advantage of the wooden tubs or *cuvelles*[2] is that they are less fragile than the *jalles*, which are expensive and break easily.

It is better to have several smaller salt crocks than just one enormous one, because if you leave a crock broached over a long period it is inevitable, despite all your best precautions, that some of the salt meat will be spoiled. In any case, in one of these [smaller] crocks you put the backfat you will use to lard the meat, in another you will have what we call the *belly*, which includes the belly strictly speaking and the spare ribs. These pieces make

1. *Jalle*, or more generally, *jale*, is a word used in the vineyards of France for a vat. It can also mean the measure of one gallon.
2. *Cuvelle* means a small *cuve* or vat. The usage seems to be restricted to Picardy and parts of Belgium.

up the *petit-salé* [1] and are most suitable for cooking. You put all the other joints in a third crock. Then you label each crock so that you are sure of finding the right piece when you want it.

You should never handle the salt meat in the brine tub; you must use a fork to choose and pick up the joint you wish to remove; joints that you put back in the tub after handling them can spoil.

A few days after salting, you should go back to the salt crocks and shake them carefully so as to pack down the meat and ensure that the salt gets into all the interstices that might exist between the joints. If this results in a void on the top surface, you should fill it with brine. To make this, you dissolve salt in water, adding salt until the moment no more can be absorbed, which is to say that after the salt has lain in the water for 4 or 5 hours it settles at the bottom without changing its form. You use this brine to refill the tubs. You can dry the salt which did not dissolve in the oven or in the sun, it will have suffered no damage.

G. — Melted fat or lard.

Once the pork is salted, you move on to melting the lard. In this melting procedure, you should not mix the trimmings from the backfat and the large mass of fat around the kidneys, which, strictly speaking, constitutes the leaf lard. Backfat trimmings that are separately melted over a very gentle flame will produce an oily fat which sets poorly and which is quite different from real lard. This fat will not keep well and should be used up first in meals for the household.

After you have removed what we call the *caul* from the flare, a net-like membrane that envelopes the fat, you divide the flare into pieces no more than a few centimetres each way and you put them in a copper cauldron adding 1 litre of water to each 10 kilograms of flare. Begin heating it very gently, stirring constantly, until some of the lard is melted. After that, you can continue to melt it without stirring. Once it gives off no more steam, and the solid parts are cooked without having changed colour too much – because it is important that they do not brown – the process is complete.

Strain the fat through a very fine sieve into stoneware crocks or white-wood tubs. In some districts, they add various herbs and spices to the lard

1.   *Petit-salé* is defined by Jane Grigson (*Charcuterie and French Pork Cookery*, 1967) as 'belly of pork and spare ribs, salted and boiled.'

while melting it. They add nothing to its conservation. As the lard will be used in the preparation of a host of dishes, all with different seasonings, it is better that it does not have a particular savour.

Lard keeps very well without being salted, so long as it is melted with all the necessary precautions. If it must be salted, the dosage should not exceed 15 grams of salt to every kilogram of lard, otherwise it will not be suitable for frying, one of its most important uses.

Lard sold by pork butchers is a very pure matt white; to obtain this level of whiteness, they melt it in a bain-marie.

H. — Pudding.

Although the pudding cannot be included among household stores, I thought I should give the recipe here because it is inevitably made at the same time as you are involved with preparing the pig's meat.

When the [large] intestines have been carefully cleaned and scraped as I described earlier, you take each piece and you blow into it to make sure it has no holes, and you cut it where it offers a natural break. Then you tie a thread around one end and you put it in water, the other end remaining open and resting on the edge of a dish. You carry on like this with all the intestines. Now there is nothing left to do but fill them with the mixture I am about to describe.

Peel and slice twelve or fifteen large onions; this amount will suffice for the blood of a normal-sized pig, weighing 100–120 kilograms. Put them on the heat with a little butter in a saucepan; cover them carefully, and let them cook, stirring frequently, until they have reduced to a purée. At the same time, wash half a kilogram of rice and cook it in about two litres of milk until the grains have burst, which will give a very thick rice milk. Put it to one side and cut up the cheeks and jowls of the pig; if this meat is not fat enough, add backfat, because it is essential that the pudding should be very fatty. This should all weigh about 2–3 kilograms, as much lean meat as fat. Take the skin off the meat and chop it up as finely as for sausage. Put this chopped meat in a cauldron, or other pan large enough to accommodate all the pudding's ingredients. Cook while stirring frequently. When the flesh seems cooked enough, add the onion and take it off the heat. However, the meat should not be too cooked or else the fat will separate out, which should be avoided at all costs. Now add the rice and mix it thoroughly with the meat, as well as backfat cut into pieces measuring about 3 or 4 centimetres long and 1 centimetre thick – in sufficient quantity that there will be two or three lardons in each pudding. Then, having let everything cool for a few seconds, pour the blood into this mixture while stirring quickly, so that the blood that was first poured in does not cook. You should pass the blood through a fine strainer at the moment you add it to the cauldron. Then you progress to seasoning: the salt should be ground to a powder, and you add what you think fitting, something that is quite difficult to specify; you add pepper and spices (also ground): cloves, cinnamon, etc. Pudding is something that should be seasoned well. Mix everything together thoroughly, then cook a small quantity of the mixture in a saucepan. When it has turned from red to black, you should taste it to check the seasoning is as you would like, and you add anything you think lacking. The mixture should taste over-salted and too spicy because when it comes to be cooked in water it will lose its salt. Now you prepare to fill the intestines. You place in the open end of the casing a small funnel made for the purpose which has a nozzle wide enough to easily take the pudding mixture. This nozzle comes to a point at its base to ease its introduction into the casing, and you insert the whole nozzle into the intestine so that you can hold it securely while filling it. You load the funnel with the mixture by spooning it out with a ladle; if there are a few bits that seem to get stuck in the nozzle, push them through with the handle of a wooden spoon.

When the casing is full, you take the end off the nozzle and you tie it with thread, having a care to leave a little gap or void. Arrange this long piece of pudding curled round in a large container such as a terrine. Successively fill all the intestines, taking care to stir the mixture at the moment you transfer it. After this you take each intestine and divide it into ordinary pudding lengths by tying it round with thread. When undertaking this part of the process, you should always stand over a large pottery bowl because it often happens that the intestine breaks and then you won't lose any of the mixture. If you have more mixture than you have intestines, you can fill the large intestines that were earmarked for the *andouilles*.

The puddings are not yet finished. You have to cook them. Put them into a cauldron large enough so that they will be covered by the water. Place the cauldron on the fire and take the water to just below boiling-point, then let the puddings cook at this temperature, without ever boiling. You can also put them into very hot water, but short of boiling. When a jet of fat, not blood, comes out when they are pierced with a pin, you take them out of the cauldron and leave them to cool on very clean cloths. When you wish to eat the pudding, you only need to heat it, rather than cook it on a grill or in a pan. None the less many who eat it prefer it well-done.

You can make an excellent onion or cabbage soup with the water in which you cooked the puddings.

I. — Andouilles.

You use the large intestines to make *andouilles*. Once you have washed them well in cold water, and scraped them lightly, you wash them in hot water; then you choose those of the best shape to wrap the others, and you leave them to macerate for twenty-four hours in salt seasoned with pepper and spices. For five or six hours you cook separately the rest of the large intestines in very salt water until they give easily under pressure from the finger. Chop them coarsely, adding backfat chopped in the same style, salt, pepper and spices. Tie one end of the casings you have chosen as wrappings and fill with this mixture. When all the *andouilles* are made, boil them on a low heat in a pot filled with water, with a few onions, salt, pepper, thyme and bay, for about half an hour, to cook the casing. Take them out of the water, drain them, and range them side by side on a plank. Cover them with another board, weighed down with a weight of about a kilogram. Let them cool like this. If you wish to make them more delicate, include some calf's mesentery that you have washed well, blanched well and cooked well.

J. — Sausages.

Pig's intestines are too large to serve as sausage casings; those which are sold at pork butchers are made from sheep's intestines; but flat sausages, called *crépinettes*, are made with caul, a transparent and fatty membrane which is located in the pig's guts and encloses the flare. Select from the meat, before it is salted, joints well layered with fat, the bits near the neck for example. Chop them quite finely and add backfat if the meat is not fatty enough. Salt and pepper suitably. When this mixture, called sausage meat, is prepared, take a piece as large as an egg and wrap it in a piece of caul while pressing it flat.

K. — Rillettes de Tours.[1]

When you propose making *rillettes*, you do not take as much care to remove every bit of meat from the lard you intend to melt, and you do not melt the lard as thoroughly. It is essential that the *rillettes* are really fatty. While the lard is melting, you cook half the liver for ten minutes before chopping it up. You take it off the heat before it is completely cooked; you take off those parts that will not chop well and you chop the rest very finely. After that, if possible, you grind it in the mortar. Then you chop and grind the scribbings from the lard, you mix everything and salt generously. Put the mixture on a gentle fire, and cook it for half an hour, stirring frequently, without it ever coming to the boil. Then let it cool, stirring it from time to time so that the fat does not separate from the flesh. When the *rillettes* are cold, put them into very dry pots. They will keep for two months in winter and one month at the most in summer. You can add pepper and even some spices; but the *rillettes* that you buy are only seasoned with salt.

L. — Rillons.[2]

Cut pieces of pork belly 15 centimetres long by 5 or 6 wide and put them in a pottery bowl for twenty-four hours with salt and a little pepper. Put them to cook with the lard as you melt it. When they are well cooked, put them in a *very dry* pot, which you fill with lard. Cover it. Usually, you do not eat cold *rillons*; you reheat them in a pan with some of the lard in which they were kept.

M. —Pork terrine [Italian cheese[3]].

Select some pork that is well marbled with fat; add some more fat and chop finely. Boil some water, seasoned with salt, pepper, onions and a few slices of carrot. When it is boiling vigorously, throw in the pig's liver. When this liver is pretty much cooked, remove it from the water and chop

---

1.   There are many terms of French *charcuterie* that translate into English coarsely at best. *Rillettes* are potted belly of pork, but the mode of their preparation is quite unlike that pursued in Britain. *Rillettes* are a particular speciality of the Touraine.

2.   *Rillons*, according to Jane Grigson, are 'small pieces of browned belly of pork.'

3.   In French, *Fromage d'Italie*, the word cheese being used in the same way as 'head cheese' or *fromage de tête*.

it very finely. Then mix it with the meat mixture. Season well with salt and pepper; then line out with thin slices of fat an earthenware or, better, an iron mould. Pour in the mixture, dotting it with lardons here and there. Cover the top with slices of backfat, put the lid on the mould and put it in the oven at the same time as the bread. After one and a half hours of cooking, take it out of the oven and leave the cheese to cool without unmoulding it. The next day, you heat the mould from the outside to release the cheese and you dress it on a dish.

You keep this preparation in the mould and serve it by slicing it.

N. — *Hams.*

It is enough to have seen a whole ham to know how to cut one. It is essential, as I have said, to avoid cutting into the ball-joint, and to take off the leg below the knuckle, which should remain part of the ham.

When the hams have been cut off, hang them by the knuckles in a dry and well-ventilated place. A certain amount of liquid will be expressed, and twice a day you should wipe them thoroughly with a clean, dry cloth. *If it remains cold*, they can stay like this without any damage for up to 9 or 10 days. They will become tender without taking on a stale flavour, which is very unpleasant and militates against the long-keeping of hams.

Before you move on to salting, trim the ham, that is, cut off anything that detracts from its proper shape, and the aitch bone which lies on its upper surface. You must take great care to cut the meat regularly, without blemish. Then firmly rub every part of it, first with a lemon cut in half, and then with a mixture of pepper, ground spices and crushed salt, mixed with saltpetre, at the rate of 125 grams for all the salt used to salt down two hams of average size. It is much better to mix these ingredients together in advance, rather than rubbing in each one separately.

Select an earthenware or wooden container large enough to take the two hams. Put a layer of the mixture I have just specified on the bottom, to which you should add generous amounts of bay leaves, small sprigs of thyme, peppercorns, cloves, and even juniper berries, all well chopped. Once the ham has been well enough rubbed, place it skin-side down in the salt tub. Cover it with the same seasonings and salt, then put in the second ham, skin-side uppermost, in such a way that the parts not covered with rind are one on top of the other, and arrange them so that they make contact at as many points as possible. Make sure that the outer edges of the tub are well provided with salt and then cover the top of the second ham with a layer of salt and seasonings. Then place on top a board that fits inside the tub, if the hams don't extend above it, and weight that board with at least 25–30 kilograms. It is better, for salting hams, to have a box 35–40 centimetres wide, the same measure deep, and long enough to accommodate from two to six hams, according to the requirements of the household. This box, which is not dissimilar to a trough, can be in white-wood, but is better in oak. You make a lid that fits exactly within the box, in which you have put the salt and seasonings already described. You place the hams side by side, rind uppermost, ensuring they are as close together as possible; then, when they have been salted and seasoned, you cover them with a small layer of bay leaves and thyme, on top of which you put the lid, which you weight evenly along its length so that it presses down on all the hams. These should remain like this for ten days to a fortnight, according to their size. During this time, the tub containing the hams should be left in a cool, dark place, well out of the way of flies. Finally, you take them out of the salt and hang them in a dry and well-ventilated spot to dry. The brine at the bottom of the tub can be used to fill up the crocks containing the salt pork.

After five or six days, when the hams have thoroughly dried, you smoke them. For this operation, I cannot propose a better arrangement than to hang them in the chimney above the mouth of the oven, because there can be scarcely any private householders who have a smoking chamber for meat as exist in regions where they make a particular business of smoked salt meat. In these chambers, the smoke is cold, which makes for a far better meat.

The hams should be hung as far away from the mouth of the oven as possible, at least three or four metres up, so that the smoke arrives as cool as possible. To install them, you can hammer in two large nails either side of the chimney and fix a wooden traverse on which to hang the hams so that they do not touch the chimney at any point and are bathed equally in the smoke. In the oven, burn green twigs of perfumed foliage and shrubs like sage, bay and juniper; you smother them by beating them, so forcing them to smoulder without flame. In this way you produce a thick white smoke that is not too hot.

This first stage can last for about three-quarters of an hour; it is better to smoke for a shorter time and repeat it three times. Once the hams have had their first blast of smoke, they should be taken out of the chimney and, while still warm, rubbed afresh with pepper, spices, bay leaves and thyme (all chopped) which will cleave to the flesh with greater facility because the fat is slightly softened. Then you return them to where they were originally hanging to cool and to dry. You smoke them again twice more, with two days between, after which they may be considered sufficiently impregnated with smoke. It is vital to hang the hams somewhere with a draught of air and, above all, inaccessible to rats. To protect them from flies which, despite the salt and the smoke, may perhaps come and lay their eggs, you wrap each one separately in a thin canvas or coarse linen bag, gathering the top of the bag carefully round the knuckle.

If you lack an oven, you can smoke the hams in the kitchen chimney, hanging them at least three or four metres above the fire. You leave them there for about three or four weeks. I prefer the smoke from the oven because the ordinary chimney leaves the hams exposed for too long to the heat, which detracts from their quality as well as their long-keeping.

O. — Smoked belly of pork.

Belly of pork can be smoked like hams. In this case, rather than cutting it into squares for putting in the salt crock, you leave each side whole. The procedures of salting and preparation are the same as for hams. Seven or eight days in salt is sufficient; after this you dry the pieces and only expose them twice to the smoke. Pork belly prepared like this is far preferable for ragouts than one which has not been so treated, but it is less satisfactory for cabbage soup.

P. — Head cheese.

Strictly speaking, this recipe should be in the *Kitchen Manual*, but as the most usual time of making it is when you have just killed a pig, I think I should give it here. The conversion of the head into cheese allows you to make use of a large part of this joint which often does not keep very well in the salt crock and which is made up anyway of so much bone that it occupies far more room than it merits. Pig's head prepared as cheese can keep for a fortnight in winter.

Break the snout in half, because you are unlikely to have a pot tall enough to contain the entire head. Split the throat and the flesh which covers the lower jaw, separate the flesh from the bone of this jaw and take out the bone carefully. Wash thoroughly and repeatedly with warm water the inside of the mouth and ears. Put the head in a stewpot with some carrots, two onions, four bay leaves, two sprigs of thyme, twenty peppercorns, four cloves; salt and pepper generously and leave to cook for eight or nine hours before a gentle fire. If the water evaporates too much, add some more, so that it always covers it, but only use boiling water. When it is perfectly cooked, draw back the pot from the fire and remove the head. Place it in a large dish and carefully detach, piece by piece, the skin which covers it. It is impossible to remove it in one piece, but try to tear it as little as possible. Arrange this skin around a bowl or salad bowl lined with a wet cloth; then place in another bowl all the meat you can find on the head, the palate, the ears, the eyes, the brain, etc.; all this will come off the bone with the greatest of ease. You cut up the largest pieces and you mix them together in this bowl. Salt, pepper, and season with spices, all quite generously; then stir with a spoon to mix the seasoning into all parts of the head. It is better not to add all the seasoning at once but to sprinkle it over as you stir. When you taste the head cheese while the flesh is warm the seasoning ought to seem rather too high because it will lose that piquancy of flavour as it cools. Now place the mixture in the bowl lined out with the skin. Once it is all in place, bring over the corners of the cloth to cover it. Put a plate or other container on the cheese and weight it with 200–300 grams. Leave it to cool. The next day, when taking off the cloth, you can take out the *cheese* from its mould. It is firm and has taken the shape of the bowl. If you would like to make this more delicate in flavour, you cook a chicken with the head and combine its meat with the pig's. To make this cheese even more sophisticated, you need only add some truffles. After washing and brushing them well, so that you leave no grit at all, you peel them and pound the peel in the mortar. Add some chopped backfat to the truffles and put everything on the fire in a saucepan to cook for half an hour, stirring often and seasoning with salt and pepper. Before you put the flesh into its mould [of skin and cloth], you mix in the truffles and the sort of stuffing [of pounded truffle peel] that you cooked with them.

You will obtain, once you have reduced it, a very fine jelly from the liquor in which you cooked the head. To colour it, add a burnt onion or a bit of caramel. When it has reduced by a half, pour it through a sieve into a bowl and leave it to cool. It will emerge as an attractive, very clear jelly which you serve chopped in pieces around the cheese. If this jelly seems not very clear, throw into it when boiling an egg white beaten to a foam with half the crushed shell and a few drops of water. Stir and, after a few bubblings, skim. So that the jelly should not be too salty, you should not salt the head much when cooking it.[1]

Q. — How to turn the remains of the salt to good account .
Before using salt meat, I like to soak it for two hours.

Once a salt crock is emptied of all its meat, there remains at the bottom plenty of salt that can be used to advantage in the kitchen. Wash it quickly by throwing cold water over it which you then let drain. Dry it in the oven or in the sunlight. As well as salt, there is a great deal of brine to which you should add the water in which you have just washed the salt. You should keep this brine to season the pig food once they are in the last stages of fattening, when they don't eat with much appetite. The salt eases their digestion.

2. — Goose legs.[2]

For this, you should only use young and very fat geese, killed not by smothering but by bleeding. These geese should be plucked and drawn while they are still warm after being killed. To pluck them, first remove the largest feathers, holding them two by two and as close to the body as possible; without these precautions, the skin will tear. After this, remove the down, which can be used to make eiderdowns. After two or three days, cut up the goose, then take out all the fat. Generously season the four joints separately, rubbing in crushed salt, pepper, chopped thyme with a few bay leaves and various spices. Pack them down tightly [in a container] one on top of the other so that there are no gaps between and weigh them down with a plate loaded with 2 or 3 kilograms placed on top. Leave them in this salt for twenty or thirty hours. After this, put all the fat you have kept aside

---

1. This seems to contradict her advice to season generously, above.
2. Although the section is headed 'Goose legs', the text leaves no doubt that the legs and the wings of the goose are dealt with in a similar manner.

into a cauldron on a gentle fire and add a little water. Stir frequently. When the fat begins to melt, put in the goose joints – having shaken them well to get rid of all the salt and spices. Let this cook until the fat has completely melted and you can pierce the joints easily with a fork. If you think there is insufficient fat from the animals themselves, you can add a little lard before proceeding with the cooking. The important point is that after they are cooked, all four joints are completely covered by the fat once placed in stoneware crocks for conservation. These crocks should be stored in a cool cellar during the summer heat.

Strain the fat through a sieve before pouring it into the pots. You can use up the scratchings left after melting goose fat as you would the pig's.

Goose legs keep for up to a year. When you wish to eat them, you reheat them and brown them a little in the fat attached to them, or in a piquant sauce. You can also eat them cold by flashing them for a moment over a hot fire so that the fat sticking to the skin melts and runs off.

Have a care to cover any joints left in the pot with fat, otherwise they spoil. To do this you take out the fat, melt it and pour it back into the pots when it is nearly cool.

SECTION XIV. — PRESERVING BUTTER AND EGGS.
I. — Butter.

When laying in a supply of butter, you need to choose the moment when it is cheapest and most plentiful, a season that will vary according to the economic conditions of each agricultural region.

There are two ways of preserving butter: the first is to salt it, the second to melt it.

A. — Salted butter.

To salt butter it must be completely free of any curd and whey. You should therefore knead it carefully, either with the hands – which must, I have no need to remark, be excessively clean – or with a wooden spoon rubbed with salt. It may be necessary to wash the butter if you cannot otherwise render it utterly pure. The amount of salt you use, which may vary according to taste and local custom, is on average 50–60 grams per kilogram if the butter is to be kept the winter through. If keeping it for one or two months, then half that amount will suffice.

When the butter is ready to be salted, put about a kilogram in a deep dish and spread it out; then sprinkle the surface with a certain amount of fine white salt and mix it in with a spoon. Spread the butter out a second time; sprinkle with salt and incorporate it once more; taste it to make sure the butter is salty enough and, if not, do it for a third time. Carefully drain the dish in which you salt the butter because the salt will take up any moisture as it dissolves. After this, take up some of the butter and put it in unglazed stoneware pots, higher than they are broad, and absolutely dry. Press it in carefully, using the spoon, so that there are no voids. Then follow this with the next portion that you have already salted. Then move on to the next batch of butter to salt, and so on successively. Finish the pot with a layer of salt, which you cover with a scrap of fine, white linen and then a paper. In order that the butter should keep well, it must be, as we have seen, more salted than that which is destined for immediate use. You should season more lightly those dishes that are made with highly salted butter.

In Belgium, when salting butter, they often use *salt kits* like the little *cuvelles* [see above] or tubs that they salt pork in. When a salt kit or pot is broached, you should cover the surface of the butter with a layer of brine several centimetres deep. Kept in this fashion away from all contact with air, the butter will last for several months in as good a condition as the day the pot was first opened.

High-fat butters, i.e. those which do not crumb when cut, nor break easily, and are a strong yellow colour, are much more suitable for salting than those without these attributes. These last can also be salted, but they keep better if they are melted. Butters from Brittany and Flanders are the best for salting.

B. — *Melted butter.*

You can melt butter in a bain-marie or over a naked flame. The first is better and hardly more difficult to effect than the second. Put some water in a large cauldron and place in this water an earthenware bowl as large as will fit and whose rim is higher than the cauldron's. It is into this bowl that you put the butter, broken into pieces.

When the water in the cauldron begins to boil, you should guard against it coming over the sides of the butter bowl. Stir the butter once or twice and let it melt until it appears transparent but not smoking. Take the cauldron off the fire, let the butter rest and cool for a few moments, and then pour it into stoneware pots, the best of all for storing butter. You only pour into the pots the clarified butter. The sediment that has formed in the bottom of the bowl is passed through a very fine sieve. The butter from this, now clear of solids, is put into a separate pot so that it may be used first. This butter can also be used to make a rather coarse biscuit, which is nice enough: you put hardly any water in the dough.

If you melt the butter over a naked flame, you must work slowly and with the fire down low. Once the butter is clear, watch that it does not brown before taking it off the fire. In the Touraine, the peasants let the butter brown a little on purpose: they find it tastier and more economical of use – and they are not wrong, given the character of their cookery. It is above all the *rillonnie* of the butter that makes a good biscuit.[1]

When the butter is cold, cover the pots and place somewhere cool and dry. The surface will become mouldy if the butter is exposed to damp.

If you do not have enough butter to fill a pot at once, there is no problem about adding some more later. The heat of the butter you add will melt the surface of that in the pot so you will never notice the conjunction.

2. — Eggs.

There are several ways to preserve eggs: the point of signal importance is to exclude them from contact with the air, and to keep them in a cool, dry place, away from any risk of frost.

Eggs from late in the season are the best and they keep longer than others, especially if you have to collect them and arrange them in a cupboard. As hens don't lay very much towards the end of the year, it is best to secure your supply in August and September.

You can keep eggs in an earthenware dish or a box, arranged in bran in such a way that every part of them is covered. Sawdust can be used in place of bran. Some people use ash. All these means are intended to exclude the air from the eggs, but they are often inadequate and the eggs spoil. The

---

1.   The word *rillonnie* does not appear in the dictionaries. It is evidently related to *rillons*, those small browned pieces of pork belly that are such a delicacy and which are a by-product of melting the lard. So, she says, *browned* butter makes for a tastier biscuit.

method I am going to describe is, I think, the best, even though it has certain drawbacks, such as softening the shell, so making the eggs difficult to handle and fragile.

Arrange the eggs in the earthenware dish you have chosen. Make a milk of lime[1] that is not too thick and, when the dissolution is complete and has cooled down, pour it over the eggs so that they are completely covered. As you take out eggs, so you draw off some of the excess water, so that they remain easy of access. The dishes called *creamers* which serve to collect the cream for making butter, are very suitable for this purpose; they have a small hole in the bottom which you can uncork to drain out any excess liquid; this means you do not have to put your hand in the lime, and you can handle the eggs with greater delicacy. I can confirm from my own experience that eggs preserved by this simple and inexpensive procedure will spoil less than by any other, and that you will be able to keep them even up to the next spring. Put the dishes in the cellar, if it is cool and wholesome, or in any other cool and frost-free place.

1.   Milk of lime (in French, *lait de chaux*) is a saturated solution of limewater, i.e. the particles are in suspension, not wholly dissolved.

CHAPTER XVI

VARIOUS RECIPES

1. — Toilet waters.

Eau-de-Cologne. — So that I might give a good recipe for eau-de-Cologne here, I have on the one hand sought innumerable recipes of greater or lesser distinction and, on the other, I have procured the actual eaux-de-Cologne of the two manufacturers with the highest reputations in Cologne and Paris. Equipped with this information, and these points of comparison, I prepared ten different eaux-de-Cologne, changing as I did so the proportions of the various ingredients which make up this cosmetic. By doing this, I was able to create a toilet water exactly like those from the most celebrated houses. However, so that there should not be an iota of difference, two factors must always be observed: 1) you must impose on yourself the rigorous obligation to always use ingredients of the first quality, at their freshest, above all alcohol of irreproachable quality; take pains, therefore, to obtain alcohol from Montpellier[1] and eschew at all costs spirit distilled from potato flour which is now so general in the trade; 2) never make less than five or six litres of eau-de-Cologne once you possess a recipe to your satisfaction. Whichever recipe is followed, it is a given that eau-de-Cologne is not at its best until at least a year has elapsed after it was made. In any case, by buying a decent quantity of the essences you are assured of getting them at the lowest price. And further, as you only need tiny quantities of these essences to make a litre of water, you are more certain of getting the quantities right if you are weighing out for six litres

---

1. Wine spirit (*esprit-de-vin*) was generally sold as *esprits de Montpellier*. The 3/6 spirit from Montpellier, rectified to a higher proof and purer, was held in particular esteem. Most French wine spirit was produced in the wine-growing areas of the Midi, particularly the departments of Hérault, Aude and Garde.

at once. You should insist that the supplier weighs each essence separately, in very small vials on very small scales. Otherwise, if he has poured out, for example, a little too much rosemary or neroli, the eau-de-Cologne will smell quite different to the one you were intending.

I would recommend anyone who makes her own eau-de-Cologne to get herself a small vial of very thin glass with a pouring spout. Each time she buys essences, she should bring the vial with her and insist that it is used to weigh out each essence separately. Thereafter, they can be poured into a single bottle, or added immediately to the alcohol.

You will find below three recipes for eau-de-Cologne.

The first gives an excellent water, simple and not costly. It might cost 5 francs the litre in Paris.

The second results in a more perfumed eau-de-Cologne, more expensive, but always a fresh and definite smell. It might cost 6 francs the litre in Paris.

The third furnishes a more sophisticated water, more attractive to some women, the perfume of which will linger a long time in a handkerchief. But the recipe involves musk and amber, and ladies of good taste abhor the slightest trace of musk or amber. On the other hand, one might ignore the musk and only add amber, which has a much lighter and less persistent smell.

The price of this eau-de-Cologne, made like this, is about 7 francs the litre.

Ingredients	*No. 1*	*No. 2*	*No. 3*
Alcohol, 1 litre	860 gr	860 gr	860 gr
Bergamot essence	5	5	5
Lemon essence	5	7	7
Portugal essence[1]	5	7.5	7.5
Citron essence[2]	7	7	
Lavender essence	2	3.5	3.5
Neroli essence[3]	1	1	1
Rosemary essence	0.5	0.5	0.5
Essence of cloves			2 drops
Essence of cinnamon			4 drops
Tinctures of musk and amber (of each)			3 drops

1.   Portugal essence is derived from the sweet orange tree (*Citrus sinensis*).
2.   i.e. the citron, *C. medica*.
3.   Neroli is the essence of the Seville orange flower (*C. aurantium*).

You can prepare a much cheaper eau-de-Cologne by cutting back on the most expensive ingredients. To this end:

1) leave out the neroli, which costs about 1 franc;

2) use the same quantity of ingredients for one and a half litres of alcohol.

In either case, the price of the eau-de-Cologne is reduced by 1 franc per litre, and this water is still very much better than those usually sold.

By using well-rectified 3/6 beet spirit, the price of this product is reduced by about 40 per cent, and the eau-de-Cologne will still be good.

The prices given here are for Paris, where excise duties greatly increase the price of spirits.

Portugal water. — This is an excellent water for the toilette, and for a handkerchief. Its composition is simple: orange essence, called *Portugal*, 75 grams; rectified spirit, 1 litre. Mix; decant off the light sediment.

This water is very sweet, and slightly coloured; but this colour is not a problem.

Some people add three or four drops of tincture of amber to it.

2. — Vinegars for the toilette.

Parfumiers have invented a host of vinegars for the toilette which have no merit save a more or less agreeable smell. Indeed, relative to the effect they have on the skin, wine vinegar would do just as well. You can easily imitate these vinegars by adding a little *eau-de-Cologne*, or *eau-de-mousseline*,[1] or *eau-de-miel*[2] to good white or red wine vinegar, according to the taste of the person wishing to use the preparation.

Dried red roses, a large handful to a litre of good vinegar, add perceptibly to its cosmetic qualities. They should macerate in it for three days.

3. — Perfumes.

In many countries in Europe, but especially in Germany, it is the custom to perfume rooms. Here is the recipe for the perfume in the most general use:

1. *Eau-de-mousseline* is a composition of orange flower, rose, carnation, and jasmine, with amber, musk and sandalwood notes.
2. *Eau-de-miel* is a toilet water made of honey and spices with floral notes from roses and orange flowers.

Chopped red rose petals	35 grams
Orris[1]	45 grams
Calamite storax[2]	45 grams
Cloves	20 grams
Cinnamon	8 grams
Lavender flowers	35 grams
Essence of bergamot	10 drops

Chop the solid materials very finely; put them in a jar; add the essence; shake well; stop up the jar.

When you wish to perfume the room, heat a shovel and throw on a pinch of the perfume.

4. — Ink.

If you use a great deal of ink, you can, for reasons of economy, make it yourself according to the following process:

Crushed oak gall	30 grams
Gum arabic	15 grams

Boil these two substances in 500 grams or half a litre of water in such a way that you end up with 450 grams of decoction; dissolve the gum; when everything is cold and strained, add:

Crystallized iron sulphate (green vitriol)	15 grams

which you have already dissolved in 30 grams of water. You can add a few drops of lavender essence.

---

1. The root of the Florentine or bearded iris.
2. Storax is a resin from the *Liquidambar orientalis* or oriental sweetgum, a tree which grew in the Levant. The best quality, which consisted of granules, was wrapped in reeds for transportation, hence was called calamite for the *calami*, from the Greek *kalamos*, reed. It was principally imported into Marseille or Holland for European distribution.

5. — English blacking.

Here is a good recipe for making a liquid blacking:

Ivory black[1]	350 grams
Treacle	350 grams
Sulphuric acid	45 grams
Hydrochloric acid	45 grams
Vinegar	170 grams
Powdered gum arabic	20 grams
Olive oil	20 grams

In a glazed terrine, let down the ivory black with treacle. Mix them together very well. Slowly pour in, while stirring with a wooden spoon, first the hydrochloric acid, then the sulphuric acid. Let this all down with vinegar. You can make the blacking more or less liquid by adding water, beer or vinegar. Use one of these fluids to moisten it when it has hardened over time.

6. — Polish.

A. — Furniture polish.

I have already advised you have, as far as possible, wax polished furniture rather than French polished. Maintaining the first is so much simpler in the country. Here is the composition of a polish that will perfectly maintain the shine on these furnishings.

Spirit of turpentine	60 grams
Yellow or white wax	30 grams

Cut the wax into very small pieces and put it in any container over a gentle fire with the turpentine, making sure you stir the mixture. As soon as the wax is melted, pour it into a jam pot and cover it with a parchment.

Spread this composition very sparingly over the wood with a woollen pad. Rub it with a wool or flannel. Commerce colours this polish red, but the tint does nothing for the appearance of the furniture.

---

1.   Ivory black is a pigment made from mixing charred ivory with oil. In view of ivory supplies today, its modern equivalent is bone char.

B. — Polish for wooden floors or tiles.

When you wish to apply wax to a wooden floor or tiles which have previously been coloured, you can use the following preparation.

Melt over the fire 125 grams of soap in five litres of water; add to it 500 grams of yellow wax cut into small pieces; heat again. Add to this mixture 60 grams of white potash, stirring constantly. Once this preparation has cooled, stir it again at intervals to really integrate the wax and make a sort of milk.

Spread this composition over the floor. The quantities I have suggested will be enough for about 50 square metres. Let it dry, then rub it.

7. — How to unstop glass bottles when the stopper has got stuck.

Pour a little water, eau-de-vie or oil in the groove between the stopper and the neck: water if the bottle contains a sweet or alkaline liquid; eau-de-vie if it is an essence or a perfume; oil if it is an oily or resinous liquid. You can also tap the stopper gently from the bottom to the top with the handle of a knife, first one side, then the other, as if you wished to extract it. These small repeated jolts are often enough to dislodge it.

Or you can dip the neck and the stopper into hot, but not boiling water. The neck, thinner than the stopper, will expand with the heat and release the stopper. You must not leave the neck in the water long enough for the heat to penetrate as far as the stopper, because that will then expand at the same rate as the neck and nullify the effect first produced.

8. — Preserving patent leather shoes.

When you wish to wear patent leather shoes in times of cold weather, you should first put them in front of a low fire to heat the varnish a little, which will loosen and become more supple. Without this precaution, the varnish, embrittled by the cold, will break and flake off when it flexes as you walk.

9. — Packing.

There are no *packers* to be found in the country. It therefore strikes me as useful to give here a few instructions on the different ways to pack various items which you may wish to send a certain distance.

By observing these rules, you will be sure to avoid any accidents caused by defective packing.

Rules to observe for a good package. — You must begin by gathering together in one place everything you are going to pack, so that you can establish as accurately as possible what capacity box you will need.[1]

The principal, I would almost say the only, definition of a good package is one which admits of no friction or movement between the objects wrapped.

The only way to achieve this object is to avoid all gaps and *to so secure all the packed items that they will weather the chaos of loading, unloading and transit.* You should never presume on the care of those who handle the packages. By these means, you can pack together in the same case the most diverse of objects provided that each item is properly separated and fixed in its position.

Those items which give most concern with respect to either friction or damage from dust should be carefully wrapped in paper and tied with string, if necessary; heavy objects should be securely fixed, either with a white-wood stay nailed to the sides of the packing case, or with other unbreakable items wedged firmly between them so that nothing can move, no matter which way up the case is left. When the goods are packed in a basket, cords, string or tape passed through the weave of the basket and pulled tight can replace the wooden stays.

Armchairs. — When packing up armchairs, you should wrap the seats, backs and arms entirely with paper, tied with string. It is possible to pack a host of smaller items in the space afforded by the shape of armchairs: but they must be secured by some means or other, such as straw, hay or cloth firmly crammed in.

1.   Mme Millet-Robinet here takes the reader very carefully through the process of packing because, as she remarked, 'there are no packers to be found in the country.' In France, the *emballeur* was a packer or packing agent. The author is specifically referring to the official *emballeurs* who operated in the various customs posts, especially in Paris. They had the monopoly (wrested in the reign of Louis XIV from the porters and casual labourers) of wrapping and tying up parcels and packages, and then properly addressing them, before they were sealed by customs officers. By the early nineteenth century, the profession was no longer official, but the larger shops and merchant houses still employed professional *emballeurs*. A related calling was that of *layetier*, the packing-case maker (*layette* is a packing-case or drawer, as well as, by metonymy, a set of clothing, etc., for a newborn child; the Old French *laie* is box or coffer). Vuitton and others now famous in the world of bags and suitcases were originally *layetiers*.

VARIOUS RECIPES

Crockery. — You pack crockery on its side with a bit of straw between each plate, and you also stuff with straw or hay the gaps between the piles and the sides of the case. Every lid is reversed on the dish it belongs to; and you put a few wisps of straw or hay between the dishes and their lids. You wrap a little straw round each drinking glass. Stemmed glasses are arranged head to foot. If the case is not entirely full up, you should fill the gap with some other object or with a pad of tightly packed straw.

If you have to put something quite light in the gaps, you should wrap it carefully if the case contains items that might damage it, and then you fix it firmly with two tapes tied crossways; fix the ends of these tapes either to the case with tacks, or to the item in which you are placing the extra object, pulling at the other two ends so that no movement can occur.

Flowers. — To pack artificial flowers, you should fix them by the stalk, either to the sides of the case, or to taut tapes. If these flowers form a bouquet, once you have fixed the stalks, you should pass thin string or tape between the flowers which you pull taut when fixing to the sides of the case.

To pack a bouquet of fresh flowers, once you have tied the stalks together tightly, sprinkle the flowers with a little cold water, then place the bouquet in an outer wrapping of two or three large cabbage leaves, their stalks joined to those of the flowers. Carefully tie the cabbage leaves around the blooms with string so that they are lightly bunched, or wrap the whole with two or three sheets of paper, also tied with string. A bouquet wrapped like this will stay very fresh for thirty hours and will arrive in very good condition.

Every winter, the town of Genoa sends a vast quantity of bouquets to Paris which arrive in the freshest condition despite a four-day journey and traversing the Alps.

Clothing. — Put bonnets, collars, sleeves, and dresses with starched panels into a case lined out with paper. Press down as much as possible without crushing; cover with paper.

Hats. — Hats are fixed to sheets of cardboard folded in a circle, with two pins inserted at the bottom of their crown at the back. These sheets are provided with three lengths of tape threaded through holes made in the sides of the case; first you join two of the tapes, then pass the third under the knot, pulling it firmly so that the whole is taut, and fixing its end with a small nail in the case. Hat boxes, and any which contain items that might suffer from the damp, should be covered with wax paper if they risk exposure to the rain.

Clock. — To pack a clock, take off the pendulum and wrap it separately in tissue paper. You should avoid touching the pendulum bob; if it is matt gilded, you handle it by its edges with Joseph paper.[1] Wedge the suspension of the pendulum and the hands on the face with Joseph paper so they cannot move; take off the bell, which is screwed on, and wrap it separately; but be sure to replace the nut and washer. The whole clock is wrapped and tied up with string. If there is a glass dome, make a compartment in the packing-case with a small wooden board and put the dome into this space on a bed of scrap paper or fine hay and wedge it with pads of Joseph paper, paper offcuts, cotton, hessian, etc. The clock should be installed in the same way. Write on the case in very large letters: *Very fragile*, and indicate which way up it should be, either by the word *Top*, or by circles drawn in ink at the four corners.

Mirror. — To pack a mirror, choose a case that measures 5 centimetres more in length, breadth and thickness than the mirror. Line the case with paper; make a sausage 5 centimetres wide of several sheets of soft paper to fix across each corner of the frame, securing it with little tacks on the underside. Then insert firmly some small wooden wedges, which you fix in the case with tacks, between these paper corner-pieces and the sides of the case. Also insert one or two cross pieces to press down on the frame. This is protected at points of contact with the wood by folded sheets of soft paper. Fix these cross-pieces to the sides of the case by nailing from the outside. Put the lid on the case and nail it down; write *Top* on one side of the case, in such a way that it will be placed *on its edge* during transportation, and write *Mirror* on the two larger surfaces [front and back].

Pictures and sculptures. — You should pack pictures just as you have packed mirrors, save that you cover pictures completely with paper. You pack sculptures in the same way but, by reason of their weight, the wedges and cross-pieces which hold them in place must be very secure.

Bottles. — You pack bottles by wrapping the necks around with a straw rope or long hay; and then you should place each bottle on a bed of straw, turning them alternately head to toe in such a way that each bottom is firmly embedded between two necks. The last bottle of the row should act

1. In French, *papier Joseph*; created by the balloonist and paper-maker Joseph de Montgolfier (1740–1810), it was a very fine paper that is today used for wrapping and cleaning silverware and for cleaning and wiping glass laboratory equipment.

as wedge; if it is not tight enough, consolidate with a tight pad of straw. Cover one row of bottles with a fairly thick layer of straw to ensure no contact between the bottles and proceed in the same with the following rows. Before you put on the lid, put on a layer of straw which should be compressed quite firmly by the lid so that all movement is avoided. Write on the case, in large letters, *Filled bottles, Top, Bottom*.

How to close the packing-case. — Before you put the lid on a case or basket, you should cover the packed items with a layer of paper, straw, hay or paper offcuts, depending on the nature of the items packed, in such a way that when you nail, close or tie down the lid, it must be pushed to make contact with the case and it presses down on the packed goods as much as possible without damaging them. You must also be sure that no item that has no give to it protrudes above the rim of the case. Anything fragile thus misplaced will be broken.

Summary. — To make up a package properly, you must:

1) Gather together in the same place all the items to be packed;

2) Supply yourself with straw, hay, paper trimmings, brown paper, Joseph paper, string, tape, tacks, white-wood cross-pieces and wedges;

3) Wrap with paper tied with string any object which might be soiled or scratched without this precaution;

4) Plan carefully in advance the placement of each object;

5) *Secure carefully* all the packed items and instal them as far as possible on their sides. Finish with a thick layer of straw or hay and make sure, before you put on the lid, that nothing will impede its sitting on the rim of the case.

6) Write as necessary the words *Top, Bottom*, and *Fragile* on the case.

7) Finally, state at departure the names of the sender and recipient, the nature of the items packed, and obtain clearance for wines, liqueurs and other items subject to duty.

Arranging items in a trunk. — Linen and clothing should be carefully folded, very tidily, well pressed down, so that there is no movement; no empty spaces should be left and the lid should only close with difficulty. Jewels should be wrapped in cotton and placed in a box where they will not move about. You can put fragile objects in a trunk so long as you follow the instructions I have already given for packing.

PART II

KITCHEN MANUAL

CHAPTER I

PRELIMINARY CONSIDERATIONS

1. — Conditions necessary for good cookery.

Cookery, on which some have bestowed the vainglorious status of art, presents no real difficulties. To do it well, you must have good supplies, care, and address. Most cooks reckon it matters not whether one ingredient goes in before another in a dish they prepare, nor if they neglect certain details in the recipe they are following: but they fool themselves. The same ingredients used in a different or an untimely manner will completely alter the taste of the dish you produce. To give just one striking example, patisserie always involves flour, eggs, butter and sugar, yet offers infinite variety thanks to their different combination and deployment.

2. — The mistress of the house must know how to cook.

It is absolutely essential that the mistress of the house knows how to cook. A thousand entirely predictable circumstances may make it necessary for even a rich woman to have to cook at some stage, especially in the country where no opportunity exists, as it does in town, of obtaining supplies from a restaurateur. Even if she does have somewhere to go for help, is it not a great blessing for the mistress who is not wealthy to be able to stand in for her cook at a moment's notice? She will thereby study economy, and avoid imposing on her family a strange and sometimes unwholesome diet; for restaurateurs of the second rank abuse their spices and seasonings to mask the poor quality of the raw materials they employ. And finally, is it not necessary to be able to give helpful advice to an ignorant cook? One can only demand what one knows how to do. The mistress will have only herself to blame for poor food being served if she knows no more than her cook. What can she answer this poor girl when she says, 'Madame, I am doing my best; I don't know how to do otherwise?' Furthermore, a whole host of little expedients may exist in a household that, when properly handled, will result in excellent foodstuffs at very little cost. It is rare that a cook knows how to take advantage of these, and even rarer that thoughts of economy will occur to her spontaneously.

The sole aim of cookery in a country household is not just the creation of fancy dishes of fresh food; it is as important to be able to take full advantage of leftovers, and plenty of other things that cookery books never mention. I have made every effort to give you the benefit of my long experience and to include dishes that can be reheated to their advantage, or without losing anything of their original quality; for in such cases there is a great economy in fuel, in time, and in flavouring.

3. — Supplies.

In a modest household, especially one in the country, the cook's time should not be spent entirely in the kitchen. The mistress, for her part, should so arrange supplies that she does not have to send or go to market every day, which simply wastes time. In winter, she can often shop for a whole week at once; in summer, two or three times a week should suffice. Planning like this will both gain her some time, and the bonus of always having tender meat or poultry on her table. What's more, she can shop on market days and thus pay much less as well as having greater choice. By working out in advance what she will serve each day, she rids herself in a trice of the daily bore of composing the dinner menu. Her supplies will always be timely, allowing every preparation; and she will also be able, thanks to this, to extend the dinner menu should there be unexpected guests, something which happens often in the country. However, she must inspect the larder daily to see what may be done with the leftovers, and to see if any of the supplies need eating up before others, or at least blanched, to avoid spoiling.

4. — Kitchen equipment.

Cleanliness *must be excessive*; it is one of the most essential foundations of the art of cookery. In the article *Kitchen* (page 177, above), I have already stated which utensils are necessary. Here I repeat that although copper pans are banished from a great many kitchens, I cannot recommend them highly enough; they are almost the only means of cooking well. I would also add that, in any given space of time, copper pans are no more expensive than earthenware. If you ensure the saucepans are properly tinned and maintained, you will always have clean and shining pots and pans which you can use without any risk whatsoever. So far as maintenance is concerned, it is straightforward for the cook once she has the habit. The pleasure she will evince from her kitchen full of lustrous saucepans, and the praise she will elicit for their spotlessness, will flatter her self-esteem and well repay her effort.

5. — The arrangement of a dinner.

To offer a good dinner to your guests, it is not enough to know what might be best to serve; you must also align the service at table to the resources at your disposal. If it is difficult enough to construct a nicely composed dinner, it is no less difficult to judge to perfection which dishes can be prepared at home, having account of the equipment, the supplies and the cook's ability. It is by tailoring the meal to the resources to hand that you will achieve something worthwhile. It is often a lack of planning that means you serve a bad meal instead of a good one.

The mistress should compose a dinner in such a way that the dishes are varied and that butcher's meat, poultry, game, fish and vegetables all have their place. If she serves several sorts of poultry, they should each have distinct seasonings; butcher's meat, just like game and fish, should be of different species. It is not fitting to place two entrées of the same colour next to each other; and the same goes for sweet dishes and dessert. A considered choice contributes greatly to the pleasure and delicacy of a meal; and the variety of dishes must be large enough so that every guest can find something to his taste.

It is important that the dishes are served properly and are nicely dressed. You must not allow the cook to send up food thrown anyhow into the first dish that came to hand. When dressing a dish, if the platter is soiled, then if necessary it must be carefully wiped or even washed before sending to table. Meat should be dressed so that the choicest cuts are on top; vegetables should be tastefully arranged, and everything must be placed on the table in proper order. A mistress must never tolerate negligence on the part of the cook or the servants on the grounds that it's just for family and would be better if there were guests, even if she does not impose on day-to-day service some of the nicer points of ceremony of a formal dinner. If the servants are not accustomed to proper service every day, the mistress can be sure that despite her best efforts they will commit the most disagreeable *faux pas* on the day she entertains strangers. It is quite enough for servants to have to remember those small points of rarely used ceremony that mark a formal dinner.

How a dinner might be arranged when guests are present depends on which style is adopted.

Dinner in the French style.[1] — The generally accepted rule nowadays is to serve at once everything which can remain on the table during the whole of the meal without risk to its quality. Sometimes a few of the entrées are removed so they might be replaced by entremets that can only be eaten when they are very hot, such as fritters, soufflés, etc. Only the dessert is held back from this first service and makes a second course.

A three-course dinner. — The oldest style is to compose a dinner of three successive courses or services. The first course consists of the soup, replaced by the remove, entrées and hors-d'oeuvre. The second consists of the roast and the entremets, to which are joined some of the hors-d'oeuvre which were not removed with the first course. The third course consists of the dessert. I prefer this style of service. The guests have a chance to relax and converse while the first course is removed and the second is served, and the servants, above all the cook, don't have to do everything at once. It is true that by serving everything at once you can better study economy, because

---

1. In French, *à la française*. In the nineteenth century, there were two predominant styles of serving dinner: *à la française* and *à la russe* (in the Russian style). These distinctions obtained throughout northern Europe, and southern too, although the rate of take-up varied between countries, social classes, and occasions.

it is obligatory in every case that the table should be well furnished, and dishes that are only eaten at the very end of the meal will adorn the table while the others are served.

I prefer a small number of dishes, but handsome, well garnished and served as they ought to be, to a clutch of measly little things, served on plates, with only the intent of making a splash by their number. For one thing, the larger joints are generally better and have a generosity which sits well with a dinner offered to several guests. If there is a great confusion of dishes, the kitchen's labours are terribly complicated, so that it is impossible to devote the care to each dish that it merits, while fewer dishes will be more considered. The result, in terms of costs, is identical.

Dinner in the Russian style. — Finally, the Russian or Italian style of dining is becoming accepted for formal dinners. It consists of covering the table, for the whole dinner long, with dishes of dessert and vases of flowers. Dishes of food do not appear on the table; they are carved by a servant in a room next door, or on a table in the corner of the dining-room, and then presented in their proper order to each guest. The dinner menu, written on a sheet of Bristol board,[1] is laid beside each place-setting. This style of service demands a larger number of servants, and one of them must know how to carve perfectly.

1.   In French, *carton Bristol*. Bristol board is a fine two-sided card used for a variety of purposes, most relevant here being wedding invitations and visiting cards. The French for leaving one's visiting card is *déposer un bristol*.

CHAPTER II

MASTERS AND SERVANTS

I. — On the conduct of masters and servants before, during and after meals.

I am going to give a few details about service at table which both masters and servants may find profitable. If these details seem overly fussy, or even superfluous, to those women who have always lived in good society and know them already, they will be, I think, of great utility to women who have come out of boarding school to get married or who, never having been in the world, know nothing of how guests are received.

The table. — The nicest cleanliness must rule service at table. The table, the tablecloth and the slip which covers it must be placed the length of, not across, the dining-room. It is customary to place a wool or cotton blanket beneath the tablecloth, to avoid any disagreeable noise as plates, dishes, glasses, etc., are put down. The table legs should sit on a carpet which, in the country, can be plaited straw or reed.

Heating. — The mistress should think of the needs of delicate people who are following a diet or who may require footstools, footmuffs or footwarmers heated with boiling water. In winter, the dining-room must be heated *in advance*; you can usually leave the fire to die down during the meal itself because the heat from the lamps, the food and the presence of guests will cause the temperature to rise a great deal. I also advise you not to forget the drawing-room fire during dinner and to keep it banked up; there is nothing worse on leaving the table than to arrive in a cold room with the fire almost extinguished. In any case, after dinner we need heat because the digestive process is always accompanied by a sensation of cold which makes the sight of a glowing fire all the more welcome.

Lighting. — The drawing-room and dining-room should be lit so that one can pass from one to the other without carrying light. However, when the guests have returned to the drawing-room, one can bring back to it some of the lights which were illuminating the dining-room. I also advise you not to stint on lighting; nothing adds more to the enjoyment and gaiety of an evening together than plenty of light.

If you give a dinner and the daylight will not be sufficient to last the whole course of the meal, it would be far better to close the shutters and light the table before starting. Lighting up in the middle of the meal is a terrible interruption, and this transition from daylight to candlelight at the very moment of sitting down is delicious: the service of dinner is always more pleasing in artificial light than daylight.

Flowers. — Flowers are a charming ornament, especially in the country. I advise the mistress of the house to decorate her table with flowers to profusion whenever she has strangers to entertain. But be sure to choose blooms that do not smell too strongly, as they may offend the guests. Arrange the flowers when you set the table. I might remark in passing that this will save you the effort of laying out dishes of dessert that are both pointless and often extravagant. The magnificent centrepieces that grace opulent tables – often in town – were once adorned with artificial flowers which good taste utterly abhors today, and which cannot hold a candle to natural blooms. If you fill a few vases with fine, damp sand (as I explained in the article *Drawing-room*, above) you can compose charming clusters of flowers which will lend much to the beauty of your arrangements. However, it is important that these centrepieces and the bouquets which grace them are not so high as to impede the view of guests seated on opposite sides of the table, which will ruin conversation and cast a gloom over the company.

Receiving the guests. — A mistress should be ready to receive her guests the moment they arrive. All orders must have been given in advance and the service well-enough organized so that she need bother no more about it. Nothing is more offensive than to arrive at a house to find the mistress not ready to receive you, nothing is more ridiculous than to see her quitting her guests (whom she should be welcoming and entertaining before the meal) to busy herself in the kitchen, pantry or dining-room. If she has no servants competent enough to be left to the task of setting the table, then she should do it herself in advance, and leave the kitchen with sufficient instruction so that it can send the food up without her.

How to lay out the place-settings, hors-d'oeuvre, decanters, glasses, etc. — Nothing detracts from the enjoyment of a dinner more than crowding guests too closely together. You should always adjust the number of invitations to the size of the dining-room and the table at your disposal: you should allow each person about 0^m,60. Each plate should be accompanied by its cutlery; the knife and spoon should go to the right of the plate and the fork to the left; the glass, right way up, in front of the plate. If you are going to serve fine wines during the dinner, the glasses for their consumption should also be laid in advance on the table. Napkins, placed on each plate, can be folded nicely, but in not too fancy a style, which has the whiff of the restaurateur about it. Unless you are serving in the Russian style, all the soup dishes should be piled in front of the mistress of the house who, usually, serves the soup. A carving knife and fork are also placed in front of her. The table is set with cutlery, salts and peppers; the hors-d'oeuvre are placed symmetrically, in such a way as to leave room for the main dishes. Plates should be arranged in piles in the dining-room so that they may be taken without opening the door. If the weather is cold, then the plates should be warmed in a plate-warmer (see figure 45) or, should that be lacking, put on a stove so they may not cool the food served on them.

Radishes should be carefully stripped, leaving but two or three little leaves, and their roots cut short. They must be served, as also the butter, in relish boats *without water*;[1] you risk, by adding water, spilling it when the relish boats are passed round; it will also soon spoil both the butter and the radishes. In the summer, a piece of ice placed on top of the butter does not suffer this defect and keeps it deliciously firm.

Well-filled decanters and bottles and small decanters of wine should be in sufficient number so that each guest can drink what he wishes without troubling his neighbours. Put these decanters on small trays with latticework to stop the decanter sticking to it when the bottom is wet.

You should never dress food in a deep dish, unless you are just family and only when dealing with a ragout of carved meat. A joint served in a

1.   Mme Millet-Robinet has here used the word *bateau*, which I have translated as relish boat (cf. sauce-boat). While a *ravier* is a small oblong hors-d'oeuvre dish, a boat or *bateau* may be taken to be oval.

dish like this is not attractive and will always appear much smaller than it is in reality.

The tureen and the dishes of food are arranged symmetrically on the table according to their contents. As soon as the guests have been served, the soup tureen is taken away and replaced by the first remove.

First course. — Serving the food should be shared between the master and the mistress. The master takes on the largest joints, which are most difficult to carve. You begin by offering the hors-d'oeuvre, which are passed round while you carve and serve the first remove; after that you serve the entrées.[1]

Second course. — When removing the first course, you leave on the table those hors-d'oeuvre that can still be eaten during the second course; you carve the roast; then you serve the vegetables and the fried foods, and you finish with the sweet dishes.[2] You pass round the salad with the roast. Before dinner, the mistress should have prepared a dressing in the salad bowl, then the salad is placed on top and is given to a servant to toss while the roast is served. If, among the sweet dishes, there are some that require a spoon for their consumption, a servant should place a certain number of spoons *on a plate* in front of his mistress. She can then place one on each plate before passing it to whichever guest she intends it.

Dessert. — At dessert, you begin by passing the cheese, on a dish with a glass dome which you lift at the moment of service. Put a knife on this dish if you have not cut the cheese in advance. After that you serve the compotes; then you pass round the light pastries and the fruit, finishing with sugar sweetmeats.

1. French dinner terminology is different to English and makes translation complicated. While the word entrée has entered English as a term common among catering professionals (who are steeped in French lore) and among Americans (who have adopted it as a synonym for main course) it was not in use in nineteenth-century English dining-rooms, where the usual term was 'made dish' or 'side dish' or, if something more substantial, 'remove' (French *relevé*), because it replaced the soup once that had been eaten. In France, the word *entrée* denoted those dishes that were placed on the table during the first course and which were consumed after the soup.

2. The dishes that occupied the table after the roast during the second course of a French dinner were generally called *entremets*. Although they were often lighter than the *entrées* of the first course, they ran the gamut of sweet and savoury, including vegetables, fried foods (*fritures*, which might include fried fish and meat), as well as the lighter and sweeter things that we also sometimes call entremets (in the thrall of *haute cuisine*) and which Mme Millet-Robinet more often called *entremets sucrés*.

Wines. — After the soup and with the entrées you serve dry wines from Madeira, Xeres [sherry], or Marsala or iced punch; claret or iced champagne with the roast, and sweet sparkling champagne at dessert. Coffee and liqueurs are usually served in the drawing-room; however, you can offer them at table.

Servants' duties. — A servant should stand behind the mistress, so he can receive her orders and be constantly on the look-out for anything the guests might require; he should have a serving cloth to hand wipe anything that might be in the slightest need of it. Otherwise he serves to keep things running smoothly. He takes away the soup dishes and spoons from each guest, one after the other, not piling them up on his left arm as is done in second-rate establishments; then he puts them down in turn on the furniture allocated for this function. He should take each plate served up by his master or mistress and deliver it to whomever it is directed, lifting with one hand the empty plate in front of this guest and replacing it with the other. Then he should take the empty plate, wiping it lightly, to the person serving out. To change a plate, he removes that which has been served out and replaces it with a clean one; then he takes the dirty plate over to the furniture designed to receive it,[1] without ever, as I have just remarked, piling the plates, clean or dirty, on his arm – a practice which causes accidents and never hastens the service. I stress this matter because the majority of servants who have not worked in properly run households have the bad habit of carrying or carrying back several plates at once. In formal dinners, it is usual for the servant to have his hands covered by white cotton or linen gloves. Each time he removes a plate from a guest, he should present him with a new one, with a clean knife and fork on it. This manoeuvre is helped by the guest who, once he has finished eating a dish, places his fork upside-down and his knife crossways because, without this precaution, the cutlery will often fall off as soon as the plate is picked up. He will usually hold out his dirty plate for the servant, who will give him a clean one. When the servant offers fine wines, he should identify them to each guest.

When serving a fish or meat joint, the mistress may put a number of pieces on one plate; the servant offers this to each guest in the order of

1. In England, this item of furniture would be either the sideboard or a side table. These discrete pieces of dining-room furniture are never referred to by name by Mme Millet-Robinet.

precedence by which they are seated, consequently beginning with the person seated to the right of the mistress; then the person seated to the left, etc.; if there is a sauce, another servant, carrying the sauce-boat, offers it immediately to each guest served. If, instead of this more rapid procedure, the mistress carves for each plate herself, indicating to the servant for whom she intends the plate as she passes it to him, she must use all her skill to share the meat fairly between her guests, for not all the joint to which she does the honours will be equally toothsome. She must anticipate the preferences of her guests, or help them in such a manner that they never suspect a difference between their plates and the others. She should send the least delicate morsels to the young people or children.

Nothing should be removed from the table, in order to serve the next course, until all the guests have a clean plate; then you only remove that which pertained to the course just finished, and you deliver the following course. Before serving dessert, the servants should remove all the hors-d'oeuvre; the salts, the peppers and any settings that furnished the table should be taken away on plates. The servant collects all the scraps of bread, and cleans the table with a curved crumb-brush before placing plates in front of the guests. Finally, he removes the napkin or slip, almost always stained, that covered the centre of the table.

At dessert, the servant puts a plate bearing spoons in front of the mistress. These will be small or large depending on what there is to serve out, unless there is dessert cutlery and knives placed on the plate of each guest.

Servants should never give anything to the master or mistress, or to any guest, in the hand, but always present bread, cutlery, glassware, or any other object that might be requested on a plate.

The mistress and the servants should always have an eye to keeping the table tidy, for it is constantly disordered during a meal.

You should insist that the servants who serve at table are nicely dressed, with perfectly clean hands, with shoes sufficiently light that you are not inconvenienced by the noise of their walking, and above all that they remain entirely removed from the conversation, or at least appear to be so; if addressed, that they reply almost under their breath, and say no more than is absolutely necessary. They should not personally greet the guests as they arrive, and certainly not ask after their health, but if they themselves are approached, they should answer politely and in a few brief words. If the servant is female, even if she normally wears a coloured apron, she should always put on a white one for service, even when it is only family; she can change it once service is over.

The role of the mistress of the house. — The mistress of the house must devote all her attention to doing the honours of the table with grace and condescension, observing that each guest lacks for nothing, and above all that no one is forgotten. She should perform this obligation in such a manner that each of the invited thinks she has only his well-being in mind. She should study to divine which dishes will please each of them, so as to offer them particularly, though without insistence or affectation, which is vulgar. The same is true for wine: although one may urge people to partake, a certain reserve should be implicit in your encouragement.

You should begin to cut into every dish that is on the table. However, while generously discharging the honours of the table by always offering the choicest morsels, a careful housewife can manage the joints she carves so they are always presentable to the family the next day and beyond. This allowable economy should be exercised with so little fanfare that no guest ever suspects it.

The mistress should also entrust the servant in whom she has most confidence with laying out dessert in its proper order on the table at the end of the meal, and also to share out the food to the other servants, so that the hostess need not leave her guests after dinner any more than she did before it. If, in spite of this arrangement, there is a certain inevitable waste, she should count it as an extraordinary cost of the pleasure she enjoyed in receiving her friends, or of the duty discharged in entertaining strangers.

The treatment of servants. — If you wish to have circumspect servants, you must not deny them everything and I do think that when you have handsomely entertained your friends and shared yourself in the festivities, you should not be ungenerous to the servants. Is it not right that they should share in the merrymaking of the household to which they are attached? It would be hard and, I think, very unwise to deny them entirely. Are they not in a some way part of the family? What's more, you can be sure that they will seek to steal that which they would not dare take in plain view, or which you would refuse them, and hence you provoke them doubly: to greed and to deceit. Look into our own hearts: would we find it easy to live a life of privation in the midst of plenty? To be content with a measly dinner in the face of a sumptuous banquet? This question of basic equality[1] is bound to cross the minds of those who find themselves, thanks to their position in society, wanting the plenty that we enjoy ourselves. There are already too many occasions when can do nothing to hinder such sentiments without adding to them wilfully. We should therefore devote all our efforts to quelling these dangerous thoughts, for the safety of society.

Formalities to be observed before the meal. — I did not wish to interrupt my earlier remarks on service by advice that I ought to give you now concerning the times before and after the meal and the usual formalities to be observed on going into and leaving the table.

As guests come into the drawing-room, so you should introduce them to anyone they have not met before. The presentation is made by naming in turn the two people you wish to introduce and, if necessary, by indicating in a few words any points of common interest to make conversation the easier. When all the guests have arrived, the host takes in turn the most important to one side and indicates where they will be placed and to which of the ladies present they should offer their arm when the moment comes to go through to the dining-room, and whom they will sit next to at table. When a servant appears and opens the double doors to the drawing-room announcing '*Dinner is served*,' the master of the house leads out to the dining-room the lady who will be placed on his right hand; the mistress of the house takes the arm of the person who will be seated on her right hand, and lets all the lady guests precede her.

Guests should find their names inscribed on a little card placed on their napkin. It is important to exercise tact in arranging the seating so as not to wound your guests' self-esteem; you should, as far as possible, observe the same precedence as would obtain at a public ceremony; if two people are of equal rank, then age gives precedence, and great age gives that person

1.   In French, *égalité naturelle*. A fundamental right of man (*Liberté, Égalité, Fraternité*) and part of the Enlightenment's bequest to our view of ourselves (see Diderot's *Encyclopédie* and the works of Rousseau). The Pétain government in Vichy France rather nicely distinguished between '*l'idée fausse de l'égalité naturelle des hommes*' (the incorrect idea of the basic equality of men) and '*l'égalité des chances*' (the equality of opportunity) putting socialists in their place. In a similar fashion, Mme Millet-Robinet seems to be summoning up the spectre of the barricades in her political commentary in this paragraph. A modern Englishman might think of the concept as one of fairness rather than equality.

the right to a higher rank, because we should all respect old age. The four seats of honour are, for women, the right and left hand of the master of the house and, for men, the right and left hand of the mistress. You should also strive to place as neighbours people likely to suit each other, and to exercise the same sort of attention to your invitations. You follow the same precedence when serving the soup, but this strict observance may be ignored in the course of dinner, when you can offer food promiscuously, breaking down any social barriers which the gaiety of dinner must serve to diminish.

Dinner's duration. — The mistress must choose the proper moment to rise from the table, once everyone has ceased eating, but in doing so must also avoid interrupting anyone speaking. You ought never seek to prolong a meal, even when there are strangers present; it is a common fault. There are without doubt some guests this would please, but they are almost always vulgar people whose manners you should in no way imitate. Meals should not last longer than one hour. There is some benefit to a formal dinner running longer, but it should never go on for more than an hour and a half. Sometimes talk among the family may prolong a meal; it would be better kept for later and you should call the table to order; often one discusses an infinity of matters in front of the servants that would be better left unsaid. It's true that we all like to chat at table; once the appetite is satisfied, we are drawn into a spirit of confidence and sweet relaxation that are the mainsprings of family contentment; but I must reiterate that you must never talk of private matters in front of the servants; they will often draw quite different inferences than those which are there in reality; hearing a word here, a phrase there, and unable to follow a conversation in all its details, they often judge and interpret things quite misguidedly, and you'll be lucky if they don't spread their distorted perspective abroad. Sometimes, too, we let drop unguarded comments that cause strife in the household; we search high and low for the wellspring of the discord, while ignoring that after-dinner banter. I am therefore of the opinion that once dessert is on the table, when just the family is dining, the servants should be dismissed. An alternative is to have the servant in the room only when serving the food itself, he can then be recalled by ringing a bell.

After-dinner formalities. — To return to the drawing-room when dinner is over, the men offer their arm to the ladies seated next to them and follow the same precedence as coming in.

Coffee and liqueurs are usually served in the drawing-room, a moment or two after the guests have returned there. I prefer this practice to that of serving them at table; this prolongs the dinner, and is tedious for those who do not indulge in coffee; what is more, it delays the servants, who cannot take anything from the table until everyone has left it. When it is only family, the same routine should be followed; I find a servant clearing the table while people are still sitting quite unacceptable.

When in the drawing-room, the mistress stands before the table on which the coffee and liqueurs have been set out; she urges her guests to come close and add sugar themselves to their cups, which she then fills with coffee. She must never carry full cups to seated guests unless, of course, they are of advanced years; she risks spilling the cup she bears, jostled by one who has not noticed her presence when they themselves are in the full flow of after-dinner conversation. Once coffee is taken, she offers liqueurs and then removes the coffee and liqueur tray.[1] As for the liqueur stand, it is best not to pass it to the servants, for fear of accidents; place it on a piece of furniture in the drawing-room. The next day, it is for the mistress herself to clean and put back the cups as well as the liqueur stand. She should not expose the servants to the worry of breaking one of these often-valuable objects.

When the guests have departed, the mistress should not retire before extinguishing the fire and the candles and imposing a little order on the room's furnishings.

2. — How luncheon-service differs from dinner-service.

There must be some difference between the service of luncheon and the service of dinner, first from the character of the food, and then from the way in which it is arranged and served forth. In this *Manual* I identify the dishes which can be served at luncheon and I am going to explain the special aspects of its service.

---

1. Mme Millet-Robinet talks here of two discrete pieces of equipment. The coffee and liqueur tray, the *cabaret*, and later, the liqueur stand or *porte-liqueurs*. The tray contains the coffee cups and liqueur glasses, and the liqueur stand is either like a tantalus or may be a more complex piece, either like an épergne or an ornate or even semi-precious box or cabinet containing both the carafes of liqueurs and the glasses from which to drink them.

Usually, luncheon is served on the bare table, without a tablecloth; when the table is not attractive, or cannot be kept very clean, then it can be covered with a wax cloth; very suitable ones are made nowadays, they cost little and they only need wiping with a wet sponge to be cleaned. Before you seat your guests, put all the dishes that make up the luncheon on the table, including dessert. Tea may be served throughout the meal, but coffee and chocolate are only served at the end.

Roast meats are rarely offered at luncheon, unless they can be eaten cold. Grilled or fried meats are, by contrast, admissible. Cold fish is also appropriate, but not fried fish. Meats in sauce or in ragouts, conceived as made dishes, are also not acceptable for luncheon, nor are hot pastries. Meats in a *rémoulade* sauce[1] and fritters, perhaps some of the vegetables, particularly those that can be eaten cold, can be served at luncheon.

The servants wait at table as they do at dinner. When they come to serve coffee, chocolate, etc., they should place before each guest a bowl or a cup and saucer on a plate together with a spoon, small or large depending on requirements. The milk, coffee, tea, etc., are put in front of the mistress, who does the honours herself. A servant should first offer the sugar bowl to each guest, for them to take what suits their fancy.

If liqueurs are drunk at luncheon, they are offered at table.

You should not, as do so many households, particularly in the provinces, serve a meal composed only of meats, even if of the most varied character; a half or third of the dishes must be fish, vegetables or dairy produce.

As a general rule, I do advise a household to adopt the practice of serving two dishes at dinner, or three at the most; one of meat, the other of vegetables, to which can sometimes be joined something from the dairy or a sweet dish. This economical and simple manner of feeding offers more than one advantage: in the first place I think it conducive to good health, of which there is no better protector than moderation – too much variety in food over-excites the stomach; and then it is rare that one does not serve too much food and I am convinced that the slight fatigue provoked each day by so doing is the source of many ailments which are otherwise ascribed to quite different causes; and finally, it spares the servants much time and effort.

1.   *Rémoulade* is a mayonnaise-based cold sauce, often with mustard and which may be bolstered with gherkins, capers and chopped herbs.

Luncheon can be made from the remains of dinner, if there is insufficient left over to provide another dinner. You can add something to that if necessary. I even advise you to accustom the children to a simple lunch, composed of a soup of some sort, usually milk-based, and a nice dish of vegetables or eggs. I am of the opinion that once wine is part of the diet, it is enough to eat meat once a day, although there are many who do not share my views. Very tasty food does not encourage child development or make them vigorous, that will come from simple, healthy food, combined with lots of exercise. As a final point, I would suggest it is good for the children to get used to being less well provided for than their parents, so long as you do it without fuss or severity.

My advice might be criticized by those people who are used to the ways of opulent households, in which the mistress is not concerned with such details, which are entrusted to able servants and performed with more ceremony; but, as I have written already, I do not address these people: they have no need for my humble knowledge; I write for good and simple housewives; I wish to be useful to them, and I hope they welcome my counsels.

CHAPTER III

HOW TO CARVE AND SERVE

1. — The carving knife.

To carve swiftly and well, it is essential to have a good knife. It should be a little larger than a table-knife, but not as large as those which are commonly sold for this purpose. The blade should be pointed and thin enough to be flexible, so that it can more easily be plunged into the meat and between the joints. The steel need not be very hard, which will make it difficult to sharpen; it should be frequently sharpened, not on a grindstone, which will quickly wear it away (and should only be used when absolutely necessary), but on a stone like reapers use. A sharpening steel, a round piece of steel across which you sweep the knife before carving, is very convenient and easy to use.

It is absolutely necessary that meats should be carved by a well-sharpened knife; the slices which look best are even, nicely formed and clean. If the eye is satisfied, it helps the food seem all the better.

2. — Butcher's meat.
A. — Beef.

The cuts of beef that are usually used for boiling are the topside, top rump, flank and brisket.[1] The topside is the best and most tender piece; the thick flank is very suitable for a daube or a beef à la mode. To carve these joints properly, you should be sure of the grain of the meat and slice across it. Stewed flank does not carve easily; usually it is best served with a spoon, because cooking breaks the flesh into gobbets which are only held

---

1. French cuts of meat differ from English so that translation occasionally distorts the meaning.

together by fat and membrane. You should always join a bit of fat to every slice before you serve it, whether you are carving for each guest's individual plate or for a common dish which is then passed round.

The loin is almost always kept for roasting; if it comes with its fillet, that is the joint you should offer in the first instance. You take it off, place it on a plate, then cut it in thin slices across the grain. The meat on the rib-bone is carved in slightly thicker slices, across the bone. Before putting the loin on the spit, you should remove any meat which extends beyond the end of the very short rib that is part of the joint. When roasted, this piece is extremely tough, so one can hardly eat it; however, in a meat or cabbage soup it is excellent.

The bones from a roasted joint of beef are excellent for making a cabbage soup or a gravy, if you add some vegetables. You will find how to do this in the articles *Cabbage soups* and *Jus and coulis*, below.

The fillet is the most desirable joint of beef; you can serve it in several ways, but you always cut it across the grain in thin slices; slices from the middle are preferable to those from the ends.

B. — Veal.

The parts of veal that are used for roasting are usually the rump, the kidney,[1] the piece after that called the loin, the chops or best end. You carve the rump in thin slices, always alert to the grain, which will change direction depending on where you start carving, and you cut across the grain. You should add to each slice a little of the browned fat to be found below the bone to which the meat is attached.

Before putting a loin or kidney of veal on the spit, you must chine it with a blow of the cleaver, without actually cutting off the piece, because veal bones are thought by some gourmets a delicacy and you will not be able to detach them without this precaution. You carve these joints in slices across the bone. You should also accompany each slice with some of the browned fat which is found under the ribs, and a piece of the kidney, if it is the joint of this name that you are carving – unless you have kept it back for an omelette. That part without any bones that comes after the ribs is much appreciated by those who enjoy fat and well-browned bits; you can

---

1. In French, *rognon*, but here referring not to the piece of offal itself, but that part of the calf which contains it, which is below the loin.

put this in a blanquette or ragout the next day, with some vegetables as I will show later. Bones from roast veal, like roast beef bones, can be used for a gravy or soup.

The leg [or cushion] of veal is not equally tender in all its parts; the most delicate are two long pieces next to the backbone, of which one is preceded by a round, tough and dry piece which appeals to people who don't like fat. You should carve these two pieces across the grain, in reasonably thick slices, and accompany them with a little of the fat from next the bone.

Shoulder of veal can be roasted, but it is dry and often tough; more usually it is eaten à la poulette[1] or stuffed; you bone it, roll it and carve it across the grain. When you prepare it à la poulette, carve it before cooking. The same goes for breast of veal.

In Paris, calf's head is a highly esteemed dish, and worthy of appearing on the best of tables because it is served with the skin on, and the hair removed with boiling water, which makes it appear perfectly white. Indeed, it is the skin – taken off in some regions – which is the best part; the skin removed, the head contains plenty of other tasty morsels, but it looks most displeasing and can only be served to family, or disassembled and produced as a ragout.

Calf's head with the skin on should be well cooked; in consequence, it is very tender; you serve it out with a spoon, only using a knife to break the skin. The eyes are the most sought-after item; after them come the temples, cheeks, ears, forehead and muzzle. Divide the brain into small portions and offer them to each guest. Calf's head should be served very hot; when cold, it is worthless.

C. — Mutton.

There are four mutton joints that can be put on a spit: the leg, the loin, the fillet and the shoulder; but the shoulder is rarely dealt with in this fashion.

The leg should either be carved across the direction of the bone you use to hold the joint, or in line with the bone, I prefer the former. The

---

1. À la poulette is a sort of fricassee, the meat served in a velouté sauce with small onions and mushrooms. It may be even simpler than this, a velouté sauce with no trimmings, or something such as hard-boiled eggs just fried in butter with herbs (see below, page 448).

slices should be very thin; take them off by passing the knife beneath them and running it along the bone. Arrange them in a dish with the gravy, which should always be heated in advance, especially in winter. Slices taken nearest the bone are less good. Some excellent slices can be found under the bone: their grain is not broken when carved and they are very tender. You should work quickly when serving a leg of mutton because the taste of mutton fat is not pleasant once it has cooled. When the meat is red in the centre, the leg is cooked perfectly; when it shows violet, then it is undercooked. When you carve a leg that has been properly cooked, the juices run freely. A leg bone makes an excellent cabbage soup.

You carve a loin of mutton like a loin of veal. You should also have a care, before cooking, to chine it with a blow of the cleaver to the large end of the bone.

The shoulder ought to be carved something like the leg; but because it has the shoulder blade running through it, you will only get small slices. Should you wish to serve it in a ragout, then you bone it.

D. — Lamb and kid.

Whether lamb is roasted or baked in the oven, it should be served up in quarters. The hindquarter is the better; however the forequarter offers small but excellent cutlets. You must chine them carefully before cooking, as I described for mutton.

Lamb must be served very hot and well browned because it is usually very fatty. The dish on which you serve it should be heated. The kidney, found in the hindquarter, is surrounded by a very delectable fat when it has been well browned. For lamb to be good, it should be neither too young nor too old; in the first instance it is too soft; in the second, it tastes too strongly.

Kid should be served exactly as lamb; it is much less appreciated.

E. — Pork.

The only pork that is roasted are the fillet and the loin. Before spitting it, the chops should be chined, as I mentioned for the loin of veal; it is also carved in the same fashion. The fillet that is found under the backbone is a much-liked joint; you take it out so as to carve it in very thin slices.

The ham must be carved with a very sharp knife in the thinnest of slices, very tidily and across the grain.

The rest of the pig is almost never served except when cut into pieces.

Sucking pig, which is a roast highly appreciated by some people, is always served whole. It must be carved with the greatest dispatch because the skin, nicely crunchy thanks to the cooking – which is the best thing about it – will soften as it cools. To carve it, remove the head by bending it backwards with a fork once you have put a knife across its neck; then take the skin off the back and sides taking great care to bring with it as much of the flesh as adheres to it. Carve the skin into pieces which you serve to each guest. The rest of this joint is only good with a sauce to relieve its blandness.

3. — Poultry and game.
A. — Wild boar.

Serve and carve as pork.

B. — Hare and rabbit.

Usually only the back half is offered as a roast, the front being used for civet. The saddle is carved in chunks by neatly inserting the knife between the joints of the backbone, or you can carve the flesh of this saddle in thin slices along the length of the joint, taking them off by passing the knife beneath them. You will find the fillet underneath the saddle and you lift out each side in a single piece which can then be divided; these are much appreciated. Lift off thin slices from the thighs, then detach the legs from the rump, which is also highly esteemed, and which you separate as I will describe for poultry.

C. — Fattened chicken, capon, chicken, boiling fowl.[1]

These four items, which are offered at table in so many forms, with so many sauces, are also perfect for roasting. The exception is the boiling fowl, which must be cooked in a sauce or in stock. To carve them, you must first

---

1. The French have a careful nomenclature for the various sorts of chicken. The gastronomic dictionaries (e.g. Larousse) do not necessarily accord with the linguistic ones (e.g. Robert). A *poularde*, which is here translated as 'fattened chicken', is a fattened bird weighing 1.8 to 3 kilograms; a capon (French *chapon*), no longer legally available, is a castrated cock, usually weighing the same as a *poularde*; the French *poulet* is the same age as a *poularde*, but not fattened up. Its free-range habits make it less fat and more savoury. Weights (in Larousse) are 600–900 grams for a *poulet de grain*, and 1000–1800 grams for a *poulet reine* at the end of the summer. This has been

take off the leg; to do this you stick the fork in the thigh and you separate it from the body with the knife reversed to cut through the joint. Then you turn to the breast on the same side. Stick the fork below the winglet, then, seeking out the joint with the knife, cut through the ligaments with care without cutting into the bones. Then work gently so that the whole breast lifts off in one piece; use a little knife work to help if necessary. If the bird is small, leave each quarter whole; if it is large, divide each breast and each leg into two or three parts. Strip the carcase of any covering flesh, then plunge the fork into the lower part of the carcase and pivoting with the knife in the middle of the spinal column at the point where it meets the ribs, bend the lower half back over the upper; the carcase is then disjointed and divided into two parts.

The wing and the breast are the choicest parts.

D. — Hen and stag turkey.

Carve them as chicken, or detach by the manoeuvre I have just described, the rump together with the two legs. You take off these three joints and hold them in reserve. You can also, without taking off the wings, carve the breast in thin slices lengthways, putting them into gravy. The oysters, which are found either side of the rump, are the most delicate parts of the turkey. Many people prefer the thigh meat to the breast which can sometimes be a trifle dry.

E. — Goose and duck.

Carve them as other poultry, or restrict yourself to taking off very thin slices, called aiguillettes, of the flesh from the breast and wings. The thigh is preferred to the wing.

F. — Pigeon.

It can be served with or without the head, however, I prefer it taken off. If left on, turn the neck in such a way that the head is on the breastbone, the beak pointing outwards. To carve a pigeon, split it down its length and then separate each half in two.

---

generally translated as 'chicken'. What we may call a spring chicken is *poulet nouveau*, and a poussin is a *poussin* in France as well. The hen or *poule* is here translated as boiling fowl.

G. — *Pheasant.*

Never pluck the head of a roast pheasant; before putting it on the spit, carefully wrap the head in three thicknesses of paper to preserve the allure of the plumage. Truss it as I have explained for pigeon, and take off the paper when the pheasant is dished up. Carve the pheasant like chicken.

H. — *Partridge.*

Truss and carve exactly like pheasant; the head should be plucked if it is cooked any other way than on the spit.

I. — *Woodcock.*

Carve it like partridge; but, to truss, you put the long beak through the breastbone. Some gourmets to not draw this bird and only eat it when it is very well hung.

You serve woodcock, partridge and pheasant with their feet on, and you leave their heads because they have never been bled and their handsome plumage identifies them.

Carve all other birds like partridge, except quail, thrush, blackbird, snipe, etc., which you cut lengthways into two halves.

4. — Fish.

A. — *Turbot, brill, etc.*

Turbot is a magnificent and delicious fish which is served boiled. It is dished white side uppermost. To serve it, split its whole length down the backbone and then divide it into square pieces. The dorsal side is preferable to the belly. If you lack a silver trowel or slice (figure 107), made especially for serving large fish, you can use a ragout spoon.

Sole, plaice, flounder, brill, in a word all flatfish, should be served in the same fashion.

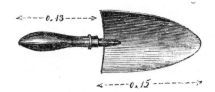

Figure 107. Silver trowel to slice up fish.

B. — Carp.

The belly of carp is preferable to its back; the head is much esteemed. The milt or soft roe is the most delicate morsel; you should share it among the guests; the eggs are good. To carve a boiled carp, split it from one end to the other with a fish slice or spoon in such as way as to obtain pieces from the back and the belly. When you have served out the flesh from one side, turn the carp over neatly and serve out the other side.

C. — Pike.

This is served like carp, but the pieces from the back are liked more than those from the belly. The head is eaten, but is less esteemed than the carp's. The eggs are so extremely indigestible that it is wisest not to serve them.

D. — Barbel.[1]

That part of the back nearest the head is the part preferred; it is served out like the carp. The eggs often cause mishaps; you must guard against eating them.

Trout and all other freshwater fish should be served like the barbel.

---

1.   In French, *barbeau* or *barbillon. Barbus barbus,* the freshwater fish named for the two pairs of barbs or beards below their mouth. There is also a Mediterranean form of barbel, usually known in France as *barbeau méridional,* but also by other names. The roe of the barbel is poisonous.

CHAPTER IV

SOUPS [1]

1. — In general.

Using rice in soups. — I strongly recommend the use of rice in soups; it improves them; ordinary bread [2] gives a broth a sour and fairly unpleasant taste, and household bread does not soak up the liquid well. Rice does not cost much more than bread; as proof of this I cite the economic soups for the poor of Paris – which are supplied to them at 10 centimes – and are made with rice. Good rice usually costs 80 centimes per kilogram; bought wholesale, you can get a discount of 10 or 15 centimes. Keep it in a really dry place, from one year to the next, but it is better purchased twice a year.

Calcutta rice costs only 50 to 60 centimes the kilogram; if you buy it in a bale of 100 kilograms it may only come to 40–45 centimes and sometimes less. I will talk about its use in making bread in my second volume.

The high price of bread in 1853 [3] caused me to seek economies and I frequently used Calcutta rice both for the household and the servants: it

---

1.   The title of this chapter in the original is *Potages ou Soupes. Larousse gastronomique* would admit to there being a distinction between the two, although that is not always apparent here. According to Larousse, a *potage* is usually based on a meat or other stock while *soupe* is made from water or milk and thickened with bread (harking back to the origin of the word, i.e. 'sop' of bread in a bowl of liquid food). A common phrase in the recipes which follow that depend on bread being laid at the bottom of the tureen and the soup poured on it to steep is, *tremper la soupe. Tremper* means to soak or steep, but the phrase in fact instructs the cook to pour the soup on the bread. If one thinks of *soupe* here referring to sops rather than soup, it makes more immediate sense.

2.   i.e. bread made with an admixture of rye and a leaven or sourdough.

3.   In the mid-1840s, harvests had been poor and bread prices high. There had been a recovery in 1847 and 1848, but not many years elapsed before a pair of very bad harvests indeed in 1852 and 1853.

is not so good as Carolina rice but very good for soup. I believe that its regular use in soup is an excellent move; our people got so used to it that they preferred soup with rice to soup with bread.

You should always wash rice before using it.

2. — Pot-au-feu.

Usually, this is made with beef; however, in some regions it is made with mutton; mutton stock has less colour than beef, but is no less good. I have already mentioned which joints are most suitable for making a good pot-au-feu. Although there is hardly a well-to-do house in France that does not make its pot-au-feu almost every day, there are plenty that do not make it well, even though it is so straightforward.

A fault of most kitchen handbooks is that their instructions are imprecise. If I am guilty of the opposite extreme, it is only because I wish my readers to lack for nothing in executing my recipes. I hope they will be indulgent enough to excuse any tedious digressions I think useful.

To obtain a perfect soup, it needs seven or eight hours *slow* cooking. Once you have trimmed, tied up and tenderized the meat, put it in an earthenware or iron pot filled with cold water; spring water or, best of all, river water are preferable to water from a well. Salt it immediately and, so that you can skim the meat, place it before a gentle fire without altogether covering it. A high fire seizes the meat and it contracts so that its juices, instead of dispersing into the stock, stay concentrated within the meat – which, in truth, makes it better to eat – but in this instance we intend above all to have a good stock, not good meat. If the water boils before all the scum has been taken off, the stock will be cloudy. When the water comes to the boil, add vegetables to it, that is to say three or four carrots (depending on their size and the size of the pot), a turnip, a parsnip, four or five leeks which you tie together so as to take them out easily when they are cooked, a very small stick of celery, one or two burnt onions, one or two cloves. If the carrots are very long, first cut them into two pieces, then split the larger piece into four. You should only put a little turnip into a pot-au-feu, its drawback is that it makes the stock taste insipid. Some people add to all this a small clove of garlic, which should be omitted if the stock is intended for invalids. When you add the vegetables, remove some of the stock to make room: it can be put back when the liquor has evaporated during cooking. Now all you have to do is to hold a steady, gentle fire to keep it simmering; if you have to stoke the fire to cook another dish, then pull the pot back until it gets just the right amount of heat.

When you are ready to serve the soup, put some bread, which you have already sliced very thinly, into the tureen; place a colander over the tureen, stir the fire and, with the help of a ladle, pour through the colander that part of the stock which bubbles the most; by doing this you avoid taking up the fat which floats on that part of the stock which boils the least; when you have filled a quarter of the tureen, you let the bread steep in it, then, at the very moment dinner should be served, you strain in the rest of the stock. In this way, the soup can always be sent up the moment it is needed and the bread is in the proper condition. You should put the vegetables that were cooked in the pot in the broth that floats above the bread, or they are served separately on a plate. The soup is better if you toast the bread first, and if you cover the bread with chopped chervil at the moment of pouring in the stock.

The carrots which are not eaten with the soup are arranged around the beef to serve as garnish; they are also excellent in a salad: crush them with a fork, making ribbons, and dress them like other salads.

The proportion of meat necessary to make a good stock is 1 kilogram for every 2 litres of water. One can make do with less.

If you wish to make the stock very much better, you can add chicken or turkey giblets to the pot, reducing the amount of beef proportionately. A piece of mutton added to the beef makes it tastier; afterwards you can grill it and eat it with a piquant sauce. One old partridge makes the stock delicious. Finally, I would suggest adding to your allocation of beef a small piece of shin of veal; this should be your preferred *makeweight*: it gives an excellent flavour to the soup and makes it most suitable for delicate stomachs. A calf's foot has the same effect; this you can eat later with a vinaigrette dressing or a piquant sauce.

You can put into the pot-au-feu all the meat offcuts and trimmings from dressed joints; you can also add a small hearted cabbage, although the stock will not be suitable for all the purposes it usually serves as the flavour of cabbage does not go with everything; furthermore, such stock will not keep well.

You should taste the stock two hours before dinner to ensure that it is salted enough; if it is not very tasty, bring it to a rolling boil, uncovered. If on the other hand, it is stronger than you would like, add a certain amount of boiling water. As this water will be boiling for another two hours, it will be totally absorbed.

It is preferable to use *rusks* as the bread to soak up the soup. These are small and very long breadsticks, thin and very well cooked. They are hardly any more costly than ordinary bread and are much better in the stock. You break, rather than cut them; they steep perfectly.

If there is any stock left over after the soup has been steeped, clarify it by passing it through the strainer and do not cover it until it has cooled completely. It will sour quickly without this precaution. When the weather is warm, you should boil it in the evening of the next day; in winter, it should keep well for two or three days. If you wish to keep it for longer, then boil it.

The fat which sets at the top of the stock is excellent for frying. It should be lifted off carefully, drained well, washed, melted, heated to a temperature when it no longer smokes then added to the deep-fat pot. (See *Fat for frying*, p. 538 below.)

You can also make a very good stock with a small proportion of meat and plenty of beef and veal bones.

3. — Stock made in two hours.

Cut the meat into pieces about as large as half an egg and crush the bones. If, rather than beef, you have a chicken, cut it up first and then chop the flesh and bones coarsely. Put everything in to a pot; salt it; have the fire hotter than when making a normal stock; skim it, having a care not to lift off any pieces of fat that may come to the top; add the vegetables cut into thin slices, including the burnt onion; after two hours strain it all. This stock is not as good as one made according to the usual method, but the flavour is none the less pleasant.

4. — Stock from the juices of roast meat.

The juice from roast meats, particularly the juices from poultry, melted in hot water, can stand in for stock, especially for a person who is unwell.

5. — Consommé.

This is stock reduced by a half, or a stock made with double the usual quantity of meat, which is the same thing.

Portable soup. — Stock is reduced until it has the consistency of a thick liquor. In this form, it can be easily transported in a bottle and it keeps a very long time – a fortnight in winter, much less in summer. You must wait until it is cold before bottling it. A dessertspoonful of this consommé dissolved in a bowl of boiling water is sufficient to make a good stock. If the journey is a long one, all you need do to have it keep for longer is to boil it briefly afresh and then put it back in the bottle. This is very convenient for an invalid who is travelling because you don't find good stock everywhere. You can provide yourself with a spirit lamp to heat the stock.

6. — Croûte au pot.[1]

Toast some slices of bread and put them in a saucepan with enough stock to cover. Let it reduce until the bread begins to gratinate. Moisten with stock and make sure they do not stick to the pan. Put these slices into the tureen and pour stock on them. Slices of *pain mollet* that Parisian bakers make is best for this.[2]

7. — Rice cooked in meat stock.[3]

The rice should first be washed to get rid of all impurities. You will need a spoonful of rice for each guest.

To cook the rice, put it in a saucepan. Pour onto it stock mixed with a third of its volume of water so the rice is completely covered; the normal proportion is to use a third of the stock which will make up the soup. When the rice has burst, that is, when the grains take the form of an x, pour the rest of the cold stock into the saucepan which will stop the rice cooking and hinder it breaking down into the stock and making it cloudy. Then to bring it back to the boil and serve immediately. You can also throw

---

1. i.e. 'Crust in the pot'.
2. *Pain mollet* is a white 'fantasy' bread (usually yeasted, not made with leaven) made in Paris. It was very light, very crusty, with large holes, and often contained milk and butter. Nowadays, it may compared to the *pain de mie* that you can buy in any *boulangerie*.
3. In French, *Riz au gras*. Here *gras* is deployed as the term for any food cooked with either meat or animal-product such as would be unacceptable for a fast-day diet. Foods that were cooked to comply with fast-day rules were termed *maigre*.

the uncooked rice into boiling stock and leave it for between a quarter and three-quarters of an hour, depending on whether you want it more or less cooked.[1]

To make a cream of rice, you let it cook longer than for an ordinary soup. When it makes a sort of porridge, you push it through a fine colander with a pestle. Put it back in the saucepan and add stock. This soup is suitable for very small children and delicate stomachs.

8. — Vermicelli with meat stock.

When the stock is at a rolling boil, throw in the vermicelli (which you have broken into lengths) and stir for a few moments. It will be perfectly cooked in 15 to 20 minutes. It should continue at full boil.

It is difficult to estimate the quantity of vermicelli to use because some sorts swell up a great deal and others very little; however, a large dessertspoonful per person is usually enough.

9. — Semolina.

You make semolina soup in the same way as vermicelli soup, but a small spoonful of semolina is enough for each guest.

You can add to this soup, as you can to rice soup, a little vegetable purée, which greatly improves it.

10. — Italian pasta soups.

It is the same dough as macaroni; it is very thin and swells a great deal. It is usually shaped as stars, or pips or crescents. These pasta make very attractive and very delicious soups because they are genuinely Italian

---

1.   Here Mme Millet-Robinet talks of cooking the rice until it bursts (*jusqu'il est crevé*). *Faire crever le riz* is a common instruction in French manuals of this era and is usually defined as cooking until the rice has released its starch (rather as you cook and stir a risotto until it releases its starch). Although she admits of the possibility that you will overcook your rice and cause it to break down entirely, the cooking of it until it 'bursts' is still quite a thorough cooking. Mary Hyman has alerted me to a remark by Mme Saint-Ange in her *Livre de Cuisine* (1927), 'We still do not know how to cook rice in French households ... To cook the rice to bursting [*faire crever le riz*] is the only goal they think one ought to aim for; and by "bursting" is meant that the grain is deformed, broken down, fluffy, turning to mush at the slightest contact, whereas rice while being perfectly tender should always preserve its separate grains' [my translation].

and of high quality, but they are double the cost of pasta made in France, from 1 franc 60 centimes to 1 franc 80 centimes the kilogram. They need a little more cooking than vermicelli, but they are prepared in the same way. When you serve this soup, you can pass round a plate full of grated Parmesan or Gruyère, from which each guest can take what he wants. You always serve Italian soups in this fashion.

11. — Macaroni soup.
You make macaroni soup in the same manner.

12. — Potato flour, with meat stock.
Put two-thirds of the stock that you intend for the soup on the fire; when it comes to the boil, mix three tablespoons of potato flour with the other third (for six people); add to that a third of the hot stock then pour it into the boiling saucepan; stir quickly in every direction; let it thicken. It should then be served immediately. If this soup is cooked a long time it will thin a great deal, to such an extent that you would doubt there was potato flour in the stock at all.

13. — Potato rice, granulated gluten.
You can cook in stock many different pasta, such as granulated gluten, potato rice, etc.[1] Do not put them in the stock until it has come to the boil.

14. — Rice with water [for fast-days].
You prepare this exactly as rice *au gras* [above]. When putting it on the fire, you can add all the cold water; this is even better, because the rice binds the soup. Season lightly with salt and pepper at the moment of service, and add a knob of butter, its size depending on how much soup you have made; you can also add two egg yolks as a liaison. Take every care to exclude any egg white from the yolks as it will form unattractive white filaments. Once the liaison has been added, you stir it but do not let it boil, because the liaison will curdle. You can successfully replace the liaison with a vegetable purée. Some people add sugar to this soup, in which case they wouldn't add the purée.

1. See the entry relating to these two indigenous 'pasta' in the previous chapter, pages 299–300, above.

A rice soup with water can be made in an earthenware pot before the fire; it is even better when made like this; but make sure the pot is always full to the brim, because otherwise the soup will take on a taste from the earthenware if the upper part of the pot remains empty and exposed to the flames.

15. — Onion soup.

Put some butter in a copper or iron saucepan, placed on a brisk fire. Peel and thinly slice one or several onions, according to how large they are and how much soup you wish to make. Add a half-spoonful of flour. Let them fry until they have all taken a nice colour. Add the correct amount of water, preferably boiling, not cold, some salt, a little pepper. Leave to boil for at least a quarter of an hour. Pour it all onto very thin slices of bread which you have placed in a tureen in alternate layers of bread and grated Parmesan or Gruyère cheese. You can strain this soup so as not to have any onion in the tureen.

One way to make this soup into an excellent pottage is to make it with a stock made from fresh podded haricots; in this case do not add flour and the flavour is very similar to a soup made with meat stock. A broth made from lentils, broad beans, dried haricots or French beans also makes something a great deal better. You can even add a purée made from the vegetables which served as a base for the broth. A little meat stock added to the water which you pour over the fried onions gives this soup an excellent flavour.

Onion soup with rice. — Make the broth exactly as I have described, but without flour. Blanch a sufficient quantity of rice; season with salt and pepper. If you wish there to be no onions in the finished soup, strain the broth before adding the rice, which you can also replace with granulated gluten or Touraine rice, indeed by any pasta intended for soups. This soup is excellent and no more difficult to make than one with bread, you just need to be a little more careful. I will reiterate frequently that good cookery depends on care and attention.

Onion soup with milk. — You make this exactly as onion soup with water. You either add nothing but milk or half milk, half water. A vegetable broth mixes perfectly with milk. This soup is excellent and little known.

16. — Plain milk soup.

Nothing is simpler: pour boiling milk onto slices of bread. Sweeten it with sugar, or not as the case may be; some people salt it like an ordinary soup. Sometimes the milk will curdle if you steep it too far in advance.

17. — Soupe à la reine [Milk soup with eggs]

Boil some milk, sweeten it. Mix two egg yolks in a cup with a little cold milk; add some boiling milk to it slowly; return this to the milk on the fire. Stir it. Steep some slices of bread in this confection. You can flavour it with a bay leaf which you boil with the milk, or with a few orange flower petals, fresh or dried, or finally with some orange flower water.

18. — Cabbage soups.

Plain cabbage soup. — Put spring or river water in a stewpan (cast iron stewpans are preferable); place it before the fire or, better, hang it off the pothook. When it boils, add carrots cut into long pieces and two onions into each of which you stick a clove, one or two turnips, depending on their size, three or four whole peeled potatoes, French beans or freshly podded white haricots, some small broad beans or large ones that you have skinned, some peas, some asparagus tips, and finally some cabbages in large pieces from which you have removed the heart and the stalk. Stir up the fire; add salt when the pot is half-cooked. If the cabbage is curly leaved, it will take less time to cook than collard greens or hearted cabbage. When all these vegetables are nearly cooked, add a lump of butter, its size depending on the dimensions of the stewpan. You can replace the butter with some good lard. Leave it to boil for half an hour. To steep the bread, first locate all the potatoes and crush them in the ladle then add them back to the broth; then pour the broth over the bread and put the vegetables on top of it.

To make a cabbage soup, you do not have to include all the vegetables I have mentioned; I only wished to acquaint you with all those which could be used to advantage; but I should state that the more vegetables, and the more varied, the better the soup. A few slices of good pumpkin, such as the Turk's turban squash, will *greatly* improve cabbage soup.

In general, soups made with water [fast-day soups, *soupes maigres*] are better when reheated; what's more, it is economical to make one for two or three days. Especially in winter, you can make almost all of them in a cast iron stewpan before the fire or on the pothook.

When there is not enough cabbage soup broth for the next day, you can add some boiling milk; this will amalgamate very readily.

If you have a vegetable stock to add to the cabbage soup, there is nothing better.

Cabbage soup with cheese. — This is much liked by some people. First you place a thin layer of sliced bread in the tureen, then some grated cheese and some vegetables, then another layer of bread, cheese and so forth. Moisten everything with the cabbage broth and leave it to steep for about three-quarters of an hour, leaving the tureen, which you must cover, very close to the fire. You should add more or less cheese depending on its quality. It should be made up of three parts: two parts Gruyère and one part Parmesan. You will need about 250 grams for a soup for eight people.

Cabbage soup with salt pork. — Belly pork is the best joint to use. Once you have rinsed it in water a few times to take the salt out, put it into cold water and skim it before it comes to the boil. It should be left on the fire for at least two hours before any vegetables are added – which are the same ones as for the soup previously described. You do not add any butter or lard.

Another cabbage soup. — When you have eaten a roast, be it beef, veal, or leg of mutton (especially if there is still flesh left on the knuckle), you can make an excellent cabbage soup with the bones. Break the bones in several places, carefully removing any splinters. They should cook in water for two hours before you add the vegetables. If you are anxious about splinters, strain the broth through a sieve before putting in the vegetables; bring it back to the boil before adding them. It only needs a very small amount of butter or lard to make this soup excellent. It is very similar to cabbage soup with meat stock. You can cook rice in this soup.

19. — Lentil or pea purée soup.

This purée can be made with lentils or [dried] green peas. Put four spoonfuls of one of these vegetables in a pot with cold water. When they come to the boil, add one or two carrots, one or two turnips (depending on their size), an onion and two or three potatoes. Salt it. For everything to be perfectly cooked, allow at least four hours. Pour it into a colander, crush and press through the vegetables. Put on the fire a bit of butter in a saucepan; let it heat up before adding the broth; once it has come to the boil, pour the soup onto bread. It is much better to make this soup with rice, as I explained under *Onion soup*, above.

You can put on to cook a larger quantity of dried vegetables than you need for the soup; what is not used makes a separate dish. If you wish to make this soup with meat, you add a piece of salt pork to the vegetables and you serve it with the purée.

20. — Soup of a purée of various vegetables.

Put some water on the fire. When it comes to the boil, add plenty of carrots, onions, some slices of Turk's turban squash, two or three turnips, four or five large potatoes (peeled and left whole). Cook this thoroughly. Push it through a large colander with a mushroom-shaped pestle. Put it back on the heat. When the broth boils, add the right quantity of rice for a soup, and some butter; salt it. Leave the rice to cook. Serve it up. This soup will keep for three or four days in winter, two days in summer. It is at least as good reheated as fresh. You can also cook some sorrel in butter to a purée before adding it to the pot. This acidity pleases many. This soup is good, health-giving, nourishing and costs little.

21. — Purée de Crécy soup for meat-days.[1]

Put any scraps of meat, the best are chicken giblets, in a pot with enough water for the soup you are making; heat it, skim it and bring to the boil. Add *plenty* of good quality carrots, *plenty* of quartered onions, one turnip, and one or two potatoes. Let them cook thoroughly. Take out all the meat; strain the broth. Crush then push through a fine colander all the vegetables (see the *pestle for purées* illustrated on page 186). These, once mixed with the broth, will thicken it considerably. Put a pat of butter in a saucepan and

---

1. Crécy is the *haute cuisine* shorthand for carrots, either in a soup or any other garnish. It was most likely named for a village east of Paris (now Crécy-la-Chapelle) where the carrots (known as *carrottes de Meaux*, a village a few kilometres to the north) were celebrated. Others, no less indeed than the poet and gastronome Charles Monselet (1825–1888) whose culinary poems included a sonnet *La Purée de Crécy*, averred that the source of the name was Crécy-la-Bataille in the Somme, site of the Battle of Crécy in 1346.

heat it without browning; pour in your soup. Let it boil; thicken it with one or two spoonfuls of the finest grade of Touraine rice [potato pasta, see above, page 300]. Serve it up. This soup is extremely delicate.

22. — Purée de Crécy soup for fast-days.

Instead of the meat scraps which were included in the soup à la Crécy for meat-days, you should cook some yellow split peas in the water destined for this soup, as I explain later in the article *Meatless stock*, and you then continue as before. This soup, although without meat, yields nothing to that which precedes it.

23. — Purée soup with croûtons.[1]

This is a purée soup to which one has added pieces of fried bread, of which I will talk later in the article *Soup à la julienne*.

24. — Leek soup.

Choose very white leeks, clean them and cut them into very small pieces. You will need a fair quantity. Brown them in butter. When they have taken a nice colour, add some well-cleaned sorrel and cover the pot so that it melts. Stir well, moisten with a little water and season with salt. You can finish this soup with bread or with rice. It is excellent.

25. — Julienne soup with bread or with rice.[2]

Cut into small cubes as large as a pea every sort of fresh vegetable, including potatoes. Brown in a fair quantity of butter without taking too much colour; moisten with boiling water; season with salt. When all the vegetables are thoroughly cooked, pour this soup onto some slices of bread dried in the oven. It is better to blanch the rice in the water and then add the julienne, which you allow to boil for a few moments. You can also blanch the rice in the julienne. You can also crush the vegetables and push

1. *Croûtons* might be translated as crusts or, when fried slices of bread, as sippets. But this last has been superseded in modern English by the French term.
2. *Julienne* is another *haute cuisine* term that has been adopted into English kitchen parlance. Strictly speaking a *julienne* is a vegetable or collection of vegetables cut into strips. But here Mme Millet-Robinet talks of vegetables cut into small squares (*petits carrés*), i.e. either *macédoine* or perhaps *brunoise*. However, in the following recipe, she does advise cutting the julienne in the conventional manner.

them through a sieve. To make this soup more delicate, cut some small, thin slices of bread (in triangles, squares or rounds) and fry them in butter before throwing them into the soup as it is served. You can add sorrel, which you cook in butter with the vegetables once you have first browned them. You should cover the saucepan so that the sorrel cooks and melts into a purée, and you should stir it frequently and vigorously.

26. — Julienne without bread or rice.

Cut some carrots, turnips and onions in very thin slices, then in strips no larger than the tine of a fork. Brown these vegetables in butter, then add some meat stock or a vegetable stock as might be made from haricots, peas or lentils. Let it cook; salt it. This soup is served without bread.

If you have no stock, you can cook three or four large peeled potatoes in a pan with water. Season it and add butter. Then strain the broth, crushing the potatoes, and use this to moisten the vegetables.

Today, there is nothing easier to obtain, at any time of the year, than the ingredients for an excellent julienne. You can find vegetables preserved according to the Masson procedure[1] at any grocer's, including among others a preparation going by the name of julienne which contains the different vegetables which make up this simple, pleasing soup. Each packet comes with detailed instructions so I do not have to delay to tell you how to use them.

27. — Sorrel soup with garden peas.

This soup is the best you can eat when fresh vegetables are in season. Carefully strip one or two handfuls of sorrel, keeping only the leaves and discarding the whole length of the ribs. Once you have washed the sorrel thoroughly, put it into a saucepan with a knob of butter and cover it. You should stir it briskly and frequently so as to break up the sorrel leaves and reduce them to a purée. If they seem to be browning before they get to this stage, add a little hot water. When the sorrel is thoroughly cooked, add water (boiling rather than cold) and when it comes to the boil, add a fair quantity of garden peas, an onion, a carrot, and a turnip if the season permits (these latter vegetables all chopped finely). You can sweat them in

---

1.   See the reference to the Masson method on page 307, above.

butter, as for the julienne soup, before adding them to the sorrel – this may be a better way to do it. Leave them to cook for at least an hour and a half, and season with salt when the cooking is halfway through. Slice the bread into the saucepan and let it boil for a few moments before serving up. This soup is better reheated; but you should not add the bread to that portion you are going to reheat. Mange-tout peas, of which you eat the pods as well as the seeds, and some French beans, give an excellent flavour to this soup. If the sorrel was too acid, you can mix in a little orach or even lettuce; but they need chopping. Small broad beans accord well with the soup too.

To make this soup even more delicate, you cook rice in it rather than adding bread. When the rice is thoroughly cooked, you serve it up. If you are doing this, once you have washed the rice in warm water, you add it to the boiling broth. If you add half meat stock [at the outset] you will have a very good soup.

You can also cook the peas and other vegetables over a bright fire in boiling water. When they are almost cooked, you melt the sorrel in butter, as I have described, and pour it into the broth. The vegetables will cook more thoroughly if you follow this method.

28. — Meatless stock.

Put in a saucepan a litre of yellow dried peas (the sort used for seed), just one or two carrots, two or three onions, and a very small stick of celery, if that flavour appeals to you. Let this boil before a low fire for six or seven hours; season with salt halfway through cooking. If you have a few small carp, or other small freshwater fish, or even the raw carcase of a carp whose flesh you have used for quenelles, add these in with the vegetables and you will greatly improve the stock. Strain it when the vegetables are cooked. It is almost as tasty as a meat stock and can be used instead of one, not only in all soups but in almost all sauces for fast-days. This is not used enough in cooking: it is the most effective tool for fast-day cookery. If the peas have cooked down well, you can push them through for a purée with the vegetables and make a separate dish. Often they do not cook sufficiently to be eaten, but they are not wasted: they are excellent for the pigs and the poultry. This stock costs very little, especially in the country where often more peas are harvested than are needed for seed. I thoroughly endorse its employment.

29. — A soup of rice and jus, and jus to replace stock in sauces.[13]

A good cook must know how to make use of everything; therefore, when there are a few offcuts of meat or bones from roast veal or roast beef left over, or even the bone from a leg of mutton on which a bit of meat remains attached to the knuckle, you can make an excellent *jus* suitable for a soup or to provide the liquid for all sauces and ragouts. If there are no leftovers of meat, then a 400–500 gram piece of beef or veal shin will make an excellent *jus*; and a little salt pork will improve it. You cut the meats into small pieces and break the bones; you prepare several carrots, especially if this is for soup, as there is nothing better for soups than carrots; a few turnips, three or four large onions; slice all these vegetables and put them with the meat and bones in a fairly large saucepan, adding a large knob of butter and a large spoonful of lard or chicken fat; then you put the saucepan on a high fire. The vegetables and meat it contains will soon turn golden; stir them around so that everything takes colour, without burning. Add a bay leaf and salt and then hot water so that everything is covered. Let it come to the boil and then stir it right to the bottom so as to scrape off anything that may have stuck to the saucepan. While you are doing this, you will have put a pot filled with water in front of the fire. When this water boils, take out sufficient to make room for the contents of the saucepan, which should be poured into the pot. Leave this to boil for two or three hours, then strain this *jus* which will be perfect for a rice soup (see the recipe *Rice cooked with meat stock*, above) or a vermicelli or semolina soup, or indeed for any sauce or ragout.

If this *jus* is not strong enough for a sauce, you can reduce it a little; if on the other hand it is very strong – which will depend on the proportion of water to the other ingredients – you can add water to the solid ingredients after you have strained off the *jus*. This will make a light broth which will be far preferable to plain water for various purposes in the kitchen. If you

1.   The French word *jus* can often be translated as gravy, when it means precisely that (a deglazing of a roasting pan with water or stock to make an enriched stock from the pan juices). But if we use the word 'gravy' indiscriminately, it distorts Mme Millet-Robinet's meaning for although she often considers *jus* to be a liquid derived from cooked or roasted bones, she also thinks of it as a variation on a standard stock, i.e. containing plenty of raw meat and vegetables, although more reduced than a *bouillon*. So the word is left in its original here, reserving 'gravy' for when it is truly a gravy in English parlance, and 'stock' for her *bouillon*.

don't cook the meat and vegetables that served to prepare the *jus* for a second time as I have just suggested, you can put them on a fireproof dish, with a bit of lard or chicken fat, or even a knob of butter, quite generous salt and pepper, and a little moistening with *jus* and put them in the fire, with coals above and below. Let them stew for half an hour and serve them up. It won't be delicious, but is perfectly acceptable. If it isn't toothsome enough for the family table, it will certainly be appreciated by the farm servants, for agricultural labourers are not accustomed to sophisticated cookery.

Every cookery book constantly recommends using a meat stock in sauces, but it is quite difficult for a small household to always have one at its disposal. This *jus* and the meat-free stock are two very serviceable and low-cost means to replace meat stock. If you want a very concentrated *jus*, you will have to use more meat. You can brown the meat first in the saucepan, then take it out and brown the vegetables in the fat which remains. While the vegetables are browning, you can start the meat cooking in the stockpot.

30. — Herb soup.

Carefully strip some sorrel, a little purslane, a little chervil, some orach and an onion; chop it all finely; reduce it to a purée in butter, as I showed in *Sorrel soup with garden peas*; add meatless stock or water; salt it. Let it boil a little. Carefully separate one or two egg yolks from their whites, according to the amount of soup; mix the yolks with a little lukewarm water; take the soup off the fire and straightaway pour in the liaison, stirring briskly. If a few strands of egg white appear, carefully remove them; they give the soup an unpleasing appearance. Soak the bread for a few moments before serving. There is no need to whiten the soup by adding milk, especially if you have made it with meatless stock.

31. — Turnip soup.

Carefully peel the turnips. If their flavour is too strong, blanch them in plenty of water, and cut them into as regularly sized pieces as possible. Yellow and white turnips from Scotland, turnips from the Limousin, and the Fosterton turnip are excellent for this purpose. When the turnips are tender, particularly the variety said to come from Freneuse, it is better to scrape rather than peel them.[1] Put them before the fire in a pot full of boiling water; let them cook, salt it, and reduce the broth. Half an hour before serving, fill the pot (in which a proportion of the water has evaporated by boiling) with good milk, and add a knob of butter; let it come to the boil again. Pour the broth onto bread and add the turnips to the tureen. Those which are not used in the soup are served with a white milk sauce, the recipe for which is found in the chapter on *Sauces*.

32. — Panada.

For this to be good, the bread should not be cut but broken and put in plenty of water, that is to say with more water than just to cover it, in a saucepan or, better, a small earthenware pot, before the fire. Cook it very gently without stirring, for at least an hour and a half or two hours. If you make the panada in an earthenware pot, from time to time you will have to detach the bread that sticks to the side of the pot nearest the fire because, without this attention, it will burn. However, you should not stir the rest of it. When you serve it up, add a knob of butter and then stir it. The bread will have become transparent and the soup, although thickened is neither cloudy nor pasty. Salt it and serve it. You can also add sugar and milk to whiten it at the moment of service. You must not boil the milk with the bread as the soup will curdle. To make this soup delicate and very good for very young children, you should strain it. You can also add a liaison.

33. — Squash or melon soup.[2]

This soup, very good when prepared as I shall explain, is more like a cream than a soup, even though it costs little. On a bright fire, put half the rice that you would need for an ordinary rice with milk, three spoonfuls for six people, in a saucepan [with the necessary milk]. When the rice has burst, but before it breaks up, add sugar and finish the cooking. While this is happening, cut the squash into pieces as large as a small egg; the

1. The Limousin has always been famed for its turnips: 'Les Limousins sont mangeurs de raves,' said Anatole France. The Fosterton (which Mme Millet-Robinet prints as 'Forsterton') is a Scottish hybrid variety. Freneuse, near Mantes in the Île-de-France, is renowned for its turnips (Potage freneuse is a turnip soup).

2. The word for squash used here is *potiron*. This is often translated in dictionaries as pumpkin, but usually refers to squash of one sort or another, the classic pumpkin being called *citrouille*.

Turk's turban, which I talk about in my *Manuel de Jardinage* [Gardening Handbook], is infinitely preferable to other varieties. Put it on the fire with very little water and some salt, in a saucepan or stewpan hung off the pothook, and let it cook thoroughly. Drain it in a colander. When the squash is thoroughly drained, sieve it – this is indispensable because of the strands that are found in many of the most common varieties. If you use Turk's turban, you will need less of it because it is very floury. At the moment of service, put this purée of squash in the tureen and pour onto it the rice and milk, which should not be cloudy, and stir it to make it all come together. If you leave this mixture close to the fire to keep it warm, the milk can curdle. If you have any soup left over, you should reheat it in a bain-marie. Even so, despite this precaution, it often curdles, which doesn't spoil it as much as you might think it would. This meat-free soup is one of the most delicate you can serve to people who like milky things. If you use melon instead of squash, even a mediocre one, the soup will be even better. You can also serve a squash soup on top of bread. To do this you add sweetened boiling milk to the squash and then pour everything onto the bread. This soup is not nearly so good as when it is made with rice.

Squash soup with onion. — Put a fairly large quantity of squash into a stewpan filled with boiling water. If you use Turk's turban, it will break down sufficiently in the cooking; if it is another variety, you will have to crush it and push it, using a mushroom-shaped pestle, through the colander. Meanwhile, cook finely sliced onions in enough butter for the soup until they are golden. When they are properly cooked, put a little stock in the saucepan. Stir briskly and pour it into the stewpan. Pour this onto the bread. It is also much better to cook rice until it bursts for this soup, which is better reheated.

CHAPTER V

JUS, COULIS AND SAUCES [1]

1. — General observations.

Using ham instead of salt pork. — One way of greatly improving one's cooking is to use ham in ragouts. I will give instruction on how to prepare hams in the article *Pork*, below. It is neither difficult nor costly; you can therefore, without increasing your expenses, make your cookery more delicate by using ham or smoked belly of pork in place of ordinary salt pork. You should not stint in your use of ham just to reduce the cost of the dish to which it is being added. This ham is never wasted, it is excellent to eat cooked with other meats, and even if it may not always be served at the family's table, it will make dinner for the servants, and the family will have had the benefit of the fine flavour it imparts to dishes. Finally, I would add that it is impossible to cook well without using salt pork or ham.

Use of flour and potato starch in sauces. — Certain cookery books advise that you can replace wheat flour, in all those instances where it is recommended, with potato starch.[2] To be sure, this starch thickens sauces

1.   The meaning of the words that constitute the (French) *fonds de cuisine* has varied over time in France itself, and they translate into English with difficulty, indeed, they have been adopted wholesale. *Jus* has been discussed in the previous chapter. *Coulis* can be defined as a purée-sauce of any foodstuff, be it meat, shellfish, fruit or vegetable. Generally, Mme Millet-Robinet treats it as a more concentrated form of *jus*. When it first was used in France, it referred to pretty much any stock (that is the definition given it by Cotgrave in 1611), but then came to be mostly applied to sauces or purées. The English translation was 'cullis', but that word has less currency today than the original French.

2.   This is the advice, for instance, of Mme Millet-Robinet's most common model, Louis-Eustache Audot's *La Cuisinière de la campagne et de la ville*. In earlier editions, he makes this recommendation without reservation, but modified it in later issues, making the same comment as Mme Millet-Robinet does here.

very well, and it only needs a few minutes' cooking; but I think it important to warn you that a sauce made with potato starch cannot be reheated, and that the sauce will *turn*, by which I mean it will become quite thin and not seem thickened at all, if you either stir a dish too often in which starch has been used or if you leave it too long on the fire. I would recommend you, therefore, only to use potato starch in a dish that is going to be eaten straightaway, or when the sauce seems too thin at the very moment of service.

Some cookery books also state that it is sufficient to reduce a sauce to thicken it, without using any flour; certainly, a very reduced sauce will be less liquid than a sauce that has not been reduced, but it will never have as much body or be as thick as one with flour or other substance which produces the same effect.

Roux.[1] — Put some butter in a saucepan, heat it until it starts to colour, add one or more spoonfuls of flour, depending on how much roux you wish to make; the melding of butter and flour must be total and it should form a thick paste. Once the flour has been absorbed by the butter, you must stir it frequently; if you don't, the roux will burn in a second. When the roux has taken on an attractive cream-colour, but not browned, add liquid and stir it, then let it boil. A roux that is too brown has an unpleasantly acrid taste. You can use dripping instead of butter; and you can also use small pieces of backfat which you melt in the saucepan before adding the flour.

Liaison.[2] — Break one or more eggs, depending on how much sauce you have to thicken; two eggs will be enough for quite a lot of sauce. Separate the yolks carefully, by tipping the yolk from one shell to the other; remove the tread; mix the yolks with a little cold water, or certainly no more than lukewarm; add to this mixture, stirring constantly, a few spoonfuls of the sauce, which should be boiling and, once you have four or five spoonfuls of sauce nicely amalgamated, pour the whole back into the sauce, stirring briskly and carefully; let the sauce thicken stirring the while; above all do not let it come back to the boil or else it will soon curdle.

---

1. Another French term that has been adopted into English. The French means 'browned', i.e. the butter, for the term is defined as butter (or other fat) blended with flour to make a thickener for sauces, etc.

2. This, too, was absorbed into English (at a relatively early date) and may be defined as a thickening or binding, usually effected by egg yolks.

2. — *Jus* and *coulis.*

Gravy, *coulis* and meat and vegetable stocks are the basis of most sauces; a spoonful or two of well-made *coulis* improves them no end.

I have described, in the recipe *A soup of rice and jus, and jus to replace stock in sauces* (no. 29, above), how to make *jus.* One made for sauces and ragouts should be more reduced; you should use more meat in it, particularly raw meat; and you should also add a bouquet garni[1] and one or two cloves. A chicken carcase well boiled with the other ingredients making up the *jus* also greatly improves it.

A *coulis* is a *jus* that has been reduced enough to begin to thicken and take on a colour that is nearly brown. To reduce it you need do no more than boil it uncovered over a high fire. If you wish to reduce a *jus* to a *coulis*, you must only lightly salt it. A reduced meat stock will also form a *coulis.*

If you wish to improve a *jus* and *coulis* a great deal you should boil with it some salt-pork rind or an old fowl cut into pieces or, even better, an old partridge.

In making a *coulis*, you put less water with the vegetables and meat than you would when making a *jus* for a soup; these vegetables and meat, if lightly seasoned, will make a better dish than the vegetables and meat from a *jus* made for soup.

If you wish to glaze a joint, then you should reduce the *coulis* a great deal and then paint the joint you wish to glaze with a feather. Although this refinement may smack of sophisticated cookery, it will lend it an excellent flavour and make it look very appetizing. However, you need very little *jus* reduced to a glaze to glaze a joint, and that will cost far more in effort than in hard cash.

The meatless stock which I described on page 426 above, and which I cannot recommend highly enough, can be made still better by the addition of small freshwater crayfish which are roughly pounded after careful washing and cleaning, as you will see in the article *Freshwater crayfish* on page 455 below. Add a knob of butter and all the fish to a saucepan on the fire and heat without browning; pour in the meatless stock and after

---

1. The term is defined by Mme Millet-Robinet in her glossary which forms Chapter XX, below.

an hour's cooking, strain it. You can add a little nutmeg. This reduced *jus* makes an excellent fast-day *coulis* which will improve any fast-day dishes when added to them.

3. — Sauces.

Béchamel sauce. — Make a white paste with good milk and wheat flour.[1] When it has thickened, leave it to boil for half or three-quarters of an hour; add salt, a little pepper and grated nutmeg, and chopped parsley. Put a large knob of butter into this paste. Stir it round until it is melted, but do not let it boil. Some people add one or two egg yolks as a liaison.

White sauce. — For this to be good, the first essential is to make it with plenty of very good butter. Put the butter on the fire in a saucepan; let it melt *while hardly heating at all*; mix in a spoonful of good flour. Add hot water while stirring to bring it together perfectly; if the fire is bright, you must not leave the saucepan on the flame. Return it to the heat for a second, stirring all the time; season with salt and pepper; pull it back off the fire; the sauce is made.

White sauce with capers. — Put the required amount of butter in the saucepan; add the flour; mix and combine thoroughly the one with the other; stir in hot water; put it on the heat for a moment to let the sauce thicken. Serve. Sometimes pepper is not added as it spoils the whiteness of the sauce; at other times, by contrast, even nutmeg is added; it depends what the sauce is for. The flour should be very white. Capers are often added to a white sauce; they work well; but beware adding a liaison because you will spoil it.

Velouté sauce.[2] — Make a roux that is not too brown; mix it into a meat or meatless stock; cook it for at least half an hour; at the moment of serving, add a knob of butter which you melt while stirring. This sauce can replace white sauce.

---

1.   The French word used here for paste is *bouillie*, which can mean paste, gruel or porridge. The recipe for *bouillie*, below, makes clear that this was made with milk and flour alone, the flour slaked in cold milk then added to the hot milk and whisked until thickened and lump free. This béchamel is not made on a roux as it commonly is today.

2.   The French is *sauce blonde.*

Maître-d'hôtel sauce. — This is simply butter that you have melted and to which you add very finely chopped parsley and some salt and pepper. Some people add a dash of vinegar or lemon juice.

Black butter sauce. — Put a large knob of butter in a frying-pan on a bright fire; if it throws a deposit when it starts to brown, pour it off carefully into a dish on a corner of the fire; clean out the pan carefully with some paper and put back the butter. Throw in a few sprigs of parsley; add one or two spoonfuls of vinegar and serve it up before the butter has got too black. As soon as the sauce has been made, you should drain everything out of the pan and wipe it with paper: the vinegar will make it go rusty.

To ascertain whether the butter is ready, take up a little in a spoon because the pan, being black, will disguise the colour of the butter and hence whether it is cooked or not. You must not use a pewter spoon for this, it will melt just like that.

Piquant sauce. — Make a roux; let it down with a meat or meatless stock, or water; finely chop two or three shallots; boil them in the sauce; you can put them in with the roux for a moment before adding the liquid; add salt, pepper, a clove and a bouquet garni. After half an hour's cooking, take it off the fire and add some gherkins, either chopped or thinly sliced, and a spoonful of vinegar. To make this sauce a lot better, you can brown some pieces of ham in the butter or fat before making the roux, and then cook them in the sauce for an hour and a half or two hours before adding the gherkins and vinegar.

Cold sauce for fish. — Pound two yolks of hard-boiled eggs; chop very finely some parsley, tarragon, chives and salad burnet; mix very slowly four spoonfuls of olive oil, one spoonful of vinegar and one of mustard, plus some salt and pepper into the egg yolks, stirring all the while; when it has nicely come together, serve it in a sauceboat or under the fish which you have cleaned and prepared beforehand.

Cold sauce for vegetables. — As the preceding recipe, but without the mustard.

Rémoulade sauce. — Put into a sauceboat a shallot, some chervil and tarragon, and a soupçon of garlic, all very finely chopped. Add some salt and pepper; mix in a spoonful of mustard, three spoonfuls of oil, and one spoonful of vinegar.

Anchovy sauce. — Make a light roux; let it down with stock or with *jus*; add a little pepper, but no salt. Let it boil for half an hour; add to it the fillets of two or three anchovies which you have finely chopped or pounded; when it comes back to the boil, serve it.

Tartar sauce. — In an earthenware bowl, put two or three shallots, and some chervil and tarragon, all of which are finely chopped; add salt, pepper, a dash of vinegar and a spoonful of mustard; pour in some oil a little at a time, stirring all the while; the sauce should come together.

Sauce Robert. — Slice ten or twelve large onions; put them on a brisk flame in a saucepan with butter; cover it. When the onions begin to soften, stir it from time to time; take the lid off so that they colour up; then add a spoonful of flour; stir it for a moment. Add meat or meatless stock or, if you have none, water; stir so that the flour is well amalgamated; season with salt and pepper. At the moment of service, add a spoonful of mustard; mix it all together. Some people add a little vinegar as well; others add neither mustard nor vinegar.

White onion sauce. — Slice a lot of onions thinly; put them on the heat in a saucepan, with a knob of butter at the bottom. Cover them carefully; let them cook on a low flame, stirring from time to time, until the onions are almost a purée. You should watch that they don't brown. If they seem a little dry and at risk of colouring, you must add a little warm water. When they are thoroughly cooked, add a spoonful of flour, stir it in, moisten with milk, stir once more and season with salt. This sauce ought to be utterly white. You can use it to reheat either sliced hard-boiled eggs as in eggs *en tripes*, or portions of cold roast chicken, or cold fish, or roast veal, or potatoes that you have sliced after they have been cooked and then let cool a little, or salsify, or artichoke bottoms. You can also add pepper, as well as nutmeg. This sauce is very good and not very well known, one would think it spicy, if not sweet.

White mayonnaise sauce. — In a terrine, place two egg yolks which have been nicely separated from their whites. Two egg yolks will be enough to make a great deal of sauce. Break the yolks and cream them thoroughly; add some salt and a *few drops* of vinegar; mix carefully; add a smidgeon more oil than vinegar; keep stirring; and then add about a spoonful of vinegar and five or six spoonfuls of oil for *each egg yolk*, adding them alternately, but always in tiny quantities; the sauce will thicken and lighten considerably if it is well made. You can add some finely chopped herbs as well as mustard;

the sauce will lose its pale tones but will be tastier. It is served with the leftovers of chicken, or of cold fish, or on a grilled eel, etc. If you can make this in a bowl set on ice, it will work even better. It is not easy to make this successfully in times of great heat.

Tomato sauce. — I have already explained, in the chapter *Concerning Provisions* (Chapter XV, page 289, above), how to preserve the juice and flesh of tomatoes. In order to use them, you should make a roux that is not too thick nor too brown, which you let down with preserved tomatoes. Season it with salt and pepper, and cook it for at least half an hour.

When the tomatoes are fresh, cut them into pieces and put them to cook down in a saucepan on the fire. Then pass them through a horsehair frame sieve or a fine strainer. You only need exclude the skin and the pips; the juice without the pulp would have no colour at all and would taste much less pleasant. The sauce is much improved by adding either *jus* or stock and reducing it somewhat. You can add tomatoes to any brown sauces, they improve them.

Provençal sauce. — Put two spoonfuls of olive oil, two finely chopped shallots and a clove of garlic, and some mushrooms cut into pieces into a saucepan; fry this; add a small spoonful of flour; add half stock and half white wine; add salt, pepper and a bouquet garni; simmer this for half an hour. If an excess of oil floats to the top, remove it.

Matelote sauce.[1] — If you want one for fast-days, without meat, then brown twenty whole small onions in butter; take them out and make a roux which you let down with a meatless stock made from dried peas or other floury vegetable (see *Meatless stock*, above). This low-cost ingredient will make your stew far better: water alone makes a very sorry fast-day stew. After an hour, add a large glass of red wine, salt, pepper, and a bouquet garni. Return the onions a quarter of an hour later and put the fish into the sauce. If you want to prepare a matelote with meat, make the roux with cured backfat or ham, and then you can use water to let it down. If you add mushrooms, the sauce will taste better. It is the more pleasing if you use just red wine as the liquid; this is what the fishermen on the Seine and the Loire do: all experts in making matelotes.

1.   A *matelote* is a fish stew (literally, a sailor's wife). It is a term often reserved for freshwater fish stews, although they make one with sea fish in Normandy. Wine is an inevitable part of the liquor.

Salmi sauce.[1] — This sauce is suitable for all roast meats except veal and white poultry. Make a roux; let it down with meat stock, *jus* or, if you have neither, boiling water; pound thoroughly the liver of whatever game the sauce is intended for and add it to the sauce; add a bouquet garni, salt and pepper; simmer in the sauce the carcases, the bones or the debris of the meats you are going to dish up with it; one hour later, add a large glass of red wine; let it boil for another hour; remove the debris. Now put in the meats, which should not boil but merely warm in the sauce. Dress them in a dish, pull the sauce off the fire and add a large spoonful of olive oil which you beat thoroughly and pour over the meats. When you roast game to make a salmi, you only half-cook it. The same is true of a domestic duck which, nicely presented in a salmi, is nearly as good as a wild one.

1. A salmi, or *salmis* in French, is defined as a game stew made from part-roasting a bird, then stewing the sliced flesh in a rich sauce (Ayto, *The Diner's Dictionary*, s.v. 'salmi') and, more generally, a ragout of roast meat. It first figured in English recipe books in the eighteenth century; Mrs Beeton called her partridge salmi a 'hash'. The English word is often thought to derive from 'salmagundi', also a hash or hotchpotch, but in this case of cold meats and vegetables.

CHAPTER VI

GARNISHES AND TRIMMINGS

Under this heading, we treat of several foodstuffs and preparations which serve to flavour or to finish other dishes but which are rarely served on their own.

1. Truffles.

The best truffles are round, fairly large, firm, very black on the outside and enclosed within a rough skin. The inside should also be very black, marbled with white. Before cooking, they must be washed in plenty of water and cleaned with a coarse narrow brush which will get into the surface corrugations. Use a pointed knife to pick off any small stones or earth that have not yielded to the action of the brush. As you wash the truffles, so you place them on a soft, clean cloth; you dry them and then remove the skin, paring it as thinly as possible. You can use this skin, pounded, in any stuffing and even in various sauces: it is the most perfumed part of the whole truffle.

When they have been prepared like this, truffles can be added to any sauce for an entrée, to which they will impart a delicate flavour, and they can also be added to poultry and feathered game (see *Truffled turkey*, below).

Truffles with wine (entremets). — Once you have washed and brushed the truffles, put them in a *court-bouillon* made up of three-quarters good white wine to a quarter of stock, with a few pieces of cured backfat or ham, some salt and pepper. The truffles should not cook for less than an hour. Leave them to cool in the *court-bouillon* and then serve them in a folded napkin. The wine in which you cooked them can be used to flavour any number of sauces with the scent of truffle.

Truffle ragout. — After you have cleaned them, slice them and cook them in a good *jus* with a little pepper; when they are half-cooked, add some really high-quality red wine; thicken the sauce with a little potato starch. You can place on this ragout every sort of game and meat.

2. — Mushrooms.

Instances of poisoning caused by mushrooms are so frequent that it is surprising anyone still dares to eat them. The excellent flavour they impart to those dishes we add them to, as well as their prolific abundance, are so many reasons for our ignoring the risks we run. Everyone claims the ability to identify wholesome mushrooms, and draws sufficient confidence from his knowledge to give himself up to the pleasure of eating them.

To put a stop to the fatal accidents that claim so many victims in France each year, the Paris police only permits the sale of three easily identifiable species: 1) the cultivated mushroom; 2) the morel; 3) the truffle. I will refrain from attempting to describe the distinctive characteristics of those other species which you can eat without coming to any harm, that would burden me with too great a responsibility, and I do not hesitate to forbid them entirely. This is also the opinion of Dr Léveillé,[1] the botanist with the greatest knowledge of mushrooms, who writes about them in the following terms in an article remarkable for its erudition and learning: 'Every day, people involved in the study of mushrooms are asked how to distinguish those which are venomous from those which are not; that question has often embarrassed me, and I confess to still not knowing how best to answer it, after twenty-five years of close study. The characteristics by which we identify edible species are so slight that you have to have great skill to perceive them; neither colour nor taste can be relied upon.... Customarily those which turn a tin or silver spoon brown, or which turn an onion black when cooked with it, are rejected: but these characteristics are of no utility.... It is generally believed that by drying mushrooms you destroy their toxicity; this is not true and it can be seen today that those species which are toxic when fresh are equally so after desiccation.... It is also said that cooking destroys the poisonous nature of mushrooms, which is true; but they must be cut up small, boiled, and the water in which they

---

1.   Joseph-Henri Léveillé (1796–1870), physician and mycologist.

were cooked must be thrown away. It is only by these means, I think, that you can consider all these plants edible. But by then they have lost all their flavour and, in any case, what could possibly be their nutritive value once they have been stripped of all their proper qualities?'

While on this topic, I should stress one particular fact that is important to know but yet seems often ignored by those who eat mushrooms. The mushrooms which are considered the most utterly harmless, like the cultivated mushroom or the morel, are only without risk for the first few hours of their development; later, but still long before they begin to decompose, they become not so much poisonous as hard to digest; they can give rise to vomiting and stomach pains – themselves indications of the start of an episode of poisoning. You should only deliver to the kitchen, therefore, mushrooms, even of the best sorts, which have been freshly harvested in the first stage of their development. Only then can you eat lots of them without fear of the slightest indisposition.

Baked mushrooms (hors-d'oeuvre and luncheon).[1] — Peel some mushrooms of the larger sort; put them on a [covered] pie plate with plenty of butter, salt, and pepper, and with a moderate fire on top and below, for an hour and a half, until the mushrooms are lightly grilled. Serve on butter that has been melted but not browned, with a little chopped parsley.

Ragout of mushrooms (hors-d'oeuvre or luncheon). — After peeling them and cutting into pieces, put the mushrooms into a saucepan and cover them so that they sweat; when they seem to have let out all their juices and you have drained them well, put them back into the saucepan with butter, chopped parsley, a scrap of garlic, salt, pepper and soft breadcrumbs you have passed through a sieve. Cooking should last half an hour. If the ragout

---

1.   In French, *champignons sur le plat*. *Oeufs sur le plat* are nowadays usually translated as 'fried eggs' but, as the recipe describes, these mushrooms are cooked in a pie plate. *Plat* is defined in French dictionaries as a plate or platter, more or less dished, on which food is served and, sometimes, cooked. *Sur le plat* therefore means something cooked on a platter. As far as open-hearth cookery was concerned, placing an item of food on a platter and cooking it on the hearth was most likely best performed if the platter was exposed to top and bottom heat, i.e. was provided with some form of lid on which or in which one could pile hot coals or embers. This is how Mme Millet-Robinet counsels you to cook the mushrooms, and many of the other dishes she describes as *sur le plat*. The equivalent in a modern kitchen, with a gas or electric stove, is simply 'baked' or, in American parlance (for eggs), 'shirred'.

begins to stick to the saucepan, add a little water or stock. You can serve this ragout under beef and under any roast.

Mushrooms on fried bread (entremets). — As you peel the mushrooms, throw them in lightly vinegared water so they do not blacken. Take them out and blanch them for a few seconds in boiling salted water; when you have drained them, put them back on the fire in a saucepan with butter, salt and pepper, stirring them briskly. Add a little flour. Moisten with some hot stock or water and throw in a little finely chopped garlic. Let it stew for half an hour. Thicken the sauce with one or two egg yolks which you have mixed with a little water. You must only add the liaison when the mushroom ragout has stopped boiling, when it has been pulled back from the fire for a few seconds, otherwise the sauce will curdle, giving it both an unpleasant flavour and an unattractive look. This is served on a slice of bread fried in butter. It is a much-appreciated dish.

3. Onions.

Glazed onions. — You can serve these as an hors-d'oeuvre. Peel ten nice onions; put them in a saucepan with half stock, half water and 200 grams of sugar; cook them on a brisk fire. When the onions are cooked, take the cover off and reduce the sauce until it looks like a fine caramel. You must watch this process closely as two minutes are enough to burn the onions. Take the onions out and arrange them on a dish. Add a little stock or water to the saucepan and boil it up for a few seconds; dislodge with a spoon any caramel sticking to the sides of the saucepan, then pour this sauce over the onions. You can serve these as a garnish round a stew or a boiled leg of mutton.

Onions in jus (hors-d'oeuvre). — Blanch some peeled, whole white onions. Cook them in a *jus* which you reduce until it is thick enough to glaze the onions.

Sugared onions. — Brown them in butter; moisten with a little water; add salt and pepper and sprinkle over some sugar; let this cook with glowing coals on top of and beneath the dish. This should be eaten hot.

Onion purée. — Peel some unblemished and really white large onions. Cut them into thin slices from top to bottom. Put them into a saucepan on a low flame with a large knob of butter and a little water; salt them, and cover. If the juice the onions throw off starts to dry up, and you fear they may be taking colour, add some water as the purée must be white. When the onions are thoroughly cooked, push them with the pestle through a colander with very small holes. Put this purée back on the fire, add a spoonful of flour and a little butter to the saucepan: stir briskly. Lighten the colour with some fresh milk. Do not let it boil much more than a minute or two.

4. — Tomatoes.

Stuffed tomatoes.[1] — You must choose large fruit, without blemish and fully red. After you have cut off the tops, remove the seeds with a teaspoon and discard them; then remove some of the flesh, which you cook and reduce before adding to it a stuffing such as is added to aubergines, and which is described on page 562, below. Stuff the tomatoes with this and cook them as the aubergines.

Tomatoes are used in many sauces and are prepared as if you were making tomato sauce (see *Tomato sauce*, page 308, above).

5. — Forcemeat to put in a hot pâté.

Chop some lean veal and some fatty pork until the mixture is reduced to a sort of paste; add some salt and pepper; mix in a whole egg, yolk and white. Cut some pork and veal into cubes about as large as half an egg; brown them in some butter; then make a roux; moisten this with water or, better, with stock; add a bouquet garni, salt, and pepper; cook the cubes of meat in this roux; add, if possible, some calf's sweetbreads, or calf's or sheep's brains cut into small pieces, some fresh or dried mushrooms, some truffles, some mushroom powder, artichoke bottoms, etc. Half an hour before serving, roll the forcemeat into small balls; dust them with flour and brown them in lard or butter, taking care not to burn them. Finish the cooking in the ragout. By replacing the veal with poultry or game, you get a more delicate forcemeat.

6. — Quenelles for a vol-au-vent.

Cut the lean meat from a leg of veal steak into small dice, and soak an equal volume of the crumb of a loaf in warm milk for an hour. Mix these

1. To all intents and purposes, this recipe is repeated by Mme Millet-Robinet on page 562, below.

together in a mortar with salt, pepper, a little chopped parsley and a little nutmeg. Pound this thoroughly; add one or two egg yolks, depending on the quantity of meat; beat the white or whites to a mousse and mix into the rest. Shape this into small balls, longer than they are round. Cook this in a boiling *jus* which you have made with meat bones (as I describe in the article *Jus*, above). You can thicken this *jus* with a little flour or a roux.

To finish off the garnish to a vol-au-vent or hot pâté, you can add calf's sweetbreads or brains cut into small dice, sheep's brains, cocks' combs, mushrooms, artichoke bottoms, crayfish, truffles, etc.

7. — Dried breadcrumbs.

To make dried breadcrumbs, you split into two a long, thin loaf and remove the crumb. Then you divide into four the two crusts and put them into the oven just before you take out the bread. They should turn a handsome golden colour. As the oven begins to lose its heat, remove one of these pieces and crush it with a hammer or small wooden mallet before finishing the process by crushing it with a bottle or a rolling pin. All the crusts must be processed like this before they have cooled. Then you pass them through a very fine strainer in order to separate, not the larger pieces, but the fine dust which arises from those bits that have been too pulverized. Then you should pass the dried breadcrumbs through a coarser strainer to remove the larger pieces, which can then be crushed again, if possible – usually, you have to put them back in the oven to reduce them to a coarse powder. A one-kilogram loaf will produce an ample supply of dried breadcrumbs; these you keep in a pot somewhere extremely dry. When they get too old, dried breadcrumbs take on a dusty flavour.

You can still buy from the baker what is called *re-cooked bread*. This is a small '*flute*' which is very slender, very long and with quite a high colour, which is often used as bread for soup. You can grate the crust, which is very thick, and thus obtain a very good dried breadcrumb.

CHAPTER VII

HORS-D'OEUVRE

1. — Eggs and omelettes.

EGGS. — Eggs are one of cookery's greatest resources. This excellent food, agreeing with all digestions and every purse, is part and parcel of all pâtisserie and of an infinite number of dishes. Eggs also have the great merit of being available everywhere, abundant in all seasons, and of very moderate cost. After meat, it is the most nutritious of our foods; what's more, you need no time at all to cook eggs and they lend themselves to a host of different flavours.

To be sure an egg is fresh, grasp it on both sides with your hands and present the unobscured part to the light. If it is thoroughly transparent, you can be certain it is fresh; if it seems spotty, then it has been laid some time ago; if a stain seems attached to the shell or if it is dull, then the egg is stale. I have explained in the chapter on *Concerning provisions*, above, how to preserve eggs.

Boiled eggs or soft-boiled eggs[1] (hors-d'oeuvre and luncheon). — The best way to cook them accurately is to have a wire egg-basket (see figure 47, above) which you plunge into a saucepan of boiling water and remove four minutes later, or a tin-plate egg-boiler with a double bottom with holes made in it into which you place the eggs: you pour in the boiling water and after five minutes the eggs are perfectly cooked, that is to say that the white is milky without any slimy part remaining . If you like them

---

1. Here the French is *Oeufs à la coque ou mollets*. The definition of *mollet* may vary. One is that it is an egg that has been cooked harder than *à la coque* and softer than *dur*. The subsequent treatment of *oeufs mollets* is not discussed by Mme Millet-Robinet. In most cases, after boiling they are briefly cooled, then shelled and the whole yet softish egg is reheated in hot salted water before being napped with a sauce of some sort.

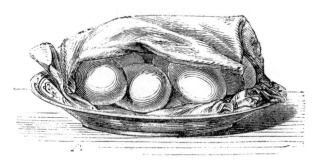

Figure 108. Eggs placed in a napkin.

somewhat better cooked, you leave them for two minutes more; but if you cook them in this fashion you will at least not have to worry that they will overcook as the water cools progressively. A just-laid egg, still warm, cooks much more quickly than one laid the day before. If you don't have an egg-basket, the best method is to add the eggs to boiling water and leave them there for three minutes while the water continues to boil. Drain the water off once the three minutes have elapsed and immediately put the eggs on the dish on which they are to be served. To keep them hot, put a napkin which you fold like a portfolio on the serving dish (figure 108) and place the eggs between the folds.

Once it is cooked, the white of an egg that has just been laid resembles a very pale boiled rice with milk; the white of an egg laid the day before is denser and grainier; the first is much more easily digested than the second.

Fried eggs, also called *mirrored eggs* (luncheon). — Put some butter in a fireproof dish or, far preferable, in a small bell-metal, three-legged saucepan. When the butter has melted, break the eggs into it, spacing them out nicely; add salt and pepper. Cover with a lid containing embers, without this the white will set on the bottom but remain soupy on top. As soon as the white has set, serve up. The yolk should be semi-liquid as with boiled eggs.

Plain scrambled eggs (first course, luncheon). — Put some fresh butter in a fireproof dish. When it is completely melted, break the eggs into it; salt and pepper them. Begin immediately to stir with a fork so as to scramble the eggs and, as they begin to cook, scrape off anything that sticks to the bottom of the dish. When the eggs are cooked, but still soft, serve them up. You can make scrambled eggs much more delicate by adding, during the cooking, either one or two spoonfuls of verjuice, or the same amount of tomato juice (for a dish of six eggs).

Some people scramble the eggs so that the yolks and the whites are thoroughly mixed; others, by contrast, prefer to mix them less so that there are parts which remain white and others which remain yellow: it is a matter of taste.

In Belgium, they generally scramble eggs in a tin-plate saucepan or a tinned copper one; they beat the eggs up before pouring them onto the butter, as if they were making an omelette.

Scrambled eggs with asparagus (luncheon). — When there are some asparagus left over from a previous meal, you cut the tender parts into small pieces. Put butter into a dish or saucepan; once it is melted, add the asparagus, salt, pepper, a little sugar and then turn the asparagus over until they are heated through; then you spread them out on a dish and break the eggs over them, which you stir about gently from time to time *with a spoon* so that you do not reduce the eggs and asparagus to a porridge, which is certain to occur if you stir them constantly with a fork. In this case, the dish looks hardly appetizing. If the asparagus were raw, you could cook them as I have described for asparagus and fresh peas, but without adding the liaison. You can also leave the eggs whole, pressing them down in amongst the asparagus and covering the dish with a lid loaded with embers.

Poached eggs or *en chemise* [1] (entremets and luncheon). — Boil up some adequately salted water in a large shallow saucepan. Into this water, break some very fresh eggs one by one, making sure they don't touch. One or two minutes later, turn them over smartly using a spoon or small skimmer; leave them for another two minutes; then take them out of the water with the skimmer (they should be *mollets* [i.e. soft but not very soft]) and place them on a dish sitting on hot embers. When all the eggs are cooked, tilt the dish to drain any water found at the bottom (holding the eggs back with the skimmer). Then pour *beneath* the eggs a white sauce, a velouté sauce, tomato sauce, sauce Robert, piquant sauce, a *jus* or a stock you have

1. *En chemise* is often used to describe something that has been wrapped in pastry or other covering. However, in this instance, the poached eggs are merely placed atop a sauce or purée.

reduced by three-quarters. This dish is excellent. You can also put the eggs on top of any purée or a forcemeat of sorrel or chicory.

Deep-fried eggs (entremets and luncheon). — When the deep fat is really hot, break the eggs into it. A moment later, turn them over smartly; take them out as soon as the white is set; serve like eggs 'en chemise'.

Eggs in black butter. — To fry eggs suitable for fast-days, you can also heat up butter [rather than lard] and, the moment it starts to turn black, break the eggs into it, then turn them over. In this case, you add salt, pepper and a dash of vinegar, and you serve the eggs up with the butter. To ascertain whether the butter has heated to the point required for putting in the eggs – something which you can't do when the butter is in the pan – as soon as the butter starts to smoke (as for the black butter sauce, above) you need to establish what colour it is by taking a little out with a spoon, made of any metal but tin.

Eggs with onions and white sauce [1] (first course, luncheon). — Peel the onions, slice them very finely, and put them in a covered saucepan with butter, salt and pepper; cook them over a low fire. Stir vigorously from time to time to reduce the onions to as smooth a purée as possible. If they seem to brown before they are cooked, add a little water; they must stay white. When they are cooked, add a spoonful of flour and stir; moisten it with fresh milk and let it come to the boil a few times. Meanwhile, hard-boil some eggs and cut them in rounds. Add them to the onions and mix everything together. Serve it up. You can replace the milk with red or white wine.

Salad of hard-boiled eggs. — Cut them into rounds, add some herbs; dress them like a normal salad.

Eggs à la poulette. [2] — Hard-boil the eggs and cut them into rounds. Put quite a lot of butter into a saucepan. When it has melted and is hot, but not browned, add the eggs with salt, pepper, chopped parsley or herbs, stir well; moisten with water or stock; let stew a few moments and then serve it up.

Stuffed eggs (first course, luncheon). — Hard-boil the eggs, cut them in half lengthwise and remove the yolks; put these yolks into a bowl with

1.   In French, *Oeufs en tripes*, often thought a Lyonnais dish, it mirrors one way of cooking tripe – with an onion sauce or *sauce soubise*.
2.   See the comments about veal *à la poulette* on page 407, above.

butter, chopped herbs, a little grated nutmeg, salt, pepper and some breadcrumbs which you have soaked for an hour in warm milk; crush and mix everything; then refill the egg whites with this stuffing so that it forms little mounds. Having done this, put some butter into a fireproof dish; spread the rest of the stuffing around the bottom of the dish; put the eggs into the dish, stuffing uppermost, and cover with the camp oven or a hot iron lid with embers on it.[1] When the eggs have coloured a little, serve them. To make this dish more delicate, take out the eggs as soon as they have coloured, then moisten the stuffing that remains in the dish with milk, meat stock or vegetable stock, or gravy. Let it boil a few seconds then serve this sauce under the eggs. You will also improve the stuffing if you put in a bit of cured backfat.

Eggs in a fast-day gravy (first course or luncheon). — Make a vegetable stock with yellow split peas, carrots, onions and turnips (see *Meatless stock*, page 426 above). Make a roux; let it down with this stock; let it stew for half an hour. You can also dispense with the roux and let the sauce reduce a great deal. Once this is done, put this sauce into a fireproof dish; when it has come to the boil, break into it as many eggs as it will hold, without them being too crowded; place embers above and below the dish. When the eggs begin to cook, loosen them from the bottom of the dish, one by one and with some address; let them finish cooking, but without letting them harden. Serve it up. You can let down the roux with one-quarter wine and three-quarters stock. You can also brown some small onions in the butter before making the roux, then put them back into the sauce to cook before you add the eggs. This is an excellent way of eating eggs as an entrée in a fast-day dinner. You can replace this vegetable stock with one made from beans or lentils.

1. Mme Millet-Robinet here refers to the camp oven or *four de campagne*, also known in the anglophone world as a Dutch oven. There have always been cooking pots, in either pottery or metal, that created an oven-like environment while being on top of or embedded in an open hearth. The means adopted were to have embers or coals heating the bottom of the vessel, while the lid was so fashioned that it would accept embers or coals on its surface, allowing the food inside the vessel to be cooked as if in an oven. This was how bread was baked in the highland zones of Britain; this was also a technique universal throughout the Mediterranean, going back indeed to the ancient world. Mme Millet-Robinet often suggests that coals or embers should be below and above the cooking vessel and she is then presuming a lid of the proper shape or a camp oven.

OMELETTES. — *Plain omelette.* — Although everyone knows how to make an omelette, they are often badly made; I would go so far to say that very few cooks know how to make them properly. Yet there is a big difference between a well-made omelette and a badly made one.

To begin with, it is almost impossible for an omelette of more than 12 to 15 eggs to be any good, unless the pan is quite enormous and thus impossible to handle: when there are several guests, it is best to make two omelettes.

Break the eggs into a bowl; add salt, pepper and a spoonful of milk; beat, but not so much that the eggs froth up. On a clear flame, melt a large piece of butter in a pan; when it is nicely hot, but not browning, pour in the eggs. Let them take for a moment; stir; let them take again; stir again, and then repeat until the eggs have partly set, but in such a way that some of it is still runny. At this point, don't meddle with the omelette any more. Reduce the heat; let the bottom colour up; serve it up quickly on a dish, folding it in half. It should be moist, that is to say that it should weep round the edges where the heat has not caused it to entirely solidify.[1] If, rather than following this procedure, you make an omelette by stirring it constantly, or if you wait until the egg has set completely before browning the bottom, the omelette will be dry and will have a crumbly texture. If you have too many eggs for the size of your pan, the omelette will be too thick, unevenly cooked or tough. If you let the butter burn, the omelette will take on a bitter flavour; if, however, you do not heat it up enough, it will have no flavour at all.

A plain omelette, served on a tomato sauce, is an excellent dish and looks most attractive.

Herb omelette (luncheon). — Prepare it like a plain omelette; when beating the eggs, add chervil, garden cress, tarragon, chives, all finely chopped. Some people replace the herbs with chopped sorrel.

Smoked herring[2] *omelette* (luncheon). — Prepare the eggs as for other omelettes, but with no salt; put one or two smoked herrings, which you

1. The French for the perfect omelette's condition is *baveuse*. This may be translated as moist, dribbling, slobbery or sloppy in other contexts.
2. The French is *hareng saur*. This general term encompasses the various forms of smoked and salted herring such as bloater, buckling and kipper. Here, Mme Millet-Robinet seems to be referring to a buckling, i.e. smoked whole, not opened like a kipper, and salted more strongly than a bloater.

have split open, on the grill for an instant; separate the flesh from the backbone and the skin and break it into small pieces. Put some butter into the pan with the herring; heat it through; add the eggs; cook as if it were a plain omelette.

Crayfish omelette (luncheon). — Cook the crayfish in the manner I will describe later on (page 456, below); take off the tails; split them and remove the flesh. Take this and pound it in a mortar; add salt and pepper; beat it up with the eggs and make the omelette as if it were a plain one.

Cheese omelette (luncheon). — Grate some Parmesan or Gruyère cheese (about 125 grams for a 12-egg omelette); add a little milk and some pepper; beat this all together; make the omelette. You can also sprinkle the inside of the omelette, before folding it, with more of the same grated cheese.

Onion omelette (luncheon). — Slice some onions and cook them in a covered saucepan with some butter, salt and pepper. Add a little milk and let it reduce, stirring frequently. Mix this purée with the eggs to make the omelette. You can also brown the onions in butter before adding the eggs to them.

Bacon or ham omelette (luncheon). — Cut the bacon or ham into very small pieces; melt them in the frying-pan; add to them the beaten eggs, seasoned with pepper, and make the omelette by stirring everything together.

Kidney omelette (luncheon). — When you have eaten a piece of roast veal that contained the kidney, there is no better way of taking full advantage of it than adding it to an omelette. Cut the kidney and all its fat into very small pieces; put it in a frying-pan with some butter to heat through, then add the eggs, beaten with some salt and pepper, and make the omelette as if it were a plain one.

'Italian cheese' omelette.[1] — Make this in the same way as the kidney omelette. It is a very pleasing dish.

Mushroom omelette. — This is made in the same way as the kidney omelette, above, but the mushrooms should be first blanched. You should cook them thoroughly and season them as I have explained on an earlier page (p. 441, above) before adding them to the beaten, seasoned eggs to make the omelette.

1.　'Italian cheese' here refers to the *fromage d'Italie* or pork terrine which is described on page 368, above.

In fact, you can add leftovers of any meat or vegetable, making sure they are already cooked before heating them in butter and mixing them with the eggs as you cook the omelette.

Truffle omelette (entremets and hors-d'oeuvre). — The truffles should be cooked in advance and sliced very thinly. You prepare and cook the omelette as I have already described. Once you have stopped stirring it, add the truffles, spreading them all over the top surface of the omelette, which you then fold in half, covering the truffles at the moment of service. You serve it as usual, just folded.

The curé's omelette (Brillat-Savarin).[1] — If the omelette is for six people, chop together two well-washed soft carp's roes, blanched by immersion in lightly salted, boiling water for five minutes, and a piece of fresh tuna as large as a hen's egg. Add to this a small and finely chopped shallot.

The chopped tuna and roe should be well mixed together; this is all put in a saucepan with a decent amount of butter; turn the mixture over until the butter is melted. This is what makes this omelette special. At the same time, pound together in a mortar a knob of butter about as large as an egg with some finely chopped parsley and chives. Put this in a long dish, squeeze a lemon over it and place the dish on hot embers. Then beat twelve very fresh eggs; carefully mix the eggs with the tuna and carp roe preparation. Then cook the omelette in such a way that it is quite long in shape, thick and runny. Spread this out quickly on the dish you have prepared for it and serve.

Jam omelette. — Make a plain omelette, but only lightly seasoned with salt and pepper; when it is dished up, but before it has been folded over, spread some jam, of any sort, over the surface; fold the omelette, serve forth; it is an excellent dessert.

You can also do no more than dust the inside and the top with grated sugar.[2]

1. This recipe comes from Brillat-Savarin's *La Physiologie du goût* (1826), 'Miscellanea', 1.

2. Mme Millet-Robinet will often distinguish between powdered sugar (*sucre en poudre*) and grated sugar (*sucre râpé*). She rarely mentions crushed or pounded sugar (*sucre concassé*). In her comments on sugar in general (Chapter XV, pages 300–1, above) she observes that 'To reduce sugar to a powder you can pound it or grate it. It is quickest to pound it in a marble mortar with a wooden pestle, but it does take on a particular, not very pleasant taste, which will be detectable in water but in no other

Brillat-Savarin's fondue.[1] — Weigh the number of eggs that you intend to use. Then take a piece of good Gruyère that weighs a third of the weight of the eggs, and a piece of butter that weighs one-sixth. Break the eggs and beat them thoroughly in a saucepan, after which add the butter and the cheese, either grated or sliced. Put the pan on a brisk fire and turn it over with a spatula until the mixture is suitably thick and soft. Put in a little or no salt at all, depending on whether the cheese is more or less aged, and plenty of pepper – which is one of the characteristics of this venerable dish. Serve it forth on a lightly warmed platter.

---

mixtures.' In later editions, she is more emphatic, more detailed and copes with different grades of sugar being available from retailers. Thus the 1893, posthumous edition reads: 'To reduce sugar to powder, you can either pound it or grate it; it saves time to pound it in a marble mortar with a wooden pestle, but pounded sugar takes on a somewhat unpleasant flavour, which is detectable in the water [in which it may be dissolved]. Much better to grate it. It is also more convenient to buy the sugar already reduced to a powder; however, you will have to go to a reliable shop as adulteration is easy.' In court proceedings in Angoulême in 1850 the curé of Saint-Germain in what is now Charente-Maritime, Laurent Gothland, was accused, with his lover and next-door neighbour Mme Marie-Laure Du Sablon, of murdering the curé's servant Mme Fanny Deguisal by administering arsenic, sometimes disguised to look like powdered sugar. The motive for the dreadful deed was that Mme Deguisal had witnessed the lovers *in flagrante* and they wished to silence her. At one stage in the interrogation, the nature of a poudrous substance added to a glass of wine and water offered to the victim was under discussion. The curé stated it to have been *sucre concassé*. Counsel fired back that he had hitherto said it was *sucre râpé*. 'How could that be?' the priest responded 'sharply' (the reporter's own word), 'As I am not a pastrycook, I don't have grated sugar in my house' (my translation). To continue this discussion of how to render your sugar a powder, I close with Alphonse Daudet's comment in his 1884 novel *Sapho*, a tale of courtesans and harlots in Paris. 'Ainsi la râpe à sucre,' he wrote. 'Conçoit-on qu'ils allaient se mettre en ménage sans râpe à sucre!....' (Then the sugar-grater, do you think they are going to set up house without a sugar-grater?) The many editions of Audot's *Cuisinière de la campagne et de la ville* have very useful illustrations of many kitchen implements. The comment about the sugar grater is that the one illustrated is a flat grater, the metal rectangle contained within a wooden frame with a handle at the end. Normally, he says, sugar graters are semi-circular metal graters so only a small section of the sugar is exposed to the corrugations at any one time. The flat grater results in four times the output. The metal grater is 24 centimetres long, by 15 wide; the holes are at 6 millimetre centres.

1.   This recipe comes from Brillat-Savarin's *La Physiologie du goût* (1826), 'Miscellanea', 16.

2. — Oysters.

You should open them, discard one shell, cut them free of the remaining shell, and serve them on dishes without tipping them up so that they don't lose any of the liquor. You should arrange them so that those that are uppermost only touch the shells of those beneath them. To open them, you should use a knife without a cutting edge, with a short blade with round tip which is firmly set in its hilt. Hold the oyster in a cloth. There are several quite ingenious small gadgets for opening oysters but, in this instance as in so many others, the simplest method – which I have just explained – is still the best.

The largest oysters are better cooked; green oysters are thought the best to eat raw.[1] At dinner, they are served before the soup; at luncheon, one should also begin with them.

Scalloped oysters (hors-d'oeuvre and luncheon). — Once you have opened and taken four dozen oysters out of their shells, you bring them to the boil in their own water, and put them to drain. Then you prepare a sauce with a piece of butter, mushrooms, chopped parsley and chives which you brown in the butter, add a spoonful of flour, and moisten with *jus* or with meat or vegetable stock and two glasses of white wine. Season with salt and pepper. Boil and reduce everything, then put the oysters in this sauce; leave them there for a few minutes, but avoid heating it to boiling-point. You should carefully reserve the twelve most handsome shells, which you wash with equal care. Each shell should take four oysters and their sauce, all sprinkled with dried breadcrumbs. Put these shells on a grill over a gentle fire. A few moments before serving, cover them with a very hot Dutch oven. Serve them as soon as the surface has browned nicely.

Grilled oysters (hors-d'oeuvre and luncheon). — After you have opened them and taken them out of their shells, bring them to the boil in their own water, then reserve. Then sauté them in butter with parsley, pepper and lemon juice. Put them four to each well-cleaned shell; put them on the grill; and when they are thoroughly heated, serve them up.

1. These are the *huîtres fines de claire vertes* from Marennes-Oléron on the west coast of France near the town of Rochefort and opposite the Île d'Oléron. The greenish tint comes from the bivalves' consumption of a particular micro-algae, *Navicula ostrea* or *Haslea ostrearia.*

3. — Salted anchovies.

After you have washed them well, open them out to remove the backbone. You should serve them in an hors-d'oeuvre dish,[1] with *fines herbes* or parsley, and with yolks and whites of [hard-boiled] eggs chopped separately and arranged symmetrically upon the anchovies (which have first been drizzled with good olive oil). You can add anchovies to a lettuce salad or one of green or yellow wild chicory.

4. — Salted sardines.

(Luncheon and hors-d'oeuvre.) — Fresh sardines have perfectly blue and white scales and the blood which exudes on pressing the gills is ruby red. As far as the fish we are discussing here, which we suppose to have been processed in the standard fashion, you must soak them for an hour or more, depending on whether they are more or less salt; then take off the head and remove the small gut, and lift off the scales with your fingers while they are still in the water. Then dry them with a dry white cloth. Shake them in flour and put them with fresh butter in a frying-pan or pie-dish for a few seconds only. The moment you serve them up, pour the cooking butter over them. Once they have been through this process, they can be placed in a pot and covered with good olive oil; they will keep for a long time.

Some people are happy simply to put the sardines on the grill without removing the head, without gutting or washing them. This way of cooking them is only acceptable the moment the fish come from the sea; in this case, serve them with fresh butter.

Nowadays, thanks to tins which are sealed after filling, there are excellent canned sardines, in either olive oil or butter, which are not at all costly. One of these tins, containing a hundred sardines, costs 4 francs.

5. — Freshwater crayfish.

After you have washed them and deveined them by carefully pulling

---

1. The French is *ravier* and denotes a small oblong dish for presenting radishes or other cold foods as hors-d'oeuvre. An hors-d'oeuvre trolley, such as used to be trundled round restaurants of a certain class, would have each of its tiers filled with such oblong dishes. By extension, the word has come to denote the trolley itself in some catering redoubts where French is still the primary professional language.

the shell at the centre of the tail, first to the right, then to the left, so as to gently detach it and bring with it the small intestine which runs up the tail and which tastes very unpleasant, put them as they are in a saucepan on a brisk fire, with some salt, plenty of pepper, some onions, some carrots sliced thinly, a little garlic, a nut of butter, and cover it. You need to turn it all over several times. When they are thoroughly red, and therefore cooked, you add half a glass of vinegar and sauté the crayfish once more. Then transfer them all to an earthenware dish and leave them to cool. You then sauté them once or twice more in this dish, and only remove them from this liquor at the moment of service, when you arrange them in a pyramid, with parsley; the liquor is then poured into the bottom of the serving dish. This is undoubtedly the best way of cooking crayfish; it has the merit of not costing very much; yet it is not very well known.

If you insist on getting rid of all the little pieces of vegetable or butter that stick to the outsides of crayfish cooked like this, you will have to heat a bottle of white wine and dip one after the other in the boiling wine so as to wash them, in a manner of speaking. But they are better straight out of their liquor, as we have just explained.

You can also cook crayfish as follows: after washing and stripping them, put them into a court-bouillon with vinegar,[1] but more strongly seasoned than a court-bouillon used to cook fish. It is best not to put any water; the crayfish do not have to be swimming in liquid – when it boils up, the court-bouillon will rise over them, and anyway, you will have a care to turn them over in the liquor.

Many people content themselves with cooking crayfish in water with a little vinegar; they will be dry and without much flavour.

Cooked crayfish are used as garnish to many dishes.

---

1.   A *court-bouillon au bleu* may indicate a *court-bouillon* with vinegar rather than wine. However, Audot (*La Cuisinière de la campagne et de la ville*, 1818 and many subsequent editions) describes a *bleu*, or *court-bouillon*, for cooking all sorts of sea-fish as follows (I quote the translation of 1846): 'Wash the fish well; then put it, without scaling, into a deep dish, and pour over it some deep-coloured vinegar; immediately cover the dish closely, so that no fume[s] escape; in a few minutes, uncover it, and put the fish into a fish-kettle of boiling water, seasoned with salt, pepper, cloves, bay-leaves, sliced onions, and cloves of garlic. As soon as the fish is done, take the kettle from the fire, put in a glass of cold water, and leave it till the moment of serving. ... This is *bleu*, or *court-bouillon bleu*; in plain *court-bouillon*, white, or distilled vinegar, is used.'

6. — Frogs.

Fried frogs' legs. — Cut off the hindquarters and skin them; then marinate the legs in vinegar for one or two hours, with salt, pepper, parsley, chives, thyme and bay leaves. Once you have drained them, shake them in flour and fry them.

Frogs' legs in the manner of chicken fricassee.[1] — Treat them in exactly the same fashion as you would chicken. To heighten the evanescent flavour of this dish, you can add a glass of white wine and use less water. Reduce the sauce; thicken it with egg yolks, then add chopped parsley.

7. — Snails.

The first essential to ensure that they are wholesome is to leave them to fast for at least two months, keeping them in any sort of container in a cool, but not damp, location. There are instances of accidents as a result of ignoring this precaution; the snails had fed on toxic plants and hence caused poisoning. Once this time has elapsed, put them into a cauldron full of boiling water (some people add a few cinders), and cook them for 20 minutes. That done, remove them from their shell; wash them in several waters; put them once more in cold, salted water; boil them briefly; take them out and drain them. The snails are then put in a saucepan with some butter and a large spoonful of flour; turn them over, and moisten with stock, or water or white wine; add thyme, bay leaf, salt, pepper, and mushrooms, if possible. Cook them until the snails are soft; bind the sauce with egg yolks, to which you can add a little verjuice, or lemon, or vinegar.

You can also do no more than sauté the snails in butter with a little flour, adding a little water, chopped onion, salt, pepper, and leaving them to cook until they are done. At the moment of service, add some chopped parsley.

---

1.   The recipe for chicken fricassee is on page 500, below.

CHAPTER VIII

BUTCHER'S MEAT

1. — In general.

All meat, poultry and game should be thoroughly tender when you wish to cook it; it needs to be *tenderized*, which is to say it should not be cooked until several days have elapsed since the animal was killed. A good housekeeper must therefore arrange her menus so that they offer only such meat as is properly ready for consumption. At the same time she must be wary of heatwaves, of stormy or humid weather conditions, and if she is brought up short by these she must at least cook her supplies to a certain degree to guard against their being lost altogether. She must give some joints a turn on the spit, parboil others, brown them, marinate them, or lightly salt them, depending on their final purpose. If, on the other hand, she fears that the meat is tough [because insufficiently hung], she should beat it vigorously with a pastry rolling-pin or a purpose-made mallet (which should be round), because the act of beating will break the fibres of the meat. It is put to cook after beating. There is no need to worry that the meat is misshapen by this beating as it will recover its original form during cooking. Such action is always appropriate for gigots, fillets of veal, beefsteaks and cutlets. If the meat is utterly fresh and you are still obliged to use it, you will have to beat it twice before cooking, and leave it in the warmest part of the house.

How to rid meat of a stale flavour or the off-taste it develops when hung too long. — To achieve this end, you should leave one, two or three pieces of charcoal with the meat all through its cooking. Embers do not produce as strong an effect as charcoal. This method is wholly efficient.

How to reheat a roast joint. — When you have eaten only a little of a roast joint and you would prefer to reheat it than convert it into a ragout or eat it cold, you should first remove any juice which surrounds it, and put it to soak in lightly salted water for three or four hours. After that, put it back on the spit to warm. Put the juice you have reserved into the dripping pan, letting it down with a little water. This roast will not be as good as it could be when coming off the spit the first time, but it is eatable. You should add a little salt to it.

If a joint intended for the spit seems likely to spoil, you should part-roast it then put it to soak as I have indicated before finishing the cooking.

Meatballs made with cooked meat. — When there are leftovers of cooked meat or poultry, you can chop them up, adding sufficient backfat and salt and pepper. Steam some floury potatoes,[1] peel them and crush them with a fork so that you have the same volume of potato as meat; mix everything together and, depending on the quantity of forcemeat, add two or three whole eggs, yolk and white. When thoroughly mixed, shape into balls a little smaller than an egg, which you flatten at each end to make a regular shape. Roll them in flour or, better, fine soft breadcrumbs. Deep fry them and, when they are nicely browned, serve them either as they are or on a tomato or any other sauce. These meatballs will puff up and are very light. They are one of the best ways of using meat leftovers.

Hash.[2] — Chop [leftover] meat very finely, after adding a piece of backfat that weighs about one-eighth of the cooked meat. Put a little butter in a saucepan on the fire; when it is well heated through, throw in the hash and mix well; then add a large spoonful of flour which you combine thoroughly, after which you moisten with stock or water. The hash should be quite thin, because it will thicken as it cooks. Add salt, pepper and bouquet garni (containing a little garlic). Bring to the boil, then damp down the fire. Stir from time to time because the hash sticks readily to the bottom of the pan. Serve after an hour's cooking, removing the bouquet garni. If you wish to dress the hash, have ready some slices of bread browned in butter, which you cut in triangles or any other shape and place around the dish in which it is served.

---

1.   Mme Millet-Robinet calls these potatoes *pommes de terre rondes* (round potatoes), to distinguish them from those of firmer, waxier flesh, which are usually elongated or oval in shape.

2.   In French, *Hachis*. This means chopped, but the dish in England eventually became minced.

2. — Beef.

The raw flesh of a good ox[1] is finely textured, soft, bright red and lightly marbled, interlarded and covered with a very firm and yellowish-white fat. Durham [shorthorn] beef is preferable to all others; this superiority is most marked when these beasts are slaughtered very young and when they have never worked. Other breeds are usually butchered when much older. Meat from bulls is very dense and dark red; its fat, very yellow and very hard, always smells rancid. Meat from cows is more densely textured and less bright red than that from an ox, and the fat is white. It is a big mistake to think that the meat of a cow is not as good as that from an ox; when it is well-covered with fat and comes from a young cow, it is just as good.

BOILED BEEF. — On page 405 above, I have indicated which are the best cuts to make good boiled beef. The joint must weigh at least 2 kilograms; if it weighs 4 or 5, it will only be better, as long as it is not cooked in too much water. For boiled beef to be good, the joint should be as rectangular as possible, it should be cooked enough so that it trembles when moved, and has a covering of fat. In many towns it is the custom to cut the leg and the rump of beef into thin slices; it is then impossible to have a good-looking boiled beef unless you take an enormous joint, some of which, it is true, can be put to other uses. If you cannot obtain a nicely dressed joint, you will need, once you have beaten it thoroughly, to tie it up firmly so as to make it a round, and then try to keep this shape when you dress it on the dish. I never serve boiled beef without an accompaniment of some sort of vegetable or a sauce. Parsley is only a satisfactory garnish when the boiled beef is not the centrepiece of the dinner. I hear you protesting at the waste; well, I do not think myself guilty of waste in counselling the mistress of the house to garnish her beef. Such a garnish costs something, I admit, but you will eat less beef; so there is no real expense. And in any event, in households where boiled beef is often the only joint of meat at dinner, you need some light relief to enable it to be eaten with pleasure, because this meat, whose juices have almost all passed into the stock, will have lost much of its savour.

Garnishes and seasonings for boiled beef. — Piquant sauce; *ibid.* with anchovies; *ibid.* with tomatoes; glazed onions; Provençal sauce; onion

---

1. In French, *boeuf,* indicating a castrated male that may be kept for work as well as for meat.

purée; cabbages seasoned in various manners; sauerkraut; seasoned young carrots or young turnips; Brussels sprouts; generally, all purées; if you want something a little more elegant, any of the elaborations of a forcemeat for hot pâté (page 443, above).

Gratin of boiled beef. — Cut the largest pieces into slices and gather together the smallest; take out any bones; arrange everything on a fireproof dish and season with finely chopped parsley, spring onion, onion, shallot or chives; season with salt and pepper. Put small pats of butter on top of the beef and all over the dish; sprinkle with dried breadcrumbs or, if you have none, the crumb of a loaf crumbled finely; moisten with water or, better, meat or vegetable stock. Place the dish on a gentle heat; cover it with an iron lid with embers on it; leave to simmer for three-quarters of an hour or an hour; serve it up in the dish it was cooked in, which you should place on the dish that would have been used for a normal service. At the moment of serving forth, you can scatter some chopped gherkins over the whole surface of the dish. A few mushrooms give a more delicate flavour to this production.

Boiled beef with onions.[1] — Peel a number of large onions and slice them. Put them in a pan with butter. When the onions turn golden, add the boiled beef cut into pieces, a small spoonful of flour, salt and pepper. Let the beef fry a little with the onions and serve it up. This is the dry *miroton*, the true *miroton*.

Another miroton. — When the onions have browned, add a spoonful of flour; stir them; moisten with stock or water; leave to cook for a few moments; add the beef, with salt and pepper. When it has heated through and is well amalgamated with the onion, take it off the fire and add a dash of vinegar and a little mustard. This *miroton* is not as good but is more economical than the first, because it comes with a sauce.

Boiled beef in the manner of haricot of mutton. — When boiled beef is used instead of mutton, giving very little flavour to either the turnips or the sauce, make a roux with ham or salt pork, as described on page 432, above. It makes the dish more substantial, saves on butter without costing any more, and heightens the flavour of the dish. (See also *Haricot of mutton*, below.)

1. The French is *Bouilli en miroton*.

Boiled beef in meatballs. — See *Meatballs*, page 459, above.

Boiled beef fried in butter or oil. — Cut the boiled beef into slices, group together the smaller pieces; melt some butter in a pan. When the butter is hot, but not brown, put in the beef and let it fry; season with salt and pepper; pour any butter that remains in the pan over the beef. You can replace the butter with oil; then you should add a scrap of chopped garlic.

Grilled boiled beef en papillote. — Cut it into large and quite thick slices, each of which is spread with butter seasoned with salt and pepper then wrapped in oiled paper and placed on the grill. You may be content with just dipping the beef into melted butter, seasoned with salt and pepper, before grilling it. Serve it on butter that has been pounded with chopped parsley.

Boiled beef used in stuffings. — See *Stuffed cucumbers* (page 561, below) and *Stuffed cabbages* (page 547, below).

Boiled beef in a hash. — See *Hash*, page 459, above.

Boiled beef in a piquant sauce. — See *Piquant sauce*, page 435, above. When you have made it, you add large, thin slices of boiled beef to reheat.

Boiled beef and onions. — Peel a fair quantity of large onions; slice them and put them in a saucepan with butter on a fairly brisk fire; cover them. When the onions are nicely softened, take the cover off the pan so that they colour up; add a little flour; turn them over; moisten with stock; season with salt and pepper; reheat the beef in these onions. If the joint is not too large, leave it whole; the dish will look more attractive.

Sirloin. — If you wish it to be tender to eat, you will have to beat it vigorously; when it is tough, it loses much of its quality. Trim it; take off the flap that runs over the flank, which remains very tough when the joint is roasted; spit it and put it to a high fire. It is advisable to pour a little water into the dripping-pan so that the juices do not evaporate. Sirloin should be served with the flesh still red. You can tell if it is sufficiently cooked from the colour of the juice which flows when you pierce the thickest part of the joint with a fine larding needle or a barding needle. The juice should be neither red as blood, nor black; but you should guard against making this investigation too frequently or else you will drain the juices from the meat, which will then be too dry.

The bone from the sirloin, once stripped of roast meat, will serve to make an excellent gravy or a good cabbage soup.

Any leftovers from this roast can be put in a salmi, or you can reheat them in a piquant sauce or a sauce Robert. They are equally good with a tomato sauce.

Sometimes a loin can be threaded with large lardons; but in my view this spoils it. And rather than just serving it with the juice that has dropped into the dripping-pan, you can season this with salt and pepper, and even add a thread of vinegar, some chopped shallots and gherkins.

FILLET OF BEEF. — This delicate and sought-after joint usually costs double the others. It can be served in several ways. To roast, it is trimmed and stuck all over with slender lardons. A competent cook will prick it symmetrically enough to make a sort of decoration with the lardons. So that it is tender enough to eat, it should be kept in the larder for a few days. You can spit it as it is (and this, to my taste, is not the worst way of serving it), but usually, having larded it, it is put in a shallow dish to marinate for twelve hours with oil, salt, pepper, bay leaf, thyme, and a few slices of onion. Turn it over two or three times so that it marinates evenly. You can also wrap it in buttered paper before spitting it. It should not be served well-done, but neither should it be too rare. Use the juices to prepare a sauce like that for sirloin; it is served either beneath the roast or in a sauceboat. The leftovers from a roast fillet will provide a very presentable dish, either reheated in a piquant sauce, sauce Robert or tomato sauce, in a salmi, or even cold.

Smothered fillet of beef. — When you want to serve a fillet as a remove, after larding and marinating it, put it on some pork rind in a little stewpan or closely covered saucepan with quarter of a glass of eau-de-vie, thyme, bay leaf, a few cloves, some whole onions and a few slices of carrot. Leave it to cook on a gentle fire for at least four hours. Serve it without the vegetables, but with its juices to which you can add a few chopped shallots a few moments before serving. A little tomato juice improves this sauce. When the fillet is dished up and the vegetables have been taken away, you can still add some chopped or sliced gherkins and a small spoonful of mustard. This remove, instead of boiled beef, is both excellent and distinguished. Fillet prepared in this manner can also be served as a main course.

Fillet of beef à la paysanne. — Once you have beaten it and larded it, put it in a saucepan with water to cover – with a little pepper, but the lardons will salt it enough. Let it cook thus for about five or six hours, covered, turning it from time to time. Half an hour before serving, if there is too much sauce, leave it to boil uncovered, stirring up the fire: the sauce will reduce and take colour; it should be thick. This is the most succulent way of cooking beef. You can eat it cold. You can add onions, which will brown round the beef. Any boneless beef joint can be cooked like this. It is excellent.

Fillet of beef as beefsteak. — Fillet makes the best, the true beefsteaks. Cut it into fairly thick slices, beat them and coat them with oil. You should do this some hours before cooking, even the day before. Put the grill on a clear fire and place the steaks on it while you are at table; you should only turn them once during the cooking. Chop some parsley which you mix with good butter that has been nicely seasoned with salt and pepper. When the steaks are cooked, dress them on a warm dish and put the butter you have prepared in equal and nicely placed pats on each one. This dish can be served at either luncheon or dinner; it may figure as either an hors-d'oeuvre or an entrée.

Usually diced potatoes fried in butter are served round the steaks; you can also replace the ordinary butter with anchovy butter.

RIB OF BEEF AND ENTRECÔTE. — This joint, although excellent boiled, does not look handsome and makes a poor soup. The best way to use it is to cut out the nut of meat and slice it up to make beefsteaks; but they will need to be beaten vigorously. With the flank piece and the bone you can make a good cabbage soup which is somewhere between one made with pork[1] and one with vegetable stock;[2] what's more this rib is very good to eat as boiled beef.

Rib of beef and entrecôte in the Flemish style (entrée). — Beat the joint vigorously; lard it with large lardons seasoned with herbs and chopped onion, salt and pepper; put it in the braising-pan on a rind of salt-pork; add a few pieces of ham, half a glass of white wine, bay leaf, thyme, a burnt onion to colour it and, when the cooking is half-finished, some whole medium-sized carrots and onions. Cook with a medium heat both under and over the pan. Serve with some vegetables as garnish but be sure to sieve the sauce, which should be thick.

Braised entrecôte (entrée). — Beat the entrecôte well; brown it in a saucepan with a few bits of belly pork or ham; take it out [and reserve].

1.   i.e. *gras.*
2.   i.e. *maigre.*

Make a roux; moisten with water or stock; put the meat back on the fire with a little salt, pepper, thyme, bay leaf, some carrots, some onions; leave to cook for five or six hours with a gentle heat above and below the pan. Serve it up. Plenty of cuts of beef, mutton, veal and pork can be prepared in this fashion. When making this dish, it is possible to omit the roux.

BEEF À LA MODE (entrée or remove). — For a beef à la mode, you should choose a piece of rump or a nicely shaped slice; beat it well; lard it with thick, seasoned lardons; put it in the braising-pan with some pieces of salt pork rind, or belly pork or ham cut into pieces, a calf's foot, some cloves, a burnt onion, an onion ball or some caramel, pepper, salt and half a glass of eau-de-vie. These quantities are right for a joint of 2 kilograms; for a greater or lesser weight, you should observe the same proportions. Cook this with a gentle fire above and beneath the pan for seven or eight hours. Three hours before serving it, add carrots that have been cut into suitable pieces; one hour after the carrots, or even a little later, put some onions to join them (which would otherwise [if added earlier] dissolve and lose their shape). When beef à la mode is intended to be on the dinner table, it is served with hot vegetables as a remove or an entrée. At luncheon, it is usually served cold; in which case, the sauce is strained into a bowl and the meat and vegetables are set aside. When everything has thoroughly cooled, the meat is dressed on a dish and the juice, by now cooled to a jelly, is put around it. The vegetables can be arranged on this jelly.

Beef à la mode is served more often cold than hot; the true purpose of this dish is to provide a luncheon that is at once substantial and enjoyable. You can, when making it, substitute water for the eau-de-vie.

FRICANDEAU OF BEEF.[1] — You cook this as you do beef à la mode. Prepare chicory and sorrel as for a fricandeau of veal and season the mixture with beef *jus*, as you usually would with veal *jus*; this fricandeau, which is not very well known, is to be preferred to one of veal. Braised rib can be served and prepared in the same fashion.

If you have no chicory, you can cook a tender cabbage in salted water; drain it and chop it very fine; season it as for chicory. This dish, which I have rarely seen served outside my own home, is really good, and I urge you to try it.

1.   A fricandeau is a larded, braised joint, often of veal. The word was adopted into English from the eighteenth century.

Daube of ox tongue (entrée).[1] — After you have washed it, boil it for an hour in water; after this, take it out and skin it. That done, stud with large lardons and put it in a saucepan, a daubière,[2] or a braising-pan, with pieces of pork skin, belly pork or ham, salt, pepper, bay leaf, thyme, a glass of white wine and half a glass of eau-de-vie. Leave it to cook for six or seven hours in this mixture. You only add carrots and onions when the cooking is half-completed.

The root of the tongue and the parts surrounding it should not be served at the master's table; they are taken off the tongue when it is half-cooked, before it is returned to the heat. The servants find it a very good dinner.

Ox tongue cooked as a pot-au-feu. — This is an excellent way to prepare it.

Smoked ox tongue (entrée and luncheon). — You can also salt ox tongue. To do this, once you have washed it, wiped it and taken off the root, you place it on a grill over hot coals. The hard skin which forms its surface will peel off quite easily. Rub it with a mixture of salt, pepper, spices (to which you add one or two pinches of saltpetre), thyme and bay leaf. Having done this, place the tongue in a container and cover it with salt. Leave it in this salt for twenty-four hours; then take it out, dry it and, to smoke it, hang it at a reasonable height in the kitchen chimney. It is best to put it in a really clean beef casing [middle], tied at both ends. When it is sufficiently smoked, you cook it in water with a few vegetables, pepper, bay leaf and thyme. At luncheon it is most often served cold, in its casing. When it is to be eaten hot, it should be stripped of its casing, split, crumbed and placed on the grill. Then serve it with a piquant sauce.

Palate of beef à la ménagère (hot entrée).[3] — Boil four beef palates for an hour. Take off the hard, black skin which covers them and wash them in cold water. Then cook them in water in a pot with some carrots, onions, salt, pepper, cloves, a clove of garlic, thyme, bay leaf and a piece of backfat. After six or seven hours' cooking, cut the palates into squares: they should be very pale. Dress them in a crown shape and pour any sort of sauce into the centre; then they can be left to simmer in this for a few moments.

1. In French, *Langue de boeuf en daube.*
2. A daubière is most commonly an earthenware pot, taller than it is broad, with a pot-belly. Its tight-fitting lid is concave, so that it will hold water. This promotes condensation within the pot and improves its function as a slow-cooker. Daubières may also be made in copper.
3. 'In the housewife's style'.

OX BRAINS WITH SAUCE (entrée). — These brains are not very delicate; they are not as good as either calf's or sheep's; however, you can still use them to your advantage by adopting the following method. Carefully wash the brain and remove the thin skin which covers it, as well as any parts which have clotted blood adhering. Leave to soak in cold water for a few hours; then put some water on the fire, to which you add a glass of vinegar, some onions, thyme, bay leaf, salt, pepper and a few cloves. When the water comes to the boil, add the brain, cut into pieces. It will be cooked in half an hour. In the meanwhile, prepare a matelote sauce (page 437, above), to which you can add mushrooms and a few pieces of ham to heighten the flavour. You can also serve ox brains with a tomato sauce, piquant sauce or Provençal sauce.

You can also, once the brain is blanched, put it on a dish with chopped up bread, dried breadcrumbs, butter and a little water, which you then let reduce so that the sauce browns.

BLANKET TRIPE.[1] — Usually, one eats beef blanket tripe with sheep's trotters. (See that article, pages 488–9, below.)

OXTAIL COATED WITH BREADCRUMBS (hors-d'oeuvre). — After you have cooked the tail in a pot-au-feu – which is the best procedure – or on its own in water with vegetables, leave to cool. Coat it with butter which you have melted; crumb it; put it on the grill and serve with a piquant or tomato sauce, or with butter squeezed together with parsley.

3. — Veal.

Veal flesh should be white and covered with white fat as well. No other meat lends itself to so many ways of cooking.

ROAST VEAL. — I have already stated that the best cuts of veal for roasting are the best end with its kidney, the joint which follows it and the *quasi* or rump.[2] Some people roast the shoulder; it is not as good as the joints I have mentioned.

---

1. In French, *gras double*. This is the flat, blanket or plain tripe from the rumen, the first stomach: less esteemed than honeycomb tripe from the reticulum or second stomach.
2. The *quasi* of veal is the rump, but explanations of this unlikely French name seem various. One derivation suggested is that it comes from the medieval Turkish *kasi* or *kasik*, the groin (of a horse or man). A less fanciful Académie des gastronomes (*Dictionnaire du gastronome,* 1962) suggests it uses the French adverb ('as if') to

The meat should be eaten when well cooked and well browned; it should not be cooked on a blazing fire; you should baste it with its juices during the cooking. Some people rub it with a piece of butter, but this procedure often gives it a taste of burnt butter, which is not very nice; others put a small spoonful of vinegar, which they let down with the juices, on the dish just before service. Halfway through the cooking, it is seasoned with fine salt.

The bone from a veal roast can be used either to make a gravy, or to prepare an excellent cabbage soup. Veal should be beaten just as you beat beef. Before spitting the best end or the joint which follows it [the loin], you should take care to roll up that part of the meat which extends beyond the bottom of the ribs.

The leftovers from a veal roast make excellent meatballs and can be incorporated in all stuffing mixtures.

BLANQUETTE OF VEAL (entrée and luncheon).[1] — You can also make excellent blanquettes with the remains from a veal roast. To do this, cut it into very thin slices, place in a saucepan in which you have melted, but not browned, a knob of butter; turn them over, then add a large spoonful of flour, and stir again. Above all, do not let it brown. Moisten with water and stir carefully. After first adding salt, and then pepper, let it simmer a minute. When the sauce has thickened, add a liaison [of egg yolks] with or without vinegar; then add finely chopped parsley and serve it up immediately. You don't need more than a quarter of an hour to make a blanquette, seeing that you will have heated the water in advance.

BEST END OF VEAL À LA BOURGEOISE (entrée). — Lard a best end with fat seasoned with herbs; place a slice of backfat[2] or a rind of salt pork and a few pieces of belly pork or ham in the bottom of a saucepan; add four spoonfuls of eau-de-vie, the same amount of stock or water, carrots, onions, salt, pepper, cloves, bay leaves, and thyme. Brown the veal in butter, then

---

identify a joint that comes after the loin and above the *gîte à la noix* or silverside (when beef). It is therefore 'as if' it were the *gîte* or lower part of the leg. *Larousse gastronomique* observes the word first appears in the eighteenth century.

1. *Blanquette* is defined by *Larousse gastronomique* as 'a ragout of white meat cooked in white stock or water with aromatic flavourings.'

2. The French for this slice is *barde*, denoting a thin slice of backfat which is often used to envelop a roast on the spit.

let it cook for four hours with a gentle heat above and below the pan. Add a burnt onion to colour it.

BREAST AND SHOULDER OF VEAL. — *Stuffed breast and shoulder* (entrée). — Choose a breast with its skin entire. Split the flesh inside and cut out and remove the bones without breaking the skin. Make a stuffing containing backfat, parsley, a chopped onion, salt, pepper, and the crumb of a loaf soaked in stock or milk. Cut off some of the meat to chop in with this stuffing; put all this in where the bones were and between the layers of flesh; roll and tie firmly. Add a few pieces of ham or belly pork [to a pan]; brown them, take them out and turn the shoulder over in their fat to give it some colour; put back the belly; moisten with stock or water; add salt, pepper and a bouquet garni; cook with a gentle heat above and beneath the pan. If the sauce is too thin, let it boil with the pan uncovered. You can add carrots and onions; in this case, it would be good to make a roux an hour before you serve it up and mix it with the sauce. You serve vegetables with it.

Shoulder of veal is prepared exactly the same way as the breast.

Breast of veal with green peas (entrée). — Cut a breast of veal into pieces and brown it in butter; add a little flour, salt, pepper, a bay leaf, and two or three glasses of stock or water, and leave to cook for an hour and a half. Then add a litre and a half of medium-sized peas, with a little salt. You need to stir up the fire the moment you add the peas because peas cooked over a high heat are better. They will need an hour to cook. If the sauce is too thin, let it boil uncovered so that it reduces by evaporation.

Breast of veal à la poulette (entrée). — Cut the meat into pieces and beat them; put butter in a saucepan; let it melt (and no more); add one or two spoonfuls of flour, depending on the quantity of meat; mix well; moisten with hot water, stir. When the sauce is thick and boiling, put in the meat. Season with salt and pepper, add a bay leaf, but no parsley (of which the slightest particle will resemble a fly in this utterly white sauce). Leave to cook for an hour; after this, add from twelve to twenty little onions (depending on their size). When everything is cooked, prepare a liaison, add it to the sauce, stirring without letting it boil. Serve.

SHOULDER OF VEAL WITH CABBAGE (entrée). — After deboning and beating the shoulder, roll it and stud with large lardons. Brown in butter one or two heads of Savoy cabbage,[1] cut into four if large, in two if they

1.   In French, *choux de Milan*.

are small. When the surface of the cabbage has turned golden, remove it and brown the shoulder likewise. Then moisten with water or, better, with stock. Add carrots, onions, bay leaf, thyme, salt and pepper. After an hour's cooking (with coals above and below the pan), make a roux which you add to the sauce – you can however dispense with this. When it is properly amalgamated, arrange the cabbage around the meat and cook with a very gentle heat above and beneath the pan. In serving, place the cabbages similarly around the meat. The carrots can also be served. This is a very good family dish. A fillet of veal [1] can also be prepared in the same way.

Veal brisket à la poulette.[2] — These [strips cut from the middle part of the breast of veal] are dealt with in the same way as breast of veal, and are eaten with the same sauce.

CHOPS. — *Chops en papillote* (entrée and luncheon). — After trimming and beating them, coat each side with a mixture of backfat, breadcrumbs, parsley, spring onion, mushrooms if possible, and even chopped truffle; season moderately with salt and pepper; cover the whole with a little slice of backfat and carefully wrap each chop in a sheet of oiled white paper: to make it easier, secure the paper to the end of the bone with a little string. Then cover the entire thing with a second sheet of white paper, or any other paper; put on the grill over a very gentle fire for between three-quarters of an hour and one hour. Take off the second paper and the string; serve without removing the first sheet of paper.

Veal chops with mixed herbs (entrée and luncheon). — Melt a knob of butter in a dish or a pie-dish; put in the chops, which you have beaten, with some salt and pepper; fry them in the butter, on both sides. Chop some herbs and some mushrooms with a few soft breadcrumbs or dried crumbs, coat the chops on one side and turn them over; leave them to cook a few moments; coat the other side in the same fashion and turn them over once more; then cover them. Leave them to cook for half an hour and serve

1. In French, *rouelle de veau.*
2. The text has *tendons* for *tendrons*, here, a few pages later and in the index. But Madame's immediate source recipe, Audot, has *tendrons.* In French butchery, that part which in England is designated breast of veal is divided into three cuts: the breast (*poitrine*) is at the front of the beast; then the middle part, below the ribs, which might in English beef butchery be called brisket, is called *tendron*, and is often cut into and cooked as slices rather than as a single piece; then towards the rear comes the *flanchet*, or flank.

them arranged like a crown. Scrape off whatever has stuck to the pan and put it in the middle of the dish.[1]

Fried veal chops (luncheon and entrée). — Put some butter in a frying-pan; once you have beaten them, dust the chops with flour and put them in the butter; brown them on one side, then the other; turn them over once or twice; add salt and pepper. Put a few spoonfuls of water in the pan; scrape off whatever juices have stuck to the pan; let it all come to the boil; pour these juices over the chops and serve. You can garnish this dish with gherkins. It is one of the quickest ways of dealing with veal chops; you can also add a little chopped garlic.

Stuffed veal chops (entrée, luncheon). — When the chops have been sliced off, they are trimmed. You should shorten the bone a lot, then remove the nut of meat which you chop up together with some backfat, mixed herbs, a little garlic, some crumb of a loaf soaked in milk (you pour over some warm milk and let it soak); then add salt and pepper. Once the stuffing has been prepared in this fashion, mix in a whole egg, then insert it into the space that was occupied by the nut, a space that will have the shape of a large ring. If the stuffing does not easily fit, force it a little; then tie it up carefully. Dust the two sides of the chops with flour, and fry them until they have taken on a nice golden colour. Some people add a little chopped garlic while the chops are browning. Moisten with a little water or, better, with stock; add the trimmings from the chops and cook with a gentle fire both beneath and on top of the pan. To serve, pour the sauce over the chops, after you have removed the string which bound them. This little-known dish is easy to prepare and excellent.

Veal chops with piquant sauce (entrée). — Brown them and put them to cook with a piquant sauce.

FRICANDEAU. — *Glazed fricandeau* (entrée). — Fillet of veal is the only joint used for this.[2] Separate out each of the parts which, as a whole, make

1. Although Mme Millet-Robinet starts this recipe by suggesting the chops are placed in a dish or a pie-dish (*un plat ou une tourtière*), she then presumes the cook will be frying them and finishes the recipe with the advice to scrape off whatever has stuck to the pan (*casserole* or saucepan). It is unclear whether she thinks her dish or pie-dish are of earthenware, pottery or metal. Audot, possibly her source for the recipe, suggests using a pan from the outset.
2. i.e., *rouelle de veau*. This joint, right at the top of the leg, is termed fillet in English butchery. It is sometimes cut into steaks or rounds, sometimes left as a single joint

up the fillet; beat them, trim them and stud them on both sides with small lardons. Brown them in butter until they have taken on a nice colour; moisten with water or, better, with stock, in sufficient quantity to cover the meat; add back any trimmings when you were larding, a few pieces of belly pork or ham, carrots cut into convenient pieces, onions, salt, pepper and a bouquet garni. Cook with a gentle fire above and below the pan for four or five hours. Halfway through the cooking, if the sauce is not coloured enough, add half a burnt onion. Half an hour before serving, take off much of this sauce and reduce it in a small saucepan over a clear fire. Dress the pieces on a dish and glaze them with the reduced sauce. Put the juices from the meat in the saucepan you used to reduce the sauce (in which a few scraps of sauce remain); mix them all up and pour it under the meat. You can arrange some of the vegetables around the edge of the dish.

Fricandeau with sorrel or with chicory (entrée). — Prepare it in the same way as glazed fricandeau; but rather than pouring the juices onto the dish, you keep them to flavour the sorrel or the chicory which is meant to be put under the meat. Keep the joints warm while you prepare the sorrel, and reduce some of the gravy to glaze the meat.

When you have stripped the sorrel, cook it in a large amount of salted water and then drain it. In a saucepan with butter, which you heat but don't brown, throw in the sorrel and stir to break it up; then add a spoonful of flour and stir again; moisten with gravy from the fricandeaux; let simmer a moment; pour the sorrel onto the dish and dress the fricandeau on this mixture.

If you use chicory instead of sorrel, after stripping it and cooking it in plenty of salted water, squeeze it in your hands in batches to extract all the water; then chop it and finish it as you would sorrel.

The remains of meat, the vegetables and the belly pork can provide a good meal for the kitchen.

FILLET OF VEAL. — *Fillet of veal cooked in its juices* (entrée and luncheon). — Choose for this type of dish a slender fillet. After you have beaten it, dust it with flour and put it to the fire with butter in a saucepan or a thin copper dish. Brown it on both sides. Moisten it with a little stock or, failing

---

encompassing the top of the leg and chump end or, more often in France, broken into its constituent parts along the muscle. The cushion of veal (the source of escalopes) is the boned and rolled *cuisse*, or leg, of the beast.

that, with water, and damp down the fire; add salt, pepper and a bay leaf; then put a lid with hot embers on the pan and leave to cook on a gentle flame for an hour or an hour and a half at the most. You can put some potatoes (which you do not let dip into the sauce) round the fillet: they will cook in the steam from the meat and absorb some of its flavour; they are then served round the edge of the dish. If the juices stick hard to the bottom of the pan during cooking, pour in two or three spoonfuls of water or stock after the meat is served up. Then, putting the pan back on the fire, the dried-on particles are detached and deglazed with a spoon and poured over the meat. You can add a small clove of chopped garlic at the moment of covering the pan. This simple dish is excellent.

Fillet of veal with mixed herbs (entrée and luncheon). — You prepare this on the dish like veal chops; you can add a little chopped garlic. You need to put heat above and below the dish and leave it to cook for an hour and a half over a gentle fire.

Fillet of veal à la bourgeoise. — Beat it well; stud it with large lardons; brown it in butter, moisten it with enough water to cover it. Put in carrots and onions; cook for two hours; add a roux and leave to cook for another hour. Serve after you have arranged the vegetables around it.

Carbonade of fillet of veal (entrée).[1] — Make quite a lot of forcemeat which you mould as a sort of dough consisting of the crumb of a loaf, backfat, salt, pepper and two whole eggs. Once you have beaten the fillet, coat it with it on both sides; tie it up well; then dust it with flour and brown it in butter; moisten with a little stock or water; cook it, with a gentle heat above and below the pan, for two or three hours, depending on the size of the joint. Dress it. Scrape off any of the stuffing which has stuck to the pan by adding a couple of spoonfuls of water or stock, and stick them back on the veal.

ESCALOPES. — *Escalopes with oil* (entrée and luncheon). — cut the fillet of veal into slices, then into rectangular pieces the size of a playing card; trim them well and beat them vigorously to flatten them and tenderize them; dust them well with flour. Put some good oil in a saucepan on a clear fire; when it is really hot, place as many escalopes as will cover the bottom

1. A *carbonade* or *carbonnade* is commonly a piece of grilled beef or other meat (fr. the Italian, *carbonata*). A Flemish *carbonade* is a piece of beef stewed with onions and beer, while a Provençal *carbonade* is a stew with red wine.

473

of the pan; when they have seared on one side, turn them. Brown all the escalopes. When they have all passed through the pan, add two spoonfuls of stock or gravy, one spoonful of dried breadcrumbs, salt, pepper, and chopped parsley; put back all the escalopes; cover; and let it simmer for an hour. You can give this dish a higher flavour by adding the juice of a lemon and a chopped clove of garlic. Serve the escalopes arranged as a crown.

Escalopes with wine (entrée and luncheon). — Prepare them as in the preceding recipe, but brown them in butter after dusting them well with flour; when they begin to take colour, add a little finely chopped garlic, salt, pepper and a bay leaf. Moisten with a glass of white wine or water: the escalopes should be covered by it. Cook it in a gentle heat, both over and under the pan; serve in a crown formation; pour the sauce over the escalopes. If the sauce seems too thin, let it boil uncovered; if it is too thick, moisten it a few moments before serving.

QUASI or *rump of veal*.[1] — You should beat this joint of meat before putting it on the spit; it makes a fine roast. You must not baste it with butter otherwise it will take on a very unpleasant burnt taste. Some people put a spoonful of vinegar in the juices, which are served under the roast.

Rump of veal with onions. — After beating it, thread it with large lardons seasoned with mixed herbs and brown it. Choose ten or twelve nice onions, which you blanch, and then lard as you have the meat. Place a piece of rind from the backfat underneath the *quasi*; add a glass of white wine, salt, pepper, a bay leaf and thyme. Cook with a gentle heat beneath and on top; when cooking is halfway through, add the onions. Skim the sauce, pass it through a sieve and pour it over the meat after arranging the onions around it.

Rump of veal à la pèlerine (entrée).[2] — Thread it with thick lardons; brown it on all sides in oil; moisten with a little water; cook it with gentle heat above and below for five or six hours. Meanwhile, glaze a dozen nice onions with sugar. When they are glazed, moisten them with the juices of the *quasi* and half a glass of white wine; add some mushrooms and simmer

1. *Larousse gastronomique* comments that the *quasi* may be used as escalopes, but will be tougher than those from the leg or cushion. It may also be cut into thicker slices for roasting, or roasted whole. *Larousse gastronomique* also notes that in Anjou it is called *cul de veau*, the term given as an alternative here, and was doubtless used in neighbouring Poitou.

2. The French word *pèlerine* means cape or cloak. This was the customary garb of a *pèlerin* or pilgrim (as well as of *gendarmes* on point duty in wet weather).

a short while. When you serve it, thicken the juices that remain in the pan with a little potato flour; glaze with this gravy; dish up the sauce and the onions and put the *quasi* in the centre.

KIDNEY. — *Fried kidney* (entrée). — Cut the kidney into fine slices and put them into a frying-pan with butter and a large spoonful of flour, then sauté. When it begins to brown, moisten it with red wine and sauté once more; then add salt and pepper. When the sauce is nicely thickened, add a little chopped parsley; mix together and serve. You won't need more than a quarter of an hour to cook a calf's kidney this way.

Calf's kidney omelette (hors-d'oeuvre). — When part of a kidney attached to a joint of veal is left over from a dinner of the day before, the next day you can use it (and the fat surrounding it) in an omelette.

MESENTERY OR FRILL.[1] — *Frill.* — The best is the whitest; blanket tripe is here included.[2] Although it will have been scalded when purchased, you will still have to soak it for three or four hours in lightly salted water, and wash it carefully in this water. Cook it in plenty of water for three or four hours, with salt, pepper, cloves, thyme, bay leaf and three or four large onions. Serve it surrounded with parsley, as hot as possible, on a dish you have warmed already. To accompany calf's mesentery, prepare a sauce with its cooking water to which you add salt, pepper, chopped parsley, chives and vinegar. Serve this sauce in a sauceboat.

Blanquette of calf's mesentery (luncheon). — Any remains of the frill, and especially of blanket tripe, make an excellent dish for luncheon. Cut it into pieces, and deal with it like blanquette of veal; but you must always add a little vinegar and only just bring it up to the boil; otherwise it will toughen.

Calf's mesentery with tomato sauce (luncheon). — Cut any leftovers into pieces and reheat them in a tomato sauce that has been a little spiced.

Fried calf's mesentery (hors-d'oeuvre or luncheon). — After you have

1.   In French, *fraise*. The word means either strawberry, dentist's drill, or frill or ruff. It is the latter meaning to which the word refers, for the *fraise* or frill of the calf is the mesentery and it takes a definitely frilly form, unlike the flat leaves or honeycombs of tripe. It is an important constituent of *andouillettes*. In the aftermath of mad cow disease or BSE the *fraise* was one of those bits of bovine offal that was excluded from the human food chain. Although the ban has been lifted from many organs, such as the brain, it has remained on the *fraise*.

2.   Her reference to blanket tripe is to *gras-double*.

cooked it as I have described, leave it to cool and cut it into pieces which you flour and fry. You could equally dip them in batter. You dress the dish with an edging of fried parsley.

CALF'S SWEETBREADS. — *Glazed calf's sweetbreads.* — You serve and prepare this most delicate part of the calf in the same fashion as a fricandeau. But before you cook the sweetbreads, you must pour boiling water over them and trim them. Calf's sweetbreads on their own have very little flavour and it is good to add a few pieces of veal to the cooking water, which you don't serve with the sweetbreads but which you can eat the next day with some sort of sauce, or which will do well for a servants' meal. You don't usually lard sweetbreads, but when you wish to do so, use a very fine larding needle.

Calf's sweetbreads à la poulette (entrée). — Prepare them as for breast of veal. It is a very delicate dish. You can join to them some chicken breasts and brains.

Calf's sweetbreads en papillote (luncheon and entrée). — Blanch them, then cut them in slices, which you coat in a forcemeat made of chopped backfat and the crumb of a loaf soaked in milk; you can add parsley and chives. Then you wrap the sweetbreads in double sheets of paper, as I have shown for veal chops (above). Cook them over a gentle heat on a grill for half an hour. Serve like the veal chops *en papillote.*

Gratin of calf's sweetbreads (entrée and luncheon). — Blanch them and put them in a dish that is at once fireproof and presentable at table. Melt a suitable amount of butter in this dish. Put between each slice of sweetbread, or over the whole thing, a forcemeat made of backfat, mixed herbs, dried breadcrumbs and finely chopped mushrooms, all seasoned with salt, pepper and a little nutmeg. Moisten with two or three spoonfuls of stock or gravy; dust with dried breadcrumbs: put embers above and beneath the pan. Serve in the dish you have cooked them in. A sauce is not necessary. Everything in the dish should be somewhat browned for it to be pronounced perfect.

LUNG. — *Calf's lung à la poulette* (entrée). — Soak it and change the water several times while pressing it like a sponge; then prepare it like veal brisket [*tendron de veau*] à la poulette (above).

Matelote of calf's lung (entrée). — Soak it and let it boil a short while in salted water with a little vinegar; finish the cooking in a matelote sauce.

476

Calf's brains [hors-d'oeuvre, entrée and entremets]. — Prepare them either à la poulette, or as a gratin or as a matelote (see *Calf's sweetbreads*, above); but most often they are eaten fried. You must start by soaking them and taking off the thin skin which covers them; then you blanch them in fairly well salted water. Let them cool to cut them into pieces, which you dip in batter before plunging in deep fat. Serve with parsley that has also been fried.

If you cannot obtain enough calf's brains to make a dish sufficiently copious for your needs, you can add sheep's brains; it's true that they are a little less delicate, but you would need to be a connoisseur to tell the difference.

You can add calf's brains to a chicken fricassee, or to forcemeat meatballs.

Calf's head. — *Plain boiled calf's head* (entrée and remove). — See what I said above relative to calf's head (page 407).

To cook it, split the skin beneath the lower jaw; strip the bones and cut them back to the large teeth; then remove the tongue. That done, turn the head over, split the palate, strip the snout by lifting off the flesh and skin without damaging it and cut the base of the upper jaw bone. Clean the insides of the ears with the utmost care by introducing a small stick with a thin damp cloth attached; finally, soak the calf's head in cold water for two hours. Once removed from the water, press the flesh back in place; reshape the muzzle; rub the entire surface with a halved lemon; then tie it up with string and wrap it in a fine white cloth. Secure this cloth with a second length of string so that it does not get displaced.

Cook the calf's head in a cauldron or, better, a large earthenware pot, filled with water to which you have added salt, pepper, an onion, a clove of garlic and a large bouquet garni. Cooking should take place over a low fire and last for at least five or six hours; during this process, you should top up with boiling water if the pot loses any by evaporation as the head should be covered at all times. It is good to put the well-washed tongue in the same pot as the head, even though it is rarely served with it. At the moment of service, remove the head from the pot with the aid of the cloth and string and place it on a dish lined with a nicely folded napkin, garnished with parsley. A few crayfish dotted among the parsley make the dish look attractive. When the head has been dished up, carefully split the skin over the skull, pull it apart to remove the two bones which cover it, then replace the skin. If you are worried that the head will then lose its shape, you can dispense with taking out these bones. Serve in a sauceboat a sauce made from the cooking liquor of the head itself, some vinegar, some mixed herbs and chopped chives, pepper and salt; some people add oil. What is left of the cooking liquor cannot be better used than to make a cabbage soup.

A calf's head cooked just so and elegantly served is a fine thing.

Calf's head in the manner of turtle (entrée).[1] — To make this as instructed in the *Cuisinier royal* [2] requires so many ingredients and so much studied elegance that a common-or-garden cook runs great risk of losing her head; what's more, the preparation demands resources not usually at her disposal. To sidestep these disadvantages, here is a recipe which may be more modest but yields a dish that is no less excellent.

Once the calf's head is in such a state that it can be served plain, cut it into pieces – having had a care to remove all the bones, but keeping the eyes whole as well as the ears. Then you simmer the whole thing a short while in a sauce prepared in the following manner.

Cut a sufficiency of smoked ham into pieces which you brown in a saucepan; moisten it with gravy or good stock. Add a bouquet garni and let it boil for two hours. Then add as much tomato sauce and good white wine as you added stock and leave it to boil for an hour; you only salt it a little because of the ham; add pepper and powdered hot pepper[3] in reasonable quantity, bearing in mind that the sauce should have a really emphatic flavour. Add to this sauce some mushrooms, sliced truffles, artichoke bottoms, cock's combs cut into pieces, and two or three brains. When all this has cooked, take out the ham while leaving all the other ingredients. Now add the pieces of calf's head and a few crayfish, and let simmer a short while. To serve, you first dress the head, skin side uppermost, terminated by

1. In French, *en tortue*. The English mock turtle soup was made with a calf's head.
2. This book, by Alexandre Viard, first appeared as *Le Cuisinier impérial* in 1806. It was a standby text for professional chefs. See the note on page 139 concerning its changes of title over the years. The recipe *Tête de Veau à la Tortue* appears on page 112 of the 1817 edition.
3. In French, *piment en poudre*. Mme Millet-Robinet's readers were probably more acquainted with Spanish *pimentón* than Hungarian paprika. She does not in fact specify whether sweet or hot. In other places, she refers to Cayenne pepper as Cayenne.

the two eyes and the two ears, placed upright. Arrange the other ingredients symmetrically around the dish and pour the sauce over everything. If it is not thick enough, you can thicken it with a little starch [1] at the moment of service; if it is insufficiently brown, you can colour it up with a little caramel or half a burnt onion.

This dish is quite fancy; it can never the less be prepared without undue expense.

Calf's head in the manner of turtle au blanc [2] (entrée). — After you have prepared the calf's head in the manner I have just described, put 125 grams of butter and 500 grams of chopped backfat, to which you add three large spoonfuls of flour, in a saucepan; stir it a short while, taking care that it does not brown; moisten with hot water and be sure to blend the flour in carefully. Once the sauce has thickened, add a bottle of good white wine, salt, pepper, six large onions, a few cloves, a piece of lemon zest, a large bouquet garni (without parsley) and chilli. This last you can add whole and remove at the moment of service. Cover with a sheet of paper and leave to cook for an hour, after which you squeeze the juice of a lemon into the sauce and add the calf's head, the brain cut into pieces, some crayfish, some sliced truffles and some mushrooms (which you should boil for a minute in plenty of salted water so that they don't darken the sauce). Cover with a sheet of paper and let cook for another hour. Then take out each piece and drain it before dressing it on the dish as I have explained in the preceding paragraphs. Serve the truffles, mushrooms, crayfish and brains around the head. Strain the sauce and put it back on the fire. When it boils, make a liaison with three egg yolks, but don't let it boil after you have added the liaison. This sauce should be very pale.

You can arrange half the head in this fashion, and the other half in the way I described earlier. You will then have a pretty contrast. Each dish is crowned by an ear placed upright in the middle.

Fried calf's head (hors-d'oeuvre). — Cut the remains of the plain boiled calf's head into pieces and after dipping them in batter, fry them.

Blanquette of calf's head (entrée, luncheon). — Melt a knob of butter

1. i.e. potato flour or cornflour.
2. *Au blanc* is the French term for something cooked in a white stock or in a cooking liquor thickened with a little flour and acidulated with lemon juice (*blanc de cuisson*).

without browning it, add a heaped spoonful of flour; stir; moisten with hot water and mix. When the sauce is thickened, put in the calf's head and salt and pepper; let it simmer a short while. Bind it with the help of one or two egg yolks. Add some finely chopped parsley. You can add to the liaison a splash of vinegar or the juice of a lemon.

CALF'S EARS. — *Ears with piquant sauce* (entrée). — Clean the ears with great care and cook them with the same seasonings as you would a whole head. When they are cooked, dress them upright on a dish and split the tips, which you fold backwards. Pour around the dish and into the centre either a piquant sauce to which you have added a few truffles and mushrooms, or a tomato sauce, or even an onion purée, a Provençal sauce or any purée you would like. You can put a truffle poached in white wine into each ear.

Fried calf's ears (hors-d'oeuvre). — When they are cooked, cut them in two down their length, pepper them and stuff them with a quenelle mixture (see *Quenelles*, page 443, above). Dip them in beaten egg (white and yolk together), dust them with fine soft breadcrumbs, and fry them.

CALF'S TONGUE. — *Grilled tongue* (entrée and luncheon). — While it is still warm, peel the skin from the tongue that you cooked with the calf's head; the next day you can serve it at luncheon. For this, split it into two without separating it entirely, holding it open with two little wooden skewers. Season with salt and pepper and place it on the grill. It should be served on a hot dish and garnished with butter rubbed into chopped parsley, salt and pepper. You can also coat it with breadcrumbs, which is very good. Several calf's tongues prepared as I have just explained make up a most presentable dish.

Daube of calf's tongues (entrée).[1] — Boil them briefly in plenty of water so that you can take off the skin and trim them; then stick them with large lardons and put them in a pan with a little butter and a few pieces of backfat, quarter of a glass of eau-de-vie, onions, carrots, salt, pepper, a few cloves, half a burnt onion, thyme, bay leaf and a little water. Cook with a gentle heat above and beneath the pan. If the sauce dries out, add a little water or stock; cook for five or six hours. When you serve it, split the calf's tongues, garnish them with the vegetables they were cooked with, and

---

1.   In the text, *Langues de veau en daube*.

pour the sauce over them. You can decorate the dish with some slices of gherkin.

CALF'S FEET (entrée, hors-d'oeuvre). — They can be prepared in all the ways suggested for calf's head. A calf's foot cooked in a pot-au-feu gives an excellent flavour to the soup; in this case, the cooled stock will jelly. Calf's foot can be prepared with a piquant sauce (entrée) and also serve as a garnish for beef. You should remove the large bone. When fried, it is an hors-d'oeuvre.

CALF'S LIVER. — *Liver on the spit* (roast). — Stick it with large lardons that you have seasoned well; marinate it for five hours in a little oil, with thyme, bay leaf, salt and pepper; turn it over so that the marinade covers everything. To cook it, wrap it in a piece of paper that you have buttered well; put it on the spit and place it in front of a gentle fire for about an hour and a half. Add to any gravy it yields some finely chopped shallots, two spoonfuls of stock, pepper, and mixed herbs. Let this boil briefly. Serve this sauce beneath the liver or in a sauceboat.

Stewed calf's liver (entrée and luncheon). — Stick it with large lardons that you have seasoned well; put it in a pan with backfat, carrots, onions, salt, pepper, a bouquet garni and a large glass of white wine; cook it for three hours with a very low fire above and beneath the pan. Serve hot with its vegetables and a reduced sauce. If you add a calf's foot to the liver, the gravy will set as it cools. A cold calf's foot coated with jelly can be served at luncheon.

Calf's liver à la paysanne. — Lard it and put it to cook in a saucepan with a little water, pepper, a little salt, a bay leaf; turn it once or twice during the cooking, which should be for two and half hours. If there is too much sauce, uncover the pan, as it should be reduced. Serve it up; it's excellent.

Calf's liver with wine (entrée and luncheon). — Lard it as in the preceding recipe and put it in a saucepan with backfat, whole onions, a bouquet garni, a large glass of red wine (or two if the liver is large). Let it cook for two or three hours at the most, with a very low heat above and beneath the pan. At the moment of service, mix a little starch into the sauce to thicken it.

Shallow-fried calf's liver (luncheon). — Cut it into thin slices about as large as half a hand's width, and put them into the pan with a knob of butter, chopped parsley and spring onions, salt, and quite a lot of pepper; put it on the fire; add a good spoonful of flour, mix it in; add a glass of red wine; cook for ten minutes, or quarter of an hour at the most. Serve immediately.

Calf's liver like beefsteak (luncheon). — Cut a few fairly thin slices of liver; brown them in butter on one side, then the other, for about ten minutes; season with salt and pepper and put them on the grill. Serve on a hot dish, with butter worked into parsley, salt, pepper and a little finely chopped spring onion. You can add the juice of a lemon or a thread of vinegar.

4. — Mutton.

Mutton flesh should be dark and the covering fat perfectly white and firm. Like all meat, it should rest for some days in the larder; it is at any rate the meat which keeps the best.

The Charmoise breed,[1] or the fast-developing English breeds, can be slaughtered at fourteen or fifteen months and provide a meat infinitely preferable to that of the old French breeds, and above all to Merinos which will only fatten at four or five years-old.

Leg. — *Roast leg of mutton.* — It should be plump, with a short knuckle and flesh that is almost black; it is the joint which keeps the best. Kept in an airy place, but away from flies, it will dry out and will keep twelve days in winter; of all supplies, it is the joint that can be sent last to the kitchen.

Before putting a leg of mutton on the spit, it should be beaten vigorously, then trimmed – that is to say, the excess of fat that sometimes covers it should be removed, it should be shaped and those bits of skin which will usually dry out in the cooking sliced off; but you should guard against touching the skin on the top surface. When the gigot comes with its tail, you stick it into the flesh, first making a hole with a knife. Give the knuckle a blow with the knife to cut the tendon and fold it over onto the leg; then take out the tendon on the shin and cut the bottom of the knuckle.

---

1.   The Charmoise is a French breed of hill sheep developed by Edouard Malingié in the mid-nineteenth century by crossing ancient French breeds onto Kentish stock. It takes its name from the Charmoise farm at Pontlevoy in Loir-et-Cher. It is hardy and of good conformation.

To spit the leg, pass the spit through the part called the knuckle and then into the heart of the leg. You can put half a clove of garlic cut in two, each piece inserted into the meat at the bottom.

The fire before which you propose roasting a leg of mutton should be laid and lit in advance and be very brisk, because this joint must be seared; without this it loses much of its quality. An hour and a half is broadly sufficient for a large leg; it will need less if it is small. The flesh of a leg cooked as it should be is red in the middle, not brown or violet. To achieve this, you should be careful, always careful; it's the way to do things properly. It's good to put two spoonfuls of water in the dripping-pan. You salt it halfway through cooking, with fine salt.

When the leg is cooked, at the moment of service you wrap the knuckle in a piece of white paper, the edge of which you have frilled. Or you put the knuckle in a purpose-made metal or wooden clamp that fixes on the bone and holds it with a set screw. You should heat the dish on which you serve the leg of mutton.

Marinated roast leg of mutton. — A marinade heightens the taste of a leg of mutton and imparts a flavour which is little different to venison. To marinade a leg of mutton, once you have beaten it, dunk it in a mixture of oil, vinegar, salt, pepper, plenty of thyme, bay leaf and cloves. Turn it over in this marinade and baste it several times. Cook it as in the preceding recipe; halfway through the cooking, add the marinade to the drippings and baste the leg. Strain the gravy before serving it.

How to use the remains of a leg of mutton. — The leg bone makes an excellent cabbage soup and not a bad gravy.

The remains of the meat can be served in paper-thin slices,[1] accompanied by a piquant sauce in which you will have boiled the cracked leg bones. You should not put the meat to the sauce until the moment of service, because all it need do is warm through; if it boils, then it will greatly toughen, unless the boiling is prolonged for about one and a half hours; then it will take on the taste and character of boiled meat, and become very tender. Take out the bone at the last minute. You can add a few slices of gherkin to the sauce.

These same leftovers are even better served in a salmi sauce [page 438, above]. The bones are also boiled in the sauce, and the meat just warmed.

1.   This, in French, is an *émincé*.

The remains of a leg in a hash make a very good dish.

You can make the leftovers from a leg into a ragout in the following manner. Cut the bone down the middle from where you have taken slices from the roast; brown a few pieces of salt pork or ham; do the same to a few rounds of carrots and a few onions in the fat which the ham or pork have produced. When you have taken the vegetables out of the saucepan, put the leftover mutton into the same fat; take this out of the pan; add a spoonful of flour and stir; moisten with warm water, and put back into this sauce the leftover meat, the vegetables and the salt pork; then leave to cook, with a gentle heat above and below the pan, for two or three hours. This dish is not done often enough and is really good.

You can also make an excellent haricot of mutton with the leftovers from a gigot.

Finally, you need do no more than cut them in slices and reheat them in the gravy, or put them on the grill with salt and pepper. In this last instance, you garnish the slices with some parsley butter, as you would beefsteaks.

Leg of mutton in its own gravy (entrée, remove, or luncheon). — After trimming it as I have described above, stud it with large, seasoned lardons and brown it on both sides in butter. Put some rind of salt pork under the leg in a saucepan, or better in a braising-pan; add at least two glasses of water, pepper, salt, thyme and bay leaf. Cook it with a gentle heat above and beneath the pan for four or five hours. You can put a few large onions around the leg. Serve it on a purée of vegetables, to which you add the gravy, or even on some whole haricot beans which you have cooked separately.

Leg of mutton in water or as a daube (entrée, remove). — Trim it as I have instructed for *Roast leg of mutton* (above), or bone it by splitting the flesh at its narrowest part so that you can open it up and remove the bones (some people don't take out the knuckle). Stud it with large lardons, roll it up and tie it firmly, ensuring it has a nice shape to it. Crush the bones, taking out any splinters. Brown the leg on all sides in butter. You could also melt a few pieces of belly pork or very fat ham and brown the leg in this fat. Moisten with a little water; place beneath the leg a rind of backfat; arrange all around the leg the ham and the leg bones, and add a little salt, pepper and a bouquet garni. Cook with a gentle heat above and beneath the pan for two hours. Now put under the bones five or six large onions and ten or twelve pieces of carrot; leave to cook for another three hours. When you are ready to serve, dress the vegetables around the leg, skim the fat off the sauce, strain it and pour it over the leg. Rather than just water, you can use either white wine, or a half-glass of eau-de-vie and a glass of water. Half an hour before serving it, you can also take out half a glass of the skimmed gravy and reduce it to a glaze in a small saucepan. Glaze the leg once it is dished up.

This can be served cold. In this case, add a calf's foot or shin split in two to the ingredients already listed, and let the gravy cool separately from the meat. It will set to a jelly which can be served around the leg.

LOIN OF MUTTON.[1] — *Loin* (entrée and roast). — Before putting it on the spit, beat it, and give a little blow with the chopper to each vertebra. The loin can be prepared in every way like the leg. You can also divide it into cutlets, which are not quite so handsome as those in the best end but which are still good.

Loin of mutton with cabbage (entrée). — Make it in exactly the same way as shoulder of veal with cabbage (page 469, above); its aroma much resembles that of game. The leg, best end and shoulder of mutton can be dressed with cabbage; it is a main course which pleases everyone. You can add a few pieces of ham around the loin.

Loin of mutton with French beans (entrée). — Beat the loin, brown it, moisten it with water, add salt, pepper and a bouquet garni. When the loin is almost cooked, skim the fat off; thicken the sauce with a little flour; boil it up briskly; add some little, nicely tender French beans, which you have blanched in plenty of salted water. Once they are cooked, serve them round the loin. This is an excellent dish. Leg of mutton or stuffed shoulder, as well as the best end, can be dressed in the same fashion.

BEST END OF MUTTON. — Use it like loin, or take chops from it.

BREAST OF MUTTON. — When you have cooked it in a pot-au-feu or a cabbage soup, let it cool and pass it through some melted butter or oil; then season it with salt and pepper; finally you coat it with breadcrumbs and put it on the grill. Serve it either on cabbage taken from the soup which you have sweated for a while in butter or dripping with salt and pepper, or on

1.   In French, *filet de mouton*.

any sort of purée, or finally with a tomato sauce. Some people are happy to eat it plain grilled, with a little vinegar.

MUTTON CHOPS. — For them to be tender, they should come from the best end. I have already observed, in the article on *Loin of mutton*, that you can take them from this joint too, but these chops should not figure in a formal dinner, even though they are as good as the others.

Plain mutton chops (hors-d'oeuvre). — Cut the chops cleanly from the best end and strip half the length of each bone; don't roll back the flesh which covers them, but remove it entirely. This meat can be put to many uses in the kitchen, for example in a cabbage soup or any sort of ragout. Beat the chops then reshape them nicely; salt and pepper them; put them on the grill over a clear fire; you should not turn them more than once and they should be served on a hot dish. They ought to be red in the centre, not violet. A little experience will teach you how much to cook them. These chops should be dressed in a crown formation, the bones uppermost. You can put them on any purée or on a tomato sauce; then they might be considered an entrée.

Mutton chops coated in breadcrumbs (entrée). — Prepare them as I have just explained; put olive oil or melted butter on a plate and pass each chop through in turn; crumb them. That done, pile them up and let them rest for at least a day. Cook them on the grill as before; only turn them once, lest they dry out. Serve as in the preceding recipe.

Smothered mutton chops (entrée). — After trimming them, cook them with a low fire above and beneath for two and a half hours in a well-covered saucepan, with stock or gravy, salt, pepper, two or three onions, thyme, bay leaf and a burnt onion. A quarter of an hour before serving, take some of the gravy and glaze it [by reduction]. The rest of the gravy will serve to flavour any purée or a sorrel stuffing. Meanwhile, the chops remain in the well-covered pan near the fire. Once the gravy is done, you glaze the chops and serve them on the purée.

Sautéed mutton chops (hors-d'oeuvre and luncheon). — When you have crumbed them, put them in a pan with a knob of butter, salt and pepper; cook them over a gentle fire; then take each chop out of the pan to keep them free of fat and dress them. Take off some of the fat and add a chopped shallot and some mixed herbs, salt and pepper to that which remains. Sauté this while adding three or four spoonfuls of stock or water which you boil briefly. Scrape whatever has stuck to the bottom of the pan and serve it on the chops. It's good to add chopped gherkins to the sauce. You should only prepare the tenderest of chops in this manner for this way of cooking often toughens them; this dish has quite a pronounced flavour.

SHOULDER OF MUTTON. — *Shoulder* (entrée). — This can be prepared in the several ways explained for leg of mutton; but it is often tough when roasted.

Stuffed shoulder of mutton. — You deal with this in precisely the same way as shoulder of veal.

HARICOT OF MUTTON (entrée). — I leave others the task of researching the etymology of this fairly odd name and concern myself solely with the ragout.[1] Brown in butter some whole small turnips; the long turnips from Freneuse or the little round turnips from Finland are the best for this;[2] if you only have rather large turnips at your disposal, cut them to a suitable shape rather than simply quartering them; you can also add some pieces of belly pork or ham. [Remove and reserve the turnips.] Pass the mutton which you are going to put in the haricot through this fat. (The loin cut into pieces is the best for this dish.) Take out the mutton and make a roux, moisten with water or stock; put the meat back on the heat with salt, pepper, and a bouquet garni; let cook for at least two hours with a gentle heat above and beneath the pan; then add [back] the turnips; leave to cook for an hour. Skim the fat off. Dress the pieces of meat in a pyramid shape and arrange the turnips around them. You can, once you have cooked the turnips, put some whole medium-sized potatoes on top of everything; they will cook without being bathed in the sauce, which you should avoid if possible as they will absorb it almost completely. Cooked thus, potatoes are excellent; serve them as a coronet round the edge of the platter.

1.　The etymology of this word (which was Englished in the course of the eighteenth century) is indeed circuitous. Ayto (*The Diner's Dictionary*) and the Centre National de Ressources Textuelles et Lexicales (www.cnrtl.fr) derive it from the medieval French word for a mutton stew, so-called because the meat was *harigoté* or cut up into chunks. Ayto suggests that this came to be transferred to beans (which often formed part of the stew by the seventeenth century) by a process of folk-etymology as the Aztec word for bean (*ayacotl*) was unpronounceable. CNRTL plumps for the more pragmatic explanation that beans (which only came to France via the Columbian exchange) were often a significant ingredient of the stew, although not of this one described by Mme Millet-Robinet.

2.　The turnips from Freneuse have been commented on before (page 429, above); small round yellow turnips came originally from Finland.

SHEEP'S KIDNEYS. — *Butterflied kidneys* (luncheon, hors-d'oeuvre). — Remove the thin skin which covers them; split them down the round side, open them out and thread their length with two small wood or silver skewers, forming a cross, to hold them open while they cook. Salt and pepper them. Put them briefly on the grill. Serve with butter worked into chopped parsley.

Fried sheep's kidneys. — Skin them and cut them in two. They are then dealt with as veal kidneys. Gourmets sprinkle them with Champagne.

SHEEP'S TONGUES. — Deal with them as you would calf's tongues; once they have been grilled, they can be served on all sorts of purées.

SHEEP'S BRAINS. — Deal with them and serve them as you would calf's brains.

DAUBE OF SHEEP'S TAILS (entrée). — Prepared in the same manner as a daube of leg of mutton (page 484, above), sheep's tails provide a reasonably delicate dish. You can also cook it in a pot-au-feu or in a cabbage soup and then put it on the grill, crumbed or not crumbed. Serve them either with a parsley butter, or on a purée, or with a tomato sauce or some other sauce.

SHEEP'S TROTTERS. — *Trotters à la poulette* (entrée). — After washing them well, they are put on the fire in the morning in a stewpan or earthenware pot with water, two onions, a large bouquet garni, salt, and a few cloves. They will need to be cooked for nine to ten hours. Once they are cooked, and they can never be overcooked, you put them in a strainer to drain their juices and then you split each of them between the two dew-claws. There is a little ball filled with hair there which you remove. You also take out the large bones and then put the trimmed trotters into a saucepan with a knob of butter and a spoonful of flour. Sauté everything well, after adding salt, pepper and a little nutmeg. Moisten with water and let it simmer a few moments, then add some chopped parsley. The liaison of one or two egg yolks should only be added when ready to serve; you can also add a dash of vinegar.

Fried sheep's trotters (hors-d'oeuvre and luncheon). — After you have cooked and prepared them as described above, you sweat them for an hour in a marinade made of salt, pepper, nutmeg and a knob of butter; let them cool; then dip each one in beaten egg, yolks and whites, carefully crumb them and fry them.

Sheep's trotters in tomato sauce (entrée, luncheon). — When they are cooked and ready to finish off, sauté them in butter with a spoonful of flour, salt and pepper; moisten this with a tomato sauce.

Sheep's trotters with cheese (entrée). — After preparing them to dress à la poulette, rather than introducing a liaison you place them in layers on a fireproof dish; between each layer of trotters you spread a layer of grated cheese, made up of three-quarters Gruyère, one-quarter Parmesan, to which you add a little butter. Finish with a layer of cheese and cover this with dried breadcrumbs. Put everything on the fire and cover the dish with the hot Dutch oven which will itself have live coals on it; when the food has nicely browned, serve it without changing the dish. It's one of the good ways to eat sheep's trotters.

5. — Lamb and kid.

Lamb and kid are dealt with identically; the following recipes, therefore, can be applied to both. When lamb is fat, it is excellent and can be compared to good mutton; but the meat is less easily digested than mutton.

ROAST QUARTER OF LAMB OR KID.[1] — Stud it on the skin side with small lardons and put it to the spit in front of a brisk fire. Pour two or three glasses of water into the dripping-pan. As the fat begins to melt, sprinkle at intervals fine soft breadcrumbs or dried breadcrumbs (which you should have mixed with chopped parsley) over the joint. This roast should be nicely browned and be crisp on the outside. Baste with the fat and juices which drip from it. Serve on a hot dish because congealed fat has no merit at all. Some people put a dash of vinegar in the bottom of the dish. The leftovers from this roast make an excellent blanquette for luncheon. Some also serve it with a tomato sauce. The roast can be served plain, but it must always be crisp on the outside.

BEST END OF LAMB À LA PÉRIGORD (entrée). — Brown it in butter, along with some slices of fillet of veal; add a little oil, chopped parsley and spring onion, salt, pepper, and pieces of ham; moisten with stock; add a few truffles or diced mushrooms; cook over a gentle flame; add the juice of half a lemon. When the best end is cooked, skim the sauce; dress it on a

---

1. A quarter (Fr. *quartier*) of lamb is defined by *Larousse Gastronomique* as half of a *baron* of lamb: this is the two legs, the saddle and, sometimes, part of the loin or *carré* prepared for roasting.

platter and put the truffles on top; strain the sauce; pour it over. Serve. The lamb is frankly a mere accompaniment.

LAMB BETWEEN TWO FIRES. — Place either a forequarter or hindquarter on a fireproof dish with a little water; dust both sides generously with dried breadcrumbs mixed with chopped parsley and spring onion; season with salt and pepper. Maintain a brisk heat above and beneath the dish; stoke the fire when it is nearly cooked so that the meat colours up nicely. It may be better to cook this in the [bread] oven to achieve perfect browning.

LAMB CHOPS. — Cooked and prepared like mutton chops, they are excellent.

LAMB WITH ONIONS. — Cut the joint into square pieces; begin by browning eight or ten large onions in butter, then add the pieces of meat; take them out. Make a roux; moisten it with water or, better, stock; return the lamb to the pan, with the onions around it; add salt, pepper, and a bouquet garni; have the fire above and beneath the pan; cook for two and a half hours. Serve the onions around the meat. You can dispense with making a roux.

LAMBS' HEADS. — You cook and serve them in the same way as calfs' heads; but you will need plenty of them to make a good show.

LAMB'S TROTTERS. — You dress and prepare them in all the ways explained for sheep's trotters, and they are infinitely preferable to them. They will take three or four hours to cook.

6. — Pork.

Good pork should have fat that is firm and absolutely white; meat from the fillet and the loin should be as pale as veal, and from the legs it should be red. The flesh should also be firm.

Several fast-developing English breeds have been introduced into France and are spreading rapidly; their flesh is much to be preferred to the old French breeds, which don't fatten until a comparatively late age, contributing to their flesh being tougher, sometimes even leathery.

ROAST FRESH PORK (entrée and luncheon). — The fillet is usually selected for a roast; sometimes, however, it is the loin. You must beat whichever joint you choose to supply the roast, lightly salt it in advance, then wait for it to age sufficiently; but watch that it does not take on an unpleasant stale flavour, which pork may contract all too easily. Cook it before a moderate fire for at least two hours; it is the meat, of all meats, that should be the most cooked; however, it should not brown too much. Skim the gravy of fat before serving it beneath the roast. This fat is excellent for cooking dried vegetables, and can replace butter in a host of ragouts; you can also eat it spread on bread. The bones from a roast joint of fresh pork make an excellent cabbage soup. This roast is perhaps better cold than hot, and can be served cold at luncheon.

How to use the leftovers from a joint of roast pork. — The most suitable sauce to dress these leftovers is a sauce Robert, in which, after slicing them, you reheat them, without letting them boil. Roast fresh pork is also very good with a tomato sauce or a piquant sauce. If the sauce Robert seems too highly flavoured, you could replace it with a purée of onions. You can use leftovers from roast pork in any forcemeat.

CHOPS. — *Fried pork chops* (entrée and luncheon). — Place them in a pan over a clear fire with a very small amount of fat, just enough to start the fat on the chops themselves melting, and lightly brown them on both sides; season with salt and pepper; then damp down the fire so that they finish cooking slowly. Dish them up and put a little water in the pan to deglaze the juices with a spoon while it is boiling. Taking it off the flame, you can add a dash of vinegar and a few sliced gherkins. You won't need more than twenty minutes or half an hour to cook pork chops in this way. If, instead of a frying-pan, you use a pie-dish [1] to prepare chops in this fashion, the cooking will take much longer.

Chops with sauce (luncheon). — Dust them with flour and brown them in a little butter or fat; moisten with water; add salt, pepper, bouquet garni, a few chopped shallots; place embers above and beneath the pan; let it cook for an hour. As you serve it, slice some gherkins and scatter them over the chops.

PIG'S HEAD (luncheon). — See the recipe for *Head cheese*, in *Concerning provisions*, in the article on *Pork* (page 371, above).

PIG'S EAR (entrée). — You must singe them carefully to take off all the hair which covers the outside, and scald their insides with boiling water. You cook them with lentils, dried haricots or green peas, two or three onions, a carrot, salt, pepper and a bouquet garni. Serve the pig's ears on

1.   In French, *tourtière*. This may be an open pie-dish such as we use today, or a covered dish with three legs so that it could sit in the coals.

these vegetables, either whole or reduced to a purée and dressed with butter or lard. Cooked with the vegetables and seasonings that I have indicated, ears can be served on their own on a tomato sauce. You can also fry them, like calf's ears.

SUCKING PIG. — In my view, this roast is more extravagant than enjoyable. This is how you prepare it. Once you have gutted and thoroughly cleaned the sucking pig, you scald it and scrape it to remove the hair, much as you would do for adult pigs. You spit it by attaching the front feet under the head and the back ones pushed up under the leg, in the same position as they would be when lying down while still alive. Once the roast is thoroughly hot, baste it two or three times with salted water which you have already poured into the dripping-pan; then remove this water and baste the sucking pig several times with oil or lard. The fire should burn briskly so that the skin gets crisp, which is the greatest merit of this particular roast. In order that the skin does not crack irregularly, which does not look very pleasing to the eye, as soon as it starts to cook, you should make evenly spaced incisions – the same number on each side. You must serve this up very hot, as soon as you take it off the spit.

PIG'S KIDNEY (luncheon). — Prepare it as you would calf's kidney; it can be moistened with red wine or white; it often retains rather an unpleasant taste when it comes from an animal that was too old when slaughtered.

PIG'S TROTTERS. — *Grilled trotters.* — Once you have thoroughly scalded them and cleaned them, cook them for five hours, like ears, and serve them in the same fashion; if they float during the cooking, they will not whiten properly; you must therefore fix them in the pot with the help of small wooden skewers placed across the inside. When they are cooked, you can also take them out of the cooking liquor when half-cooled, split them, crumb them and put them on the grill to serve at luncheon or as an hors-d'oeuvre; this is the best way to eat them.

Between the two dew-claws there is a little gland full of hair which you should make sure you remove.

Stuffed pig's trotters. — Cook them as the ones above; split them and remove all the bones. Chop some of the flesh with parsley, salt, pepper, a little soft breadcrumb, and some well-cleaned truffle peelings. Cut the truffles themselves to add to the rest of the flesh, which you mix with that you have chopped; wrap everything in pig's caul and put the stuffed trotters on the grill just before you serve them as an hors-d'oeuvre or at luncheon. This is a very dainty dish.

HAM (luncheon or opposite a roast at dinner). See, in the chapter *Concerning provisions*, the article *Pork* (page 358, above).

With the help of a ham, you can greatly improve your cooking, and at little cost. You can buy a raw ham without yourself having to kill a pig. I advise you to choose small, round, firm hams, coming (whenever possible) from an English breed. If they are just killed, you should wait a few days before salting them. (See the article *Hams*, under *Salted meats*, page 369, above.) I have already, on several occasions, recommended the use of ham; I repeat, it is one of the most important foundations of good cookery. There are many bits that need removing from a ham before it is cooked; anything black or rusty should be sacrificed; these are not just unpleasant to eat, but they will spoil the rest and give it a disagreeable flavour. Once you have very carefully cleaned it, tie it up securely from every angle before placing it in the pot. To eat it cold, cook it with water, carrots, onions, a large bouquet garni, pepper and a few cloves. Some people add a bottle of white wine; this wine gives the ham a slightly acid flavour which is not to everyone's taste.

The fire should be quite gentle and cooking can last from eight to ten hours, depending on the size. You will need less time if you only cook a part of it. When it is cooked, which you will recognize by being able to plunge a match easily into it, place it on a normal dish; take out the bone, then transfer the joint to a deep dish so that it assumes a nice shape, with the fat uppermost, and pour the cooking liquor over it. Leave it to cool like this and serve it with the rind uppermost; this you take off and replace with nicely coloured dried crumbs. When you have arranged the ham on the dish, surround it with parsley.

There is another way of dressing ham. When you take it out of the vessel it was cooked in, take off the rind and carefully lift off the fat which covers the meat. Put this leaf of fat in a deep dish or a salad bowl which you have lined with a damp cloth. Then take the flesh and chop it very finely, or even pound it in the mortar while it is still hot, mixing in any bits of fat that came away from the main piece as they will make the meat more delicate. Now place this meat on the leaf of fat and gather everything into the damp cloth. Cover with a plate or dish (according to the size of the bowl which contains everything) and place a weight of 4 or 5 kilograms on it. Let it cool like that. The whole will compact together so that the lean does not appear to have been chopped; it is infinitely more tender and more suitable for making sandwiches; it is never stringy, and the joint can be carved from any direction. You can cook just a part of the ham this way and yet give it the same form as a whole one.

Usually, the knuckle end is not cooked with the ham; the dish would be too large. Cook it on its own, as you would the ham. If you wish to serve the ham with the knuckle end, you must cut through the flesh and saw through the bone below the knuckle, not take the bone out after cooking, and decorate the end with a white paper frill.

The cooking liquor from a ham is perfect for a cabbage soup; but it is often very salty and strongly flavoured; add water to it.

Fried ham (luncheon). — Cut the ham into very thin slices and put them into a pan with a little butter and two or three crushed lumps of sugar; when the ham has browned on one side, turn it over and brown the other in like manner, but not too brown as it will toughen. Place the ham on a dish. Then add a little wine to the fat in the pan, let it boil up and serve it beneath the ham. You will need a quarter of an hour to cook ham in this fashion. You can dispense with the sugar and, in place of the wine in the fat, just add a little water, but the first method is the best.

Pudding. — *Black pudding* (hors-d'oeuvre and luncheon). — See how to prepare it in the article *Pork* in the chapter *Concerning provisions*, page 365, above. — You can cook the pudding in a frying-pan or on the grill, but always over a gentle flame so that it doesn't split; you should have a care to prick it before cooking. You can serve it on its own, or with a purée, or even with sausages.

White pudding (luncheon and hors-d'oeuvre). — Carefully chop together the flesh of raw fish (having removed the skin), calf's sweetbreads, chicken breasts, brains, and carp's soft roes, and add to this a fair amount of backfat, as well as some crumb of a loaf soaked in warm milk for an hour. Add to this mixture a few spoonfuls of rice cooked in milk without sugar, three or four egg yolks, salt, pepper and nutmeg. When everything is sufficiently chopped up, pound it in a mortar to achieve a perfect blend. You will thus obtain a sort of dough of great finesse. Let this down with fresh milk, as if making a porridge, and fill intestines with this, in the same way as has been explained for making black pudding. Tie them in suitable lengths; cook them in plenty of water, without salt; leave them to cool. A few minutes before service, place the lengths of pudding on the grill, having a care to prick them all over because they will split very easily when cooking. You can make this even more delicate by adding a few pistachios.

White pudding may be made with fewer ingredients and you can limit yourself to chicken breast, rice with milk, egg yolks and brains, all well chopped; if you pound the forcemeat in a mortar after chopping it, it will have more finesse.

SAUSAGES (luncheon and hors-d'oeuvre). — (See how to prepare these in the article *Pork* in the chapter *Concerning provisions*, page 367, above.) You cook them on the grill, over a low fire, or in the frying-pan and, using a spoon, you scrape up the juice, which you pour over the sausages. You can serve them on cabbage that has either been buttered or passed through the pan with the juices from the sausages; you can also serve them on lentils, peas, haricots, potatoes or on purées of any of these vegetables.

Sausages with apples. — Halve some medium-sized apples; put them, without peeling, in a frying-pan with a little butter and sausages; let everything cook together. If, when the sausages are cooked, the apples are not done enough, you finish their cooking in lard and then serve them round the sausages. Then put a quarter of a glass of water in the pan and boil it up briefly; pour all this over the sausages.

This dish, which is little known in France, is excellent for luncheon. It is much more common in Belgium; but it is not prepared as I have just described: they stew apples as usual; they cook the sausages separately, either on the grill or in a pan; they then serve them on the apples. Sometimes, instead of sausages, they place fresh pork chops on a similar purée. This dish also makes a really enjoyable luncheon.

CHAPTER IX

POULTRY

I. — General remarks.

Dressing poultry. — Poultry must not, in any circumstance, be served at table with the head and neck. In any event one rarely eats these parts roasted. They could be served in a ragout, but then they are presented detached from the animal's body; they look, therefore, less offensive.

To dress a bird, split the skin on the top of the neck with a pair of scissors, which are better than a knife; then you can take out the neck at its base. After that, having cut the skin to a convenient length, fold it over the back of the bird and fix it with a piece of string. The handsome round shape given to the bird when dressed like this looks far better than leaving the head and the neck, which one never knows how to arrange, and whose bloody aspect and beak are so repellent.

Leave the feet, which you can rid of the scales which cover them by passing them through the fire. You can leave them extended when roasting the bird; but you will have to remove them or fold them back on the drumstick when the bird is dressed as a ragout; to fix them like this, pass them under a little strap of skin; but you should not hide the whole limb in the stomach cavity; the bird in this case looks much less attractive. You need to make a little knife cut on the joint to sever the nerve which causes the feet to spread.

Geese or ducks' feet must never appear on the table, but you should not take them off with the chopper: the joint should be disarticulated in such a manner that, when cooking, the flesh does not retract, leaving the bare bone, which is really disgraceful. To avoid this solecism, cut the skin a little below the joint and lift it off when separating the knuckle.

From the turkey-hen and turkey-cock, the duck and the goose, remove the first two phalanges of the wing,[1] which you cook with the offal. It is not the same with the winglets of chicken, capons, hens and boiling fowl; their wings should remain intact; fold them back by passing one end through the winglet which secures them on the back of the bird.

I should also advise you against a practice I have sometimes witnessed of threading the liver and gizzard onto the feet, or placing them beneath the winglets. The liver should be cooked in the bird's carcase; the gizzard can only be served with the giblets or added to some other ragout.

How to draw poultry. — In almost every region, save those where fine poultry is raised for the Paris market, birds are only drawn as they are made ready for cooking. However, the practice of drawing them as soon as they are killed is better in every respect; if poultry is only drawn at the point of cooking, it is very difficult to remove the giblets without breaking them, because they have softened; and when broken, they impart an off-flavour to the insides of the bird. What is more, leaving the giblets inside the bird means it goes off more rapidly.

This is how you proceed to avoid these defects. Once the bird is dead, turn it immediately onto its side and take hold of the large intestine (having broken the membrane that covers it); pull it out slowly, and all the intestines will follow. If this is done with address, they will not break. If they do break, look again for the end which should be located without much trouble. Once all the giblets have been removed, only the liver and the gizzard remain in the carcase. These do not affect its keeping qualities and are removed by the cook as she dresses the bird for cooking.

In Le Mans, they fill the void left by the removal of the intestines by replacing them with brown paper. The paper maintains the shape of the bird and improves its keeping. You should avoid using paper that has a wool content as it imparts an undesirable flavour

You should *never* put onions, either whole or cut up, in a bird intended for the spit; they will infuse it with an odour – to be counted among the most unpleasant – which becomes apparent as the bird is carved. It is a mistake to think that onions heighten the flavour of poultry; they spoil it, and that's that. Nor should you put butter on a roast: butter only results

---

1. The first and second phalanx, which may also be called digits, are the first and second bones at the end of a bird's wing.

in a burnt taste which you should in fact be avoiding; if the bird seems to lack fat, it is better to bard it with some backfat.

2. — Pigeon.

Dressing pigeons. — You dress them as you do partridge (see the following chapter), but you pluck the head. Bard them and wrap them in vine leaves; it makes a dainty enough roast when the birds are young and fat. It is better to smother than to bleed pigeon.

Pigeons with fresh peas (entrée). — In a saucepan, brown a few pieces of belly pork, salted backfat or ham; then add to them the whole pigeons so they too can colour a little. Take them out; put back the salt pork and a little flour; stir, and add liquid. Let the salt pork cook for an hour and a half, then put back the pigeons. Once it has come back to the boil, add a sufficiency of fresh peas (a litre for a pair of pigeons), salt, pepper, and a bouquet garni. Give it heat above and beneath the saucepan. An hour and a quarter should be enough to cook it. You can either serve the salt pork with the pigeons or omit it.

Spatchcocked pigeons (entrée and luncheon).[1] — Split the pigeons down their backs, open them out, rub them inside and out with salt, pepper and oil. Make a stuffing with breadcrumbs soaked in warm milk, the pigeon livers, a little backfat, spring onion[2] and parsley. Fill the pigeons with this stuffing; coat them in oil and crumbs; wrap them in paper, and put them on the grill over a very low heat. You can also cook them on the grill without the paper, but in that case some of the stuffing will escape and be wasted.

Pigeons in a pie dish (entrée and luncheon). — Make a stuffing with the same ingredients as in the foregoing, adding, if you wish, a little sausage meat and breaking an egg into the mixture. Stuff the pigeons with this, and cook them in a dish with heat from above and below so that they brown. Take them out, moisten the dish with a little stock, scraping up any stuffing that has stuck to the dish, which you can serve beneath the pigeons.

---

1.   In French, *à la crapaudine.*
2.   In French, *ciboule.* An alternative name for spring onion (or scallion in America) is *cive.* The chive is *ciboulette* or *civette.* Although chives play a role in her larger mixtures of *fines herbes,* Mme Millet-Robinet comments in her gardening section (in volume II of *La Maison rustique*) that chives are not often used in French country households, while spring onions are very useful indeed.

Stewed pigeons (entrée). — Cut the birds in quarters; brown a dozen whole small onions in butter; then pass the quartered pigeons through the same fat. Prepare a roux, moisten it with liquid; put back the pigeons and the onions, with salt, pepper and a bouquet garni; cover. After an hour and a quarter's cooking, serve it up.

Braised pigeons (entrée). — Prepare the pigeons as if they were to be stewed, but moisten them with half wine and half water or stock. Usually, they are served on pieces of toast.

Fried pigeons (entrée and luncheon). — Cut them in quarters; put them in the pan with butter; let them cook, turning them over from time to time; take them off the heat. Serve them with a sauce made at the last minute with a little water, a spoonful of vinegar or verjuice, and some chopped parsley.

3. — Chicken, fattened chicken, capon.[1]

For these birds to be considered top quality, they must not only be fat, but the fat must be very white and the skin finely textured. To be sure that a live chicken is fat – while always bearing in mind its weight – you must examine the bone at its rump, near the tail;[2] if it is nicely rounded and plump with fat, you can be certain the bird is fat. Look also at the top of the neck, close to the body; the skin should be thick and almost form a roll. It is essential, when drawing poultry, to take the greatest care that the body cavity contains not one scrap of the intestine and none of the grain that was fed to the bird: nothing is more repugnant.

Roast chicken. — Once it has been drawn and singed, cut out the neck by splitting the skin on the top side and turning this skin over the back, which you also do with the winglets, which you tie with a piece of string; pass the feet over the fire to strip them, and take off the spurs; then, once you have salted the insides, tie the legs either side of the parson's nose with some string, with the feet sticking out, and put the liver back inside the body (once you have taken out the bile duct). Once all this has been achieved, you can spit the bird. If it is not very fat, you can bard the belly with backfat. If the contrary is the case, then cook it before a very gentle fire, keeping a watchful eye that it colours neither too much nor too little;

1. See the note on page 409, above, on the French terminology for chicken.
2. When cooked, this is termed the parson's nose.

however *it absolutely must not be dark brown* (nothing smacks more of the 'village inn'), even worse is if it should blacken; it should be golden on its peaks, white in its folds, such as the insides of the legs and under the wings. Beware of basting it with butter, as is often done; this butter will brown and spoil not only the juices but also the bird itself, which will taste fricasseed, not to speak of tasting of burnt fat. The many occasions I have experienced this only confirm my argument.

You can present poultry on a dish with a garnish of watercress that you have first lightly dressed with vinegar and which you toss in the dressing before serving.

Chicken fricassee (entrée). — A chicken fricassee should be *utterly white* – something you achieve by following my instructions exactly. The bird should be prepared as for roasting, but you break the knee joint so as to fold it, together with the foot, between the drumstick and the belly, fixing it there with string. Or you can pass the leg through a small loop of skin, which looks better, even though you will still need a string tie. Once you have done this, put a large knob of really fresh butter into a saucepan; when it begins to melt, add two heaped spoonfuls of flour and mix it thoroughly; then add enough hot, but not boiling, water to come half-way up the chicken when it is put in. Use a spoon to stir the sauce, and cook it until it has thickened. When it is ready and nicely boiling, put in the chicken on its side. You can place around the bird its gizzard, liver, neck and head (which should have been carefully washed of any blood). A bay leaf, a little shred of lemon peel (which is not, however, essential), pepper, and *a little* nutmeg can be added to the seasoning, but thyme and parsley should be rigorously excluded. Cover the pan with a circle of paper or a really clean lid. Leave it to cook for three-quarters of an hour at most; then turn the chicken over onto its other side, and surround it with a score of little onions, left whole and carefully peeled. Once cooked some more, dress the chicken on a dish, making sure you empty any sauce from inside the body back into the pan. If the sauce is too thin, boil it down, stirring it the while so that it does not grain while it reduces. If you have to do this, take out the onions and arrange them round the chicken, which you should cover. Put the neck, liver and gizzard to one side as they should not appear at table, even though they are excellent to eat. Then add a liaison of an egg yolk (which you have carefully separated from the white and the germ), stir it without letting it boil. Pour it over the chicken, it will be perfectly white and excellent.

To this fricassee, you can add mushrooms which you have previously blanched, artichoke bottoms (also blanched), Jerusalem artichokes, and even sliced truffles. All these ingredients will improve a chicken fricassee.

You should not cut up the chicken in advance, and most emphatically not chop it with a cleaver, as do some cooks who know nothing of their craft. However, if the chicken was very scrawny, to disguise its inadequacy you can cut it up without breaking any bones (which always has a regrettable effect); but you will be able to convince yourself that you have a nice white fricassee.

You can bulk out the fricassee by cooking with the chicken some brains which you have already blanched, or even calf's sweetbread: this will never spoil it. You can also leave the chicken liver inside the bird.

Making a perfectly white chicken fricassee is often a stumbling block for mediocre cooks; I confess I don't understand the reason. It is as easy as any other dish to prepare, it just needs care and attention. Never the less, a chicken fricassee that is not utterly white will still be very presentable and of excellent flavour.

Chicken sauté (entrée and luncheon). — Joint a chicken, put in a frying-pan with butter; brown it lightly on a reasonably brisk fire; then let it cook more gently. A few minutes before serving, add chopped parsley, a little tarragon, salt and pepper. Arrange the pieces of chicken on a dish; moisten the sauce with a little water or stock; bring to the boil for a second; serve it beneath the chicken. This is a very fine way of eating young, unfattened pullets.

Chicken with tarragon (entrée and remove). — Put a knob of butter that you have mixed with chopped tarragon and salt inside the chicken. Sew up the stomach cavity; truss the chicken as for a fricassee. Put it on its side in a saucepan so that it is half covered by water, together with salt, pepper, carrots, onions, some backfat or very fat ham, a few cloves, thyme, bay leaf, and one or two stalks of tarragon without their leaves. Cover with a sheet of paper and cook for two hours, or even more if the chicken is large. When the cooking is halfway through, turn the bird onto its other side. Half an hour before serving, take out some of the sauce and reduce it on a brisk fire until it has coloured up enough. Then mix in the rest of the sauce.

Add a few tender sprigs of tarragon and let them boil a few seconds in this same sauce. Serve the chicken with the tarragon around it and the sauce beneath. The chicken should be white and the sauce have a nice colour to it.

Chicken with jus (luncheon and entrée). — After preparing the chicken as for a fricassee, brown it in some butter; put a sheet of backfat above and beneath it and add some onions, carrots, parsley, a bouquet garni, salt, pepper and a little bay leaf. Moisten with stock or *jus*; cook it over a gentle heat for two hours. Half an hour before serving, glaze some of the sauce. Dress the chicken on a dish, glaze it, then dilute the rest of the glaze with the sauce which you should then sieve. Serve the sauce beneath the chicken. You can garnish the edges of the dish with slices of lemon.

Chicken en papillote. — Both the preparation and seasoning are the same as for pigeon or veal chops en papillote (pages 498 and 470, above).

Chicken en gibelotte.[1] — Prepare this as you would *gibelotte* of rabbit (page 512, below).

Capons, fattened chicken. — The preceding paragraphs, so far as they relate to the various ways of preparing chicken, may apply in every instance to fattened chicken and capons. In addition, you may truffle them. You will find how to go about this in the article *Truffled turkey-hen* (page 505, below).

Capon or fattened chicken with sea-salt. — Once you have prepared and trussed the bird as if you were going to fricassee it, cook it in an earthenware pot of a size that the bird fills it almost entirely, with water, carrots, onions studded with cloves, a bay leaf, salt and peppercorns. Cooking, which should be over a gentle heat, should last between two and four hours, depending on the age of the fowl. Before you serve it, put some of the cooking liquor in the dish and arrange slices of lemon around its border. You can reduce this liquor somewhat over a brisk flame before serving it beneath the fowl (which should be held in the pot under cover so that it does not cool down).

Capon, fattened chicken or boiling fowl with rice (entrée). — Brown the bird in butter; after trussing it as for a fricassee, moisten it with water; add some belly pork or ham, onions, carrots, salt, pepper, thyme, and a burnt onion; cook with heat above and beneath the pan for four hours if it is a boiling fowl; three hours should be enough is it is a reasonably tender

1. A *gibelotte* is a stew with white or red wine, most often of rabbit. Larousse informs us that the word derives from the O. Fr. *gibelet*, a platter of birds.

capon. At least an hour before serving, remove all the vegetables; leave the salt pork. Wash 100–110 grams of good rice in hot water and put this around the fowl; cover and stir the fire. When you serve this, remove the salt pork, skim off any fat, and serve the rice with the fowl on top. If the rice is too stodgy, you should moisten it before serving it up with a little water or, better, stock. The rice must not be so stodgy that it sticks together closely around the fowl. A few spoonfuls of good gravy adds greatly to the savour of the rice which accompanies the fowl.

Capon or fattened chicken with celery. — Prepare the bird as you did for cooking with rice; blanch eight or ten whole heads of celery in salted water once you have stripped them of any substandard sticks, cut them to a length of about 20 centimetres and peeled any skin off the root. When the celery yields to pressure from a finger, drain it in a colander, then remove any vegetables that you have cooked round the bird and replace them with the celery, which will then finish cooking there. If any water runs out of the celery and dilutes the sauce, you should reduce this by boiling with the cover off.

Galantine (luncheon). — See below (page 508), *Turkey-hen galantine.*

Daube of capon and *fowl* (entrée and remove). — After dressing as for a fricassee, lard and brown it lightly. Make this in the same way as daube of leg of mutton (page 484, above).

Boiled capon and *fowl* (remove). — Dress the bird as for a fricassee; put it in the pot three hours before dinner, or earlier if it is not young. Serve with some of the stock, salted a second time and a few slices of lemon arranged around the dish. These birds make a fine soup; their flesh can be used to prepare very delicate meatballs (see this recipe, page 459, above).

Chicken mayonnaise. — Any remains of chicken can be served with mayonnaise. (See the recipe on page 436, above.) Cut them up nicely and dress them on a platter, then pour the sauce over them. You may add lettuce hearts and hard-boiled eggs.

Rémoulade of chicken (luncheon). — Take out the bones and cut the flesh of a cold roast chicken into thin strips. Make a sauce with oil, vinegar, salt, pepper, mixed herbs and mustard beaten together. When the sauce has come together, add the chicken; turn it over in the sauce and dress it, serving it as tidily as possible.

Marinaded or fried chicken. — Cut the breasts and the boned legs of a roast chicken into pieces longer than they are wide. Salt them, pepper them, even rub them with a little vinegar if you like its flavour; then dip them in a normal but very light frying batter and fry them like any other fritter. You should heap this on a dish and decorate the pyramid with some nice green fried parsley.

4. — Turkey-hen and turkey-cock.

These birds should have handsome black feet and white fat and flesh. Reddish-black feet are a sign of maturity in turkeys.

The turkey-hen is far more delicate to eat than a turkey-cock. To gauge how fat a live bird is you must, as with other poultry, examine the bone next to the tail at the end of the rump, the underside of the wing and the topside of the neck, where you will find an accumulation of fat.

Spit-roasted turkey-hen. — Remove the neck, the feet and the winglets; take care that as far as possible, when you cut through the joints at the feet and the winglets, you leave some skin from the side you are removing so the bone is not exposed during cooking. You can bard the bird. When dealing with a stuffed bird, you will need two hours to cook it. It should not brown too much; nor should the skin be blistered, which may happen if the fire is too brisk. The bird should be a golden brown. You should no more baste this with butter than you do any other bird: it will have the consequences that I have already indicated. During winter cold spells, so that it should be tender, the turkey-hen should not be cooked until eight days have elapsed from killing; when it is warmer, three or four days suffice.

Turkey-cock stuffed with chestnuts and potatoes. — For the stuffing, you chop the liver with some backfat, the crumb of a loaf, parsley, salt and pepper. Put this stuffing in the cavity and in the skin of the neck, called in some districts the *crop*.[1] You can add to this stuffing (and you will thereby obtain a most pleasing dish) one or two litres of roast chestnuts, or even, instead of chestnuts, some pieces of good potatoes. A potato stuffing is less delicate than the chestnut stuffing, but is good none the less. This is a family dish. Skim the fat off before serving up, but keep the fat as it is excellent to eat spread on bread, and even better for giving flavour to every sort of vegetable.

---

1.   In French, *jabot*.

The leftovers from a roast turkey can be eaten cold, or with a piquant sauce, a mayonnaise, a tomato sauce, as a blanquette, grilled, with parsley butter, or finally on a split pea purée. The parson's nose is particularly good grilled. These leftovers can also be used in all forcemeats. With the carcase you can make an excellent cabbage soup; you add some of the fat that you have skimmed from the sauce; in a pot-au-feu it gives the stock an excellent flavour.

Truffled turkey-hen (roast). — After preparing it as if you were roasting it on a spit, keep all the neck skin (which you have split along the top to remove the neck – of which you keep a small part to hold back the stuffing and the truffles), and stuff it with truffles prepared in the following manner.

A fine turkey could hold two or three kilograms of truffles; but you can manage with much less, even – if your ambition is to do no more than produce a more elaborate family dinner than usual – half a kilogram of truffles, placed in the body in advance, will result in an excellent aroma. You must wash the truffles twice in plenty of running water and brush them with the utmost care so that not a speck of dirt remains; use a knife when necessary to pick out any earth that lurks in those parts the brush cannot reach. This should be done quickly because if the truffles soak for a long time, they lose much of their perfume. As they are cleaned, place them on a sieve or a dry white cloth; when they have all been cleaned, wipe them and peel them, having a care to take as little of the flesh as possible, you need a really sharp knife for this; cut any that are too large into pieces; were you to leave them whole, they would cook unevenly and stay dry in the middle. Then you should cover the truffles and turn to chopping the skins very finely, or pounding them in a mortar, to reduce them to a sort of paste. Also chop 500 grams of good backfat, to which you add the turkey liver and one or two other poultry livers if they are available. Then rub a fair amount of stale bread in a coarse white cloth and sieve it [to make crumbs]. Proceed to mix the pounded truffle skins, the backfat, the chopped livers and the breadcrumbs. Season with salt and pepper. You should have seasoned the truffles previously. Now mix everything and put in a saucepan on the fire, stirring as it heats up. When this sort of hash has cooked long enough, you proceed to the truffling of the turkey by stuffing this hot farce into the body cavity and the skin of the neck. You should divide the farce so that the turkey appears quite extended and of even diameter from one end to the other. Once the stuffing has been completed, sew up the openings and adjust the crop so that it looks attractive. Once truffled like this, if the turkey was recently killed and the weather outside is chilly, it can be kept for a week; but only keep it for a couple of days if the weather is damp or close.

A large turkey well stuffed with truffles needs three hours in front of a low fire; baste it with the juices and fat which will flow abundantly from it. Before serving up, skim the fat off the sauce; this fat, spread on bread, is even better than the fat from a turkey that has not been truffled; and is no less good in any sort of ragout.

I do not think there is a more suitable way of truffling a turkey. Some people don't peel the truffles, but then they will stay hard and dry; others dispense with the truffle peelings: they are quite mistaken, because the greater part of the aroma resides in the peel; still others don't bother to make a stuffing but simply put raw truffles in the body cavity; but then the truffles will remain dry as they need to be impregnated with fat. Some will perhaps object to the breadcrumbs which I have included: but they, too, will be wrong as the crumbs absorb the fat and hold it close to the truffles – and when they have been thoroughly mixed with the truffle peelings, you will hardly notice their presence.

Truffled turkey can be served as a remove just like the capon with sea-salt, or turkey cooked as a daube or in its own gravy.

Turkey-hen stuffed with mushrooms. — After preparing the turkey as if you were to truffle it, peel the mushrooms and blanch them in salted water. Prepare a stuffing with backfat, breadcrumbs, a little finely chopped parsley and a little pepper; the backfat will salt it enough. Add the thoroughly drained mushrooms and put everything into the body cavity and the crop of the turkey, which you tie up and cook as truffled turkey. It is excellent.

Daube of turkey-hen (remove and entrée). — This is a good way to use an old turkey-hen. After studding it with large, seasoned lardons, you can stuff it as I have described for spit-roasted turkey-hen; you will need to truss it, then put it into a daubière on a piece of salt-pork rind, with some slices of backfat, a calf's foot, salt, pepper, thyme, a burnt onion, bay leaves, a small clove of garlic, ham, some carrots and some onions. Moisten it with two glasses of water or, better, with stock, to which you add the third of a glass of eau-de-vie. Cover it tightly,[1] and maintain a gentle fire above and below the pot. When the cooking is halfway through, turn the bird. When cooked enough, dress it on a platter and arrange the vegetables around it. You must skim the sauce of its fat and strain it as you pour it over the turkey. This bird served cold, with its juice all jellied (which you have cooled separately in a bowl and then arranged round the bird), is a very handsome dish for luncheon. The calf's foot which was cooked with it is excellent eaten hot. An old turkey will need at least five hours' cooking, three or four hours will suffice for a young one.

You can also use the turkey juices to prepare some chicory or sorrel, as I described for fricandeau, and serve the turkey on top of them; it is an excellent dish. Equally, you can replace the chicory with a nice cabbage cooked in salted water. This extremely enjoyable dish is not widely known.

Boiled turkey-hen (remove).[2] — This is a rarely undertaken yet excellent way of eating a turkey. After trussing it nicely, put it in a stewpan, which it should fill almost completely, with some carrots, onions, salt, pepper, thyme and bay leaves. Fill the pot with water and cook over a gentle heat for three hours if the bird is young, four or five hours if it is old. If the water reduces too much, you should top the pot up with boiling water. This is a really good and distinctive remove. If you have prepared a gravy soup, you can add the turkey stock to it at the moment of service. If you leave the turkey covered after drawing the pot off the fire, it will stay hot enough until you are ready to serve it. It is advisable to keep back a little of the stock, reduced over a brisk flame, to garnish the bottom of the serving platter after you have poured it over the bird which you ring with slices of lemon. You can also serve a turkey cooked like this on a tomato sauce.

The leftovers of a daube of turkey or boiled turkey are excellent as meatballs or in any forcemeat, as well as with a tomato sauce.

Turkey giblets in chicken fricassee. — (See *Chicken fricassee.*) Cooking should take at least two and a half hours.

Boiled turkey giblets. — Serve this with a little of the reduced cooking liquor or with a tomato sauce. Turkey giblets cooked with beef in a pot-au-feu greatly improves the stock.

1.   In French, *hermétiquement.* This is often achieved by seating the lid on a strip of cold-water paste with egg white placed on the rim of the opening.

2.   In French, *dinde au pot.*

Haricot of turkey giblets. — (See *Haricot of mutton.*)

You prepare the turkey-cock and the turkey-poult as you would the turkey-hen. As the turkey-poult is never fat, you have to bard it if you wish to roast it.

When only the family is dining and the turkey-cock or turkey-hen is too large, you can cut the bird in two, that is to say separate the front from the back end about two-thirds of the way down the spine[1] then put the front end to the spit and the back in a daube or in the boiling-pot. One or two limbs from the turkey in the pot-au-feu improves the stock no end.

Turkey-hen galantine (luncheon and opposite the roast). — You can make this dish with an old turkey quite as well as with a young one; but you need to know to wait until it has hung enough, especially if it is a very old bird. Once you have drawn it and removed the feet, legs and winglets, you must debone it. To do this you split the skin down the back from one end to the other and quickly separate all the flesh from the carcase. Then you cut through all the limb joints from the *inside* and leave on each side the limbs, which remain attached by the skin. Continue cutting away the breast and the rest of the meat, until you have separated *the whole* carcase, which is not nearly as difficult as you might think. Now there only remains the flesh of the four limbs. Split the thighs down the *inside*, not touching the outside skin at all, which must remain everywhere intact; split the skin and flesh of the drumsticks in the same manner. Then remove the large thigh bone as well as the leg bone by parting them deftly from their flesh. The same manoeuvre for the wing, which you also split down the inside, and scrape the flesh carefully from the bone. Now the bird is entirely boned and flat on the table, skin side down. You take some of the breast meat and all the meat you can find off the crop-bones and chop it all up with ham, backfat or fresh pork (fat and lean, but more fat than lean), adding to all this 500 grams of fillet of veal, salt, a fairly large amount of pepper, mushrooms, and even truffles, of which you chop the peelings for the forcemeat and put the whole truffles, salted and peppered some time previously, in the bird itself with this same stuffing. Once the stuffing, which should have quite a pronounced flavour, is ready, you cut into the turkey flesh, without disturbing the skin, and you spread the stuffing evenly

1.   Mme Millet-Robinet calls this point of division *à la jointure des reins* – where the kidneys are.

between all the various parts which you have boned. Once the stuffing is in place, bring up the two sides of the skin so they join once more down the centre and sew them together. At each end, you do the same, ensuring a nice shape to the turkey and continuing with your sewing. You must then carefully tie up the turkey along its length and place it in a braising-pan, in which you have lain a rind of salt pork. Add a calf's foot cut in pieces, carrots, onions, salt, pepper, thyme and bay leaf. Moisten with enough water to cover, and cook with a gentle fire above and below the pan for five hours. If the jellied stock is pale, colour it with a little caramel; let it set in a bowl after straining it. You serve the galantine with the jellied stock in which it was cooked. The vegetables, salt pork or ham which were cooked round the turkey are excellent eaten hot or cold.

Any poultry with white meat can be treated in the same way.

5. — Goose.

Everything I will remark about duck, in the following chapter, may be applied to goose. Some people prefer it roasted in the oven. On the spit, this bird ought to cook for two hours. It may be stuffed, either like a duck, or with potatoes. Equally, geese are often cooked solely to obtain supplies of their excellent fat.

Preserved legs and breast of goose.[1] — (See, in the chapter *Concerning Provisions*, at page 373, above, the way to prepare them.) To use them, cook them for a few seconds in a frying-pan with mixed herbs and a little fat; take care not to let them dry out. Cooked in a cabbage soup and served cold, they are just as good as ham and taste somewhat similar. You can also eat them cold, after removing them from their [preserving] fat and flashed them before a brisk fire to melt off any fat sticking to them (without thereby heating them), and serve them surrounded with parsley; they are not dissimilar to ham; you can also serve them on a piquant sauce or on an onion purée after you have put them on the grill.

1.   i.e. *confit.*

CHAPTER X

GAME

1. — Furred game.
A. — Wild boar.

The fillets, head and cutlets are the only parts of wild boar that should figure on the table. The hams can be prepared in the same way as domestic pig. This meat should not be eaten immediately after it has been killed, the more so as it is often old and tough. The head is dealt with in the same way as a pig's; the fillet and the chops are served as a roast.

B. — Venison.

The haunch is the most desirable venison joint; it should be marinated for a shorter or longer time, depending on whether the animal was killed more or less recently. The marinade consists of oil, pepper, salt, thyme leaves, bay leaves and sliced onions. The haunch is spitted, once larded, in the same way as marinated mutton, and it is served unaccompanied on the platter. Make a sauce consisting of finely chopped shallots, the strained marinade, and the roasting juices. This sauce is served separately in a sauce-boat.

Venison fillet and cutlets (entrée). — You can put them on the spit, like the haunch or, once you have larded them, you can cook them in a casserole with stock, some onions, a few carrots and a bouquet garni; you should have heat above and below the pan. Reduce the cooking juices to a glaze before pouring them over the meat. This dish is often accompanied by a piquant sauce.

Civet of venison. — The shoulder and breast of venison should be dealt with as a civet. (See *Civet of hare.*)

C. — Hare.

Roast hare. — Large hares are not good spit-roasted; it's better to put them in a pâté or in a civet; however, left in a good marinade for a few days, they can be really good roasted. Should you have to eat a large hare that has just been killed, skin it and beat all the flesh with light taps of a rolling pin, taking care not to break any bones. It will recover its shape nicely in the cooking, and will seem as tender as if killed several days before.

Spit-roast hare or leveret (roast). — Only the hindquarters are roast, which you lard finely and marinate in a mixture of oil, vinegar, pepper, salt, bay leaf and thyme; put it on the spit a good hour before service. It should be basted with its juices, to which you add the marinade, a few shallots, chopped spring onions and tomato. Before larding it, and after skinning, you should remove the shining white skin that is found on the fillets.

Daube of hare (entrée or remove). — Prepare this as a daube of leg of mutton (page 484, above).

Civet (entrée, luncheon). — Disarticulate into pieces the parts you wish to cook in a civet; don't use a chopper or you will have splinters; brown a few pieces of salt pork or, better, ham, and remove them from the pan. Put the hare into this ham fat and colour it slightly. Once you have removed the hare, lightly brown in their turn in the same fat fifteen or twenty whole small onions. Take out the onions; brown a little flour in the fat; moisten with some meat or vegetable stock, or even with water; finish cooking the salt pork. After an hour's cooking the sauce should have reduced; put to it the hare with some pepper and a bouquet garni. After another half-hour of cooking, add a large glass and a half of good red wine; let it cook for three-quarters of an hour, or even as much as two hours if the hare is an old one; at the end of this, add in the blood and the little onions and let it cook again for half an hour. Serve on a few thin slices of well-toasted bread.

Adding mushrooms and truffles greatly improves a civet. You can also cook it with wine alone, but many find the flavour a little too pronounced.

Quick civet.[1] — This civet can be cooked on the pot-hook in a cauldron,[2] and very quickly. In this case, beat the flesh of the hare, brown the joints

---

1. In French, *civet à la galopade*, literally 'at the gallop'.
2. The French is *à la crémaillère*, on the pot-hook in a hanging cauldron over a high flame, rather than in a saucepan or casserole with a low fire above and below it as in the longer-cooked civet, above.

in butter or lard; add flour to it, which you let colour up; then moisten with red wine and add the blood. Let it boil vigorously then add fifteen or twenty small onions; season; let it cook another half-hour; serve it on toast.

Hare pâté (luncheon). — See the article *Pâté*.

Sauté of leveret. — After skinning and gutting it, cut it into pieces as when making a civet, and put it in a saucepan or frying-pan with a knob of butter, salt, pepper and other spices; fry it until it has coloured up nicely; then add mushrooms, parsley, chopped shallots and two spoonfuls of flour. Fry it again, moisten it with white wine, and let it bubble for a few seconds. Only pour the sauce over the leveret at the moment of service. You can content yourself with just frying the leveret with butter, salt and pepper; when it has browned nicely, add a little water to deglaze the pan and a little chopped parsley; give it two or three shakes; serve; it is excellent.

D. — Rabbit.

To prepare domestic rabbit, you should gut it as soon as it is killed, and stuff the cavity with thyme, bay leaf, sage, basil, pepper, salt and a few cloves before removing it later and preparing the animal as if it were hare.

Many people prefer to bleed the rabbit rather than killing it by striking it between the ears; the flesh is whiter and more delicate; if you wish to make a civet, then keep the blood. The best way of killing a rabbit is to make it drink a decent-sized glass of eau-de-vie; it will die in a few seconds, and the eau-de-vie will make the flesh more tender.

Fricassee of rabbit (entrée).[1] — Prepare this exactly as a civet, but don't use wine and don't add the blood.

When the rabbit has been bled, you can prepare it *à la poulette* like breast of veal.

Baby rabbit en papillote.[2] — A very young rabbit is excellent *en papillote*. After skinning and gutting it, stuff it with a mixture of backfat, breadcrumbs, salt, pepper, parsley, and chopped onions; bard it all over and wrap it in two sheets of paper before cooking it over a very gentle flame on the grill.

Sauté of rabbit is excellent. See *Sauté of leveret*.

---

1. In French, *Gibelotte de lapin*. Usually, a *gibelotte* is a rabbit stew with wine.
2. In French, *lapereau*. *En papillote* is the standard French method of wrapping in sheets of paper or, later, putting in a paper or a foil bag.

2. — Feathered game.

Before anything else, we must alert readers that no feathered game should be salted before the cooking is half-way through.

A. — Pheasant.

Roast pheasant. — This uncommon and magnificent bird appears but rarely on tables as modest as those of the households for which this book has been written; however, if some happy huntsman makes a present of one to our mistress of the house, then she must absolutely know how she should serve it. In the first place, if the pheasant is an old one it should not be cooked until several days have elapsed after death; if it is put on the spit straight away it will be tough and dry rather than the delicate, fine dish it should be. You should wait therefore for eight or ten days when the weather is cold, or just three or four when warm. Some people lard the whole breast of the pheasant with very slender lardons; I myself think it preferable to bard it and to cover the fat with a vine leaf, if it's the right time of year. The head is not plucked; place it on the wishbone, turning the neck, and fix it there with string; in addition, you should wrap this handsome plumage in a sheet of paper folded in three, which is removed at the moment of serving. You can also quite simply remove the head before putting the bird on the spit and, as it is only kept feathered for the show of it, it can be fixed by means of a small wooden skewer pushed down through the beak onto the breast of the animal when it is ready to be served. The custom is to leave the feet extended and to fold the wings under the back.

Pheasant should be cooked before a low fire for three-quarters of an hour at the most. The gravy is served under the roast, not separately in a sauce-boat.

A few slices of truffle placed in the dripping-pan, or even in the bird itself, give this a nice flavour.

Should the pheasant be extremely old, it will have to be prepared simply with cabbage. (See *Partridge with cabbage* or *in a daube*, pages 514 and 515, below.)

B. — Partridge and young partridge.

The red-legged partridge is more highly esteemed than the grey; however, I consider that this last is only inferior to the first by dint of its size; its aroma is more pleasing and its flesh is less dry. Young partridge are distinguished from the old by holding them up by their beaks; the young birds' beaks will bend, the old will not.[1] You should not expect any young partridges after 1 October; the hunters' proverb is relevant here: 'On St Remy's day, all young partridge are old.'[2]

Spit-roasted young partridge (roast). — Dress it like the pheasant, but it only needs half an hour in the cooking. When you have two young partridge, you can lard one and bard the other. Any young partridge which you wish to truffle, should be truffled four, five or six days in advance; one pound of truffles is sufficient for two young partridge. (See the article *Truffled turkey-hen*, page 505 above, to read how to prepare them.) With the young roast partridge you can serve slices of orange arranged all round the platter.

Salmi of young partridge (luncheon, entrée). — This is sometimes made with partridge that have already appeared on the table; however, if you are putting them on the spit with the sole intention of making a salmi, you should cook them much less and should crush the liver into the salmi sauce. (See that sauce.) Normally, a salmi (which is greatly improved by truffles) is made with a woodcock or a wild duck as well as young partridge.

Young partridge with a mayonnaise sauce. — Joint the cold roast partridge and dress them on a dish, then cover them with a mayonnaise sauce.

Partridge with cabbage (entrée). — Dress the partridge as if you were going to roast them, but fold in the feet and pluck the heads; you can lard the partridge, but this step is not essential. Brown some pieces of salt belly pork, or even of ham, and then take them out; pass several heads of Savoy cabbage through the fat that has been rendered. If the head is large, cut it into four; if small, then in half; take out the heart for fear that it may have the slightest odour of musk. In the absence of Savoy cabbage,[3] use very tender white cabbage, or even better a St-John's-day dwarf cabbage,

1. In French, *Perdrix et perdreaux*. The French make a linguistic distinction between the mature birds and those aged up to one year, which take a good deal less cooking.
2. St Remi or Remy is St Remigius (*c.* 437–533), the Archbishop of Reims who converted Clovis, the king of the Franks. 1 October is the feast of the translation of his relics; 13 January is his day in Reims itself.
3. The names of various sorts of cabbage can be problematic in translation. *Choux cabus* are hearted cabbages, with either smooth or curled leaves. The *chou cabu commun* is the common-or-garden hearted white cabbage. The *chou pancalier*, translated here

which I reckon the best of all; remove the hearts. Brown the partridge; moisten them with water or, better, with stock. Arrange the cabbage and the ham [or salt pork] around the partridge; add four or five onions, four or five pieces of carrot, salt, pepper, and a bouquet garni. Ensure there is heat above and below the saucepan. Half an hour later, make a pale roux, moistening it with the liquor from the partridge; pour it over the partridge without disturbing them in the pan, shake them to mix in the roux, then let them cook for three hours over a low heat. You can leave out adding a roux; if the sauce is thin, you can boil it uncovered [to reduce]. If you are using white cabbage, put them to cook with the other ingredients an hour before adding the partridge because they are harder to cook than the curly cabbage and the partridge and because they produce a great deal of water which needs to be evaporated by boiling. Serve the cabbage with the partridge in the centre. The carrots, onions and salt pork should not be sent to table, unless you cut the carrots into ornamental shapes to decorate the serving-dish. A few slices of cervelas sausage cooked with the cabbage improves things and can be served on the cabbage as a garnish.[1]

Daube of partridge (entrée). — Lard them and cook them as daube of mutton; it is an excellent dish. It requires at least four or five hours cooking. Rather than serving them with vegetables, they can be arranged on top of a purée of some sort that has been finished with their gravy, or better still on some chicory that has been prepared as for a fricandeau (page 472, above).

---

as Savoy, is a curly-leafed hearted cabbage, most often found in the Touraine. Mme Millet-Robinet in fact prefers the *chou de Genillé*, which I have followed Vilmorin-Andrieux in translating as the St-John's-day dwarf cabbage (St John being St John the Baptist, whose day was 24 June, midsummer – if sown then, it would be harvested as a winter cabbage). The French synonyms for this variety are *chou Joanet hâtif, chou nantais, chou Jaunet, chou de Chenillet, chou de Genillé, chou Colas, chou pommé d'Angers*. It may be noticed that the place-names are all in the Touraine-Poitou area. Genillé is just south-east of Tours, and is where Mme Millet-Robinet lived through the 1850s. The variety's description stresses the shortness of its stalk, the dark colour of its outer leaves, the tightness of its heart, the difficulty it has over-wintering in colder parts of France, and the normal practice in the Touraine of sowing it in autumn for a spring harvest.

1.   Cervelas sausage is a generic term for a seasoned pork sausage for cooking. The name is related to brains (*cervelles*) but commonly the sausage did not contain any (save in Switzerland). The name *cervelat* is also found in Germany: a common etymology but a very different sausage. In English, saveloy is the related word.

I have already noted that an old partridge added to the pot-au-feu greatly improves it. Cooked like this, it can be served with a piquant or a tomato sauce, or on a purée.

C. — Duck, Teal, Moorhen.

Wild duck is more highly esteemed than the domestic sort;[1] it is sometimes tremendously fat, and the best way to deal with it is to cook it on the spit: cooked in a ragout, it will be too oily. Duck fat is excellent for cooking dried vegetables, or for making naturally dry meats more toothsome.

Duck with cabbage. — This is prepared exactly as partridge with cabbage; it is an excellent dish.

Fricandeau of duck. — You dress it as in the preceding recipe. Prepare chicory as for fricandeau of veal (page 472, above); moisten it with the duck sauce. This dish is not very well known but none the less very good. You can replace chicory with a cabbage of the right sort, which you cook in advance in salted water and then chop up once it is cooked.

Duck with apples. — In Belgium and northern France, the duck is cooked either in the oven or on the spit; a compote of very well-cooked pippins[2] is prepared separately, pressed through a fine sieve and mixed with the duck gravy; the duck is then served on this compote.

Duck with celery. — You dress it as in the previous recipe. Blanch in plenty of water either heads of normal celery or a celeriac. Take out the vegetables which you have cooked with the duck and replace them with the celery; finish cooking it with the duck. This is a very good dish.

Spit-roast duck (entrée). — Cut off the winglets and the feet; split the skin of the neck down the back; take out the neck and fold the skin back between the two shoulders so that the wishbone is nicely rounded. You should salt the inside before spitting it. You can stuff it with either roasted chestnuts and sausage meat or with a forcemeat made of liver, backfat, parsley and breadcrumbs. If the duck is very fatty, it will need cooking

1. Mme Millet-Robinet does not include domestic duck recipes in her chapter on poultry, all her duck recipes are in fact contained within this section. Some of them certainly appear more suited to a large and fat domestic breed than the smaller wild ducks that are usually available from the game dealer.
2. i.e. dessert apples.

for an hour and a half, before a very gentle fire. You should guard against searing it too fast, so that it takes on a nice colour.

Salmi of duck (entrée). — What I have said about other game salmis is applicable to duck.

Duck with green peas (entrée). — The same as for pigeons; but, as duck takes longer to cook, you only put the peas on the fire an hour after the duck (if it is a young one), or an hour and a half if it is old. If it is very fat, it is pointless to add the belly of salt pork. It is wise to skim the fat off the sauce before serving.

Duck with turnips (entrée). — Brown the duck in butter first of all, then the turnips, preferably whole small ones rather than large ones that have been cut up. The Freneuse turnip or the Finland are the best to accompany duck.[1] Remove the turnips and add back the duck. Moisten with water or stock; turn it over. Make a small and well-browned roux; add to the sauce a bouquet garni, salt and pepper and put hot coals above and below the pan. If the turnips are very tender, three-quarters of an hour will suffice to cook them; if the duck is very old, it will need three hours, or an hour and a half if it is young. Skim the fat off the sauce. If the sauce is too thin, let it boil down uncovered.

Duck with onions (entrée). — You prepare duck with onions in exactly the same way as duck with turnips; the only difference being that you replace the turnips with ten or twelve large onions, which you need to take off the heat as soon as they are cooked, otherwise they will cook down to a purée.

Duck with olives (entrée). — Brown the duck, then a few onions; take out the onions and put back the duck. Moisten with water or stock. Make a roux and add it to the sauce. You can, however, leave out the roux. Add back the onions, a little salt, pepper and a bouquet garni; leave to cook, for longer or shorter, depending on whether the duck is young or old. A quarter of an hour before service, take out the onions and put in their place some olives, which you have stoned, with their flesh cut in a spiral. Let it boil briefly. Serve the olives around the duck: 250 grams will be sufficient to garnish a medium-sized duck.

Daube of duck. — The same method as for daube of mutton. You can lard the duck and serve it on a purée.

1.   See above, page 429, for comments on turnips. The Finland turnip is the swede or rutabaga.

Teal. — This is a type of waterfowl little different from a duck save that it is much smaller; you prepare teal just like duck.

Moorhen. — This is hardly edible except in a salmi.

D. — *Plover.*

The golden plover is the most desirable: it is put to the spit; it should be roasted before a gentle fire for half an hour. Those who like it do not gut it. Slices of toasted bread should be placed in the dripping-pan.

E. — *Lapwing and grouse.*[1]

The lapwing is roughly the size of a pigeon; grouse is one-third larger; both are served either roasted or in a salmi. They are dressed in the same way as partridge.

F. — *Wood pigeons and turtle doves.*

These birds are very delicate when young. They are served spit-roasted, barded with lard and a vine leaf, or in a salmi. They can also be dealt with in the same way as pigeons. They are dressed like partridge.

G. — *Woodcock and snipe.*

The woodcock is as large as a partridge, the snipe the same size as a thrush. Both are served spit-roasted, either barded or larded. Those who like them do not gut them; you should place pieces of toast beneath them as I have mentioned for plovers. They are nicer in a salmi. You dress them like partridge; you stick the beak through the wishbone.

H. — *Quail.*

This delicate small bird is spitted, wrapped in a bard and a vine leaf; twenty to twenty-five minutes is enough to cook it. Quail are excellent *en papillote.* (See *Baby rabbit en papillote*, above.) You can also cook them in a frying-pan or saucepan with butter, salt and pepper. When they are cooked and dressed, throw a little water in the saucepan or, better, stock,

---

1.   In French, grouse is *gélinotte* and usually refers to the hazel grouse or hazel hen, *Tetrastres bonasia.* Sometimes it is specified *gélinotte des bois.* The red grouse (*Lagopus lagopus scotica*, a member of the ptarmigan family), familiar in Scotland and northern England, is not the species hunted in France.

and let it bubble up for an instant. Serve this sauce under the quail, dressed like partridge.

I. — *Larks, thrushes and blackbirds.*

Larks. — I reckon to gut larks, contrary to the advice of most cookery books. The gizzard harbours stones, which are most disagreeable to encounter in the mouth; the liver contains a very bitter gall. Stick the beak into the wishbone; take the skin off the head and cut off the feet. Roast larks should be barded and threaded onto a small wooden skewer which you attach to the spit; you can also cook them in a frying-pan or saucepan. Once they have been dressed, line them up in a pan with some butter; in addition, put some thin pieces of backfat between the larks, which should be cooked quite briskly; ensure that you turn them. When they are cooked and seasoned with salt and pepper, take them out of the pan and add a little water or stock in their stead, let this boil up for a few seconds, and serve the larks with this sauce. This makes very good fare. The little lardons are served with the larks.

You can also make very good pies or pâtés with larks. (See that article, page 610, below.)

Thrushes and *blackbirds.* — You prepare them as you do larks; you can bard them and wrap them in a vine leaf.

CHAPTER XI

SEA FISH AND FRESHWATER FISH

I. — In general.

How to prepare and keep sea fish. — As soon as it comes into the kitchen, wash it with care, scale it and gut it; then wipe it and wrap it in a really dry cloth before placing it in the coolest spot in the house. Arranged thus, it will keep perfectly. If you are dealing with small fish, place them in a row on a kitchen cloth, fold the cloth in such a way as to wrap them up then place a second row and carry on thus. You can also improve the keeping qualities of your fish with a fair degree of success by placing it between two layers of coarsely crushed charcoal (from which you remove any dust) and then wrapping the whole in a dry cloth. The best way still is to surround it with ice, but then you have to cook it as soon as it is removed from this.

It would be a great mistake to think that fish can be kept cooler by leaving them in water: they will spoil much faster than in the open air.

Court-bouillon for fish. — Usually one cooks sea fish in a water *court-bouillon*, to which sometimes white wine is added: this is a bad method. Almost all sea fish are better, and their flesh is whiter and firmer, if they are cooked in a *court-bouillon* of half milk, half water, a little salt and pepper. However singular this recipe may appear to many cooks, it is none the worse for that; it is common practice in Nantes and many seaports. Once the two methods of cooking have been compared, you can make your choice, but I don't doubt that the *court-bouillon* with milk will be found the better.

It is quite different with freshwater fish, whose flavour is dull, and which are often cooked with their scales; in this case you need a very tasty *court-bouillon*; I also make it with half water and half white wine, at the very least; you can replace the wine with vinegar, but the result is not so good. Before adding the wine, you boil carrots, onions, a clove of garlic, a few cloves, peppercorns, thyme, several bay leaves, salt and pepper in the water for an hour. Strain everything, put it back on the fire and at the moment you put in the fish, add the wine or vinegar. Red wine does not make a good *court-bouillon*; it pleases neither the taste-buds nor the eye. When wine dominates in a *court-bouillon*, you can put it on the fire after you have put the fish in; this will give it a very fine flavour. You can keep a *court-bouillon* for ten or fifteen days in winter; it can serve a second time if you add some more wine. We call a fish cooked in *court-bouillon* cooked *au bleu*.

It will not be possible to touch on every species of fish; you will easily be able to assess the best way to cook them by comparison with those I do discuss. There are ways of preparing fish that are particular to certain regions which are unknown to me, although much appreciated by gourmets. I consider that a good cook is able to make a fair fist of any fish she is asked to prepare without this special knowledge.

To cook very large fish, you need vessels made for the job: a long fish kettle with a removable double bottom, or a square or round kettle with the same device. In the absence of these, you can use a small cauldron, which is better than a basin or a jam pan, provided it has a double bottom – which can be in tinplate and therefore not expensive.

You can even cook large fish in a cauldron without a double bottom but before you put the fish in the *court-bouillon* you should wrap them in an old piece of white calico; it will then be easy enough to lift them out of the cauldron without breaking them.

How to soak salted fish, meats or vegetables. — One often uses salt cod or other salt fish, salted meat or even vegetables preserved in brine in the kitchen.

Generally, to get rid of the salt from these foods, one is content to place them in a pot with water, which you change from time to time. This procedure is defective. In fact, because salt water is heavier than fresh water, as soon as the liquid which surrounds the object being soaked has taken up some salt it sinks to the bottom of the container where it saturates and ceases to dissolve any new salt. The object therefore finds itself in a liquid as salty as it might ever possibly be. It will not satisfactorily get rid of the salt.

This defect can be avoided by a simple procedure. Place the meat, fish or salted vegetables in a net or fine cloth and put them in a water-filled container filled large enough so that they hang in it. By this means, as the water takes up the salt, so it sinks to the bottom and is replaced by fresh water. The process is much quicker and the result as thorough as possible.

An even better method, based on the same principle, is much practised in the north. It consists of placing the salt cod and other salted foods in very small baskets arranged like laundry bucking-tubs so that the foods are in contact with a constant flow of fresh water which you pour over them, pushing the salt water out through the drain hole at the bottom of the container.

2. — Sea fish.

A. — Sturgeon.

The same preparation as for salmon.

B.— Tuna.

Tuna (hors-d'oeuvre) is a Mediterranean fish; it is prepared in several ways particular to the coasts where it is fished. Tuna conserved in oil can be found everywhere. It is a very good hors-d'oeuvre.

C. — Turbot and Brill.

Turbot and brill au bleu (entrée or remove). — Turbot, like brill, should be cooked in a milk *court-bouillon* that has been lightly salted. After thoroughly gutting, washing and scaling the fish, and cutting off the end of the tail and the edges of the fins, place it on its back on the double bottom of the fish kettle. Cook it over a very gentle flame for at least an hour and a half, if the fish is a large one, without letting it boil, to avoid it breaking up. In the summer, you may speed up the cooking, because the fish can spoil before it is cooked. As soon as the *court-bouillon* starts to bubble, reduce the heat. To serve the fish, you slide it gently off the rack onto a folded napkin of the right size, taking care that the stomach, that is the more convex side, is uppermost. Garnish with parsley. If there are any tears in the skin, these are disguised with parsley. Send round the table at the same time a jug of oil or a white caper sauce in a sauce-boat.

Turbot with a béchamel sauce (entrée). — The leftovers or a piece of turbot or brill can be served with a béchamel sauce in a crust such as you use for hot pâtés, or even, at luncheon, with a mayonnaise or, finally, fried.

D. — Dabs, Plaice and Soles.

All these fish are prepared in the same manner.

Soles au bleu (entrée). — Soles are often not scaled carefully enough. The scales are, it's true, extremely small, you can barely see them, but it is none the less unpleasant to find them in your mouth. To scale a sole properly, you must lay it on a board, scrape the scales against the grain, and not neglect the edges, near the fins.

Cook the soles in a milk *court-bouillon* when you wish to eat them with a white sauce or with oil and vinegar.

Fried soles (entremets*)*. — Once you have thoroughly scaled them or, perhaps which is better, skinned them, wiped them with a white cloth and floured them, drop them in plenty of very hot fat. Sometimes you may add sprigs of parsley. The fish should take on a nice colour, without being burnt, and be crisp round the edges. Serve lemons at the same time, each guest squeezing as much juice on his fish as he desires. Sometimes, before serving the soles, they are split, the fillets lifted and cold butter insinuated beneath them. They are served as soon as the butter has melted. If you wish to have something a little more refined, you can take off the fillets and then fry them, serving them garnished with parsley. The debris can then be cooked in the vegetable stock which I have described on page 426, above. This will greatly improve it and it can then be used in a matelote or other, different sauces. (See *Fried foods.*)

Gratin of soles (entrée). — Once you have prepared them as you did before frying, but without flouring them, put them in a heatproof dish with butter on the bottom, a little chopped spring onion and parsley, salt, pepper and dried breadcrumbs. You top the fish off with the same accompaniments and then moisten, either with water or with stock. It must be cooked with heat above and below the dish. Serve it in the dish it was cooked in. You can only prepare a gratin with fillets of sole.

Grilled soles (entrée). — Once you have thoroughly washed and scaled them, wipe them carefully and put them on the grill – which you have heated in advance so that the soles' skin does not stick to it. Serve them with a white caper sauce or with oil and vinegar. It is one of the best ways to eat them.

Soles with oysters (entrée). — You fry them until they are half-cooked, then you finish the cooking in a sauce made with a roux moistened with a vegetable or meat stock to which you add mushrooms, two dozen oysters (without their liquor, for two medium-sized soles), pepper and a little salt. This little-known dish is first-rate and pleases almost all lovers of fish.

Matelote of soles (entrée and luncheon). — This is a really good way to eat small soles. Prepare a matelote sauce and cook them in it.

Baked soles (entrée).[1] — Put some butter in the dish and add the soles; scatter some dried breadcrumbs over them, as well as chopped parsley and spring onion; add a glass of white wine, salt and pepper; cook this with a gentle heat above and below the dish.

Fillets of sole in jus. — Once you have skinned the soles, fillet them, that is, divide the flesh down the middle then lift off the fillets with a thin, sharp knife. Roll them up and put them to cook with a good, reduced meat *jus*. Arrange the fillets on their edge and keep them warm; reduce the *jus* and pour it over the fillets. You can cook these in water, to which you add butter, salt, pepper and mixed herbs. Take the fillets out, keep them warm, then reduce the sauce over a high flame. You can add lemon juice or vinegar before you pour it over the fillets.

E. — Cod.[2]

Cod au bleu (entrée). — It is better cooked with milk than any other way, and it is eaten with a white sauce, or oil and vinegar, or with a béchamel sauce, in which you put potatoes that have been boiled in water, then cut in two and roasted on the grill.

You can slice it into steaks and make a gratin, or make a matelote. Served whole, it can make a very fine remove. In Holland, they cook cod in lightly salted water with a bouquet garni. At the same time they serve melted butter (very lightly salted) and some boiled potatoes.

F. — Mackerel.

Mackerel à la maître-d'hôtel (entrée). — You need to split it down the back to the bone, and marinate it for one or two hours in oil with salt and pepper. Put it on the grill wrapped in a sheet of oiled paper – which is replaced in Flanders and northern *départements* by a layer of fennel held

---

1.   The French is *Soles sur le plat*.
2.   Mme Millet-Robinet's section head here is *Cabillaud ou Morue fraîche*. The French have two words for cod, although *morue* used alone usually means salt cod.

in place with string. When the mackerel is dressed, you insert some butter worked with chopped parsley, salt and pepper into the gills and serve it surrounded with the same butter.

Mackerel with black butter (entrée). — Cook it on the grill as in the preceding recipe and brown about 125 grams of butter in a pan; when it is very hot, throw in a few sprigs of parsley, salt and pepper, and let the butter colour up, but not too much; add a spoonful of vinegar. Serve over the mackerel. Sometimes the fish is put in the pan for a few minutes.

G. — Ray.

Ray au bleu (entrée). — There are quite a lot of species of ray; thornback ray is to be preferred to all the others; it is at once firmer, whiter and more tender. The bucklers are small hooks, with a larger base, which appear on the surface of the skin; you should handle it with some care. After washing it well, cook it in a *court-bouillon* composed as follows: water, salt, pepper, carrots, onions, bouquet garni. You can add white wine or vinegar, but the skate is itself quite flavoursome. When it is cooked, drain off the *court-bouillon*. Then take off the skin carefully, as well as the head and the tail (which both, however, contain some morsels of flesh which are excellent to eat). Then reverse your serving-dish over the top of the pan in which your ray was cooked and turn it over, so that the skate is dressed for service without breaking. Then remove the skin from the other side, which now finds itself uppermost, and clean the edges of the dish. The side with the black skin should be served uppermost because it is the side which contains the most meat. Brown some butter, as I have explained for mackerel, and pour it over.

Ray with butter sauce (entrée).[1] — After cooking it as in the preceding recipe, and dressing it in the same fashion, melt some butter with salt, pepper and chopped parsley and pour it over at the moment of service.

You can also eat it with a white sauce.

Fried ray (entrée). — Small rays are good cooked in deep fat; you will have to take the skin off both sides before frying.

---

1.   i.e. *beurre blanc.*

H. — Herring.

Fresh herring (luncheon). — Scale and wash the herring; place them on the grill, which you have heated in advance so they do not stick to it. Serve with a white sauce or a parsley butter with salt and pepper.

Fresh herring with mustard. — After cooking them on the grill, pour into a saucepan a sauce made from a knob of butter and some flour which you have melted and mixed; moisten with a little stock and bring it together on the fire; then add a spoonful of mustard.

Smoked herring (hors-d'oeuvre, entremets, luncheon, entrée).[1] — You can eat pickled herring either cooked on the grill and dressed with oil, or with a salad of wild chicory, escarole or dandelion with hard-boiled eggs. You can also mix the flesh with beaten eggs to make an omelette. (See *Smoked herring omelette*, page 450, above.)

I. — Thick-lipped grey mullet and Grey mullet.[2]

Thick-lipped grey mullet with a white sauce (entrée). — Gut them through the gills, then make a stuffing with breadcrumbs, chopped parsley and spring onion, oil, salt and pepper and insert it in the stomach. Wrap it in oiled or buttered paper. Put it on the grill, over a gentle fire. If it is not wrapped like this, you must heat the grill up beforehand. You can also cook it with milk. Serve it with a white sauce with capers.

J. — Whiting.

Baked whiting (entremets). — After gutting and washing, put it on a flat dish with butter, chopped parsley and spring onion, salt, pepper, a little water or vegetable or meat stock, and dried breadcrumbs. You give it heat above and below the dish. If you wish to make it a gratin, put the same

---

1.   This, as on page 450 above, is *hareng saur*, a general term indicating a smoked and salted herring such as buckling.
2.   The section heading is *Meuil et Mulet. Meuil* is the name used in the Vendée, close to Mme Millet-Robinet's home, for the thick-lipped grey mullet (*Chelon labrosus*). Alan Davidson, in his *North Atlantic Seafood*, suggests the usual French for this species is *muge noir. Meuil* does not figure in French dictionaries, however, *Statistique ou description générale du département de la Vendée* (1844), where its fishery was important, offers *meuil* as the local name. *Mulet* refers to the grey mullet (*Mugil cephalus*). The red mullet in French is *rouget*.

accompaniments beneath the fish and, when it is cooked, take the cover off to reduce the sauce and brown it more quickly.

One often cooks whiting more simply on a flat dish with butter, to which is added parsley, salt and pepper.

Fried whiting (entremets). — After carefully cleaning the whiting, wipe them with a dry cloth and slash them diagonally; sprinkle with flour and fry them. This fish is much nicer when fried in a very light batter.

K. — Gurnard.

Gurnard au bleu (entrée). — It is usually cooked in milk; eat it with either a white sauce or oil and vinegar.

L. — Red mullet.

Red mullet is a very delicate fish; prepare it exactly like the mackerel.

M. — Mussels.

Boiled mussels (entrée). — You must begin by scrubbing them carefully to remove all the small barnacles that cover them, wash them thoroughly, then put them dry in a saucepan over a brisk fire (to force them to open). When the mussels contain no crabs, you need do no more than add soft breadcrumbs that have been pounded and sieved, pepper, no salt and chopped parsley, and let the whole simmer for quarter of an hour, then serve. But, if you have grounds for thinking that they do contain crabs, you will have to take them one by one, take off the shell, open the mussel, look for any crabs and remove them; for this small crustacean is terribly indigestible and can even give rise to accidents which seem very akin to poisoning.

Mussels à la poulette (entrée and luncheon). — Once you have caused the mussels to open, pour any liquor they have given off into a bowl so the impurities they may contain sink to the bottom; then take one shell off each mussel; arrange them regularly on a dish you have placed on the hot embers. In the meanwhile, melt and heat a knob of butter without browning it, throw in one or two spoonfuls of flour, depending on how many mussels you have; stir it and moisten with the mussel liquor you have carefully decanted and passed through a fine muslin. Season generously with pepper, but don't add salt. Let this boil up for a few seconds; then add some chopped parsley and a liaison [of egg yolk], without letting it boil.

Pour this over the mussels. You can also put the mussels in the saucepan with the butter and flour; they will shrink a certain amount, and some will be shed from their shells, but they will still taste excellent.

Gratin of mussels (hors-d'oeuvre and luncheon). — Clean the mussels as if they were going to be boiled, then put them as they are in a saucepan over a brisk flame. Shake them frequently to force them to open. Separately, prepare a gratin mixture of dried breadcrumbs with the same ingredients as you would need to cook a gratin of sole or whiting. Then take some large oyster shells (almost every kitchen in Flanders is equipped with these large ribbed shells for just this purpose) and coat the bottom with prepared breadcrumbs (which a little butter will inhibit from dropping down to the bottom of the shell) and arrange one mussel (completely rid of their shells) next to the other. Cover them with the breadcrumb mixture as I have already described; add some good butter; then place the filled shells on a grill over a medium flame. Cover the whole thing with a Dutch oven, with very hot embers on top. As the cooking is half-complete when the mussels are put into the large shells, all that is needed is that the gratin takes on a nice colour for them to be good to eat.

This dish, little known in France but frequently prepared in Belgium, is excellent.

Mussel salad. — This is one of the best ways to eat mussels. After cleaning them, inspecting them and causing them to open as I have already described, you serve them in a salad bowl without their shells. You can combine them with lettuce or chicory.

N. — Lobsters, Crayfish and Crabs.

You need to cook these on a high fire in a good *court-bouillon* with a little butter; when they are thoroughly red, they are cooked; leave them to cool in their *court-bouillon*. To serve them, crack the claws, split the tail and dress them on a napkin garnished with parsley. Make an oil and vinegar sauce or a rémoulade sauce.

When they are bought cooked, it is good to finish cooking them for a few seconds in a *court-bouillon*.

O. — Dried and salted cod.

There are two sorts: dried cod [stockfish] and salt cod. The last is the most used in *cuisine bourgeoise*, although the other is highly esteemed by some people. The best is that with white flesh, divided into large flakes, with a thoroughly black skin. You should split the flesh in several places and put it to soak (see the method on page 522, above) in cold water which you change several times. When you have soaked the cod enough, which you can test by tasting it, put it on the fire with a milk *court-bouillon*. Let it simmer, without rapid boiling, for three-quarters of an hour; boiling toughens it. It is preferable to put the cod in a deep dish and to pour over boiling water before covering it. After half an hour you empty out the water and repeat the procedure. That will be enough to cook the cod perfectly, and it will not toughen up. Serve it with a white caper sauce. You can also eat salt cod with oil and vinegar. Often one arranges boiled potatoes that have been passed over the grill around the cod.

Salt cod with béchamel sauce (entrée). — Once you have cooked it as in the preceding recipe, divide it into pieces and take off the black skin (the white skin is much liked); then leave it for five or six minutes in a béchamel sauce. It is also excellent in a crust such as you use for hot pâtés.

Gratin of salt cod. — Cook it as in the preceding recipes, break it into pieces, and put it in a gratin as you do soles. Salt cod in a gratin is almost always very tough.

Salt cod with cheese. — Prepare it like gratin of salt cod; you add grated Gruyère cheese and Parmesan cheese.

Salt cod à la maître-d'hôtel. — Cook as above; after breaking it up, put it on a flat dish with some butter, chopped parsley and pepper; turn it over in the butter while it melts, then take it out straight away. You can add a little vinegar, verjuice or lemon juice; you can also add some slices of cooked potato.

Salt cod with potato. — Prepare it like fresh cod, once you have cooked it as we have just described.

Matelote of salt cod. — Make a matelote sauce with a stock made from split peas, haricots, lentils or green peas. (See *Meatless stock*, page 426 above, and *Matelote sauce*, page 437 above.) Simmer in the sauce for half an hour, without letting it boil, the cod cut into pieces. This little-known way of preparing salt cod is excellent.

Salt cod fried in oil. — After cutting the salt cod into small square pieces, soak it as instructed earlier. A moment before frying, take it out of the water and dry it in a white cloth. Then put some oil in a frying-pan on the fire; when it is thoroughly hot, sprinkle the pieces of salt cod with flour and drop them in the oil. They should take on a nice colour. Serve with the oil. You can use walnut oil; this, when freshly pressed, gives a particular flavour to the salt cod which agrees with many people.

Cod tongues. — Prepare them like salt cod. They are generally more esteemed than any other part of this fish because they are fattier and more tender.

3. — Freshwater fish.
A. — In general.

River fish are more highly regarded than fish from ponds; and golden fish are more valued than brown. We are assured that by giving a muddy-smelling carp a few spoonfuls of vinegar it will exude a sort of perspiration which will be taken off when the fish is scaled, thereby eliminating the unpleasant flavour it had at the outset. I have not myself experimented with this method. Freshwater fish should be bought live; if it comes from muddy ponds, you rid the taste of mud by holding it for a few days in clean water that is frequently renewed.

Matelote. — Although a matelote is usually made with carp or eel, most freshwater fish can be treated in this manner. You must place the carp on a board to scale it thoroughly and cut it into chunks: skin the eel and cut this into chunks, disposing of the head which doesn't look very nice. Some people don't take the skin off the eel, which becomes very tender when cooked and very tasty, although a bit fatty.

Although I have described how to prepare a matelote in the article on *Sauces* (page 437, above), I will repeat it here.

Brown twelve to twenty whole small onions in butter; set them to one side. Make a roux; moisten it with a vegetable stock made with split peas, failing that a haricot stock, or one made with lentils, or a meat stock. Water should not be used unless you have no vegetable or meat stock. Add salt, pepper and a bouquet garni; leave to boil for half an hour; add as much red wine as you did stock, then the onions, mushrooms, artichoke bottoms and Jerusalem artichokes. When all this is half-cooked and boiling away, throw in the fish cut into chunks and let it finish cooking. Put the soft and hard roes into the pan a few moments after the fish itself as they cook more rapidly. The fish will thin the sauce; you will need to reduce it. Serve it on a few small crusts of dried bread.

To make a matelote for meat-days, you can brown a few pieces of belly pork or ham to begin with; then make the roux; then let it cook for at least an hour before adding the onions. This way of doing things greatly improves the matelote.

Some people make a matelote in a cauldron on the open hearth. In this case, brown the onions as I have explained, make a roux, moisten it simply to let it down, then straight away add the onions and the wine, salt, pepper and a very large bouquet garni. When the onions have half cooked, throw in the fish; soon after this, add half a glass of eau-de-vie and set it alight. You also need not make a roux but thicken the sauce with some butter worked into flour.

A few crayfish in any matelote will give it an excellent flavour and decorate the dish. A reheated matelote is excellent.

White matelote. — Prepare and cut up the fish as I have explained; in a saucepan, heat up some vegetable stock and twice its volume of white wine. Let it boil for a moment; take it off the heat; sauté some onions and mushrooms in butter, without them browning; add two spoonfuls of flour; moisten with the stock and let cook for a few seconds. Add the fish, salt, pepper and nutmeg. When the fish is cooked, dress it on a dish; thicken the sauce with egg yolks; sieve it then serve it on the fish.

B. — Carp.

Carp for the roast course. — When the fish is a handsome one, cook it *au bleu* and it can be served hot. If you wish it cold, you need to leave it to cool in a high-flavoured *court-bouillon*. Don't scale it, and gut it through the gills.

Fried carp (entremets). — The fish should not be too large. Gut it and split it through the stomach; pass it through some flour and plunge it into some very hot and plentiful oil. Throw some sprigs of parsley into the fat for the few seconds it takes to drain the fish after taking it out; serve the parsley around the fish. You should salt the fried fish at the moment you take it out of the pan.

Stewed carp. — You prepare this in the same way as a matelote, except you only add wine.

Fishballs of carp (entrée). — Make a good vegetable stock with split peas (see *Meatless stock*, page 426 above), in which you cook the carcase of the carp after scaling it and removing all the flesh. Chop this flesh very finely. Soak some bread crumb in warm milk for an hour; add it to the carp flesh, with some finely chopped parsley, salt and pepper. For a medium-sized carp, add two whole eggs, the white and the yolk. A few truffles chopped in with the fish will greatly improve the balls. Mix everything together, which should produce quite a loose forcemeat; put it on a dish. Make a roux; moisten it with the vegetable stock in which you have boiled the carp carcase; add, if possible, some mushrooms, artichoke bottoms, salt, pepper, a bouquet garni and let it simmer at the outset over a low flame; then quickly bring it up to the boil over a high heat. Take two spoons; take up the forcemeat in one; with the other, give the same form to the top of the forcemeat as it has from the bottom spoon; put the spoon and its forcemeat in the sauce. In an instant, the fishball will stiffen up; then push it off the spoon so it falls in the sauce. Continue in this fashion until all the forcemeat has been converted into fishballs; reduce the heat, add the soft roe, and leave to cook for half an hour. Serve. These balls are excellent in a crust as used for hot pâtés. The forcemeat is better if the ingredients are pounded rather than chopped. You can cook some crayfish in the sauce, and add a few sliced truffles.

This has such a good flavour and is so delicate that most people who eat it can scarcely believe it is a fast-day dish. These balls can replace the pâtissier's quenelles in all their sauces, as well as in vol-au-vents. You can add other fish to the carp.

This is one of the best ways of using the flesh of freshwater fish that have too many bones, because these become undetectable when pounded or thoroughly chopped.

Fish balls made with sea fish are no less delicate.

Gratin of carp. — Once you have scaled it, proceed exactly as for sole. (See *Gratin of soles*, page 523, above.)

Matelote of carp. — See *Matelote*, above.

C. — *Perch.*

Perch au bleu (roast course). — Take out the gills and gut it; cook it *au bleu*; when it is cooked, scale it; dress it on a dish with parsley all round. You eat it with oil and vinegar.

Fried perch. — Scale and gut the perch; snip the flesh along their backs; flour them and fry them.

Baked perch. — The same preparation as for soles.

D. — Trout.

Trout au bleu (entrée). — Trout is a fish which merits its reputation. Those called *salmon trout*, sometimes very large, are rightly esteemed the most; cook them *au bleu* and serve them surrounded with parsley, to be eaten with a white sauce or with oil and vinegar. When they have been cooked, you can also put some butter in a pan, with chopped parsley and shallots; let them brown an instant, then add a crust of bread which you crush after cooking in the *court-bouillon*. Sieve all this to make a purée, on which you serve the fish.

Fried trout (entremets). — To prepare these in this way, they should not weigh more than 25 grams each. Fry them in oil or butter. [On the table,] they will do very nicely opposite a roast.

E. — Tench.

Fried tench (entremets). — This is the best way to eat them. Their delicate flesh resembles soft roes.

Matelote of tench (entrée). — Prepare them as you do carp.

Tench with mixed herbs. — Plunge them in boiling water and take them out immediately. Then you will be able to easily remove the few scales that they have. Once you have gutted them, marinate for an hour in oil, salt, pepper, chopped parsley, spring onion and shallots, thyme and bay leaf. Cook them on the grill, over a gentle fire, after wrapping them in a double sheet of paper into which you insert some of the marinade. To serve, take off the paper and serve a white or piquant sauce with the fish.

F. — Pike.

Pike au bleu (roast course). — You don't scale it, but you do remove the gills with a cloth, so you don't hurt yourself as they are armed with prickles. You gut the pike through the gills and cook it *au bleu* in a strongly spiced *court-bouillon*, in which you leave it to cool. The hard roe of pike is not eaten; its flavour is not very pleasant and it is considered, not without reason, very indigestible.

Fried pike (entremets). — Small pike are excellent fried. I don't need to say that they are prepared as all other fried fish.

Pike à la maître-d'hôtel (entremets). — Small pike are also prepared à la maître-d'hôtel; they are stuffed with a mixture of bread crumb, oil, mixed herbs and mushrooms and, after they have been wrapped in a double sheet of oiled paper, placed on the grill. Serve with a white sauce or a tomato sauce.

Leftovers of pike are served with a mayonnaise, or in a salad, or in a gratin, like sole.

G. — Barbel.

The *barbillon* and the *barbeau* are one and the same fish;[1] but the first name refers to it when small, while the other name refers to it when it is more fully developed. A large barbel is served *au bleu.* The hard roe should be rejected, it is very indigestible.[2] Made into a matelote, this fish tastes a little too strong; it is better cooked on the grill, with a stuffing such as I described for the small pike. You can make fish balls of barbel and pike.

H. — Gudgeon.

After washing, gutting and rolling them in flour, you fry them with parsley sprigs and serve them, in a manner of speaking, in a thicket.

All the other small fish of the same size are served in similar fashion, but they are less delicate than gudgeon. Usually they are dipped into a runny batter before being deep fried.

I. — Eel.

You should select eels with a slate-blue back and nice white belly.

To skin the eel, attach a small cord round the neck and hook it on a nail; cut the skin round the neck with a knife and, with a dry cloth, pull it down all the way to the tail; cut off the head, which should never be served, and then gut the eel.

---

1. As this sentence implies, the section title contained the two names. There are in fact several sorts of barbel, which may add to the complexity of nomenclature. There is the English barbel (*Barbus barbus*), found in northern rivers, and there is also the Mediterranean barbel (*Barbus meridionalis*) which is found in southern Europe and Ukraine. In France this is called, among other names, the *barbeau truité.*
2. Some would say that they were poisonous.

Eel with a tartar sauce (entrée). — Once you have skinned it, marinate it for a few hours in a mixture of oil, salt, pepper, chopped shallots, thyme and bay leaf, to which you add a little vinegar; arrange it in a circle in the dish and turn it over in the marinade once or twice. To cook it, put it with the marinade in a pie-dish which you cover with a Dutch oven; baste it from time to time with the marinade. When it is cooked, serve it with a tartar sauce. You can also take the eel out of the pie-dish before it has cooked entirely and coat it with breadcrumbs and place on the grill, which you have heated up in advance. An eel thus prepared can be eaten with a tomato sauce, or à la maître-d'hôtel, instead of the tartar sauce.

Matelote of eel (entrée). — You prepare this like the carp or, better, with the carp. (See *Matelote*.)

Eel à la poulette (entrée). — After skinning it and cutting it into chunks, throw it for five minutes into boiling water, mixed with a few spoonfuls of vinegar. Melt a knob of butter; add a spoonful of flour, stir without letting it colour; moisten with a glass of boiling water and as much white wine; add salt, pepper, a bouquet garni and mushrooms. Cook the eel for half an hour in this sauce, which you thicken with an egg yolk. Serve. Cooked like this, you can serve it in a pastry case such as you would use for a vol-au-vent.

Fried eel (entrée and luncheon). — When the eel is a large one, cut it into pieces 10 centimetres long, then place in a saucepan with white wine, slices of onion, carrots, thyme, bay leaf, a little knob of butter, salt, pepper and a few cloves. When it is almost cooked, take it off the heat and coat it with breadcrumbs, then let it cool. You can serve it like this without any further preparation. If you want something a little more elaborate, you can fry it. Put a knob of butter in a saucepan with two spoonfuls of flour; mix them together; moisten with the liquor from cooking the eel and add three egg-yolks, then the eel; stir it once more and let it cool. Then take out each piece coated with some of the sauce and crumb it. Dip it in the sauce again and crumb once more. Then you fry it. Serve it on a tomato sauce.

You can also fry the eel without this long and difficult preparation, that is to say just as it is, once it has been skinned and dipped in flour.

If the eels are small ones, skin them, cut them into chunks, dip them in flour and fry them. You can leave them whole and bend them round in the fat.

Grilled eel (entrée and luncheon). — Cut the chunks a little long, sauté them in butter for five minutes over a brisk fire; tip them into a deep dish. Add salt, pepper, nutmeg, parsley or mixed herbs, chopped shallots or spring onion, some mushrooms (if possible) and two spoonfuls of oil. Let the eel marinate for two or three hours; then coat with breadcrumbs and put on the grill. Serve on a tomato sauce or a piquant sauce, or with a parsley butter.

J. — Lamprey.

(Entrée). — You can fry it like eel or cook it on the grill. It is also stewed or in a matelote; in this case, add some cooked prunes, their stones removed.

Baked lamprey. — The same preparation as soles.

K. — Shad.

This excellent fish is not found in all parts of France. It is the freshwater fish which spoils the quickest; it should be cooked as soon as it comes out of the water. After washing, scale and gut it through the gills, which you remove. Wrap it in two sheets of paper, the first of which should be white and oiled, and attached at both ends. Cook the fish on the grill over a very gentle heat. If the shad is large, it must be left there for at least an hour. Serve it with a parsley butter. You can also place it on a purée of sorrel, or on a white sauce, or with black butter. A stuffing made of fine breadcrumbs mixed with butter or oil, chopped mixed herbs, salt and pepper placed in the stomach of the shad gives it flavour and softens it.

Matelote of shad. — This is a very delicate dish. (See *Matelote*, pages 530–1, above.)

L. — Salmon.

Salmon au bleu (remove, luncheon or entrée). — Salmon is classed as a freshwater fish, even though it goes down to the sea every year, where it spends about a month before going up through the broad estuaries and on to the rivers and streams. It is perhaps the fish which admits of the most varied flavours; it is also, in France, one of the most esteemed. It is quite the opposite in Scotland, where servants lay down in their terms of engagement the number of times each week that they will be obliged to eat salmon.

The whole salmon, or cut into large pieces, is most often cooked *au bleu*; then it is served with a white caper sauce. It is also eaten with oil and vinegar, or with a sauce made with melted butter, pepper and chopped parsley.

Grilled salmon. — Put on the grill salmon cut into fairly thin steaks. After salting and peppering them, wrap in some oiled paper and place over a gentle heat. If the slice is thick, it will need half an hour to cook. You can marinate the salmon for two hours in oil with salt and pepper before placing it on the heat; you take off the paper to serve it and accompany the salmon with a white sauce.

Matelote of salmon (entrée). — Make a matelote sauce (see that recipe), and cook a whole slice of salmon in it. It is an excellent dish.

Salmon salad (luncheon and entremets). — The leftovers of a salmon cooked *au bleu* can be served in a salad; slice them and mingle with lettuce hearts and a few hard-boiled eggs, also sliced. This salad can be coated with a mayonnaise.

Salmon in jus (entrée). — Cook a salmon in a good consommé of meat *jus*, this is perhaps the best way to prepare this fish. Generally speaking, fish are very good with a meat-based flavour. Placed in a crust such as you would make for hot pâtés, it is a very distinguished dish. You can bind the sauce with a little potato starch.

Salmon is also served with a béchamel sauce, or a rémoulade sauce and many other sauces.

Salted salmon. — You should prepare a salted salmon like salt cod; it is much to be preferred and much more costly. (See the articles *Dried and salted cod* and *How to soak salted fish, meats or vegetables*, pages 521 and 528, above.)

CHAPTER XII

FRIED FOODS

Fat for frying. — In many households, when they want to fry something, they put a knob of butter, oil or lard in a frying-pan; but the fish or other things they wish to fry are not immersed in this fat, which is thus never kept for re-use and is almost entirely absorbed by the fried substance. This method is defective and wasteful; it is much preferable to have a fat pot, which contains a frying medium which is kept for whenever you need it, in sufficient quantity so that whatever is being fried is immersed. After frying whatever item, any fat that has not been absorbed is poured back into this pot; it will keep indefinitely, and you can top it up from time to time with whatever fats make it up, so that you always have enough.

You can have two frying mediums, one meatless, one of animal fats: the second is to be preferred.

The meat-based medium is made up of various fats, of which the best, without doubt, is the fat taken off a meat stock once it has cooled. This gives fried foods a nice colour, never scums up in the pan and does not give the foods any particular flavour. Every time a stock needs to be kept from one day to the next, you should lift off the fat, wash it, put it on the heat, warm it until it stops smoking, let it rest, then decant it into the fat pot. However, as it will take a long time and be complicated to create a fat pot from this alone (for it should contain at least a litre and a half of fat), you can start by buying some fat from round the ox kidney and from the marrow, from which you cut off small pieces which you throw into boiling water to melt. Leave them in this for four or five hours; sieve them together with the water, then leave to cool. The fat will congeal on the surface. You should prepare this fat like the pot-au-feu fat; you can also melt it down like pig fat. Lard added to this foundation, and even butter melted over heat and sufficiently cooked so that all the cheese-like particles which it normally contains fall to the bottom of the bowl, then sieved as you pour it into the fat pot, make a mixture which will be perfect for a good frying medium; finally you can add the fat from various roasts (except those of mutton which give a most unpleasant flavour to anything fried), but always after washing it, melting it once more and decanting it.

A frying medium that is not meat-based can consist of either butter prepared in the way I have just described, or a not-too-fruity olive oil; such a fat will ensure anything cooked in it has a fine appearance, but oil lends a particular flavour that does not appeal to everybody. If using oil, every time you fry something, you top up the fat pot so that you always have the same amount of fat at the ready; if you have used butter, which needs rendering before use, you cannot top up after each occasion, but you should not let the fat pot get too low before replenishing it with fresh butter. Oil and butter mixed together also make a good frying medium. When you use the same fat for any sort of fried food, it can happen that fried meats, for example calf's ears, brains, or calf's sweetbreads, can take on a fishy flavour, and vice versa. The fat that has been used once for fish should be set aside and never used to fry anything else but fish.

Once you have put the fat on the fire, which should be clear and brisk, you must watch it carefully because, if it heats up too much before anything you want to fry is added to it, it will brown and burn. Once you reckon it sufficiently hot, dip your finger in water and flick a drop into the pan: if the fat is hot enough, it will spit vigorously: immediately lower into it whatever you are wanting to fry. You can also test it with a sprig of parsley or any other leaf; but you must never put anything into the pan without being sure the fat is really hot, as that is the essential precondition for any fried food being crisp and golden and not impregnated with fat – which will give them a foul flavour and wastes fat into the bargain. The fire should be kept very bright and brisk all the time you are frying. If the item being fried is not wholly immersed in the fat, you should turn it over with a skimmer; otherwise, you should refrain from touching it, judge the right moment when it seems nicely browned to take it out, and then drain it in a colander you have placed over the fat pot. While doing this, take the pan off the heat lest the fat burns. Sprinkle salt on the food you have fried before serving it. After that, pour the fat into the pot, leaving behind any food residues that may lurk at the bottom of the pan. To prevent fat from dropping into the fire (the chimney can easily catch alight), you must place the pan on a pot-stand or trivet and support the handle with the cord I mentioned when describing the kitchen fireplace (page 179, above). You can also support it on the back of a chair laced in the corner of the fireplace, but this arrangement is not very reliable. You must never support the pan on a log. If the chimney catches alight, you should scatter ashes on the fire rather than water, and if the pan itself catches fire, you must remove it from the fireplace and throw a well-wetted cloth over it.

Before using the fat, you must put the pot in which you keep it close to the fire for half an hour; failing this, you will have great difficulty extracting it to put in the pan, especially in winter, because the fat gets very hard. If you use tin spoons to try to get it out, they will most likely break.

A fat that has been properly prepared can be kept for more than twelve months without spoiling; it will keep indefinitely so long as you have a care to top it up from time to time after using it.

Batter. — Here are the proportions, which you can increase or diminish according to the nature of what you wish to fry. You must, however, make up the batter an hour before using it. Put into a deep dish three spoonfuls of flour, two egg yolks and a little salt; add liquid; add as much water as needed to make a thin gruel. When you wish to use the batter, beat the two egg whites to a snow, add them, combine carefully. Dip whatever you wish to fry into this batter.

For fritters and other light, sweet confections, it is a good plan to add a spoonful of eau-de-vie at the same time as the egg yolks.

Here is a list of some of the things which can be deep-fried; it is enough to list them as we give details of preparation of some of them in their relevant articles; the others present no problem at all: Eggs; — Frog's legs; — Meatballs; — Beef; — Calf's mesentery; — Calf's brains; — Calf's head; — Sheep's brains; — Sheep's trotters; — Lamb's trotters; — Pigeons; — Poultry or marinade of poultry; — Trout; — Sole; — Plaice; — Lemon sole; — Skate; — Whiting; — Salt cod; — Smelt; — Carp; — Perch; — Tench; — Gudgeon; — Eel; — Cauliflower; — Artichokes; — Salsify; — Potatoes; — Potato croquettes; — Jerusalem artichokes; — Sweetcorn; — Buckwheat fritters; — *Bouillie* or cream; — Rice croquettes; — Fried pastries; — Various fritters.

CHAPTER XIII

VEGETABLES

1. — In general.

Using vegetables. — This chapter is no less important than any that has come before: a dinner without vegetables is a dinner ill-conceived. I urge the mistress of the house to offer them to her family not just once but twice each day. I have already advised that the usual meal should consist of one meat dish, or two if one is too light, and one dish of vegetables: I repeat this recommendation. To me, this routine is as advantageous to good health as it is to the budget: moderation agrees with all digestions. To serve more dishes than this is an intolerable extravagance to the careful housewife, who in any case does not have an unlimited income at her disposal. She might add a milk or cheese dish to the vegetables, particularly on fast-days; but, I reiterate, it is always better to offer fewer dishes, yet make them good, abundant and to the taste of the whole family.

In most cookery books, vegetables are reckoned to be *entremets*,[1] because they are eaten in the entremets, after the roast. However, a great number of households have adopted the practice of passing round the dish of vegetables while the roast is being carved; they are therefore eaten after the first course and before the roast. The dinner is terminated by the sweet *entremets*, which follow the salad. To put it bluntly, is there not too great a gulf between a plate of cardoons in gravy and a chocolate cream for them

---

1. The word *entremets* usually indicates the second course in a meal, served with or after the roast and before the dessert of nuts, fruit, etc. This second course was often a mixture of sweet and savoury dishes but this paragraph alerts the reader to the shift that was occurring in dining habits, so that the word became restricted to sweet foods (unless it was a 'savoury', in the English meaning of the word, in which case it would be an *entremets salé*).

to be put in the same category? So I believe I have sufficient grounds for taking *vegetables* out of the classification *entremets*, and I think my action conforms with the good sense of – and the reality obtaining in – most middle-class households, which usually designate as *entremets* creams and other *sweet entremets*.

How to cook dried vegetables and green vegetables. — To cook vegetables properly, you need river water or spring water; should you have only well water, and when it is what is called *very hard*, you have to add a little bag of wood ash, no larger than a walnut: it will make cooking vegetables much easier.

All dried vegetables *must be put into cold water*, and should not be salted until they are half-cooked. In some regions, they only add enough water to cover, and top it up as need be during cooking, so that when fully cooked there is only as much liquor as may be needed to dress them. I do not reckon this a sound way of doing things: in the first place, dried vegetables have an astringency which, accentuated by this method of cooking, becomes more perceptible and causes a disagreeable sensation in the throat. By using too little water, you deprive yourself of the excellent stock you will obtain by cooking the vegetables in plenty of water. This meatless stock can be used either to improve a multitude of sauces or to make excellent soups. The mistress of the household is often at a loss for good soups when she does not make a pot-au-feu. This single point should cause her to always embrace the practice of cooking her dried vegetables in plenty of water.

Green vegetables can never be eaten too fresh; they should be put into *plenty* of *boiling* water that is salted in advance. If you wish to preserve their green colour, salt the water heavily. The cooking liquor from many fresh vegetables can be used, like that from dried vegetables, either in a soup or in making sauces. A small, tinned copper cauldron is the best vessel for cooking fresh vegetables. They also cook well in a cast iron pot, but cauliflower and sorrel will blacken unless the cast iron is enamelled on the inside.

Almost all vegetables are suitable for service at luncheon, especially when only the family is present; however, there are certain ways of preparing them that are more suited to this meal than to dinner. In these cases, I will take care to mention the fact.

2. — Fresh vegetables.

A. — *Green peas* [Petits pois].[1]

You can be sure the peas are tender if, when you shell them, you notice that they still have the little stalk which connects them to the pod, and if they are also not too dark a green in colour. You will know they are extremely delicate if, when splitting the shell, a drop of sap appears.

When the peas have been shelled, put a knob of butter on a high fire and pour the peas into the saucepan as the butter melts; add a spoonful of flour (some people do not do this); stir them around. When the butter has completely melted and everything is well mixed, *without letting the butter brown*, moisten with a little boiling water. You only need to add a very small amount; you can even dispense with it altogether if the peas are very fresh. Mix everything and cover. Half an hour later, add a little salt and pepper; add sugar if you wish, and let them continue cooking. In one hour they should be cooked; if you leave them longer they go hard. If the liquor is too thin, reduce it by boiling with the lid off. This is the best way of dealing with fresh peas.

Gratin of fresh peas [Petits pois]. — Deal with them as in the preceding recipe, but let them cook over a low fire for two hours and reduce the cooking liquor enough so that they begin to brown.

Fresh peas [Petits pois] *with lettuce.* — Prepare them as in the first recipe, but add some whole small onions and one or two heads of hearted lettuce; no sugar. When the peas are thoroughly cooked, you can add a liaison. This way of doing things is suitable for peas past their best.

Peas with a roux (luncheon). — Make a pale roux, moisten it with water; when it is boiling vigorously, throw in the peas; cover, and continue cooking over a brisk flame. Add salt, pepper, bay leaf. This way of doing things is suitable for slightly larger peas.

Peas English-style. — Bring to the boil in plenty of water; salt them; let them cook for about half an hour. Pour into a colander. Put a knob of butter into a shallow dish; add the peas and turn them over in the butter. A little pepper will not go amiss. You need plenty of butter; the liquor is excellent.

---

1.   Mme Millet-Robinet makes two distinctions with regard to peas: they are either fresh (green) or dry; and they are either small (*petits*) or large (*gros*). I have indicated where she is referring specifically to *petits pois*, which is generally an expression of youth rather than variety.

You can also prepare peas *English-style* in the following manner. Put the *cooked* peas in a saucepan with the butter; turn them over; make a liaison with two or three egg yolks; take them off the heat; let the sauce thicken while stirring constantly. Serve. With the water in which you cooked the peas, you can make an excellent herb soup.

Peas with backfat or ham (luncheon). — Cut the backfat into pieces; brown it so that half the fat melts; moisten it with hot water. Let this sauce cook with the salt pork for an hour; add the peas, with a bouquet garni, pepper, but not salt. The fire should be very brisk. When the peas are almost done, thicken them with some potato starch which you have first slaked in cold water and then add the sauce to it bit by bit before pouring it back into the saucepan; if you ignore this step it will form lumps.[1]

Large peas [Gros pois] as a salad and [or] with butter (luncheon). — Cook them in plenty of salted water. Drain them in a colander, then pour them into a salad bowl; when they have cooled, dress them as a salad, adding the vinegar first, and more of it than for a normal salad; or else, while they are still warm, add a knob of butter, salt and pepper; stir them briskly in this. It's an excellent dish. The cooking liquor makes an excellent herb soup.

Dried peas are only useful for a purée or for a meatless stock. (See *Purées*, page 574 below.)

B. — Broad beans.

You eat these either very small without being *skinned* (peeled), or large and skinned.

Baby broad beans à la maître-d'hôtel. — Throw them into salted boiling water; when they are cooked, drain them and put them in a saucepan with a knob of butter, salt, pepper, and a little flour; stir them round; moisten with water or milk; leave to simmer for while; add a liaison if you wish. Serve. Some people introduce a small sprig of savory, removed at the moment of service.

---

1. The word Mme Millet-Robinet uses for 'to form lumps' is *mottonner*. This is not listed in French dictionaries, but derives from the noun *motton* which is a French-Canadian usage. It means lumps or clods and is a variation of the French word *motte* which on the one hand refers to the mounds on which were raised early medieval keeps and castles, and on the other to clods of earth, or to *mottes* of butter such as you see on the counter of an old-fashioned *crèmerie*.

The cooking liquor has an unattractive colour and a pronounced flavour; however, let down with water, it is perfect for a herb soup, an onion or a cabbage soup.

Sauté of broad beans. — Cook them and drain as in the previous recipe; add a knob of butter, salt, pepper and chopped parsley. Serve.

Large broad beans. — Peel off the skin; put some butter in a saucepan at the same time as the peeled beans; stir them if they do not split of their own accord; add a spoonful of flour, salt, and pepper; moisten with milk or water; leave to simmer. Serve.

You can also cook them in plenty of boiling water, drain the cooking liquor and dress them with a knob of butter.

The liquor can be used in the same way as that from baby beans, to which it is much to be preferred.

Broad beans in a roux. — Make a roux, moisten with water; skin the beans and put them in the sauce when it comes to the boil, with salt and pepper. Some people add savory. (See *Purées*, page 575 below.)

C. — Beans.

You will find an indication of the best varieties of beans to eat fresh in the *Gardening manual* (Volume II). When they have grown too large, you should split them in two down their length after topping and tailing them.

Plain French beans. — When the water is well and truly boiling, salt it heavily so the beans keep their green colour; they must cook *in plenty of water*. When they are done, pour them into the colander then, as soon as the water has drained off, put them in a saucepan with butter, pepper and, if you wish, a spoonful of flour; turn them over in this. Let them simmer for a few minutes. You can moisten them with some meat stock and leave them to simmer for half an hour: this is very good. Serve, adding chopped parsley, if you wish. The cooking water can go to making a soup, but because it is extremely salty you should let it down with half its volume of fresh water.

French beans à la poulette. — Proceed as in the previous recipe; but add a liaison seasoned with a little vinegar.

Browned French beans.[1] — Cook them as before; put in a saucepan with

---

1. In French, *Haricots verts rissolés. Rissoler* means to brown, often in the oven. This dish might be translated as 'Sauté of French beans', but the instruction is to leave them to catch (*gratiner*) on the bottom of the pan, so I have been literal.

butter, salt and pepper; leave to simmer over a low flame until they begin to catch.

French beans in black butter. — After cooking them as before, brown some butter in a frying-pan; add the beans, with salt and pepper; flip the beans; add a thread of vinegar. Serve.

Salad of French beans. — The same cooking as before. You will need more vinegar than in a normal salad; you can add chopped parsley and even chives or spring onion. It is good, if you are serving it cold, to sprinkle the vinegar an hour in advance, then let some of it drain off when finishing the dressing.

French beans for meat dishes. — French beans can also be served as an accompaniment to mutton. (See *Loin of mutton with French beans*, page 485 above.)

Fresh haricot beans, shelled.[1] — Cook them in plenty of boiling water, less salty than for French beans. You can make an onion soup with this cooking liquor that tastes almost as if it were made with a meat stock; this vegetable stock lends quality to any sauce in which it is used.

Shelled haricot beans à la maître-d'hôtel. — When they are cooked, drain them; put them in a saucepan with butter, a little flour, salt and pepper; toss them; moisten with a small quantity of stock; add chopped parsley. Serve. To prepare them for a meat-day, add enough stock to cover, then reduce it. They are even better with gravy.

Haricot beans with milk. — Cook as before, moisten with milk, let it simmer. Serve.

Fried shelled haricot beans. — The same cooking as before. Heat a knob of butter in a saucepan without colouring; add the well-drained haricots, with salt and pepper; when they start to colour a little, sauté them until they have all turned a golden brown. They are excellent like this; it is the most refined way of serving them.

Salad of shelled haricots. — The same as for French beans.

Coloured haricots. — Prepare these as if they were white haricots, they do not look as nice, although they taste as good. Coco or chestnut beans are very good fresh.[2] You can moisten them with red wine rather than milk or stock.

1.　In French, *Haricots en grain, écossés.* These are navy or lima beans picked fresh and shelled, rather than being left to dry.

2.　The coloured coco bean is also known as the borlotti. Cocos de Paimpol (in Brittany) are not in fact coloured, but are a popular autumn bean, sold semi-dried all over modern France. The chestnut bean is most likely the chestnut lima bean.

D. — *Cabbage.*

This precious vegetable is used in a vast number of ways: as a vegetable, as a way of dressing meat, in a soup, and as sauerkraut.

There are two distinct sorts: the curly-leafed cabbage and the smooth-leafed. The first is usually more tender, but has less flavour than the second, and sometimes tastes musky in quite an unpleasant manner.[1] In addition, the heads are not so large as the smooth-leafed cabbage and can't be used for the same purposes. There are several varieties of smooth cabbage, some of which are more delicate than others. I will indicate in each recipe which variety of cabbage you should use for best effect.

When the curly-leafed cabbage has a musky odour, this can be reduced by taking out the heart.

For the use of cabbage in soups, see the article *Cabbage soups*, page 421 above.

Stuffed cabbage (*entrée*). — Choose a nice smooth-leafed cabbage, hearted but not too dense. Take off the green leaves and wash the head if necessary. Fill a cauldron with water; when it boils, put in the cabbage, stalk side down, and boil vigorously. When the leaves seem to have softened, spread them out with a spoon and let the water penetrate to the heart; then take the cabbage out and place it on a nice clean table. Continue to spread the leaves out, without tearing them. The cabbage should soon be completely opened out and flat; take out the central part, which is about as big as a large hen's egg, and it is ready to stuff.

You should have prepared a forcemeat in advance, of either cooked or raw meat, thoroughly chopped, to which you add a little backfat, salt, pepper, and two eggs (the white and the yolk); mix everything well together. Leftovers of meat: poultry, beef, mutton or veal, are all fine for this stuffing. You can also use sausage meat, to which you should add two eggs.

Begin by putting a small nut of meat in the middle of the cabbage, and cover it with a few leaves by lifting them, stretching them and restoring them to their original position. To the ball that you have thus created, add

---

1.   The scent of musk is reflected in the English variety, the musk cabbage, highly regarded in the eighteenth century, but almost lost by the mid-nineteenth. Various French authorities considered the hearted cabbage to have a musky scent, though the Milan or Savoy cabbage was thought to avoid this defect.

a layer of three or four millimetres of stuffing, taking care to push it *right down to the bottom of the leaves*. This may not coat the entire surface of the ball. Cover this farce with more leaves by drawing in each one, stretching it and restoring it to its original place. Lay down another layer of stuffing and leaves, and continue until no more stuffing and leaves remain. The final layer of leaves should be quite thick. The cabbage prepared like this should be roughly the same size and shape as it was when raw. Having done this, carefully tie it all up by winding string round the cabbage and gathering it all up in the middle, just like a ball of thread. Then put the stuffed cabbage in a saucepan, sit it on a rind of salt pork; pour in enough water or, better, stock, so that it covers the cabbage. Add some pieces of belly of salt pork or ham, the bones of the meat (raw or cooked) used to make the stuffing, some carrots, onions, salt, pepper and a bouquet garni. Cook with a gentle heat above and below the pan. An hour before serving, make a roux which you mix with the sauce: you can however dispense with this. You can add a burnt onion to the vegetables and then, at the moment of service, thicken the sauce with potato starch. If the cabbage is a large one, it will need at least five hours' cooking from the time it is put in the saucepan after being stuffed. The longer this dish is cooked, the better it is. A few little cervelas sausages cooked with the cabbage greatly improve it; you can use them instead of the salt pork. Serve the vegetables and the salt pork around the cabbage, or only serve the sauce. As the cabbage shrinks in the cooking, there is more meat than cabbage: you can blanch a second head at the same time as the first and then break off its leaves to insinuate them between those of the cabbage which has been stuffed: in this case you turn the leaves so that the rib is uppermost and you push the edge of the leaf between the ribs of the stuffed cabbage, which helps it to preserve its proper shape. The rest of the second cabbage can be sliced up and served in the sauce.

This method of preparing cabbage not only provides a matchless and very economical dish but it is also one of the best ways of using up leftovers of meats that would otherwise not be presentable. Its only drawback is the length of time required to prepare it.

Stuffed cabbage cooked in the pot-au-feu. — Chop together a piece of beef and salt pork; also chop up a head of white cabbage parboiled with two onions; mix everything together; add three eggs, a small spoonful of flour, salt and pepper. Blanch a few cabbage leaves; spread them out on a net which you have cut to size; pile the chopped mixture on top; gather the cabbage leaves around it and bring it all together with the net. Cook this in the pot-au-feu. The stock will take on a particular flavour, but it will be none the worse for that and the cabbage will be excellent. You serve it with a little of the stock.

Cabbages with white sauce. — Cut some cabbage hearts in two; cook them in plenty of salted water. Prepare a sauce by working a knob of butter into some flour, salt, pepper and nutmeg. Let this down with hot water, which you should add little by little; let it thicken on the heat. Once the sauce has thickened, add a liaison with a splash of vinegar; don't let it boil. Drain the cabbages, pour over the sauce.

Cabbages cooked like chicory. — Cook them as before and drain them well; chop them finely; drain them a second time. Put a knob of butter in a saucepan; when it has melted and got hot, add the cabbages with a spoonful of flour; mix; moisten with milk or stock; add salt, pepper and nutmeg; leave to simmer. Serve. Cabbage prepared in this fashion can replace chicory either as a dish in its own right, or when intended to be placed under joints of meat. (See *Fricandeau*, page 471 above.)

Cabbages with sausages (luncheon). — Cook them as before, or even, when you are cooking a cabbage soup, put in more cabbage than the soup requires, and once they are cooked, put some to one side. To dress this cabbage, put some butter in a fireproof dish, then the cabbages, salt and pepper; let them cook gently. Cook the sausages in a frying-pan, set them to one side and cover them. Add a little water to the sausage juice and fat that remain in the pan; stir briskly. Add this sauce to the cabbages; turn them over gently so that you do not break them up. Serve the sausages dressed on top of the cabbages. This is an excellent family dish.

You need do no more than add the cabbages to the pan once the sausages are cooked; moisten them with some of their cooking liquor, adding salt and pepper. The cabbages will absorb the juices and fat the sausages have left in the pan.

Salad of cooked cabbages. — After you have removed them from the soup, or after cooking them separately, leave them to cool and drain them completely; dress them like a salad. Like the haricot beans, you can add a thread of vinegar in advance, which you let drain before adding the rest of the dressing. You can serve them hot or cold, according to taste.

Buttered cabbages. — Once they are cooked and well drained, put them in a saucepan with some butter, salt, pepper and nutmeg; let them stew gently for half an hour. Serve.

Larded red cabbage. — Choose quite a hard [i.e. dense] red cabbage; trim it; take out as much of the centre as you can, without affecting the shape of the cabbage; put it into boiling salted water for a few minutes. When it begins to soften, take it out of the water. Lard the cabbage through and through, from one side to the other, with large, closely set lardons. Tie it up with string. Put some belly pork or ham in a saucepan. Brown it and add water. Put the cabbage in, seated on a rind of salt pork. Add carrots, onions, salt, pepper and a bouquet garni round the cabbage. Leave it to cook for three or four hours, depending on the size of the cabbage. Reduce some meat juice to a glaze; thicken the cooking liquor with a roux – the roux is not essential. Dress it. Pour the meat glaze over the cabbage and the sauce underneath. Cut it into slices, through the lardons.

Salad of raw red or white smooth-leafed cabbage. — Choose a hearted cabbage that is at once quite dense and quite tender; cut it in two, and then shred it as finely as possible; leave out the heart and the stalk. Put the shreds in a salad bowl with salt, pepper and tarragon vinegar; toss it; let it macerate for an hour. After this is done, remove any moisture the cabbage may have expressed and add a little vinegar, then oil. This salad is usually very tender and does not taste of raw cabbage: it resembles an excellent chicory salad.

Cabbage is cooked and eaten with various sorts of meats. (See *Partridge with cabbage, Veal, Mutton,* pages 514, 469, 485, above.) It is also served with beef, after being tossed in butter or dripping.

Brussels sprouts. — This excellent small variety of cabbage, the easy cultivation of which I describe in the *Gardening manual,* has the great merit of providing a delicate fresh vegetable all winter through. It is so frost-resistant that the rigours of the season will rarely deprive you of a supply. In Belgium, whence they originate – as might be seen by their name – they leave them exposed to the frost on purpose. They are prepared several ways.

After trimming each little sprout separately, throw them into salted boiling water; ten minutes is enough to cook them. When done, drain in a colander; then transfer them immediately to a saucepan with butter and a spoonful of flour; toss them, because stirring with a spoon will crush them;

then moisten with milk or stock; add salt, pepper and nutmeg; leave to stew gently for a few minutes while the sauce thickens; serve.

It is also enough to drain them for a few minutes the moment you have taken them out of the boiling water in which they were cooked, then add a knob of butter, to which you add salt and pepper. They are very good dressed simply like this. These cabbages are extremely tender and agree with all digestions: it is a suitable dish for invalids. When you have cooked a piece of meat in its own juice or in a daube, you can take some of the juice and add the sprouts (which you have already cooked). They are then served, like chicory or sorrel, under the meat.

In spring, when they are growing, the young stalks are excellent in soup, or blanched or chopped then prepared in ways I have described for hearted cabbage; they are no less good eaten like asparagus, with a white sauce, or with oil and vinegar.

Sauerkraut. — In the chapter *Concerning provisions* (page 309 above), I have already explained how to prepare sauerkraut. Here is how to cook it. After washing it in several waters, as soon as the sun is up you should put it in a pot (which it should fill) with some lard or a piece of backfat and place it before a gentle fire. It should have enough water so the sauerkraut is completely covered. Boil it so that the water barely moves; stir it frequently so that it does not stick to the side of the pot exposed to the heat. If it dries up, add more boiling water. If you have a few cervelas sausages, cook them with it. After seven or eight hours' cooking, draw it back from the heat; taste; if it does not seem fatty enough, put it in a saucepan with some good lard and whatever seasoning is needed if it is not tasty enough; add some stock or meat juice and let it reduce. Serve it with salt pork and cervelas sausages, which you place on top. Or serve it under a stew. If you wish to eat it with sausages, cook them in a frying-pan, then pass the sauerkraut through the same pan. Sauerkraut is also very good eaten cold as a salad, but with very little vinegar in the dressing. Cooked, it will keep for at least eight days in winter. The more it is reheated, the better it is. You can say that of many vegetables, but this is especially true of all sorts of cabbage.

Asparagus kale.[1] — See *Asparagus*.

Sea kale. — See *Asparagus*.

1.   In French: *Choux-asperges*. See the note under asparagus, below.

E. — Cauliflower.

Cauliflower with white sauce. — Some people do not separate the cauliflower heads into florets before cooking them; they run the risk of missing the caterpillars and snails that have slithered to the centre of the head: and more, the stalks, not being peeled, remain tough and are even sometimes inedible, though they have a flavour much to the taste of many, and will soften if peeled. You must therefore break each head into little bunches, and peel the stalks of each bunch by taking the skin off from the bottom of the stalk up towards the flower: it comes off easily in strips. Once that's done, throw the cauliflower into boiling salted water and keep an eye on it, because a few minutes' inattention will mean it is overcooked. The cooking water should be thrown away some distance from the house because it gives off a bad smell. However, some people use it to make a soup of bread, sorrel and some other vegetable, such as haricots for example; we have never tried this. When the cauliflower is sufficiently cooked, drain it in a colander; then take each floret and arrange them on a platter in the shape of a dome. You can also arrange them head down in a deep dish or a colander; when they are all in place, put the serving platter on the bowl of cauliflower and reverse it: the dome will appear in perfect shape. Pour over it either a white sauce to which you add, if you wish, a liaison and a splash of vinegar, or a velouté sauce, or a tomato sauce.

Cauliflower salad. — Cauliflower can also be eaten cold with oil and vinegar and some mixed herbs. Nutmeg goes well with cauliflower.

Cauliflower with jus. — Just blanch the cauliflower, then put it in a saucepan with a knob of butter and a spoonful of flour; toss lightly so that you do not break the florets; add enough *jus* so that it covers the cauliflower; add a little nutmeg; leave it to boil so that the *jus* reduces by about half. Serve.

Buttered cauliflower. — Cook the cauliflower a little, then put it in a saucepan with butter, salt and pepper; cover, leave to seethe. Serve.

Fried cauliflower. — Cook the cauliflower a little; drain it; put the florets on a dish with salt, pepper and a little vinegar; toss them; then dip them in a batter and throw them into the deep-frying pan.

Gratin of cauliflower. — When the cauliflower is cooked, place them in a heatproof dish; scatter small pats of butter over the florets as well as fine soft breadcrumbs; sprinkle with salt and pepper. Cover the dish with a

Dutch oven. To start with, the dish should be put on a gentle heat, let that cook gently until the cauliflower has taken on a golden tint. Serve in the same dish. This is one of the good ways to prepare cauliflower.

Cauliflower cheese. — Cook the cauliflower as usual; butter the bottom of a fireproof dish and scatter grated cheese over the butter; put in a layer of cauliflower with pepper and a little salt; put in another layer of cheese, then cauliflower, and so on, finishing with cheese. Sprinkle some stock or a little water; scatter dried breadcrumbs; put the fire above and below the dish, using the Dutch oven; let cook gently for a good half-hour, so that the top takes on a nice colour. Take out any fat; serve in the same dish. Some people mix a white sauce in with the cauliflower, but it almost always curdles, though it is not a bad idea. The grated cheese should consist of three-quarters Gruyère and one-quarter Parmesan.

F. — Artichokes.

I wrote earlier about how to preserve artichoke bottoms: they serve their purpose as an agreeable and flavoursome support to a multitude of dishes.

Artichokes with white sauce. — To cook artichokes, you cut the stalk very close to the bottom, then you remove all the small leaves that surround it of which not a single part is edible; then, with some scissors, you cut the ends off all the other leaves a few centimetres from their bottoms. If you wish the cooked artichokes to remain green, you must cook them in plenty of very salty water. When they are cooked, press them lightly to expel all the water and then remove the heart to get rid of the choke. That done, put the heart back where it was. You can dispense with this procedure. Serve them with a white sauce, a tomato sauce or a velouté sauce, or with oil and vinegar; or in fact cold with any sauce suggested for cold vegetables. The sauce is always served separately, in a sauce-boat. (See *Sauces.*)

Fried artichokes. — You can fry them with or without a batter. Trim them; blanch them; then cut them into eight. Take out the choke and the small leaves in the middle; dredge the sections in flour; fry them until they have taken on a nice colour. In another way, after seasoning with salt and pepper and tossing them in a little vinegar, dip the sections in a batter; plunge them into boiling deep-fat; when they have turned a nice colour, remove them and salt them again. Serve.

Artichokes à la barigoule.[1] — Trim them; cut the leaves very short; put some water in a saucepan or small cauldron, with salt, pepper, carrots, sliced onions and a few pieces of backfat or ham; let this boil for an hour; add the artichokes. When they are almost cooked, take them out of the stock; remove the hearts and chokes, and replace them with a stuffing of soft breadcrumbs, backfat, chopped parsley and chives, salt, pepper and all the tender parts of the hearts you took out earlier (which will add greatly to the goodness). If you wish to cook it for a fast-day, you can replace the backfat with oil or butter and mix two or three chopped or pounded hard-boiled egg yolks to the breadcrumbs. A little finely chopped garlic added to the stuffing heightens the flavour. Arrange the artichokes in a dish that will withstand a brisk flame; put some olive oil, or butter if you have none, in the bottom of the dish. So that the artichokes brown on both tops and bottoms, cover the dish with a Dutch oven with lots of embers on top. While this is doing, strain the stock in which they were cooked and reduce it over a high flame. When the artichokes are nicely browned, moisten them with the reduced stock; let it bubble up once or twice, not more. Serve with the sauce underneath: it should be thick.

This is an excellent dish which doesn't cost a great deal; it might almost take the place of a dish of meat.

Stuffed artichokes (entrée). — Prepare and cook the artichokes as you would to dress them à la barigoule, but fill the insides with a stuffing made from cooked or raw meat, the nibs of the leaves from the hearts, parsley, salt, pepper, and one or two eggs (whites and yolks) depending on how much stuffing there is. You can use either oil or butter on this occasion; you must also have the heat above and below the dish so that they brown. After taking them off the heat, moisten the bottom of the dish with the cooking liquor or meat juices. Serve the sauce beneath the artichokes. This is an extremely good dish which can do service as an entrée or be part of luncheon.

---

1. The usual presumption is a dish cooked with mushrooms, named for the Provençal word for a certain sort of mushroom. Although many nineteenth-century recipes include mushrooms, not all do. Nor does Mme Millet-Robinet.

G. — Chicory.[1]

This is eaten either raw, in a salad, or cooked, with or without meat.

To eat as a salad, you can add a small crust of bread rubbed with garlic, and mix in crushed cooked potatoes; made in this manner, this salad is more nourishing than usual and is very good; it needs quite a lot of vinegar.

To cook it, after stripping and washing it, you put it in a saucepan with plenty of salted water; you drain it well in a colander; when it is no more than warm, you squeeze it in clumps with your hands or in a cloth, then you chop it as finely as possible. Put some butter in a pan and fry some small pieces of the crumb of a loaf cut into triangles. When they are fried, if there is not enough butter left, add some more and heat it up (but do not brown). Put in the chicory with a spoonful of flour and stir; then heat it up. Moisten this with milk or stock, or with the sauce of whichever ragout you propose to serve the chicory under. Mix carefully, add salt, pepper and nutmeg. If the chicory has been finished with milk, you should let it simmer. Serve the croûtons on top.

H. — Lettuce.

This is eaten, like chicory, raw in salad, or cooked, dressed in a variety of ways.

Lettuce for fast-days. — Choose nice tight-headed lettuces; only keep the heads; cook them in salted water, then drain them; squeeze them gently. Put some butter and a spoonful of flour in a saucepan; mix well with water; add the lettuce; stir; add salt, pepper and a little nutmeg; cover; cook over a low heat. You can add a splash of vinegar, or some milk and a liaison.

Lettuce with jus. — Prepare it as before; blanch, then drain it; squeeze

1.   The French words for chicory are sometimes confusing. The common chicory, *Cichorium intybus*, is a green-leaved plant that is consumed as a salad or cooked, it looks something like a cos lettuce. The most common variety is the sugarloaf or *pain de sucre*. This may be called *chicorée* in France and is what Mme Millet-Robinet is writing about here. The Belgian witloof chicory, with tight heads of blanched white leaves (*C. intybus* var. *foliosum*) is often called *endive* in France, or *chicon* in northern France. The *chicorée frisée* and the *chicorée scarole* are the true endive. They are two varieties of *Cichorium endivia*, the first var. *crispum*, the second var. *latifolium*. These may be referred to as *scarole* or *frisée*, or as *endive* in the case of Mme Millet-Robinet. The red chicories and the *puntarelle* of Italy are varieties of *C. intybus*. The root which is used as a coffee-substitute is another variety (*sativum*) of the same species.

it. Finish cooking in *jus* or a good stock; thicken it with potato starch or a roux. You should let it boil uncovered so that the sauce evaporates somewhat, because the lettuce will give off some water, even though they have already been blanched and squeezed dry.

Lettuce with a velouté sauce. — Cooked in salted water, they can be served with a velouté sauce.

Stuffed lettuce. — Blanch them in salted water; open them up; place a ball of forcemeat or fish (see *Fishballs of carp*, page 532 above); lift the leaves back in place; tie up. Cook in a vegetable or meat stock. Three-quarters of an hour before serving, thicken the stock with a roux or potato starch.

Chicory-lettuce. — There is a type of lettuce, also called scarole or endive, the cultivation of which you will find described in the *Gardening manual*, which can in most cases, although not in all, replace the lettuce and be dressed in like manner. You need very little vinegar in a lettuce salad, unless you are adding hard-boiled eggs.

I. — Romaine lettuce.[1]

This is treated and served exactly as the tight-headed lettuce.

J. — Cardoons.

Cardoons au blanc.[2] — This excellent vegetable, which has much in common with artichoke, is usually expensive in the markets; but when you have a kitchen garden you can grow cardoons for very little cost. When the cardoon is fresh, in autumn or at the beginning of winter, it needs no more than a quarter of an hour to cook; but when it has been stored for a long time in the cellar, it needs sometimes three or four hours, sometimes even more; in this case the cardoon loses much of its flavour.

To prepare cardoons, you must reject any hollow stems and cut the rest in lengths of 10 centimetres. After scraping the sort of fluff that is found on the insides of the ribs, as well as stripping the sides and the strings on their

---

1.   Romaine lettuce (*Lactuca sativa* var. *longifolia*) is also known as cos lettuce.

2.   The culinary term *au blanc* means that something is either cooked in a white stock or in a liquor designed to prevent the discoloration of foods. 'A simple *blanc* is made by blending a little flour with water, then adding more water, with lemon juice or vinegar to acidulate it. Butter is another possible addition, to float on the surface and insulate the vegetables from the air' (Larousse). In fact, Mme Millet-Robinet seems to have omitted the essential acidulation, and she omits too the flour.

outsides, place them in a bowl with plenty of water as you go, to stop them blackening; you also remove all the skin from the root and the heart and cut these lengthwise into slices. Cook everything in salted boiling water when the cardoon is fresh, but it should be put into cold water when the cardoon is old – you can even add a little dripping or beef marrow, and not salt it until half-cooked. When it is done, lift out the pieces with a skimmer and arrange them on a dish, all lying the same way. Serve it on a white velouté sauce.

Cardoons with jus. — When they are cooked, as before, put them in some *jus* or a very good stock and thicken the sauce with a roux or with potato starch. Leave to simmer for at least an hour. If the sauce is too thin, reduce it by boiling without a cover; serve as soon as the sauce has reduced enough.

Buttered cardoons. — After cooking them, put them in a fireproof dish with butter, salt and pepper. Let them simmer for at least an hour.

Cardoon salad. — Cardoons cooked as described, and cold, are excellent with oil and vinegar.

Cardoons with cheese. — You can dress cardoons with Parmesan and Gruyère cheese as you did cauliflower, and fry them with or without a batter.

Chard stalks. — You cook and serve chard stalks in the same way as you do cardoons; but they are far from them in quality.

K. — Celery.

You can put celery in a salad, either on its own or with other vegetables. When it is on its own, mustard is most often added to the dressing; it is also served as an hors-d'oeuvre, with no dressing, in an hors-d'oeuvre dish. You must take off all the green stalks, and any that are full of holes, as well as all the skin from the root.

Celery with jus. — Its preparation is exactly the same as the cardoon. Often, after blanching it, you put it to cook round a chicken. (See *Capon or fattened chicken with celery,* page 503 above.)

Celery is also eaten with a white sauce, after cooking in plenty of water.

Celeriac. — There exists a variety of celery called celeriac, of which you only eat the root, which is large and round. You serve it cooked like ordinary celery, to which it is definitely to be preferred. You can put it in a dish in *jus*, between two heats, and leave it to cook until the sauce has thoroughly reduced; you glaze it with that sauce and serve it. You can also prepare it without meat by first cooking it in boiling salted water, then putting it to finish between two heats with butter, salt and pepper.

It is an excellent vegetable. It is to be regretted that its cultivation, although very straightforward, is not more generally adopted because it provides a precious resource.

L. — Sorrel.

Sorrel forcemeat. — Sorrel is really only worthwhile in spring and autumn: in summer, it has an acrid flavour; in winter, preserved sorrel is normally used. Choose the best sorrel, strip it carefully, removing the large central rib; wash with the greatest care in plenty of water, failing which particles of sand and soil will surely persist. Throw it in a cauldron and cook in plenty of salted water. After it has bubbled a few times, drain it. Put some butter in a saucepan; when it has melted, add the sorrel; stir it and add a spoonful of flour. You should stir it for a long time to make the sorrel a smooth purée. Moisten it with fresh milk and add salt and a little pepper. Thicken with one or two egg yolks mixed into a small amount of milk; don't let it boil once you have added the liaison. Serve halved hard-boiled eggs or poached eggs en chemise on this farce. Instead of milk, you can use stock or some of the juices from the meat under which the farce will be served. Sorrel is used in soups and in omelettes.

You can select large sorrel leaves, wipe them well without removing the stalks, dip them in a fairly stiff batter and fry them.

M. — Spinach.

Strip the leaves and clean them like sorrel; so that they remain green, which is essential, throw them in a cauldron containing a large quantity of salted boiling water and cook them over a high fire. When they are cooked, drain them; to get out all the water, squeeze small handfuls in a white cloth, then chop them very fine. As I have described for chicory, fry some small triangles of the crumb of a loaf in a saucepan. Remove them as soon as they have taken on a nice colour. Put the spinach in the butter together with a spoonful of flour; let it heat up while stirring; moisten with good milk; add sugar; leave to simmer for at least half an hour. Serve with the croûtons nicely arranged on top. The spinach should not be so thick or stiff that it holds itself together in a lump; it should be as soft as a purée. Instead of milk, you can moisten it with meat juices; but then you must not add sugar. Spinach is better reheated.

N. — *Asparagus.*

In some districts it is not standard practice to scrape the asparagus stalks before cooking them; this is mistaken, because this small action cleans them and removes a thin skin which toughens them. Take the asparagus by their tips and scrape the stalk with a knife; put them in cold water as you go. Then tie them into small bunches with the tips all in line and cut the bottoms so that they are all the same length. In the country, asparagus comes in all sizes, which is not the case when they are bought at market where they have been sorted; you have therefore to choose spears of approximately the same size to make up each small bundle. When dressing them, you put the most handsome ones on one side of the dish and the smallest on the other: thus making it easy for the mistress to hand the largest spears to the people she wishes to honour at the meal.

The youngest asparagus, whose tips are still violet, are far preferable to green asparagus.

Asparagus with white sauce. — The asparagus should cook in plenty of very salty boiling water, otherwise they will not be green, marring their quality.

When asparagus are fresh, they will cook in five minutes; watch them, therefore or the tips will drop off if cooked too long. To avoid this, you can put the bundles in vertically, the tips out of the water; this will only cover them as it bubbles in boiling, they will therefore cook less than the rest of the bundle. To arrange them on a dish, untie the bundles and place the tips towards the centre; arrange them in two piles, then drain off any water they may give off. They are usually eaten with a white sauce or a velouté sauce, or indeed with oil and vinegar, hot or cold. Serve the sauce in a boat.

Asparagus with meat stock (luncheon and entremets). — After cooking them as before, make the sauce with a very good meat *jus* or *coulis* to which you add a knob of butter, salt, pepper and a little potato starch to thicken the sauce. This is the best way to dress asparagus.

Asparagus in the style of petits pois. — You should choose greener spears than those you would eat with a sauce. Break all those parts of the stalks which offer no resistance into small pieces and put them in a saucepan with butter and a spoonful of flour. As the butter melts, you should stir. Once everything has mixed well, moisten with water and stir some more; then add a little sugar, pepper and salt and cook over a brisk fire. At the moment of service, thicken the sauce with an egg yolk, although many people dispense with this. Others boil the asparagus in water before finishing them.

Asparagus can be eaten cold, with oil and vinegar. Asparagus also can be cooked with scrambled eggs. After cooking them, cut them into small pieces and pass them through the butter before adding the eggs.

Asparagus kale.[1] — You treat these exactly as asparagus; they yield little to them in quality.

Sea kale. — The same preparation as asparagus.

O. — Hops.

The young shoots of hops are prepared in the same way as asparagus; it is an extremely delicate dish. In Belgium, they give them a preliminary boil in lightly salted water so as to rid them of the hop's natural bitterness.

P. — Cucumbers.

Cucumbers with a white sauce. — The white cucumber is preferable to others. To dress them with a white sauce, you split them in four and peel them carefully, as the skin is bitter, especially at the stalk and the flower end. Take out the seeds and cut the cucumbers in pieces a little bit longer than they are wide. Then throw them into salted boiling water. Cooking

---

1. Vilmorin-Andrieux, in *Les plantes potagères* (1904 ed.), makes reference to the *Chou branchu du Poitou*, a variety of kale still known in England as asparagus kale. Its young stalks can be eaten as asparagus and it is reported to be called 'poor man's asparagus' in Mme Millet-Robinet's home-turf of Poitou. Vilmorin-Andrieux comments: 'Dans tout l'Anjou et les pays avoisinants, on emploie couramment au printemps, les jeunes pousses de ces variétés, notamment du Chou branchu du Poitou, soit comme légumes, soit pour faire la soupe dite « *aux choux verts* ».' (In the whole of Anjou and neighbouring districts, particularly in spring, the young shoots of these varieties, notably the Chou branchu du Poitou, are used either as a vegetable or to make a soup called 'spring green soup'.)

will be complete in a few minutes. When cooked, they are put in a colander to drain; they must be covered so they stay hot. You pour the sauce over them when they are dished. You can, after peeling and preparing them as described, put them raw into a saucepan in which you have melted enough butter to dress them. Sauté them well in this butter; add a spoonful of flour and sauté them again; add a few spoonfuls of water, salt and pepper; leave to cook for an hour, uncovering the saucepan if the sauce is too thin (which will often happen as the cucumber gives off a great deal of water). The sauce should be very thick.

Cucumber à la maître-d'hôtel. — Once they are cooked and thoroughly drained, put them in a saucepan with some butter; sauté them and add chopped parsley, pepper, salt and a thread of vinegar. Serve.

Cucumber à la poulette. — When they are cooked, melt some butter; add the cucumber and a spoonful of flour; sauté the cucumber; moisten with milk; season with salt and pepper; thicken the sauce with egg yolks.

Cucumber with meat jus. — Melt some butter, add the cooked cucumber and a little flour; sauté them; moisten with meat *jus*; let the sauce thicken. Serve.

Stuffed cucumbers (entrée). — Peel them whole; [for each cucumber,] cut off one of the ends; empty it all the way to the bottom using a wooden spoon, then fill with a forcemeat made of backfat and raw or cooked meats that have been quite highly seasoned and which have been mixed with one or two eggs (depending on the quantity of stuffing). Replace the end you cut off and fix with a small wooden peg.

Once prepared in this fashion, cook them in water or, better, stock, with some ham, salt, pepper and a bouquet garni; once it has come up to the boil, take the cover off the vessel containing them because they will give off a lot of water which needs to evaporate. When they are half cooked, make a roux, which you moisten with the liquor, add it to the ragout and leave to finish cooking.

This is a very good way of using up leftovers of cooked or raw meats. You can serve vegetables around it.

Salad of raw cucumber (hors-d'oeuvre and luncheon). — Once you have peeled and emptied them, cut them across into extremely thin slices; then let them marinate for two hours with salt and vinegar; drain them thoroughly and dress them as you would a normal salad, but without mixed herbs.

Q. — Aubergines.

Stuffed aubergines. — They should not be fully ripe, otherwise their flesh will be woolly and the seeds hard.

Split them in two; take out some of the interior flesh and chop it coarsely; put this into a dish with salt; squeeze it. Make a stuffing with this flesh to which you add backfat, the crumb of a loaf soaked in stock or warm milk, and some mixed herbs such as chervil, a little tarragon and chives; season with salt and pepper; chop everything well together; then fill the aubergines with this stuffing and sprinkle over dried breadcrumbs. Arrange them in a fireproof dish, add butter or, better, good olive oil and put some heat above and below the dish. When they are cooked, serve. They should have browned a little.

You can add a little meat to the stuffing; or you can replace the backfat with butter and one or two eggs (the white and the yolk), then you have a dish for fast-days. A little garlic in the stuffing heightens the flavour.

Fried aubergines (entremets and luncheon). — Cut them into slices 1 centimetre thick. After dredging them in flour, fry them. Salt them as you take them out of the fat. This is a delicate dish.

R. — Tomatoes.

Stuffed tomatoes. — You should choose large ones, nicely shaped and a good red colour. After cutting off their tops, you remove the seeds, which are good for nothing, with a small spoon; then you take out some of the flesh, which you cook and reduce separately and which you add to a forcemeat similar to that for the aubergines (see the previous paragraph); you fill the tomatoes and you cook them in the same way as the aubergines. The tomato skins, when done like this, become pretty tough which lessens the value of this dish.

Tomatoes are used in a multitude of sauces. When you like their flavour, you can add them to almost every dark sauce, preparing them as you would for tomato sauce.

S. — Pumpkins, Squash, Melons (young).

These three fruits are excellent when harvested very young and consequently under-ripe and treated as if they were cucumbers. When you grow them yourself, you often need to cut back plants that have fruited too heavily and it would be frustrating not to know how to take advantage of this. You can also stuff them and prepare them like aubergines.

T. — Winter squash.[1]

Purée of winter squash with onion (entrée). — As I state in the *Gardening manual*, the best squash is that called Turk's turban. It is a small *giraumon*, but much sweeter and more delicate than all the varieties of so-called squash. Peel it, cut into chunks, and cook it covered with very little water and a little salt; drain it and sieve it. Then brown one or two finely sliced onions in butter; when they are nicely coloured, add the purée and leave to simmer a little.

Purée of winter squash with milk. — After cooking it as I have just described, and sieving it, put it in a saucepan in which you have melted and made very hot (but without browning) a knob of butter. Stir it and add a little flour. Moisten with milk and add sugar. Instead of flour, you can add an egg yolk mixed in some milk at the moment of service. Do not let it boil after this. This is a very delicate purée.

Vegetable marrow.[2] — The young fruits are prepared and eaten like the cucumber.

U. — Turnips.

The best turnips are small, firm and floury; the variety called *de Freneuse*, which possesses all these characteristics, is one of the most sought-after. However, we do not think it pointless to alert our readers to Scottish turnips, whose culinary qualities are little known, but which yield little to the Freneuses in point of quality, despite the size they sometimes achieve.

1. In French, *potiron*. The previous section touched on pumpkins, in French *citrouilles*. The distinction is often muddy. I have taken *potiron* to refer to *Cucurbita maxima*, not dissimilar to pumpkins, but less regular in shape, often flatter, and often of a darker hue – but there are countless cultivars. The classic pumpkin, such as may be made into lanterns, is *Cucurbita pepo*, the summer squash. The previous section (S) also referred to squashes as *giraumons*. These might be translated as butternut squashes, the principal type known in France was the Turk's bonnet squash. This is also *Cucurbita maxima*, although in the francophone West Indies, the *Cucurbita moschata* or *courge musquée* is referred to as *giraumon*.
2. In French, *Moelle végétale*. A synonym is *Courge à la moelle*. This is recognized as an English import. The term is mostly found in Canadian French; it is not listed in standard French dictionaries.

Rutabagas, or Swedish turnips [swedes], are also very good and very tender; they only take on a *strong*, and therefore unpleasant flavour when they do not grow vigorously enough. They are known in some regions as *roots*;[1] they can be kept until May; their flesh is white or yellow. Sometimes they weigh up to 3 kilograms.

Turnips à la poulette. — Cut them into pieces of rounded shape yet a touch longer than broad, and no bigger than a pigeon's egg. Melt a knob of butter; add the turnips with a spoonful of flour; sauté them, without letting them colour; moisten with water, milk or stock; add a little sugar; cook them gently, uncovered, to reduce the sauce. If the turnips are watery, add a liaison. Serve.

Turnips with a meat jus. — Choose larger turnips than in the preceding recipe; shape them like a pear, then blanch them in boiling water and put them in a saucepan, the pointed end uppermost. Moisten with stock or meat *jus*; add a little sugar; season with salt and pepper; cover with a circle of paper.[2] At the start, boil fairly briskly, then more gently. If the sauce is too thin, uncover and let it reduce a lot. To serve, dress the turnips on the dish the same way up they were placed in the saucepan.

Turnips with ham (luncheon). — Cut them a suitable size and shape; brown some pieces of ham or salt pork, then remove them from the saucepan. Brown the turnips in the fat; remove them as well. Make a roux, which you moisten with water or, better, with stock. Add the ham and let it cook for two hours. Then put in the turnips; leave to cook. Serve everything together. You can add a few potatoes; this is a family dish.

Sugared turnips. — Brown them lightly in some butter; moisten with water; add a little salt and quite a lot of sugar; leave to cook over a gentle heat. The sauce should be concentrated.

Sugared turnips au blanc. — Peel them and shape them nicely; put some butter in a saucepan; when it has melted, put in the turnips, with a spoonful of flour; stir; moisten with boiling water; season with enough sugar. You need very little salt. If the sauce is too thin, leave it to boil uncovered.

Turnips with white sauce. — After cooking them in a mixture of milk and water (which will serve as a soup to pour on bread), you pour a white sauce prepared with milk over them. (See *Purées*, page 576 below.)

1. In French, *raves*.
2. This, in modern culinary parlance, is called a cartouche.

V. — Carrots.

The best are the short carrot of Holland and England, the white Belgian carrot,[1] and the yellow carrot of Flanders. They should be smooth, nicely shaped and healthy. If carrots are clamped for winter storage, it is important that the collar of the root is removed because they can grow and take on a strong flavour if this precaution is omitted. The carrot is one of the most serviceable vegetables for cookery. It is used in a host of ragouts and soups.

Baby carrots in milk. — When carrots have got to a quarter or third of their full size, they can be used in a very delicate dish. After scraping them, sauté them in butter with a little flour; moisten with milk; add a little sugar – which can be omitted if the carrots are of a good variety; let it cook over a gentle heat. Serve. You can also eat fully-grown carrots cooked in this way, but often they have too strong a flavour. You should cut them into suitable chunks; you will need to increase the amount of sugar.

Carrots à la poulette. — When they are very young, scrape them and cut them into rounds on the thick side of medium. Put them in a saucepan with some butter. Sauté them. Add a little flour; add salt, a small quantity of pepper, half their depth in water, and a little sugar; cook over a gentle flame; the sauce should be concentrated; it is excellent. It is difficult to give you an idea of the quality of this simple dish without your tasting it.

Carrots à la maître-d'hôtel. — When they are young, cook them in water with salt and a little butter; then drain them. Afterwards, melt some butter; sauté the carrots in this with salt, pepper and chopped parsley. Serve. The cooking liquor can be used to make soup.

Carrots with ham (luncheon). — (See *Turnips with ham*.)

Pan-fried carrots. — Slice them and put them in a frying-pan with butter; brown them. Then add a spoonful of flour and moisten with water; put in salt, pepper and a little bay leaf. Serve. This is a pleasing dish when the carrots are tender.

Carrot salad. — Carrots that have been cooked in a pot-au-feu, a cabbage soup or in any ragout are extremely good as a salad. When they have cooled, crush them with a fork so they form small strands; then dress them like a normal salad; they need nothing else other than a little parsley or chervil. (See *Carrot purée*, page 575 below.)

---

1.   In French, *carotte blanche à collet vert*.

W. — Beetroot.

The best varieties for the kitchen are the white and yellow Silesian beets, or even the round yellow beet;[1] many other red and yellow varieties are also used. The red is not so good, but a mixture of red and yellow beetroot makes a nice decoration for a salad.

Beetroot is difficult to cook in the oven. You have to put it in with the bread and take it out long afterwards and even so any larger ones have to be buried in the ash from the embers that you have left in a corner of the oven or at its mouth. You can also boil the beetroot in water for four hours in advance of putting it in the oven with the bread – or just after if the oven is very hot – this is the best method, though it lessens some of the sweetness of the root.

To be more or less sure of having good beetroots, you should choose specimens of medium size (that is, weighing about 2 kilograms), nicely shaped (not forked), having a smooth skin, then wait until the end of October before eating them. Like carrots, you need to trim them off at their necks [where the green stalks sprout] before you store them, otherwise they start to grow and lose much of their quality.

Beetroot salad. — When they have been cooked in the oven, as I have described, you should peel and slice them thinly; add them to a salad, or even eat them on their own, but dressed like a salad.

Beetroot in milk or wine. — You use baked beetroot; slice them and sauté in butter with a spoonful of flour. Salt them; add a little sugar if the beets don't seem sweet enough; moisten with fresh milk; leave to simmer. Serve. You can add a few onions, cut into thin slices so they cook quickly.

You can replace the milk with wine.

Beetroot with wine. — Peel them raw and cut them into very thin slices. Put some butter into a saucepan, add the beetroot and three sliced onions; cover tightly; cook over a low flame. You can moisten this with a little boiling water so that the beetroot do not stick to the pan. Leave to cook for three hours. Then add a spoonful of flour, some salt and a little pepper; stir. Moisten with one or two glasses of good red wine; leave to simmer for

1. It was from the white Silesian fodder beet that Franz Karl Achard began to breed the sugar beet from 1784. The yellow globe beet is identified by Vilmorin-Andrieux, *Les Plantes potagères* (1883), as primarily a forage beet, known in England as the yellow globe mangold.

two hours. Serve. This is an extremely good dish, which is even better when reheated. You can cut the beetroot into very thin slices indeed and fill an earthenware pot with them, pressing them down as you do so. Then fill with water to cover and leave to cook over a low heat for four or five hours; season with salt halfway through cooking. When the water evaporates, top up with boiling water. As the beetroot are pressed down together, you will need very little water; when they are cooked there will be hardly any left. You dress them at the end with milk or wine; they have a vanilla flavour, particularly when dressed with milk.

This vegetable is not cooked widely enough. It is hardly ever eaten in a salad; but you deprive yourself of a really useful winter resource, at the very moment that the supply of vegetables is restricted.

X. — Salsify and scorzonera.

Salsify are white and can be eaten in the same year that they were sown. Scorzonera have a black skin and are only good to eat in their second or third year, sometimes their fourth; they are larger and more tender than salsify.[1]

Salsify with sauce. — Scrape them and throw them into some cold water mixed with a little vinegar to stop them browning; cut them into suitable lengths and cook them in plenty of boiling salted water. Make a white sauce with water or, which would be better, with milk, or a tomato sauce, and pour it over them. The cooking liquor from salsify makes good soups for fast-days.

Salsify à la poulette. — Scrape them and wash them as in the previous recipe. Put a knob of butter and a spoonful of flour in a saucepan; stir. Moisten with water; stir again. When the sauce has thickened, add the salsify, salt and pepper. When they are cooked, add a liaison. Serve.

Salsify with meat jus. — Make a roux; moisten it with stock; add a bay leaf; add the raw or cooked salsify to this sauce; if the latter, leave to simmer for an hour. You can simply cook the salsify in meat *jus* or stock, which you let reduce a great deal. You colour this with caramel if the sauce is too pale.

---

1. Salsify (*Tragopogon porrifolius*) is a biennial and scorzonera (*Scorzonera hispanica*) a perennial. Both can be eaten in their first year of growth, but the scorzonera will grow larger in time and be therefore more useful to the cook.

Fried salsify. — After cooking them in boiling salted water, leave them to cool; then fry them. Serve really hot, sprinkled with salt. You can also dip them in a very thin batter before putting them in the fat.

Y. — Potatoes.

This precious vegetable may be dressed in the greatest number of ways; it agrees with the most delicate of digestions. The diverse and innumerable varieties of potato each possess particular qualities. Round ones break up easily in cooking; flat ones, shaped like a parrot's beak and variously coloured, hold together better even though they are very easy to mash; long, red ones rarely break up but are difficult to mash. You will find the article *Potato* in the *Gardening manual* indicates the best varieties; yellow ones are more floury, and red ones are often bitter. In the following recipes, I indicate the most suitable variety for each suggestion.

Sound potatoes have few eyes, are of medium size, and their skin is chapped. You should guard against keeping them anywhere too light; on the contrary, they should be deprived as far as possible of light and air. They can lose condition in four or five days. When stored in disregard of the conditions I advise they go green and take on a bitter taste which renders them inedible. If they get frosted, and you notice in time, they should be eaten straightaway, otherwise they will be lost. Potatoes that are cooked and then cooled acquire a strong flavour of soap which is really quite unpleasant; however, I am at pains to suggest ways of dressing them which allow you to eat them cold or reheated.

When you wish to avoid potatoes breaking up while cooking, you must cut them into small pieces; cook them whole if you seek the opposite effect.

Smothered potatoes. — In the lower part of a cast-iron cooking pot, arrange small pieces of wood in a criss-cross; they should be of a length that they do not rest on the actual bottom; fill with water to the point where they rest. Carefully wash the potatoes in plenty of water to rid them of all the soil still clinging to them, then place them on this sort of trellis. Salt them and cover with an old white cloth, then with the pot lid. Hang this on the pot-hook over a fire that is not burning too high. In about half an hour the potatoes will be perfectly steamed or smothered, retaining all of their goodness. To present them at table, cover them with a napkin. They can stand in for bread, or will eat nicely with butter and a little salt. Each diner peels them at the moment of consumption. This is an excellent way to serve potatoes at luncheon. If you make a habit of eating smothered potatoes, instead of the small pieces of wood I mentioned, you should have a double-bottom of metal lattice work made up to put in the pot under the potatoes. This way of cooking potatoes is better than all the others when they are intended to be dressed with some sort of sauce. Under no circumstances should they be cooked with water covering them; it is enough that the pot is half filled; the water will rise as high as the potatoes when it boils.

In Belgium and Holland, where they eat more potatoes than bread, they are never cooked with their skins still on; they are always peeled, cut into large chunks and cooked in plenty of heavily salted water.

Potato casserole (luncheon).[1] — A *cocotte* is a cast-iron saucepan with three feet and a tight-fitting lid on which you can place burning embers. They exist in earthenware, but to cook potatoes you should only use cast iron. Wash the potatoes, peel them and wipe them well. (You should never wash potatoes once they are peeled.) Place them in the casserole, sprinkling each layer with salt. When the casserole is full, cover it and put some embers on the lid. Make a fire on the hearth in the corner of the fireplace and place the casserole on it. Watch the fire, because it is on the floor it can easily go out. In an hour at the most, if you are cooking a lot of potatoes, they will be cooked and partly grilled, as if they had been cooked in the embers, but because they have been peeled they are nicer and much, much cleaner. Serve them accompanied by fresh butter; many people prefer these to smothered potatoes. Every variety of potato is suitable for these two ways of cooking them, provided that they are floury and not bitter. However, the best variety for this purpose is the long, flat, ash-leaved kidney.[2]

Potatoes à la maître-d'hôtel (entremets). — To prepare them in this fashion you need red, parrot's beaks or ash-leaved potatoes. After you have cooked them, peel them, slice them and leave them to cool a little. Then put them in a saucepan with butter, add salt and pepper. Let the butter

---

1. In French, *à la cocotte*.
2. The most famous English variety of the ash-leaved kidney was Myatt's, introduced in 1804, but made much of in the 1830s as especially prolific. It is described as a second early, 'long, yellowish and waxy'. Vilmorin-Andrieux has it in French as *Pomme de terre royale* or, in Picardy, *Pomme de terre cornichon*.

melt; sauté the potatoes; add chopped parsley; some people add a thread of vinegar. Serve. You can also heat the butter and stew the potatoes gently; they will brown somewhat and are, in my opinion, much nicer, but they will break up to some extent. If you do this, dispense with the vinegar.

Potatoes English-style (entremets). — Prepare them as before, but add neither parsley, nor spring onion, nor vinegar.

Potatoes with white sauce (entremets). — The variety is not important here. Steam them; peel them and cut them in two; salt them and put them on the grill. When they are toasted enough, lay them out on a dish in a seemly manner. Pour over them a white sauce made with milk or a velouté sauce.

Potatoes à la poulette. — Put a knob of butter in a saucepan; when it has melted, add a spoonful of flour; stir; mix with fresh milk; add nutmeg, salt, a little pepper; stir until the sauce begins to boil. Peel the cooked potatoes; slice them; put them in this sauce; let it simmer for half an hour; add a liaison. Serve.

Potatoes with backfat (luncheon). — Cut some backfat into small pieces; melt it over the heat and add a spoonful of flour; stir; moisten with water; add a little salt, pepper, a bouquet garni and a little garlic. When the sauce boils, add the potatoes – peeled, wiped and cut into chunks. Serve very hot. Any variety of potato can be dressed like this.

Potatoes with a roux (luncheon). — Make a roux with butter; moisten with water; add salt, pepper, a bouquet garni and a little garlic; put into this sauce some potatoes prepared in the same way as above.

Stewed potatoes (entremets and luncheon). — Cook some red potatoes or those called parrot's beak; peel them and slice them. Put some butter in a saucepan with pepper, salt, chopped parsley and chives and a little flour; stir; moisten with equal parts meat or vegetable stock and red wine; add the potatoes. Let them simmer for half an hour. Serve.

Potatoes in water (luncheon). — Put some uncooked potatoes cut into chunks into a pot filled with salt water placed before the fire; add two or three sliced onions, salt, pepper and bay leaf. When they are almost cooked, add a knob of butter, or some chicken fat or lard. Give the potatoes time to absorb this fat.

Potatoes with milk. — After peeling them and cutting them into chunks, cook them in a saucepan with salt, a little nutmeg and enough milk to cover them. You can add a liaison to this.

If you cook whole potatoes like this, they will partly break up; before serving, therefore, you should smash any other parts that have not done so. You can add sugar. The round potato is the variety best to cook in milk.

There is another way of preparing potatoes with milk. Cook, peel and slice the potatoes; put some butter in a saucepan. When it has completely melted and is hot, without browning, add the potatoes; sauté them; add a spoonful of flour; sauté them again; moisten with milk, salt them and leave them to simmer for half an hour, stirring them gently from time to time. You can add a liaison, but you must not let it boil or it will curdle. You can sweeten potatoes cooked the previous two ways.

Buttered potatoes. — This is the best way to prepare potatoes when they are still new and small. As the skin comes off easily, scrape them and carefully wipe them; then put them into a saucepan on a brisk fire with a knob of butter. You should not cover them. Turn them over so that they colour evenly and salt them at the moment of serving.

When the potatoes are very large, you cut them into chunks and turn them to a potato shape.

Potatoes cooked in this way can be served on their own, or under beefsteaks, cutlets, with poultry or with beef. Sprinkled with sugar after cooking, they are a very delicate entremets.

Potatoes with oil. — Peel some large potatoes and cut them into little cubes of about 1 centimetre. Put some olive oil or fresh walnut oil in a pan; when it is hot, throw in the potatoes; stir from time to time; let them brown; salt them. Serve. Potatoes fried like this are extremely good and, what's more, they are most attractive.

Potato salad. — The red potato is the best for salad. Cook the potatoes smothered; peel and slice them, then place them in a salad bowl while still hot. Add three or four spoonfuls of water, mixed herbs or parsley. Dress them like a salad; but you will need much more vinegar. You can add potatoes to every sort of salad.

Potatoes are used in a host of ragouts; in cakes, pancakes, etc.; cooked in the embers of the oven or on the hearth, they are excellent with butter; but I believe they are best cooked in a casserole [à la cocotte] as I have already indicated.

Z. — Jerusalem artichokes.

This root, which never freezes, is a useful winter resource. After washing it well to get rid of the soil which adheres to the knobbles which cover it, peel and wipe it. You can use it in chicken fricassees, matelotes and several coloured sauces in place of artichoke bottoms, which it resembles in taste.

Jerusalem artichoke gratin. — After washing, peeling and wiping them, cut them into thick slices and put them into a fireproof dish with butter, chopped mixed herbs, salt and pepper. Moisten with stock or water, and scatter dried breadcrumbs over the top. Put a medium heat above and beneath the dish and leave to cook gently for an hour. Serve them in the dish in which they were cooked.

Fried Jerusalem artichokes. — Cut them into thick slices and fry them like potatoes; you can dredge them with flour or dip them in a thin batter before deep-frying them.

Jerusalem artichokes cooked in the embers. — Jerusalem artichokes cooked in the embers and eaten with butter taste very pleasant. You can also cook them in boiling salted water, leave them to cool and eat them with oil and vinegar.

3. — Dried vegetables.
A. — Beans.

Dried beans. — Put them in a saucepan with *cold* water; they will need four to six hours' cooking, depending on the water or the time that has elapsed since the beans you are using were harvested. Two-year-old beans take a lot longer to cook than those from the previous year. All dried beans are excellent dressed with the fat either from poultry or from roast fresh pork. You treat them as if they were fresh podded beans but you must never fry them.

Stewed red beans. — The best variety of bean for this dish is the small Swiss flat haricot, very red, with a black and white eye. Put together in a pot the beans, water, a piece of salt pork belly and some onions. When they are cooked, put a knob of butter in a saucepan; let it heat; add the beans; if they have not broken up at all, add a little flour; moisten with red wine; season with salt and pepper; leave to simmer. Serve with backfat.

Beans à la poitevine. — Put some butter and finely sliced onions in a frying-pan; let the onions cook and brown somewhat; add the beans after they have been cooked as in the previous recipes; mix everything; season with salt and pepper; moisten with a little water; let it simmer. Serve. It is a somewhat coarse dish but very good however.

The cooking liquor from dried beans greatly improves sauces made with it; it can also be added to all soups.

B. — Lentils.

The best are large and an attractive golden colour; their skin is perfectly smooth. There are some which have small greenish lines, they are just as good. Those called *à la reine*, smaller, are more delicate.[1] Lentils are only available for consumption as a dried vegetable; they should be put into cold water to cook. To make them taste better, you can add a piece of salt pork. They will need three or four hours of cooking. The cooking liquor is put to the same sort of use as bean liquor.

When the lentils have been cooked and drained, put a knob of butter into a saucepan; when it is hot, add the lentils with a spoonful of flour; stir; moisten with milk or with meat stock. You can replace the butter with poultry fat or fat from roast fresh pork.

Lentil salad. — This is one of the best ways to treat them. You should add mixed herbs, salt, pepper, oil and vinegar.

Lentils à la poitevine. — See *Beans à la poitevine*.

Purée of lentils. — See *Purées*.

---

1. The first variety of lentil Mme Millet-Robinet mentions is probably the *lentille large blonde*, the most widely cultivated in France. Those she describes as *à la reine* are either the *lentillon de Mars* or the *lentillon d'hiver* (Vilmorin-Andrieux, *Les Plantes potagères*, 1883).

CHAPTER XIV

PURÉES

As purées can be served as a garnish under either meats or eggs, or as dishes in their own right in the entremets, I have devoted a separate chapter to them.

1. — Green split pea purée.

Sort and wash some dried green split peas; put them with some cold water in a pot in front of the fire. A litre of them will provide you with one very large dish or two normal-sized dishes. When the peas start to boil, add a carrot, two onions and a turnip and let them cook before a low fire for at least four hours; season with salt when the cooking is halfway through; pull the pot back from the fire and leave it for a moment so that the purée settles; decant. The stock can be used to prepare various soups. Then sieve the purée, mashing the vegetables. Put some butter or fat into a saucepan; fry a few thin slices of bread cut into small triangles; when they are nicely golden, take them out and reserve them. Add some more butter or fat if there is insufficient remaining for the purée; add the purée; stir well to mix with the dressing; add pepper. If the purée is too thick and you have finished it with butter, you can thin it down with milk or some of the stock you have reserved; if you used fat, you thin it with that same stock, or even with meat stock, or indeed a meat *jus*. Let it boil for a quarter of an hour; serve with the croûtons around the dish.

2. — Yellow split pea purée.

As they take longer to cook than green split peas, they need to boil for two more hours; a little fat or backfat helps their cooking. Chickpeas are employed more often than ordinary peas for this purpose. During the cooking, you put a tightly tied linen bag full of ash into the pot. (See *Meatless stock*.) You finish this purée like the one before.

3. — Purée of large fresh peas.

When the water is bubbling nicely, throw in the peas; salt them and add just one onion. When the peas are thoroughly cooked, leave them to rest [and settle]; [strain off and] reserve the stock: it is excellent and very suitable for making several soups; sieve the peas; finish them with butter. If this purée is not thick enough, you can add an egg as a liaison.

4. — Broad bean purée.

Choose large beans, but not those which have turned yellow; skin them and throw them into boiling water which you have quite strongly salted before adding the beans so that they keep their green; add a bunch of parsley to which you can add a few sprigs of savory, neatly tied so that it doesn't come apart. When the beans are cooked, leave them to settle; decant the stock; sieve them and finish them like the other purées. Bean stock has quite a strong flavour; you will need to add water to it, especially if you have used savory. It is most suitable for herb soup.

5. — Haricot bean purée.

You make this like the dried green pea purée; but you add neither carrots, onions, nor turnips, which doesn't stop the stock from being very good. For preference, you use red or coloured haricots.

6. — Lentil purée.

You make this like the split pea purée, but without carrots, turnips or onions. In washing through the skins that remain in the sieve with the cooking liquor, this will pick up enough of the purée to make good onion or rice soups.

7. — Carrot purée.

You can only make a purée with carrots that do not have too strong a taste, which is the hallmark of some varieties. In a pot before the fire, you cook them cut in chunks, covered with water, with a little butter and an onion. When they are thoroughly cooked, pour them into a colander and drain them, then sieve them. You finish this purée like the others, but you add a spoonful of flour just when you stir them into the hot butter. The stock will serve for a soup.

8. — Onion purée.

Prepare it like the carrot purée.

9. — Turnip purée.

Yellow and white Scottish turnips, Freneuse turnip and the Limousin root[1] can all be served as a purée, which is prepared like the carrot purée.

10. — Celeriac purée.

The celeriac is naturally pasty and very suitable for making an excellent purée. Peel it and cook it in *plenty* of boiling, salted water. Crush it and sieve it, using the pestle for purées. Finish like the other purées; it will need a little flour. Adding some stock or meat *jus* makes this an excellent purée.

11. — Pumpkin purée.

Cook the pumpkin as if you were making soup with it, then drain it and dress it as if it were a normal purée. You can add a spoonful of flour and some milk, then some sugar: this will make this purée a very delicate dish.

Pumpkin purée with onion. — Fry an onion in butter; when it has coloured nicely, add a little flour, the pumpkin, salt and pepper; it is very good.

12. — Potato purée.

Cook as smothered potatoes some large and floury potatoes; peel them; crush them while they are still very hot, one by one with a fork in a plate. Put some butter in a saucepan; when it is hot, add the purée; stir; thin with stock, milk or water; add a little pepper. You can sweeten this purée.

13. — Purée of chestnuts and candied chestnuts.

Prepare them like the potato purée.

1.   In French, *la rave limousine*, also known as the *rabe de Sologne* and sometimes *la rabioule* (although that can also be a Provençal word for cabbage). It is usually likened to an English turnip by French gardening writers. See the note above (page 429) about turnip varieties.

CHAPTER XV

FLOURS AND PASTA

1. — Pancakes.

Put a litre of flour into a bowl; break six eggs into the centre; add a spoonful of olive oil, two spoonfuls of eau-de-vie, two spoonfuls of orange flower water or grated lemon zest, and a little salt; mix together; thin it down with half milk, half water, while stirring briskly, until the batter is like a thin gruel; leave it to rise for three hours. To make it lighter, you can hold back two of the egg whites, whisk them to a snow and mix them into the batter at the moment you make the pancakes. Put butter or lard the size of a walnut, or a half-spoonful of oil, into a pan on a brisk flame; when the fat you have chosen is thoroughly hot, use a large spoon to pour in enough batter to cover the bottom of the pan with the thinnest of layers. When this layer has taken nicely, give a sharp blow to the pan handle to toss the pancake and turn it over to cook on the other side. Sprinkle with sugar and serve promptly.

2. — Dry pancakes.[1]

Make the dough in the morning for the evening or at the crack of

[1] The original title of this recipe is *Crêpes sèches*. Were this in Brittany, a *crêpe sèche* would be a plain pancake, with no garnish, perhaps cooked longer than a normal *crêpe*, and dunked in buttermilk on consumption. In the later 1873 edition, Mme Millet-Robinet gives an alternative name for the dish: *Rousseroles. Rousserolle* is the French for a Eurasian warbler and it has not been easy to find a culinary use of the word. However, in one instance located, a synonym was suggested: *roussette. Roussette* may be a name of a variety of grape, a dogfish (rock salmon to the English fish and chip trade), a fruit bat or a flying fox, but it is also a regional name for a beignet such as the *bugne* of Lyons, the *merveille* of Gascony, and the *oreillette* of Languedoc and Provence. The recipe for *roussette* in *Larousse gastronomique* has many similarities with the one here, although Mme Millet-Robinet's is plainer.

dawn for luncheon. Break six eggs into a well you have made in a litre of flour tipped onto a pastry board; add about 30 grams of butter and the same amount of leaven; season with salt. Begin to mix it, then add enough water to wet the flour and make a very stiff dough; then place this in a dish, covered with a cloth, in a warm place, so that it rises. When you wish to make the pancakes, take a piece of this dough and push it out on the pastry board with a rolling-pin until it is about one centimetre thick. Dust it with flour and make it long, oval, round – the shape does not really matter – or cut it into leaf-shapes if you have a pastry-cutter of the right sort. If the dough is too soft, you can dust it with a little flour, because it really must be firm. Heat up the deep fat; throw in these leaves of dough; let them take on a nice colour; drain them. Serve in a heap; dusted with sugar. In the fat, the dough will puff up and take on the most unexpected shapes. These pancakes are extremely good and less heavy than the first recipe; you can serve them with tea and eat them hot or cold.

3. — Noodles (a German dish).[1]

Place half a litre of flour in a mound on a pastry board, make a depression in the centre; break three eggs into it; mix well, absorbing as much flour as you can so as to obtain a fairly stiff dough. Knead it quickly, then let it rest for a moment. Tear off a piece of dough as large as an egg; dust the board with flour and roll out the dough to a thickness of 1 millimetre at the most; stretch this out over the back of a chair that you have protected with a white cloth; it will look like a piece of buffalo skin. Repeat this process. Let it dry, but not so much that the dough becomes brittle. Roll up these sheets of dough and cut them into ribbons 4 or 5 millimetres wide; unroll them as you go, spread them out, and leave them to dry for an hour. In a cauldron, boil some fairly salty water; when it comes to the boil, add the noodles, and let them cook in the water for half an hour; take them out and drain them in a colander. Heat some butter or fat in a pan, add the noodles and season with salt and pepper. Shake the pan from time to time, but it is good if some parts of the noodles brown. Serve.

You can cook sausages, dress the noodles with their fat, then serve the sausages on the noodles; this is even better.

1.   Mme Millet-Robinet has called this dish *Noudles*. The German word she is reflecting is *Nudeln*.

Noodles as macaroni. — You can perfectly well replace macaroni by noodles; macaroni is by no means superior.

You can also eat them as a salad; dress them as if they were a normal salad, but while they are still hot.

4. — Macaroni.

With this pasta, quality is an important factor. French macaroni is markedly inferior to Italian. You can find this in some commercial houses. It is no more expensive than the French.

Macaroni with meat stock (entremets). — Put a litre of stock for 500 grams of macaroni on the heat; the moment the stock comes to the boil, add the macaroni with a little pepper; cover; leave it to cook over a low heat. When the pasta has absorbed all the stock and seems very soft, mix in 200 grams of good Gruyère cheese, 125 grams of grated Parmesan and a knob of butter; shake the pan to combine it all together: if you use a spoon, you will break the macaroni. Gourmets add 375 grams of cheese and, when that has entirely melted, serve forth the macaroni; but usually it is left longer to form a crust. To do this, put some butter in a fireproof dish; pour in the macaroni; mix in the cheese as I have explained; scatter grated cheese and dried breadcrumbs over the top; leave it to simmer for half an hour on a low heat, having ensured it's covered with a lid and hot embers. Serve in the same dish.

Macaroni for fast-days (entremets). — You prepare this exactly as macaroni with meat stock, only you cook the pasta in water or, better, milk.

Timbale of macaroni. — Cook the pasta and dress it as in the previous recipes. Make some pastry containing 125 grams of flour, 100 grams of butter, an egg yolk – which you break into the centre of the flour after you have first added the butter – and half a glass of water. Knead it all together; flatten it out; then knead again; roll out the pastry to the thickness of half a centimetre. Trim the pastry to a circle the same size as the bottom of the tin you are using for the macaroni; grease the bottom and sides of the tin with butter; put the circle of pastry in the bottom, then line the sides with the pastry you have left; damp the joints with water to bring them together. Pour the macaroni into the tin; put this in red-hot embers on the fire and put a lid with its own embers on the top; keep the fire lively so that the pastry colours up. Serve by turning it out onto a dish. When the pastry is thoroughly cooked, this sort of cake holds together well and makes a very attractive entremets. A little time and care: that's all it needs. You can make the pastry several hours in advance.

5. — Maize flour bouillie, or Gaudes.[1]

This excellent flour has so pleasing a taste that when made into a porridge, with no extra flavouring, it is a very fine dish. You moisten it in the way I explain on page 584 for a *bouillie* made with ordinary flour; but you will need three times the quantity of flour, because it only thickens a little. You can add sugar, although that is by no means necessary. You must let it cook over a low heat for at least two hours; and the crust on the bottom of the pan is delicious. You should add a little salt, even when you sweeten it.

You can make excellent soups with maize flour, either with a meat stock, or with water and butter, with or without the addition of milk.

6. — Buckwheat flour or sarrasin.[2]

Buckwheat can be grown successfully in almost every part of France; however the use of its flour is not generally known, even though it lends itself to many excellent recipes; people in districts where it is common eat it with pleasure. It has the double advantage of being very digestible as well as inexpensive. I urge the mistress of the house to introduce the cultivation of buckwheat on her farm, and the use of its flour.

Groux.[3] — This is the name given in Brittany to a buckwheat-flour *bouillie* made with water. To obtain a thick *bouillie*, you must mix water

1. As defined by *Larousse gastronomique*, *gaudes* is the word used in the Franche-Comté and Burgundy for a porridge of maize flour not dissimilar to polenta.
2. In French, buckwheat is also called *blé noir*, or sometimes *froment noir*. The name *sarrasin* means 'saracen corn', like the Italian *grano saraceno*. Although the route of buckwheat into France was from Russia and the east via Germany, the name seems to indicate early adopters deemed it to come from Muslim Spain, where a word derived from Arabic denoted the grain.
3. The French word *gruau* means either groats or oatmeal, or a gruel made from such. The French *bouillie* is usually defined as a mixture of flour (of whatever nature) and milk or other liquid boiled together to a certain consistency. This might be a pap as is made for infants, or a thicker substance which we might describe as porridge, although in Brittany particularly, the *bouillie* may often be stiffer than an English porridge. I have usually left the word *bouillie* untranslated as it should not be

into the flour. You will need three times as much buckwheat flour as wheat flour. This how you proceed. Put the flour in a saucepan and begin to mix it with cold water. When all the flour is wetted and has formed a thick paste without lumps, you finish by mixing with boiling water. Then you place it over a decent fire and stir. After a few moments, the porridge will turn lumpy, but soon, as you continue to smooth and stir, it will form a smooth and thick paste. Season with salt and damp the fire so that it boils gently for an hour. From time to time you should stir it. This sort of cooked porridge, or *groux*, is eaten with cold milk, which each guest adds to his plate of *groux*, taking a little of the porridge and some milk with each spoonful. *Groux* is served at luncheon, instead of soup. You can put a knob of fresh butter in the middle of the *groux*: this would replace the milk; you can even sweeten the milk.

Buckwheat pancakes.[1] — To make these, you must have a cast-iron *galette-maker*[2] with a handle. A galette-maker is a form of frying-pan without a raised edge, or an edge that is very small indeed. When it has no feet, you place it on a trivet. You should add to the cast-iron handle a piece of wood long enough to be fixed in place with wire so that you don't burn yourself when handling the metal. You will also need to equip yourself with a thin iron palette knife, looking like a large kitchen knife but with a rounded end, with a blade 6 or 7 centimetres wide and 30 to 33 centimetres long, it too having a handle; and finally a small wooden stick round the end of which you wind a little white linen to form a sort of brush, about the size of a finger.

Once you have equipped yourself with all these tools, you prepare the batter which will be made into galettes in the following manner. Put a litre of flour into a bowl; break four eggs into the centre; mix them into the flour, adding milk, so that you end up with a batter that looks like one you would use for deep-frying or like a very thin porridge. Season with salt. You can leave out the eggs; the galettes will be a little less delicate, but still good.

---

confused with the English porridge. The Scots oatmeal porridge is not the invariable French form, which is made with a more finely ground flour and hardly ever of oatmeal. The masculine form *bouilli* is used in the kitchen to denote boiled meat, particularly beef.

1. Mme Millet-Robinet here gives two words for the same thing: *galettes ou crêpes de sarrasin. Galette* is the Breton term for these buckwheat pancakes.

2. The French word is *galettoire*.

Put the galette-pan on the fire; when it is thoroughly heated, take a knob of butter about the size of half a walnut and spread it over the pan using your wooden 'brush'. Straightaway, use a ladle to pour a generous-enough spoonful of batter so that it covers the whole surface of the pan in a very thin layer as you turn it this way and that. Let it cook; lift it with the palette-knife to check that it has coloured nicely. When you are satisfied, slip the palette-knife smartly beneath the galette; lift it up and turn it top to bottom. Let the other side cook. Serve. Some gourmets spread a bit of fresh butter on the galette before eating it; others add grated sugar as well. You need to eat galettes as they are cooked. As soon as one is lifted out of the pan, so you spread more butter, then more batter, and you carry on until there is no more batter left. The fire should be very moderate, above all on the handle side of the pan; in the middle it really doesn't need much.

These galettes are excellent, and much less heavy than ordinary pancakes. Often, the first to come off the pan is a failure; but usually the second is successful; subsequent ones present no problem; all this is a matter of practice; but you must keep the fire burning correctly, and particularly know where to direct it to best advantage to give the galette an even, handsome colour.

When it is only family at table, each galette, as it comes from the pan, is split into three or four portions so that as many people as possible can be satisfied. Although little-known in much of France, it is a luncheon dish that deserves to be more popular.

You can also leave galettes to cool, cut them into pretty shapes with a pastry-cutter, then fry them in butter. This is an excellent entremets, which looks most attractive. Dust the pieces with sugar as they come from the pan.

7. — Waffles (dessert and tea).

You can only make waffles in a cast-iron mould made for the purpose.

Put 250 grams of flour into an earthenware terrine; make a well in the middle; add a pinch of salt, a spoonful of eau-de-vie, a spoonful of olive oil, three eggs (the white and the yolk); mix together with a wooden spoon, leaving not a single lump. Let this down with milk until the batter is the consistency of a thin gruel. Prepare this batter two hours in advance. Heat the waffle-iron evenly on both sides over a clear fire (no smoke); once hot, but not glowing, grease the inside with a brush dipped in oil or melted butter. Fill the iron with batter, using a spoon that holds the quantity you need; put the iron back into the fire for two minutes, one side as long as the other. Stand the iron up; open it and take out the waffle with the tip of a knife-blade; dust with sugar. With a little practice, you will soon get to know how hot the iron needs to be.

8. — Fritters.[1]

Mix thoroughly together about 60 grams of flour, 30 grams of butter and as much sugar; add a little ground cinnamon; put everything on a table and break an egg into it. Once the dough is well worked, roll it out, then cut it up, either into ribbons or with a pastry-cutter. Fry this.

This dough is dry and can be eaten cold.

Here is another way. Put three whole eggs plus five yolks and 500 grams of sugar, 500 grams of flour and 125 grams of fresh butter into an earthenware terrine; you should make sure you have softened the butter to make it easier to work the dough, which should be thin and light and which you leave to rest overnight. Flavour it with whichever ingredient seems to you the most pleasing. The next day, pass this dough through some beaten egg whites, then dredge it with dried breadcrumbs; cut it into little fish shapes and fry it.

Finally, you can also make excellent fritters in the following manner. Beat four eggs with four spoonfuls of fresh cream, two spoonfuls of orange flower water, sufficient sugar and 30 grams of butter. Add as much flour as is needed to make a dough soft enough to roll easily. After rolling it out and folding it over a first time, roll it out thinly again and cut it into pretty shapes. Fry them.

---

1.   The title of this recipe is *Pâte frite. Pâte à frire* is batter for frying. This *pâte*, however, is stiffer than a batter.

CHAPTER XVI

SWEET DISHES[1]

There is an infinity of sweet dishes; I will not discuss all of them because, as I have already observed, my *Kitchen manual* cannot possibly be comprehensive; it is pitched to meet the needs of the mistress of the house as I see them.

1. — Bouillie.

A well-made and well-cooked *bouillie* is an excellent sweet. It is also eaten at luncheon; among family, it is served quite simply in the saucepan in which it was cooked, because the crust on the bottom of the pan is the most enjoyable part. Put three-quarters of the milk you will be using to make the *bouillie* on the fire; when it has nearly come to the boil, carefully slake the right amount of flour in the cold milk: practice will teach you how to judge the correct quantity; add some boiling milk and stir it in; then pour this mixture into the saucepan containing the rest of the hot milk, stirring it briskly so that it doesn't form *lumps*.[2] When the *bouillie* has thickened and begun to boil, add sugar, damp down the fire and let it simmer for at least an hour; add a little salt half an hour before serving. If you wish to make the *bouillie* more delicious, mix in two or three egg yolks and two spoonfuls of orange flower water at the moment of service. This *bouillie* cooled, sliced and served on a sauce of *oeufs à la neige*[3] makes the most delicate of sweets.

---

1. In the original: *Entremets sucrés.*
2. In French, *mottons.*
3. i.e. custard.

2. — Fritters.

Fritters of bouillie or fried cream.[1] — Make a fairly stiff *bouillie* (see the preceding recipe); let it cool somewhat; add four egg yolks; mix them in well; pour this out to a suitable thickness on plates; let it cool completely. Cut the *bouillie* into diamonds; dip them in beaten egg, to which you have added sugar and lemon zest; crumb them, then dip them in the egg again and crumb them a second time. Fry them. If the deep fat is not hot enough to seal the fritters straightaway, they may sometimes break up.

Apple fritters. — Peel some nice apples, cut them into slices 1 centimetre thick. Once you have taken out the core, marinate them in eau-de-vie. Make a thin batter which should consist of the necessary amount of flour, a spoonful of olive oil, a little salt, four egg yolks and two whites, a spoonful of orange flower water and two spoonfuls of eau-de-vie. Mix everything together well while adding enough water to give it the consistency required; leave the batter to rest for two or three hours. When you wish to use it, beat two egg whites to a snow and mix it into the batter; heat the deep fat; dip the apples in the batter and take them out to put them in the pan. Leave them there until the fritters have coloured nicely. Dredge with sugar and serve in a pile.

A simpler way to make the batter is to mix water into flour, with two spoonfuls of eau-de-vie and a little salt.

Peach fritters. — These fritters, which might at first sight seem much nicer than those made with apple, are, on the contrary, inferior – in my opinion at least. Whatever the case, this is how to make them:

Cut the peaches into four and marinate them in grated sugar moistened with eau-de-vie. You can fry them without dipping them in batter and merely dredging them with flour.

Sorrel fritters. — Choose some nice sorrel leaves, leaving the stalks on. Wipe them, then dip them in batter to deep-fry them. As soon as they have taken on a nice colour, take them out and pile them on a dish; then dust them with sugar. The sorrel gives the batter a most pleasing slight sharpness.

Black locust flower fritters.[2] — Choose nice clusters of locust flowers, dip in a batter, deep-fry them like the sorrel fritters. The fat should be very hot.

1. In French, *Beignets en bouillie ou crème frite.*
2. In French, *fleurs d'acacia.* This is the source of acacia honey. The tree is a native of North America, *Robinia pseudoacacia.*

You leave the fritters in the fat until they have coloured sufficiently. Heap them on a dish and then dust with sugar.

The fragrance of the locust flower, which resembles that of the orange flower, is partly preserved in this confection; what is more, the finished article looks charming.

Beignets soufflés.[1] — Put a litre of water into a saucepan, with a lump of sugar, salt and some lemon zest; boil it so that the water takes up the fragrance, then remove the lemon. Then, with one hand sprinkle flour little by little into the boiling water while stirring with the other hand, continuing until the paste is extremely thick; continue to stir for a good half an hour, making sure you stop any of it sticking to the bottom. The more the paste is cooked, the lighter it will be; it will become transparent. Pull back from the fire; continue to stir for a minute, then leave to cool. Break an egg into the paste, stir and beat it in every direction to achieve a perfect combination; break in another egg, beat again, and so on until you have used eight eggs. Once the dough is satisfactorily completed, put it on a dish and wait for dinner to be served before you fry it. First, heat the deep fat. Take a piece of dough the size of a walnut, let it fall into the fat by tapping it on the side of the pan; take another piece and do the same thing, and continue until the surface of the fat is half-covered. This dough will puff up, leaving it hollow inside. Because the beignets float, turn them over with a skimmer so they brown on all sides. Then drain them in a colander; pile them up in a dish; dust with sugar. Serve. It is an excellent sweet. The quantities given above will make an enormous platter.

3. — Maize cakes.[2]

Make a *bouillie* as I have explained in the article *Bouillie*, sweeten it; when it has cooled, add three egg yolks and about 60 grams of melted butter; mix it all together; flavour it with orange flowers or the grated zest of lemon (you can omit these ingredients). Grease a pie-dish with butter;

---

1. This is also called 'nuns' farts', *pets de nonnes*, a name Mme Millet-Robinet did not acknowledge until later editions.
2. Mme Millet-Robinet omits any mention of maize flour in this recipe, a failing rectified in later editions where she points out that the *bouillie* should be prepared with that substance, not wheat flour. She should perhaps have cross-referred not to the article *Bouillie*, but to the recipe for *Maize flour bouillie, or Gaudes* in the previous chapter (page 580).

heat up the Dutch oven or a dished lid that will accommodate embers; beat the egg whites to a froth; fold them into the *bouillie*. Pour this all into the pie-dish; smooth the surface; put it on a gentle heat and place over it the warmed Dutch oven, with sufficient embers to provide top heat. Let it rise and take on a nice colour. Serve very hot and quickly. It is one of the most delicate sweet dishes you could ever eat. You need not beat the egg whites to a froth and can content yourself with adding just one egg to the *bouillie*, rather than the three that I suggest; in that case you let the bottom and the top form a gratin so that there is a sort of thick crust all over the cake. If the butter you put in the pie-dish before adding the *bouillie* is really hot, but not burnt, the cake will slide off the pie-dish and can be served as a biscuit, without being quite so crisp. It is then a golden brown and excellent.

4. — Soles de guérets.[2]

Make a well-cooked and thick *groux* [buckwheat *bouillie*] (see *Buckwheat flour*, page 316 above); let it cool in a shallow dish; cut it into slices 2 centimetres thick; dust them with flour; deep-fry them in really hot fat; dust with sugar. Serve very hot. It's an excellent dish.

1.   In later editions, Mme Millet-Robinet explains her interpretation of this name for fried buckwheat *bouillie*. The element *guéret*, she says, refers to fallow land, in which the buckwheat was sown as a catch crop. The *sole*, in her view, comes from the shape the *bouillie* takes when it is poured into a shallow dish or soup plate and then removed to be sliced: a little like half a flatfish or sole. This explanation is confirmed by the folklorist Paul Sébillot in his *Coutumes populaires de la Haute-Bretagne*, Paris 1886, p. 336. He writes (in translation), 'They also fry slices of cold *bouillie* in the pan, which are cut into squares or thin slices which resemble small soles in shape. So they amusingly call them "*soles de guéret*".' The Norman historian Jean Seguin, in his *Vieux mangers, vieux parlers bas-normands* (Avranches, 1938), suggests the name is specifically Avranchin. Another from the same province, André Guérin in his *La Vie quotidienne en Normandie au temps de Madame Bovary* (Hachette, 1975), makes reference to salmon, saying, 'Cold, the left-over *bouillie* is fried the next day as "salmon" browned in butter [my translation].' An alternative view of the phrase is entirely agricultural. A three-course rotation (in French, *assolement*) saw the arable land divided into three sectors or *soles*: the *sole de blé* was that part sown with winter grains (wheat, rye, or a mixture of the two); the *sole de mars* is sown in spring with oats, barley, peas and so forth; and the *sole de guéret* is the fallow or *jachère*. So the name of the dish may simply refer back to where the grain, buckwheat, was sown as a catch crop or *surcharge*. Or, indeed, the name may refer to both possibilities at once.

5. — French toast.[1]

Cut bread into slices 2 centimetres thick and the width of a hand; trim them to a rectangle. Heat some milk to lukewarm; sweeten it and flavour it, if you wish, with orange flowers or lemon zest. Place the slices of bread in a deep dish and pour the milk over them; leave them to soak for an hour. Beat some eggs as if you were making an omelette, but without pepper; put a knob of butter in the frying-pan; when it is hot, take the slices of bread, lay them in the eggs, lift them out with a skimmer and place them side by side in the pan. Fry one side, then turn it over. Do the same for the rest of the slices. Serve hot, after dusting them with grated sugar.

6. — Bread mould.[2]

Boil some milk and pour it over a small 250-gram loaf that you have sliced; let it soak for two or three hours; stir it around in such a way that you mash the bread thoroughly. Flavour it with powdered vanilla, or grated zest of lemon or some orange flower water. Add six egg yolks and two whites to a litre of milk; sweeten with powdered sugar. Beat the other four whites to a froth [and fold them in]; pour this mixture into a mould that you have lined with caramel, like you do for a rice cake;[3] cook in the bain-marie, placing some embers on the lid. Let it cool in the mould; serve with or without the sauce for *oeufs à la neige*.

7. — Apple pancakes (entremets).

Prepare a batter as if for plain pancakes; then peel some nice *reinette franche* apples;[4] take out the cores; cut them in slices or thin rounds; add them to the batter: you should have five or six rounds to each pancake. Cook in the frying-pan; dust (or not) with grated sugar. These pancakes are excellent.

8. — Cherries.

Cherry pie. — Make a shortcrust with two eggs (the whites and the

1.   In French, *Pain perdu*.
2.   The recipe is entitled *Gâteau de mie de pain*.
3.   Mme Millet-Robinet is mistaken in her cross-reference; she should have referred the reader to her recipe for *Cake à la neige* (page 593, below).
4.   The *reinette franche* is a Norman variety. The English variety Ribston pippin is a *reinette*, and was first raised from pips sent from Normandy in 1708.

yolks), 5 grams of salt, half a glass of lukewarm water, 125 grams of butter and sufficient flour: the pastry should not be too firm. Beat the dough with a rolling-pin, then roll it out to a thickness of 5 millimetres. Butter a pie-dish, or even an earthenware platter, and lay in the sheet of pastry, trimming off any that hangs over the edge of the dish. Take off the stalks and take out the stones of 1200 grams of best-quality cherries. Place a small jam jar upside down on the pastry and arrange the cherries around and on top of the jar, in a pyramid, with 250 grams of sugar. Bring together again the pastry you trimmed from the edges and roll out another sheet. Lay it over the top of the pie; crimp the edge, which you seal with a little water, with a pastry wheel. Gild the pastry with a little egg yolk which you have reserved for the purpose. Put it in the oven half an hour after the bread. Three-quarters of an hour should be enough to cook this pie, which you can also cook on a trivet set in a corner of the hearth. Keep a low heat underneath it. You can serve it hot or leave it to cool; in the latter case, you take it off its pie-dish and serve it on a porcelain dish.

At the moment of eating, you break the top crust and remove the jam jar which will contain much excess juice from the cherries; when this returns to the filling, it greatly improves the pie.

If you hadn't taken this precaution of having the jam jar there, the abundance of juice could have broken the crust during the cooking and either flowed into the dish or even spilled over its edges.

You can make a similar pie with plums, apricots, even apples or pears; but in these cases, the jam jar is not needed: these fruits do not have the great abundance of juice that might fracture the crust. You can also make it with gooseberries – either green or half-ripe: the latter's natural acidity will mean using much more sugar.

Cherry soup. — Take 1 kilogram of sweet black cherries and take off the stalks. Put 60 grams of butter in a saucepan; let it melt; add the cherries; stir. Sprinkle it all with flour; sauté; add a glass of water and 125 grams of sugar; leave to cook.

Fry in butter some crumb of a loaf cut in dice; when well-cooked, drain them; then put them in a bowl; pour over the cherries, and serve it forth quickly and very hot, so the croûtons do not soften.

You can reheat this sort of soup; but then the croûtons will no longer be crunchy.

9. — Creams.

Chocolate cream. — Cut 200 grams of chocolate into very small pieces; moisten with water and melt it while stirring; add a litre of milk and let it cook for half an hour; sweeten it. At the end of this time, take it off the heat and let it cool down somewhat. Mix eight egg yolks into this milk chocolate; sieve the mixture and fill some little pots or a bowl; put it to set in the bain-marie, remove it when the cream is firm; let it cool. You can serve this cream runny; in which case, instead of cooking it in the bain-marie, you slake the egg yolks (without whites) with a little milk and then add them to the boiling chocolate, which you stir briskly without letting it return to the boil. When the cream has thickened, you pour it into the pots. This cream is the most expensive of all creams, but is one of the best. The quantities indicated will suffice for ten people.

Vanilla cream. — Boil a litre of milk flavoured with a vanilla pod or powdered vanilla sugar. If you use a vanilla pod, you should take a length of about 3 centimetres and cut it into four. Remove the vanilla and then sweeten the milk. If you wish to thicken the cream, whisk eight egg yolks and mix the milk into them, sieving everything when it is nearly cold. Then let it set in the bain-marie, as if it were the chocolate cream; or thicken it over the heat while stirring, but not letting it boil. If you want the cream to be runny, serve it cold.[1]

Laurel cream. — Instead of vanilla, you can infuse two leaves of the almond or cherry laurel in the milk. It would be dangerous to use too much laurel: a strong dose is poisonous.[2]

Caramel cream. — Make some caramel; when it has turned a lovely colour, let it down with boiling water and allow it to boil until everything has dissolved and become liquid. When it has done this, pull it back from the heat and leave to cool. Boil a litre of milk, add lots of sugar because the caramel is slightly bitter. Whisk eight egg yolks and mix them into the

---

1. In later editions, Mme Millet-Robinet clarified this last, slightly opaque instruction. If you wish to serve a more liquid cream, she says, you do not set it by cooking in the bain-marie, but you stir the mixture of egg yolks and milk over the heat, without letting it boil. Then you serve it cold.

2. Almond or, more usually, cherry laurel (*Prunus laurocerasus*) is the Victorians' favourite shrub laurel, of glossy, funereal foliage and a persistent habit. The leaves give off an almond flavour but contain cyanide. It should not be confused with the bay tree (*Laurus nobilis*).

milk, add the caramel; sieve; cook it to set in the bain-marie. Serve it cold. If you add the caramel when it is still hot, the milk will curdle.

Tea cream. — Make some very strong tea and proceed as if you were making a caramel cream.

Black coffee cream. — The same procedure as the preceding recipe.

Raw coffee cream. — Boil 30 grams of good-quality raw coffee in a glass of water;[1] then proceed as you would for a caramel cream.

10. — Eggs.

Sweet omelette. — First whisk the whites, after you have separated them from the yolks; add some powdered sugar to the yolks; beat them too, then mix everything together; season sparingly with salt; add a little lemon zest. Make the omelette as you would a normal one; but pay attention as it burns easily.

You can also prepare this omelette as you would a normal one, and cook it the same way, then sweeten it with grated sugar before you dish it up, folding it as you serve it, sprinkling the top with a little sugar. This is a better way of doing things, in my opinion, particularly if you are only using two or three eggs rather than making an omelette with lots of eggs. If there are quite a few diners, then you make several omelettes.

Jam omelette. — Make it as you would an ordinary omelette, placing it on the dish and filling the inside, which should not be too set, with one jam or another; then fold the omelette over. You can replace the jam with an apple *marmelade.*[2]

Omelette soufflée. — For six people, break six eggs; separate the whites and whisk them to a firm peak: the addition of a drop of water helps the whisking. Beat the yolks well with 125 grams of powdered sugar; add some grated lemon zest and a pinch of salt. In a dish over a low fire, melt 60 grams of really fresh butter, and at the same time, heat up a Dutch oven; the bottom heat does not need to be very high. Mix the yolks and whites together quickly and thoroughly; pour them into the melted butter; cover with the Dutch oven, loaded with plenty of bright embers. Five minutes

1.   i.e. unroasted beans. Other people's recipes suggest that the raw coffee is first ground.

2.   i.e. a purée. *Marmelade* is defined by *Larousse* as a thick purée of fruit cooked with sugar in which the pieces of fruit, by the end of cooking, are no longer identifiable.

are enough to cook it. You will know that the omelette soufflée is cooked when you see it has risen well when lifting off the Dutch oven. Take the oven away, dust with lots of sugar; dish it up *rapidly*, because the omelette *soon* collapses.

If the kitchen is a long way from the dining-room, you have to make the omelette in a room close by. There is nothing simpler than to make a nice omelette souflée: you just mustn't linger, that's all. It is an inexpensive dish, but much esteemed. There is something to be gained by mixing a spoonful of potato starch in with the egg yolks: it holds the omelette up.

Baked egg custard.[1] — Break six eggs, take away two whites, and mix the rest with 125 grams of powdered sugar and a litre of milk; sieve it; pour it into a bowl. Cook it in a bain-marie, covered with a Dutch oven with coals on top. When the mixture has set, sprinkle the surface with sugar and pass a red-hot shovel over it.[2]

You can make *eggs with water* in a similar fashion; you should add a little lemon zest or two spoonfuls of orange flower water. This dish can be served hot or cold.

If you increase the number of eggs, always leaving only two whites, the dish will be much more delicate.[3]

Moulded egg custard with caramel.[4] — Whisk the whites of six eggs to a froth; whisk the yolks with 60 to 80 grams of powdered sugar; mix this all together. Add a glass of fresh milk which you have brought to the boil; mix once more. Prepare a liquid caramel by putting 60 grams of sugar and a spoonful of water in a small saucepan; when it has turned a nice colour,

1. In French, *oeufs au lait*.
2. The red-hot shovel, *la pelle rouge* or *la pelle rougie*, is the means by which some foods were browned on the top or glazed before there were salamander grills of the sort that grace most modern kitchens. The cook would plunge the kitchen shovel into the hot coals until it was itself red-hot. Its heat was sufficient to glaze sugar, for instance. A purpose-built tool was developed, and is still used by some chefs. It is illustrated in some editions of Audot where the comment is that it is far more convenient for fitting inside dishes than the standard kitchen shovel which Mme Millet-Robinet advised. It is called a *fer à glacer*, or indeed, a salamander. The part that is heated in the fire is a cast-iron disc of 10 centimetres.
3. It is not quite clear if her first instruction (to break 6 eggs and take away 2 whites) was intended to be thus, or to agree with this later recommendation to leave only 2 whites, whatever the number of eggs.
4. In French, *oeufs au lait en forme*.

pour it into a copper or tin mould (without a handle) and turn it all about so that the caramel covers everything; pour the eggs into this mould; cook it in a bain-marie. When this has set, put the mould in cold water and, when everything has cooled, turn it out gently onto a dish which you have placed on the mould itself [so that you can turn it over and avoid damaging the custard].

Oeufs à la neige. — Put a litre of milk into a shallow saucepan and add a piece of vanilla pod or some lemon rind; sweeten it generously; bring it to the boil. Break six eggs; separate the whites; whisk them to a high peak and add two heaped spoonfuls of powdered sugar; mix together. Use a spoon to lift some of this white and place it in the boiling milk: as you dip the spoon in, so the white will slip off. Take another spoon and repeat this until the surface of the milk is covered with large flakes. Then turn the first one from top to bottom so that it cooks equally on both sides; do the same successively for all the others. Don't let them cook more than an instant; take out those which have cooked with a skimmer and arrange them on a dish. Carry on thus with all the egg white; then pour back into the saucepan any milk that may have ended up in the dish under the whites. Slake the egg yolks by slowly adding some spoonfuls of the same milk and then pouring it all into the saucepan; stir it until it thickens, *without letting it boil*. When the liquid has thickened, remove the lemon rind or vanilla; quickly pour the cream under the egg whites, which will rise and float on it. It's a dish that looks most attractive, is inexpensive and is excellent.

Cake à la neige.[1] — Whisk eight egg whites to a very firm peak, add to it 100 grams of grated sugar. Prepare in advance a nicely coloured caramel with 100 grams of sugar moistened with a little water, but only enough so that it stays quite thick. Coat a mould with this caramel; pour in the beaten egg whites and cook it in a bain-marie so that when you test it with a straw, it comes out dry. With the eight egg yolks, make a caramel cream but, instead of setting it in the bain-marie, stir it over the fire until it has thickened. Turn the cake over onto a dish as soon as you have taken it out of the boiling water; tap the mould to make it come out; pour the sauce around it. Serve. It is a very pretty dish.

1. Most modern recipes for this dish, called variously *Gâteau neige* or *Gâteau de neige*, appear to have a modicum of flour cooked with the egg whites. Louis-Eustache Audot however, Mme Millet-Robinet's model, follows the same procedure as Madame.

II. — Apples.

Apple charlotte. — Peel some decent apples which cook easily; take out the cores (for this there are small tin cutters which greatly ease the task, they are known by ironmongers as *apple corers* [1]); place the prepared apples in a saucepan with a little water, cinnamon, and enough sugar so that they are properly sweet: the amount will vary depending on the sort of apple you have used. Cover; let them cook until they have formed a purée; add a small knob of butter. Cut the crumb of a round loaf in slices the thickness of your little finger; shape from this crumb a circle the same size as the bottom of the mould, and cut the rest into slices equal to the height of the mould; butter the mould generously; line it completely with the circle and slices of bread; pour in the purée; cover the surface with slices of bread that you have spread generously with butter; cook it like a timbale of macaroni. Serve hot. Rather than buttering the mould, you can soak the bread in melted butter. You can also cut the crumb at the bottom into long triangles whose apexes come together at the centre with no gaps between. And finally, if you want the charlotte to be more delicate in flavour, you can add 250 grams of redcurrant jelly or apricot *marmelade* to the apple purée.

Apple meringue. — Make a *marmelade* as you would for a charlotte; line the bottom of a fireproof dish with slices of the crumb of a loaf fried in butter; place the *marmelade* on top, giving it a slightly conical shape. Whisk three egg whites stiffly; add 65 grams of grated sugar; cover the apple with these whites; dust with sugar. Put the dish on hot embers: porcelain will withstand the heat without breaking; cover with the Dutch oven, preheated and provided with coals. When the whites have risen and coloured slightly, serve.

Marmelade of apples with boiled rice pudding. — Prepare on the one hand a *marmelade* of apples, and on the other a boiled rice pudding (page 599, below) which you have quite heavily sweetened and with which you have boiled some lemon rind. Put a layer of *marmelade* in a dish, then a layer of rice, a second of *marmelade*, a second of rice, and so on; give the whole a slightly conical shape; cover this with egg whites sweetened and whisked to a froth; cook it like the apple meringue. This is a very delicate dish.

You can also cook whole apples in butter on the dish, once they have been peeled, cored and sweetened. Spoon round the boiled rice pudding,

---

1.   In French, *vide-pommes*.

dust them with sugar and leave them for a few minutes under the Dutch oven.

Buttered apples. — Peel the apples whole and core them. Cut slices of bread the same size as the apples. Butter the bottom of a pie-dish and place the slices of bread with the apples on top. Put butter in the holes where the cores were; dust everything with grated sugar; put on a gentle heat and cover with a lid filled with coals. After about three-quarters of an hour, the apples will be cooked. Serve them in the pie-dish. You can, at the moment of service, put a little redcurrant jelly in the centre of each apple.

12. — Potatoes.

Potato cake (entremets). — Peel some round potatoes, wipe them and put them whole in a saucepan: they will mash more easily; add enough milk to cover; let them cook. While they are still hot, sieve them, or mash them one by one on a plate with a fork. Add three whites and yolks of egg, powdered sugar, some orange flowers or lemon zest, or even ground vanilla, a little salt, a large knob of butter, and a spoonful of potato starch; mix together. Thoroughly grease a copper mould with butter and dust the whole of the inside with sieved soft breadcrumbs; the crumbs should stick everywhere on the butter; you can use flour instead of crumbs; then pour the potatoes into the mould; it should be half full. Assemble a large heap of red-hot ashes mixed with embers, make a depression in the middle and place the mould there; cover with the Dutch oven well provided with embers; leave it to cook for three-quarters of an hour. When the cake has risen nicely, take the mould out of the fire and put a plate over its top; turn it over. If the cake has been cooked properly, it will hold its shape; however, not infrequently it collapses. To avoid these accidents, you can make the potato cake in a deep dish, in which you serve it at table once it's cooked. When the cake has risen nicely and has been dusted with grated sugar, you put the dish on another porcelain dish. This cake is extremely good cold.

Souffléed potatoes cooked in milk (entremets and luncheon). — Cook and sieve them as in the previous recipe; put them back on the fire with butter, sugar and a little milk, if they are too stiff; add a little salt and either vanilla, orange flowers or lemon zest. When this purée comes to the boil, slake three egg yolks with some milk; mix them in; stir for a few seconds, then withdraw the pan from the heat. Add the egg whites, beaten to a froth; mix everything together well; put it in a dish. Smooth the surface, dust with sugar and glaze with a red-hot shovel. Serve quickly. This is one of the best ways to serve potatoes.

Fried potato balls. — Steam some large round potatoes; peel them and mash them thoroughly; add a knob of butter, some chopped parsley, salt, pepper, and three eggs, whites and yolks; mix everything together thoroughly. Use your fingers to shape pieces of this dough to look like a slightly elongated small egg; dredge this ball in flour. While doing this, heat up the deep-fat on the fire; when it is really hot, add the potato balls; they will swell up a great deal. Serve when they are a nice colour, with fried parsley arranged around them.

Potato croquettes. — Prepare them as if you were making potato balls but, instead of adding pepper and parsley, sweeten them and flavour them with orange flower water or lemon zest. Dust with sugar. Serve. These croquettes are much more delicate when made with potatoes that have been pounded in the mortar. You can cook them in a saucepan with butter, but you only add them to the pan when the butter is hot.

13. — Pudding.[1]

Bread pudding. — Slice a small loaf of no more than 250 grams as if you were cutting bread for soup and arrange the slices in a deep dish or bowl with 250 grams of powdered sugar. Break four eggs into another bowl; beat them lightly; add 1 gram of ground cinnamon, the grated zest of half a lemon, 5 grams of salt, 2 spoonfuls of rum and half a litre of warm milk. Mix everything well together and pour it onto the bread. The *next day*, mix thoroughly and add 325 grams of Malaga raisins which you have deseeded, and 125 grams of currants.[2] Carefully mix again. Butter well a copper or wrought iron mould or, failing a mould, a saucepan; line the bottom and sides with a circle and a band of paper; pour in your mixture; put it in the oven just after the bread, or cook it in hot ashes on the hearth, covering the mould with a Dutch oven well-provided with embers. One hour's cooking usually suffices. To be sure the pudding is cooked, test it with a wooden skewer; it should come out dry when the pudding is done to a turn.

1. The original title is '*Pouding*'.
2. *Raisins de Malaga* are dried muscat grapes; currants, in French, are *raisins de Corinthe*.

Rum pudding. — Cook 125 grams of very fine vermicelli in enough milk for it to become very thick: you will need about 1 litre; into this you mix 1 spoonful of flour, 2 or 3 spoonfuls of grated sugar, 3 egg yolks plus one white, 4 spoonfuls of rum, a pinch of salt. Finally you add 60 grams of Malaga raisins, 60 grams of currants, 60 grams of Cuba raisins,[1] a piece of citron cut into very thin slices. Mix everything thoroughly and pour the mixture into a mould that you have greased well with butter and previously dusted with powdered sugar. Cook in a bain-marie for two hours; the water should always be boiling. You should watch the water does not get into the mould, and from time to time add some more boiling water because what is in the bain-marie can evaporate quite quickly. When cooking is done, turn the mould out onto a dish and anoint the pudding with four or five spoonfuls of rum. Light it and serve while the liquor burns brightly.

Cream pudding. — Prepare the vermicelli mixture as I have just described; make a richly coloured and fairly thick caramel, and use it to coat the whole interior of the mould. Pour in the pudding mixture and then place the mould in the bain-marie. Cook for three-quarters of an hour; take off the heat and leave to cool in the mould. Having done this, make a sauce like the one that accompanies *oeufs à la neige*; serve the pudding cold, in a dish, with the sauce around it. This is extremely pretty and very good.

Rice pudding. — Cook 60 grams of good Carolina rice (carefully washed two or three times in boiling water) in half a litre of milk; continue cooking until the rice forms a porridge. Let it cool, stirring the while, so a skin doesn't form. Add some powdered vanilla and grated sugar so that it is well-flavoured and sweet.

On the fire, dissolve in half a litre of water 10 grams of good isinglass which you have chopped into small pieces. Let it cook until the liquid has reduced to a quarter of its original volume.

Whip about a quarter of a litre of good fresh cream until thick. (See *Whipped cream for meringues*, page 620, below.) Add this cream, now light and frothy, to the rice and the isinglass. Mix everything together. Put this mixture into a mould which you leave in a cool place until it has set; it will

---

1.   In French, *raisins de Cuba*. English gardening manuals of the time liken them to Black Lombardy grapes. In later editions, reference to *raisins de Cuba* is suppressed and their weight distributed between Malaga and Corinth raisins (i.e. currants).

need two hours. Turn out the pudding onto a platter and pour over half a pint[1] of redcurrant or raspberry syrup. If the syrup is too runny, you can reduce it a little by cooking it. Only pour it on the pudding once it has cooled. This is an extremely handsome dish; the quantities given should be enough to serve ten people.

14. — Purées.

Chestnut purée. — Remove the outer skin of nice chestnuts or *marrons*,[2] cook them in plenty of water with a little salt. As soon as they are cooked, pour off the water, leaving just enough to cover the chestnuts; take them out one by one to peel them more easily. Throw them into the mortar and pound them; thin the paste with a little milk so that you can sieve it like a purée. Then melt some really fresh butter in a saucepan; add to it the purée and some powdered sugar; stir; thin down with a little milk; you can add some grated zest of lemon. The purée should be reasonably thick. Let it simmer for a quarter of an hour, making sure the purée doesn't burn; dust with sugar and glaze with a red-hot shovel. Serve. You can colour this purée with a little cochineal. This sweet is little known and really good; adding a little powdered vanilla makes it more delicate still.

Chestnut purée vermicelli. — Cook the chestnuts as I have just described: pound them in a mortar; flavour them with lemon zest, vanilla, or crushed candied orange flowers.[3] Sweeten with powdered sugar; mix everything well to make a firm paste which you push through a fine colander with a mushroom-shaped pestle; by doing this it will form little strands like fine vermicelli which fall from the colander into the dish you use to present them at table. In this way the chestnut purée appears as light as can be; but as you serve the purée, the strands stick together and clump up wherever they are subject to pressure from the spoon: never the less it is a very pretty

1. The measure given in the text is *une demi-chopine*. A *chopine* is usually a half-litre bottle.
2. The sweet chestnut, in French, is *châtaigne*. The outer shells usually contain twin or triplet nuts. The *marron* is the same species, but a cultivar (not wild) that has been bred to deliver larger nuts and only one nut to each shell. The *marron*, therefore, is better for creating *marrons glacés* or for gracing the tables of the rich. The wild nuts are of good flavour and lend themselves to chestnut flour and other by-products.
3. In French, *la fleur d'oranger pralinée et pilée*, i.e. the same method as used to make almond pralines deployed with orange flowers.

and very satisfactory dish. You can divide the purée into several parts: one coloured with cochineal, one left its natural colour: you will need to use two colanders for this; take first one, then the other, to create a two-tone pyramid to delightful effect.

Pumpkin purée. — The best sort, we have stated on several occasions, is called *Turk's turban*, its true name being winter squash;[1] you should always, therefore, choose it before any other. Peel a quantity of squash and cut it into pieces; cook it covered, with very little water and a pinch of salt. When it is cooked, drain and sieve it. Put a knob of butter into a saucepan; when it is hot, add the pumpkin and a little flour; stir; moisten with milk and add sugar. When you serve it, you can dust the top with sugar and pass a red-hot shovel over it. Or you can thicken the purée with egg yolks, which would be better than flour.

15. — Rice.

Boiled rice pudding.[2] — The quantity of rice is determined by the number of diners; you need a spoonful of rice per person. Having previously sorted the rice, washed it in warm water, then drained it, put it in a saucepan with half the milk that should be required; put the pan on a brisk fire. When the rice has burst, that is to say each grain forms an *x*, add the rest of the cold milk: it stops the rice cooking and the grains from splitting; sweeten, lightly salt. You can also sweeten the rice as you put it on the heat; this is perhaps the better course. Once it comes to the boil, damp the fire so that it cooks gently. The rice should not be too thick. To make it more delicate, when you come to serve it, take it off the heat and add three egg yolks, which you have slaked with a little cold milk before mixing in with the rice; let them thicken the rice, while stirring. A little lemon zest or orange flower water gives this dish a pleasing flavour. If you serve it up in a porcelain casserole or in a deep dish, dust it generously with sugar and glaze it with a red-hot shovel.

By flavouring the rice with a cup of good black coffee, you get a very elegant and excellent dish; but you will have to add more sugar. You can also add chocolate, which is just as good.

1. *Giraumon.*
2. The title of the recipe is *Riz au lait.*

Rice soufflé. — Cook the rice as you would for boiled rice pudding; sweeten it, lightly salt it; cool it to lukewarm. Break three eggs; add the yolks to the rice and the whites beaten to a froth. Butter a fireproof dish, fill it half-full with the rice; have a gentle heat beneath it and cover it with a heated Dutch oven with hot embers on the lid. When the rice has risen nicely, serve quickly after dusting the top with grated sugar.

You can also cook the rice for a long time so that the grains break up in all the milk at once, then sieve it to make a purée.

Rice cake. — Prepare some rice as I have just explained, with a lot of sugar and really thick. Put in a strip of lemon rind or vanilla, and a little salt. When it is cooked, take out the lemon rind. First, add a knob of butter which must be left to melt; then, when the whole has cooled down a little, add six eggs, less two whites; mix it all together. Carefully butter the bottom and sides of a mould, line it with soft breadcrumbs which you have crushed and sieved, or with flour. That done, pour the rice in; put the mould in the centre of a heap of red embers and cover it with a hot Dutch oven with embers on the top. The breadcrumbs should brown and form a crust. Carefully turn it out onto a dish; serve. This dish is equally good hot or cold.

You can flavour the cake with a cup of very strong black coffee, like the boiled rice pudding. In this case, add the coffee during the cooking and add less milk, because it is essential that the batter should be very stiff. You can substitute chocolate for the coffee. You can serve the sauce for *oeufs à la neige* around this cake.

Rice pudding. — See *Pudding*, page 597, above.

16. — Various sweet dishes.

Blancmange. — Blanch 250 grams of sweet almonds mixed with three or four bitter almonds; reduce it all to a paste in a mortar by adding little by little, with a spoon, about two glassfuls of cold water; sieve through a muslin, squeezing hard; sweeten the almond milk with 200 grams of sugar. Beat six egg whites short of them rising to a peak, pour them with the almond milk into a saucepan, which you put on hot ash to give a very gentle heat. Beat with twigs until the cream has thickened. Serve cold, in a crown of halved sponge fingers placed upright all round the dish.

You can make blancmange another way: make an almond emulsion as in the previous paragraph, but instead of moistening the pounded almonds with water, boil a calf's foot in a litre of water for five hours: the pan should always be kept full so that you still have a litre of stock when the calf's foot is cooked. Sieve then moisten the almonds with this stock; sweeten; flavour with vanilla, or orange flower, or lemon zest. Let the mixture warm slightly in the bain-marie, then pour it into a mould and leave it to cool; then turn it out onto a dish, placing a crown of biscuits around it. If you surround the mould with ice half an hour before adding the sugar, the blancmange will be better.

Clafouty,[1] *a Limousin dish.* — Take: flour, 200 grams; grated sugar, 100 grams; salt, 5 grams; fresh fruits, 750 grams; egg yolks, 4; milk, ½ litre. Put the flour in a bowl; add the egg yolks and the salt; pour and mix in the milk.

If the clafouty is prepared with stone fruits such as plums, cherries, apricots, you should take out the stones.

Pour the batter into a well-buttered pie dish which you place on a fairly brisk fire. When the butter appears to have melted and you reckon the bottom has started to firm up, place the fruits that you have already mixed with grated sugar on the batter. Cover with a really hot Dutch oven with embers on top. In principle, the cake will rise, then fall. You let it cook for about an hour, taking care that the bottom does not burn. Take off the Dutch oven as soon as it is cooked. The cake should have browned beautifully. Take it off the heat and let it cool a little; free it from the edges of the pie-dish with a knife; then turn it out onto a dish to serve cold.

You can substitute 500 grams of prunes for the fresh fruits (but you must cook them in advance), or raisins, or even sliced apples or pears. You can also increase the amount of sugar, especially if you are using greengages.

Prune cake à la bouillie. — Make a thick *bouillie*; sweeten it with powdered sugar (sugar in pieces will not melt), or even, which is better, sweeten the milk before you add the flour (see how to mix in the flour in the article *Bouillie*, page 584 above); let the *bouillie* cool and add some egg yolks. Cook some nice prunes, sweeten them to taste; remove the stones. Melt a knob of butter in a pie dish; when it begins to melt, put in a layer

---

1. More usually spelled *clafouti* or *clafoutis*. A dialect word of Poitou and the Limousin. The etymology of the name suggests a part-derivation from the Old French *claufir*, to fix with nails, in the sense that you scatter something which shows up as the nail heads on the surface of the dough or batter.

of *bouillie*, then a layer of prunes, a new layer of *bouillie*, another of prunes, and so on; dust with sugar; cover with the Dutch oven with plenty of embers on top. When everything is nicely set and browned, serve.

Fried Turk's turban squash. — Cut a piece of a good sort of Turk's turban into slices 1 centimetre thick. Dust the slices lightly with flour and fry them. Dust with sugar at the moment of service.

You can also dip the slices of squash in batter.

Boiled milk of Ernée (Mayenne).[1] — Put 2 litres of good fresh milk and 100 grams of sugar in a copper saucepan on a brisk fire which you need to carefully maintain. While it boils, stir it frequently to prevent a skin forming on the surface of the milk, which you need to watch anyway so that it doesn't boil over. Reduce it by about two-thirds. (It is better to reduce it a little less than a little more.) The milk thickens and takes on a tint similar to that we call salmon-pink. Serve cold, in a compotier or similarly shaped dish. In summer, the colder this dish is served the better it seems.

This sweet, little known but excellent, costs nothing and is a good resource for the country above all, where milk is worth very little.

Pears in a roux. — Peel the pears, cut them in quarters and put them to cook in a saucepan with enough water to cover; add a little sugar if the variety of pear you are using is not naturally sweet. When they are half-cooked, make a roux with a fairly high proportion of butter in another saucepan; moisten it with the pear cooking liquor; add the pears to the roux; let them finish cooking. The sauce must be nicely thickened and not too transparent. Toast some small, thin slices of bread: arrange them in the bottom of a dish; place the pears on top. Serve. It is an excellent dish.

Pumpkin soufflé. — Cook and drain the pumpkin as if you were making purée. Sieve it and sweeten it; add some egg yolks (three egg yolks are sufficient for quite a large dish), two spoonfuls of potato starch, a knob of butter. Whisk the egg whites into very firm peaks, mix everything together. Butter a fireproof dish; pour in the mixture; you will need not much heat below, but a lot from above. When the soufflé has risen well, dust the surface with sugar and serve immediately, before the soufflé collapses. It is an inexpensive sweet and yet highly esteemed.

---

1. In French, *Lait cuit d'Ernée*. Ernée is a small town in the Mayenne department, east of Fougères on the Breton border. It is a centre of dairying.

Chestnut surprise. — Take off the outer skin of fifty nice chestnuts;[1] cook them in water with a little salt; peel them and mash them with a pestle or a spoon; then put them in a saucepan, with 125 grams of good butter and 125 grams of grated sugar, over a gentle heat. Stir and mix well. Let this cool to lukewarm and put spoonfuls of the mixture into a colander with reasonably large holes; push it through with a mushroom-shaped pestle; the purée will take the form of vermicelli.

Carefully arrange this vermicelli, without crushing it, in a heap on a dish; use a spoon to cover it with whipped cream. Place the dish on some ice and leave it there until you have to serve it.

You can flavour the purée and the cream with vanilla, orange flower water or lemon.

Fifty chestnuts prepared like this will make a dish enough for 12 people. In Paris, the amount of whipped cream needed for this dish could cost 60 centimes.

This is an extremely delicate and highly rated dish, even though it is very simple to make.

---

1.   These are *marrons*, i.e. the cultivated, larger chestnuts.

CHAPTER XVII

PASTRY AND CONFECTIONERY[1]

1. — In general.

I do not pretend to offer here a complete guide to confectionery; it is a difficult skill, quite distinct from that of the cook, which demands a certain study and particularly much practice and experience. I have confined myself to providing confectionery recipes, which are in no way inferior to those made by professional pastry cooks, that may be achieved without trouble in a domestic kitchen.

To undertake pastry, it is essential to have several thin iron baking-sheets, with or without raised edges, and pie dishes of varying dimensions. These last will, in any case, lend themselves to other culinary purposes, and you will also use them to hold different confections when you bake them in the oven. You should also have at your disposal a small flat, iron pastry pincer with jagged ends used to pinch the pastry together to seal it, or to decorate it. I have explained in the article *Kitchen* (page 188, above) the other equipment necessary to make pastry goods.

The most difficult element of this sort of work is the cooking itself, for only practice will tell you how to get the oven to the correct temperature: which is to the crucial to the success of the operation.

A pie containing meat should be put in the oven at the same time as the bread; it should stay in the oven for one or two hours, depending on its size.

---

1.   The original chapter title is *Pâtisserie*. Generally, the French word is now accepted in English, but I have translated it in keeping with the professional distinction between bakery (concerned with bread) and confectionery (concerned with fancy breads and other flour-based products that are often, if not always, combined with sugar). The use of the word confectionery to describe sugar-based creations such as humbugs, chocolates, etc., is ignored here.

The ideal moment to put biscuits and tarts into the oven is when you move the bread round, that is to say five or six minutes after it has been put in the oven. You should note that having bread in the oven makes it much cooler than if you bring the oven up to heat and then don't put in any bread, yet still wait for the same time to elapse before putting in your biscuits.

To cook pastry goods, it is always advisable to heat the oven as if you were going to bake bread: that way you can determine the temperature from a given point. At the same time, when the oven is not lit every day, it is essential that it should be thoroughly heated, even should you need a temperature much lower than that will entail, because, ignoring this, only the surface of the oven will get hot and it will cool much too quickly.

When pastries have been put in the oven, you must check them every so often to make sure that they are browning sufficiently, without, however, browning too much. If they are not colouring enough, you might add embers, either inside the oven, along the sides, or in the mouth, outside, whichever is best. If, on the other hand, the pastries have browned too much, you can open the oven door.

If you cook pastry in one of those large ovens used to bake loaves of 10 to 12 kilograms, you should not put it in after you have moved the loaves around (above): the oven will be too hot. A small oven specifically intended for pastry is extremely convenient for the country; however, it should not be too small; the heat will not stay in for long enough.

2. — Pies.[1]

When you plan to make a pie, you must gather together and prepare in advance the meats that make up its filling. If ham is involved, you should cook it the day before, as I have instructed in the article *Hams* (page 369, above); but you cannot make a decent pie with ham alone; you will need

---

1.   The original has *Pâtés*. The French name is a classic of metonymy, where the container (or process) gives its name to the whole (e.g. casserole) as a *pâté* is contained in *pâte*, pastry. The English don't think of the French making pies but *pâtés*, but the dish which Mme Millet-Robinet describes in the following pages is not far distant from our veal and ham pie. And the method of fashioning the crust is akin to our own raised piecrusts. It is worth noting that Jules Gouffé, in his very popular *Le Livre de cuisine* of 1867, which was written for household cooks as well as grander chefs, does not suggest hand-raising a pie crust, but always uses a mould such as Madame proposes later on in this recipe.

to combine it with veal, some sort of poultry, and cured pork fat. The commonest pies are veal and ham. You can supplement them with poultry or game.

We take as an example a pie made with ham, cured pork fat and veal. Usually, the fillet [top rounds from the leg] is used. It must be very tender; this is a *sine qua non* for all meats enclosed in a pie. Cut the ham into neat pieces, leaving out any which would not be perfectly tender or which are but scraps attached to the main cuts; you add these to the pâté or forcemeat that layers the meats contained in the crust. Prepare the veal in the same way, that is, cut the most tender and neatest bits into cubes, roughly the same as you did the ham; prick them with large lardons placed very close together and season them with pepper and salt. All the other parts of the veal, save the skin and bone, are used in the forcemeat. Break the bones and put them in a saucepan with the skin, sliced carrots, one or two sliced onions, a bay leaf, a little thyme, salt and pepper, a little butter or lard, and a cured pork rind or two. Brown everything, add water and leave to cook for three hours; after which you strain it to obtain the *jus*, which you finally reduce to the consistency of a *coulis*. This concentration of the *jus* adds greatly to the quality of the pie, but is not essential.

Gather together on the block the meats intended for the forcemeat, add an equal weight of backfat and chop it all about as finely as for sausages; season quite liberally with salt and pepper, unless the outside of the backfat is very salty itself, a consideration which will affect the amount of salt added to the forcemeat; the interior of the backfat is never very salty, and a pie should be highly seasoned. Add the *coulis* to this chopped meat and mix it in thoroughly, kneading with your hands. This *jus*, in combination with whatever comes out of the meat, will form an excellent jelly round the inside of the pie; it will also stop the meat from drying out, which will inevitably occur if you don't do something to inhibit the pastry from absorbing the juices into the crust.

Once all the pie-filling has been prepared, you proceed to make the pastry to contain it. For this, you can use either fresh or clarified butter, or melted pork fat or lard. Once the pastry is cooked, it is difficult to taste which was used; however, I prefer butter to lard. A mixture of lard and butter is even better. If you use fresh butter, you need to work it well to rid it of the water and milk that it usually contains and to make it more compact. This precaution is essential. The amount of butter or fat used should be about half the weight of the flour.

Arrange the flour in a circle on the pastry board; leave a large well in the middle, making sure you create a perimeter wall of flour of an even depth, which you firm up by tamping with your hands. Put into the centre all the butter, cut in pieces; then the water, in winter heated to more than lukewarm, in summer almost cold, in which you dissolve enough salt to season all the pastry. It is very important to add in one go the right amount of water for making the pastry because, if you have to add some in the middle of the operation, this pastry will never be as short as one where you added the right amount of water at the outset. You need a little practice to be able to guess the quantity accurately, but you must study all manner of things before you become adept. Mix the butter carefully with the water, incorporating the flour little by little from the perimeter wall without, however, breaching it. Little by little all the flour will be absorbed, finishing with a dough that should be firm. Knead it by bringing the edges into the centre then pushing the centre back out to the edges with the palm of the hand, keeping the board well dusted with flour so that the dough does not stick. Once you have a nice smooth dough, you can beat it. For that, you gather it into a ball and then flatten by hitting it sharply with the rolling pin. Bring it back into a ball, and flatten it again; after this you can progress to raising the pie.

While you have been doing this, you should have lit the fire in the oven so that it will be hot at about the time you finish preparing the pie.

Put to one side the quantity of pastry needed to make the pie lid; then form the dough into a nice circular shape before creating a depression in the centre by using the fingers to pull most of the dough to the edges; this depression may be oval or round, whichever you fancy. Then thin down what is to be the base [the depression formed in the centre] by pressing it with your clenched fist so that it is no more than half a centimetre thick. The pastry has now assumed the shape of a pie, with a thin bottom ringed by a thick roll of dough. Pick it all up neatly and place it on a clean iron baking sheet. Nudge it back into shape, a little disturbed by this operation, then start to raise the sides of the crust with your fingers, taking care to slim down the lower part, next to the bottom. If you don't do this, the crust will be much thicker there than anywhere else.

In summer, when high temperatures make the dough softer than in winter, it is difficult to raise the crust right up to the rim in a single stint. So you can start to put in the meat, which you should have arranged on three plates. First you lay down a layer of forcemeat, taking care to push it well into the angle between sides and bottom. Then you arrange the cut pieces of ham and veal, mixing them up at random; you fill the edges and any spaces with forcemeat and finally you top it all off with a layer of forcemeat. Give the pile of meat a nice shape, the same width at the bottom as at the top, and then compact it with your hands to be sure that there are no voids or spaces remaining in the mass that will be the pie filling. Once you have done that, use your fingers to extend the pastry sides to enclose the meat and make your crust. Raise them carefully, little by little, so they are of even thickness and turn over the top of the meat, without, however, covering it entirely. Once the whole outer edge of the piecrust is at this point, there will be folds over the top of the meat. You fold these back to the edge so that you form a roll around the outside of the meat. Make this roll as even and regular as possible, taking off any surplus that may arise at certain points. Moisten the outside of the crust below this roll and crimp it together using the small pincers I have referred to. Finally, give the whole pie a nice shape, handling it carefully and trying hard to reduce its size at the base so that the bottom is not much broader than the top. You should keep the top edge shapely, standing proud above the meat, so that you can continue with preparing and placing the lid.

Gather up the ball of pastry you set aside for this and flatten it out with the rolling-pin in such a way that none of it is more than half a centimetre thick. Moisten the *inside* edge of the top roll; then use a knife to cut out a piece of pastry about the same size as that part of the pie which is yet to be covered; moisten similarly the *outside* edge of this piece, then place it on the pie, close to the top roll and aiming to pinch them together with wetted fingers. If the lid is too large, cut off the surplus with a knife and wet it so that you get adhesion; if, on the other hand, it is too small, pull it gently to stretch it so that it reaches the top roll. Once the lid is properly seated and joined to the edge, make a hole the size of a franc piece in the centre to serve as a chimney, then move on to the decoration. You can cut out of the bits of pastry left over, which you roll out so that they are very thin indeed, leaves shaped like bay leaves, the ribs of which you mark with the back of a knife, which you place on the lid, either attached to little rolls of pastry to represent the stalks, or around the chimney, which you should dress for this purpose with a little roll of pastry. You can also cut out a number, or make up little fruits, such as cherries, which you place on the lid. Then you crimp the whole of the pie in a criss-cross with your little pastry pincers.

Once this whole edifice is complete, if the oven has reached a suitable temperature, close it for a few minutes so that the heat loses some of its edge, which might otherwise brown the crust too fiercely. Then glaze the whole surface of the pie with an egg yolk mixed with water, wetting it generously either with your fingers or with the barbs of a feather dipped frequently into the eggwash. Finally, put it in the oven on the baking sheet. You should check the pie five or eight minutes after putting it in to see if it is browning nicely; if it is too much, you can cover it with a piece of paper; if not enough, you can surround it with some of the embers from the oven itself.

By following my instructions exactly, you will always succeed in making a good pie. To ease the problems of raising a piecrust in the proper fashion, you can get a tin mould in which you raise the pastry and which holds it in shape, making the task much easier. You cover the pie as I have described and, once it is cooked, you let it cool in the mould, which opens thanks to a small locking pin, allowing you to extract the pie. This is a very good device.[1]

When you wish to put a hare in a pie, you can omit the ham but not the veal from the forcemeat. After skinning and gutting the hare, cut it up, that is to say, take the saddle off the bone, then the fillets; you can leave the legs whole, but debone them. Prick these joints with large lardons, and season them. All the other parts of the hare are put into the forcemeat. You can boil the hare bones with the veal bones and vegetables to obtain the *jus* I have mentioned; or else you can make a civet with all the debris that still has a little meat adhering to it. If partridge are to be added to hare in the pie, then pluck and dress them as if you were wishing to spit-roast

1.   These tin moulds, which could be opened after baking was finished thanks to a hinge on one side and a removable pin holding the two halves together on the other, were popular in both England and France. One advantage they had was that the pastry need not be so thick or robust if support was offered the raw pie by the tin itself. A pie raised in such a mould was termed, in both countries, a pie *en timbale*.

them; stuff them with forcemeat, then arrange them in amongst the pieces of hare, mixed with the forcemeat. You can leave the heads on top, which you push through the pastry lid, wrapped in triple papers fixed round the neck so the plumage is kept in good shape.

You make a lark pie the same way as a partridge pie. You must be careful to gut them all and stuff them with forcemeat; but you pluck the heads, or better you take them off: you insert forcemeat (always made with veal and backfat) between the larks.

You can also put a chicken or duck into a pie. It is always better boned.

Veal can be replaced by chicken in the forcemeat: you make the *jus* with the bones; but chicken flesh is drier than veal and is not as good in a forcemeat for pies.

If you wish to add truffles to a pie, wash and prepare them exactly as you would when truffling a turkey. You add the pounded peelings to the forcemeat, and disperse through the pie the truffles which are cut into suitably sized pieces. If you mix two or three finely chopped chicken livers into the forcemeat, or even a piece of calf's liver prepared in the same way, you will have a pie that tastes much like many Strasbourg *pâtés de foie gras*. Half a kilogram of truffles is enough to correctly flavour a pie of two or three kilograms.

Pie in a terrine.[1] — Prepare the meats exactly as you did for raised pie (above), and arrange them in a terrine of suitable shape for this purpose.

---

1. In French, *Pâté en terrine.* I have continued to translate this as pie, rather than *pâté*, because, as the recipe indicates, the meats contained in the pie are cut larger than those we normally associate with a terrine (a word we use in current English to describe a coarse country pâté, as do the French). I have left the French word *terrine*, to denote an earthenware pot. The pâté described here, however, is no different to Mrs Beeton's raised veal and ham pie. In England, the pastryless pie-dishes developed by the pottery firm of Wedgwood, manufactured in caneware with handsome external ornament and a glazed interior together with a fine decorated lid, were first introduced at the end of the eighteenth century at the suggestion of Richard Lovell Edgeworth, the father of the novelist Maria Edgeworth. The notes made by the Wedgwood Museum on these dishes remark that they 'came into their own during the Napoleonic blockades of British ports, which resulted in a flour famine. This is commented on in the biography of Beau Brummell — "The scarcity two years after Brummell's retirement, viz, in July, 1800, was so great, that the consumption of flour for pastry was prohibited in the Royal Household, rice being used instead; the distillers left off malting, hackney-coach fares were raised twenty-five percent, and Wedgwood made dishes to represent pie-crust."' Terrines were less ornamented than this.

Cook it in the oven. Serve it in the terrine. Various pieces of butcher's meat, even beef, prepared as a pie like this are very useful for luncheon. Meat cooked in a pie keeps much better than in any other fashion. A raised pie or one *en timbale* is also an excellent provision for a journey.

Calf's liver pâté in a terrine. — Cut the liver, which should be light in colour, into pieces; carefully remove the nerves and the hard parts in the middle of the liver. Chop it up, then pound it in the mortar, seasoning it with pepper, salt, four-spice mix,[1] chopped parsley, a little thyme, chopped shallots, two egg yolks and a piece of the crumb of a loaf as large as your fist, soaked in warm milk or stock; grate 400 or 500 grams of cured backfat with a knife; you can also add a little beef bone marrow, so that you create a fairly runny paste.

Take a pig's caul and line the mould you are going to use for the pâté, making sure it extends over the rim. At the bottom of the mould, but on top of the caul, place a few thin bards of pork fat. Pour the mixture into the mould; cover it with the caul. Place on the top a round piece of white paper large enough to cover the whole; cover the mould, which you put in a cauldron or saucepan filled with boiling water. Keep the water boiling for four hours, taking care to add fresh water to replace whatever evaporates.

Watch that the boiling water does not get into the mould: you can weigh down the lid to avoid this mishap.

Once the pâté has cooled completely, you can take it out of the mould.

This pâté is really good and quite unlike any other dish of this sort; a few truffles will make it taste something like a *pâté de foie gras*.

A pie should not be cut into until it is utterly cold. A reasonably large pie will not have completely cooled until it has been out of the oven for twenty-four hours.

The pastry you choose to make the lid of a pâté can be puff: this is even to be preferred. Below, I give the different methods of preparing such a pastry.

---

1. In French, *quatre épices*. The classic mix contains pepper, cloves, nutmeg, ginger. English 'mixed spice' is a sweeter blend, found in Holland and the USA, of predominantly cinnamon, nutmeg and allspice.

3. — Puff pastry.

Work 350 grams of butter, as I explained for piecrust (above), so that it becomes soft and dense, holding together, and all its milk and water is expelled: this is important. Put 500 grams of flour on the pastry board; make a well in the centre; add enough salted water to make, with the flour, a dough that is about as firm as the butter: this consistency is very important too. Knead it briskly: gather the pastry into a ball; let it rest for a quarter of an hour; then flatten it, first with your fists, then with the rolling-pin, so that you have something no more than half a centimetre thick; make this sheet square, as far as you are able. Spread the butter over the pastry, in such a way that it is not too close to the edges; press it down so the butter adheres to the pastry. Take two corners [top and bottom] of the pastry, pull them over by one third of the breadth; fold the other third over the top; you will thus have a thick slab with the paste and the butter forming alternate layers. Fold this slab again, but lengthwise, as you did first when it was a single sheet; the result will be something more or less square. Roll this out gently, so you do not break the layers of paste, until it is no thicker than one centimetre, keeping it always, as far as possible, a square. Fold again as you did the first time; roll it out again and fold the paste again; mark it with two lines, to remind you that it has been rolled out and folded twice, then leave it to rest for half an hour. Give it two more turns, just as I have explained, but without adding any more butter. On the last turn, make the pastry the shape and thickness it is meant to have for the job in hand; in the cooking, it will rise to three or four times the height it was before it encountered the heat of the oven.

To make a vol-au-vent crust, or for a hot pie, you lay two or three thicknesses of pastry on top of each other and cut them as they are with a knife. You can make the bottom with flaky pastry (see the following article); the lid is made from a single thickness of puff pastry.

You can cut little diamonds or circles out of this pastry to make little millefeuille cakes. Glaze them with an egg yolk mixed with water and put them in the oven at the moment you move the bread around. Twenty minutes is enough to cook puff pastry. Later, I show different uses for this sort of pastry; you will have then to refer back to this recipe; but I should warn you that the slightest deviation from the rules I have laid down for making this paste will utterly change its nature.

4. — Rich puff pastry.[1]

Take 500 grams of flour, 500 grams of butter and 10 grams of salt. With the flour and warm water in which you have dissolved the salt, quickly make a dough that is neither too soft nor too firm; pull it together into a ball. Work the butter in such a way that you get rid of all the water and milk it may retain; if it is too hard, knead it after warming your hands on a stove that still has some hot cinders; if it is too soft, take it down to the cellar. Once you have worked the butter to the *same consistency* as the dough (this point is important), roll out the paste to a circle that is large enough that when you put the butter in the middle, you can fold it over to cover it *completely*. Use a rolling-pin to very carefully roll out this ball of paste and butter, so that the butter does not escape, until you have a sheet about half a centimetre thick: its length will depend on the size of the original ball. Fold this sheet in four. If the butter is too soft, take the dough down to the cellar and wait until it has firmed up; in summer, you may sometimes have to use ice. Roll it out again to the same thickness, and fold it again into four, observing at all times the same care [that the butter does not escape]; this sometimes means that making the paste this way takes a long time.

After these two stages, roll the paste to a circle, always the same thickness. Fold it up by bringing the edges to the centre, as if you were wrapping a ball. Roll it out again, always carefully, and fold it up again. Repeat this twice. The paste, including the first two stages, will now have had six turns. Fold it up for the last time into a ball; then place it on an iron baking-sheet and roll it out until it is two centimetres thick and is the shape you wish for the job in hand: a bit of practice with the rolling-pin and you will soon get the hang of this. Use a knife to etch diamonds on the pastry; mark the centre of the pastry with the point of the same knife; gild with an egg yolk mixed with a little water and put in the oven a few seconds after the bread. Half an hour will be enough to cook this biscuit; you must check it during this time to make sure it is colouring as it should. If it gets too brown, leave the oven open; on the other hand, heap embers around it if it remains too pale.

1.   In French, *Pâte feuilletée brisée*. It has more butter than the first puff pastry recipe.

The quantities I have suggested will make a very large galette[1] which should be eaten hot to be appreciated at its best.

You can use the same pastry to make a host of cakes, either by cutting it into different shapes before putting it in the oven, or by spreading jam on a very thin sheet of pastry, then topping it off with another sheet. You could also leave the jam or fruit uncovered while placing several layers of pastry round the perimeter to create a thicker border which will rise considerably in the oven. This pastry can also be used to make little meat pies or vol-au-vents.

Pastry made in this fashion is finer, yet no more expensive, than that you will achieve by following the earlier recipe. It only needs a little more effort. If you put in a little less butter, it will be drier. It is not more difficult to make, but when you are working during the hotter months you will often have to devote more time to it.

5. — Patties.

You make these with two thicknesses of puff pastry which you simply cut out of a single sheet of this paste by pressing with the rim of a drinking glass, used here as a pastry cutter. Put a little chopped cooked meat, or better a little meat or fish quenelle mixture (also, of course, cooked) in the centre of the round which will serve as the bottom. Once the forcemeat is in place, moisten the edge of the paste and cover with the second round, which you stick to the first; gild it and put it in the oven. Serve these little patties hot and as an hors-d'oeuvre.

6. — Fried patties (hors-d'oeuvre, luncheon).

Make a shortcrust, roll it out to no more than 5 millimetres thickness; cut rounds a little larger than the rim of a standard glass. Put in the middle a little chopped meat, cooked or raw, and mixed with backfat and seasoned, or some quenelle mixture. Fold the pastry over to cover it and crimp it with the pastry pincers; fry it until it has browned nicely. Serve hot. By using a fish filling, you will have a really appetizing hors-d'oeuvre for fast-days.

---

1.   The word galette has entered into English, defined by *SOED* as 'a broad round cake, usually of pastry'. Because we usually reckon cakes to be made from a sweet batter rather than a pastry, 'cake' does not seem an apt translation. However, more traditional English cakes, such as Eccles cakes, are made of pastry too (the word cake is in origin a description of shape – small, round – not ingredients).

7. — Kidney mould.[1]

This is how they prepare this excellent *gâteau* in Belgium. Take the kidney from a cold roast veal joint; leave the fat with it; pound it in a mortar until reduced to a fine paste. Soak a large piece of the crumb of a loaf in milk (about 200 grams), and pound it with the kidney; add 250 grams of powdered sugar, three eggs (white and yolk), and the grated zest of half a lemon or some orange flower water. Mix everything thoroughly together. Butter a mould carefully and dust all the buttered surface with flour; pour in the mixture; then put the mould in the oven half an hour after the bread, or cook it at the mouth of the oven, like a pudding. At the moment of service, turn it out of the mould and, above all, serve it hot.

8. — Piecrust galette.

You make this pastry exactly like the one intended for a pie; adding egg yolks makes it more delicate. Make the galette three or four centimetres thick, and then prick it with a fork here and there, but regularly from side to side. If you want a sweet galette, dissolve a modicum of sugar in the water you mix with the flour, and reduce the amount of salt. Sweetened galettes will burn more readily than those which are not. This cake, although a trifle dull, is none the less extremely good.

9. — Tarts.

Tarts can be made with shortcrust or puff pastry. When you make them with puff pastry, the bottom does not rise when cooked; just the edges will grow higher. Whichever sort of pastry you use, you lay several layers of paste round the border, which should be of a certain thickness, so that you are able to place either cooked or raw fruits or some sort of cream or boiled rice in the middle. If you use *shortcrust*, you can put it in an iron mould with raised edges.

You can cover the surface of any tart with strips of pastry arranged in diamond formation; this makes a pretty decoration. These little strips, which will get crisp and dry in the baking, are very dainty.

You won't need more than three-quarters of an hour to cook a tart; put it in the oven when you move the bread around. Thirty-five to forty minutes will be enough if the filling is already cooked.

1.   The French title of this recipe is *Gâteau de rognon*.

Fruit tarts. — When you want to make an apple tart, you cook the apples first to a purée[1] which you sweeten and flavour with a little cinnamon or lemon peel. Spread this purée all over the tart, right up to the raised edge; dust with sugar and put it in the oven.

If you think of using pears for this, cook them as a compote before putting them in place; however, if they are juicy summer or autumn pears, you can put them in raw. They need less sugar than apples.

You can use raw cherries. It is better to take out the stones and drain off as much of the juice as possible. When you cook them in advance, you also stone them, and don't add sugar until they are almost completely cooked; then you drain off the juice, add sugar and finish the cooking. You wait until they are cool before placing them on the pastry.

For plums, you split them in two and take out the stones. If you are using greengages, put them in a colander as you stone them so that their juice drains out, and add lots of sugar as cooking brings out the acid in them. Then place them very close to each other in the tart case because they will lose much of their original volume. When cooked, mirabelle plums, St Catherine or Agen are less juicy and much sweeter than greengages.

Apricots make an excellent filling for tarts but you need to add a lot of sugar. Split them in half to take out the stone; you should choose very ripe specimens. You can cook them a little in advance, as I have explained for cherries.

It is not wise to put raw currants, strawberries or raspberries into tarts; you have to make them into a jam first before using them. However, the large strawberry called either 'pineapple' or 'capron'[2] is one of the best fruits to fall back on for this purpose.

In England and Belgium, unripe *gooseberries* are often used in pastry work. They are cooked before they are combined with the pastry. Their extreme sharpness demands the use of lots of sugar. It is a very good way of using gooseberries, which are otherwise scarcely conceivable as a dessert.

Custard tart. — Fruit tarts are without doubt the best; however, you can, if necessary, substitute a custard for the fruit filling: here is the recipe.

1. In French, *marmelade*.
2. The pineapple strawberry is usually thought to be the cultivated garden strawberry (*Fragaria ananassa*), first hybridized in Brittany in the middle of the 18th century. The 'capron' strawberry (*Fragaria moschata*) is commonly thought to be a cultivated 'hautbois' or wood strawberry.

Make quite a thick milk *bouillie*, with plenty of sugar and flavoured with lemon zest, orange flower water or, even better, vanilla. Leave it cooking for a long time, then cool it to lukewarm, stirring it from time to time so that a skin doesn't form on the top. Add two, three or four egg yolks, depending on how much bouillie you have, and mix them in thoroughly. Then pour all this onto the pastry until you judge it to be thick enough. You can dust it with sugar before putting it in the oven, however this is not essential; but when you take it out of the oven you will have to dust it with a little sugar ground to a fine powder.

Rice tart. — Rice boiled in milk, cooked to bursting and sufficiently thick, can be used in exactly the same way as the *bouillie*.

Pumpkin tart. — A pumpkin purée, to which you add two or three egg yolks and the right amount of sugar, also makes an excellent tart.

Frangipane tart. — Finally, you can fill tarts with an almond paste. After you have blanched the almonds by pouring boiling water over them, you pound them in a mortar while adding the required amount of sugar; they will then form a paste which you spread on the tart, and which two or three bitter almonds will flavour nicely.

10. — Cream flan.

Make a small amount of shortcrust pastry, making doubly sure you do not omit adding an egg yolk. Roll this pastry out so it is half a centimetre thick; put it on a pie-dish which you have already buttered and which has a raised edge. Then mix two spoonfuls of flour into half a litre of milk, with a little salt; sweeten generously; thicken it on the heat while stirring, then take it off the fire; let it cool to lukewarm. Now add three egg yolks; mix thoroughly.

Before pouring this into the pastry, you add a little cup of very strong coffee to this cream. Once you have done this, whisk the four egg whites to a snow, which should be very stiff. Sweeten them the right amount with powdered sugar (about three spoonfuls); spread this meringue over the surface of the cream. Then place the pie-dish on a stove with a moderate, but still hot, fire, and surround it with hot ashes still containing some small embers. Let it get really hot on the bottom, then dust the egg whites with very finely pounded sugar and place over the whole thing the Dutch oven with *hot cinders* on its lid. The whites are meant to rise and take on a nice colour without burning. Cooking should take at least an hour. But you should also check its progress from time to time. If the fire beneath the pie-dish is too lively, you will have to damp it down: this may be particularly necessary when the cooking is half over; if, on the other hand, it seems to be nearly extinguished, you will have to get it going again. When the pastry round the edge of the pie-dish seems to be colouring and is firm to the touch, and the egg whites seem to be of the right consistency, the cake is cooked. Leave it in the pie-dish to cool a little so that it firms up before taking it out.

This cake is delicious. You can flavour it with various things: for example, vanilla, chocolate, tea, orange flowers or orange flower water, or even a laurel leaf which you boil in the milk. You can also boil a few finely pounded bitter almonds in the milk; you strain the milk just as you use it in the cream.

11. — Thousand-year cakes (for tea).[1]

Place a litre of good flour on the pastry board; make a well in the middle and break three or four eggs into it; add a little fine salt and 125 grams of good butter. Mix everything in quickly so that all the flour is absorbed, because the dough needs to be very firm and well kneaded. Leave it to rest for an hour; then use a rolling-pin to reduce it to a thickness of a centimetre on the board dusted with flour. Cut out rounds of pastry using a tin pastry-cutter, or if you have none, a wine or liqueur glass. Knead the offcuts back together and do the same again, until there is no pastry left. Leave to dry for an hour; deep-fry them so that they are a nice colour. You can put powdered sugar in the pastry. These cakes will keep a long time and are very good with tea. You can cook them in the oven on an iron baking sheet, in which case you should eggwash them before putting in the oven.

12. — Anise cake.

Take two eggs, a knob of butter as large as an egg, four large spoonfuls of powdered sugar, and a few grams of lightly crushed fresh green anise. You can melt the butter. With all the ingredients, make a dough with

1. In French, *Gâteaux de mille ans*. Earlier texts where this recipe appears suggest that the original name may have been *Gâteaux de Milan*, although they all admit that because they keep very well, they are also called *de mille ans*.

as much flour as you can make it absorb. Roll out the pastry to half a centimetre thick; cut it out either with a tin cutter, or with the rim of a dessert-wine glass. Knead the offcuts together, roll that out and cut out shapes again, until all the pastry is used up. Gild with an egg yolk mixed with a glass of water. Put the cut shapes on sheets of paper and put them in the oven as soon as the bread comes out.

These small cakes keep well; they are as good reheated as fresh.

13. — Colinette (entremets and tea).[1]

Place eight eggs in the scale pan; weigh on the other side an equal weight of butter, sugar and flour in equal parts; separate the yolks from the whites; beat the yolks with the sugar reduced to a powder until they turn pale; add the butter, melted in a bain-marie, a little salt and the flour little by little, making sure it does not form lumps; finally, add the egg whites whisked to a snow. Having done that, butter a mould and dust it with sugar; then pour in the mixture until it is half-full; put it in the oven a little before you take out the bread and let it cook for an hour; let it cool in the mould. The quantities I have suggested produce a very large and very good cake.

Colinette has the advantage of keeping for at least three weeks; it is even better when stale. Cooked in small tins, it can replace madeleines. You can add grated zest of lemon.

14. — Almond galette (entremets and evening reception).

Make a shortcrust paste, as if you were preparing a pie, but sweeten it; after blanching some sweet almonds and a few bitter almonds, pound them in a mortar; knead them in with the paste. When rolling this out, give it a suitable shape, but always allow it a fair thickness. Trim the edges or crimp them; gild the surface. Put it in the oven before taking out the bread.

1. Mme Millet-Robinet's name for this cake, *Colinette* (not found elsewhere), may be merely a use of the diminutive feminine name, deriving in turn from the male name Colin (which is a development or diminutive of Nicolas). Colin and Colinette are often found as characters, in for instance Mother Goose, French nursery rhymes and other theatrical works. The name may also refer to a form of nightcap, or a bonnet worn by women at home *en déshabillé* or undress. This name seems to figure most prominently in northern regions such as the Pas de Calais, French Flanders and Normandy.

15. — Meringues (entremets, evening reception).

Beat eight egg whites to a froth firm enough to support a whole egg without it sinking; quickly mix in 200 grams of sugar reduced to a very fine powder and then sieved. The mixture once achieved, take a spoonful of this and throw it onto a sheet of white paper; take a second and sling it likewise, and continue thus, keeping the meringues well spaced – they must not touch. When the egg whites [in the bowl] no longer offer an even surface allowing you to take up a well-formed spoonful, beat them a little with the spoon before loading it. As soon as all the egg whites have been laid out on the paper, *put them into the oven immediately*, after the bread has been taken out. However, if you are using an oven designed to accommodate large loaves, you should not put the meringues in until at least an hour has elapsed after the bread has come out. *Leave the meringues in the oven for twelve hours.* If they seem to be getting too brown, open the oven door.

The most difficult thing about making meringues is throwing them onto the paper in the proper manner. So that they should be nicely shaped and the right size, you must not use too much force, nor flick the spoon back up too sharply. Success comes from a little practice. Cooking may also be a little problematic, at least if you want to have meringues of a nice colour. You take them off the paper as they come out of the oven. If they stick fast, you have to wet the paper from the underside and let it absorb the water; then they will come off very easily. One disadvantage of meringues is that they go soft after a few hours; if you wish to keep them crisp, you have to leave them in the oven until the moment of service. These problems push up the price of meringues, because otherwise they cost very little. Use the yolks which are a by-product of making meringues either in making a custard, or an omelette, or in cakes that exclude whites. The quantities I have given can make thirty shells which, sandwiched with cream into pairs, makes fifteen meringues.

In most cases the sole of the oven is too hot when the meringues are put in, caramelizing the sugar underneath and causing them to stick to the paper. To avoid this nuisance, place the sheets of paper on a thin board and place them in the oven on this board.

Whipped cream for meringues. — In summer you will have to resort to ice, or have an extremely cool cellar, to make this cream successfully; in winter, or even when it is not actually hot, it is much easier to make. This is how you proceed.

Take yesterday evening's milk, or this morning's; let the cream rise. It is easy to tell cream from milk by its colour. Skim this cream off and put it into a bowl (with a glass of cream you will get quite a large whipped cheese), whip it with twigs or a fork until it comes up into a mousse.

Once the cream has come up, sweeten it with very finely grated sugar; you can flavour it with powdered vanilla or with a piece of vanilla that you boil in a very small quantity of water, which you add to the cream before whipping.

Just when you serve them, place a spoonful of this cream between the two halves of the meringues. Moreover, you can prepare the cream a couple of hours in advance. If the cream doesn't froth up enough, you can beat an egg white stiffly and add it to the cream.

16. — Macaroons (dessert).

Pound in the mortar 125 grams of blanched sweet almonds, to which you add three or four bitter almonds, and 250 grams of sugar, which you add little by little. When the almonds and sugar form a nice fine paste, whip eight egg whites to a froth stiff enough to support a whole egg; mix these whites with the almond paste. Lay out this paste in little rounds on sheets of paper; put them in the oven straight away and cook them like meringues.

Little macaroons without almonds for tea and dessert. — Beat one and a half egg yolks with 200 grams of sugar until the mixture is pale; add 200 grams of flour, which will make a very firm paste. Once you have beaten two egg whites to a very stiff froth, incorporate them in the paste. Roll out a little bit of this paste to the shape required; then put them as you make them onto an oiled or lightly buttered iron baking sheet. Once all the macaroons are shaped, mix the half-yolk you have kept back with a little water to gild all the macaroons which you put in the oven on the baking sheet after the bread has been taken out. If the floor of the oven is still too hot, which happens if it has been heated to cook very large loaves, you should place a couple of small pieces of wood under the sheet to insulate it from the floor. Fifteen or twenty minutes' cooking is enough.

17. — Apple turnover (entremets).

Make some shortcrust or puff pastry; roll it out, making it round; line half of this round with slices of peeled apples; dust generously with sugar; fold the pastry over in such a way that the apples are covered and enclosed within an envelope, the edges sealed by rolling them over a little and pinching them with your fingers. Gild, and put to cook in the oven when the bread is half-way through baking.

You can also use the following method. Put the flour on a pastry board; make a well in the centre, into which you break an egg; add a large pinch of salt, 100 grams of butter, and half a glass of warm water; knead it together to make a dough a little firmer than for bread; roll it out until it is at most half a centimetre thick. Cut rounds from this sheet, about ten centimetres across; cover half of each round with pieces of peeled eating apples, add a spoonful of powdered sugar. Fold the pastry over, seal the top to the bottom; you will then have something like a small turnover. Repeat this until you have used all the pastry. With the quantities indicated above, you will get six or seven turnovers. Butter a pie-dish well; place the turnovers in this; put them in the oven five or six minutes after the bread; check them from time to time. When they are firm to the touch and seem cooked, take them out. Usually there is a sort of caramel in the bottom of the pie-dish; if it is hard, add a few drops of water to detach it from the dish; remove this and use it to gild the tops of the turnovers; put them back in the pie-dish and pop them for a few seconds in the oven again to glaze.

You can make cherry, plum or apricot turnovers. You can also cook them on a stove over a gentle fire, covered with the Dutch oven

You can also line a buttered pie-dish with this same pastry and fill it with fruits, or almond paste, or a really sweet *bouillie*, or milk rice, etc., and cook it under the Dutch oven as I have just described.

18. — Pithiviers cake (entremets and evening reception).

Make some puff pastry; let it rest. Blanch 250 grams of sweet almonds and two or three bitter almonds; pound them in a mortar with 250 grams of sugar and the zest of half a lemon; bring them together into a paste. Roll out half the puff paste to a circle until it is no more than 5 millimetres thick; spread the almond paste over it, making sure it is not too thick at the edges. Prepare the other half of the puff paste in the same way as the first;

use it to cover the cake; after wetting the edges of the two sheets of pastry, crimp them together with the help of the pastry pincers or your fingers; then mark out squares or diamonds on the top of the cake with a knife. Gild; put it in the oven when the bread is half-cooked. Half an hour's cooking will be enough.

You can also line a shortcrust with almond paste and lay thin ribbons of pastry in a diamond grid over the top.

19. — Apple tartlets (entremets and evening reception).

Make some puff pastry or shortcrust; roll it out to a thickness of 3 millimetres. Butter the bottom of a pie dish; line it with this pastry; pour on top an apple purée such as you make for a charlotte; cover this with pastry and stick the edges together. Having done this, score the surface in diamonds or some other design, pressing down hard on the pastry with the back of a knife; gild. Put the pie-dish over a gentle heat; cover it with a Dutch oven. Usually, half an hour's cooking is enough.

20. — Little choux buns (entremets and evening reception).

Make a paste like that for *beignets soufflés*; cut small pieces which you round off on the bottom and which you place on a sheet of buttered paper or even on an iron baking sheet; gild. Put into the oven quarter of an hour after the bread; keep an eye on whether they are cooked because they may be done in an instant.

You can dust the tops of these little buns with crushed almonds which will be partly grilled by the heat of the oven. To make them even daintier, split them on one side and fill them with jam or whipped cream. This is a really inexpensive cake.

21. — Baba (evening reception, luncheon, tea).

Place a litre of flour on a pastry board; make a well in the centre; add 10 grams of salt, four or five eggs, 200 grams of kneaded butter,[1] a little

---

1. In French, *beurre manié*. Today, this is usually understood as butter kneaded together with flour, deployed as a way of thickening sauces, etc., without going to the trouble of a roux. *Beurre manié*, also meaning kneaded or worked, is butter that has been kneaded to exclude all traces of water and whey. Mme Millet-Robinet is referring to her recommendation to knead the butter to get rid of those two impurities in her

powdered saffron, 100 grams of dried raisins (the pips of which must be removed), 100 grams of currants, and a piece of brewer's yeast the size of a walnut. Mix everything with warm water; knead. The dough should be slightly soft; place this in a saucepan or buttered mould and let it sit near the hearth for five or six hours in winter, less time in summer. When it is well risen, take it out of the mould and place it on a sheet of buttered paper; then put it in the oven when the bread is half-way through its baking.

22. — Brioches.

Place 500 grams of the best flour on the pastry board; make a well in the centre into which you put some bread leaven the size of a small egg or, which is much to be preferred, some brewer's yeast the size of a walnut; this last you can obtain easily enough from cafés or establishments which sell beer, because it is to be found at the bottom of the small barrels in which the beer is delivered. Add to all that a quantity of warm milk sufficient to dissolve the leaven and to make a dough with the flour that is about as firm as a bread dough (you will need about a glass of milk). Carefully dissolve the leaven or yeast in the milk and then incorporate all the flour. When the dough is made, form it into a ball and place it in a napkin which has been generously dusted with flour, or in a small bowl, also floured and warmed in advance. Cover this dough so that the cold cannot penetrate; then put it in a warm place if it's cold weather, in the dough trough if it's hot. When you use brewer's yeast, you must let it rise for two hours; when you have relied on bread leaven, you must wait six hours.

Knead 750 grams of very fresh butter so that all the whey is extracted and to make it as soft as possible. In winter, you do this with your hands; in the summer, with a wooden spoon, in a dish. Place 1 kilogram of flour on the pastry board; make a well in the centre and put the starter dough there when you think it has risen enough. Add a spoonful of grated sugar, 15 grams of crushed salt, half a glass of quite warm milk; work the starter dough into the milk, and add twelve eggs and the butter, which you have cut into

---

earlier recipes for pie crust and rich puff pastry (pp. 606 and 613 above), or in the recipe for brioche which follows. Nowadays, concentrated bakers' butter is a product made by putting raw butter through a centrifuge to achieve the same end. This is widely used in *boulangeries* and *pâtisseries*.

small pieces. Mix all these ingredients together, thoroughly incorporating as you do so all the flour; when doing this, knead vigorously.

As soon as the mixing is complete, you must stop kneading because if you knead too much or too slowly you risk seeing the dough *blown* (technical term) and it will not rise as it should. Bring the dough together in a ball, dusting it lightly with flour as you pull it off the pastry board; then wrap it in a napkin, also well dusted with flour. Place the napkin in either a bread basket or a bowl, and cover the whole with a woollen blanket, placing it in a warm place if you are working in winter; in the summer, it is enough to put it in the dough trough, once you have wrapped it as I instruct; if it is really very hot weather, it is even better to take it to a cool place, still covered as I mentioned.

An iron baking sheet is essential for baking a brioche in the oven. If you want a ring-shaped brioche, you must lightly dust the middle of the sheet with flour and place the ball of dough on top. Then you pull apart the centre of the dough with your fingers so that you fashion a hole which goes all the way through to the baking sheet, of a width to give the ring of dough the size and thickness you want.

To make a brioche of the usual shape, you take a small piece of the dough and roll it into a ball, then flatten the main piece slightly and place the ball on the top. If you want several smaller brioches, divide the dough into as many as you wish, and then treat each of these as you do a single larger example.

When making several brioches, you must space them out on the baking sheet, otherwise they will stick to each other because they swell up when baking. You gild them with an egg yolk mixed in water or, if you have no egg, with milk, and you put them in the oven about ten minutes after the bread, depending on how hot the oven is. Cooking a large brioche takes three-quarters of an hour; half an hour is enough to cook a ring, or small brioches.

The quantities I have suggested will make a very large brioche, enough for twenty people; success is more difficult with smaller quantities, for instance with a quarter of those indicated. However, if you cut the recipe by a half, you will achieve your goal relatively easily.

Brioche should as far as possible be served hot; you can reheat it in the oven after the bread has come out. When there is some left over, cut it into thin slices which you put in the oven just before you take the bread out; they will toast and make an excellent sort of cake to go with tea, and which children greatly appreciate.

23. — Pumpkin bread.

Cook and drain a piece of nice Turk's turban squash, then sieve it; add 125 grams of butter, 125 grams of sugar or 200 grams of honey, and a little salt. Mix everything thoroughly while keeping it warm.

Place flour in a circle on the pastry board; make a well in the centre. Take a piece of bread leaven as large as two eggs (the *fresh starter* you made for the bread the day before is very appropriate for this purpose); put this piece of leaven in the middle of the flour. Mix everything together with half a litre of more-than-lukewarm milk, then add the pumpkin prepared as I have just described. Mix this in vigorously with the leaven, flour and milk to make a dough as firm as a bread dough. Butter an iron mould with a raised edge, place the dough in the centre and flatten it so that it fills the mould. Having done this, put it in a warm place, having covered it with a warm napkin and a woollen blanket so that the dough does not chill. Let it rise as long as the bread. (I am assuming that you are preparing the pumpkin bread while someone else is preparing the ordinary bread.) Gild, either with an egg yolk or with milk, and put it in the oven as soon as the bread has gone in. Let it cook for an hour; once this time has elapsed, take the mould out of the oven and let it cool a little. This *bread-cake* will have risen, but not as much as bread. It is excellent hot, still good when cool, and even when stale; moreover, you can grill the slices, which makes it seem fresh again.

This cake for family consumption, very inexpensive, is most suitable for children; it is always digestible. You can sweeten it more or less, or even not at all; in this last instance, increase the proportion of salt.

24. — Milk bread and Rusks.

Proceed exactly as for pumpkin bread but, to replace the pumpkin, increase the proportion of milk.

To make rusks, you place the dough in strips on an iron baking sheet, where it will rise, as we have seen above. When it is cooked and stale, you cut thin little slices and put them back in the oven just before you take out the bread. The rusks will colour nicely, dry out, and keep for a very long time in a box. For them to be light, the dough must be well risen. Honey is not suitable as a sweetener for rusks; you can dispense with sugar altogether, which is what you should do if the rusks are going to be used instead of bread in all sorts of soups, whether for fast-days or not.

25. — Savoy biscuit.[1]

Crack eight eggs and carefully separate the yolks from the whites, which you put in a bowl large enough for you to whisk them stiffly. Keep back two yolks; put the other six into an earthenware dish with 500 grams of powdered sugar and a little salt; beat them with a wooden spoon until you have a nice paste which is quite thick and almost white. This will take about half an hour. Add 250 grams of potato starch or the finest white wheat flour,[2] and the grated zest of half a lemon and a little powdered vanilla. (You can do without any flavouring.) Whisk the egg whites stiffly enough to support a whole egg. Lightly butter a tin or copper mould; dust it all over with powdered sugar; pour in the mixture to half-fill it and put it in the oven without delay, the moment you take the bread out; then close the oven.[3] To check how far cooking has progressed, try to insert a straw into the cake. You can easily gauge whether it is cooked enough by how the straw behaves. When it seems right, take it out of the oven; let it cool somewhat in the mould before trying to extract it, then turn it out onto a dish.

You can easily do without an oven by surrounding the mould with hot cinders, even glowing ones, mixed with small embers which you have taken out of the oven after baking the bread. Even the day after, if the oven was heated with small sticks and the ash was gathered together into a single heap, there will be enough residual heat to cook a biscuit. Put an iron lid on the mould and heap on it hot ash and embers.

If you desire a biscuit that is less sweet, you can reduce the amount of sugar to 350, or even 250 grams instead of 500. If, instead of eight egg whites, you use ten (which means four more whites to the number of

1. The actual volume used to make this translation was annotated at this point by the [original?] owner, Dr B. Vogelweid of Altkirch (Haut-Rhin), just south of Mulhouse. In any event, the user increased the quantities to make a larger batch.
2. In French, *fleur de froment*. Nowadays, this is defined as Type 45, used for pâtisserie.
3. Mme Millet-Robinet has omitted to instruct the reader to combine the egg yolk and sugar mixture with the egg whites.

yolks), the biscuit will be lighter, but a little drier. This is then left a little longer in the oven. The quantities I have given will give you a very large biscuit. It is an inexpensive cake.

Rather than using a mould, you can pour the mixture into a pie-dish that you have buttered and dusted with sugar. Dust as well the top surface of the biscuit with sugar, then put it in the oven. Half an hour, three-quarters at the most, will be enough to cook it. In this case, you have a flat biscuit. Leave it to cool, then split it into two halves, top and bottom. Then you have two very flat biscuits. Spread a layer of apricot jam on the bottom half; place the other half on top; the result is a delicious cake.

If you put this mixture into paper cases, you will have *biscuits in cases*.[1] To make *fingers*,[2] drop them onto a sheet of paper from a spoon; you begin at one end of the paper and, when the batter sticks slightly to the paper, quickly draw the spoon back to yourself. Dust the surface lightly with sugar and put into the oven immediately. Ten minutes will be enough to cook them.

26. — Almond cake.

Place eight eggs in a scale pan; and place an equal weight of sugar in the other pan; add half this weight of flour or potato starch, plus 125 grams of blanched sweet almonds which you have pounded in a mortar or chopped *very finely*, and 250 grams of butter. Break the eggs and separate out the whites. Use a wooden spoon to beat together the yolks and the sugar, which you have reduced to a fine powder, until they form a smooth and almost white paste; add the *melted*, but *not browned*, butter, the flour and the ground almonds; mix everything together. Beat the whites to a stiff froth, so that it supports a whole egg; mix them in. Grease a pie-dish with butter; dust it with sugar; pour in the mixture. Fill a stove with still-glowing cinders; place the pie-dish on top; surround it as well with glowing cinders; then cover it with a hot iron lid also loaded with glowing cinders mixed with a few embers. The cake is cooked when it resists your finger as you prod it. Let it cool somewhat in the pie-dish; then turn it out onto a grill covered with a white cloth; dust the top with grated sugar. This is an excellent cake.

1.   In French, *biscuits en caisse*.
2.   In French, *biscuits à la cuiller*. These are the sponge fingers used in charlottes, etc.

You can also proceed as follows: melt 350 grams of good butter; take 250 grams of sweet almonds and as much grated sugar, plus 5 grams of salt and 3 eggs. Blanch and pound the almonds finely – and you can add a few bitter almonds too. Break the eggs; add the yolks and whites to a dish with the salt, almonds, sugar and butter; mix everything together. Pour this mixture onto flour and knead it until you have a very firm dough. Roll this out so it is no more than 5 millimetres thick; give it a nice shape. Mark it out in diamonds or other patterns; gild it with egg yolk. Put it in the oven on an iron baking sheet, a little after you have installed the bread. When the biscuit has dried out, it is cooked; it keeps fairly well.

27. — Croquets.[1]

Their confection is little different to that of the almond biscuit above; save that the flour is added before the almonds, which are not pounded but shredded as if for making nougat; they are mixed thoroughly into the dough which is then rolled out to a thickness of no more than 1 centimetre and cut into strips which are then divided into long rectangles and baked in the oven like the almond cake. These croquets keep for a long time.

28. — Nougat.[2]

Take 250 grams of sweet almonds; blanch them in hot water, then shred them lengthwise. (Each almond into four.) Pound or grate 250 grams of sugar; put the sugar and almonds over a brisk fire; sauté them to begin with, then stir them with a spoon. The sugar will soon melt and turn a caramel colour; the moment the colour is just right, that's to say when it's golden brown, you put the nougat into a mould. You should have ready a mould whose inside has been coated all over with sweet almond oil, or olive oil if you have none. Pour in some of the nougat so that it spreads out in a thin layer on the bottom, using a spoon frequently dipped in almond oil to help. When the bottom of the mould is covered, pour the rest in little by little, spreading it across the mould in the same way, trying

1. This is the French name for these crisp almond biscuits. It derives from the verb *croquer*, to crunch.
2. This type of nougat is identified as *nougatine*, made without the addition of egg whites. It is therefore a more brittle confection than the *nougat de Montélimar* that we commonly buy today.

not to compact the mixture but still working quickly enough so that the sugar doesn't start to harden. Success comes easily with a little dexterity. If some caramel sticks to the spoon, take another one – being always sure to moisten it with oil from time to time. The nougat will harden immediately. When it is *thickened* and hard, turn the mould over and, if necessary, give a light tap to the edge of the mould to turn out the nougat. If it sticks to the mould anywhere, you can pour a little oil between the nougat and the mould and, turning this last in all directions so that the oil circulates, the nougat will come away. If it persists in sticking, flash the mould over a brisk fire; it will heat up and the nougat will come out. All these small problems will be surmounted with a little practice.

You can also make up the nougat in a saucepan or an earthenware bowl which is really well glazed and perfectly dry, which is coated all over with almond oil. All you must watch for is that the mould is wider at the top than the bottom so that the nougat will come out easily.

This sweetmeat is really not expensive and is excellent.

You can also put just the sugar on the heat; when it starts to caramelize, you add the almonds and let it finish cooking. For the rest you do as I have explained. If you make it in this fashion, the nougat is perhaps easier to lay out because the almonds have not dried out so much in the cooking and are thus less brittle. However, the result is not so good and is less crisp.

By splitting the mixture between two moulds, one smaller, one larger, you will have two nougats to pile one on the other, making an extremely elegant gâteau.

29. — Trottoirs et croquignoles (dry cakes to accompany tea).[1]

Put flour on the pastry board, make a well in the centre; add three egg yolks, 125 grams of powdered sugar, as much butter (which you melt), and 5 grams of finely crushed salt. Mix everything, drawing in the flour little

1. The French name defies translation: *trottoir* means pavement; *croquignoles* are small dry cakes, the most famous being (according to *Larousse gastronomique*) from Paris and Navarrenx in the Pyrenees. Larousse notes that a *croquignole* also denotes a flick of the finger (to the nose or the face) and suggests that the name may have been applied to the cake as it was thrown or projected by participants in various festivals or fairs, in rather the same way as confetti, originally comfits, is thrown over bride and groom. As the recipe explains, the *trottoirs* are the dough rolled into lengths, while the *croquignoles* are the dough shaped as round buttons.

by little; add half a glass of tepid milk; then finish kneading it, making a dough firmer than a bread dough. Work this dough intensively; take a portion and roll it with the hands so that you make a roll about the thickness of a finger. Make a measure of between 10 and 15 centimetres with a small wooden dowel; cut the rolls to this length and place them on an iron baking sheet. Continue until you have used all the dough; cover the sheet and the rolls and leave them in a warm place: let them rest for about an hour and put them in the oven ten minutes after the bread. Fifteen minutes baking will be enough if the oven is heated to the right temperature. If the 'pavements' do not brown enough, you should put a few embers in the mouth of the oven.

By cutting this dough into small pieces which you then roll between the hands you can make *croquignoles*, which are popularly called *breeches' buttons* or *gaiters' buttons*.[1] This confection will keep at least a month.

30. — Drumsticks (dry cake for tea).[2]

Warm a glass of milk and melt 125 grams of butter. Put some flour on the pastry board; make a well in the centre into which you place a piece of bread leaven as large as a hen's egg, 15 grams of finely ground salt and a little milk; dissolve the leaven very carefully; add the butter and the rest of the milk. Swiftly draw in enough flour to make a dough that is slightly firmer than a bread dough; tear off a piece; roll it on the pastry board until it is about the size of a lady's little finger; cut it to a length of 30, 40 or even 50 centimetres and place it on an iron baking sheet. Carry on like this for all the dough, spacing the sticks on the sheet so that they do not stick to each other while baking; cover with a white cloth, then a blanket, and take it to a warm place. Let it rise as long as bread; put it in the oven, on the sheet, ten minutes after the bread. Check the sticks to make sure they are colouring up nicely; if they remain too pale, put a few embers at the mouth of the oven. Fifteen or twenty minutes will be enough to cook them.

1. In French, these last are *boutons de guêtres.* This is also a name of a small, black mushroom (*Bulgaria inquinans*), which is not edible, as well as the very edible *faux mousseron* or Scotch bonnet *Marasmius oreades.* The biscuits are sometimes called *patiences.*
2. In French, *baguettes de tambour.* In a later (1893) edition, this confection is also called *Cressini.* This is the name which can be found for the same thing in *Cookery for English Households,* by a French Lady (Macmillan, 1864). It is a variant of the Italian *grissini.*

These very crisp sticks keep for a very long time. By making rolls with the same dough, splitting them as you put them into the oven, you will get excellent milk rolls.

31. — Jaw breaker (cake from Poitou).[1]

Put some rennet in two litres of milk that has just been drawn from the cow and put the container in another one full of water hot enough so that you can plunge your hand in without scalding; cover it. Once the milk has set, that is to say after one or two hours, put it to drain either hung in a napkin you have wetted in advance or in a cheese strainer.

The next day, pour this curd into a bowl and add a little salt and six whole eggs which you have thoroughly beaten; mix everything carefully together then add flour to it until you make a dough that is firm enough so that you can pick up a bit as large as half an egg on the end of your finger – which you then place on a chestnut leaf, and then cover with another leaf – and then put immediately into the oven using a small peel with a long handle, or some such implement, just after the bread. Carry on until you have used all the dough; the quantities stated will make a fair number of *casse-museaux*. While they are baking, which will take about 15 minutes, this little cake will rise considerably. You can put the dough onto an iron baking sheet rather than a chestnut leaf.

32. — Burgundy cake (for tea).[2]

Put a spoonful of cream in a little pile of flour; knead it so that you absorb as much flour as possible into the cream; roll out this paste to a thickness of 2 millimetres. Butter a pie-dish; lay the pastry in it; dust with

1.   In French, *casse-museau* (*museau*: muzzle, snout). *Larousse gastronomique* describes this as a hard biscuit now rarely made. It derives its name not only from its toughness, but also from the custom of 'tossing the biscuits at the face during certain popular festivals, such as the Rogation Procession held in Poitiers.' It goes on to remark that in Corsica, these same biscuits are called *sciappa-denti*: tooth-breaker. In Poitiers, the Grand'Goule ('Bigmouth') is a mythical dragon that lived at the bottom of the river Clain (which flows through Poitiers) at the time of St Radegonde in the 6th century AD. An effigy, which was carved in the 17th century, is paraded through the streets on St Radegonde's day (13 August), as well as Rogation days, and onlookers would throw these biscuits at the dragon's gaping mouth: a bullseye meant good fortune in the coming year.
2.   In French, *Gâteau bourguignon*.

sugar that you have pounded coarsely, and flavour it with a little lemon zest. Put it in the oven a moment after the bread; as soon as the pastry is cooked and has coloured up nicely, take it out of the oven. This little cake, which will puff up or blister here and there, is crisp and really good.

You can make up a larger amount of dough and line several pie-dishes, or use the same pie-dish repeatedly because it takes no time at all to cook such a thin cake and the oven will hold its heat for plenty of time to bake it.

CHAPTER XVIII

DESSERT AND EVENING RECEPTIONS

1. — Marrons and chestnuts.[1]

How to roast marrons. — Remove the outer skin of the marrons and put them in the coffee roaster over a lively fire; turn it as if you were roasting coffee; in a quarter of an hour, if the roaster is not too full, the marrons will be perfectly cooked and nicely grilled. The thin skin still covering them is easily removed, without the fingers getting blackened. You can roast marrons without taking off the outer skin but they will take much longer to cook. When cooking marrons still in their outer skin, you must be sure to split them across on the round side, not near the germ. If you fail to splice them, you run the risk of explosions which may not be entirely accident-free. To serve marrons, arrange them in the folds of a napkin placed on a dinner plate; they will retain their heat for a fairly long time.

Some flower-pot manufacturers produce pots that are ideal for cooking marrons. These vessels, shaped something like a ewer, have two handles, and below the shoulder are pierced with large holes like a chestnut-pan or a large-holed colander. Place this pot on a small trivet over embers in the hearth; put in the marrons spliced the way I advised; stir them about from time to time, holding the pot by one of the handles – which you should purposely turn towards the room so it barely gets warm. If the fire is maintained as it should be, the marrons will be perfectly cooked in a quarter of an hour, won't blacken the fingers, and will peel easily. This pot,

---

1.   Mme Millet-Robinet here preserves the distinction between *marrons*, the cultivated, larger chestnut and the unimproved sweet chestnut referred to in note 2 on page 598, Chapter XVI, above.

made from the same clay as flower-pots, is utterly fireproof, indeed it will toughen in the heat.

Boiled marrons and chestnuts. — When you wish to eat boiled marrons, you should remove the outer skin and cook them in water with a little salt. Some people add fennel or celery. Serve them in a bowl with a tight cover; they peel very easily. Cooked thus and eaten with milk, they are extremely good.

To keep chestnuts, they should be stored somewhere cool, not too damp, and well ventilated, otherwise they blacken and dry out. You can also bury them in sand, in the cellar. This last method is very successful.

Chestnuts and marrons in good condition should usually be brown, round and firm.

2. — Cooked compotes.[1]

Compote of prunes. — The first article in this section must be devoted to *prunes*, which of all fruits are the most often put in a compote. After washing, put them in enough water to cover and cook them either in a little earthenware pot before the fire or in a saucepan on the stove. You should add sugar almost at the outset. If the juice is not thick enough when the prunes are cooked, take them out and reduce the juice until it is a syrup; if, on the other hand, it is very thick, you can add some water or some red wine, which will greatly heighten the flavour of the compote. Some people even make it with wine alone, but I feel that this lends the prunes too pronounced a flavour; moreover, the acidity of the wine cooked with the prunes means the quantity of sugar must be doubled.

Apple compote. — Choose medium-sized dessert apples;[2] peel them, take out the centre with an apple-corer, leaving the apples whole, and throw them into cold water. Once they are all prepared, arrange them side by side in a saucepan; add two glasses of water and sufficient sugar. To keep them white, squeeze the juice of a lemon on the apples and at the same time add

---

1. In French, *Compotes cuites*. While we might translate this as 'stewed fruit', the idea of a compote of fruit, made with a prepared syrup, was universal in England and referred to as such by both Eliza Acton and Mrs Beeton. *Compote* means no more than mixture (deriving from the Latin) and is usually composed of whole fruit or at the least identifiable pieces of fruit. A dish where the syrup and fruit form an indeterminate whole would be a *marmelade*. A *compotier* is a wide, flat, stemmed dish in which compotes are served.

2. In French, *pommes de reinette*, in English 'pippins', e.g. Cox's Orange Pippin.

a strip of lemon peel and a little cinnamon to the saucepan. Cover the pan with a sheet of white paper and then put on the lid; cook on a fairly brisk fire. Check the apples when you think them nearly cooked, that is to say after about half an hour on the heat at the most; cooked too long, they will be reduced to a *marmelade*. Put the apples in a compote dish, lifting them out carefully with a spoon; if the juice is too thin, reduce it by cooking for a few minutes more; strain it over the apples, around which it will form a very clear and pale jelly. Put a glacé cherry or some redcurrant jelly in the centre of each apple, this will bring out their whiteness.

Compote of pears. — This will be red or white, depending on the variety of pear you use. The best pears to eat raw always make the best compotes. If they are large, cut them in four; peel them and throw them into cold water; if they are small, leave them whole and keep the stalk, which you trim by a half after scraping it. Put the pears in a saucepan with enough water to cover, this is especially necessary when the pears are a firm-fleshed variety. Sweeten; cover the pan if the compote should be white; leave to cook. You need not fear that pears suffer the same drawback as apples in the cooking; they need at least two hours, and often more. When cooking whole pears, stand them upright; if you have cut them up, arrange the quarters in a circle, one next to the other. Reduce the juice; pour it over the compote. To make it excellent, take the juice off the fire when it is reduced and leave till nearly cold; add a small glass of kirsch and pour it immediately over the pears. If you want to have a nice red compote, add good red wine during the cooking.

Cherry compote. — The best cherries for this are sour, English, morello, from Holland, or pearly.[1] Reduce the stalks to half their length; put the cherries on the fire with a few drops of water; add sugar, cover. When they have rendered some of their juice, take them off the heat and make up the compote. Reduce the juice before pouring it over the cooked cherries.

Other red fruits are not good in a compote, at least when it involves heating them.

Compote of verjuice.[2] — The muscat is the grape that makes the best

1. The French for 'pearly' is *nacrée*. This is perhaps a reference to 'white heart' cherries.
2. The use of the word verjuice (*verjus*), together with the advice to use more sugar than in other compotes, indicates that the grapes used here were unripe, as they would be for making verjuice.

compote. Pick them off the bunch, remove the pips from each grape; cook like other compotes, but with more added sugar.

Quince compote. — Wipe them; half-cook them in boiling water: without this precaution the compote will not have a nice colour; take them out, peel them and cut them in quarters. Finish the cooking as for a compote of pears.

Plum compote. — Greengages make a nice compote. Once you have cut the bottom off the plum stalks, cook them whole in a syrup of half a glass of water and 200 grams of sugar. When they are cooked, dress them in a dish. Reduce the juice a little before pouring it over the compote.

Apricot compote. — Prepare it in the same way as the plum compote; the juice will jelly. You should remove the stones.

Peach compote. — The same procedure as the previous ones. You must wipe the peaches before adding them to the syrup. Cooked peaches do not taste very pleasant.

Compote of marrons. — After removing the outer skins, blanch fifty nice marrons in boiling water; leave them to cook until you can pierce them easily with a pin; then peel them and throw them into some water acidulated with lemon juice. Drain the marrons and put the acidulated water on to heat; add 375 grams of sugar and three spoonfuls of orange flower water, or else rub the outside of a lemon with some of the lumps of sugar. When the syrup has heated to soft-ball,[1] add the marrons and heat them gently until they are done enough.

3. — Raw compotes.

Peach salad. — Peel the peaches and slice them. Put them in a compotier after coating both sides well with powdered sugar; sprinkle a little decent eau-de-vie over everything.

You do the same for excellent cold compotes of juicy pears, apricots and tender apples.

Orange salad. — Cut them in slices without peeling them; arrange them in a compotier, dusting them generously with sugar; sprinkle over eau-de-vie, rum or kirsch.

All these compotes need to be tossed like a salad at the moment of service.

1.   118–125°C.

Peeled cherries. — Choose some nice sour cherries; peel them: this is not difficult when the fruit is ripe enough; shorten the stalks by a half; roll the cherries in powdered sugar so that they are covered by a thick layer; leave them spaced out in a single layer on dinner plates in the sun. Bring them in, keep them in a cool place until the moment of service. It is a most superior dessert.

Pearled currants. — Choose some nice bunches of red and white currants; dip them in water, then in powdered sugar; leave them out in the sun; keep them in the cool.

4. — Hors-d'oeuvre for an evening reception.

Sandwiches.[1] — These are prepared with the crumb of a loaf large enough to yield little slices about the size of a playing-card. In large towns, bakers make loaves especially for this purpose.

The bread should not be too fresh. Take off the crust and cut the crumb to the size you want for your slices. Spread the surface of the bread with a layer of very fresh butter. As a preliminary, you should have secured a piece of ham of the first quality with very firm flesh. This ham should be cut into slices as thin as possible with a well-sharpened knife. Ham that has been prepared as I have already explained, that is chopped and reformed, is very suitable for sandwiches. One of these slices is laid on the butter, and the slice of bread is then taken off the large piece of crumb – it should be no more than 4 or 5 millimetres thick. You then prepare a second slice of bread and butter, but without ham, and stick it on the first, that is to say the one where the buttered surface received the slice of ham. Thus you will have two slices of bread and butter with a slice of ham in between. You can substitute the ham with thin slices of *pâté de foie gras* or salmon.

As you prepare them, you pile these slices on a platter and cover them with a damp napkin folded in four so that they do not dry out. You only uncover them at the moment of serving.

Sandwiches are excellent with tea; and they are also served at dances, when they are usually welcomed.

Slices of buttered rye bread. — Prepare these like sandwiches, but they are not interleaved with ham. You must be sure to cover them with a *damp*

1.   In the text, *Sandwish*, with no plural form. In later editions the spelling was *sandwich*, pl. *sandwichs*.

napkin because if they dry out, the lose much of their merit. You will need *almost* as much butter as bread.

Canapés. — This is what you call small rolls that have been made for this purpose, which are split in two and have their middles filled with a thin slice of *pâté de foie gras*, or ham or galantine. It is a very elegant form of sandwich.

5. — Hot drinks.

Punch. — Make a strong infusion of tea. Rub the peel of one or two lemons with several lumps of sugar with sufficient force that you take off the yellow part. Put all the sugar in a porcelain tureen or silver bowl. Pour in the boiling tea, in sufficient quantity that you have a *very sweet* liquor. When the sugar has dissolved, add a little rum, tasting from time to time, to give the punch the strength you wish for. Ladies, with very few exceptions, do not like a very strong punch. Serve hot in stemmed glasses.

Here are some satisfactory quantities: tea, 15 grams; 2 lemons; sugar, 1 kilogram; boiling water, 3 bottles; rum, about 1 bottle. You can replace the rum by a good eau-de-vie. Some people add to all this the juice of a lemon, but then you will have to almost double the quantity of sugar.

You can set the punch alight, which makes it less intoxicating and imparts a most pleasing caramel flavour. To do this, you heat it up, then bring a lighted piece of paper close to its surface and keep stirring with a silver spoon. You extinguish it when you think it has burnt enough, or you just stop stirring when it will go out by itself.

Mulled wine. — Over a hot fire, heat a good red wine to which you add 10 to 15 grams of cinnamon to every litre. Add sugar. As soon as it comes to the boil, take it off the heat; serve in stemmed glasses.

Coffee. — You must not grind it too finely, otherwise it will pass through the holes of the filter and make the coffee cloudy. Porcelain filter coffee pots, or fine earthenware pots with a pewter filter are better than coffee-makers with tinplate filters; the iron is oxidized by the coffee and affects both the colour and the taste. The price of porcelain coffee-makers is not high: those which hold six cups cost 2 or 3 francs; they are usually red or black earthenware with yellow edges, or brown porcelain. True gourmets will never take coffee made with a tinplate device once they have tasted it from a china coffee-maker. But in my opinion, the best way to prepare coffee is with a coffee-maker with a spirit lamp: there are several models and various arrangements, all of which are much to be preferred.[1] I find coffee prepared in these coffee-makers is much better than any made by other means; it loses not the smallest fraction of its aroma.

Nowadays, certain commercial houses specialize in coffee and have pretty ingenious roasting equipment which preserves the aroma. The sale price of this coffee is higher than raw beans, but as these last lose a fifth of their weight by torrefaction, roasted coffee is not in fact any more expensive, and is sometimes very good. I can recommend the coffee sold at 53 rue Constantine, Plaisance, near Paris, under the name of coffee extract of the Compagnie des Antilles.[2] By mixing equal quantities of this and other coffee prepared as I have already instructed, you will get a very good coffee at moderate cost. They have agents in almost every town.

Mocha coffee is without doubt the best; however you can mix it with equal quantities of good Martinique coffee, especially when it is going to be served with milk.

I have already described the particular characteristics of the principal varieties of coffee in the chapter *Concerning provisions* (page 302, above); here, therefore, I have only to advise on how to prepare it.

A properly roasted coffee should be *not black* but a handsome dark reddish-brown.[3] If it is roasted too much, it loses its aroma and becomes bitter; if not enough, it is acrid. If when checking the roaster you find that it is almost the desired colour, you should not put it back on the fire but rather complete the roasting by turning it over in the roaster. Once it is roasted, you should put the coffee in an earthenware pot, better than china,

---

1.   Mme Millet-Robinet does not go into detail about this last class of coffee-maker. She is correct, however, that there were myriad different designs. In their principle, they resemble the Cona system of making coffee that used to be seen widely in British restaurants and hotel dining rooms until the 1960s.

2.   Plaisance is a district in the 14th arrondissement of Paris; rue Constantine is now called rue Vercingetorix. The *Journal de chimie médical, de pharmacie et toxicologie*, 4th series, vol. 4, 1858, reporting on criminal proceedings against various adulterators of foodstuffs, etc., gives an account of proceedings brought against the Compagnie des Antilles for adding sugar to the coffee beans which it then roasted. The defendants protested that this addition was not an adulteration inasmuch as it was not harmful to health, but the judges ruled none the less that it was a fraud and condemned the manager to a short prison sentence and a fine.

3.   In French, *roux*.

and cover it while it cools; when cold you can store it in a standard tinplate canister with a tight lid or a properly stoppered glass jar, which is perhaps even preferable. You should only grind it as and when you need it.

This is how to make coffee: if you are going to drink it black, put a *large spoonful per cup* in the filter: many people only take a demitasse so you do not need as many spoonfuls as there are diners; three will usually be enough for six people. When the coffee is in the filter, press it down a little with the small tamper (which is usually tinplate but which is much better made from wood because of the propensity of coffee to oxidize iron which I mentioned earlier); leave the tamper in place while you pour on boiling water. Pour on just a little water at first and let the coffee absorb it; then add the right amount of water for that quantity of coffee; remove the tamper. Cover; pour hot water into the outer lining of the coffee pot. As soon as the coffee has passed through the filter, remove it, cover the coffee pot and serve.

An economical measure is to throw the grounds into boiling water on the next day, leave it to infuse for two or three hours, then decant it. In this case, you add less coffee to the filter for a fresh pot because you will be using the infusion from the grounds of the day before, which you will bring to the boil. However, a better way to proceed is to leave the grounds in place once the first coffee has gone through the filter, then add a little more boiling water to them. This coffee can then be heated in a bain-marie and added to the second day's.

Many people boil coffee, but I do not think it possible to obtain good coffee by this means. Others are used to making a large quantity all at once and storing it in a bottle for later; but this will darken it and make it acrid and bitter. They deprive themselves of the pleasure of smelling freshly made coffee for the want of a little effort.

You should never heat coffee over a naked flame; the bain-marie is the only way to warm it up.

When you make coffee to drink with milk, it must be much stronger than if you are drinking it black; otherwise you will be merely adding water to milk. This milk should be boiling. After dinner, some people add a little milk to their coffee; in this case, you should usually serve cold milk, as creamy as possible. If you wish to serve it hot, it must be heated in a saucepan made of porcelain, wrought iron or silver, and *only used for this purpose.* It should heat extremely slowly and stay on the fire for a long time. By doing it this way, the water in the milk, even if it is fresh and unadulterated, will evaporate, and the milk will noticeably thicken; what's more, a cream will adhere to the sides of the pot which is much esteemed by enthusiasts.

To serve coffee, you present the sugar bowl to your guests; once they have helped themselves to sugar, you pour out the coffee first, then the milk.

The coffee habit has spread widely in France, even to country districts. This is much less extravagant than you might think; it is even a source of economies when you take it with milk and you dunk lots of bread in it, as do some people. A standard small cup of black coffee,[1] sweetened as it should be, will not set you back more than 8 or 10 centimes, even using high-quality coffee. You will see in the second volume how you can obtain an even lower price for orders in bulk.[2] I will also describe in that place how I have managed to replace wine by coffee in the farm servants' diet. The high cost of wine over a number of years has encouraged me to think about substituting another stimulating, but cheaper drink. I think I have succeeded. My readers can profit from my experience.

Tea. — Over the last twenty years, the consumption of tea has become more general in France; however, in most regions tea is drunk less commonly than in Paris or in port cities; furthermore, grocers usually have nothing better than green tea, acrid, very strong, an irritant, with barely a hint of perfume. I really do recommend my readers obtain their supplies from Paris or a seaport, even if only to use as medicine; because green tea stirs everything up a lot and, taken as medicine, can do as much harm as good.

To have a nice tea, you should make it up like this: three-quarters Souchong and one-quarter Russian white-tip tea.

How much tea to use is difficult to work out because some people prefer theirs strong, while others like it lighter; thus it may be better to have a very strong infusion in the teapot and hot water in the kettle; you can mix these two liquids in each cup according to the desires of each guest; if however you reckon to prepare the same tea for all the guests, a

1. In French, *demi-tasse.*
2. Mme Millet-Robinet discusses the costs and benefits of coffee in her second volume when treating of the food and drink to be supplied to the farmworkers.

large tablespoonful[1] per litre of water seems right to me. To prepare an infusion, the teapot must first be scalded so that the boiling water which is poured on the tea does not cool down too quickly by coming into contact with a cold pot; discard the water used for this preliminary, put the tea in the teapot and pour a little *really boiling* water on it; five minutes later, add the right amount of water, always boiling, for the tea dispensed; leave to infuse for five minutes, after which you can serve it. If you need to make more tea, add some more fresh leaves to the pot without removing what was already in there and carry on as before. You should add less tea the second time.

As with coffee, everyone takes sugar before the tea is poured; then the mistress offers cold, creamy milk. If anyone wants it hot, you should heat it following the same procedure I advised for warming it to add to coffee.

When you wish to take tea with milk only, that is with boiling milk, you can throw some leaves into boiling milk; but even in this instance, I think it preferable to prepare it with water, making it very strong, and mixing this aromatic infusion into the milk.

Usually, little thin slices of bread covered with butter are served with tea; you take two, one on top of the other with the butter in the middle. You can also serve little dry cakes or brioche.

Orange flower tea. — At the time of year when the orange trees flower, the blossoms are picked, the petals detached and then dried somewhere airy in the shade. A pinch of these petals infused in water or milk produces a hot drink consumed like tea. It is very good, soothing and much more delicate than orange flower water. Its perfume is slightly different.

I highly recommend orange flower tea; mixed with ordinary tea, it produces the best effect.

Chocolate. — In recent years, the consumption of chocolate is more widely accepted. It is quite wrong to think you can have good chocolate at a very low price: cocoa, the raw material, always commands a fairly high price when of decent quality. I am therefore sure that it is impossible to get a good chocolate for less than 4 francs a kilogram; and to have a very high quality vanilla chocolate you will need to pay 6 or 8 francs the kilogram. Chocolates that come in under this price are made either with mediocre

---

1. In French, *cuillerée à bouche*. It may also mean soup spoon, but the size – it seems generally agreed – is 15ml, the same as an English tablespoon.

cocoa beans or with those that have had their fat content or cocoa butter extracted.

High-quality chocolate is not very sweet; lower-quality chocolate, by contrast, is very sweet indeed, given that as sugar is much cheaper than cocoa, there are notable economies to be made by introducing it in large quantities to the manufacture of chocolate; and you will be fortunate if you don't also find it mixed with other adulterants which taste unpleasant, even if they are not harmful.

Only taste will inform you of a chocolate's quality, and you need much practice to become a connoisseur. The best guarantee is the honesty of the manufacturer.

To make chocolate with water, you must divide it into pieces with a knife; add a little water and place it on the heat. You must stir it until it is completely melted; then you add as much water as will give you the desired consistency. Gourmets beat it in a chocolate pot which makes it more unctuous.

To prepare it with milk, you melt it in water then add milk instead of water.

You will often need to sweeten good chocolate.

You cannot keep chocolate a long time; in the end it tastes dusty and goes rancid.

Chocolate soup. — Chocolate soup is very enjoyable taken in the morning, when you cannot last until luncheon without eating something. Cook half a bar of chocolate in a little water. Add a sufficient quantity of milk and a lump of sugar; cut a little bread to fit an appropriate bowl and pour the boiling chocolate over it. Let it soak for about quarter of an hour. This soup is healthy, enjoyable, and not much more extravagant than any other soup, if you use chocolate costing 4 francs the kilogram in the making of it.

Cocoa bean husk. — Cocoa bean husk has very little value: it costs no more than 80 to 90 centimes the kilogram; however, boiled in milk, it makes a nice hot drink for luncheon; children usually like it a lot. None the less, it has a certain astringency so does not agree with everyone's digestion. It is widely adopted in some countries, for example Flanders; they import it from Spain, where a great deal of chocolate is consumed. To cook this very light husk, once you have washed it you put a glassful in a small saucepan with an equal amount of water; this quantity will be enough for four people. Let it boil for twenty minutes; then strain the liquor, which will be the colour of chocolate, and pour it into a litre of boiling milk. Leave it to continue boiling for a few minutes, then serve. The taste is quite pleasant and not dissimilar to chocolate.

CHAPTER XIX

HOME-MADE SWEETS[1]

A small oval frying-pan made of untinned copper, with two handles, is pretty much indispensable for making almost any sweet; in the first place, it is an inexpensive piece of equipment; in the second, it can be put to other uses. A saucepan is no substitute for a small pan because of its shape and the fact that it is tinned.

1. — Orange flower soufflé.[2]

Cook 125 grams of good crushed sugar in 3 spoonfuls of water to *hard ball*;[3] throw in 31 grams of fresh orange flower petals; let it cook to *hard crack*;[4] pour it on to white paper in little dots the size of a five-franc coin; lift off the sweet as soon as it sets. The quantities I have proposed will be barely enough to cover a plate; repeat the process to make a second batch. If you put larger quantities into the pan, the sugar will harden before you have time to pour the mixture on to the paper. You can use a smaller weight of orange flowers.

2. — Violet soufflé.

Prepare this exactly as the orange flower soufflé; you need only put in 15 grams of violet petals. It is excellent.

These two sweets, placed in boxes in a dry place, can be kept for a year.

1. The original title is *Bonbons de ménage*. Although most recipes are for *bonbons* or sweets (or candies), there are some which are for sweet dishes or drinks.
2. The name *soufflé* refers here, not to the sweet or savoury dish made with egg whites that swells up in an oven when baked, but rather to a stage in sugar-boiling which may be indicated in English by the term 'large pearl', i.e. 113–115°C.
3. *Grand boulé*, 121–124°C.
4. *Cassé*, 149–150°C.

3. — Almond milk.

Crush 5 almonds with their shells. Put them in half a litre of milk. Boil; strain through a fine sieve or something similar. Sweeten. It is an excellent *bavaroise* which smells of vanilla, and very soothing.[1]

You can make a decoction of almonds in a little water; strain it; add boiling milk and sweeten.

4. — Liqueur bavaroise.

Boil some milk; sweeten; add a liqueur such as kirsch, rum, eau-de-vie, anisette, orange flower liqueur, etc. Put more or less liqueur, according to taste. This *bavaroise* is excellent, even when you soak bread in it.

5. — Orange flower or violet macaroons.

Cook 500 grams of sugar to *hard ball*. In the meantime, coarsely chop 125 grams of orange flower petals and beat three egg whites to a very firm froth; throw the orange flower into the sugar and mix well; add the egg whites and mix again. Take off the fire; with a small spoon, quickly transfer spoonfuls of the mixture, sufficiently spaced out, on to paper; put straight into the oven. You need to time the operation so that you can put them in the oven two hours after you have taken out the bread. One hour later, bring out the sheets of paper, which you dampen to detach the macaroons; place these upside down on dishes or on paper in the same oven, so that they can dry out. These macaroons will keep for a year packed in a box in a dry place. You can do some with violet petals which are just as good and, when mixed with the others, make a charming dessert dish at little cost.

6. — Orange flower praline and violet praline.

Carefully pick over 500 grams of orange flowers, that is to say, keep only their petals. Put 500 grams of crushed sugar and a glass of water in the pan; cook to *hard ball*; throw in the orange flowers; they will be quite bulky and will at first mix with some difficulty with the sugar. When the mixture has boiled for a minute, take it off the heat and pour it into a china bowl; then let it rest; the next day put it back on the fire in the pan; bring it back up

---

1.   Describing this preparation as a *bavaroise* is to use the word to denote a drink of 'milk, eggs and tea, often with some sort of spirit', cf. the following recipe. A *bavarois* (n.m.) is a custard or cream dish set with gelatine.

to the boil then do the same as the day before. The next day, put it back on the fire and take it to *hard crack*; pour it into a large, deep dish and make it into praline, that is, stir it with a wooden spatula until the sugar sticks fast to the orange flower petals; use your fingers to separate any which stick together. Then lay out this confection on sheets of paper and put it in the oven at least three hours after the bread has been taken out; leave it there for four or five hours; take it out and leave to cool. Pack it into glass jars with tight stoppers in a dry place.

Violet praline is prepared in the same way.

7. — Pralines.

Put 1,500 grams of sugar broken into pieces into the pan with a glass of water; let it dissolve; add 500 grams of shelled almonds. Cook to *hard ball*, nearly to *hard crack*, stirring frequently with a spatula; take it off the fire and stir neither too fast nor too slowly with the spatula until the sugar looks like demerara. Then put it back on a brisk fire; stir thoroughly and in every direction without interruption until the sugar sticks firmly to the almonds; take off the heat; pour out either onto a metal sieve or on to a dish and separate any almonds that have stuck to each other.

You can colour the sugar with a little cochineal and perfume it with rosewater the moment you put it on the fire. You can also glaze the pralines when they are made. To do this you add a little water and sauté them briskly in the pan over the heat; then you decant them into a sieve in which you leave them to dry out in the oven – where you should put them three hours after you have taken out the bread.

8. — Maréchal MacDonald's coffee cream sweets.[1]

Put half a litre of milk on the heat and reduce it slowly by three-quarters, stirring it frequently so that a skin doesn't form on the surface. Reduce as well a demitasse of strong black coffee. Break 500 grams of

---

1. In French, *Bonbons du maréchal Macdonald, au café au lait*. Maréchal Jacques Etienne MacDonald (1765–1840), 1st Duke of Taranto, was a revolutionary and Napoleonic military leader. This may one of the very few 'personal' recipes recorded by Mme Millet-Robinet – in the style of manuscript recipe collections which often recorded the source of each new set of instructions. Marshal MacDonald was a colleague of François Millet, Mme Millet-Robinet's husband, and had appointed him *chef de secrétariat* of the grand chancery of the Légion d'honneur.

sugar into lumps; put it in the reduced milk; let it cook over a low fire until the mixture bubbles up a lot; add the coffee little by little, stirring the while. Cook it to *hard crack*, stirring often so that the mixture does not boil over the edges of the pan. When you reckon that matters are near their conclusion, throw a few drops of the liquid on a plate; if they firm up nicely, without exactly hardening, the sweet is cooked. Take off the heat and stir briskly with a wooden spatula; then pour it while still hot into one or several paper cases to a depth of at least half a centimetre. Before the sweet is altogether cold, mark out the top with the back of a knife in little diamonds. When it almost cold, detach the paper (by moistening it underneath). You can pour the mixture on to a marble slab – that you have thoroughly yet lightly oiled – otherwise the sweet will stick to any part of the marble you have not coated with oil. Let it cool completely and break it into diamonds along the lines you have marked; this is very simple. This sweet, which might cost 1 franc for half a kilogram, is just as good as that which confectioners sell at a very high price.

9. — Coffee or chocolate creams.

Put 250 grams of demerara sugar or crushed sugar with 100 grams of fresh butter in the pan over a brisk fire; let it boil for ten minutes while stirring the mixture. Add a cup of very strong black coffee and a glass of very fresh cream; let it boil for another ten minutes, stirring all the while; when the mixture froths up a lot, it is almost cooked. You should not stop stirring. To determine whether it is done, throw a few drops of the mixture in a glass of cold water; if they harden immediately, it is cooked enough. Pour the contents of the pan on to a lightly and evenly oiled marble slab; score the sweet with a pointed knife so that you can separate it into squares when it has cooled completely.

To make this with chocolate, grate two cups of good chocolate and, instead of the cream, add half a glass of water when you add the chocolate to the mixture. You finish this off as you did the preceding one.

10. — Angels' hairs (dessert or sweet entremets).

You must cut hearts of carrot into half-centimetre strips, add an equal weight of sugar and put everything into a saucepan with enough water to cover; for 500 grams of sugar, you add the juice of two oranges or two lemons, plus the amount of zest required to flavour the whole. You can break the sugar into lumps and briskly rub the whole orange or lemon, enough zest will stick to the sugar this way. Cook this until the syrup glazes easily; but you must take care not to let it caramelize. Pour it onto a dish and carefully mix it with a fork to make it cool more quickly, and in such a way that the carrot strips remain on the surface. It is an excellent sweetmeat, very similar to crystallized fruits and very inexpensive. You can keep it for a little while by leaving it in a dry place.

CHAPTER XX

EXPLANATION OF DIFFERENT CULINARY TERMS[1]

Assiette (small plate). This is what you call the small entrées, hors-d'oeuvre or desserts which can be served on an *assiette*.

Bain-marie (bain-marie). One means by this a way of cooking which consists of placing the food you wish to prepare in a bain-marie: in a bowl or vessel which you plunge in another, larger one filled with water kept at boiling-point. This procedure protects the dish from the direct action of the fire, which might otherwise burn it or cook it too quickly.

Barder (to bard). This is to cover with a thin slice of backfat, called bard, the breast or the back of poultry or game. The slice is held in place with a thread or a skewer.

Battre (to beat). This is to place meat on a block and strike it forcefully with a rolling-pin or something similar; a flat beater is much less suitable than a round one.

Blanchir (to blanch). This is to plunge meat, fruits or vegetables into boiling water and to leave them there for only a few seconds, or to simply pour boiling water over them.

Bouquet garni (bouquet garni). This is the name for a bunch of parsley, bay leaf, thyme and sometimes garlic, which you bind together to add to some ragouts to flavour them. You don't put parsley in white sauces. You always remove the bouquet before service.

Chausse (straining bag). A piece of thick woollen cloth in the form of

1.   For this glossary, I have retained the original French headwords; the alphabetical order is thus not disturbed. It might be remarked that Mme Millet-Robinet does not make constant or repeated use of all the entries in this glossary; some, indeed, are barely seen at all, or are referred to by other terms.

a cornet provided with a small hoop at its top. The bag serves to strain liquids in order to refine them.

Désosser (to bone). To remove the bones from any bird or joint of meat, avoiding as far as possible any damage to the flesh of whatever you are boning.

Faire écumer (to skim). This is to put a piece of meat into water, to salt it and place it on the heat so that you can take off any scum before it comes to the boil.

Étouffer (to smother). This is to cook something in a tightly stopped container to inhibit any evaporation.

Flamber (to singe). This is to light a paper and to pass a bird or a piece of game over it to take off the small hairs or down that cannot be otherwise removed.

Garniture (garnish). This is what you call the vegetables, sauces, ragouts, hashes, purées, fritters, croutons, parsley, etc., which you serve on the dish around the principal joint.

Glacer (to glaze). This is to spread over meats a sauce or *coulis* to which you have imparted a certain consistency by boiling for a long enough time; or to anoint a cake or compote with a layer of grated or melted sugar which you then caramelise, either by passing a hot shovel over it, or by some other means.

Lits (beds). This is what you call a purée or slices of various vegetables served beneath a joint of meat or some poultry.

Mijoter (to simmer). This is to cook over a low fire.

Mitonner (to cook/soak bread in soup). This is to soak bread for a long time in soup, even to boil it in it.

Mouiller (to moisten). This is to add water or any liquid to a roux or a sauce.

Paner (to crumb). To crumble the crumb of a loaf, mix salt, pepper and sometimes finely chopped parsley into it, and cover some meats, which have first been passed through oil or melted butter so that the bread adheres: this is what we call paner. To crumble the crumb of a loaf, you wrap it in a clean and slightly coarse cloth and rub it, while pressing it down on the table, as if you were washing linen; you then sieve it through a colander with large holes, pressing with the hand when necessary. You put any that did not go through the colander back in the cloth, to crush it again. You should always use the crumb of a stale loaf.

Parer (to dress or trim). This is to remove from any foods used in cooking all that should not be served and everything that detracts from their quality or form.

Piquer (to lard). This is to introduce small strips of backfat, called *lardons*, larger or smaller according to circumstance, in the flesh parts of poultry, game or meat.

Faire revenir (to brown). This is to pass meats, poultry, game or vegetables which you want to flavour through butter, fat or oil in a saucepan over a brisk fire in order to give them a golden colour. When you worry that a piece of meat is turning, you brown it; it will then keep almost as well as if it had been completely cooked. To brown meats or other foods with lots of juice, which will inhibit their browning, you really heat the butter, fat or oil you are going to use (but without burning it) before you add the substance you wish to brown.

Rapprocher (to reduce). This is to reduce a sauce by boiling, either to achieve a higher flavour, or to obtain a consistency that will allow you to glaze a dish.

Sauter (to sauté). This is to move in a saucepan or a frying-pan, without the help of a spoon but merely by a short upward jerk, whatever foodstuff it contains; or it means to cook something very quickly.

Trousser (to truss, to tie). This describes the treatment you give a bird or item of game before you put it to cook; this term also refers to how you dress a joint of meat.

MENUS
FOR
LUNCHEONS AND DINNERS

I hope to be of help to my readers by adding to this new edition menus for a dozen luncheons and forty-nine dinners, of which thirteen are for fast-days; one of these last can be served in Holy Week. The composition of fast-day dinners being so much more difficult than those for meat-days, I think that many housewives will be grateful for my small labour which will save them from several long and complicated calculations.

I have adopted a monthly arrangement for my menus so as to show what supplies are available in each season.

If you find yourselves unable to procure or to execute all the dishes in a menu, you can choose something similar. This substitution is easy to achieve by consulting the table below which lists dishes by their group.

I have written the menus with sufficient dishes to satisfy the needs of a table of eighteen. By halving the menus, that is to say by only taking two entrées, not four, a single remove, a single soup, and so on, you will have a more modest dinner; but you must remember not to choose two entrées of the same colour or two entremets of the same sort. You can reduce the number of dishes still further, bearing in mind the same rule when making your choice of which items to preserve.

I have suggested more elaborate menus in January and February, months when one gives more dinner parties and which usually includes the pre-Lenten carnival. The month of March includes three fast-day dinners because it is always Lent.

I cannot advise the mistress of the house strongly enough to ensure she has all the supplies necessary for the menu which she chooses, and not to delay to the day of the meal itself anything that might be prepared the day before or the day before that; there is always too much to do on the day of a formal dinner.

You will find on page 388, under the heading *Part II, Kitchen manual, Preliminary considerations*, and on page 393, under the heading *On the conduct of masters and servants before, during and after meals*, details which the mistress should study in advance if she wishes to receive guests in the proper manner.

In my book *On Fruit Preserves*, you will find a host of recipes for fruits, sweetmeats, jams, ices, etc., etc., which ought to figure in a dessert.

LUNCHEONS

(Note: dishes marked with an asterisk should be placed in the middle of the table.)

JANUARY

Butter, celery, olives, marinated tuna,[1] Lyon dried sausage, pickles,[2] sardines; Oysters; Truffled pig's trotters; Sausages with cabbage; Breaded mutton chops; Fried calf's kidneys; Fish mayonnaise; Salt cod with cheese; *Pâté de foie gras;** Potato croquettes; Sugared turnips; *Oeufs à la neige*; *Marmelade* of apples with boiled rice pudding; Savarin; Little choux buns; Moulded whipped cream;[3] Gruyère cheese; Prune compote; Apple compote; Fresh

---

1. In French, *thon mariné*. The reader may presume Mme Millet-Robinet means a marinated raw fish such as we are now familiar with, but she makes no reference to such a preparation, or any other manner of serving tuna in her short section on the fish (remarking reasonably enough that it is something people near the Mediterranean shore set great store by). She does, however, comment that 'Tuna conserved in oil can be found everywhere. It is a very good Hors-d'oeuvre.' I assume, therefore, that wherever she lists 'marinated tuna', she really means canned tuna in oil.

2. In this instance and throughout the menus, *achars*. In the section on pickles in the chapter on provisions (page 304, above), she spells this word *aschards*. There it describes a piccalilli. A wordlist for 1845 gives as many as four different spellings. Although she gives a recipe for *achars/aschards*, the word can also refer generically to anything pickled.

3. In French, *fromage à la crème fouettée*. The note relating to *fromage glacé* in the second dinner menu of February has some relevance to this item. Mme Millet-Robinet is here identifying the dish we know better as *crémets*: double cream whipped with egg whites then poured into little moulds. In later editions, she extends her description of whipped cream (which in this volume she discusses only in relation to meringues) to take in the idea of a moulded and drained whipped cream: the mould being the critical factor which lends its name, *fromage*.

apples; Fresh pears; Two plates of *petits-fours*; Two plates of biscuits; White coffee; Drinking chocolate; Buttered toast.

FEBRUARY

Butter, celery, shrimps, lobsters, pickles, tuna, sardines, olives; Black and white puddings; *Andouillettes*; Sheep's kidneys; Veal chops *en papillote*; Chicken mayonnaise; Roast wild duck; Galantine of truffled turkey;* Sugared spinach; Salsify fried in batter; Apple meringue; Rice soufflé; Cake; Brioche; Gruyère cheese; Roquefort cheese; Preserved plums;[1] Preserved cherries; Pears in eau-de-vie; Plums in eau-de-vie; Two plates of sweets; *Mendiants*;[2] Oranges; Fresh apples; White coffee; Tea with cream.

MARCH (suitable for fast-days)

Butter, radishes, marinated tuna, sardines preserved in oil,[3] anchovies, pickles; Oysters; Boiled eggs; Little fried patties; Brillat-Savarin's cheese *fondu*; Sea fish vol-au-vent with béchamel sauce; Cold turbot,* with cold sauce; Buttered potatoes; Lentil salad; Potato cake; Cream flan; Gruyère cheese; Preserved cherries; Prunes; Two jams; Two plates of orange

---

1. In French, *prunes conservées*. It is not always clear what Mme Millet-Robinet means precisely by this. She suggests three methods of conserving fresh fruit: drying, canning and bottling. Later in the menus, she will specify *en bouteilles* for bottled fruit, so we have to presume that her *fruits conservés* are often dried after harvest. We have also to assume that when she suggests a compote of fruit out of season, the fruit is either dried or bottled, even if she does not specify.

2. *Les mendiants* or *les quatres mendiants* (*mendiant* means, literally, beggar, but also refers to the mendicant orders of friars of which the four principal ones are the Franciscans, Dominicans, Augustinians and Carmelites) was the name given to a plate of almonds, figs, hazelnuts and raisins, the foodstuffs representing, it was said, the colours of their respective habits. The usage dates from at least the seventeenth century. It was often part of the grand dessert of the Provençal Christmas feast. *Jane Grigson's Fruit Book*, p. 191, has more information. Nowadays, a *mendiant* consists of those fruits and nuts on a circle of chocolate (in similar fashion to the florentine biscuit). A *mendiant* is also a sweet confection from Alsace somewhat akin to a bread pudding, made with stale bread and fruits (often cherries). Its local name is also *bettelmann*, i.e. 'beggar'. There is no recipe for *mendiants* in this volume.

3. In French, *sardines confites*. Mme Millet-Robinet's recipe for salted sardines (page 455) goes on to explain how to fry them then pot them up with olive oil. She also points out that commercially available canned sardines are excellent and it is quite possible that she expects the reader to use these.

salad; *Mendiants*; *Nonnettes de Reims*;[1] White coffee; Drinking chocolate; Burgundy cake.

APRIL

Butter, radishes, olives, marinated tuna, sardines, pickles; Truffled sausages; Head cheese in slices; The curé's omelette from Brillat-Savarin; Lobster; Fried pigeons; Fillets of sole with mayonnaise sauce; Ham pâté from Lesage;*[2] Asparagus with white sauce; Haricot bean salad; Boiled rice with chocolate; *Soles de guéret*; Lemon *galettes*; *Gâteau Quillet*;[3] Cream cheese; Pineapple; Gruyère cheese; Orange salad; Jams; Two plates of biscuits; White coffee; Tea with cream; Drumsticks.

MAY

Butter, radishes, *rillettes* of Tours, Lyon dried sausage, fresh sardines, pickles; Stuffed pig's trotters; Fried ham; Fillet steak; Fried calf's kidney; Lobster; Scrambled eggs with tomato sauce; Head cheese;* Sugared asparagus in the manner of *petits pois*; Small potatoes fried in butter; Rum pudding; Rice soufflé; Piecrust *galette*; Brioche; Cream cheese; Strawberries; Dutch cheese; Pineapple; Oranges; Two jams; Two plates of sweets; White coffee; Tea with cream.

1. *Nonnettes de Reims* are small round cakes made with honey and mildly spiced, i.e. *pain d'épices*. There is no recipe for this in the volume here printed.
2. This specific pâté is not referred to elsewhere in the book. Lesage (or more correctly Proton-Lesage) was a pâtissier in the Rue Montorgueil, Paris. His pâtés were celebrated from the end of the eighteenth century – recorded by the Goncourt brothers in their *Histoire de la société française pendant la Révolution* as well as celebrated by Grimod de la Reynière who noted that M. Lesage procured thirty thousand hams from Bayonne each year and these still did not suffice for his truffled pâtés which 'melt in the mouth'. Restif de la Bretonne's narrator also enjoyed a pâté from Lesage in his novel *Monsieur Nicolas*. The closing chorus of a theatrical nonsense called *Pâté de Chartres* by Eugène Grangé, Selme-Davenay and Abel (1840) begins: 'Nous avons les pâtés d'Lesage, / Nous avons les pâtés d'Amiens, / Les p'tits pâtés d'certain passage, / Et puis l'pâté des Italiens'. Unfortunately, M. Lesage's matchless pâtés caused serious food-poisoning in 1824, an episode reported in the *Journal de chimie médicale* (a journal co-founded by Mme Millet-Robinet's brother Stéphane Robinet) where the problem was put down to verdigris from cooking vessels being inadequately tinned.
3. Gâteau Quillet is named after the maker, a pâtissier in rue de Bucy, Paris. It was described in Joseph Favre's *Dictionnaire universel de cuisine pratique* (1894) and in the first edition of *Larousse gastronomique*. It was a fairly plain but rich vanilla genoise sponge with lots of butter icing.

JUNE

Butter, radishes, small broad beans, baby artichokes,[1] fresh sardines, marinated tuna, pickles; Melon; Omelette with a tomato sauce; *Matelote* of salmon in pastry; Veau escalopes; Grilled shad with caper sauce;* Fried calf's mesentery; Young garden peas; Small buttered potatoes; Bread pudding; Baba; Cream cheese; Strawberries; Meringues; *Calottes*;[2] Brie cheese; Cherries; Currants; Two plates of *petits-fours*; White coffee. Tea with cream.

JULY

Butter, radishes, baby artichokes, fresh sardines, dry-cured sausage, pickles; Melon; Kidney omelette; Eggs à la poulette; Mutton chops; Salmon salad; A whole cold ham;* Pyramid of freshwater crayfish; Fried calf's head; Artichokes à la barigoule; French beans; Cherry cake; *Gâteau Quillet*; Goat's cheese; Cream cheese; Strawberries; Peaches; Apricots; Two plates of *petits-fours*; Two plates of biscuits; White coffee; Tea with cream; Drumsticks.

AUGUST

Butter, radishes, baby artichokes, cucumber salad, fresh sardines, ripe figs; Melon; Sardine fillet omelette; Sugared fried ham; Sausages with cabbage; Steaks of calf's liver; Pyramid of freshwater crayfish; Deep fried gudgeon; Cold beef à la mode with aspic;* Young garden peas; Shelled haricot beans; Peach fritters; Plum *clafoutis*; Brie cheese; Goat's cheese; Fresh strawberries à l'eau-de-vie; Apricots à l'eau-de-vie; Peaches; Pears; Plums; Fresh almonds; White coffee; Tea with cream; Burgundy cake.

SEPTEMBER

Butter, radishes, cucumber salad, baby artichokes, fresh sardines, ripe figs, dry-cured sausage, pickles; Melon; Beefsteak with potatoes; *Andouillettes*;

1.   These are named by Mme Millet-Robinet as *poivrades*. She is referring to young artichokes eaten raw with salt.
2.   The French *calotte* is the word for a priest's skullcap (and for a baker's cap). By extension, it may also mean the cranium and is equally the word for a dome-shaped bowl or cover used by chefs and bakers. A *calotte bretonne* is a cottage loaf, perhaps because of the spherical topknot. *Calottes* are also very simple sponges (the weight of three eggs in flour and sugar) that are spread out quite thinly for baking, making a tea-biscuit-style dry confection.

Quail *en papillote*; Salmi of partridge; Hare pie;* Potatoes à la maître-d'hôtel; French beans; Boiled rice pudding with coffee; Peach fritters; Plum tart; Brioche; Brie cheese; Goat's cheese; Cream cheese; Strawberries; Plums sprinkled with eau-de-vie; Peaches sprinkled with eau-de-vie; Pears; Peaches; Grapes; Fresh almonds; White coffee; Tea with cream.

OCTOBER

Butter, radishes, celery, baby artichokes, fresh sardines, figs, anchovies, pickles; Oysters; Puddings and sausages; Sheep's kidney; Fillets of fish with mayonnaise sauce; Sauté of chicken; Partridge pie;* Macaroni gratin; Fried brains; Potatoes à la maître-d'hôtel; Cold artichokes dressed with oil; Little cabbages; Rum pudding flambé; Brie cheese; Cream cheese; Strawberries; Fresh peaches with eau-de-vie; Fresh pears with kirsch; Pears; Figs; Grapes; Cracked walnuts; White coffee; Tea with cream; *Calottes*.

NOVEMBER

Butter, radishes, celery, sardines in oil, marinated tuna, olives, dry-cured sausage, pickles; Mushroom omelette; Beefsteak with potatoes; Pieces of cold turkey poult, with mayonnaise sauce; Gratin of soles; A whole ham on spinach; Game pie; Roast thrush;* Fried cauliflower; Fresh haricot beans; Chestnut surprise; Rum pudding; Gruyère cheese; Cream cheese; Pear compote; Apple compote; Pears; Apples; Grapes; Green walnuts; Roast chestnuts; Two plates of biscuits; White coffee; Chocolate; Bread rolls.

DECEMBER

Butter, celery, olives, tuna, anchovies, sardines, dry-cured sausage, pickles; Oysters; Scalloped oysters; Stuffed truffled pig's trotters; Mutton chops; Mayonnaise of sea fish; Cold boned leg of mutton cooked in a daube; Cold chicken rémoulade; Truffled Ruffec pâté;*¹ Potato croquettes; Cardoon salad; Kidney mould; Apple tartlets; Brie cheese; Pear compote; Chestnut compote; Pears; Apples; Grapes; Oranges; Roast chestnuts; White coffee; Chocolate; *Trottoirs*.

---

1. Ruffec is a town about halfway between Poitiers and Angoulême to the south. It is in the department of Charente. The proprietor of the Hôtel de la Poste, one Thurel, began making pâtés according to a Strasbourg recipe for *pâté de foie gras truffé* from about 1820. He built up a considerable trade, sending out partridge and capon pâtés

DINNERS

[*For convenience, I repeat Mme Millet-Robinet's remarks at the end of the first chapter of her kitchen manual on the various ways of serving dinner. The reader will observe that in these menus she ignores any idea of serving dinner 'à la russe'. Her words are:* 'Dinner in the French style. — *The generally accepted rule nowadays is to serve at once everything which can remain on the table during the whole of the meal without risk to its quality. Sometimes a few of the entrées are removed so they might be replaced by entremets that can only be eaten when they are very hot, such as fritters, soufflés, etc. Only the dessert is held back from this first service and makes a second course.*

'A three-course dinner. — *The oldest style is to compose a dinner of three successive courses or services. The first course consists of the soup, replaced by the remove, entrées and hors-d'oeuvre: The second consists of the roast and the entremets, to which are joined some of the hors-d'oeuvre which were not removed with the first course. The third course consists of the dessert. I prefer this style of service. The guests have a chance to relax and converse while the first course is removed and the second is served, and the servants, above all the cook, don't have to do everything at once. It is true that by serving everything at once you can better study economy, because it is obligatory in every case that the table should be well furnished, and dishes that are only eaten at the very end of the meal will adorn the table while the others are served.*

'I prefer a small number of dishes, but handsome, well garnished and served as they ought to be, to a clutch of measly little things, served on plates, with only the intent of making a splash by their number. For one thing, the larger joints are generally better and have a generosity which sits well with a dinner offered to several guests. If there is a great confusion of dishes, the kitchen's labours are terribly complicated, so that it is impossible to devote the care to each dish that it merits, while fewer dishes will be more considered. The result, in terms of costs, is identical.*

---

as well. A travellers' directory for 1846 comments (my translation): '[the Hôtel] de la Poste, held by M. Thorel; handsome establishment, renowned for the pâtés *de foie gras truffés*, partridge, and capon, which M. Thorel sends out in large quantities.' A local historian remarks that his partridge pâtés were pure partridge, with no admixture of pork.

'Dinner in the Russian style. — *Finally, the Russian or Italian style of dining is becoming accepted for formal dinners. It consists of covering the table, for the whole dinner long, with dishes of dessert and vases of flowers. Dishes of food do not appear on the table; they are carved by a servant in a room next door, or on a table in the corner of the dining-room, and then presented in their proper order to each guest. The dinner menu, written on a sheet of Bristol board, is laid beside each place-setting. This style of service demands a larger number of servants, and one of them must know how to carve perfectly.'*]

JANUARY

FIRST MENU

Soups: Rice, with meat stock; Crécy with vegetable stock.

Hors-d'oeuvre: Butter, olives, celery, marinated tuna, anchovies, pickles, gherkins, dry-cured sausage.

Hot hors-d'oeuvre: Stuffed truffled pig's trotter; Sheep's kidneys.

Removes: Turbot with white sauce; Beef à la mode.

Entrées: Venison chops; Capon with celery; Calf's head in the manner of turtle *au blanc*; Lamb's trotters à la poulette.

Roast: Truffled turkey.

Salads: Red cabbage; *Chicorée frisée* with beetroot.

Vegetables: Brussels sprouts; Fried potatoes.

Entremets: Timbale of macaroni; Partridge pie.

Sweet entremets: Buttered apples; Rice soufflé; Crème caramel; Almond cake.

Dessert: Roquefort cheese; Brie cheese; Angels' hairs; Chestnut surprise; Pear compote; Bottled raspberries; Pears; Apples; Oranges; Grapes; Two jams; Two plates of *petits-fours*; Candied angelica; Candied citron; Two plates of biscuits; *Mendiants*; Malaga raisins;[1] Roast chestnuts.

SECOND MENU

Soups: Meat stock, with Italian pasta; Pumpkin.

Hors-d'oeuvre: Butter, celery, sardines preserved in oil, marinated tuna, pickles, gherkins, mortadella, olives.

---

1. These were the dried muscatel grapes of Malaga. The season for the fresh grapes is very short (from the end of August) so, although Mme Millet-Robinet does not call these *raisins secs*, she doubtless means this.

Hot hors-d'oeuvre: *Andouillettes*; Scalloped oysters.

Removes: Capon with sea-salt; Smothered fillet of beef.

Entrées: Duck with onions; Leg of mutton in its juice, on a bed of lentils; Thick-lipped grey mullet or bass with a white milk sauce; Veal chops *en papillote*.

Roasts: Fattened chicken; Truffled partridge.

Salads: *Scarole* with beetroot; Wild chicory (*barbe du capucin*) with fillets of pickled herring.

Vegetables: Mashed potatoes with croûtons; Fried salsify.

Entremets: Fried sole; Pears in a roux.

Sweet entremets: *Marmelade* of apples with rice; Meringues; Chestnut purée; Nougat.

Dessert: Rich flaky pastry *galette* with a bean;[1] Chester cheese;[2] Gruyère cheese; A centrepiece of baskets of fruit;[3] Apricot compote; Cherry compote; Raw apple compote; Orange salad with rum; Two plates of biscuits; Two plates of *petits-fours*; Two plates of sweets; Pear jam; Strawberry jam; Two compote dishes of fruits in eau-de-vie; *Mendiants*; Dried Agen prunes;[4] Dried flattened pears; Grasse figs;[5] Roast chestnuts.

THIRD MENU

Soups: Meat stock, with macaroni and cheese; Pumpkin with onion and rice.

Hors-d'oeuvre: Butter, olives, smoked salmon on small slices of buttered bread, sardines preserved in oil, pickles, gherkins.

Hot hors-d'oeuvre: Little patties; Baked larks.

Remove: Boiled beef with glazed onions.

Entrées: Grilled soles, with white milk sauce; Hot pie filled with quenelles

---

1. This is *Gâteau* or *galette des rois*, served on Twelfth Night. He or she who has the bean has good fortune in the coming year.
2. We know this better as Cheshire cheese.
3. The French for centrepiece is *pièce montée*.
4. Agen, Lot-et-Garonne, is 75 miles south-east of Bordeaux. It is famous for its dried prunes.
5. Grasse, Alpes-Maritimes, is a town 6 miles north of Cannes. It is most celebrated for its perfumes. It also produced dried figs. In 1844, the *Journal d'agriculture pratique* reported that dried figs from Grasse were fetching 48 francs the 100 kilograms at the port of Sète.

and truffles;[1] Calf's head in the style of turtle *au blanc*; Salt cod in béchamel sauce in pastry.

Roasts: Sirloin with tomato sauce; Capon.

Salads: Lettuce; Chicory.

Vegetables: Pumpkin purée; Celery in meat *jus*.

Entremets: Truffles cooked in wine; Fried whiting.

Sweet entremets: Potato cake; Apple meringue; *Beignets soufflés*; Coffee cream.

Dessert: Roquefort cheese; Dutch cheese; Whipped cream; The sugar bowl; Pear compote; Apple compote; Agen prunes; Quinces; Lady apples;[2] Oranges; Two plates of raisins; Violet soufflé; Orange flower soufflé; *Nonnettes* of *pain d'épices*; Macaroons; Two plates of biscuits; *Mendiants*; Dried flattened pears; Apricot cheese; Roast chestnuts.

FOURTH MENU (for fast-days)

Soups: Crécy, with vegetable stock; Rice with sugared water.

Hors-d'oeuvre: Butter, celery, sardines preserved in oil, pickles, gherkins, olives, anchovies.

Hot hors-d'oeuvre: Smoked salmon on bread and butter; Grilled oysters.

Removes: Cod with white milk sauce; The curé's omelette from Brillat-Savarin.

Entrées: Mussels à la poulette; Hot pie of sea fish in a béchamel sauce; Eggs *en chemise* with a fast-day gravy; *Matelote* of soles.

Roasts: Lobster; Truffle omelette.

Salads: Celery with mustard; Lettuce.

Vegetables: Bottled garden peas; Potatoes à la maître-d'hôtel.

Entremets: Fried whiting; Timbale of macaroni.

Sweet entremets: Eclairs; *Gâteau à la neige*; Angels' hairs; French toast.

Dessert: Brie cheese; Dutch cheese, *Tête de mort*;[3] Jams from Bar;[4] Chestnut

---

1.   There is no single recipe for this dish in the book, but it may be created by following the instructions on page 612 for a hot pie crust made of puff pastry in a similar fashion to vol-au-vents and then filling it with the quenelles which are described (for vol-au-vents) on page 443.

2.   In French, *pommes d'api*: a small, hard winter variety.

3.   *Tête de mort* was a generic name for the large red waxed Edam cheeses.

4.   Bar, now known as Bar-le-Duc, in the Meuse department is especially known for its red or white currant jellies which are potted up with the whole, seeded fruit. Recipes for the jellies are on page 324, above.

surprise; Apple jelly; Plums à l'eau-de-vie; Cherries à l'eau-de-vie; Apple compote; Prunes; Oranges; Apples; Savoy biscuit; Nougat; Maréchal MacDonald's coffee cream sweets; Fruit pastes; Two plates of *petits-fours*; Two plates of *mendiants*.

FEBRUARY

FIRST MENU

Soups: Meat stock with granulated gluten; Crécy.

Hors-d'oeuvre: Butter, olives, anchovies, sardines preserved in oil, celery, radishes, pickles, gherkins.

Hot hors-d'oeuvre: White pudding with pistachios; Fried calf's ears.

Removes: Calf's head; Smothered fillet of beef with truffles.

Entrées: Salmi of woodcock and wild duck with truffles; Daube of venison fillet with a purée of lentils; Grilled salmon, with a white caper sauce; Capon with sea-salt in a ring of truffles.

Roasts: *Pâté de foie gras de Strasbourg*; Fattened Bresse chicken.

Salads: Red cabbage; Lettuce.

Vegetables: Fried potato balls; Bottled garden peas.

Entremets: Lobster; Fried soles.

Sweet entremets: Meringues; Kidney mould; *Beignets soufflés*; Chocolate cream.

Dessert: Roquefort cheese; Chester cheese; A centrepiece of pâtisserie; Apricot compote; Raspberry compote; Chestnut surprise; Orange salad; Two plates of *petits-fours*; Two plates of mixed sweets; Two plates of biscuits; Pears; Apples; Two plates of raisins; Two plates of biscuits; Two plates of *mendiants*; Quince cheese; Apricot cheese; Honey from Narbonne;[1] Roast chestnuts.

SECOND MENU

Soups: Crécy with meat stock; *Soupe à la reine*.

Hors-d'oeuvre: Butter, radishes, anchovies, marinated tuna, olives, pickles, gherkins, dry-cured sausage.

Hot hors-d'oeuvre: Slices of ham mixed with slices of turkey, stuffed with truffles; Filet steaks of beef.

---

1.   Narbonne, in the Aude department, has been celebrated for its honey since Roman times. Rosemary and other wild flowers from the *garrigue* (Mediterranean scrub) are its principal flavours.

Removes: Finely larded turkey with sea-salt on tomato sauce; Beef à la mode.

Entrées: Veal escalopes with garlic; Duck with olives; Hot sea fish pie with béchamel sauce; Chicken fricassee.

Roasts: Truffled pheasant; Turbot *au blanc*.

Salads: Lettuce; *Scarole*.

Vegetables: Brussels sprouts; Fried salsify.

Entremets: Fried calf's head; Macaroni in a vegetable stock.

Sweet entremets: Chestnut surprise; Apple turnovers; Vanilla creams; Nantes cake.[1]

Dessert: Roquefort cheese; Gruyère cheese; Moulded ice;[2] Chestnut compote; Apricot compote; Apple compote; Raspberry compote; Pears; Apples; Two plates of oranges; Two plates of biscuits; Two plates of *petits-fours*; Fruit pastes; *Mendiants*; Grasse figs; Malaga raisins; Roast chestnuts.[3]

THIRD MENU

Soups: Meat stock with vermicelli; Turnip.

Hors-d'oeuvre: Butter, celery, sardines preserved in oil, tuna, pickles, gherkins, dry-cured sausage, small radishes.

Hot hors-d'oeuvre: Sausages with apples; Little fried patties.

---

1. *Gâteau nantais. Larousse gastronomique* suggests this is a small almond cake flavoured with kirsch. The town of Nantes is insistent that its cake represents its links with the Atlantic trade and that it should be flavoured with rum and vanilla. It was claimed by the Breton historian Paul Eudel (1837–1911) that the first commercial version was elaborated by a baker at the beginning of the nineteenth century. In the twentieth century it was taken up and distributed extensively by the Nantes biscuit manufacturer LU.

2. In French, *fromage glacé*. This does not mean 'cheese ice' but is the use of the word *fromage* in its more literal sense (see *Larousse gastronomique*). *Fromage* is a metonym deriving from *forma* or mould. Cheeses, of course, were always moulded. Hence the use of the word *fromage* in charcuterie, *fromage de tête* or head cheese for example, is due to its being moulded. The English 'cheese' derives from the Latin *caseus* which is related to earlier forms which imply some connection with fermentation or souring. Mme Millet-Robinet does not have any instructions for making ice-creams or sorbets.

3. This item in the original is '*Marrons rôtis circulant*'. It is not clear what this means, or how it differs from the more usual '*Marrons rôtis*'. One can only presume she means that the chestnuts are passed round.

Removes: Boiled beef on sauerkraut, with slices of cervelas sausage; Skate with black butter.

Entrées: *Fricandeau* of veal with chicory; Hot pie filled with quenelles and truffles; Sheep's trotters à la poulette with cheese; Grilled sole with white sauce.

Roasts: Turkey stuffed with chestnuts; Ham pie.

Salads: Chicory; Beetroot and celery.

Vegetables: Cardoons with *jus*; Brussels sprouts.

Entremets: Brillat-Savarin's *fondu*; Fried calf's brains.

Sweet entremets: Boiled rice pudding with coffee; Charlotte russe; Apple fritters; *Colinette.*

Dessert: Brie cheese; Gruyère cheese; Well-sweetened slices of orange, apples and pears sprinkled with kirsch; Chestnut compote; Pear compote; Apple compote; Two compotiers of fruits in eau-de-vie; Narbonne honey; Two plates of assorted sweets; Two plates of jams; Two plates of *petits-fours*; Two plates of biscuits; *Mendiants*; Prunes from Agen; Dried flattened pears; Chestnuts.[1]

FOURTH MENU (for fast-days)

Soups: Crécy with vegetable stock; Onion with milk.

Hors-d'oeuvre: Butter, radishes, anchovies, sardines preserved in oil, olives, pickles, gherkins, salmon sandwiches.

Hot hors-d'oeuvre: The curé's omelette from Brillat-Savarin; Mushrooms on fried bread.

Removes: Pike *au bleu* with anchovy sauce; Lobster.

Entrées: *Matelote* of small soles; Eggs with a vegetable *jus*; Salmon with a caper sauce; Brillat-Savarin's *fondu.*

Roasts: Brill with oil; Truffled teal.[2]

Salads: Lettuce; Wild chicory (*barbe du capucin*) with fillets of sardines.

Vegetables: Buttered celeriac; Bottled garden peas.

Entremets: Fried oysters; Gratin of Jerusalem artichokes.

Sweet entremets: Meringues; Savarin; Apple charlotte with apricot jam; Maize cake.

Dessert: Roquefort cheese; Chester cheese; Moulded ice-cream; Two

---

1. In the original, '*Marrons circulant*'.
2. As teal is waterfowl, it was allowed on fast-days, although farmyard duck would be forbidden.

centrepieces of pâtisserie; Pralines; Dragées; Quince compote; Cherry compote; Apple compote; Agen prunes; Two plates of *petits-fours*; *Mendiants*; Malaga raisins; Pears; Apples; Two plates of oranges; Two compotiers of fruits in eau-de-vie; Roast chestnuts.[1]

MARCH
FIRST MENU

Soups: Rice with meat stock and a little lentil purée; Onion with milk.

Hors-d'oeuvre: Butter, radishes, anchovies mixed with chopped egg, marinated tuna, pickles, gherkins.

Hot hors-d'oeuvre: Mutton chops; Noodles with sliced cervelas sausage and sausage.

Removes: Boiled beef on tomato sauce; Grilled shad with white sauce.

Entrées: Veal chops *en papillote*; Mackerel with black butter; Calf's brains and sweetbreads in the manner of a chicken fricassee; Loin of mutton with cabbage.

Roasts: Marinated leg of mutton; A whole ham.

Salads: Cress; Lettuce.

Vegetables: Asparagus; Potatoes à la poulette.

Entremets: Gratin of macaroni; Poached sea fish with mayonnaise sauce.

Sweet entremets: *Gâteau à la neige*; Savarin; Apple fritters; Chocolate cream.

Dessert: Brie cheese; Gruyère cheese; Viry cream cheese;[2] Agen prunes; Preserved mirabelle plums; Orange salad; Dried flattened pears in a compote; Two plates of *petits-fours*; Two plates of biscuits; Orange flower praline; Violet soufflé; Pear jams; Strawberry jams; *Marrons glacés*; Candied fruits; *Nonnettes* of *pain d'épices*; Macaroons.

SECOND MENU
Oysters.

Soups: Meat stock with Italian pasta and cheese; Sweetened panada with egg yolks.

Hors-d'oeuvre: Butter, radishes, cress dressed with vinegar, sardines preserved in oil, marinated tuna, pickles, gherkins, horseradish.

---

1.   In the original, '*Marrons rôtis circulant*'.
2.   Viry is now a suburb of Paris, and called Viry-Châtillon, in the department of Essonne. For centuries, it supplied Paris with fresh cream cheese (see Andrew Dalby, *Cheese: A Global History*, 2009).

Hot hors-d'oeuvre: Confit of goose legs; Little patties with gravy.

Removes: Boiled beef with sauerkraut; Brill with white milk sauce.

Entrées: *Matelote* of salmon in a pie crust; Fillet of veal in a carbonade; Lamb's trotters à la poulette; Stuffed eggs.

Roasts: Best end of lamb; Ruffec pâté with truffles.

Salads: Cress; Lettuce with hard-boiled eggs.

Vegetables: Potato croquettes; Split pea purée with croûtons.

Entremets: Fried sheep's brains; Lobster.

Sweet entremets: Eclairs; Crème caramel; Rice soufflé; Rich puff paste *galette*.

Dessert: Roquefort cheese; Gruyère cheese; Viry cream cheese; Prune compote; Cherry compote; Two compotes of orange salad; Two plates of jams; Two plates of preserved fruits; Two plates of biscuits; Two plates of *petits-fours*; *Mendiants*; Hazelnuts; Walnuts; Apricot cheese; Quince cheese.

THIRD MENU (for fast-days)

Soups: Lentil purée with rice; Onion with milk.

Hors-d'oeuvre: Butter, radishes, marinated tuna, sardines preserved in oil, pickles, gherkins, anchovies, olives.

Hot hors-d'oeuvre: Slices of smoked salmon on small buttered pieces of best wheaten bread; Little fried patties for fast-days (with a fish filling).

Removes: Sturgeon with provençale sauce; Grilled thick-lipped grey mullet with a white milk sauce.

Entrées: Poached eggs with a tomato sauce; Brillat-Savarin's *fondu*; Gratin of whiting; Mussels à la poulette.

Roast: Hot carp *au bleu* with oil.

Salads: Lettuce; Cos lettuce.

Vegetables: Green pea purée; Potato balls.

Entremets: Lobster; Fried tench.

Sweet entremets: Bread pudding; Boiled rice pudding with coffee; Meringues; Apple fritters.

Dessert: Roquefort cheese; Brie cheese; Decorated cake; Prunes; Compote of preserved apricots; Orange salad; Apple salad with rum; Two plates of *mendiants*; Dried flattened pears; *Brugnolles*;[1] Two plates of biscuits;

---

1.   Mme Millet-Robinet uses here a variant spelling for a town we know better as Brignoles, in the Var department in Provence, which was once famed for its sun-dried, late-season plums. They were laid out on tiles, dried and flattened so that they

Pralines; Dragées; Two jams; Two compotiers of fruits in eau-de-vie; Two plates of *petits-fours*.

FOURTH MENU (for fast-days)

Soups: Green cabbage and cheese; *Soupe à la reine*.

Hors-d'oeuvre: Butter, cress with a salad dressing, radishes, anchovies, marinated tuna, pickles, gherkins, fish sandwiches.

Hot hors-d'oeuvre: Well-fried noodles; Scalloped oysters.

Removes: Poached salmon, sauce mayonnaise; Skate with black butter.

Entrées: Fishballs of carp; Eggs in a fast-day gravy; Salt cod béchamel in pastry; Baked fillets of sole.

Roasts: Grilled stuffed shad with a white sauce; Lobster or crayfish [*langouste*].

Salads: Lettuce; Cos lettuce.

Vegetables: Bottled garden peas; Potatoes with milk.

Entremets: The curé's omelette from Brillat-Savarin; Plain macaroni.

Sweet entremets: *Oeufs à la neige*; Boiled rice pudding with chocolate; *Colinette*; Eclairs.

Dessert: Gruyère cheese; Dutch cheese; Savoy biscuit; Prunes; Bottled raspberries; Orange salad; Compote of dried flattened pears; Two plates of sweets; Two plates of *petits-fours*; *Mendiants*; Figs from Grasse; Malaga raisins; Pistachios; White nougat from Marseille;[1] *Marrons glacés*; *Nonnettes* of *pain d'épices*; Macaroons.

FIFTH MENU (for fast-days; Holy Week)[2]
Oysters.

Soups: Vegetable stock with croûtons fried in oil; Onion fried in oil and rice.

Hors-d'oeuvre: Radishes, cress with a salad dressing with fillets of pickled herring, anchovies, smoked salmon, pickles, gherkins.

---

resembled a large coin, the pistole – an alternative name. In point of fact, the town saw all its orchards destroyed during the Wars of Religion and the speciality migrated to Digne further north, in the department of Alpes-de-Haute-Provence.

1. White nougat is made with egg whites. The first manufacture of nougat in France was at Marseille in the seventeenth century. Montélimar displaced Marseille as the principal site of manufacture in the eighteenth century.

2. The rules of the Catholic Church meant that butter and dairy foods were not to be consumed during Holy Week.

Hot hors-d'oeuvre: Soft carp roes fried in oil; Sardines preserved in oil.

Remove: Lobster, sauce rémoulade.

Entrées: Sturgeon with oil; Skate with tartar sauce; Fillets of sole with anchovy sauce (make the roux with oil and vegetable stock); Hot potatoes dressed as a salad.

Roasts: Grilled stuffed shad with oil, sauce rémoulade; Turbot *au bleu* with oil.

Salads: Cos lettuce; Wild chicory (*barbe du capucin*) with fillets of pickled herring.

Vegetables: Potatoes fried with oil; Preserved truffles.

Entremets: *Soles de guérets* fried in oil; Small pike fried in oil.

Sweet entremets: Rum jelly; Blancmange; Angels' hairs; Nougat.

Dessert: In the centre, fruit basket with pineapple; Prunes; Compote of preserved cherries; Compote of preserved apricots; Chestnuts; Pistachios; Grasse figs; Malaga raisins; Two plates of *mendiants*; Dried flattened plums; Two jams; Two compotiers of fruits with eau-de-vie; Violet soufflé; Marseille nougat; *Nonnettes de Reims*.

APRIL
FIRST MENU

Soups: Meat stock with Italian pasta and cheese; With rice and a purée of green peas.

Hors-d'oeuvre: Butter, radishes, grated cheese, mixed herbs dressed with vinegar, sardines preserved in oil, marinated tuna, olives, pickles, anchovies, dry-cured sausage.

Hot hors-d'oeuvre: Fried calf's mesentery; Stuffed pig's trotters.

Removes: Plain calf's head; Boiled beef with tomato sauce.

Entrées: Fresh pork chops with sauce; Daube of ox tongue; Mackerel in butter; Calf's sweetbreads and brains in the manner of a chicken fricassee.

Roasts: Quarter of a lamb; A whole ham.

Salads: Cos lettuce; Cress.

Vegetables: Purée of haricot beans with croûtons; Lettuce with meat *jus*.

Entremets: Fried tench; Timbale of macaroni.

Sweet entremets: Tea cream; French toast; Little choux buns; Savarin.

Dessert: Pineapple; Gruyère cheese; Dutch cheese; Cream cheese; Agen prunes; Compote of preserved apricots; Compote of preserved cherries;

Orange salad; Pears; Apples; Quince cheese; Apricot cheese; *Marrons glacés*; Candied angelica; Two plates of biscuits; Two plates of *petits-fours*; Two plates of jams; Two compotiers of fruits with eau-de-vie.

SECOND MENU

Soups: Meat stock with vermicelli; Rice with sweetened water.

Hors-d'oeuvre: Butter, radishes, mixed herbs, olives, marinated tuna, sardines conserved in olive oil, pickles, gherkins.

Hot hors-d'oeuvre: Fried calf's kidney; Puddings and sausages.

Removes: Daube of calf's liver; Capon with sea-salt.

Entrées: Calf's head in the manner of turtle; Beef à la mode; Grilled shad; Calf's mesentery.

Roasts: Fillet of beef; Two small chicken à la reine with watercress.

Salads: Lettuce with hard-boiled eggs; Cos lettuce with mixed herbs.

Vegetables: Asparagus; Lettuce with meat *jus*.

Entremets: Fried brains; Lobster.

Sweet entremets: Rum pudding; Meringues; Rice cake; Jam omelette.

Dessert: Chester cheese; Roquefort cheese; Cream cheese; Compote of dried flattened pears; Orange salad; Compote of mirabelle plums; Two plates of *petits-fours*; Two plates of biscuits; Two plates of *mendiants*; Two plates of candied fruits; *Nonnettes de Reims*; Macaroons; Marseille nougat.

THIRD MENU

Soups: Meat stock with Italian pasta, with a little lentil purée; Sugared panada.

Hors-d'oeuvre: Butter, radishes, mixed herbs, marinated tuna, anchovies, pickles, gherkins, olives.

Hot hors-d'oeuvre: Fried calf's mesentery; Small patties.

Removes: Skate with white sauce; Boiled beef with tomato sauce.

Entrées: *Matelote* of salmon; Veal chops with mixed herbs; Eel à la poulette; Cheese omelette.

Roasts: A whole cold ham on sugared spinach; Carp *au bleu* with a very concentrated *jus*.

Salads: Cos lettuce; Small green chicory.

Vegetables: Asparagus in the manner of garden peas; Potatoes with milk.

Entremets: Lobster or crayfish [*langouste*]; Macaroni with meat stock.

Sweet entremets: Charlotte russe; Savarin; Sorrel fritters; Omelette soufflée.

Dessert: Gruyère cheese; Brie cheese; Cream cheese from Viry; Dried flattened pears; Prunes; Orange salad with rum; Orange salad with eau-de-vie; Two plates of biscuits; Two plates of jams; Two compotiers of fruits in eau-de-vie; [Candied] angelica; [Candied] citron; *Mendiants*; Malaga raisins; Two plates of *petits-fours*; Nougat; *Croquets*.

FOURTH MENU (for fast-days)

Soups: Vegetable stock with Italian pasta and cheese; Rice with water.

Hors-d'oeuvre: Butter, radishes, mixed herbs, marinated tuna, fresh sardines, olives, gherkins, pickles, anchovies, grated cheese.

Removes: Poached salmon with a white sauce; Pike *au bleu*, with an anchovy sauce made with vegetable stock.

Entrées: The curé's omelette from Brillat-Savarin; Eggs à la poulette; Fishballs of carp in pastry; Salt cod béchamel in pastry.

Roasts: Brill with white sauce; Lobster with a rémoulade sauce.

Salads: Cos lettuce; Small green chicory.

Vegetables: Asparagus with a tomato sauce; Purée of haricot beans with croûtons.

Entremets: Fried soles; Well-fried noodles.

Sweet entremets: Bread mould; Rum jelly; Meringues; Chocolate éclairs.

Dessert: Pineapple; Roquefort cheese; Dutch cheese; Prunes; Compote of bottled apricots; Compote of bottled raspberries; Two compotiers of fruits in eau-de-vie; Two jams; Raisins; Oranges; Apples; Marseille nougat; Candied fruits; Pistachios; Two plates of *petits-fours*; Two plates of biscuits; *Mendiants*; Malaga raisins; *Croquignoles*; *Nonnettes de Reims*.

MAY

FIRST MENU

Soups: Meat stock with granulated gluten; Sorrel, with a purée of very green peas and croûtons.

Hors-d'oeuvre: Butter, radishes, mixed herbs, fresh sardines, marinated tuna, olives, pickles, gherkins.

Hot hors-d'oeuvre: *Andouillettes*; [Confit] legs of geese.

Removes: Boiled beef with piquant sauce; Leg of mutton in its own *jus*.

Entrées: Shad on a sorrel forcemeat; Veal chops *en papillote*; Best end of lamb à la Périgord; Spatchcocked squabs.

Roasts: Calf's kidney; Head of wild boar.

Salads: Lettuce with hard-boiled eggs; Cos lettuce with mixed herbs.

Vegetables: Asparagus in the manner of garden peas; Small artichokes à la barigoule.

Entremets: Fried calf's head; Timbale of macaroni.

Sweet entremets: Boiled rice pudding with chocolate; Prune cake; Charlotte russe; *Beignets soufflés*.

Dessert: Gruyère cheese; Brie cheese; Cream cheese; Savoy biscuit; Compote of bottled apricots; Compote of cherries; Prunes; Orange salad; Two jams; Two compotiers of fruits in eau-de-vie; Two plates of *petits-fours*; Two plates of biscuits; Two plates of sweets; *Mendiants*; Marseille nougat; [Candied] angelica.

SECOND MENU

Soups: *Croûte au pot*; *Soupe à la reine*.

Hors-d'oeuvre: Butter, radishes, mixed herbs, fresh sardines, marinated tuna, pickles, gherkins, olives, baby artichokes, grated cheese.

Hot hors-d'oeuvre: Slices of ham mixed with slices of pig's head, decorated with mixed herbs; Brains.

Removes: Plain calf's head; Smothered fillet of beef; Melon.

Entrées: Capon with rice; Carbonade of fillet of veal; Grilled salmon with a white sauce; Calf's sweetbreads and brains à la poulette in a pastry crust.

Roasts: *Pâté de foie gras en terrine*; Two chicken à la reine.

Salads: Cos lettuce; Young chicory with sardine fillets.

Vegetables: Young garden peas with sugar; Baby broad beans in milk.

Entremets: Crayfish [*langouste*]; Fried lamb's trotters.

Sweet entremets: Coffee cream; Cakes; *Oeufs à la neige*; Nougat.

Dessert: Brie cheese; Gruyère cheese; Cream cheese; Strawberries; Prunes; Orange salad; Dried flattened pears; Bottled cherries; Honeycomb cake; Two nougats from Marseille; Two jams; Two compotiers of fruits in eau-de-vie; Pistachios; *Mendiants*; Malaga raisins; Two [plates of] *petits-fours*; Two [plates of] sweets.

THIRD MENU

Soups: Meat stock with Touraine rice; Herb.

Hors-d'oeuvre: Butter, radishes, baby artichokes, fresh sardines, marinated tuna, pickles, gherkins, olives.

Hot hors-d'oeuvre: Fried lamb's trotters; Fried ham with wine and sugar; Melon.

Removes: Boiled beef with tomato sauce; Chicken with sea-salt.

Entrées: Veal escalopes; Daube of leg of mutton; Calf's head in the manner of turtle; Lamb's trotters with cheese.

Roasts: Fillet of pork; Plaice with white milk sauce.

Salads: Cos lettuce; Lettuce.

Vegetables: Small potatoes with butter; Small carrots with milk.

Entremets: Sweet omelette; Fried brains.

Sweet entremets: Cakes; Vanilla cream; Kidney mould; Kirsch jelly.

Dessert: Gruyère cheese; Dutch cheese; Cream cheese; Strawberries; Prunes; Bottled apricots; Marseille nougat; Honeycombs; Two jams; Two compotiers of fruits in eau-de-vie; Two plates of *petits-fours*; Maréchal MacDonald's sweets; Fruit cheeses; *Mendiants*; Savoy biscuit; Nougat.

FOURTH MENU (for fast-days)

Soups: Sorrel with garden peas and rice; Onion with milk.

Hors-d'oeuvre: Butter, radishes, little broad beans, baby artichokes, olives, pickles, fresh sardines, gherkins.

Hot hors-d'oeuvre: Cheese omelette; Little patties; Melon.

Removes: Barbel with white sauce; Lobster with rémoulade sauce.

Entrées: Stuffed eggs, served on asparagus tips cooked as garden peas; Eggs poached on a vegetable *jus*; Baked plaice; Grey mullets à la maître-d'hôtel.[1]

Roasts: Salmon with white sauce; Trouts *au bleu* with oil.

Salads: Cos lettuce; Lettuce with mixed herbs.

Vegetables: Small carrots with milk; Sugared spinach.

Entremets: Sorrel fritters; Gratin of macaroni.

Sweet entremets: Iced cakes; *Colinette*; Flambéd rum omelette; Boiled rice pudding with coffee.

Dessert: Brie cheese; Gruyère cheese; Cream cheese; Pineapple; Strawberries; Orange salad; A very sweet compote of gooseberries; Two plates of *petits-fours*; Two plates of biscuits; Two plates of jams; Two compotiers of fruits in eau-de-vie; Savoy biscuit; Nougat; Pistachios; Almonds à la reine; Two plates of sweets.

---

1.   Here, Mme Millet-Robinet refers to the grey mullet as *mulet*. In keeping with the distinction I propose on page 526 between thick-lipped grey mullet (*Chelon labrosus*) and ordinary grey mullet (*Mugil cephalus*), I have listed this as grey mullet.

JUNE

FIRST MENU

Soups: Meat stock with stale bread and small young carrots cut in rounds; Sorrel with young garden peas.

Hors-d'oeuvre: Butter, radishes, little broad beans, baby artichokes, fresh sardines, marinated tuna, olives, pickles, gherkins.

Hot hors-d'oeuvre: Little patties; Breaded lamb cutlets in the manner of mutton cutlets.

Removes: Boiled beef surrounded by buttered new potatoes; Plain calf's head; In the centre, melon.

Entrées: Two gurnards with white sauce; Lamb's trotters à la poulette; Veal escalopes with garlic; Ox tongue with piquant sauce.

Roasts: Barded squabs; Calf's kidney.

Salads: Cos lettuce with mixed herbs; Lettuce with a cream dressing.

Vegetables: Sugared young garden peas; Artichokes à la barigoule.

Entremets: Pyramid of freshwater crayfish; Stuffed pig's head.

Sweet entremets: Crème caramel; Eclairs; *Beignets soufflés*; Jam omelette.

Dessert: Brie cheese; Gruyère cheese; Frozen cream cheese; Gooseberries; Wild strawberries;[1] Pine strawberries; Cherries; [Red or white] currants; Two compotiers of fruit in eau-de-vie; Two plates of sweets; Two plates of *petits-fours*; Two plates of biscuits; *Nonnettes de Reims*; Macaroons; Two decorated cakes.

SECOND MENU

Soups: Julienne; Meat stock with vermicelli.

Hors-d'oeuvre: Butter, radishes, little broad beans, mixed herbs, baby artichokes, fresh sardines, pickles, gherkins, anchovies; Melon.

Hot hors-d'oeuvre: Sausages and pudding; Fried calf's ears.

Removes: Boiled beef with asparagus cooked like garden peas, with meat *jus*; Leg of mutton cooked in its own juice, with baby carrots.

Entrées: *Matelote* of carp and eel; *Fricandeau* [of veal] with sorrel; Pigeons *en papillote*, or spatchcocked; Sweetbreads and brains à la poulette.

Roasts: A whole ham; Pâté in a terrine from Ruffec.

Salads: Cos lettuce with nasturtiums; Lettuce with hard-boiled eggs.

Vegetables: Small broad beans; Fried artichokes.

Entremets: Pyramid of freshwater crayfish; Fried frog's legs.

1.   In French, *fraises des quatre saisons.*

Sweet entremets: *Oeufs à la neige*; Bread mould; Cherry cake; Boiled rice pudding, iced or soufflé.

Dessert: Gruyère cheese; Brie cheese; Cream cheese; Orange salad; Gooseberries; Two compotiers of fruits in eau-de-vie; Two plates of *petits-fours*; Two plates of biscuits; Two plates of sweets; Cherries; Strawberries; *Mendiants*; Two jams; Savoy biscuit; Nougat.

THIRD MENU

Soups: Meat stock with rice and garden peas; *Soupe à la reine*.

Hors-d'oeuvre: Butter, radishes, little broad beans, mixed herbs, baby artichokes, fresh sardines, marinated tuna, pickles, gherkins.

Hot hors-d'oeuvre: Fried brains; Small slices of ham, stuffed tongue, boar's head, etc; Melon.

Removes: Smothered fillet of beef served on baby carrots with meat *jus*; Salmon *au bleu*.

Entrées: Calf's head in the manner of turtle; Carbonade of fillet of veal; Grilled sole with a white milk sauce; Eel with tartar sauce.

Roasts: *Pâté de foie gras* in a terrine, from Toulouse;[1] Salmon trout *au bleu*.

Salads: Cos lettuce with mixed herbs; Lettuce.

Vegetables: French beans; Small potatoes with butter.

Entremets: Crayfish [*langouste*]; Freshwater crayfish omelette.

Sweet entremets: Savarin; Strawberry tart; Chocolate cream; Omelette soufflée.

Dessert: Brie cheese; Gruyère cheese; Moulded ice; Peeled cherries; Pearled currants; Strawberries; Compote of large strawberries with rum; Cherries; Red and white currants; Two plates of biscuits; Two plates of *petits-fours*; Two compotiers of fruits in eau-de-vie; *Calottes* with jams; Nougat.

FOURTH MENU (for fast-days)

Soups: Cabbage, with garden peas, baby carrots, French beans, young broad beans; Vegetable stock with granulated gluten.

Hors-d'oeuvre: Butter, radishes, baby artichokes, little broad beans, fresh sardines, marinated tuna, pickles, gherkins; Melon.

Hot hors-d'oeuvre: Fried lamprey; Little fried meat-free patties.

---

1.   The *foie gras* from Toulouse was more usually duck; goose was the norm in Strasbourg.

Removes: Plaice with white sauce; Eggs with vegetable *jus* and artichoke bottoms.

Entrées: Fishballs of carp in a pastry crust; The curé's omelette of Brillat-Savarin; Frog's legs in the manner of a chicken fricassee; Fried eggs with a tomato sauce.

Roasts: Brill *au bleu* with a cold sauce; Whole fried eel.

Salads: Cos lettuce; Lettuce.

Vegetables: French beans; Fried aubergines.

Entremets: Pyramid of freshwater crayfish; Small potatoes with butter.

Sweet entremets: Strawberry tart; Cherry cake; Vanilla cream; Boiled rice pudding with coffee.

Dessert: Roquefort cheese; Brie cheese; Cream cheese; Gooseberry compote; Cherry compote; Strawberry compote; Strawberries; Cherries; Red and white currants; Two plates of *petits-fours*; Two plates of biscuits; Two plates of sweets; *Nonnettes de Reims*; *Croquets*; Two compotiers of fruits in eau-de-vie; Two jams.

JULY
FIRST MENU

Soups: Meat stock with large green pea purée and twice-cooked bread; Onion with milk.

Hors-d'oeuvre: Butter, radishes, baby artichokes, little broad beans, fresh sardines, marinated tuna, pickles, gherkins, anchovies, black mulberries.[1]

Hot hors-d'oeuvre: Fried calf's kidney; White puddings and sausages; Melon and figs.

Removes: Daube of rump of veal; Boiled beef with glazed onions.

Entrées: Pigeons with garden peas; Daube of calf's liver; White *matelote* of eel and carp; Chicken fricassee.

Roasts: Pâté in a terrine, from Ruffec or Toulouse; Fillet of beef.

Salads: Cos lettuce; Lettuce.

Vegetables: French beans; Cauliflower with white sauce.

Entremets: Fried brains in pastry; Pyramid of freshwater crayfish.

---

1. Other families may have had mulberry trees in their back garden, but the reader should remember that Mme Millet-Robinet, her husband and her brother were all three great advocates of, and practitioners and experts in, the raising of silkworms, which of course depend on the (white) mulberry tree.

Sweet entremets: Cherry *clafoutis*; Strawberry tart; Black coffee cream; Peach fritters.

Dessert: Gruyère cheese; Cream cheese; Peeled cherries; Pearled currants; Very thin, very sweet slices of melon, sprinkled with eau-de-vie; Savoy biscuit; *Calottes*; Two plates of *petits-fours*; Two plates of biscuits; Two plates of sweets; Blanquette pears;[1] Monsieur plums;[2] Cherries; Red and white currants; Two compotiers of fruits in eau-de-vie.

SECOND MENU

Soups: Meat stock with rice; Sorrel with garden peas.

Hors-d'oeuvre: Butter, radishes, baby artichokes, mixed herbs, fresh sardines, pickles, gherkins, marinated tuna, figs, black mulberries, melon.

Hot hors-d'oeuvre: Truffled [pig's] trotters; Little patties with meat *jus*.

Removes: Skate with black butter; Beef à la mode.

Entrées: Escalopes of veal; Daube of ox tongue, served on a sorrel purée; Freshwater crayfish omelette, served on a parsley butter; Frog's legs à la poulette.

Roasts: Ham pâté from Lesage; Spit-roast calf's liver.

Salads: Cos lettuce; Potato.

Vegetables: Artichokes à la barigoule; New potatoes with milk.

Entremets: Fried calf's head; Pyramid of freshwater crayfish.

Sweet entremets: Strawberry tart; Cherry cake; Vanilla cream; Rice soufflé with coffee.

Dessert: Brie cheese; Gruyère cheese; Moulded ice; Peeled cherries; Pearled currants; Small, sweet slices of melon with kirsch; Compote of green apricots; Two different sorts of strawberries; Two different sorts of cherries; Peaches; Apricots; Plums; Pears; Two plates of *petits-fours*; Two plates of sweets; Two plates of biscuits; Two plates of macaroons.

THIRD MENU

Soups: Crécy with meat stock; Melon [soup].

Hors-d'oeuvre: Butter, radishes, baby artichokes, borage with vinegar, fresh sardines, pickles, gherkins, tuna, anchovies, figs, melon.

Hot hors-d'oeuvre: Stuffed aubergines; Mutton chops.

1. A small summer pear with white skin.
2. *Prunes de monsieur* are defined in the *Dictionnaire de l'Académie* (8th edition) as a round plum 'd'un beau violet'.

Removes: Boiled beef with tomato sauce; Plain calf's mesentery.

Entrées: Fillet of veal à la bourgeoise; Beef fillet steaks with potatoes; Perch with white sauce; Grilled shad with parsley butter.

Roasts: Sucking pig; Two chicken.

Salads: Green and variegated cos lettuce.

Vegetables: Fresh haricot beans; Artichokes with white sauce.

Entremets: Fried tench; Chicken mayonnaise.

Sweet entremets: Cherry *clafoutis*; Eclairs; Moulded egg custard with caramel; Omelette soufflée.

Dessert: Goat's cheese; Gruyère cheese; Cream cheese; Cherry compote with kirsch; Apricot compote with rum; Plum compote; Two sorts of strawberries; Two sorts of cherries; Apricots; Peaches; Pears; Plums; Macaroons; *Croquignoles*; Nougat; Savoy biscuit; Two plates of sweets.

FOURTH MENU (for fast-days)

Soups: Rice with water and a purée of large fresh peas; Cherry.

Hors-d'oeuvre: Butter, radishes, baby artichokes, fresh sardines, marinated tuna, pickles, gherkins, figs; Melon.

Hot hors-d'oeuvre: Freshwater crayfish omelette; Little meat-free patties.

Removes: Shad *au bleu* with oil; Grilled plaice with white sauce.

Entrées: Fishballs in pastry; Grilled tench; Poached eggs, on a purée of large fresh peas; Eel à la poulette.

Roasts: Perch *au bleu* with cold sauce; Carp *au bleu* with mayonnaise sauce.

Salads: Lettuce; Variegated cos lettuce.

Vegetables: Gratin of young peas; Sugared spinach.

Entremets: Fried frog's legs; Potatoes served on parsley butter with lemon juice.

Sweet entremets: Cherry cake; Apricot *clafoutis*; Meringue;[1] French toast.

Dessert: Gruyère cheese; Goat's cheese; Three macédoines of fruits; Four vases of flowers; Two plates of sweets; Two plates of *petits-fours*; Two plates of biscuits; Two plates of jams; Two compotiers of fruits in eau-de-vie.

---

1.   Here, *meringot*. I have not been able to find this form in French dictionaries. It figures as an entremets in a menu printed in the *Nouveau manuel complet de maître-d'hôtel, ou L'art d'ordonner les dîners et autre repas* by A. Chevrier (Roret, 1842), and the pâtissier Jean-Claude Montauriol remarks in his Internet blog that they used to call meringue *meringot* when he was an apprentice at Claude Monvoisin in Talence, a suburb of Bordeaux.

AUGUST

FIRST MENU

Soups: Rice with meat stock and a purée of sorrel and young garden peas; Sugared panada.

Hors-d'oeuvre: Butter, radishes, baby artichokes, dry-cured sausage, fresh sardines, pickles, gherkins; Figs; Melon.

Hot hors-d'oeuvre: Fried brains; Stuffed aubergines.

Removes: Boiled beef with tomato sauce; Rump of veal à la pèlerine.

Entrées: Fillet of veal cooked in its own juice; Grilled tench; Young chickens with tarragon; Calf's head in the manner of turtle *au blanc* in pastry.

Roasts: Barbel with oil; Young turkey.

Salads: Cos lettuce; Chicory.

Vegetables: Fried shelled white haricot beans; Stuffed artichokes.

Entremets: Fried gudgeon; Jam omelette.

Sweet entremets: Waffles; Iced boiled rice pudding soufflé; Plum *clafoutis*; Peach fritters.

Dessert: Goat's cheese; Gruyère cheese; Moulded ice; Compote of raw peaches in kirsch; Compote of plums; Compote of apricots; Pearled currants; Pears; Apricots; Peaches; Strawberries; Two plates of *petits-fours*; Savoy biscuit; *Calottes*; Two plates of sweets; Two compotiers of fruits in eau-de-vie.

SECOND MENU

Soups: Meat stock with rice; Onion with milk.

Hors-d'oeuvre: Butter, radishes, celery, baby artichokes, tuna, fresh sardines, pickles, gherkins; Figs; Melon.

Hot hors-d'oeuvre: Little patties; Sausages with cabbage.

Removes: Chicken with sea-salt; Leg of mutton *à l'eau*.

Entrées: Daube of calf's liver; *Matelote* of carp; Forcemeat in pastry; Chicken mayonnaise.

Roasts: Trout *au bleu*; Spit-roasted duck.

Salads: Cos lettuce; Chicory.

Vegetables: Sugared garden peas; Fried shelled haricot beans.

Entremets: Pâté from Lesage; Salmon salad.

Sweet entremets: Apricot tart; Bread mould; Boiled rice pudding with coffee; Peach fritters.

Dessert: Gruyère cheese; Brie cheese; Cream cheese or moulded ice;

Strawberries; Small, highly sweetened slices of melon sprinkled with rum; Compote of apricots; Raspberries; Pears; Peaches; Plums; Apricots; Grapes; Nectarines; Two plates of *petits-fours*; Savoy biscuit; *Calottes*; Two [plates of] sweets; Fresh hazelnuts; Fresh almonds.

THIRD MENU

Soups: Crécy with meat stock; *Soupe à la reine.*

Hors-d'oeuvre: Butter, radishes, baby artichokes, mixed herbs, fresh sardines, marinated tuna, pickles, gherkins, black mulberries; Figs; Melon.

Hot hors-d'oeuvre: Fried ham with wine and sugar; Fried pigeons.

Removes: Smothered fillet of beef; Plain calf's head.

Entrées: Mutton fillet with French beans; Red mullet with white sauce; *Fricandeau* of calf's sweetbreads with chicory; Chicken fricassee.

Roasts: Pâté in a terrine; Turkey poult.

Salads: Lettuce; Variegated cos lettuce.

Vegetables: Fried potatoes; Cauliflower in meat *jus.*

Entremets: Pyramid of freshwater crayfish; Fried aubergines.

Sweet entremets: Apricot cake; Rice cake; Meringue; Savarin.

Dessert: Goat's cheese; Gruyère cheese; Macédoine of fruits; Flowers; Apricot compote; Verjuice compote; White grapes; Black grapes; Pears; Plums; Peaches; Nectarines; Strawberries; Apricots; Two plates of biscuits; Two plates of *petits-fours*; Two plates of sweets; Two compotiers of fruits in eau-de-vie.

FOURTH MENU (for fast-days)

Soups: Crécy with vegetable stock; Sugared panada.

Hors-d'oeuvre: Butter, radishes, baby artichokes, celery, fresh sardines, marinated tuna, pickles, gherkins; Melon; Figs.

Hot hors-d'oeuvre: Crayfish [*langouste*]; Fresh sardine omelette.

Removes: Carp *au bleu*; Plaice with white sauce.

Entrées: Fishballs of carp in pastry with freshwater crayfish; Stuffed eggs; Frog's legs in the manner of chicken fricassee; Grilled salmon.

Roasts: Trout *au bleu*; Pyramid of freshwater crayfish.

Salads: Lettuce with hard-boiled eggs; Cos lettuce.

Vegetables: Artichokes with white sauce; Cauliflower with tomato sauce.

Entremets: Sweet omelette; Fried small pike.

Sweet entremets: Chocolate cream; Potato soufflé; Eclairs; Apricot tart.

Dessert: Goat's cheese; Gruyère cheese; Cream cheese; Compote of plums with eau-de-vie; Compote of apricots with eau-de-vie; Verjuice compote; Raspberry compote; Two sorts of strawberries; Pears; Peaches; Apricots; Plums; Fresh hazelnuts; Fresh almonds; Two plates of *petits-fours*; Two plates of biscuits; Two plates of sweets; Meringues sandwiched with cream; Macaroons.

SEPTEMBER
FIRST MENU

Soups: Rice with meat stock and two partridge in the pot; Pumpkin.

Hors-d'oeuvre: Butter, radishes, baby artichokes, celery, cucumbers dressed with vinegar, pickles, gherkins, dry-cured sausage, shrimps, fresh sardines; Melon; Figs.

Hot hors-d'oeuvre: Little patties; Sauté of young rabbit.

Removes: Boiled beef with glazed onions; Partridge on a piquant sauce.

Entrées: Stuffed cucumbers; Chicken mayonnaise; Civet of hare; *Fricandeau* with chicory.

Roasts: Pheasant; Chicken.

Salads: Cos lettuce; Chicory; Celery.

Vegetables: Artichokes à la barigoule; Shelled haricot beans.

Entremets: Fried brains; Mushrooms on fried bread.

Sweet entremets: *Colinette*; Boiled rice pudding with chocolate; Plum *clafoutis*; Little choux buns.

Dessert: Brie cheese; Gruyère cheese; Cream cheese; Compote of plums with eau-de-vie; Compote of apricots with eau-de-vie; Verjuice compote; Peach compote; Pears; Peaches; Currants; Strawberries; Fresh almonds; Fresh hazelnuts; Two plates of *petits-fours*; Two plates of sweets; Biscuits; Macaroons.

SECOND MENU
Oysters.

Soups: Rice with meat *jus*; Julienne.

Hors-d'oeuvre: Butter, radishes, baby artichokes, cucumber salad, fresh sardines, pickles, gherkins, shrimps.

Hot hors-d'oeuvre: Cutlets; Little patties.

Removes: Daube of pig's head; A whole ham served hot on sugared spinach.

Entrées: Partridge with cabbage; Gurnard with white sauce; Veal escalopes; Calf's ears.

Roasts: Quail; Fillet of beef.

Salads: Lettuce with hard-boiled eggs and mixed herbs; Cos lettuce with nasturtium.

Vegetables: Cucumber à la poulette; Browned French beans.

Entremets: Fried gudgeon; Baked mushrooms.

Sweet entremets: Savarin; Green coffee bean cream; Dry pancakes; *Gâteau à la neige.*

Dessert: Brie cheese; Gruyère cheese; Peach salad; Melon salad; Strawberries; Cream cheese; Plums; Two sorts of pears; Grapes; Fresh almonds; Fresh hazelnuts; Two plates of sweets; Two plates of *petits-fours*; Macaroons; *Calottes*; Compotes of fresh fruits in eau-de-vie.

THIRD MENU

Soups: Vegetable purée; Pumpkin with onion and rice.

Hors-d'oeuvre: Butter, radishes, celery, cucumber salad, fresh sardines, pickles, gherkins, dry-cured sausage.

Hot hors-d'oeuvre: Mutton chops; Chicken sauté.

Removes: Daube of ox tongue; Hot carp *au bleu* with provençale sauce.

Entrées: Salmi of partridge; Vol-au-vent; Stuffed cabbage; Chicken fricassee.

Roasts: Pig's head with sauce; Turkey poult.

Salads: Cos lettuce with mixed herbs; Celery; Chicory.

Vegetables: Cauliflower with butter; Fried potatoes.

Entremets: Pyramid of freshwater crayfish; Fried brains.

Sweet entremets: *Colinette*; Plum tart; Laurel cream; Small cakes.

Dessert: Brie cheese; Gruyère cheese; Cream cheese; Verjuice compote; Peach compote; Plum compote; Pear compote; Green walnuts; Fresh almonds; Two sorts of pears; Strawberries; Peaches; Grapes; Currants; Two compotes of fresh fruits with eau-de-vie; Two [plates of] *petits-fours*; Savoy biscuit; *Calottes*.

FOURTH MENU (for fast-days)

Soups: Vegetable stock with granulated gluten; Sorrel with garden peas.

Hors-d'oeuvre: Butter, radishes, celery, cucumber salad, fresh or marinated sardines, pickles, gherkins, shrimps.

Hot hors-d'oeuvre: Little fried patties; Ragout of mushrooms.

Removes: Brillat-Savarin's the curé's omelette; Pike *au bleu*.

Entrées: Eggs with a vegetable *jus*; *Matelote* of fish; Fish vol-au-vent; Skate with white sauce.

Roasts: Grey mullet with cold sauce; A ring of whole fried eel with a large bunch of parsley in the centre.

Salads: Cooked cabbage; Cos lettuce.

Vegetables: Fried cauliflower; Sugared spinach.

Entremets: Pyramid of freshwater crayfish; Mushroom omelette.

Sweet entremets: Babas; Plum tart; Boiled rice pudding with coffee; Meringues.

Dessert: Brie cheese; Gruyère cheese; Cream cheese; Strawberries; Pear compote; Plum compote; Plums; Two sorts of pears; Two sorts of grapes; Peaches; Two plates of *petits-fours*; Two plates of biscuits; Two plates of sweets; Almonds; Green walnuts.

OCTOBER

FIRST MENU
Oysters.

Soups: Cabbage with salt pork; Rice with meat stock.

Hors-d'oeuvre: Butter, radishes, celery, cucumbers with vinegar, anchovies, marinated tuna, pickles, gherkins.

Removes: Salt pork served with the cabbage from the soup and surrounded with sausages; Boiled beef with ragout of mushrooms.

Entrées: *Fricandeau* of mutton with sorrel; Grilled soles with white sauce; Fried fresh pork chops served on a sauce Robert; Capon with celery.

Roasts: Partridge and quail; Spit-roast goose, stuffed with potatoes.

Salads: Potato; Cos lettuce.

Vegetables: Sugared turnips; Podded haricot beans with tomato sauce.

Entremets: Fried brains; Pears in a roux.

Sweet entremets: Potato cake; Pumpkin soufflé; Crème caramel; Eclairs.

Dessert: Brie cheese; Gruyère cheese; Moulded whipped cream; Peach salad with kirsch; Pear salad with rum; Verjuice compote; Plum compote; Strawberries; Grapes; Two sorts of pears; Apples; Green walnuts; Two plates of *petits-fours*; Two plates of sweets.

Soups: Rice with meat *jus*; Onion with milk.

Hors-d'oeuvre: Butter, radishes, celery, figs, sardines, anchovies, pickles, gherkins, shrimps, dry-cured sausage.

Hot hors-d'oeuvre: Scalloped oysters; Baked larks or thrushes.[1]

Removes: Daube of hare; Pike *au bleu*.

Entrées: Salmi of game; Sea fish with a béchamel, served in pastry; Stuffed cabbage; Chicken fricassee.

Roasts: Quarter of venison; Bresse chicken with watercress.

Vegetables: Sugared garden peas; Cauliflower with meat *jus*.

Entremets: Fried whiting; Mushrooms on fried bread.

Sweet entremets: Pumpkin soufflé; Buttered pears; Savarin; Meringues.

Dessert: Brie cheese; Roquefort cheese; Cream cheese; Strawberries; White pear compote; Red pear compote; Apple compote; Chestnut compote; Two sorts of grapes; Two sorts of pears; Two sorts of apples; Green walnuts; Two plates of *petits-fours*; Two plates of biscuits; Two plates of sweets; Two compotiers of fruits in eau-de-vie.

Soups: Crécy with meat stock; Turnip with milk.

Hors-d'oeuvre: Butter, radishes, celery, cucumber with vinegar, figs, pickles, gherkins, tuna, dry-cured sausage, shrimps.

Hot hors-d'oeuvre: Stuffed pig's trotters; Little patties.

Removes: Daube of leg of mutton; Capon with sea-salt.

Entrées: Civet of rabbit; Grey mullet with white sauce; Stuffed cucumbers; Calf's sweetbreads and brains à la poulette.

---

1. In the text, *alouettes ou mauviettes*. *Larousse gastronomique* (1936) remarks that the usual culinary designation of *alouette* is *mauviette*, which may also imply that they are fattened. The *Nouveau dictionnaire de cuisine, d'office et de pâtisserie*, edited by Borel (1826) has this to say (my translation): '*Mauviettes* are sorts of small thrushes which resemble quite closely larks [*alouettes*] for colour, but which have a shorter tail; they are often confused with these last. They are not very common, and almost always roasting-chefs or cooks will seek to pass off fat larks as *mauviettes*. The manner of preparing and dressing them is the same as that employed for larks and the gourmand will need a very fine palate to detect the difference that exists between these two birds.' As Borel is closer in time to Mme Millet-Robinet than is Larousse, I would suggest that his is the more accurate definition. The word *mauviette* (which in modern French means a wimp or weakling) itself derives from *mauvis*, a thrush. Shakespeare called his thrushes 'mavises'.

Roasts: Spit-roasted woodcock; Game pie.

Salads: Celery; Cos lettuce.

Vegetables: Celeriac with meat *jus*; Sugared spinach.

Entremets: Pears in a roux;[1] Battered and fried cauliflower.

Sweet entremets: Potato cake; Chestnut surprise; Angels' hairs; Small cakes.

Dessert: Brie cheese; Gruyère cheese; Moulded whipped cream; Savoy biscuit; *Calottes*; Compote of fresh pears with eau-de-vie; Apple compote; Strawberries; New season's prunes; Two sorts of pears; Two sorts of grapes; Two sorts of apples; Green walnuts; New season's hazelnuts; Two plates of *petits-fours*; Two plates of orange flower and violet praline.

FOURTH MENU (for fast-days)

Oysters.

Soups: Vegetable stock with granulated gluten; Cabbage, with cheese.

Hors-d'oeuvre: Butter, radishes, celery, cucumber with vinegar, figs, pickles, gherkins, anchovies.

Removes: Skate with black butter; Gurnard with white sauce.

Entrées: Omelette with tomato sauce; Gratin of fillets of sole; Scrambled eggs served on a mushroom ragout; *Matelote* of mackerel.

Roasts: Lobster; Pike *au bleu*.

Vegetables: Sugared turnips *au blanc*; Fried fresh haricot beans.

Entremets: Pears in a roux; Plain macaroni.

Sweet entremets: Chocolate cream; Bread mould; Rum jelly; Pear tart.

Dessert: Gruyère cheese; Roquefort cheese; Cream cheese; Angels' hairs; Chestnut compote; Pear compote; New season's prunes; Pears; Apples; Two sorts of grapes; Strawberries; Currants kept in straw mats;[2] Two plates of *petits-fours*; Two plates of sweets; Fresh walnuts; Two compotiers of fruits in eau-de-vie.

---

1.   The printer has misprinted *purées* for *poires*.

2.   In the section relating to fruit bushes in her second volume, Mme Millet-Robinet remarks that ripe currants can be held in suspended animation on their bushes by wrapping the plants in straw when they ripen. Another writer on these topics, publishing her book in 1834, was Élisabeth Celnart (Élisabeth-Félicie Bayle-Mouillard, 1796–1865), author of several manuals, including one on charcuterie, mostly for the publisher Roret. In her *Manuel des habitans de la campagne et de la bonne fermière* she advises that fruit-heavy bushes should be wrapped in straw and this will keep them in perfect condition until the first frosts.

NOVEMBER

FIRST MENU

Soups: Meat *jus* with rice; Vegetable.

Hors-d'oeuvre: Butter, radishes, celery, baby artichokes, cucumber with vinegar, gherkins, pickles, sardines preserved in oil, marinated tuna, olives.

Hot hors-d'oeuvre: Sausages with apples; Breaded mutton chops.

Removes: Smothered fillet of beef; Turbot with white sauce.

Entrées: Soles with oysters; Chicken fricassee; Partridge with cabbage; Veal chops *en papillote*.

Roasts: Hare; Chicken galantine.

Salads: Chicory with beetroot; Cos lettuce.

Vegetables: Cardoons with meat *jus*; Celeriac with butter.

Entremets: Pears in a roux; Fried battered artichokes.

Sweet entremets: Potato cake; Buttered apples; Boiled rice pudding with coffee; *Gâteau à la neige*.

Dessert: Gruyère cheese; Roquefort cheese; Moulded whipped cream; Compote of pears with kirsch; Chestnut compote; Prune compote; Apple compote; Two sorts of pears; Two sorts of apples; Two sorts of grapes; Two plates of *petits-fours*; Savoy biscuit; *Calottes*; Green walnuts; New season's hazelnuts; Orange flower praline; Violet praline; Roast chestnuts.

SECOND MENU

Soups: Meat stock with potato starch; Pumpkin with milk.

Hors-d'oeuvre: Butter, radishes, celery, sardines preserved in oil, marinated tuna, gherkins, pickles, olives.

Hot hors-d'oeuvre: Pig's trotters stuffed with truffles; Small fried patties.

Removes: Boiled beef served on Brussels sprouts cooked with meat *jus*; Capon with sea-salt.

Entrées: Civet of rabbit; Calf's sweetbreads and brains cooked as a chicken fricassee served with truffles and in a pastry crust; Stuffed cabbage; Grilled soles with white sauce.

Roasts: Turkey poult stuffed with chestnuts; Game pie.

Salads: Celery with beetroot; Cos lettuce.

Vegetables: Beetroot with wine; Salsify à la poulette.

Entremets: Fried sheep's trotters; Timbale of macaroni.

Sweet entremets: Chocolate cream; Waffles; Various small cakes; Rum jelly.

Dessert: Dutch cheese; Gruyère cheese; Cream cheese; Strawberries; Pear compote; Apple compote; Quince compote; Chestnut compote; Two plates of pears; Two plates of apples; Two plates of biscuits; Two plates of *petits-fours*; Dragées; Pralines; Two jams; Two compotiers of fruits in eau-de-vie; Prunes; Dried flattened pears; Roast chestnuts.

THIRD MENU

Soups: Crécy with meat stock; *Soupe à la reine*.

Hors-d'oeuvre: Butter, radishes, celery, sardines preserved in oil, anchovies, gherkins, pickles, olives.

Hot hors-d'oeuvre: Puddings and sausages; Herrings with mustard.

Removes: Ham served hot on sugared spinach; Daube of turkey.

Entrées: Duck with turnips; Mackerel with butter; Beef à la mode; Calf's head cooked in the manner of turtle *au blanc*.

Roasts: Truffled chicken; Lapwings and grouse.

Salads: Chicory and celery; Lettuce.

Vegetables: Sugared turnips; Celery with meat *jus*.

Entremets: Pears in a roux; Small fried pike.

Sweet entremets: Buttered apples; Rice cake; Crème caramel; Various little cakes.

Dessert: Brie cheese; Roquefort cheese; Decorated cake; Moulded whipped cream; Chestnut surprise; Compote of pears with kirsch; Compote of whole apples; Two sorts of pears; Two sorts of apples; Two sorts of grapes; Two sorts of jams; Two sorts of *petits-fours*; Macaroons; Biscuits; *Mendiants*; Dried flattened pears; Candied fruits; Roast chestnuts.

FOURTH MENU (for fast-days)
Oysters.

Soups: Vegetable stock with rice; Sugared panada.

Hors-d'oeuvre: Butter, radishes, celery, sardines preserved in oil, marinated tuna, pickles, gherkins, olives.

Hot hors-d'oeuvre: Fried fresh herring; Truffles in a napkin.

Removes: Skate with black butter; Grey mullet with white sauce.

Entrées: Hot pie of *matelote* of sea fish; Poached eggs with a vegetable *jus*; Mussels à la poulette; Truffle omelette.

Roasts: Whiting; Lobster.

Salads: Celery with mustard; Chicory with beetroot.

Vegetables: Cauliflower with tomato sauce; Potatoes maître-d'hôtel.

Entremets: Fried soles; Macaroni cooked in vegetable stock.

Sweet entremets: Pumpkin soufflé; *Colinette*; Savarin; Meringues.

Dessert: Mont-Dor cheese;[1] Brie cheese; Chestnut compote; Apple compote; Pear compote; Quince compote; Two sorts of pears; Two sorts of apples; Grapes; Medlars; Two jams; Two compotiers of fruits in eau-de-vie; Two plates of *petits-fours*; Savoy biscuit; Nougat.

DECEMBER

FIRST MENU

Soups: Meat stock with granulated gluten; Julienne.

Hors-d'oeuvre: Butter, radishes, olives, celery, sardines preserved in oil, anchovies, pickles, gherkins, dry-cured sausage.

Hot hors-d'oeuvre: Pig's trotters stuffed with truffles; Baked larks or thrushes.

Removes: Boiled beef on tomato sauce; Truffled turkey cooked with sea-salt.

Entrées: Salmi of woodcock and partridge; Béchamel of sea fish in pastry; Duck with olives; Capon with rice.

Roasts: Snipe; Chicken.

Salads: Red cabbage; *Scarole* with celery.

Vegetables: Cardoons with meat *jus*; Cauliflower with white sauce.

Entremets: Potato croquettes; Mushrooms on fried bread.

Sweet entremets: Apple charlotte; Charlotte russe; Boiled rice pudding with chocolate; Chestnut purée.

Dessert: Roquefort cheese; Dutch cheese; Decorated cake; Moulded whipped cream; Angels' hairs; Quince compote; Compote of pears in kirsch; Two sorts of pears; Two sorts of apples; Two sorts of grapes; Two sorts of *petits-fours*;[2] Two sorts of biscuits; Two sorts of fruits in eau-de-vie; Two sorts of sweets; Roast chestnuts.[3]

SECOND MENU

Soups: Meat stock with macaroni; Cheese.

---

1.   i.e. Vacherin de Mont-d'Or.
2.   Where the printer has printed 'Two sorts of…' he meant either 'Two plates of…' or 'Two compotiers of…'.
3.   In the original, '*Marrons rôtis circulant*'.

Hors-d'oeuvre: Butter, black radishes, celery, olives, marinated tuna, anchovies, pickles, gherkins.

Hot hors-d'oeuvre: Sausages with cabbage; Beefsteak with potatoes.

Removes: Daube of hare; Turkey with sea-salt.

Entrées: Hot pie with quenelles and truffles; Béchamel of salt cod in pastry; Sheep's trotters with cheese; Chicken fricassee.

Roasts: *Pâté de foie gras*; Venison fillet or haunch.

Salads: Red cabbage; *Scarole* with beetroot.

Vegetables: Celeriac with meat *jus*; Potatoes cooked with milk.

Entremets: Potato balls; Fillets of sole with sauce mayonnaise.

Sweet entremets: Rice mould flavoured with coffee, with a custard sauce as for *oeufs à la neige*; Little apple turnovers; Meringues; Rum jelly.

Dessert: Roquefort cheese; Chester cheese; Moulded ice; Compote of bottled apricots; Compote of cherries; Compote of pears in kirsch; Chestnut compote; Two sorts of apples; Two sorts of pears; Candied angelica; Candied citron; Orange flower praline; Maréchal MacDonald's sweets; *Mendiants*; Malaga raisins; Two plates of *petits-fours*; Two compotiers of fruits in eau-de-vie; Roast chestnuts.

THIRD MENU

Soups: Meat stock with Italian pasta; Julienne.

Hors-d'oeuvre: Butter, black radishes, celery, anchovies, sardines conserved in oil, olives, pickles, gherkins, shrimps, dry-cured sausage from Lyon.

Hot hors-d'oeuvre: White pudding with pistachios; Pig's trotters stuffed with truffles.

Removes: Boiled beef served on sauerkraut with cervelas sausage; Brill with white sauce.

Entrées: Duck with apples; Veal escalopes; Stuffed cabbage; Chicken fricassee.

Roasts: Plovers; Truffled chicken.

Salads: Wild celery with pickled herring; Beetroot.

Vegetables: Scorzonera à la poulette; Brussels sprouts.

Entremets: Gratin of macaroni; Small fried pike.

Sweet entremets: Kidney mould; Apple charlotte; Vanilla cream; Small cakes.

Dessert: Gruyère cheese; Mont-Dor cheese; Agen prunes; Apple compote; Quince compote; Preserved cherry compote; *Marrons glacés*; Angels' hairs; Two plates of biscuits; Two plates of *petits-fours*; Two plates of sweets; *Mendiants*; Malaga raisins; Nougat; Decorated cake; Two sorts of apples; Two sorts of pears.

FOURTH MENU (for fast-days)

Soups: Crécy with vegetable stock; Onion with pumpkin and rice.

Hors-d'oeuvre: Butter, black radishes, celery, olives, smoked salmon, marinated tuna, pickles, gherkins.

Hot hors-d'oeuvre: Herrings with mustard; Little fish patties.

Removes: Pike *au bleu* with oil; Cod with tomato sauce.

Entrées: Sole with oysters and a vegetable *jus*; Fishballs of carp in a hot piecrust with truffles; Mackerel with butter; Brillat-Savarin's the curé's omelette.

Roasts: Fried soles; Truffled teal.

Salads: Chicory with celery; Wild chicory with beetroot.

Vegetables: Cardoons *au blanc*; Fried potatoes.

Entremets: Well-fried noodles; Truffles with wine.

Sweet entremets: Chestnut surprise; Jam tart; Apple meringue; Rice soufflé with chocolate.

Dessert: Chester cheese; Roquefort cheese; Fruit basket with pineapple; Quince compote; Apple compote; Pear compote; Chestnut compote; Two plates of *petits-fours*; Two plates of biscuits; Two plates of *mendiants*; Two plates of sweets; Two compotiers of fruits in eau-de-vie; Two compotiers of jams; Angels' hairs.

INDEX

This index is to the text of *The French Country Housewife*, not to the introduction. The model luncheon and dinner menus in the final section have also not been indexed. Figures in bold type refer to the illustrations.

INDEX

of, 511; in pies, 609; quick civet of, 511-12;
roast, 511
Harel stoves, 264
haricot beans, dried, purée, 575; coloured,
546; shelled, 546; shelled, à la maître-
d'hôtel, 546; shelled, fried, 546; shelled,
salad of, 546; with milk, 546
haricot of mutton, 487; of leftovers of leg
of mutton, 484; of turkey giblets, 508
hash, 459; of leftovers of leg of mutton,
484
haslet, pig's, 360
hats, packing of, 385
head, calf's, blanquette of, 479-80; calf's,
fried, 479; calf's, in the manner of turtle,
478-9; calf's, in the manner of turtle, au
blanc, 479; calf's, plain boiled, 477-8;
pig's, 491
head cheese, pork, 371-3
heads, lambs', 490
heather for fires, 291
herb(s), mixed, fillet of veal with, 473;
mixed, tench with, 533; mixed, veal
chops with, 470-1; omelette, 450; soup,
428
herring, fresh, 526; fresh, with mustard,
526; smoked, 526; smoked, omelette,
450-1
hip-bath, 176
Holland, carrots from, 565; cherries from,
636; cod in, 524; potatoes in, 569
hooks for dresses, 109
hops, 560
horn, cleaning of, 222
hot water bottles, 171
hot water cylinder, 173-4
indigo, 292; see also blue
indoor greenhouse, **10**, 161
ink, 381; stains, removing, 246-7
insecticidal powders, 227-8
ironing, 263ff.
isinglass, 277
jacket and bonnet, **1**
jam, 321-37; cherry, 328; grape, 334;
greengage, 330; marrow, 334; mirabelle

plum, 329-30; omelette, 452, 591; pear,
331-2; pots, covering, 336-7; strawberry,
329; whole apricot, 326-7
jardinière, **7**
jawbreaker, 632
jelly, 321-37; apple, 332-3; apricot, 327-8;
currant, 322-3; currant, uncooked, 324;
quince, 333-4; raspberry, 325; white
currant, 323-4
Jerusalem artichoke(s), 572; cooked in
embers, 572; fried, 572; gratin, 572
jug, stoneware, **20**
jugs, 189
juice, currant, bottled, 340-1
julienne of vegetable soup, with bread or
rice, 424-5; without bread or rice, 425
jus, 431ff.; cardoons with, 557; cauliflower
with, 552; celery with, 557; cucumber
with, 561; lettuce with, 555-6; onions in,
442; salmon in, 537; salsify with, 567; to
replace stock in sauces, 427-8; turnips
with, 564; with chicken, 502
kale, asparagus, 551, 560&n
kettle, **32**, 180
kid, carving of, 408, 489; see also lamb
kidney(s), calf's, fried, 475; calf's, mould,
615; calf's, omelette, 451, 475; pig's, 492;
sheep's, butterflied, 488; sheep's, fried, 488
kitchen, arrangement, 177ff.; equipment,
390
kitchen cloths, 235-6; washing, 254, 257
kitchenware, cleaning of, 217
kneading, 280-1; machine, Eeckman's, 286
knife, carving, 405
knife board, 187
knives, kitchen, 187
lamb, baked between two fires, 490; best
end of, à la Périgord, 489; carving of,
408; chops, 490; roast quarter of, 489;
with onions, 490
lamb's trotters, 490
lambs' heads, 490
lamp(s), Carcel, 218-9; hanging, **12**;
maintaining and cleaning, 218-22;
moderator, **63**, **64**, 219-20; self-levelling,
65, **66**, 220